Marketing Research:
An International Approach

Visit the *Marketing Research: An International Approach* Companion Website at **www.pearsoned.co.uk/schmidt** to find valuable **student** learning material including:

- Data files in both SPSS and Excel format
- A number of appendices with additional enrichment material

PEARSON
Education

We work with leading authors to develop the
strongest educational materials in marketing,
bringing cutting-edge thinking and best learning
practice to a global market.

Under a range of well-known imprints, including
Financial Times Prentice Hall, we craft high quality
print and electronic publications which help readers
to understand and apply their content, whether
studying or at work.

To find out more about the complete range of our
publishing, please visit us on the World Wide Web at:
www.pearsoned.co.uk

Marketing
Research

An International Approach

Marcus J. Schmidt
Svend Hollensen

FT Prentice Hall
FINANCIAL TIMES

An imprint of **Pearson Education**
Harlow, England • London • New York • Boston • San Francisco • Toronto • Sydney • Singapore • Hong Kong
Tokyo • Seoul • Taipei • New Delhi • Cape Town • Madrid • Mexico City • Amsterdam • Munich • Paris • Milan

Pearson Education Limited
Edinburgh Gate
Harlow
Essex CM20 2JE
England

and Associated Companies throughout the world

Visit us on the World Wide Web at:
www.pearsoned.co.uk

First published 2006

ISBN-13: 978-0-27364-635-8
ISBN-10: 0-273-64635-4

British Library Cataloguing-in-Publication Data
A catalogue record for this book is available from the British Library

Library of Congress Cataloging-in-Publication Data
A catalog record for this book is available from the Library of Congress

10 9 8 7 6 5 4 3 2 1
10 09 08 07 06

Typeset in 10pt Times New Roman by 3
Printed and bound by Bell & Bain Ltd., Glasgow

The publisher's policy is to use paper manufactured from sustainable forests.

Contents

Supporting resources
Visit **www.pearsoned.co.uk/schmidt** to find valuable online resources

Companion Website for students
- Data files in both SPSS and Excel format
- A number of appendices with additional enrichment material

For instructors
- Answers to end-of-chapter questions and selected case questions
- PowerPoint slides with key figures from the book
- Additional animated PowerPoint slides

For more information please contact your local Pearson Education sales representative or visit **www.pearsoned.co.uk/schmidt**

Foreword

Every few years a really excellent and innovative text is published. More often than not it seems the most interesting books are on introductory as opposed to advanced topics. I am pleased to say that *Marketing Research: An International Approach*, co-authored by Marcus Schmidt and Svend Hollensen, is the exception to this pattern. The text goes beyond the basic idea of showing how marketing research approaches and tools can be applied in solving marketing problems and creating business opportunities. It actually provides some very practical examples of specific tools and techniques and how they can be usefully applied. The premise is that with both large and small businesses moving toward globalization of marketing practices, today's and particularly tomorrow's information requirements will be much more challenging than those we have relied on in the past. The text does an excellent job of demonstrating the ability of marketing research approaches to meet the information requirements of successful global companies.

The book begins by providing an excellent foundation in the fundamental principles of marketing research. The critical role of the internet as well as other secondary data sources is examined early to demonstrate their increasing importance in marketing decision-making. Moreover, unlike many books there is extensive coverage of qualitative research approaches. Finally, the critical issues underlying the development of scale measurements and information properties are discussed in detail, as are the important concepts of validity and reliability.

From my review of the text there are several competitive advantages of this book beyond the initial coverage of the internet, secondary data sources, questionnaire design and data collection. First, it does an excellent job of covering the challenges of conducting marketing research on a global scale. These unique challenges are illustrated with examples that bring the discussion to life. Another strength of the text is its extensive coverage of statistical analysis techniques. To make accurate business decisions in today's increasingly complex environment, marketers must analyze and understand intricate relationships with many intervening variables. The statistical techniques covered in the text are powerful analytical tools that enable marketing researchers to identify interesting, non-obvious patterns hidden in databases and data warehouses that have a high potential for improving decision-making and creating knowledge. An understanding of the power of these tools is increasingly needed by business decision makers, and the applied approach used by the authors makes otherwise complex techniques understandable.

The book is positioned as an advanced coverage of marketing research topics. But for students needing to review the fundamentals, material is provided in several appendices on the book's website that will refresh their recall of these topics. My own text on marketing research is positioned at a lower level, has limited coverage of the challenges of global marketing research, and less coverage of the advanced analytical techniques. If I were teaching an advanced marketing research course covering international perspectives and advanced analytical techniques, I would definitely consider this text.

Most marketing research books are readable, but perhaps a more important question is "Can students comprehend what they are reading?" For this text, I believe the answer is definitely "yes". The market the text is targeted at should find the book to be a very useful and informative reference for the latest in marketing research techniques.

Joseph F. Hair, Professor of Marketing at Kennesaw State University, Georgia. Formerly Alvin C. Copeland Endowed Chair of Franchising and Director, Entrepreneurship Institute, Louisiana State University, and the Phil B. Hardin Chair of Marketing at the University of Mississippi.

Preface

Why conduct marketing research in the international environment?

Internationalization is no longer a choice for a company. It has become a necessity for survival. Global marketing has become a fact of life. Even if companies are not engaged in selling goods and services abroad, they are affected by what happens in the global marketplace.

As firms push the geographic frontiers to take advantage of growing opportunities, they need to collect information from a broader and more diverse range of markets. Increasingly, this entails conducting research in unfamiliar and distant markets. This poses a number of challenges, not only in collecting cost effective, accurate and reliable information on existing behaviour patterns, but also in predicting responses to new and unfamiliar stimuli and interpreting the implications for marketing strategy. Conducting successful research requires both understanding and sensitivity to differences in the market environment as well as an ability to deal with the lack of a well-developed market research infrastructure. The accuracy of results hinges, in part, on the respondent's ability to understand the questions being posed.

The role of marketing research cannot be overestimated, especially in times of uncertainty. Managers have to take a closer look at what constitutes good research and how it can be used to help businesses cope in difficult situations. Marketing research does not replace management skills; it reinforces thinking by testing conventional wisdom and commonly held assumptions in business. In short, marketing research provides managers with new perspectives in strategic planning.

Target market/book objective

Marketing Research: An International Approach is intended as a text for graduate and advanced undergraduate courses in Marketing Research, International Marketing Research, or as a supplementary text for any International Marketing course. The main objective is to help students develop an in-depth knowledge of the marketing research issues. The book offers the reader a comprehensive, analytic, decision-oriented framework to assist the market researcher in developing research needed to make business decisions.

Book overview

The book is divided into two parts. The first part (chapters 2–7) looks at Qualitative Research Methods. The second part (chapters 8–17) explores Quantitative Research Methods. The flow chart on page xiii provides a clear overview of the book's structure.

Key features

Written from the perspective of the firm conducting marketing research in national and international markets irrespective of its country of origin, the book has the following key features:

- Emphasis on marketing research in the international setting
- Comprehensive and detailed description of the market research process and advanced research techniques
- Coverage of online/internet surveys
- Coverage of database marketing, including data mining and data warehousing.

To reinforce learning, each chapter contains learning objectives, exhibits from the real world, marketing models, end-of-chapter summaries, discussion questions, endnotes, and references.

Robust website

Both students and lecturers should visit **www.pearsoned.co.uk/schmidt** to access the following:

- Selected end-of-chapter appendices with in-depth discussions on selected technical details
- SPSS and Excel files that are referred to in the book
- Suggested answers to end-of-chapter questions and case studies
- PowerPoint slides
- Multiple-choice tests in Business Statistics
- Links to other sites.

A crash course on Business Statistics which includes:

- Appendix A – four real-life, large scale cases, including data sets in SPSS and Excel format
- Appendix B – Multiple choice questions
- Appendix C – Cola brand case study with questions and an Excel file containing the data set
- Appendix D – Detailed suggested solutions to all questions.

A note regarding software

When we started writing this book almost a decade ago, versions 7 and 8 of SPSS were still in widespread use. When the book went into print, version 14 had just been released. Presently, new versions of SPSS appear once or twice each year. This makes it extremely difficult to include figures of screenshots in a textbook that are still up-to-date and valid once the book is published.

In our effort to keep our pedagogical journey state-of-the-art, we will upload information to readers concerning new versions of SPSS to our book's website. On the site we intend to discuss how the changes impact the methods and analyses that are covered in the book: Screenshots of input settings that have changed, alterations in how output looks, how it is to be interpreted and so on. Therefore, it is recommended that the reader visits the book's website for such new information.

We have tried to employ consistency when reproducing numbers. A full stop ('.') is used as a decimal separator and a comma (',') is used as a thousand separator. However, in the screenshots in the book and on the website a comma is used as a decimal separator.

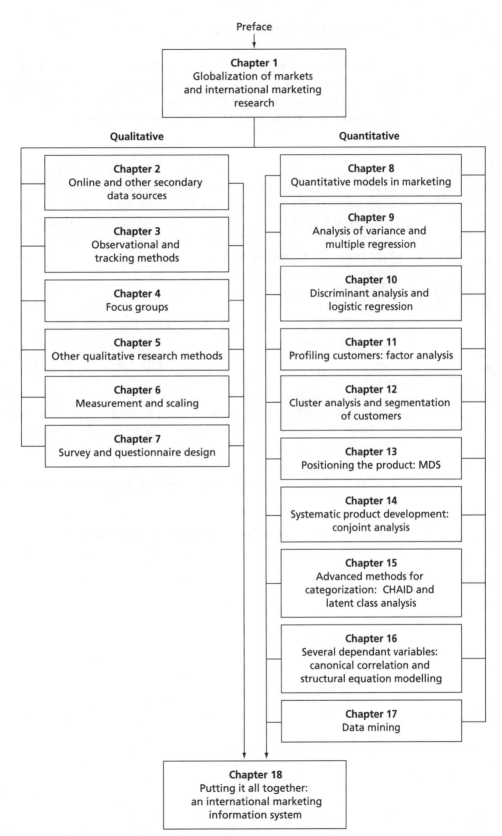

The structure of the book

Acknowledgements

Writing any book is a long-term commitment and involves time-consuming efforts. The successful completion of this book depends on the support and generosity of many people. We wish to thank the many scholars whose articles, books, and other materials we have cited, quoted or used as references. We are indebted to the following for their contributions:

Aase Simonsen and Charlotte Hansen, University of Southern Denmark
Claus V. Jacobsen, associated with Copenhagen Business School
Frank Carmone, Wright State University, Dayton, Ohio
John Von Briesen Raz, University of Chicago/Smallwaters Corporation
Axel Schultz-Nielsen, Copenhagen Business School
Lene Hansen, GfK Denmark
Karsten Dalsgaard, SPSS Worldwide Services
Uffe Wolffhechel, Danish Foreign Ministry

We are grateful to our publisher, Pearson Education. We would like to thank Senior Acquisitions Editor, Thomas Sigel, and Senior Desk Editor, Sarah Wild, for their encouragement and professionalism in transforming the manuscript into the final book. Thanks also to copyeditor, Tony Quinn, and Jann Hadfield for their work on editing the manuscript.

We also extend our greatest gratitude to our colleagues at Copenhagen Business School and University of Southern Denmark for their constant help and inspiration.

Finally, we thank our families for their support through the writing process. We are pleased to dedicate this book to Jonna, Nanna, and Julie Hollensen and to Anette Schmidt.

Marcus Schmidt, Center of Market Economics, Copenhagen Business School, marcus.schmidt@cbs.dk

Svend Hollensen, University of Southern Denmark, svend@sam.sdu.dk

March 2006

About the authors

Marcus Schmidt

Marcus Schmidt is an Associate Professor of Marketing Research and Business Statistics at the Copenhagen Business School (Center of Market Economics). For almost two decades he has served as an analytical consultant for big companies and market research agencies, GfK Denmark in particular. He regularly teaches at PhD seminars and provides lectures for market managers on multivariate analysis in Denmark and abroad.

His research has been published in the *International Journal of Advertising, Futures, Qualitative Market Research, Tourism Analysis, International Journal of Opinion Research, Journal of Services Research* and *European Advances in Consumer Research*.

Marcus is a three times winner of the Best Paper Award in Research Methods at the AMA Summer Educator's Conference (1990, 1992 and 1998). He has written a frequently cited book on direct democracy (in Danish). He is currently working on a book about the Danish judicial system.

Svend Hollensen

Svend Hollensen is an Associate Professor of International Marketing at the University of Southern Denmark (Mads Clausen Institute in Sønderborg). He has practical experience as an International Marketing Coordinator in a large Danish multinational enterprise as well as an International Marketing Manager in a company producing agricultural machinery.

He was awarded his PhD in 1992 from Copenhagen Business School (CBS).

He has published articles in international journals and is the author of *Marketing Management: A Relationship Approach*, published by Financial Times Prentice Hall in 2003, as well as *Global Marketing: A decision-oriented approach*, which was published in its third edition by the same publisher in 2004. This book has been translated to both Chinese and Russian.

Svend has also worked as a business consultant for several multinational companies, as well as global organizations such as World Bank.

Publisher's acknowledgements

We are grateful to the following for permission to reproduce copyright material:

SPSS for use of the screen images, copyright © SPSS Inc. SPSS is a registered trademark and the other product names are trademarks of SPSS Inc.; Other, non-SPSS, screenshots reprinted by permission from Microsoft Corporation; Figures 1.2 and 2.2 from *Marketing Management: A Relationship Approach*, Financial Times Prentice Hall, (Hollensen, S. 2003), reprinted with permission from Pearson Education Ltd.; Figure 2.1 from *Marketing Research, sixth edition,* John Wiley & Sons Inc, New York, (Aaker, Kumar and Day 1998), reprinted with permission of John Wiley & Sons, Inc; Figures 2.3, 5.1, 6.10 and 18.3 from Global *Marketing: A Decision-Oriented Approach*, Financial Times Prentice Hall, (Hollensen, S. 2004), reprinted with permission from Pearson Education Ltd.; Figures 2.4, 2.5, 2.6 and Tables 2.3, 2.4 from Windenergienutzung in der Bundesrepublik Deutschland in *DEWI Magazin*, German Wind Energy Institute (Ender 2004); Figure 8.8 reprinted from *International Journal of Research in Marketing*, 17(2–3), (Leeflang, P.S.H. and Wittink, D.R. 2000), Building models of marketing decisions: past, present and future, pp. 105–26, Elsevier Ltd, with permission from Elsevier; Marketing Research in Action box on pp. 454–60 and Figure 4.10 reproduced with permission from GfK, Denmark.

In some instances we have been unable to trace the owners of copyright material and we would appreciate any information that would enable us to do so.

1

Globalization of markets and international marketing research

Learning objectives

After studying this chapter you should be able to:

- Understand the differences between domestic and international marketing research.
- Explain how changes in the global market environment affect the need for international marketing research.
- Define the role of international marketing research.
- Describe the company's need for information in the different phases of the internationalization process.

1.1 Introduction

The basis of all marketing activities is the "marketing concept." This management philosophy suggests that companies should first determine the wants and needs of their target customers and only then create products and services that satisfy those needs. The extent to which an organization satisfies customer needs better than its competitors determines the degree of success in meeting organizational objectives. The marketing concept therefore identifies the ultimate goal of an organization as that of creating customer satisfaction. To determine customer needs and to implement marketing strategies aimed at satisfying those needs, information is vital. Managers need information about customers, competitors, and other forces in the marketplace. The role of marketing research is to assess the information needs and provide managers with relevant and up-to-date information to help them make decisions. Using appropriate information will reduce or remove uncertainty and so improve outcomes. However, there are instances when a decision must be made quickly, and the lengthy process of extensive market analysis cannot be carried out. For example, even though Amazon.com's Jeff Bezos prefers to rigorously quantify users' reactions before rolling out new features, he did not test the company's 'search-inside-the-book' offering, but applied it to a critical mass of books. In this case, Bezos trusted his instincts and took a flier. The feature proved to be popular when it was introduced (Davenport, 2006).

EXHIBIT 1.1 PILLSBURY'S PROGRESSO SOUP

The problem

Consumers in the US weren't ladling out enough Progresso soup. During the 1997–98 "soup season" (September to March), sales of Progresso slipped 6 percent from the year before. How could Pillsbury get more people to try the brand and boost revenue?

The marketing research

After reviewing existing research, Pillsbury went out to talk to consumers, primarily women aged 25 to 54, including those who bought Progresso products and those who did not. In focus groups, researchers learned which attributes or feelings people associated with Progresso. Some participants mentioned Progresso's distinctive flavours and premium ingredients; others talked about its Italian-sounding name. The qualitative research also found that most consumers who bought Progresso had discovered it as an adult. The Progresso label, with its appetizing picture of steaming soup, caught their eye and they just bought a can to try, they said. After one spoonful, they were converted.

However, not enough shoppers were crossing over from condensed soups. Progresso requires no additional water or milk and condensed soups account for two-thirds of the market, according to AC Nielsen data. Many focus group respondents who didn't eat Progresso recalled fond childhood memories of slurping down alphabet soup on wintry days. For the most part, their pantries were stocked with the same condensed offerings that they enjoyed when growing up. Progresso didn't make children's favourites, such as alphabet soup. Advertising was needed to remind consumers that Progresso was a soup for adults, a step up from the condensed varieties of their childhood.

Solving the problem

Nelson-Henry developed 30 advertising ideas for Progresso, and focus groups helped narrow the list to three campaigns. Further qualitative research uncovered what worked with consumers. First, people loved humour. One spot, called "The Lunchbox," featured a young male office worker eating a bowl of a competitor's condensed chicken noodle soup. Next to him is a child's lunchbox. An older female colleague teases him about what he's eating and for clinging to things from his childhood. "You're an adult now," she says, and suggests that he try her bowl of Progresso chicken noodle, with its all-white-meat chicken and chunky veggies. There's even a side-by-side comparison of Progresso and its condensed-soup competitor. The tagline "Discover the Better Taste of Progresso" reflected insights from consumers about how they felt like they had "discovered" the brand.

With Ipsos-ASI, Pillsbury tested the copy for two campaigns with consumers in 1998. "Discover the Better Taste of Progresso" relayed the intended message and persuading participants to try the brand. A national television campaign was launched in October, the prime soup season, aimed at women aged 25 to 54. To complement the TV spots, Pillsbury sponsored a "Great Discovery" contest and invited consumers to

EXHIBIT 1.1 CONTINUED

submit recipes for homemade soup. The main prize-winner would inspire a future Progresso offering. The brand's blue label also sparked an idea for a "Blue Is Better Sweepstakes," in which all of the prizes had a connection to the colour blue (the main prize was a blue Volkswagen Beetle).

The payoff
During the 1998–99 soup season when the advertising was on air, Progresso sales rose 12 percent. Statistical analysis (regression models) indicated that 60 percent of that gain was due to the campaign. Tracking by Winona Research also showed that awareness for Progresso hit 48 percent, an increase of 17 percentage points following the campaign.

Sources: Adapted from: www.bettycrocker.com/products/prod_progresso.asp; and Hansson (2000)

The Progresso experience leads us to a definition of "marketing research" by the European Society for Opinion and Marketing Research (ESOMAR):

Marketing research is a key element within the total field of marketing information. It links the consumer, customer and public to the marketer through information that is used to identify and define marketing opportunities and problems; to generate, refine and evaluate marketing actions; and to improve understanding of marketing as a process and of the ways in which specific marketing activities can be made more effective.

The phrase "total field of marketing information" recognizes that marketing decisions are not only supported by marketing research. Further information sources are now competing with the "traditional" view of marketing research. Among these are data suppliers, such as call-centres, direct-marketing agencies, database-marketing firms, customer loyalty programmes and internet database providers.

Furthermore, the ESOMAR definition points out two important phases in the marketing-research process (Malhotra and Birks, 2003):

1. **"Define marketing opportunities and problems" (problem-identification research):** Undertaken to help identify problems that are not immediately apparent, but are likely to arise. For example, problems with marketing strategy, such as the product being rejected too quickly by customers, or problems with the product design. Appropriate research will help diagnose the problem.
2. **"Generate and refine marketing actions" (problem-solving research):** Once a problem or opportunity has been identified, "problem-solving research" is undertaken to help develop a solution. The findings are used to support decisions that tackle specific marketing problems.

Problem-identification research and problem-solving research go hand in hand. **Exhibits 1.1 and 1.2** in this chapter are examples of projects that combine both types of research.

The "International Market Information System" should reflect the increasingly complex environment

Information and knowledge are key to developing successful international marketing strategies. Yet, while knowledge exists in most organizations, it is often difficult to access. Lack of customer, competitor and market environment information, coupled with the growing complexity and diversity of international markets, makes it increasingly critical to collect information about these markets.

An international researcher has to deal with a number of countries that may differ considerably. Therefore, many marketing decisions are concerned with priorities and allocating resources between countries. Globalization represents the growing interdependence of national economies – involving consumers, producers, suppliers, and governments in different countries.

The function of an information system is to provide information to improve decision-making – see Figure 1.2 later.

The distinction between a multinational operation and a global operation has become more important to the design and implementation of marketing information systems (decision-support systems). The following describes the development of a company from one that is home-market-oriented (ethnocentric) to one that is globally oriented, measured against four orientations (Wind, Douglas and Perlmutter, 1973; Shoham, Rose and Albaum, 1995). This is the Ethno-Poly-Regio-Geo model (EPRG):

- Ethnocentrism: The lowest level of international commitment. At this stage a company focuses on its home market and tries to dump excess goods on occasional ad hoc export markets.
- Polycentrism (multinational/multidomestic firm): International marketing programmes are designed independently to match the needs of each individual country.
- Regiocentrism: International marketing programmes are designed independently to match the needs of areas or regions (e.g. the EU or NAFTA), emphasizing similarities that transcend national boundaries.
- Geocentrism: The global marketing programmes are based on the perception that world markets are progressing toward a converging commonality and that the "global marketing" approach represents the prevailing trend in conducting business.

Figure 1.1a and Figure 1.1b show how the four strategic EPRG concepts are related to company size and company ownership. The plots of Figure 1.1 are based on an empirical sample – personal interviews with 456 export managers. Exhibit 1.2 contains technical details on how the plots were produced. (This exhibit includes terms that may be unfamiliar to some readers, but it can be passed over without any loss of context. The statistical method employed to produce the plots (correspondence analysis) is addressed in Chapter 13.)

EXHIBIT 1.2 HOW THE PLOTS IN FIGURE 1.1A AND FIGURE 1.1B WERE PRODUCED

Data concerning both plots are taken from the file *Danish_exporters.sav* (www. pearsoned.co.uk/schmidt). The file has an SPSS format. The EPRG-variable is called "eprg," while the company-size variable is called "employed" (since the latter variable is a metric or rather a discrete measure, it had to be recoded into a categorical format). The company ownership variable is called "owner." The variable "employed" (ratio scaled) is called "employx" in its recoded nominal scaled form.

This is how the plots were obtained (assuming that the file *Danish_exporters.sav* has been loaded into an SPSS screen editor).

1. In SPSS, tap *[Analyze]*, *[Data Reduction]*, *[Correspondence Analysis]*.
2. Click "owner" (or "employx") into *[Row]*.
3. Tap *[Define Range]*, plug in "1" for *[Minimum]* and "3" for *[Maximum]* – the "owner" variable has 3 levels.
4. Tap *[Update]* and *[Continue]*.
5. Next, click "eprg" into *[Column]*. Once more click *[Define Range]*. This time plug in "1" for *[Minimum]* and "4" for *[Maximum]* – the "eprg" variable has four levels.
6. Click *[Update]*, *[Continue]* and *[OK]*.

The resulting plot (at the bottom of the output) should resemble Figure 1.1b.

As expected, Figure 1.1a shows that large companies are associated with geo- and poly-centric strategies, and medium-sized companies seem more related to a regiocentric strategy. Small companies appear to be statistically unrelated to any of the four strategies.

From Figure 1.1b, while national companies are associated with a regiocentric strategy, subsidiaries of foreign companies appear to pursue a geocentric strategy. Finally, the

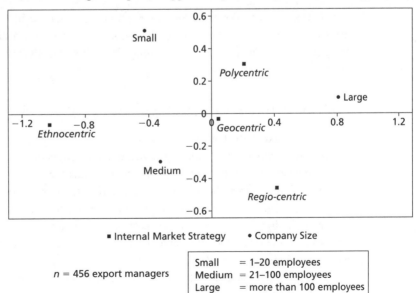

n = 456 export managers

■ Internal Market Strategy   • Company Size

Small	= 1–20 employees
Medium	= 21–100 employees
Large	= more than 100 employees

Figure 1.1a EPRG and company size

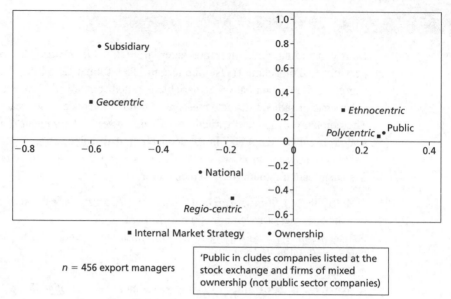

Figure 1.1b EPRG and company ownership

public companies are related to poly- and ethnocentric market strategies. This makes sense since the group of public companies includes some that are listed at the native Stock Exchange.

1.2 Changes in the global environment

Boundaries between domestic and international markets are becoming less relevant as firms increase their profiles abroad. In Europe, North America and Asia, international competition has intensified, precipitating the following changes in global marketing research.

Changes in the international market focus

In the 1970s and 1980s the country was typically used as the unit of analysis for research design, for developing the sampling frame, and data collection. Owing to economic, political, linguistic and cultural barriers, the country was the focal point of entry decisions. Equally, the firm's international operations were often organized by country. Marketing research agencies were also typically national organizations, with relatively few having the capability to conduct research across several countries.

However, the issues facing companies in the 1990s have changed dramatically, as have research and information needs. In industrialized regions, such as North America, Europe and Japan, regional market integration and the removal of trade barriers, the growth of a regional and global market infrastructure as well as increased mobility of consumers have created pressures to consolidate and integrate marketing strategies across countries.

Consequently, increased attention is focused on conducting studies covering several countries to examine differences and similarities in behaviour and response patterns.

Changes in communication technology

Developments in mass communications technology and global and regional media, have created certain segments of the population worldwide with a common set of expectations, familiarity with a common set of symbols, similar preferences for products and services, and an overall desire to improve their standard of living. Market segments such as teenagers share common interests in clothing, music, films and sports, as trends and related products are rapidly spread through global media.

Increasing discretionary spending also expands choice and increases the role of services in consumer decisions. This trend, coupled with the multiplicity of shopping modes available, results in more emphasis on examining the role of the shopping environment on choice behaviour. Situational and contextual variables, such as the effect of store ambience on shopping mood have to be considered.

Dramatic changes in the global environment, coupled with technological advances in data collection, analysis and dissemination, imply that researchers need to broaden their capabilities in order to design, implement and interpret research. New tools need to be mastered and creative approaches to understanding behaviour in differing cultural contexts developed. The ability to interpret and integrate complex data from diverse sources and environments will also be critical to providing meaningful recommendations for a company's global marketing strategy.

In emerging markets, conditions not only are changing rapidly, but are also different from those in industrialized countries. Not only are consumer standards of living and purchasing power much lower, but attitudes towards foreign products are often extremely complex, sometimes ambivalent and difficult to predict. This, coupled with the lack of a research or technological infrastructure to collect and analyze data, poses a challenge not only in designing research, but also in developing and implementing the collection of data. This in turn adds to the complexity of conducting marketing research as the range and nature of research contexts become increasingly heterogeneous.

As a result of these trends, more timely and relevant information is essential for day-to-day decision-making as well as to chart a firm's path in an increasingly turbulent and competitive environment. The speed of business, the flood of information provided by the new technologies, and flatter organizational structures are driving this trend. In short, managers need help in processing more issues without the help of mid-level managers. The marketing researcher is accessible and is informed about these issues; therefore managers increasingly involve them in decision-making. Managers want well-reasoned recommendations, not just information about the issue or descriptions of possible courses of action.

Information needs are changing in both developed and developing countries. Established markets are becoming more geographically integrated, as direct vertical links and information flows are established between customers, retailers, and suppliers. As a result, there is a growing need for research spanning country boundaries, in order to identify regional or global market segments, or to examine opportunities for integrating and co-ordinating strategies across borders. At the same time, speed in collection and interpretation of results from multiple and geographically diverse sources becomes imperative.

As firms push the geographic frontiers of their operations, they need to collect information from a broader and more diverse range of markets. Increasingly, this entails conducting research in unfamiliar and distant markets. This poses challenges, not only in collecting accurate and reliable information on existing behaviour in an expeditious and cost-effective way, but also in predicting responses to new and unfamiliar stimuli, and interpreting the implications for marketing strategy.

Advances in technology both facilitate and at the same time render more complexity in the collection of global data. Better communications enable faster data collection on a much broader and diverse geographic scale. Yet, at the same time, managers have to master these tools and understand their inherent limitations and implicit biases.

In addition to these trends, two main reasons are cited for the growth of marketing research. First, the speed of doing business has increased due to the diffusion of information technologies, enabling firms to be more responsive to customers through flexible manufacturing, and reduced cycle times in channel operations. Instant communication has become a prerequisite to developing viable markets. Marketing has assumed a new significance, as the costs of misreading signals from the marketplace become higher. As the interpreter of signals and clues from the marketplace, marketing research has a critical role in providing "the voice of the customer" to managers. Advances in technology have enhanced the scope, effectiveness, and efficiency of marketing research leading to its increased use.

One of the first academics to identify the challenges and opportunities of globalization was Theodore Levitt (1983) with his seminal article "The globalization of markets." No doubt, the homogenization of consumer habits and lifestyles, caused by the tremendous progress of communications technology and worldwide tourism, came true. Moreover, intensified competition and growing investments in research and development seem to force companies to operate globally, enforcing the marketing of global products, services, and brands.

Implementing a pure global strategy does not only mean offering and marketing products or services that are standardized. A global strategy includes linking the dispersed units of the globalized firm plus addressing all functions of the value chain, especially marketing, distribution and the design of products or services, which can also demonstrate the limits of globalization. As differences between products and services in any given industry are vanishing and global standards become the rule, consumers will appreciate the value of offers specific to a country.

1.3 Consequences of "de-globalization"

The growing variety of market needs forces managers of global brands to run locally adapted strategies. One such company, which is famous for practising globalization at its best, is running a more and more locally oriented strategy. Nearly everyone thinks that Coca-Cola offers its soft drink Coke in an identical quality worldwide, but this is not true.

For example, in the Arab world, consumers prefer soft drinks to be sweeter than in Europe. So Coca-Cola had to adapt its products for Arab countries. In a similar vein, Coca-Cola of Germany no longer implements the global marketing strategy developed by its headquarters. The German subsidiary developed a country-specific series of commercials, which show a "hidden" kind of eroticism. These commercials intend to attract more teens and "tweens" by emphasizing the connection between the soft drink and the "coolness" of younger German consumers. Coca-Cola could not show such "erotic" commercials on US television.

As a consequence of mad-cow disease in Europe, international fast-food-giants such as McDonald's and Burger King have been forced to modify their global strategic orientation. Hamburgers are no longer the focus of marketing campaigns. Instead of "Big Macs" and "Whoppers," European markets emphasized "Chicken Wings," "Fish Weeks," and "Bacon Toasts." Although this strategic redesign is not driven by a return to country-specific values and attitudes, it is the consequence of a similar cause. Such a redesign implicitly demonstrates the long-term effect of practising "monocultural" strategies (Macharzina, 2001).

Firms relying only on pure global strategies will have to learn the lessons of falling profits in a diversifying world market. Various cases illustrate the need for a high degree of flexibility and the ability to adapt to local specifications.

Taken together, these forces could be viewed as indicators of an economic and social future that is by no means a one-way road towards global products, services and brands. On the contrary, "de-globalization" is likely to occur. As the history of cultural dimensions such as arts, architecture or literature shows, long-term development in these fields has followed a pattern, which is similar to the swing of a pendulum.

International marketing research needs to consider local differences and nuances in design, respondent availability, field execution, and data quality. Data collection methodology may have to vary from country to country.

Interviewing services with facilities in shopping centres don't exist in most countries. Interviewing is done at home with interviewers going door-to-door; by street intercepts where the respondent is invited to a meeting room or hall; or by pre-recruitment. The use of telephone interviews in individual homes varies a lot; in some countries it is as low as 10 percent. In Japan, where telephone interviews are not a problem, it is considered discourteous to conduct a lengthy interview.

The way in which respondents interact with interviewers varies greatly; in some lesser-developed countries, there is a desire to please the interviewer. This, along with other cultural differences, results in the variation in scaling. Differences also exist between "no answer" and "refused."

While Western Europe has different social classes, the lines between them are less distinctive than in other countries. In Latin America, it is difficult to approach the upper socio-economic classes because of physical barriers such as houses with gates and the intervening servants. Always check with locals about the dynamics and nuances of different socio-economic groups. This holds true in qualitative research in which mixing of social classes will at minimum be unproductive. In some countries, mixing genders does not work, and in some Middle Eastern countries males are not allowed to interview females (Frevert, 2000).

Before defining the international marketing research problem, the researcher must isolate and examine the effect of the self-reference criterion (SRC), or the unconscious reference to one's own cultural values (Lee, 1966; Malhotra, Agarwal and Peterson, 1996). For example, attitudes to time vary considerably across cultures. In Asia, Latin America, and the Middle East, people are not as time-conscious as westerners. This influences their perceptions of and preferences for convenience foods such as frozen foods and prepared dinners.

1.4 The changing role of the international market researcher

Formerly, marketing research was regarded as a staff-function and not a line-function. Marketing researchers had little interaction with marketing managers and did not participate in decision-making. Likewise, external providers of research had little interaction with managers. However, this demarcation between marketing research and marketing, and thus the distinction between researchers and managers, is becoming thinner.

As the line authority and staff boundary blur, marketing managers are becoming more involved in research, making research more of a line function. This is likely to continue and even accelerate as "sense and respond" increasingly characterizes a firms' approach to business. Thus, the traditional marketing researcher focused on producing presentations and reports for managers will become a rare breed. Increasingly, the marketing manager is becoming a part of an integrated, decision-making team. Some of the most effective researchers of customer satisfaction are not only participating in decision-making, but are also deployed as part of the team to implement organizational changes in response to customer satisfaction surveys.

The availability of better decision tools and decision support systems is helping managers become better decision-makers. Senior managers can now directly access internal and external secondary data from computers and websites around the world.

In this millennium, good marketing researchers will be good marketing managers and vice-versa. If either fails to do so, they will both be swept away by sudden shifts in the marketplace, as consumers become increasingly empowered through rising incomes, technology, and information access (Malhotra and Peterson, 2001).

Marketing research as a continuous operation

Another change is that more marketing research will be undertaken as part of normal business operations, rather than in response to specific marketing problems or opportunities. A traditional approach to research started with a definition of the marketing research problem, formulation of a research design, analysis of secondary data, development of a questionnaire and the collection of primary data, data analysis, report preparation and presentation. In the future, marketing research will be a continuous activity. This will be true for secondary data obtained from syndicated sources as well as primary data collected exclusively by or for the firm.

Trend towards secondary data

As decision-support systems become more pervasive and managers become better at handling information, this trend to continuous research will accelerate. More and more marketing research problems will be addressed based on secondary data alone. In the past, collection of primary data was an integral part of marketing research. However, this need not be the case because of the extensive nature of secondary data available online. Given the time and expense associated with the collection of primary data, the use of secondary data will continue to grow. Evaluation of secondary data is even more critical for international than for domestic projects. The need to evaluate data systematically before using it will become even more crucial. Different sources report different values for a given statistic, because of differences in the way the unit is defined. Measurement units may not be equivalent across countries. Data from highly industrialized countries such as England or Sweden are likely to be more accurate than those from developing countries. Business and income statistics are affected by the taxation structure and the extent of tax evasion. Population censuses may vary in frequency and year in which the data are collected.

The need for information in the stages of an internationalization process

Before going abroad a company has to evaluate the information needed in the different stages of the internationalization process. It must gather relevant knowledge and then it

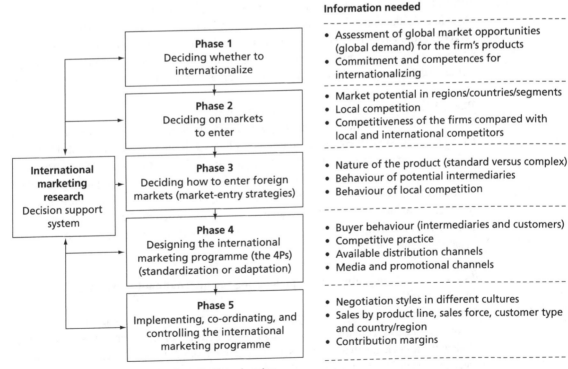

Figure 1.2 Phases in international marketing planning
Source: Hollensen, 2003

can make a commitment of resources. Figure 1.2 shows what kind of knowledge and information are needed in the five phases of the decision-making process in international marketing.

Phase 1: Deciding whether to internationalize[1]

Firms need a motivation to go international. They may be looking for external sources of increased competitive advantage, following a competitor's moves, asked explicitly by their customers, or need a larger market potential for economies of scale. But motivation does not come spontaneously: the company must be alert and keep gathering the relevant information that will indicate when the moment has arrived. Not all firms will find internationalization to be the best strategy, but all must constantly question themselves as to whether the right moment has arrived or is about to arrive.

Phase 2: Deciding which markets to enter[2]

When the motivation for internationalization has arisen, companies start doing more intense research to select appropriate markets. Knowledge in this stage is key, because a fit must be obtained between the firm's objectives and capabilities and the destination that will be chosen. After the information has been gathered the international market must be chosen. Probably the most important consideration at this stage is the fit between the foreign market's demand characteristics and the company's competences. A country that is attractive for a specific company might not be the optimal one for another company, or a country might present extremely convenient operational conditions, but not fit the company's strategy at different levels, for example organizational, political, or financial. This makes the selection of the final destination different from that of researching market conditions. The information gathered in the stage of market research has to be put in the broader context of the company's strategy. It is likely that no market will be optimal in all dimensions of a company's strategy, so the final decision must be taken by comparing the overall implications of each candidate.

Phase 3: Deciding how to enter foreign markets[3]

When a firm knows where it wants to go, how should it go there? Entry modes – export strategies, licensing, franchising, marketing alliances, joint ventures, and subsidiaries – differ in the degree of control over foreign operations. No particular mode of entry gives a higher probability of success than another *a priori*. Each situation requires a thorough analysis of the best way to enter the specific foreign market, but no general solutions can be given. The final decision often involves a trade-off between the firm's desire for control and the desire to maintain flexibility. Also factors such as risk preferences, resources, and capabilities may be included.

Phase 4 and 5: Designing and implementing the international marketing programme[4]

When a firm has reached a foreign market with the help of the chosen entry mode, resources must be committed. Furthermore, a high level of involvement is necessary to update the knowledge that will be used for later international involvement. A fundamental decision regarding the international marketing strategy across countries is the degree to which managers should standardize or adapt their international marketing mix. The standardization of the marketing mix is concerned with the extent to which individual elements of the 4Ps can be unified into a common approach for different national markets.

1.5 Summary

Conducting international marketing research is much more complex than domestic marketing research. Different methodological issues confront the cross-cultural researcher, as well as different practical considerations, such as the legal aspects of conducting research, and the culture's norm about sharing opinions with strangers. The viability of global marketing programmes will increasingly be assessed through multi-country marketing research studies. When conducting international marketing research, it is important to realize that, given the environmental differences, a research design appropriate for one country may not be suitable in another.

Questions

1. Define and describe marketing research and explain how it is related to the marketing concept.

2. Which factors would fuel the growth of international marketing research?

3. Which factors will determine whether a firm decides to "make-or-buy" – that is to outsource most of the market analysis tasks or conduct it themselves?

4. How might the following use international marketing research? Be specific.

    (a) Harley Davidson penetrating the Asian market.

    (b) IKEA opening a store in Brazil.

    (c) Absolut Vodka reviewing its market possibilities in Eastern Europe.

    (d) Heineken considering entering the market in the Middle East and trying to find an alliance partner.

    (e) The manufacturer of a female condom, the Female Health Company (www.femalehealth.com) is evaluating markets in Africa.

References

Craig, S.C. and Douglas, S.P. (2001) "Conducting international marketing research in the twenty-first century." *International Marketing Review*. Vol. 18, No. 1. 80–90.

Davenport, T. H. (2006) "Competing on analytics". *Harvard Business Review*. Vol. 84, Issue 1. 98–107.

Frevert, B. (2000) "Is global research different?" *Marketing Research*. Spring. 49–51.

Hansson, P. (2000) "Progresso soup tells soup lovers what they're missing." *American Demographics*. March. 10.

Hollensen, S. (2003) *Marketing Management: A relationship approach*. Financial Times/Prentice Hall. 362.

Hollensend, S. (2004) *Global Marketing: A decision-oriented approach*, 3rd edn. Financial Times/Prentice Hall.

Lee, J. A. (1966) "Cultural analysis in overseas operations." *Harvard Business Review*. March–April. 106–14.

Levitt, T. (1983) "The globalization of markets." *Harvard Business Review*. May–June. 1–11.

Malhotra, N. K., Agarwal, J. and Peterson, M. (1996) "Methodological issues in cross-cultural marketing research: A state-of-the-art review." *International Marketing Review*. Vol. 13, No. 5. 7–44.

Malhotra, N. K. and Birks, D. F. (2003) *Marketing Research: An applied approach*, 2nd edn. Financial Times/Prentice Hall, Harlow.

Malhotra, W. K. and Peterson, M. (2001) "Marketing research in the new millennium: emerging issues and trends." *Marketing Intelligence & Planning*. 19/4. 216–235.

Macharzina, K. (2001) "The end of pure global strategies." *Management International Review*. Vol. 41, No. 2. 105–108.

Shoham, A., Rose, G. M. and Albaum, G. S. (1995) "Export motives, psychological distance, and the EPRG-framework." *Journal of Global Marketing*. Vol. 8, No. 3–4. 9–37.

Wind, Y., Douglas, S. P. and Perlmutter, H. V. (1973) "Guidelines for developing international marketing strategy." *Journal of Marketing*. Vol. 37, April. 14–23.

End notes

[1] See Hollensen (2004), chapters 1–4.

[2] See Hollensen (2004), chapters 5–8.

[3] See Hollensen (2004), chapters 9–14.

[4] See Hollensen (2004), chapters 15–20.

2 Online and other secondary data sources

Learning objectives

After studying this chapter you should be able to:

- Define the secondary data sources used in international marketing research.
- Understand the advantages and disadvantages of secondary data.
- Evaluate the "quality" of secondary data sources.
- Describe some of the ways international marketers use secondary data.
- Understand the search process for secondary data.
- Explain the difference between "data warehouse" and "data mining."
- Explore the opportunities for searching secondary data using the internet.
- Discuss the problems associated with secondary data in international marketing.

2.1 Introduction

Secondary data is information that has been gathered by someone other than the researcher and/or for some other purpose than the project at hand. This chapter is concerned with externally available secondary sources, for which the specification, collection, and recording of the data are done by someone other than the user. This becomes evident when census data are used to analyze market demand. We will also look at secondary data that are collected especially for a set of information users with a common need. Such data are both purpose-specific and expensive, but still cheaper than each user gathering the information independently.

The amount of secondary data available is overwhelming, and researchers have to locate and use the data relevant to their research. Most search procedures follow a distinctive pattern, which begins with the most available and least costly sources. Figure 2.1 shows the various sources of secondary data.

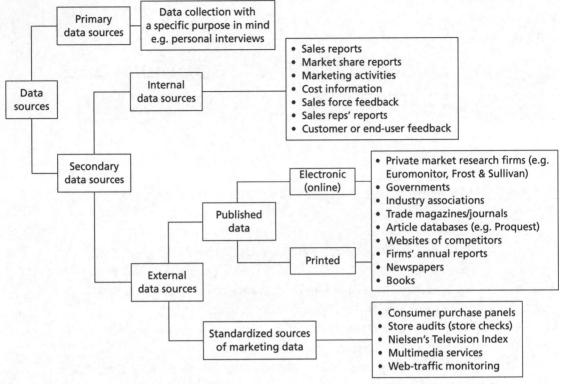

Figure 2.1 Sources of secondary data
Source: Adapted from Aaker, Kumar and Day (1998)

2.2 Advantages and disadvantages of secondary data

Table 2.1 provides an overview of the advantages and disadvantages of secondary data.

The most significant advantage secondary data offers is savings in cost and time. Secondary data research involves spending time in a library extracting the data and compiling relevant information. This involves little time, effort, and money compared with

Table 2.1 Advantages/disadvantages of secondary data

Advantages	Disadvantages
Quick way of obtaining data	Collected for some other purpose
Low cost	No control over data collection
Less effort expended	May not be accurate
Less time taken	May not be reported in the required form
Sometimes more accurate than primary data	May be outdated
Some information can be obtained only	May not meet data requirements
from secondary data	A number of assumptions have to be made

primary research. Even if the data are bought from another source, it will be cheaper than collecting primary data, because the cost of data collection is shared by all those using the data.

Certain research projects may not be feasible and in such cases, secondary data will be the only option. Historical data is always secondary data. If a firm wants to obtain information on incidents that happened in the past, it cannot conduct primary research to obtain it.

In some cases secondary data can be more accurate than primary data. For example, if a company wants information on the sales, profits, and so forth, of other companies, it can get more reliable and accurate information from government-released sources than from the companies themselves.

Despite the advantages of secondary data, there are also disadvantages. By definition, secondary data has been collected for purposes other than the current research. Hence, problems of fit are likely to occur between the data required for current research and the available data. The available data may have different units of measurement from those required. For example, consumer income can be measured and reported at the individual, family, or household level. Even assuming that the data use the same unit of measurement, there still may be differences in the class definition.

The researchers have no knowledge of how the data was collected, nor do they have any control over it. Therefore, they do not know anything about the level of accuracy or bounds of error, and so must make assumptions before they can do any analysis. It is also difficult to evaluate the accuracy of the data, because one can only gauge the level of accuracy by assessing research characteristics, such as the methodology or evidence of conscientious work. In many cases the secondary data may not be sufficient to meet the data requirement for the research at hand. In these cases, researchers may have to use primary research.

Secondary data may also be outdated, and hence cannot be used in current research. Some secondary data may only be published once. However, even for secondary data published at regular intervals, the time passed since the last publication can be a problem. Another issue frequently faced by researchers using secondary data is that the time from data collection to data publication is often lengthy; hence, the data is outdated even when first available. An example is a government census, which takes years to be published.

2.3 Evaluating secondary data

All information gathered must be evaluated before it is used as a basis for decision-making. To determine the reliability of secondary data, marketing researchers must evaluate it. This is done by answering these questions:

- What was the purpose of the study?
- Who collected the information?
- What information was collected?

- How was the information collected?
- How consistent is the information with other sources?

A discussion of each of these questions follows.

What was the purpose of the study?

Studies are conducted for a purpose and will indicate why the data was collected. However, studies are sometimes conducted in order to "prove" some position or advance the special interest of those conducting the study.

Who collected the information?

Even when convinced there is no bias in the purpose of a study, a researcher should question the competence of the organization that collected the information. Why? Because organizations differ in terms of the resources they command and also in their quality control. But how do you determine the competency of the organization that collected the data? There are several mechanisms for evaluation:

- Examination of the report. Competent firms provide carefully written and detailed explanations of the procedures and methods used in collecting the information.
- Ask others who have more experience in a given industry. Typically, professional organizations have a reputation based upon their credibility and experience.
- Ascertain customer satisfaction levels by contacting previous clients of the firm. Have they been satisfied with the quality of the work performed by the organization?

What information was collected?

There are many studies available on topics such as economic impact, market potential, feasibility, and the like, but what exactly was measured in the studies that constituted impact, potential, or feasibility? There are many examples of studies that claim to provide information on a specific subject but, in fact, measure something quite different. The important point here is that the user should discover exactly what information was collected.

How was the information collected?

Before evaluating *secondary* data, it should be remembered that it was gathered as *primary* data by someone. Therefore, the options for gathering the data had an effect on the nature and quality of the data. It is not always easy to find out how the secondary data was gathered.

Therefore researchers should be aware of the methods used to obtain information reported in secondary sources. What was the sample? How large was the sample? What was the response rate? Was the information validated? There are many ways of collecting primary data and each may influence the information collected.

Reputable organizations who provide secondary data also provide information about their data collection methods. If this information is not readily available and the use of the secondary data is very important to a research project, you should make the extra effort to find out how the information was obtained.

How consistent is the information with other sources?

In some cases, the same secondary data is reported by several different organizations, which provides an excellent way to evaluate secondary data sources. Ideally, if two or more independent organizations report the same data, you can have greater confidence in the validity and reliability of the data.

However, if all independent sources report very large differences of the same variable, then you may not have much confidence in any of the data. You should look at some of the factors already discussed to help understand why these differences may occur.

2.4 Sources of internal secondary data

The answers to many problems often lie within the files of an organization or in published material.

Internal data refers to data that has been collected within the firm. Such data includes sales records, purchase requisitions, and invoices. Obviously, a good marketing researcher always checks for internal information.

Internal databases are often available. These typically hold information gathered about customers. Think about the information you may have provided to marketing agencies: your name, address, telephone number, fax number, e-mail address, and so on. Coupled with a knowledge of what products you have purchased and other information provided by government and commercial sources, many companies know quite a bit about you. Although there are issues here regarding the privacy rights of consumers, companies do use their internal databases for direct marketing and to strengthen their relationships with customers.

Records of frequent customers and their transactions are maintained, and the companies use this data to identify trends among customers. This data can also be used to find out about customers' product preferences, form of payment, and so on. Holiday Inn has created a customer database for its Priority Club members to track their activities and transactions with the company. Such customer databases are used extensively by marketing managers for formulating relationship marketing strategies.

Increasingly, companies are augmenting internal records with systematic compilations of product returns, service records, and customer correspondence, in a manner that permits easy retrieval. Responding to the customer has become critical to maintain or increase sales. Complaint letters are being used as sources of data on product quality and service problems. One reason is the insight they can provide into the problems of small groups with unusual requirements, reactions, or problems. Complaint letters, however, can present an incomplete and distorted picture. People who write such letters are not typical clients or customers. They are most likely to be highly educated, articulate, and fussy, with more than average amounts of free time. A letter of complaint is an infrequently used method of resolving dissatisfaction; instead, people are more likely to switch brands, shop in a different store, or complain to friends.

Sometimes insightful analyses based on internal data are difficult because of limitations in the accounting system and distortions in the data. The first problem is that accounting systems are designed to satisfy many different needs. As a result, the reporting formats tend to be rigid and inappropriate for marketing decisions. Often the accounting data is too highly aggregated into summary results and not available for managerial units, such as geographic areas, customer types, or product types. Efforts to break down sales and profitability data by different units may involve special, time-consuming studies. Production, sales, and profit figures are each measured in slightly different time frames, which are all at variance with external data such as bimonthly store audit data.

Another problem is the quality of data in internal records. On the input side, the reports of salespeople's call activities may be exaggerated if they are being evaluated in this way, and the well-known optimism of sales staff may unconsciously pervade all such data. Even accounting data is not exempt from such problems. The usual interpretation of a sales invoice is compromised if liberal return privileges are permitted or if the product is purchased at one location, but delivered to or used in another. In general, whenever there is a long distribution channel, with several places where inventories can be accumulated, the data on orders received or invoices billed may not correspond to actual sales activity.

Global marketing and sales departments are the main points of commercial interaction between an organization and its foreign customers. Consequently, a great deal of information should be available, including the following:

- *Total sales*. Every company keeps a record of its total sales over a defined time period: for example, weekly or monthly records.
- *Sales by countries*. Sales statistics should be split up by countries. This is partly to measure the progress and competence of the export manager or the salesperson (sometimes to influence earnings because commission may be paid on sales) and partly to measure the degree of market penetration in a particular country.
- *Sales by products*. Most companies sell several products and keep records for each kind of product or, if the range is large, each product group.
- *Sales volume by market segment*. Such segmentation may be geographical or by type of industry. This will give an indication of segment trends in terms of whether they are static, declining or expanding.
- *Sales volume by type of channel distribution*. Where a company uses several distribution channels, it is possible to calculate the effectiveness and profitability of each type of channel. Such information allows marketing management to identify and develop promising channel opportunities, and results in more effective channel marketing.
- *Pricing information*. Historical information relating to price adjustments by product allows the organization to establish the effect of price changes on demand.
- *Communication mix information*. This includes historical data on the effects of advertising campaigns, sponsorship, and direct mail on sales. Such information can act as a guide to the likely effectiveness of communication expenditure plans.

■ *Sales representatives' records and reports.* Sales representatives should keep a visit card or file on every "live" customer. In addition, representatives often send reports to the sales office on such matters as orders lost to competitors and possible reasons why, as well as on firms that are planning purchasing decisions. Such information could help to bring improvements in marketing strategy.

Data warehouses

A data warehouse can be seen as a "super-database." It contains a collection of integrated databases designed to support decision-making.

Customer data warehouses can be seen as "gold mines" of information about the customer, from sources both internal to the company and from the customer and third sources, such as the government, credit bureaux and market research firms. Data can include behaviours, preferences, lifestyle information, transactional data and data about contact with the firm before, during and after the sale. It may include information about customer profitability, satisfaction, retention, loyalty, and referrals.

Customer data warehouses can be described in terms of the processes and layers needed to automate and add value to communications with the customer and to facilitate mass customization.

Data warehousing enables companies to extract information from the underlying data to develop a better understanding of the most profitable relationships. The process of exploring the databases uses data mining techniques. Data mining relies on statistical modelling and the other tools discussed below to turn information from a data warehouse into rules and patterns.

Data mining

Data mining is a process that employs information technology to uncover previously unknown patterns of behaviour, trends and issues from assessment of warehoused data (Thelen, Mottner and Berman, 2004).

The focus is on finding consumers' buying patterns to help marketers make better decisions. One example of data mining is the process of classification of customers into specific segments that are meaningful to decision-makers. The use of data mining may depend on a series of interactive, structured databases (data warehouse).

With the explosion of supermarket scanner data, data-mining techniques were developed to analyze sales data. The results portrayed the most important changes in a particular product's volume and market share, indicating location, product type, price level or other factor.

Still other knowledge discovery tools have concentrated on the movement of stock at a point of sale. Such information can support decisions about shelf-space allocation, store layout, promotional effectiveness, product location, and product turnover.

With data mining, the decision-maker discovers more from the data and explores new areas, integrating other sources of data, going through an iterative process to dig deeper. The statistical method underlying data mining is further addressed in chapter 17.

The customer information file

The benefits of keeping a customer information file, internal in the company, include (Gordon, 1998):

- Marketing effort becomes more efficient and more effective because a marketer is able to identify the most important customers and then present to them the right offer, product, or service at the right time.
- Information technology is harnessed to manage the vast amounts of data the marketer requires to interact with customers in a personalized manner.
- A true "dialogue" can be maintained with consumers by tracking interactions over time, identifying changes in purchasing, and allowing the marketer to anticipate changes.
- Product development is facilitated by knowing who has purchased a product, how satisfied he or she is and whether any changes would enhance the performance of the product.

In the following example, a customer information file (from the business-to-business market) is presented (only the most important data are shown):

EXHIBIT 2.1 A B2B CUSTOMER FILE

Identification
- Account or identification number
- Company name
- Main telephone number/fax/e-mail
- Website address

Background
- Business demographic
- Industry classification code (SIC)
- History of company
- Geography

Sales, profitability, cash flow and financial position
- Size: total sales
- Growth rate: total
- Size: relevant products
- Growth rate: relevant products
- Profitability: overall
- Profitability: relevant products
- Cash flow: overall
- Return on investment
- Operating profit on net sales

EXHIBIT 2.1 CONTINUED

Market position
- Market size for customer's products
- Market segment participation
- Market share
- Customer's major customers

Suppliers
- Big suppliers to this company
- Duration of relationships with big suppliers

Pre-sale contact
- Number of "touches" or contacts prior to purchases
- Types of information sought
- Channels of communication initiated by customer (telephone, online, interactive voice response, etc.), by type of information sought
- Call history: personal sales calls, by date, by audience

Purchases
- Purchase behaviour

Frequency
- Frequency with which purchases are made (per day, week, month, year)

Monetary value
- Amount spent on purchases
- Average margin on customer's purchase

Decision-makers
- Names, titles
- Our staff who have relationships with these people

Decision-making process/Buying centre
- Decision-initiators (users)
- Decision-influencers (influencers)
- Decision-makers
- Executors of decision (buyers)
- Gate-keepers

Purchase cycle
- Time required to make decision, by type of decision:
  - New buy
  - Modified rebuy
  - Rebuy

EXHIBIT 2.1 CONTINUED

Customer's buying criteria
- Vendor selection criteria
- Product selection criteria
- Main selection and patronage criteria, overall company
- Perceptions of our company in respect of criteria
- Perceptions of competitors in respect of criteria

Post-purchase behaviour
- Services required
- Items returned
- Condition in which returned
- Purchase amounts of returned product
- Tone and manner of return, customer
- Customer complaint frequency
- Customer satisfaction
  - Overall company satisfaction
  - Specific product/service satisfaction

Distribution channels used by customers
- Intermediaries used for product/service, type and name
- Customer satisfaction with channel intermediaries

Pricing
- Pricing history
- Pricing expectations
- Win/loss assessments: prices of winning vendors

Creditworthiness
- Debt history
- Receivables on account
- Payment schedule
- Credit scoring and rating

Selected relevant information
- Customer's customers
- Business strategies

Source: Adapted from: www.scip.com; www.companiesonline.com; Rothberg (1999)

Customer databases, data warehouses and the use of data-mining techniques promote a wider and shared use of data, with graphical ways of presenting data breaking down barriers for decision-makers, who have previously resisted formal statistical analyses.

2.5   Sources of external secondary data

Secondary data can be useful in exploratory work, as a news source or in marketing decisions. When used as part of an exploratory study, secondary data are often associated with long-range considerations, such as whether to consider developing a new product or service.

Published data sources (printed or electronic)

Published data is the most popular source of marketing information, being readily available, and often sufficient to answer many research questions. Studying the growth trends of production data over a period of years, for example, can help a manufacturer to identify new product lines or additions to a product line.

A marketing manager studying developments in the beer industry will use trade association data to learn how the total consumption of beer is broken down, by type of customer, geographic area, type of beer, brand, and distribution client. The data is available annually and sometimes quarterly, so trends can be isolated.

A person opening a shop will use census data on family characteristics and income to find a likely location. Demographic data would also be useful. Furthermore, a firm may establish territories for its sales staff using the population census.

The prospective user of published data is often confronted with the problem of matching a specific need for information with an array of secondary data sources of variable and often indeterminate quality. What is needed first is a flexible search procedure to ensure that no pertinent source is overlooked, and secondly, some general criteria for evaluating quality.

Search procedure

How should someone who is unfamiliar with a market or research topic proceed? In general, two basic rules are suggested: start with the general and go to the specific; and make use of all available expertise.

Step 1: Identify what you wish to know and what is known
This is the most important step in searching for information. Without having a clear understanding of what you are looking for, you will have difficulties. Clearly define your topic; the relevant facts; names of researchers or organizations associated with the topic; key papers and other publications; and any other information.

Step 2: List the main terms and names
These terms and names will provide access to secondary sources. Unless you have a very specific topic in mind, keep this initial list long and general. Use business dictionaries and handbooks to help develop the list.

Step 3: Begin the data search using the "easiest" sources
The best starting point is someone else who has conducted research on the same subject. Trade associations and specialized trade publications are particularly useful, for they often

compile government data and collect additional information from their subscribers or members. If information about a specific geographic area is sought, the local chamber of commerce is a good place to begin.

Types of external secondary sources

The key to obtaining census data in the industrial and services market is the **Standard Industrial Classification** system (SIC). This is a uniform numbering system for classifying establishments according to their economic activities. The total economy is first divided into 11 divisions, such as mining, manufacturing, retail trade, and public administration. Within each of these divisions, the main industry groups are classified by two-digit numbers, e.g.:

Classification	SIC number	Description
Major group	57	Home furniture, furnishings, and equipment stores
Industry sub-group	571	Home furniture and furnishing stores
Detailed industry	571.1	Furniture stores
	571.2	Floor covering stores

The SIC is often used by companies in order to segment their markets.

Compilations are intermediate sources that provide access to original sources. This is particularly desirable with statistical information. A standard work in this area is the *Statistical Abstract of the United States,* which contains selections from the various censuses as well as data collected by other agencies.

Private research firms are often overlooked by researchers yet they provide valuable information on trends and conditions in specific markets. Example companies include Frost and Sullivan, Predicasts, Euromonitor, Economist Inteligence Unit, Stanford Research Institute, and A. D. Little. Although their reports may be expensive, they are usually much cheaper than primary research.

Source databases provide numerical data, complex text, or a combination of both, and include the many economic and financial databases and textual source databases that contain the complete texts of newspaper and journal articles. As opposed to the indices and summaries in the reference database, source databases provide complete textual or numerical information. They can be classified into: full-text information sources; economic and financial statistical databases, and online data and descriptive information on companies.

For example, Lexis-Nexis has three services. Tracker scans thousands of publications daily and delivers relevant news for only those topics designated by the customer. PubWatch allows users to scan a publication's table of contents and select only the stories they want to read. AM News Brief provides news summaries every day. Market research reports from more than a dozen brand names such as Data Monitor, Find/SVP, and Nielsen are also available on Nexis.

Online databases can be accessed in real time directly from the producers of the database or through a vendor. To access online databases, all one needs is a personal computer, a modem, and a telephone line. These databases greatly reduce the time required for a search and bring data right to the desk.

Standardized sources and syndicated services are agencies that collect information and report their findings to subscribers. Usually, the data are not problem-specific, but are provided in a standardized format. Service providers include A.C. Nielsen for its television ratings in the US. Another example is Roper Starch, which uses a standardized approach to evaluate the effectiveness of print advertisements through its US readership survey.

From www.pearsoned.co.uk/schmidt you can be linked to relevant online international marketing databases.

2.6   Competitive intelligence (CI)

Competitive intelligence (CI) is a systematic way to identify and gather timely and relevant information about existing and potential competitors. Information gathered from relevant sources is analyzed to identify competitors' strategies. Maintaining an understanding of competitors' strengths and weaknesses puts an organization in a better position to exploit opportunities and alleviate threats, as well as to anticipate and respond to competition.

Competitor intelligence is based on published material and other types of information on competitors, current and potential, which provides an important basis for formulating strategy. No general would order an army to march without knowing the enemy's position and intentions. Likewise, before deciding which competitive moves to make, a firm must be aware of the perspectives of its competitors. CI includes information beyond industry statistics and trade gossip. It involves close observation of competitors to learn what they do best and why and where they are weak.

Most western countries have seen an intensification of competitor analysis. The reasons are:

- Increasing competition between companies
- Deregulation
- Liberalization of trade
- Globalization
- Periods of economic recession
- Reduced product and service differentiation.

Factors inhibiting the growth of CI include:

- Data protection
- Different legislation in various countries
- Fears that competitive intelligence is unethical
- Fears of counter intelligence
- Failure of competitive strategies to yield the expected gain.

The increasing use of CI is not a process that occurs in a single step. Rather, it takes place over a period of time during which there is a growing awareness of the need to have a competitor strategy, which is every bit as important as the customer strategies that are already commonplace (West, 1999).

Stages of "competitive awareness" development

Characteristics of the three stages of competitive development

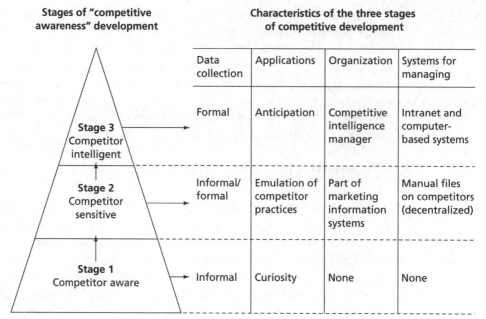

	Data collection	Applications	Organization	Systems for managing
Stage 3 Competitor intelligent	Formal	Anticipation	Competitive intelligence manager	Intranet and computer-based systems
Stage 2 Competitor sensitive	Informal/ formal	Emulation of competitor practices	Part of marketing information systems	Manual files on competitors (decentralized)
Stage 1 Competitor aware	Informal	Curiosity	None	None

Figure 2.2 Development of competitive intelligence
Source: Hollensen (2003)

In terms of their use of competitive intelligence, companies seem to go through a series of stages (see Figure 2.2). The first stage is competitor awareness. This begins soon after a company is formed, or even before, when the start-up is being planned. Being competitor aware means that competitors are known and that there is some knowledge – usually incomplete and certainly unverified – about their products, their prices, the clients they have won business from, the market sectors they service and the staff they employ.

The organization that is competitor-aware rarely uses the data that it holds other than for occasional tactical exercises, such as competitive pricing decisions, or as an input to a business plan that has to be submitted to an external organization, such as a bank, or a contractual tender bid.

As companies grow they tend to become competitor sensitive – both in terms of their awareness of the damage competitors can inflict on their business and the need to win orders by competing more effectively. Unfortunately, being competitor sensitive does not always increase the demand for information on competitors. An alarming proportion of competitor-sensitive companies continue to rely exclusively on informal information flows through their sales forces, business contacts and scans of the trade press, rather than a structured programme. When they do step outside the informal information channels the prime motive is usually emulation, seeking to copy what they perceive to be the best of their competitor's practices. There is nothing wrong with emulation as a business process, providing it is factually driven using such techniques as reverse engineering and competitor benchmarking, but it represents a limited application for the data that can be derived about competitors.

The organization that is competitor intelligent devotes resources to studying competitors and anticipating their actions. This includes: identifying competitors' physical and intangible resources; studying their organizations and their methods in as much detail as is practical; and developing knowledge of their strategies and potential game plans. The competitor intelligent organization is continuously aware of the threats posed by competitors, the nature and seriousness of those threats and what needs to be done to counteract them. They recognize the need to look forward to anticipate competitive actions and to predict the likely responses to actions they are proposing to take themselves. They are also aware that the most serious threats may arise from companies that are not yet active in their business sector.

There is a close parallel between the growth in competitor analysis and the development of customer analysis. There was a time when organizations were only customer aware.

Interest in competitive strategy was nurtured by books such as Michael Porter's *Competitive Advantage* and *Competitive Strategy* in the 1980s. This was accompanied by a short flirtation with marketing warfare that focused on beating the competition by adopting military tactics.

Competition is good for the customers because it means that companies have to try harder or lose their customer base. In many markets competition is the driving force of change.

Strategic and tactical levels

Strategic intelligence is future-oriented and allows an organization to make informed decisions concerning future conditions in the marketplace and/or industry. **Tactical intelligence** focuses on the present. This level of intelligence provides decision-makers with the information necessary to monitor changes in the company's current environment and proactively helps them search for new opportunities. To maximize the benefit of CI, the strategic and tactical levels must be co-ordinated and all partner companies treat co-ordination as a priority. These companies believe that co-ordinating strategic and tactical intelligence with sales and marketing has led to a strengthening in competitive positions as well as increases in customer satisfaction and customer retention.

Questions for competitive intelligence can include the following:

- Who are our competitors?
- How do we learn about our competitors? (How do we gather competitor information?)
- What are the strengths and weaknesses of our competitors (competitor audit)?
- What are the objectives and strategies of our competitors?
- What are the response patterns of our competitors?
- How can we set up an organization for competitive intelligence?

Gathering competitor information

The information-gathering techniques summarized below are all legally used to gain competitive insights, although some may involve questionable ethics. A responsible company should carefully review each technique before using it to avoid practices that might be illegal or unethical.

- Information from own staff and employees of competing companies. Firms can collect data about their competitors through interviews with new recruits or by speaking with employees of competing companies. When firms interview, e.g. students for jobs, they may pay special attention to those who have worked for competitors, even temporarily. Job-seekers are eager to impress and often have not been warned about divulging what is proprietary information. Companies send engineers to conferences and trade shows to question competitors' technical people. Another tactic in corporate intelligence gathering is to hire executives from competitors to find out what they know.
- Information from competitors' customers. Some customers may give out information on competitors' products. The co-operative relationship that is cultivated with the customer may encourage these customers to divulge competitor activities.
- Information from competitors' suppliers. A firm and its main competitor are sometimes supplied by the same subcontractor. As many firms today have close relations to their suppliers some information exchange may be possible.
- Information from observing competitors or by analyzing physical evidence. Companies can get to know competitors better by buying their products or by examining other physical evidence. Companies increasingly buy competitors' products and take them apart to determine costs of production and even manufacturing methods.
- Published materials and public documents. Examples of published material include: financial reports of the company; government reports; company presentation brochure; profiles in industry journals. Much of this information may be found on the web.

Why the web is a good source of competitive intelligence

Online resources will provide an array of basic information. However, just because something is on the web does not mean it is accurate. "www" is not the source of the data, it is just part of an electronic address. The analyst must document the author, method of data collection, date, publisher location, and purpose of publishing the data.

Experienced researchers question the authenticity of data until there has been an opportunity to assess the reliability of the online (and any other) data source. Although sales exaggerations affect few people, such a practice on the web could lead to vastly different conclusions unless the information and source credibility are questioned by those who use information in making important strategic decisions.

Falsifying data on the web is rare. However, the inability to police the internet could lead to inaccurate if not intentionally false data inputs. Always keep in mind the fact that it is up to the data collector to verify the quality of information found using the internet.

Types of competitive intelligence

In the broadest sense, data sources are either free or available for a fee. Paid-for services are of three types:

- A database that charges a monthly fee for access to data.
- Services that provide data to subscribers on a per-inquiry basis.
- Reports from research firms.

Subscription services

Numerous online data links give subscribers access to special databases. A subscription to Lexis-Nexis is one possibility. Subscribers get up-to-date information direct from www.lexisnexis.com. Lexis-Nexis is one of the leading business intelligence providers. More than 30,000 sources are covered with three billion searchable documents. Over a million documents are added every week. Nexis will provide regular reports (such as Lexis-monthly). Each of these updates would show any new article on this subject published in the past month.

There are many other online subscription services. Others include:

- Dun & Bradstreet, (www.dnb.com). There is also Dun & Bradstreet On-Line giving selected operating ratios by SIC code, credit reports, etc.
- Hoovers (www.hoovers.com) provides profiles of companies. A great deal of financial data is available.
- Moody (www.moodys.com) is useful for checking out the credit ratings of competitors.
- Database America (www.databaseamerica.com) provides current information on competitors' products and strategies.
- Euromonitor (www.euromonitor.com) publish market and competitor research reports.
- Phoenix Consulting Group (www.intellpros.com) provides competitive intelligence and counterintelligence services.
- Fuld & Company (www.fuld.com) is a pioneer in CI – in the US. It offers detailed descriptions of competitive intelligence, seminars and consulting services.
- Aware (www.marketing-intelligence.co.uk) provides CI for businesses in Europe and the UK.
- Datamonitor (www.datamonitor.com) provides market and competitor analyses.
- Current Analysis (www.currentanalysis.com) brings action-oriented CI to clients within 24–28 hours of a significant development.
- Free internet sources. High on any list of sites for those who want to start building CI systems using online sources should be industry or trade associations. Similarly, professional associations can provide valuable data.

Sources for general information

Perhaps one of the more interesting CI developments can be found when one looks at any of the various free global news retrieval services. These online services are of special interest because they are delivered to a computer as often as every 15 minutes. In some cases, the material is available before it is in print. Suppose a company is doing business throughout Europe or the US. How can it track news of special interest to its business? Here are some of the possibilities:

- Corporate Information (www.corporateinformation.com) allows searches on company names (250,000 company profiles) and industry in the US.
- Comfind (www.comfind.com) is a US service on industries, companies, and their products.
- Society of Competitive Intelligence Professionals (www.scip.org) offers assistance, articles, and advice.

Online annual reports

Several services provide free access to company annual reports, in PDF format so they look exactly like the printed version.

EXHIBIT 2.2 SHADOW TEAMS IN COMPETITOR INTELLIGENCE

Shadow teams provide a way to integrate a company's internal knowledge with external competitive intelligence. Shadow team members should represent a cross-functional composite, drawn from the organization's best and brightest employees. Each team's mission is to "shadow" a competitor and to learn everything possible about the rival from published data, firm personnel, contacts, etc. As information is collected and analyzed, the shadow team becomes a knowledge base that may soon operate as a think tank.

Case study: a pharmaceutical company

A medium-size US pharmaceutical company structured shadow teams around ailment classifications. During scanning activities, a shadow member heard a rumour from a FDA contact, which was corroborated by a field sales person, that a new drug positioned to rival the firm's market-leading product was close to receiving approval. An upcoming conference gave the shadow team an opportunity to gather intelligence and validate, or refute, the rumour. Personal contacts identified the academic institution conducting the competitor product trials. During an evening cocktail party, shadow team members independently engaged scientists in discussions about chemistry and related topics. In time, they learned about the trials, (although the product or sponsor was never noted by name), confirmed the FDA rumour and, just as important, identified new procedures employed in clinical testing.

Result 1: The firm acted on the information and launched a campaign to bolster its product's market share.

During this time, the shadow team was charged with finding out why competitors were constantly beating the firm to market with new drugs. Experience with competitor scientists at the conference prompted the team members to launch a counter-intelligence investigation of their own firm. They learned that their own scientists, both in-house and those contracted to run clinical trials, behaved similarly in terms of letting slip information to other scientists at conferences.

Result 2: A programme was created to develop awareness of protecting intellectual property and competitive information throughout the organization. The shadow team drove home the importance of not only learning, but of guarding knowledge.

Source: Adapted from Rothberg (1999); www.scip.com; and other public sources

- Report Gallery (www.reportgallery.com) has over 3,000 annual reports on US companies.
- Investor Relations Information Networks (www.irin.com) also covers US companies.
- Company Annual Reports On-Line (www.carol.co.uk) hold UK and European company reports.
- Corporate Direct, for Japanese companies, go to www.c-direct.ne.jp. There is a Japanese and English version.
- Get the Report (www.getthereport.com) provides all annual reports of German AGs.

Setting up an organization for CI

Competitive, or business, intelligence enhances a corporation's ability to succeed in global markets. It provides early warning intelligence and a framework for understanding and countering competitors' initiatives. Competitive activities can be monitored in-house or assigned to an outside agency.

Within the organization, competitive information should be acquired both at the corporate level and at the business division level. At the corporate level, CI is concerned with competitors' investment strengths and priorities. At the divisional level, the main interest is in marketing strategy, that is, product, pricing, distribution, and promotion strategies that a competitor is likely to pursue. The true payoff of CI comes from a divisional review.

The CI task can be assigned to various individuals but, whoever is given the task of gathering competitive intelligence should be allowed adequate time and money to do a thorough job.

2.7 Special problems and methods associated with secondary data

Two main problems are associated with secondary data in international marketing research: the accuracy of the data and the comparability of data obtained from different countries (Engle, 2005).

Different sources often report different values for the same macroeconomic factor, such as gross national product (GDP), or per-capita income. This casts doubt on the accuracy of the data. This may be due to different definitions and interpretations, for each of those statistics in different countries. The accuracy of data also varies from one country to another. Data from industrialized nations is likely to have a higher level of accuracy than data from developing countries, because of the difference in the sophistication of the procedures adopted. The level of literacy in a country also plays a role in the accuracy of the macroeconomic data.

Business statistics and income data vary because different countries have different tax structures. Hence, it may not be useful to compare these statistics across countries. Population censuses may not only be inaccurate, they also may vary in frequency and the year in which the information was collected.

Another problem is that the measurement units are not necessarily equivalent. For example, the cost of buying a television in Germany would be classified as an entertainment expense, whereas in the US it would be a furniture expense.

Use of secondary data

Secondary data is particularly useful in the screening of potential international markets in order to select the most attractive new markets. Once the appropriate markets have been selected and the initial market-entry decision has been made, the next step is to make an explicit evaluation of demand in those countries or markets. Because of the high costs and uncertainty associated with entering markets, management has to make an initial estimate of demand potential, and also project market trends. Four types of methods and data analyses are discussed here, regarding demand estimation in an international context.

Lead–lag analyses

This uses time-series (yearly) data from a country to project sales in other countries. This technique is based on the use of time-series data from one country to project sales in other countries. It assumes that the determinants of demand in the two countries are the same, and that only time separates them. This requires the diffusion process, and specifically the rate of diffusion, to be the same in all countries. Of course, this is not always the case, and it seems that products introduced more recently diffused more quickly (Craig and Douglas, 2000).

Figure 2.3 shows the principle behind the lead–lag analysis by an illustrative example in the DVD market. By the end of 2003 it is assumed that 55 percent of the US-households have at least one DVD in their home, whereas it is assumed that "only" 20 percent of Italian households have a DVD. If we were to estimate the future penetration of DVDs in Italian households (and as a consequence also demand) we could make a parallel displacement of the US penetration S-curve by two years, as illustrated in Figure 2.3. This also shows how rapidly products are diffused from market to market. The difficulty in using the lead-lag analysis includes the problem of identifying the relevant time lag and the factors that influence future demand. However, the technique has considerable intuitive appeal to managers and is likely to guide some of their thinking.

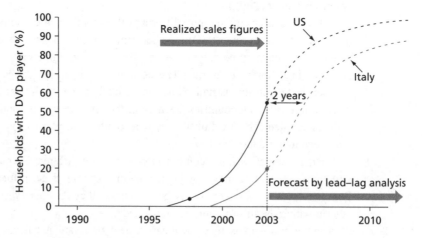

Figure 2.3 Lead–lag analysis of penetration of DVD players
Source: Hollensen (2004)

Table 2.2 Global installed generating capacity for wind power in 2003

Country/region	Generating capacity (MW) installed by end of 2003	Capacity installed MW during 2003
USA	6,361	1,687
Canada	351	81
South and Middle America	193	50
Total America	6,905	1,818
Germany	15,371	2,674
Spain	6,420	1,572
Denmark	3,076	218
Netherlands	938	233
Italy	922	116
Greece	538	76
Sweden	428	56
Austria	415	285
Portugal	311	107
France	274	91
Ireland (Rep.)	230	63
Norway	101	4
Belgium	78	33
Poland	55	1
Finland	53	9
Turkey	20	1
Switzerland	6	0
Other European countries	65	10
Total Europe	29,301	5,549
India	2,125	423
Japan	761	275
P.R. China	571	98
Other Asian countries	33	8
Total Asia	3,490	804
Australia & NZ	294	70
North Africa	211	63
Middle East	71	39
Gulf States	24	2
Other countries	5	1
Total other continents	605	175
Total worldwide	40,301	8,346

Source: Adapted from public sources; including BTM Consult (www.btm.dk); Deutsche Windenergie-Institut (www.dewi.de); and Ender (2004a)

Figure 2.4 shows the total generating capacity of wind turbines in Germany (curve with scale to the right), together with added generating capacity each year (left scale).

Furthermore, information is needed about the potential geographic segment(s) in Germany. The report cited earlier provides the figures for Table 2.3.

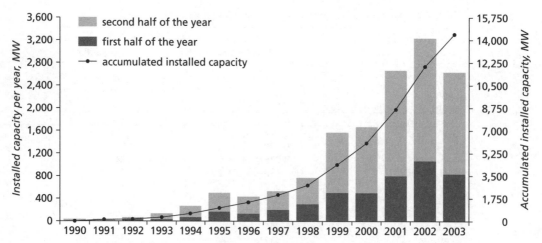

Figure 2.4 Market growth of installed wind turbines in Germany
Source: Ender (2004), 9

Table 2.3 Installed wind turbines (WT) and generating capacity in each *Bundesländer* (2003) (WEA = WT = Wind Energie Anlagen)

Bundesland Federal State	In 2003 errichtet WEA WT installed in 2003		In 2003 abgebaote WEA WT pulled down in 2003	
	Anzahl der WEA Number of WT	Installierte Leistung Installed Capacity MW	Installierte WEA Durchschnittsleistung Average Installed Power per WT kW	Anzahl der WEA Number of WT	Installierte Leistung Installed Capacity MW
Niedersachsen	381	603.10	1,582.9	25	6.60
Brandenburg	339	550.12	1,622.8	0	0.00
Nordrhein-Westfalen	279	377.60	1,353.4	2	0.58
Sachsen-Anhalt	164	303.70	1,650.5	0	0.00
Schleswig-Holstein	139	229.76	1,662.9	40	22.00
Mecklenburg-Vorpommern	88	137.90	1,567.0	0	22.00
Thüringen	81	132.95	1,641.4	0	0.00
Sachsen	59	102.45	1,736.4	0	0.00
Rheinland-Pfalz	59	92.40	1,566.1	1	0.00
Hessen	30	34.60	1,153.3	0	0.50
Bayern	29	34.55	1,191.4	0	0.00
Baden-Württemberg	25	32.40	1,296.0	0	0.00
Saarland	7	10.80	1,542.9	0	0.00
Hamburg	3	2.20	0.0	0	0.00
Bremen	0	0.00	0.0	0	0.00
Berlin	0	0.00	0.0	0	0.00

Source: Ender (2004), 12

From adding up the "Number of WT" column, it appears that the biggest market for Monitoring Systems exists in the northern part of Germany. The number of turbines installed in Germany (2003) was 1703.

Figure 2.5 Total number of turbines (WEA), installed MW and average capacity (kW/turbine) (end of 2003)
Source: Ender (2004), 11

Figure 2.5 shows the number for wind turbines in each state, installed generating capacity (MW), and the average size (in kW) of the turbines in the different *Bundesländer*.

To develop a strategy for targeting the manufacturers, information is needed on their market shares (see Figure 2.6). So, to target the northern part of Germany, it is a good idea to contact turbine makers that are strong in that region.

The market leader in 2003 was Enercon, followed by Vestas (which merged with NEG Micon in May 2004) and GE Wind Energy.

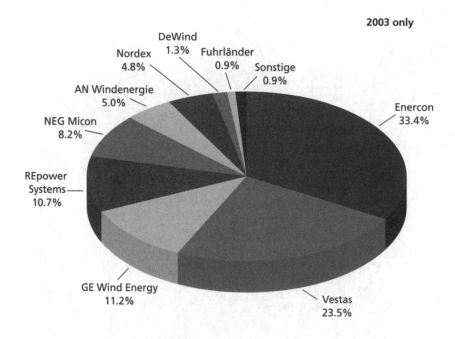

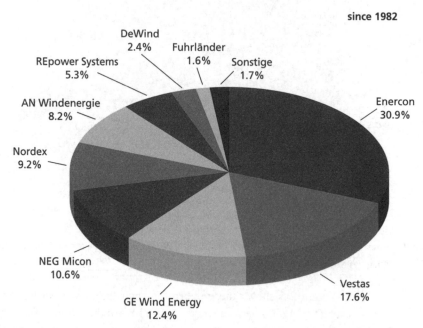

Figure 2.6 Market shares of turbine makers in Germany: 2003 only; and since 1982
Source: Ender (2004), 16

In terms of regional market shares, the leader in the northern part of the country is Enercon, followed by two Danish manufacturers, Vestas and NEG Micon (which merged in May 2004) (Table 2.4).

Table 2.4 Regional distribution of market shares

	Market shares 2003						
	AN Winden.	Enercon	GE Wind Energy	NEG Micon	REpower	Nordex	Vestas
Niedersachsen	9.3%	54.7%	8.2%	4.7%	1.5%	4.5%	16.4%
Schleswig-Holstein	9.6%	15.7%	0.0%	5.5%	27.9%	10.0%	31.3%
Nordrhein-Westfalen	2.8%	41.3%	21.2%	3.5%	8.1%	2.4%	16.8%
Mecklenburg-Vorpommern	0.0%	1.7%	27.2%	2.4%	21.8%	3.6%	43.3%
Hessen	0.0%	18.5%	0.0%	0.0%	34.7%	4.3%	0.0%
Sachsen-Anhalt	11.8%	22.3%	10.9%	18.4%	3.1%	1.1%	32.4%
Brandenburg	1.3%	20.9%	10.4%	18.9%	12.0%	5.3%	30.4%
Thüringen	1.0%	28.4%	3.4%	0.0%	36.1%	11.3%	18.7%
Rheinland-Pfalz	0.0%	42.1%	21.1%	0.0%	0.0%	11.9%	14.9%
Sachsen	0.0%	50.8%	14.6%	0.0%	3.4%	0.0%	18.5%
Sonstige	0.0%	52.8%	0.0%	0.0%	14.0%	3.8%	5.0%

Source: Ender (2004), 17

Table 2.5 Summary of target market for Monitoring Systems

Target market: Bundesländer	Number of turbines installed in 2003 (Table 2.3) (manufacturer market)	Total number of turbines at end of 2003 (Figure 2.5) (after-installation market)
Niedersachsen	581	3,982
Brandenburg	339	1,556
Sachsen-Anhalt	184	1,335
Nordrhein-Westfalen	279	2,125
Schleswig-Holstein	139	2,612
Top 5 wind energy *Bundesländer*	1,522	11,610
Total Germany	1,703	15,387
% Top 5 wind energy *Bundesländer*/Total Germany	89%	75%

The following keywords in Google: "wind turbines" AND Germany AND manufacturer AND statistics AND "market share" generate a link to the website: http://reisi.iset.uni-kassel.de/wind/reisi_dw.html

From here, Monitoring Systems can see where the turbines are located in northern Germany. This information is important if the company chooses to follow an after-installation strategy. The main market is in the north-western part of Germany.

Conclusion

The resulting target market is summed up in Table 2.5.

Implications for future marketing activities

Based on this analysis, a *dual marketing strategy* can be recommended:

- On the *manufacturer (OEM) market*, where the monitoring system is sold as an integral part of the turbine, Monitoring Systems should concentrate on the following manufacturers:
  - Enercon (www.enercon.de)
  - Vestas (including Micon from May 2004) (www.vestas.dk)

  Though the German manufacturer, Enercon, is the market leader, its exports are limited. By approaching the Danish manufacturer, Vestas, Monitoring Systems gains access to an internationalized company with a large percentage of exports. Vestas would also provide a ready-made export route to countries other than Germany.
- On the *after-installation* market, Monitoring Systems should concentrate on the northern part of Germany. Nearly 90% of the market is concentrated in five northern *Bundesländer*.

2.9 Summary

The chapter has considered the various sources of secondary data and suggested systematic ways of searching for appropriate data or information relevant to a marketing problem. There is a surprising amoung of material available for little effort. Even if they are not entirely suitable, secondary data sources can provide useful pointers on how to design a research study.

Many management problems can be resolved by access to the firm's internal records or to secondary sources such as government statistics, trade association reports, periodicals, books, and the various databases accessed via the internet.

In terms of secondary consumer intelligence data, numerous resources are available to market researchers on the web. General characteristics of consumer markets can be obtained from the many government-based and private statistical services and many of these are online. This information can be used to generate a situational analysis of select target markets and design strategies according to the characteristics of consumers in that specific market. Product and media consumption data are increasingly in demand, especially due to the growth of new media. Such data can help marketers make strategic marketing decisions about new and existing products and the appropriate media vehicles to use for promotion.

The web has opened up opportunities for organizations to set up a competitive intelligence system in-house, so it is both cost-effective and timely. There is a vast number of resources that can be accessed online. The abundance of information may create problems for researchers who do not have the skills to filter relevant information.

Questions

1. Why is it important to know the purpose of a study based on secondary data?

2. Why should a company use all potential sources of secondary data before initiating primary data research?

3. Why is secondary often preferred to primary data?

4. What pitfalls might a researcher encounter in using secondary data?

5. What is the difference between internal and external secondary data?

6. On what criteria should secondary data be evaluated?

7. What are the major sources of competitive intelligence?

8. How would you design a CI system?

9. Collect data on beer consumption in your country for the latest available year. Calculate the per-capita consumption for your country and compare it with other countries, where data is available. What accounts for possible differences?

10. What is the difference between "data warehouse" and "data mining"?

11. Why is the internet of such great value to researchers seeking secondary data?

References

Aaker, D. A., Kumar, V. and Day, G. S. (1998) *Marketing Research*, 6th edn. John Wiley, New York. 106.

Craig, C. S. and Douglas, S. P. (2000) "Configural advantage in global markets." *Journal of International Marketing*. Vol. 8, no. 1. 6–27.

Ender, C. (2004) "Windenergienutzung in der Bundesrepublik Deutschland." *DEWI Magazin*. DEWI, Wilhelshaven, no. 24. 6–18.

Ender, C. (2004a) "International Entwicklung der Windenergie nutzung mit." *DEWI Magazin*. DEWI, Wilhelshaven, no. 25. 26–30.

Engle, R. L. (2005) "Global Marketing: A tale of two multinational companies". *Problems and Perspectives in Management*. No.3, 128–360.

Gordon, I. (1998) *Relationship Marketing*. John Wiley, Canada.

Hollensen, S. (2003) *Marketing Management: A relationship approach*. Financial Times/Prentice Hall, Harlow. 169.

Hollensen, S. (2004) *Global Marketing: A decision-oriented approach*, 3rd edn. Financial Times/Prentice Hall, Harlow. 142.

Neuborne, E. (2003) "Know thy enemy." *Sales and Marketing Management.* January. 29–33.

Rothberg, H. N. (1999) "Fortifying strategic decisions with shadow teams: a glance at product development." *Competitive Intelligence Magazine.* April–June, vol. 2, no. 2. 6–10.

Thelen, S., Mottner, S. and Berman, B. (2004) "Data mining: on the trail to marketing gold." *Business Horizons.* 47/6. 25–32.

West, C. (1999) "Competitive Intelligence in Europe" *Business Information Review.* Vol. 16, no. 3 (September). 143–150.

3 Observational and tracking methods

Learning objectives

After studying this chapter you should be able to:

- Understand the characteristics of observational methods years.
- Determine appropriate tracking research methods to be used as an alternative to questionnaires.
- Describe the types of mechanical observation.
- Explore the way retail scanner research has changed the marketing research industry.
- Discuss the main type of human observation: "mystery shopping."
- Explain the advantages and limitations of observational methods.

3.1 Introduction

Observation is the process of watching actual human behaviour, phenomena or events and recording them as they occur. Like many marketing research tools, modern observational research has its roots in anthropology and sociology. The technique began as participant observation around the turn of the century when anthropologists began collecting data first-hand. Observation does not often appear as a research methodology in the marketing literature: this may be because it is sometimes hard to quantify the outcomes of observational research at the outset, or because it is considered time-consuming, or sometimes, it may be difficult to generalize the findings. Nevertheless, in cross-cultural market research, observation may be the only way to obtain data on consumers' behaviour in some situations. A researcher with no knowledge of the culture may not know what questions to ask in a questionnaire. In such a situation, videotaping of consumers ensures that a visual record is compiled, and helps to bring home issues relating to a specific cultural context. Videotaping also provides a wealth of information about visual cues and their role in product evaluation and purchase behaviour. These cues are not easily obtained from other forms of data collection.

3.2 Criteria for using observation

Observation is an appropriate methodology for conducting market research when at least one of four criteria is met (Boote and Mathews, 1999).

1. The phenomenon is easily observable

For example, if a researcher wants to know why an individual or a family purchased a certain car, observation research may not provide the answer. This is because the consumer behaviour being studied is public, rather than private, behaviour. **Public behaviour** refers to behaviour that occurs in a setting the researcher can readily observe. Actions such as cooking, playing with one's children, or private worshipping are not public activities and are therefore not suitable for observational studies.

One of the main advantages of observational research is the way it gives direct access to social interaction. It is a flexible technique, and can be used very effectively to enrich and supplement other methods. It can also be used profitably at the start of a study to uncover promising areas of investigation. From the respondents' point of view, it is probably the most convenient form of data gathering because it requires no effort on their part. In the case of covert participant observation, however, there may be an ethical dimension to be considered if the actions of the individual being observed are criminal or reprehensible.

2. The phenomenon is a social process or a mass activity

Observation is useful in the analysis of large-scale social processes, or mass-activities, where a pattern of activity is under investigation, and aggregate statistics are all that is required. The behaviour of interest must be repetitive, frequent, and of relatively short duration. This means that the event must begin and end within a reasonably short time. Suitable examples include a shopping trip to a supermarket, waiting in a queue at a bank, buying an item of clothing, and observing children as they watch television.

Some decisions take a long time, and it would be unrealistic to observe the entire process. Observation of the entire decision-making process for purchasing a house, which might take months, is not feasible. Because of this, observational research is usually limited to scrutinizing activities that can be completed in a relatively short time or to observing certain phases of activities with a long time span.

3. The phenomenon occurs at a subconscious level

Observation is useful for examining subconscious influences on consumer behaviour, for example, the studies linking music to shopping behaviour. Leicester University's Music Research Group reported that the *type* of music played can influence the *type* of product sold (Hawkes, 1997). Such research is best investigated by observation because respondents to a questionnaire would probably regard themselves as being too sophisticated to allow music to influence their speed of shopping and the type of products they buy. Observational techniques, being unobtrusive, can uncover links between subtle influences and subconscious changes in shopping and buying behaviour; linkages that may not be uncovered through other methodologies. Also, what people say is often different from what they do. Observation can provide an accurate record of individuals' actions in situations where they do not wish to reveal their behaviour or where they genuinely do not have a "conscious" reason for their behaviour.

Faulty recall occurs when actions or activities are so automatic that the respondent cannot recall specifics about the behaviour under question. Observation is necessary under such circumstances to understand the behaviour at hand. For instance, an observation technique called "actual radio measurement" using a high-gain antenna, digital frequency scanner and computer, can be used to determine which radio stations were listened to by commuters in their cars.

4. Consumers are either unable or unwilling to communicate directly with the researcher

For a television programme such as *Postman Pat*, which is aimed at pre-school-aged children, any research aimed at gauging their reactions would have to be observationally based because the children themselves are still learning to communicate. More information could be gleaned by observing the children watching the programme than by attempting to ask them even simple questions.

3.3 Classification of observation methods

Qualitative techniques include the class of **observation methods** – techniques in which the researcher relies on powers of observation rather than communicating with a respondent in order to obtain information. Observation requires something to watch and because our memories are faulty, researchers depend on devices such as videotapes, audiotapes, handwritten notes, or some other tangible record.

At first glance, it may seem that observation studies can occur without any structure; however, it is important to adhere to a plan so that observations are consistent and comparisons or generalizations can be made without worrying about anything confounding the findings. There are strong arguments for considering the observation of continuing behaviour as an integral part of the research design. Some of these are the following:

- **Casual observation** is an important exploratory method. Managers continually monitor such variables as competitive prices and advertising activity, the number of customers waiting for service, and the trade journals on executives' desks, to help to identify problems and opportunities.
- **Systematic observation** can be a useful supplement to other methods. During a personal interview, the interviewer has the opportunity to note the type, condition, and size of the residence, the respondent's race, and the type of neighbourhood with regard to locality and qualities of homes. Seldom is this data source adequately exploited in surveys.

- "Simple" observation may be the least expensive and most accurate method of collecting purely behavioural data such as in-store traffic patterns or traffic passing a certain point on a road. Thus, people's adherence to safety rules before and after a safety campaign can be measured most easily by counting the number of people who cross against a red light.

Sometimes observation is the only research option. This is the case with physiological phenomena or with young children who cannot articulate their preferences or motives.

Note that each observation technique is unique in how it obtains observations. There are two general ways of organizing observations:

- direct versus indirect,
- disguised versus undisguised.

Direct versus indirect observation

Observing behaviour as it occurs is called **direct observation**. For example, to find out how often shoppers squeeze tomatoes to assess their freshness, researchers can watch people actually picking up the tomatoes.

Observing types of hidden behaviour, such as past behaviour, relies on indirect observation. With **indirect observation**, the researcher sees the effects or results of the behaviour rather than the behaviour itself. Types of indirect observations include archives and physical traces.

Archives are secondary sources such as historical records. These sources contain a wealth of information and should not be overlooked or underestimated. Many types of archives exist. For example, records of calls may be inspected to determine how often salespeople make cold calls.

Physical traces are tangible evidences of some event, consumption or conducted behaviour. For example, "garbology" (observing the trash of subjects being studied) as a way to analyze household consumption patterns. See Cote, McCullough and Reilley (1985), Ritenbaugh and Harrison (1984).

When questionnaire-based methods appear to provide invalid results, the analyst will need to look for other means of gathering data. Research based on retail scanners and software for tracking surfers' behaviour on the web (see below) are sophisticated ways of gathering data.

Alternative techniques of data gathering usually imply that the respondent is not aware of the behaviour being researched. Therefore such methods are sometimes called **nonreactive** or **unobtrusive** techniques in an attempt to differentiate them from reactive or obtrusive ways (questionnaire-based methods).

"Classical" examples of empirical unobtrusive studies are (Webb et al., 2000, 35–52):

- The wear of floor tiles in a museum indexed by the replacement rate was used to determine the relative popularity of exhibits.
- The setting of car radio dials brought in for service was used to estimate share of listening audience of various radio stations.

■ Cigarette butts collected after a football game were treated as indicator of market shares of selected brands.

Advantages of unobtrusive methods, according to Kellehear (1993) are:

■ The study of actual rather than reported behaviour.
■ Safety (they are regarded as discreet and harmless).
■ Repeatability (re-checking is possible).
■ Non-disruptive, non-reactive.
■ Research access is easy (co-operation of others is rarely needed).
■ Inexpensive.
■ Good for analysis over time.

Disadvantages of unobtrusive methods, according to Kellehear (1993) are:

■ The records may be of poor quality or distorted.
■ Records are seen from the point of view of the stranger (de-contextualizing).
■ Intervening (exogenous) variables may distort data.
■ Recording is selective and may be biased.
■ Over-reliance on a single method.
■ The application (interrogation) range is limited (the focus is narrow).

Marketing research in action
Unobtrusive indirect observational research

A sample of nationally distributed flyers was collected at recycling centres and analyzed for fingerprints by an expert, for an empirical study aimed at determining the readership patterns of sales flyers.

A total of 117 sales flyers was collected across seven different retailers/distributors (column I). The flyers were of different sizes, ranging from six to 120 pages (front and rear pages were ignored). The total number of pages analyzed was 4,370. Some 32 percent (38/117) flyers contained at least one valid fingerprint. The 4,370 pages revealed 395 fingerprints corresponding to 9 percent. The "readership" of a flyer was estimated by dividing the number of issues with a positive identification of at least one valid fingerprint (column II) by the total number of issues of the flyer (column I). While the fingerprint approach to assessing readership appears to be inappropriate for flyers that do not have many pages, it seems to work for voluminous flyers like Flyer 1. Flyers of more than 100 pages appear to contain several fingerprints provided they have been studied. When reading a catalogue, the reader needs to wet her/his finger several times. When the wetted finger is used for flipping the page, a trace consisting of 98 percent water and 2 percent amino acid is left on the page. Amino acid can be made visible using chemical materials. The study is described in Schmidt and Krause (2000, 2001); www.mic.cbs.dk/marcus/GBPapers/38_FPs/38_Fingerprints%20JMR.htm   ➤

In addition, a telephone survey conducted by a research agency had shown that 59 percent of respondents had reported reading Flyer 1 regularly. However, according to Table 3.1, 76 percent of the issues analyzed contained fingerprints. The company that distributes the flyer sells advertising space in its pages to a lot of producers of brands. The cost of advertising space corresponds closely to the readership as reported by the research agency (59 percent). Assuming that the fingerprint method is a valid measure of readership, the distributor of the flyer is charging too little for the advertising space.

Table 3.1 Assessing readership of sales flyers by identification of fingerprints (FPs) on pages

	I	II	II	IV	V	VI	VII	VIII
	No. issues	+ FPs	− FPs	Valid pages per issue	Total no. pages (I × IV)	Total no. with valid FPs	Fraction of pages with FPs (VI/V)	Readership (II/I)
Flyer 1	25	19	6	118	2950	324	.11	76%
Flyer 2	16	5	11	22	352	34	.10	31%
Flyer 3	13	4	9	22	286	11	.04	31%
Flyer 4	44	5	39	14	616	12	.02	11%
Flyer 5	9	3	6	6	54	6	.11	33%
Flyer 6	6	1	5	4	24	1	.04	17%
Flyer 7	4	1	3	22	88	7	.08	25%
Totals	117	38	79	–	4370	395	.09	32%

Disguised versus undisguised

Disguised observation is another method where the subject is unaware of being observed. In contrast to unobtrusive techniques that deal with traces of *past behaviour*, disguised methods analyze respondents' *current* behaviour. An example of this is "mystery shopping," where researchers pose as customers to record and report on staff. One-way mirrors and hidden cameras are other ways of preventing subjects from becoming aware that they are being observed. This disguise is important because if the observed were aware of the observation, they might change their behaviour, resulting in observations of atypical behaviour.

Sometimes it is impossible for the respondent to be unaware of the observation, and this is a case of **undisguised observation**. Laboratory settings, observing a sales representative's behaviour on sales calls, and people meters (a device that is attached to a television set to record when and to what station a set is tuned), must all be used with the subject's knowledge. Because people might be influenced by knowing that they are being observed, it is wise to minimize the presence of the observer to the maximum extent possible.

Machine versus human observation

Observation is often analyzed in terms of who (or what) is doing the observation. Where the observation is less structured, particularly in the initial stages of a research project, a person, rather than a device, is often considered to be appropriate because, while a device is superior in terms of speed, a human-being is superior in terms of interpretation. Large-scale, statistically-driven observation often necessitates the use of a mechanical device as the observer – such as an electronic point of sale scanner, which is used to track sales. It is also the case that certain observable phenomena may not be visible to the naked eye – hence the development of equipment such as the pupilometer and the psychogal-vanometer.

3.4 Mechanical observation methods

In many situations the use of devices is more suitable than a person collecting primary data. Such devices may reduce the cost and improve the flexibility, accuracy and other functions of data collection. For example, it would not be feasible for researchers to sit in people's homes to record television viewing habits. Cameras and audiovisual devices can record behaviour more objectively and in greater detail than human observers. Several types of devices are used to measure and collect physiological actions and reactions of consumers.

Traffic counters

Together with retail scanners, this is perhaps the most common form of mechanical observation research. As the name implies, the devices are used to measure the vehicular flow over a particular stretch of road. In countries where billboards are used, outdoor advisers rely on traffic counts to determine the number of exposures per day to a specific hoarding. Retail chains use the information to ascertain where to place a particular type of store. For example, convenience stores require a moderately high traffic volume to reach target levels of profitability.

Retail scanners

Scanners at grocery checkout counters, read a product's bar code (which holds the universal product code) and automatically print out the price. The result is a cash register receipt prepared, in the ideal case, entirely without manual data entry.

The information scanned not only provides pricing information, but is also stored in a computer where it is used to update inventory records and trigger necessary reorders. A shop no longer needs to rely on average sales or a time-consuming physical inventory to determine which items to order each day, because it has a daily record of what was sold the day before. The data have value beyond the individual store and store chain as well.

A manufacturer that has access to scanner data from a random sample of shops has an instant access to the market share of his brands. This scanner data enables the manufacturer to assess in which stores the products do well and where more effort is needed. Third, a retail chain can quickly react to changes in demand for the products it sells.

Marketing research in action

Wal-Mart's quick reaction

On the afternoon of 11 September 2001, managers at Wal-Mart were alerted to a sudden and significant rise in demand for US flags by the company's information system and data mining software. Immediately, a large order for flags was made. Because of the size of the order, US production capacity was absorbed by Wal-Mart for several days. When the managers of competing retailers a day or so later became aware of the same increase in demand for flags at *their* stores, they also ordered more flags. However, all capacity for the next days was occupied by the order from Wal-Mart. Some days later, Wal-Mart managers noticed a decline in the demand for the flags. Consequently, they resold most of the flags still on stock to producers who took them back so they could meet orders from Wal-Mart's competitors. When the competitors finally received the flags they found out that demand for them had almost vanished. *Source*: Roussel-Dupre (2002)

The ability to correlate scanner-recorded sales with special offers, advertising and displays could yield insights into the effectiveness of each of these marketing tools (Ghosh, 1997). Scanner-based technology is expected to replace consumer purchasing diary methods within a decade.

A **scanner-based panel** typically consists of between 2,000 and 6,000 representatively selected households. Panel members shop, using a unique bar-coded identity card, which is presented at the tills in scanner-equipped stores. In this way, it is possible to track each household's purchasing, item by item. The system allows researchers to build an extensive purchase behaviour database on each household. With such a measure of household purchasing, it is possible to manipulate marketing variables, such as TV advertising or consumer promotions, or introduce a product and analyze changes in consumer buying behaviour.

For strategic tests of potential marketing plans, the scanner-based panel can be split into two or more subgroups. Then, through direct marketing, a different treatment can be delivered to each group. Resulting sales and profits are analyzed. For advertising issues, one half of the panel could view a test commercial, the other half a control advert. In summary, scanner-based panels allows the marketing manager to answer critical marketing questions such as:

- What volume level is possible with my brand?
- Who are my brand's buyers and what else do they buy?
- How many consumers will try my new brand and how many will try it again?
- Will a product line extension "steal" market share from my existing brands?
- What are the sales implications of a change in advertising, price, package, or shelf placement?

Pupilometer

This device observes and records changes in the diameter of a person's pupils. The subjects view an advertisement at a constant brightness and distance. The assumption is that increased pupil size reflects positive attitudes, interest, and arousal in an advertisement. A pupilometer may help the manufacturer to find out if consumers perceive the message of an advertisement in the way it was intended. Assume, for example, that the pupilometer-test of an advertisement for potato chips reveals that the consumers' interest centres on a delicious steak that appears in the advertisement along with the chips. The insight obtained by the pupilometer-test may motivate the producer to change the advertisement, say, by making the chips look more appetizing.

Eye-tracking monitor

This device observes and records a person's unconscious eye movements. The monitor can determine which parts of the stimulus (e.g. a magazine advert, TV commercial, package design) are seen and which are ignored. This data can provide insights to alter selling points in advertising. Assume that a sample of consumers is asked to monitor an advertisement for an expensive healthcare product. However, the eye tracking shows that the respondents focus on the attractive model and on the price, but that they ignore the product specification and the brand's name. This finding may cause the producer to reconsider the advertising layout.

Electroencephalogram (EEG)

This device measures rhythmic electrical fluctuations of the brain. It is probably the most sensitive procedure for detecting arousal, but it also involves expensive laboratory equipment, and complex data analysis using sophisticated software. Market researchers claim EEG can be used for evaluating, among other effects, viewers' attention and their understanding of an advertisement.

Galvanic skin response (GSR)

The device resembles a lie detector and measures changes in the electric resistance of the skin associated with activation responses. A small electric current of constant intensity is applied to the skin via electrodes attached to the fingers. Changes in the voltage between the electrodes indicate the level of stimulation. GSR is a popular device for measuring activation, because the equipment is portable and not expensive. It is used primarily to measure stimulus response to print adverts or TV commercials.

People meter

This device is a microwave-based device, that replaces passive meters and handwritten diaries. The device is connected to the television set and the data it provides are used to measure the size of television audiences. It provides information on what shows are being watched, the number of households watching, and which family members are watching. Activity is recorded automatically; household members only have to indicate their presence in the room by pressing a button.

Website tracking

Website visitors leave traces, cookies, which are small files stored on a web surfer's computer that identify the user's computer. Tracking software can examine people's browsing and interactive website behaviour, so measuring the popularity of websites. The software is installed on participating consumers' computers. The system may also be employed by the management of a company for analyzing the workforce's usage of a corporate intranet. In both settings the person's choice of pages and the keystrokes made can be saved in a so-called weblog file that can subsequently be loaded into statistical software or a spreadsheet.

Videotaping shopping behaviour

Filming can trace the flow of shoppers through a store. By comparing the flows of a representative sample of shoppers, the store managers can determine where best to place such items as impulse goods. Also, the store can change layouts and see how this modifies shopping patterns. For example, supermarkets typically place necessities towards the rear of the store, hoping that shoppers place more items in their basket on impulse as they move down the aisle to reach the milk, bread, and other necessities.

3.5 Human observation: mystery shopping

In order to reach service excellence, customer satisfaction data based on surveys are needed; however, they will not be sufficient for continuing the change process over time. To achieve that, mystery shopping can be a useful instrument in addition to the more often-used survey methods (Wiele et al. 2005).

Mystery shopping is a process for measuring service quality, with feedback, that is understandable to the frontline people in retailing. It is a form of participant observation that uses researchers to act as potential customers to monitor the quality of processes and procedures used in the delivery of a service. The need for specific performance information stems from the increasing emphasis being placed on service performance. While standards are invariably set by head office staff and senior management, the task of delivering these standards falls to individuals at the service encounter. Variations in service performance can have a big effect on customer satisfaction.

Step 1: The objectives

1. Know what you want to get out of the shopping programme.
2. The objectives should be related to having satisfied customers as well as satisfied employees.

3. Mystery shopping is meant to reinforce positive behaviour and modify improper behaviour, but not to punish.

Objectives for mystery shopping programmes include:

- to act as a diagnostic tool identifying failings and weak points in an organization's service delivery, especially the customer contacts of frontline personnel;
- to encourage, develop and motivate service personnel by linking with appraisal, training and reward mechanisms, and to enable marketers to scrutinize and fine tune the human element;
- to assess the competitiveness of an organization's service provision by benchmarking it against the offerings of others in an industry in order to identify areas that need training or further training. It can also be used to reveal how employee contact with customers is positive.

Step 2: The evaluation form

The use of employees to define and set the measurable standards to be met. Determine what customers value and incorporate these into the evaluation form.

Often a significant amount of effort is put into implementing the mystery shopping research within an organization before the research is undertaken. Seminars, presentations, and newsletters are used to explain the purpose of the research, the standards against which the service is being measured, and the manner in which the result will feed into appraisal and reward systems. Such briefings encourage a high degree of staff acceptance.

In principle, there are two ways of evaluating service quality:

- Mystery shoppers visit the shop, posing as a customer, blending with other customers, while observing customer service and the sales skills of staff. After leaving the shop, they file a report, which is sent to the client.
- Another way for mystery shoppers to obtain information from frontline employees is to meet them in focus groups or individually to discuss the employee's impressions and experience with the customer and the service delivery system. Results from these interviews are then used to prepare a list of characteristics the employees view as important to customers.

Which method to use is up to the company, but staff acceptance of mystery shopping is seen as critical if the results are to be taken seriously and if industrial relations within the organization are not to suffer.

Shopper evaluations can be in the form of a checklist or an open, made-to-order format, which is more time-consuming to complete. In formulating the shopper questions, open-ended questions probing for more information are suggested, such as: "How did the employee describe the product or service?"

The service rating gives points on a scale of ten on the overall standard of service. Points are given for a specific action or attributes. For example, a welcoming smile is worth four points, a well-dressed server is worth two points. Service standards that are to be evaluated must be identified to the employee and should be easily measurable by the internal or external mystery shopper.

Step 3: The mystery shopper

Select, inform, and train the mystery shopper in line with the company's objectives. The shopper must match a customer profile that is appropriate for the scenario that they are being asked to enact.

In selecting the mystery shopper, the company must decide whether it will use in-house personnel or external shoppers. In-house shoppers are usually quality control experts from corporate headquarters. The advantages with this type of shopper may be lower cost and better knowledge of the company's objectives and products. However, the cost of using corporate personnel may be hidden in the overall budget and there is a stronger chance of the shopper being recognized.

The use of external mystery shoppers may have certain drawbacks. Obtaining consistent shopping evaluations from external shoppers requires the preparation of the shopper. A high turnover of mystery shoppers may also influence the quality of the shopping evaluation.

Training and informing the mystery shoppers is important, with regard to the briefing and data collection skills. Shoppers receive a detailed briefing on the scenario that they are to enact, focusing on their personal characteristics, the questions they should ask and the behaviours they should adopt. They are then tested on these elements to ensure that the service encounter is realistic and reduce the opportunity for the true identity of the mystery shopper to be detected.

The training of data collection skills focuses on identifying the elements of the service to be observed as well as the retention and recording of information. Retention and recording of information is particularly important, as the shoppers cannot complete an assessment form during the service encounter. Therefore shoppers should receive memory testing and training.

Step 4: Conducting the shop visit

Produce an unbiased, mainly objective evaluation (but include a limited amount of subjective information) of the shopping experience.

With the objectives of the shopping visit in mind, an evaluation checklist or more subjective information collection form in hand, and any training that might be necessary, the mystery shopper is ready to conduct the visit.

Branches and employees involved in the programme could be forewarned of the visit. Some companies remind their employees continuously of the mystery shopper by using posters behind the counter where customers cannot see them. Other companies use stickers attached to workstations to remind employees of service standards.

Bose Corporation (US) makes loudspeakers and other audio equipment. To ensure employees extend the pursuit of excellence to the retail setting, Bose has been using mystery shopping since 1995 to monitor performance of salespeople at its factory stores, and at its showcase stores. Mystery shops are also conducted at department stores and electronic superstores where Bose products are sold.

For Bose, it is important for employees to greet customers within ten seconds of their arrival. They should introduce themselves, or, if they're busy with another customer, acknowledge the customer's presence with a nod or other gesture. Once with the customer, they must be friendly, helpful and demonstrate product knowledge.

One of the things customers have told Bose is that salespeople can increase satisfaction by making them feel welcome.

The Bose mystery shopping has two elements. It begins with a phone call, in which the shopper calls to ask questions on specific products. Shoppers indicate if the employee performed tasks such as answering questions clearly. Employees are also rated on their friendliness, helpfulness, etc., using an excellent–satisfactory–unsatisfactory scale. Finally, shoppers have space to write about their interaction and support the ratings they gave the employee. Mystery shoppers are instructed to complete the forms immediately, while everything is still fresh in their mind.

Each Bose shop receives a quarterly summary showing the staff's overall performance. The district and store managers also get copies. The stores use the data as a tool to bring awareness of where they're doing well and where there are opportunities to do better. They can use it as a basis for a staff meeting, to look at things they can do to improve.

Depending on each store's performance, the employee team, including managers, are awarded a customer satisfaction bonus. Individual employees are also noted only for outstanding service; however, they are not singled out if they perform poorly.

Source: Adapted from www.bose.com and Rydholm (1998)

Step 5: The analysis

Identify gaps in the service delivery and determine origin.

The information obtained from the shopping visit is matched to the pre-established objectives and standards to determine outstanding performance as well as any gaps that might exist. Identifying the reasons for the gaps is the challenge for managers and employees participating in the programme.

Results from mystery shopper visits should be analyzed with the history of previous shopper visits in mind, not as a one-off event.

To increase the reliability, the mystery shopper evaluation can be cross-checked with results from other sources such as customer contact cards, management reports, and customer satisfaction surveys.

Step 6: Action needed

Develop a reward and incentive scheme related to employee performance in mystery shopping programmes. Provide coaching to develop employees' technical and behavioural skills. Work on the service delivery system if gaps exist because of poor design. Repeat the shopping experience.

The results of individual shopping visits should not only go to top management, but to the people directly involved, especially the contact employees. Feedback must be relevant to those involved and be made in a positive manner. Once the programme has been completed with a series of visits, and results have been tracked, recorded, and improvements made, a report of the mystery shopper study should be sent to top management. Management must be informed of the value that has been obtained from the shopping programmes (Morrall, 1994) and any changes needed to improve customer service.

Coaching is the key to dealing with service delivery problems arising from lack of training. Mystery shopping evaluations provide information on what skills need to be developed. Employees can attend off-site training programmes in small groups where they play out roles and work on service delivery.

In terms of motivation, the mystery shopping results can be used to reward those service teams that are performing well against the standards set. Rewards can range from simple forms of recognition through to team league tables with team awards associated with sales performance in determining levels of financial reward. Financial rewards and incentives are seen as becoming more common, particularly in financial services, travel agents, and shops.

In general, mystery shopping tends to lead to improvements in service quality. However, in the longer term, the novelty of being "shopped" can wear off, leaving personnel complacent about their service and lacking motivation to take steps to improve it further. To overcome this, standards need to be constantly updated, and staff need to understand the benefits of mystery shopping.

3.6 Advantages and limitations of observational research

Observational data collection methods have several specific advantages and limitations worthy of discussion.

Advantages of observational data

- The researcher collects observed and actual behaviour patterns of marketing events rather than response data relating to consumers' intentions or preferences.
- Reduction or elimination of recall error. The researcher gathers and records data as it is observed, whether the respondent's recall of past experiences is accurate is not an issue.
- Observation methods allow researchers to obtain information from people who are

unable to communicate in written or oral form. This can be an advantage when collecting data on young children, and it can also be an advantage in cross-cultural and cross-national research if the researcher has problems with the foreign languages.

■ Normally, observational data can be collected in less time and at lower costs than through other types of collection procedures.

Limitations of observational data

Some limitations of observation are the limitations inherent in qualitative research in general.

■ It is difficult to generalize data. With direct observation, typically only small numbers of subjects are studied and usually under special circumstances, so their representativeness is a concern. This factor, plus the subjective interpretation required to explain the observed behaviour, usually forces the researcher to treat the conclusions as tentative.

■ Inability to explain behaviours or events. The greatest drawback of all observational methods is the researcher's inability to pry beneath the behaviour observed and to interrogate the person on motives, attitudes, and all of the other unseen aspects of why what was observed took place. This can be especially problematic where observation is conducted in different cultural contexts by a researcher with little familiarity with these cultures. The researcher may tend to interpret the data in terms of his or her own cultural self-reference (CSR).

■ It may not be possible to engage in observational methods in all countries. For example, in Saudi Arabia it will be nearly impossible to observe shopping behaviour of women, because they are not supposed to accept any kind of monitoring of their behaviour.

■ Observation research can be time-consuming if the behaviour occurs infrequently. For example, if the observer in a supermarket is waiting to observe people selecting a certain cereal brand.

The general limitations of observation methods are that motivations, attitudes, and other "internal" conditions cannot be observed. Only when these feelings are relatively unimportant or readily inferred from the behaviour is it appropriate to use observational methods. For example, facial expression might be used as an indicator of a child's attitudes or preferences for various types of fruit drink flavours because children often react with conspicuous physical expressions. But adults and even children usually conceal their reasons and true reactions in public, and this fact necessitates a direct questioning approach because observation alone cannot give a complete picture of why and how people act the way they do.

3.7 Summary

Ideally, the subjects of observational research are unaware they are being studied. Because of this they react in a natural manner, giving the researcher insight into actual, not reported, behaviours. As previously noted, observational research methods reduce the occurrence of recall error. The subjects are not asked what they remember about a certain action. Instead, they are observed while engaged in the act. In some cases, observation may be the only way to obtain accurate information. For instance, children who cannot yet verbally express their opinion of a new toy will do so by simply playing or not playing with the toy. Retail marketers commonly gather marketing intelligence about competitors and about their own employees' behaviours by hiring the services of mystery shoppers who pose as customers, but who are actually trained observers. In some situations, data can be obtained with better accuracy and less cost by using observational methods as opposed to other means. For example, counts of in-store traffic can often be made by observation more accurately and less expensively than by using surveys.

Such advantages of observational research methods should not be interpreted as meaning that this technique is always in competition with other approaches. A resourceful researcher will use observation techniques to supplement and complement other techniques. When used in combination with other techniques, each approach can serve as a check on the result obtained by the other.

Questions

1. In which situation would you recommend using observational methods in cross-national market research?

2. What is the difference between mechanical and human observational methods?

3. Explain the relative advantages and disadvantages of observation methods.

4. What kind of observational method should a supermarket manager use if he would like to know the popularity of a new cereal brand produced by Kelloggs?

5. How may electronic observations be used in supermarkets?

6. Describe a marketing research problem in which an observation method could be used in combination with another marketing research method.

7. Explain how mystery shopping can be used by:

   ■ store chains managers;

   ■ producers of brands sold in the store chains.

8. What do you see as being the main ethical problems of

   ■ mystery shopping;

   ■ analysis of people's garbage?

References

Boote, J. and Mathews, A. (1999) "Saying is one thing doing is another: the role of observation in marketing research." *Qualitative Market Research*. Vol. 2, no. 1. 15–21.

Cote, J. A., McCullough, J. and Reilley, M. (1985) "Effects of unexpected situations on behavioral-intention differences: a garbology analysis." *Journal of Consumer Research*. Vol. 12, September. 188–94.

Erstad, M. (1998) "Mystery shopping programs and human resource management." *International Journal of Contemporary Hospitality Management*. Vol. 10, no. 1. 34–38.

Ghosh, S. (1997) "Targeted promotions using scanner panel data." *Journal of Product & Brand Management*. Vol. 6, no. 6. 405–416.

Hawkes, J. (1997) *Music in the Grocery Store*. Voice of America, 222.voa.gov. 20 November 1997.

Hollensen, S. (2003) *Marketing Management: A relationship approach*. Financial Times/Prentice Hall, Harlow.

Kellehear, A. (1993) *The Unobtrusive Researcher: A guide to methods*. Allen and Unwin. St Leonards, Australia. 5–8.

Morrall, K. (1994) "Mystery shopping tests and compliance." *Bank Marketing*. Vol. 26, no. 2. 13–15.

Ritenbaugh, C. K. and Harrison, G. G., (1984) "Reactivity of garbage analysis." *American Behavioral Scientist*. 28. 51–70.

Roussel-Dupre, S. (2002) "Where Did Kmart GO Wrong?: – Retailers need to differentiate themselves and cater to a specific and loyal customer base to compete in today's marketplace". *Integrated Solutions for Retailers*. March Issue (online), www.ismretail.com/articles/2002_03/020305.htm.

Rydholm, J. (1998) "Extending excellence: mystery shops help Bose make sure its customer service matches its reputation for quality." *Quirk's Marketing Research Review*. January. 3–6.

Schmidt, M. and Krause, N. (2000) "Investigating an unobtrusive data gathering technique: estimating readership of circulars by analyzing fingerprints," in Gundlach, G. T. and Murphy, P. E., *AMA Educators Proceedings*. Vol. 11. 322–223. See also Hansen, F. and Hansen Y. L. (eds.) (2000) *Advertising Research in the Nordic Countries*. Samfundslitteratur, Copenhagen, 228–243.

Schmidt, M. and Krause N. (2001) "Using unobtrusive methods in consumer research: an assessment." *European Advances in Consumer Research*. Vol. 5. 180–186.

Webb, E. J., Cambell, D. T., Schwartz, R. D. and Sechrest, L. (2000) *Unobtrusive Measures*. Thousand Oaks, CAL, Sage Classics. 35–52.

Wiele, T. van der, Hesselink, M., Iwaarden, J. van (2005) "Mystery shopping: a tool to develop insight into customer service provision." *Total Quality Management and Business Excellence*. Vol. 16, Issue 4. 529–41.

Wilson, A. M. (1998) "The role of mystery shopping in the measurement of service performance." *Managing Service Quality*. Vol. 8, no. 6. 414–420.

4 Focus groups

Learning objectives

After studying this chapter you should be able to:

- Explain the purpose of focus groups.
- Understand the different steps in conducting focus group research.
- Describe the different types of focus group research.
- Explain in which context online focus groups can be used.
- Discuss the advantages and disadvantages of conducting traditional and online focus group interviews.
- Provide an overview of challenges and prospects concerning quantitative analysis of qualitative data.
- Explain how a software-supported quantitative analysis of a focus group can improve target-marketing strategy.

4.1 Introduction

Focus group interviews represent an array of techniques and methods that have been used by social scientists for several decades. Originally termed the "focused interview," the method was quickly adopted in marketing research as a means of product testing and has become the predominant qualitative method in this field. A focus group can be described as a research technique that collects data through group interaction on a topic or topics.

The distinguishing feature of focus groups is the explicit use of the group interaction to produce data and insights that might be less accessible without the interaction found in a group. The focus group is one research technique in which participants are encouraged to interact. Focus groups can be relatively structured, with specific questions asked of each member, or extremely unstructured, depending on the research purpose. They can be used as a stand-alone technique, or as an integral part of a more complicated design in which they precede, supplement, or triangulate design from other methods. For example, focus groups are useful for generating research hypotheses, testing research methods, or interpreting other survey results.

There are four main objectives of focus groups:

1. To generate ideas: to use the focus group as a starting point for product or service ideas, uses, or improvements.
2. To understand consumer vocabulary: using the focus group to stay abreast of the words and phrases consumers use when describing a product so as to improve products or service communication with them. Such information may help in writing advertising copy or in the preparation of an instruction pamphlet. This knowledge refines research problem definitions and also helps structure questions for later quantitative research.
3. To reveal consumer needs, motives, perceptions and attitudes on products or services: using the focus group to refresh the marketing team as to what customers feel or think about products or a service. This application is useful in generating objectives to be addressed by subsequent research.
4. To understand findings from quantitative studies: using focus groups for better comprehension of data gathered from other surveys. Sometimes a focus group succeeds in uncovering why the findings came out in a particular way.

Focus group research is becoming more widespread worldwide. In fact, differences among the world's populations necessitate that the research be tailored to the specific culture and people. The focus group approach will remain a popular and influential marketing research technique, because focus groups are easy to interpret; are reasonable in cost terms when compared with large-scale quantitative surveys involving a thousand or more respondents; are adaptable to managers' concerns; and capable of yielding immediate results. They are a unique research method because they permit marketing managers to see and hear the market.

Marketing research in action

Executives at General Motors and Chrysler did not use information from the focus group

When Chrysler was going to launch the PT Cruiser in 2000, its sales estimate for the first six months was set at 60,000 units, but, in fact, it took orders for twice that number.

On the other hand, General Motors set its sales estimate at 80,000 units for the introduction of the Pontiac Aztek later in 2001, but never sold more than a quarter of this volume.

Both car manufacturers were using focus groups as a basis for their estimates, but neither of them was estimating the right figure.

The irony of the slow-selling Pontiac Aztek and sold-out Chrysler PT Cruiser is that both represent a focus group process that failed. In the case of Aztek, the product development team and numerous focus groups failed to alert management that the styling was a turn-off to the target audience. And in the case of PT Cruiser, Chrysler's planners missed the fact that the car had a much broader appeal than intended. The bottom line: neither car was selling according to plan.

The cause of the problem was the lack of information flowing from focus groups up to the executive level. What was the reason for this? By the time focus groups were done, so much money had been spent that it would have been a disaster for a product representative, to inform management that the vehicle had missed the mark.

Ideally, GM should have stopped Aztek in its tracks, but the poor performance in the focus groups was never shown to senior managers. So the inventory and marketing costs ended up outweighing what it would have cost to fix the problem earlier.

In Chrysler's case, focus groups told it that the PT was a huge success, but Chrysler viewed it as a niche car and moved cautiously on volume. The results were staring them in the face, but senior managers were sceptical because they knew it was hard to sell a niche vehicle to somebody that doesn't want one.

One of the ways to solve these problems is to try to hold the focus groups earlier.

Sources: Adapted from: www.gm.com; www.chrysler.com; Kobe, G. (2001); public sources

4.2 Framework for focus groups

All research methodologies, including focus groups, benefit from a rigorous framework and planning. The following sections present some useful steps and guidelines in the planning process.

Step 1: Define the problem

Quality is affected when the purpose of a focus group is not clear. So the first step in preparing for a focus group is to gain a thorough understanding of the problem or issue and to express it as a concise question or topic for discussion.

Step 2: Establish the groups and plan for the sessions

This stage requires the researcher to determine the number of groups, the number of participants in each group, the length and timing of each session, and finally the recruiting of participants.

Step 2.1 Determine the number of groups

Selection for focus groups is deliberate rather than being a random selection. Participants are selected (screened) for their suitability and ability to provide insights that are relevant to the particular problem.

The number of focus groups to be conducted depends on the nature of the issue being investigated, the number of distinct market segments, and the number of ideas generated by each successive group. A secondary factor may be time and cost, but this should not be a primary concern for restricting the number of groups. A general guideline is to continue conducting focus groups until little additional information is gained and the moderator can predict what is going to be said in the next group. This occurs usually after three to four groups.

Step 2.2 Set the size of a focus group

There is no consensus in the literature as to the number of participants in a focus group. According to industry wisdom, the optimal size is six to ten people. A small group (fewer than eight participants) is not likely to generate the necessary energy and group dynamics. With fewer participants, it is common that one or two of the participants do most of the talking despite the moderator's efforts.

Often, a small group will result in awkward silences and force the moderator to take too active a role in the discussion. Similarly, a group with more than twelve will ordinarily prove too large to be conducive to a natural discussion. As a focus group becomes larger in size it tends to become fragmented. Participants may become frustrated by the inherent digressions and side comments. Irrelevant small talk may break out among two or three participants while another is talking. This situation places the moderator in the role of disciplinarian who has to maintain order rather than focusing the discussion on the issues.

Unfortunately, it is often difficult to predict the exact number of people that will attend the focus group interview. Ten may agree to participate and only six may show up or fourteen are invited, in the hope that eight will show up, and all fourteen will arrive. Of course, if this occurs, the researcher faces a judgement as to whether or not to send some home. In the worst case, a researcher may run into a situation in which no one attends, despite promises to the contrary. There is no guaranteed method that will ensure a successful participation ratio. Incentives (which will be discussed later) are helpful, but definitely not a foolproof way of gaining acceptance. So although six to ten is the ideal size range, it is not uncommon to have bigger or smaller groups.

Smaller groups may also be more productive. With twelve panellists, for example, after subtracting the time it takes to warm up (usually about three minutes) and the time for the moderator's questions and probes, the average member of a ninety-minute focus group has three minutes of talking time. The experience becomes more like a group survey than an exploration of experiences, feelings, and beliefs. It is also a very expensive form of survey, so cutting the group size makes sense.

Step 2.3 Who should be selected?

It is generally believed that the best focus groups are those in which the participants share characteristics. This requirement is sometimes automatically satisfied by the researcher's need to have particular types of people in the focus group. A heterogeneous group will enable broad and general discussion and a wide variety of opinions to be expressed without prejudice or pre-judgement. Most focus group research, however, will seek some element of homogeneity, so that opinions reflect some element of commonality among participants. This can be as simple as commonality of age group, lifestyle, consumption patterns, expertise or experience.

The need for similar demographic or other relevant characteristics in group members is accentuated by the fact that the participants are strangers, and many people feel intimidated or at least hesitant to voice their opinions among strangers.

Participants typically feel more comfortable once they realize they have something in common, such as their age, job situations, family composition (they may all have pre-school children), purchase experiences (they may all have bought a new car in the past year), or even leisure pursuits (they may all play tennis). Furthermore, by conducting a homogeneous group, the researcher is assured that differences in these variables will be less likely to confuse the issue being discussed.

Another approach to selection is to allow focus groups to be self-selected so that members know each other and will talk openly, for example a group of managers in the same distribution channel who communicate regularly and who perhaps have become friends.

Whilst focus group participants may be experts in a field, their deliberations are about issues outside their immediate sphere of responsibility and influence.

Step 2.4 How to recruit participants

The selection of participants is determined by the purpose of the focus group. For instance, if the purpose is to generate ideas on product packaging, the participants must be consumers who have used the brand.

It is necessary to contact prospective participants by telephone initially to vet them, and then to obtain their co-operation in the focus group. Occasionally, a focus group company may recruit by requesting shoppers to participate. Exhibit 4.1 addresses some problems that may be overlooked.

EXHIBIT 4.1 PROBLEMS OF RECRUITING TARGET CUSTOMERS FOR FOCUS GROUPS

Screening is an important task in focus group research. To collect relevant information, focus groups must contain people who have knowledge about the topics at hand. If Disneyland wants to conduct focus groups to understand better children's perception of its attractions, it needs to use the children of families who have recently visited a Disneyland. It can be difficult to find enough families who meet such specific criteria. Once a prospective participant is identified, contacted and qualified for group membership, the next task is to secure that person's willingness to join the group. This is not an easy process.

Assume that a planned focus group must address a brand that has a market share of 1 percent. This may be the case if the brand's share has been due to decline or if it has been launched recently but does not meet expectations. In such cases managers may wish to keep the product on the market and consider a revival of the brand. Assuming that the company intends to carry out four focus groups with ten persons each, then, according to probability theory, at least 4,000 screening interviews need to be carried out. Since far from every call is successful (respondents will not be home, busy, refuse to participate, etc.) one will probably need to carry out 10,000 or so screening calls. Usually then, the screening question is put on a research agency's computer-aided telephone interview system for several months.

There are easier ways to recruit, however. For instance, if a bell rings each time a supermarket's scanner encounters the barcode of the appropriate brand at the checkout, an employee could approach the customer and ask her/him to participate in an interview, and request the completion of a questionnaire. This technique has been used by a Danish market research agency called Factivator.

Researchers have at least two strategies to entice prospective participants. First, incentives of various types are used. These range from paying for the participant's time to free products or gift certificates. Second, many focus group companies call prospective participants the day before the event to remind them that they have agreed to take part. If one prospective participant cannot be there, it is then possible to recruit a replacement. Neither approach works perfectly, and anticipating how many participants will show up is always a concern. Some focus group companies have a policy of over-recruiting, and others have lists of people they can rely on to participate, given that they fit the qualifications.

Step 2.5 Selecting the venue

The venue should be neutral and one in which participants feel comfortable and at ease. Moreover, it should be easy to get to.

For a focus group to be successful, the room is just as important as the venue. The environment should be free of distractions and as relaxed as possible to encourage informal off-the-cuff discussion. The most common option is a quiet room with a circular or round conference table, which allows participants to lean forward and be less self-conscious about their bodies. Others prefer a living-room atmosphere with coffee tables and easy chair.

Aside from a circular seating arrangement where participants can all see one another, the second requirement is to select a meeting place quiet enough to permit an intelligible audio- or videotaping of the sessions.

The ideal setting is a **focus group facility**. These are rooms designed for focus groups at a marketing research company. The focus group room contains a large table and comfortable chairs, a relaxed atmosphere, and a one-way mirror so clients can view the interviews. Ample space for video and audio equipment should be provided.

Microphones may be built into the walls or ceiling, or set in the centre of the table, and videotape equipment often resides behind a one-way mirror. One-way mirrors also allow clients to observe the focus group as it takes place.

Step 2.6 The timing of sessions

The time of day that a focus group is held can affect the extent to which participation is achieved. For example, early evening (5.30 to 7.00 p.m.) is often the most appropriate time to conduct sessions. The primary justification for this timing is that holding the sessions after normal business hours minimizes disruption to the daily routines, so removing a possible obstacle to attendance.

Step 2.7 Selecting moderators

The quality of focus group research depends on the abilities of the moderator/facilitator/catalyst because that person is the instrument in the focus group interview. Here, we emphasize the use of the researcher as the moderator, and also discuss the role of the assistant moderator.

A **focus group moderator** conducts the session and guides the flow of discussion on topics suggested by the client. The moderator must strive for a delicate balance between stimulating natural discussions among all of the group members while ensuring that the focus does not stray too far from the topic. A good moderator must have excellent observation, interpersonal, and communication skills to recognize and overcome threats to a productive group discussion. He or she must be prepared, experienced, and armed with a detailed list of topics to be discussed. It is also helpful if the moderator can eliminate any preconceptions on the topic from his or her mind. Finally, the moderator should be empathetic or sensitive to the participants' situations and comments.

The focus group's success depends on the participants' involvement in the discussion and in their understanding of what is being asked of them. Productive involvement is largely a result of the moderator's effectiveness, which in turn is dependent on understanding the purpose and objectives of the interview. Unless the moderator understands what information the researcher is interested in and why (the managerial agenda), she or he will not be able to phrase questions effectively. It is good policy to have the moderator contribute to the development of the project's goals so as to guide the discussion topics, aiding in the formation of the topics (questions), and so be better prepared to conduct the group. It is important when formulating questions that they be in a logical sequence and that the moderator follow this sequence as much as possible. With an incompetent moderator, the focus group can become a waste of time and money.

The moderator's introductory remarks are important because they set the tone of the session. All subsequent questions should be prefaced with a clear explanation of how the participants should respond. For example, how they really feel, not how they think they should feel. This allows the moderator to establish a rapport with participants and to lay the groundwork for the interview's structure.

It is recommended having an assistant moderator if one can be found. Although the subject is not often addressed in the literature, the advantages of having an assistant moderator are numerous. Primarily an assistant moderator prevents the moderator from being distracted by housekeeping duties and environmental issues, so enabling total concentration on the discussion. For example, the assistant moderator can take care of the refreshments, control the audio equipment, and make notes about the proceedings and participants' reactions, which are helpful in the post-meeting analysis of each session.

The following are critical moderating skills:

- Ability to establish rapport quickly by listening carefully, demonstrating a genuine interest in each participant's views, dressing like the participants, and avoiding the use of jargon or sophisticated terminology that may turn off the group.
- Flexibility, observed by implementing the interview agenda in a way the group finds comfortable. Slavish adherence to an agenda means the discussion loses spontaneity and degenerates into a question-and-answer session.
- Ability to sense when a topic has been exhausted or is becoming threatening, and to know which topic to introduce to maintain a smooth flow in the discussion.
- Ability to control group influences to avoid having a dominant individual or subgroup that might suppress the total contribution.

Step 3: Conducting discussions

Common techniques for conducting successful focus group interviews include the chain reaction, devil's advocate, and false termination. In the **chain reaction** technique, the moderator builds a cumulative effect by encouraging each member of the focus group to comment on an idea suggested by someone else in the group, by adding to or expanding on it. When playing **devil's advocate**, the moderator expresses extreme viewpoints; this usually provokes reactions from group members and keeps the discussion moving forward in a lively manner. In **false termination**, the moderator falsely concludes a focus group interview, thanks group members for participating, and inquires whether there are any final comments. These "final comments" frequently lead to new discussion avenues and often result in the most useful data obtained.

Step 3.1 The level of moderator involvement

The level of the moderator's involvement is governed by the objectives of the research and the structure of the groups. The focus group researcher is best considered not as an interviewer but as a catalyst for discussion. The true ability of a focus group researcher is in being able to introduce a topic in such a way that participants are stimulated to respond. A further skill is in managing the balance of opinions. Every focus group will have a variety of personality types, some will be extrovert or dominant and perhaps jump in with opinions frequently and early, while others will be introvert or be inclined to think privately about an issue and may or may not offer their opinions.

Any new focus group researchers must be acutely aware of their role and function. Experiential learning will enable a researcher to stabilize discussion to achieve an adequate balance of participants' opinions. Experiential knowledge will also ensure that the researcher does not dominate the focus group through too much involvement and direction.

The moderator can control the group dynamics so that the desired high level of involvement is planned and achieved. This control prevents one person from dominating the conversation, as well as allowing stimulation of quiet respondents to participate. Furthermore, unproductive discussion can be carefully interrupted without imposing the moderator's personal biases or putting words in respondents' mouths.

In brief, the moderator needs to strike a balance between having too much structure, which prevents the participants' own ideas surfacing, and not enough structure, allowing some participants to dominate and some research issues or topics to be ignored.

Step 3.2 The number of topics in a session

The number of topics covered determines the level of moderator involvement, and contributes towards the structure of the interview. But there appears to be little consensus as to what constitutes a structured group. In addition, it is not necessary to adhere rigidly to the order of topics and the moderator may adjust the sequence according to the flow of the discussion. As well as having the freedom to rearrange the order of topics, the moderator needs to be involved, to ensure that all topics and surrounding issues are discussed. This prevents problems that may occur with low levels of moderator involvement, such as failure to discuss some topics, and difficulties in analyzing disorganized data.

Deciding on the number of topics to be addressed in a session is often difficult, as one group may react enthusiastically to a topic while another group may be uninterested, affecting the length of the session.

Another approach is to develop a rolling interview guide, where the list of topics is revised for the next group, based on the outcome of the previous group. This method may result in difficulties when trying to make comparisons between groups. But this difficulty may be outweighed by the progression of in-depth understanding.

Step 3.3 Questions or topics for discussion

Quality data is directly related to quality topics, which typically follow a prescribed format so that the maximum amount of useful information can be gained. Consequently, careful forethought is needed to be given to the wording of the topics in the sessions, to ensure that respondents are not placed in embarrassing or defensive situations.

Quality topics for focus groups are those that are *open-ended*, thereby providing a stimulus to the participant. Start with some general issues and then funnel in to more specific ones. If the researcher decides to use questions, these should begin with words such as *what, which* and *how. Why* questions must be used cautiously in recognition that respondents often rationalize answers when asked "why" or may become defensive. Therefore, *why* issues are best addressed as discussion points, coupled with phrases such as, "could you explain that a little more" and similar probes. This approach indicates to the respondents that the moderator is interested not only in facilitating the discussion, but also in the complexity of their answers.

Step 3.4 Test the moderators' guide

The focus group interview guide or protocol should be tested to eliminate obvious problems. This allows the nature and wording of the interview topics to be evaluated to ensure that the wording of questions is appropriate, to ascertain whether the right topics have been selected and addressed properly.

Step 4: Analyzing the information

Analysis of the information is a challenging part of focus group research. Two important factors must be remembered. First, the researcher must translate the qualitative statements of participants into categories and then report the degree of consensus apparent in the focus groups. Second, the demographic and buyer behaviour characteristics of participants should be judged against the target market profile to assess to what degree the groups represent the target market.

The focus group report reflects the qualitative aspect of this research method. It lists all themes that have become apparent, and it notes any diversity of opinions or thoughts expressed by the participants. It will also have numerous verbatim excerpts provided as evidence. In fact, some reports include complete transcripts of the group discussion. This information is then used for further research or even for more focus groups. If the information is used for subsequent focus groups, the client uses the first group as a learning experience, making any adjustments to the discussion topics as needed to improve the research objectives. Although focus groups may be the only type of research to tackle a marketing problem or question, they are also used as a beginning point for quantitative research efforts. That is, a focus group phase may be used to gain a feel for a specific survey that will ultimately generate standardized information from a representative sample.

Several features of group interactions must be kept in mind during the analysis. An evaluation of a new concept by a group tends to be conservative; that is, it favours ideas that are easy to explain and not necessarily very new. There are further problems with the order of presentation when several concepts, products, or advertisements are being evaluated. If group participants have been highly critical of one thing, they may compensate by being uncritical of the next.

4.3 Types of focus groups

Focus groups can be classified into three types:

- *Exploratory focus groups* are commonly used early in the market research process to help define a problem precisely. Exploratory groups can also be used to generate hypotheses for testing or concepts for future research.
- *Clinical focus groups* involve qualitative research in its most scientific form. The research is conducted as a scientific endeavour, based on the premise that a person's true motivations and feelings are subconscious in nature. The moderator probes under the level of the consumer's consciousness. Obviously, clinical groups require a moderator with expertise in psychology and sociology. Their popularity is limited because of the difficulty of validating findings from clinical groups and because unskilled operators sometimes attempt to conduct clinical groups. The reality in the kitchen or supermarket differs drastically from that in most corporate offices.
- *Experiencing focus groups* allow the researcher to experience the emotional framework in which the product is being used, and explores the "experience" of a consumer.

An emerging trend is the two-way focus group. This allows one target group to listen to and learn from a related group. In one application, physicians viewed a focus group of arthritis patients discussing the treatment they desired. A focus group of these physicians was then held to determine their reactions. The cost of this option, of course, is high. Some research firms are planning an international network of focus facilities. Thus, global focus groups will be possible.

Role of the observer(s)

Backroom observers have a different perspective from the moderator – they can listen in a way that the moderator cannot, since the moderator is often concentrating on a specific issue being discussed. The client's representatives (e.g. marketing people) may function as observers, to benefit from "experiencing" the consumer. Marketing people are often isolated, making assumptions about their users. Seeing and hearing consumers acts as a reality check.

Sitting behind a mirror or in front of a video screen and observing focus groups might sound simple, clients should be quiet, and open-mindedly listen to and look at respondents. However, even if they do this, it may be difficult to sort out all the fast-flying comments. The clients' presence has the advantage of being able to indirectly or discretely intervene in a discussion: either the client can communicate with the moderator through a covert earphone, or the setup of the focus group meeting may include one or more short breaks. These breaks are then used for a brief conference between client and moderator where the client can ask the moderator to raise follow-up questions or even new topics.

With the growing popularity of focus group research, there is increased pressure for organizations using the technique to get the most possible out of each session. One over-looked area is the dynamics of the backroom, and what each of the people attending a focus group should do to ensure they get the maximum out of each session. The following suggestions will enable the backroom observer to get more information from each session.

First, the backroom observer should be totally familiar with the discussion guide before the groups begin. This will provide the opportunity to concentrate on the discussion rather than checking the discussion guide to figure out whether the moderator will be covering some topic of interest later in the session.

Second, the observer should decide how to communicate with the moderator during the session. There are many ways to do this. For example, many moderators would prefer to come to the backroom during a group, to talk with the observer, as they find this less dis-tracting than receiving notes. The important thing is that the observer should get a chance to talk with the moderator a few times during the session to share ideas, suggest topics or ways to approach a subject.

Third, before the group starts, the observer could write down the three to five most important things that he would like to learn from the participants. While the group is in progress, he should make sure that the moderator covers these topics.

Fourth, the observer should focus on the overall picture rather than the comments of the minority during the discussion. He should not listen only to the one or two people who are the most dominant, but most positive or the most negative about the subject being dis-cussed. It is easy to gain a false sense of the group due to the aggressive behaviour of one or two participants. The best way to focus on the inputs from the full group is to write down brief notes on the comments made regarding a particular topic by each participant.

Fifth, the backroom observer should note the body language of the participants. In addition to the person that speaks, the observer could note whether other respondents are nodding agreement or shaking their heads. Also, focus group members are sometimes saying what is acceptable rather than what they believe. Therefore the observer should listen for the tone of voice (for example, flatness suggests lack of conviction).

Sixth, at the conclusion of each focus group, the observer could write a brief summary, which would indicate the following thoughts:

- The most important things learned during the group session.
- Things that were not learned, but which should be covered in subsequent sessions.
- Suggestions for changes in the discussion guide for future focus group sessions.

Finally, a debriefing is important to ensure that there is good communication between the backroom observer and the moderator on the quality and nature of the content the session generated. The observer and the moderator should also talk about any changes to the guide that seems warranted.

4.4 Advantages and disadvantages of focus groups

Advantages of focus groups

There are four main advantages to using focus groups as a form of qualitative research.

Generate ideas

Creative and honest insights are often the result of focus groups. Because the respondents are not alone with the interviewer, they feel more at ease and free to express honest opinions rather than the ones they think will please the interviewer. The effect of "snowballing," or of one comment triggering another, is also common in focus groups. A "group creativity" factor is often observed in brainstorming sessions in which one person's idea stimulates others to generate their own ideas. Focus groups are excellent arenas for this sort of effect.

Allow clients to observe the group

A frequent complaint of marketing research clients is that they have difficulty understanding the complex quantitative techniques used and the statistical results produced. This lack of understanding invariably leads to an under-utilization of the information provided. However, because managers can be involved throughout the process by helping with the design of objectives and by observing the focus group, the results make more of an impression on them and are more likely to result in action. In fact, managers sometimes formulate and begin executing action plans based on their focus group observations even before the data are analyzed and submitted as a formal report.

Generally versatile

There is little to limit the number of topics and issues that can be discussed in a focus group interview. It is even possible to incorporate the use of other qualitative techniques such as role-playing, so increasing the productivity of the discussion. Prototypes of products can be demonstrated, concepts can be described, and product performance test results disclosed. Even advertising copy can be evaluated. Moreover, a focus group is a great forum for unravelling prejudices concerning products and people, such as politicians and actors. The moderator is allowed to probe deeper into the opinions of participants, something not allowed in highly structured quantitative methods.

A different aspect of this advantage is the flexibility afforded by technology. Some companies regularly conduct focus groups with participants in different places through the use of videoconferences. Some services can run focus groups across the internet where respondents enter "chat rooms" where certain topics are identified and the participants can submit their comments and reactions in a public forum. Some online focus groups take place over extended time periods using newsgroup postings.

Work well with special respondents

Focus groups permit the researcher to study respondents that might not respond well under more structured situations. In some situations, such as those involving hard-to-interview groups such as lawyers or doctors, the format gives them an opportunity to associate with their peers and to compare notes. Otherwise, they might refuse to take part in a survey. Creative variations of focus groups are successful in studies on children. The toy maker Lego has for decades run focus groups with children for assessing the target age of their products.

Disadvantages of focus groups

No research technique is flawless, and focus groups are no exception. Some weaknesses are readily apparent, whereas others are less obvious. There are three major weaknesses.

May not represent the population

Focus group results should not be viewed as conclusive research because the participants are not likely to be representative of the population the researcher is studying. Generally, those who agree to participate in focus groups are more outgoing than the average person. They are more accessible and probably more compliant. Coupled with the small sample size and homogenous group design, these characteristics render many focus groups unrepresentative of the marketer's target population. Furthermore, because it is not possible to ensure that all of the participants who agree to take part will show up, semi-professional respondents are sometimes "on call" for last-minute emergencies. Consequently, tight controls and a sober evaluation of the "representativeness" of focus groups' participants are vital.

Interpretation is subjective

Selective use of the data collected by focus groups is a typical problem. Individuals with preconceived notions can almost always find something to support their views, ignoring anything that does not support their opinions. So focus group analysts are constantly on guard against bias. The subjectivity problem is compounded by involvement of management personnel during the design and conduct of the focus groups. It is not uncommon for a manager to enter the process with a preconceived notion of what the research will find (or what it should support). Because focus group research typically allows managers to suggest topics and to add specific questions, as well as to observe the groups in progress, a danger exists that preconceptions will affect their impressions of the findings. They may even take these impressions and convert them to action before the focus groups are analyzed and the summary report delivered. A researcher who senses that premature actions are a danger should advise the client to wait until an analyst has interpreted the transcripts, and experienced researchers know that this takes time.

Cost-per-participant is high

A variety of expensive items contribute to the high cost-per-participant:

- Participant recruitment (comprehensive screening by telephone, etc.)
- Incentive costs/compensation for participants showing up (food, wine, gifts, etc.)
- Moderator's salary for participation in developing the objectives, conducting the focus groups, transcribing the videotapes, and writing and presenting a full report. The moderator often possesses a university degree in psychology.

- Rental of the focus group venue. Sometimes the client wants focus groups carried out in different places. In such situations, the agency may need to rent rooms at a hotel or conference centre.
- Hidden costs. Such costs include time spent by the clients working and travelling that are not necessarily assigned as a direct cost to the focus groups.

4.5 Online focus groups

As the web became popular, offering the chance to discover people's views remotely, researchers were excited about the possibilities, even for qualitative research. Not having to get a group of people together in a room potentially offers substantial savings on both costs and time.

Online focus groups are ideal for locating and researching markets that are hard to recruit, touch on sensitive topics, are online based, and geographically dispersed. For instance, high-level executives may be willing to participate in an online focus group but would never consider expending the amount of time required to attend a traditional focus group.

Online qualitative studies have been conducted to evaluate online and offline advertising, test mock websites, get feedback on existing websites, test and evaluate products (mailed in advance to the groups), uncover competitive website information, evaluate training programmes, explore decision-making, uncover imagery, evaluate concepts, evaluate package visuals, generate ideas, and ascertain customer and employee satisfaction.

The two most common online methodologies are real-time virtual focus group rooms where six to eight respondents participate simultaneously, and asynchronous online bulletin boards with, ideally, 12 to 20 respondents lasting over a period of days. Both allow respondents to participate from their desired location. There are many real-time and asynchronous virtual facilities offering different formats. The features, capabilities, and sophistication will vary according to which provider is selected.

The use of either methodology requires a re-thinking and re-application of qualitative design and techniques. Some activities and techniques used with in-person groups work as well (e.g., sentence completion, brain dumps, pantry recall/checks, brand verification) with online groups. Other activities and techniques need to be adjusted (e.g., brainstorming, imagery exercises), do not work as well (e.g., mind mapping, picture sorts), or do not work at all (e.g., controlled sensory tests, paired assignments).

The design and development activities necessary to conduct online groups are similar to offline groups, specifically: establishment of objectives, screeners, discussion guides, moderation, analysis and report writing. However, there are crucial differences, reflecting the influence of the technology, that require expertise beyond the skills required for in-person groups.

Important characteristics of online focus groups

Recruiting online groups requires specially crafted screeners that are similar in content and depth to those used for traditional focus groups. Online groups can be initiated by contacting a specialist moderator or company. Most will provide virtual rooms as well as recruitment services. Respondents can be recruited electronically from established panels, compiled online lists, targeted websites, or client-provided lists. Sometimes telephone recruiting is used to recruit audiences less likely to respond online.

Respondents and observers who are invited to the group receive invitations with login and passwords. If there are complications or questions during the session, the respondents should be able to contact technical support during the group session.

To avoid the online discussion becoming less focused, the group discussion should last ninety minutes at most. Ideally, thirty to forty questions are written in advance for input during the discussion. A ninety-minute group session leaves enough time to insert additional spontaneous questions.

Online focus groups demand that a moderator possesses strong and fast keyboard skills or is willing to hire an assistant who does. Also, moderating online groups requires someone who relates to the online venue and recognizes that respondents are excellent at developing relationships in this medium. Many respondents have participated in chat rooms and feel comfortable online. At the same time, it is the responsibility of the moderator to ensure that less-experienced respondents feel comfortable and valuable.

During the group session respondents see all of the moderator's questions and the comments of other respondents as they are input. Each respondent has a name, often a pseudonym, that identifies them and sometimes the responses are colour coded. They do not see any of the comments from the observers or observer notes to the moderator. In a study of cross-national online focus groups Scholl, Mulders and Drent (2002) noticed that the respondents are inclined to respond primarily to the moderator, and that interaction between respondents is lower than with face-to-face groups. The moderator can stimulate interaction by inviting respondents to react to each other's comments, such as; "Peter, what do you think of the answer Mary gave on this question?"

Regarding analysis and reporting of the focus group, transcripts are available quickly. The final report covers areas similar to traditional reporting of focus groups, such as objectives, methodology, conclusions, and findings. Typically, reports can be turned around quicker because of the immediate availability of transcripts (Sweet, 2001; O'Connor and Madge, 2003).

Technologies for online focus groups

Until a few years ago, the only way a qualitative researcher could remotely view a live focus group was through videoconferencing, and that required a special venue and dedicated phone lines carrying the video to the researcher's office. Now internet video streaming (also called webcasting or internet video broadcasting) is growing rapidly in acceptance. Webcasting now comprises about 15 percent of the market for focus group video broadcasts, and is growing steadily.

Videoconferencing is familiar to most researchers. At its most basic, a video camera records the focus group's discussion, and the picture is sent over digital phone lines to a monitor watched by the client's executives. Although they are not on-site, with videoconferencing, remote viewers still may be able to communicate with moderators by audio or video during or after the session.

Internet video streaming is a better option with the widespread deployment of broadband technology. The picture quality is better, although the size of the picture, seen on a computer screen, is small. Also, remote viewers typically can communicate with the moderator only via two-way text chat.

Whereas videoconferencing can accommodate a potentially unlimited number of viewers, video streaming can be viewed by a maximum of fifteen to twenty people at one time. But the biggest disadvantage of videoconferencing – and one of the strengths of video streaming – is geography; videoconferencing has to happen at a specially equipped venue, but video streaming can be seen on any computer with a broadband network, and in future also by mobile phones and handheld computers.

The cost of internet video streaming for a single, two-hour focus group session is similar to videoconferencing but the computer equipment is far cheaper than a dedicated videoconferencing unit.

Advantages and disadvantages of online groups

There are numerous advantages to online focus groups as compared to face-to-face focus groups (Reid and Reid, 2005). First, they are inexpensive and eliminate the costs of travelling, lodging, and renting venues. The research can also be completed in a shorter time as travelling time and time needed to arrange venues are eliminated. Although participants may not have a chance to touch a product or its prototype in the case of product research, 3D images and graphics of prototypes can be sent electronically, or test samples mailed in advance. More importantly, because the discussion is conducted electronically, the researcher has an accurate record. Also, analysis of the information obtained in an electronic focus group can be faster because there is no need to go through the transcription process. Because the internet is global, research can be conducted internationally. Advertisements can be put in appropriate newsgroups to invite people to participate in paid focus group sessions. This is very attractive to researchers who are interested in cross-cultural studies using focus group techniques.

Another advantage of an electronic focus group concerns the lower level of stress on the part of the participants. They can take part in the discussion in a familiar (home) environment, and there is no need to worry about appearance, so they feel more relaxed in expressing themselves. Someone joining a discussion at home is more likely to make a contribution. There are no interviewer/interviewee biases, nor social desirability biases that would distort the results because the discussion is conducted in a faceless and anonymous situation. That is, other participants' tone of voice, dress and gestures are normally not seen by the interviewee and cannot influence the interviewee's responses.

Removing the need to travel can be crucial to those participants who may have restricted mobility. Also, since every participant can enter an opinion into the system at any time, electronic focus groups can avoid the problem of a particular participant dominating the talking, a common problem in traditional focus groups. Those individuals who are shy and reticent to speak in face-to-face group interactions may find the virtual environment a liberating one in which they can "speak." Finally, it is easier to recruit hard-to-find target respondents (Tse, 1999).

Disadvantages of online focus groups

It is difficult to attract an online sample that truly reflects the domestic population. The feasibility of online data collection depends on the level of internet usage among potential respondents. Generally speaking, surveys have found that the online community is predominantly white, affluent executives and professionals and that college graduates are over-represented. Hence, participants in online discussions will most likely be those who are higher in socio-economic status, and those who are familiar with the technology. Like traditional focus groups, editors of online groups may therefore be unable to get representative participants unless the target sample is of higher-than-average socio-economic status.

Another disadvantage is that since the discussion is conducted in a faceless environment, the moderator will not be able to read the facial expressions and body language, make eye contact, nor hear the tone of voice of participants. However, a researcher can solve this problem by arranging the discussion in premises where videoconferencing facilities are available, otherwise only participants with video conferencing software or a PC-mounted web camera should be invited to participate. Of course, the researcher must be willing to tolerate a lower degree of openness in expressing opinions when participants know that they are being observed.

Since online participants cannot touch the product and can only see images of it, the method may not be suitable for some products.

Some people may have poor keyboard skills. This problem may be particularly difficult in an environment when English is not the mother tongue and when software that uses the local language has not been developed.

There are other, technological difficulties. For example, the speed of typing dominates interaction rather than the most vocal personality and this may change the rules of engagement. Those with slower typing speeds, or participants who prefer more time to consider their replies may find themselves lagging behind, still preparing an answer to an earlier question and finding the discussion has moved on. This may result in the loss of valuable data as the respondent deletes the reply and moves forward to join the continuing discussion.

Furthermore, the participation in the virtual interview requires a far higher level of motivation and interest from the interviewee than would be the case in a conventional interview. The interviewee has to provide the relevant equipment (the computer), bear the financial costs of being online for the interview and be prepared to take part in a physically quite demanding interview involving typing and reading. There is a need to think, type, look at the screen, read the text and maintain a logical thread of answering. The same is true for the interviewers, who also have to cover all relevant questions, probe unclear answers and ensure that everyone is still taking part, while under considerable time pressure to get a response on the screen (Tse, 1999).

4.6 Quantifying text: methodological challenges and available software

Recent advances in computer hardware and software have improved both speed and value of data analysis. Nevertheless, it is still a tedious and time-consuming task to quantify qualitative data. Text is a tremendously complicated construction – much more complicated than numeric data. A two-hour discussion of eight to ten people contains approximately 5,000 words, so there will be 5,000 data points. While many words are unique, others appear frequently. It is reasonable to assume that such a focus group contains something like 1,000 unique words. If we consider text as a statistical measurement problem, this corresponds to 5,000 observations of a single variable. Unfortunately, the variable is nominally (categorically) scaled and has 1,000 different levels. See Harwood and Garry (2003) for an overview of content analysis methods.

Before computer-analyzing a text, one first needs a typewritten excerpt of the input material (i.e., a video of a focus group interview). Theoretically, one could use speech recognition software and let respondents talk into microphones. Unfortunately, even the most powerful software is inadequate for automatic statistical conversion: it is easier to retype the manuscript than edit the automatically recognized text. Once the text has been typed and refined it is ready for analysis.

Figure 4.1 provides an overview of the steps involved in quantitative analysis of text. These steps are detailed below.

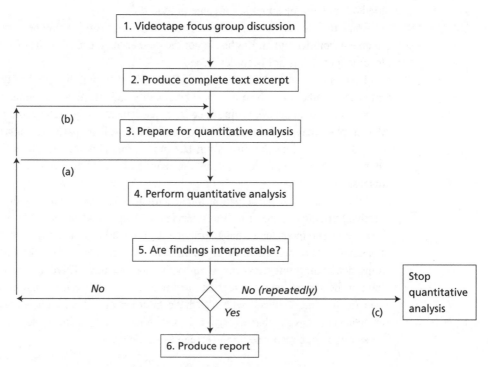

Figure 4.1 Steps in quantitative analysis of focus group interview

1. Record the focus group discussion, preferably using a video (a voice recorder will not record non-verbal communication). Although quantitative techniques cannot register nodding, smiling, etc., the researcher has the opportunity to inspect the video and use non-verbal communication for his qualitative report.
2. It is necessary to produce a complete text excerpt of the verbal communication.
3. The input text has to be prepared appropriately before the quantitative analysis can begin.
4. A series of quantitative runs needs to be performed. If the findings seem interpretable, the analysis ends and the findings can be documented and published.
5. If step five produces results that make no sense, one of several interventions is possible:
   (a) The researcher can try again by varying the options and parameters that come with the software, or choose other software. If other systems do not work, the researcher may be forced to move one step back.
   (b) The reseacher can continue working on the coding of the text (step three). Maybe the preparation phase was not handled properly. This procedure is both cumbersome and time-consuming, but it may prove necessary.
   (c) If new runs do not provide satisfactory results, the researcher probably is advised to abandon further quantitative analysis.

Table 4.1 Software for analyzing qualitative data

Category	Facilities	Software
1 Text retrievers	Advanced search, identifying synonyms and similar words, establishing bookmarks and hyperlinks to related documents and files, etc.	WordCruncher, Metamorph, Zyindex, Sonar Professional, Orbis, Text Collector
2 Textbase managers	Database-indexing, inclusion of pop-ups for memos, notes, comments, etc.	AskSam, FolioViews, Max, Tabletop
3 Code-and-retrieve programs	Coding, structuring and sorting of text-fragments, construction of hierarchic relations, etc.	Ethnograph, Qualpro, HyperQual2, Kwalitan, Martin
4 Code-based theory-builders	Building of theories about the text, primitive causal analysis and hypothesis-testing	NUD*IST, Atlas/ti, Aquad, HyperResearch, QCA
5 Conceptual network-builders	Graphical modelling, construction of relations, establishing of word-matrices and lists, certain statistical analyses	Inspiration, MECA, MetaDesign, SemNet SPSS Text Mining Builder
6 Content analysis programs	Content analysis assisted by encyclopedias concerning values and social-psychological phenomena	Textpack (Zuma), General Enquirer III
7 ANN-based programs	Neural network analysis	Catpac

Source: Adapted from Catterall and Maclaran (1998)

Researchers can choose from a wide array of software for analyzing text. Table 4.1 provides an indication of what is available.

Table 4.2 lists useful websites for various quantitative analysis tools.

Textual computer programs have been plagued by two main weaknesses. One important drawback, of course, concerns processing time, as it is a very time-consuming and cumbersome task to manipulate the input file and ready it for analysis. Higgins, Ford, and Oberski (1996) report that it took them a minute to code each half line of text when first working with the well-known NUD*IST program (developed by Richards and Richards, 1991). Another fundamental problem concerns basic methodological philosophy. Most scholars agree upon what constitutes a powerful quantitative model: a scientific algorithm should provide the researcher with clues about "hidden" patterns in the data. Moreover, a capable program ought to include options to automate this part of the procedure. It should not be necessary that the researcher has to make all the model-building assumptions. Unfortunately, that is exactly how many text analysis programs work. One of the above programs, Catpac, addresses the latter problem in an interesting way (Woelfel, 1993). (However, it is still time-consuming to use.) Appendix 4-A at www.pearsoned.co.uk/schmidt provides an introduction to Catpac based on a text fragment from a focus group. For a software review of Catpac and related software for quantative analysis of text see Chakrapi (1995); Moore, Burbach and Heeler (1995); Belisle (1996); Catterall and Maclaren (1998); Maclaren and Catterall (2002); Schmidt (1999b, 2001).

Table 4.2 Websites for quantitative analysis software

Software	Link to site
Metamorph	www.thunderstone.com/texis/site/pages/metamorph.html
Ethnograph	www.qualisresearch.com/
Kwalitan	www.kwalitan.net/engels/
NUD.lst/NVivo/N6	www.qsr.com.au/
SPSS Text Mining Builder	www.spss.com/lexiquest/index.htm
Textpack	www.gesis.org/en/software/textpack/
Catpac	www.terraresearch.com

Industry applications of Catpac

Peacock and White (1994) have used Catpac for analyzing respondents' responses to an open-ended question concerning the popularity of radio shows. They detected that the week that was used for field interviewing might have been atypical. This important finding had not been detected prior to running the neural network analysis on the data. In a separate study the authors concluded that the neural network program was capable of finding the most frequent types of comments by diary keepers as recorded by an experienced researcher of qualitative interviews.

Wassmann (1992) analyzed responses to an open-ended question with the help of Catpac. The focus of the study was people's attitudes towards low-emission cars and the data were gathered from visitors to an electric car display. After a series of runs with different options he found several stable "word clusters" used by respondents to explain the reasons for buying electric cars.

Marketing research in action
Quantitative analysis of focus group discussion of a tourist catalogue

A quantitative analysis was performed on a transcript of two focus groups. The overall theme of both discussions was the respondents' attitude towards the annual catalogue distributed to all households by the Danish Tourist Board.

Selection of the respondents was based on the following criteria:

Group 1: parent with youngest child less than seven years old
Group 2: parent with youngest child between seven and thirteen years

Five males and five females were selected for each group. The two focus groups contained about 6,000 and 8,000 words, respectively, and both contained approximately 1,200 unique words (the moderator's comments were eliminated). Table 4.3 shows a list with ten (out of forty-two) keywords used in the final analysis. The table shows how many times each word was used across both groups. Moreover, the results are broken down by: age of youngest child; by gender; and by both background characteristics simultaneously. While the analysis was based on Catpac, only the word-count facility in the program was used. Detailed results of the analysis are reported in Schmidt (1998) and Schmidt (1999a).

What does Table 4.3 tell us?
1. Families with small children in general and females in particular use the terms "children" and "amusement park" much more frequently than, say, males with children who have started in school.

Table 4.3 Frequency of use of keywords by focus groups participants broken down by demographic background characteristics

Keyword	Total	Child age < 7	Child age 7–13	Gender Males	Gender Females	Males Age of youngest child < 7	Males Age of youngest child 7–13	Females < 7	Females 7–13
Children	51	37	14	16	35	16	0	21	14
Holiday	55	19	36	30	25	13	17	6	19
Advertisement	56	16	40	29	27	7	22	9	18
Pictures	12	7	5	0	12	0	0	7	5
Catalogue	55	26	29	38	17	20	18	6	11
Camping	15	10	5	11	4	7	4	3	1
Read	25	8	17	13	12	6	7	2	10
Confusing	14	3	11	0	14	0	0	3	11
Interest	18	11	7	6	12	2	4	9	3
Amusement-park	26	16	10	6	20	5	1	11	9
Total	327	153	174	149	178	76	73	77	101

Note that keywords here include different versions of the word. For instance "children" covers: "child, child's, children, children's, kid, kids, kid's, kids', son, sons, son's, sons', daughter, daughters, daughter's and daughters' " But the majority of occurrences were "children" and "child."

➤

2. Females use the terms "pictures," "interest" and "confusing" more often than males.
3. Families with school-children use terms "holiday" and "advertisement," "read" and "confusing" more frequently than families with one or several small children.
4. Males use terms such as "catalogue" and "camping" more often than females. Not a single male mentions "pictures."

A chi-square test for homogeneity shows that the differences both between males and females, and between the two groups of parents are significant, way beyond the 99 percent level (the same holds for the double-split displayed in the last four columns).

What do these general findings indicate?

■ Females are concerned with the comfort of their small children. Whenever they encounter holiday-related topics or issues, they immediately start thinking about what serves the child best: playing grounds, swimming pool, nearby amusement park, events, a zoo and so on. Consequently, the term "children" is often on their mind.

■ According to conventional wisdom, females are more attracted by pictures than males are. Note also the growing usage of the terms "catalogue," "read" and "confusing" when moving from females with small children to females with schoolchildren. Why? Most probably because mothers begin reading tourist catalogues aloud in front of their literate child or encourage the child to read from the catalogue. Mothers use the catalogue as a means of discussion and for involving or engaging the child directly in the holiday decision-making process. Therefore, it is important for the mother and child that the catalogue is interesting and *not* confusing. It is reasonable to believe that this pedagogical trend is more prevalent among mothers with children that have started in school than among those with very small children.

■ Generally, families with schoolchildren seem to perceive the term holiday as leisure and not just as "how do I arrange a fun time for my children?" Again, these families tend to involve the children in the decision-making process.

■ Males are more prone to non-figurative information, and perhaps more interested in camping.

These findings are suppositions and need to be confirmed by quantitative analysis. One way of doing this would be to regard them as hypotheses and operationalize them, say, by constructing a number of interval-scaled statements (1 = totally agree to 5 = totally disagree), and then include them in a questionnaire. Next, a random sample could be drawn, stratified such that the demographic characteristics concerning gender and age of children matched the appropriate target population. Data could be collected using phone or face-to-face, and finally data could be analyzed and findings be compared with the suppositions, thereby either confirming or disproving them.

Assume this has been done and that the quantitative analysis confirms the above suppositions. Table 4.4 lists words that have been used (at least once) by female respondents but not by males, and vice versa. It also summarizes a few gender specific phenomena.

Table 4.4 A selection of words used exclusively by one of the sexes

Females	Males
packed lunches, picnic, meals, cook, menu, bedclothes, toilet-paper, horses, shark, sea-lion, icebergs, zoo, museum, roller-coaster, playground, nature, environment, reusable, beautiful, happy, in love, cute, nice, negative, spoil, unhappy, pictures, coupon, competition, win, gift, pictures, frustrating, irritating, difficult, confusing, odd, system, systematic, classify, group, categories, simple, orderly, well-planned	railway station, bus stop, airline, airport, charter, petrol station, kiosk, freeway, road, pull-in, map, bridge, glove compartment, cigarettes, beer, relax

Females used sixteen different references to family relations (daughter, cousin, parents, father-in-law, grandmother, etc.) compared with four used by males.
Females referred to seven different colours (compared with two for males).
Males mentioned seven foreign countries (compared to 0 for females).

Question

Presume that the marketer, say the national tourist organization, has been treating all families with children up to 13 years as one single segment and as target for the same undifferentiated advertising campaign, the core of it being a catalogue mailed to all household with children up to 13 years. Based on the above, the marketing manager decides to change the company's perception of the target segment and promotion strategy. Why should the strategy be changed? What are the premises of your opinion? Next, say how the strategy should be changed.

4.7 Summary

A **focus group** is a small number of people brought together and guided by a moderator through an unstructured, spontaneous discussion about a topic. The goal of a group is to drag out ideas, feelings, and experiences about a certain issue that would be obscured or stifled by more structured methods of data collection. The use of a small group allows the operation of group dynamics and helps make the participants feel comfortable. It is called a "focus" group because the moderator serves to focus the discussion on the topic and does not let the group dwell on irrelevant points.

Focus groups are a useful and often cost-effective method of gathering insight about a topic. Efficiency can be enhanced by following a clearly defined framework:

Step 1: Define the problem
Step 2: Establish the groups for the sessions:
- The number of groups
- The size of a group
- Who should be selected for the group?
- How should participants be recruited?
- Selection of the venue
- The timing of sessions
- Selection of moderator and assistant

Step 3: Conducting discussions:
- The level of moderator involvement
- The number of topics in a session
- Identifying questions or topics for discussion
- Pre-test the moderator's guide

Step 4: Analyzing the discussion

All stages of the discussion are of equal importance.

Focus groups are a versatile research methodology, but can be misused unless a well thought-out planning process is followed.

An appropriate number of respondents in each group is six to ten. A critical element is the moderator, who must be careful not to bias participants' responses.

Focus groups are most useful when they produce new results. However, the results of focus groups cannot be generalized to the larger population, as the participants may not be representative of the target population. Emphasis is on analytic generalizability, rather than statistical generalizability.

Technology is increasing the range and types of measurement tools and respondent pools available to market researchers. With the internet, not having to get a group of people together in a room potentially offers substantial savings. Conducting qualitative research online in chat rooms is becoming more popular as a way of collecting insights and information. Online focus groups are ideal for locating and researching markets that are hard to recruit, touch on sensitive topics, and geographically dispersed.

After a discussion of traditional qualitative interviews, other approaches of quantifying bodies of text are introduced. Today, several programs can be used for quantitative assessment of text. One is assessed. Catpac is a self-organizing neural network. It begins with a set of artificial neurons: one for each word in the text it is reading. The analysis is initiated by passing a "scanning window" of n consecutive words through the text. The structure thus established can be represented by a square matrix of numbers. Each row and column represents a neuron (word), while each number (an updateable weight) represents the strength of connections of the neurons corresponding to the row and column of the number (cell entry). The resulting matrix resembles a covariance or correlation matrix and can be used as an input matrix for multivariate statistical analysis. Results are scrutinized using cluster analysis and perceptual space analysis. It is concluded that the software can be of value for the marketing, provided appropriate time is dedicated to the analysis.

Questions

1. In which business situations are focus groups a relevant research tool?

2. What are the advantages and disadvantages of focus groups, compared with other methods?

3. Why is the focus group moderator so important?

4. What are the advantages of online focus groups?

5. The Coca-Cola Company has asked you to conduct an online focus with worldwide heavy users of soft drinks. What problems would you foresee in starting up such a group?

6. Section 4.6 shows how to quantify an excerpt from a focus group discussion. Are there other forms of marketing communciation that could be used for quantitative analysis?

References

Belisle, P. (1996) "CATPAC – neural network for qualitative analysis of text." *Imprints*. May. 6–10.

Carson, D. and Coviello, N. (1996) "Qualitative Research Issues at the Marketing/ Entrepreneurship Interface," *Marketing Intelligence and Planning*. Vol. 14, no. 6. 51–58.

Carson, D., Gilmore, A., Perry, C. and Grønhaug, K. (2001) *Qualitative Methods for Marketplace Research*, Beverly Hills, CAL: Sage.

Catterall, M. and Maclaran, P. (1998) "Using computer software for the analysis of qualitative market research data." *Journal of the Market Research Society*. Vol. 40, no. 3. 207–222.

Chakrapani, C. (1995) "Neural net analysis of qualitative data." *Canadian Journal of Marketing Research*. Vol. 14. 110–111.

Harwood, T. G. and Garry, T. (2003) "An overview of content analysis." *The Marketing Review*. Vol. 3. 479–498.

Higgins, S., Ford, K. and Oberski, I. (1996) "Computer-aided qualitative analysis of interview data: some recommendations for collaborative working." *British Educational Research Conference*, Lancaster, September.

Jarvis, S. (2002) "Two technologies vie for piece of growing focus group market." *Marketing News*. May 27. 4.

Kobe, G. (2001) "How focus groups failed Aztek, PT Cruiser," *Automotive Industries*. February. 9.

Langer, J. (2001) "Behind the mirror – get more out of focus group research." *Marketing News*. September 24. 19.

Maclaren, P. and Catterall, M. (2002). "Analyzing qualitative data: computer software and the market research practitioner". *Qualitative Market Research*, Vol 5. No. 1. 28–39.

Moore, K., Burbach, R. and Heeler, R. (1995) "Using neural nets to analyze qualitative data." *Marketing Research*. Vol. 7, no. 1. 34–39.

O'Connor, H. and Madge, C. (2003) "Focus groups in cyberspace: using the internet for qualitative research." *Qualitative Market Research*. Vol. 6, no. 2. 133–143.

Peacock, J. D. and White, T. W. (1994) "Participants say the darndest things." *Second Worldwide Electronic and Broadcast Audience Research Symposium*, Paris.

Reid, D. J. and Reid, F. J. M. (2005) "Online focus groups." *International Journal of Market Research*. Vol. 47. Issue 2. 131–62.

Richards, T. J. and Richards, L. (1991) "The NUD.IST qualitative data analysis system." *Qualitative Sociology*. Vol. 14, no. 4. 307–324.

Schmidt, M. (1998) "Quantitative analysis of qualitative interviews: theoretical considerations and empirical analysis." *AMA Educator's Proceedings*. Vol. 9. 168–177.

Schmidt, M. (1999a) "Multivariate analysis of focus groups." *EMAC-Proceedings*. www.mic.cbs.dk/marcus/GBPapers/EMAC99/EMAC99.htm

Schmidt, M. (1999b) "Software review: CATPAC for Windows." *Tourism Analysis*. Vol. 4, no. 2. 121–128.

Schmidt, M. (2001) "Using an ANN approach for analyzing focus groups." *Qualitative Market Research*. Vol. 4. No. 2. 100–11.

Scholl, N., Mulders, S. and Drent, R. (2002) "On-line qualitative market research: interviewing the world at a fingertip." *Qualitative Market Research*. Vol. 3, no. 3. 210–223.

Sweet, C. (2001) "Designing and conducting virtual focus groups." *Qualitative Market Research*. Vol. 4, no. 3. 130–135.

Tse, A. C. B. (1999) "Conducting electronic focus group discussions among Chinese respondents." *Journal of the Market Research Society*. Vol. 41, no. 4. 407–415.

Wassmann, David A. (1992) "Using CATPAC to read qualitative data." *Advanced Research Techniques Forum of the American Marketing Association*, Lake Tahoe.

Woelfel, J. (1993) "Artificial neural networks in policy research: a current assessment." *Journal of Communication*. Vol. 43, no. 1. 63–80.

5 Other qualitative research methods

Learning objectives

After studying this chapter you should be able to:

- Explain the difference between individual, in-depth interviews and focus groups.
- Understand why and how qualitative researchers develop theory through a grounded approach.
- Explain other forms of qualitative research, for example projective techniques and action research.
- Understand the ethical issues involved in collecting qualitative data, especially through in-depth interviews.
- Understand how a Delphi study and the scenario planning process is conducted.

5.1 Introduction

The purpose of qualitative research is to find out what is going on in a person's mind. Although focus group interviews are the most frequently used qualitative research methods, they are not the only type of non-structured research. Frequently, decision-makers need current information that can be obtained by directly asking people questions, i.e. making use of in-depth interviews. Other popular methods include grounded theory, protocol analysis, various projective techniques, and physiological measurements. Besides various techniques this chapter also deals with the internal and external use of the Delphi method as a research tool.

5.2 Individual, in-depth interviews

Individual in-depth interviews are non-directive or semi-structured interviews in which the respondent is encouraged to talk about the subject rather than to answer "yes" or "no" to specific questions. Like the group discussion technique to which it is closely related, an interview endeavours to understand the nature of the area being researched, rather than gauge its size.

In **non-directive interviews**, the respondent is given freedom to respond, within the bounds of topics of interest to the interviewer. Success depends on:

■ establishing a relaxed and sympathetic relationship;
■ the ability to probe to clarify and elaborate on interesting responses, without biasing the content of the responses; and
■ the skill of guiding the discussion back to the topic when digressions are unfruitful, always pursuing reasons behind the comments and answers.

Such sessions normally are one to two hours long and may be tape-recorded (with the permission of the respondent) for later interpretation.

In **semi-structured** or **focused individual interviews** the interviewer attempts to cover a specific list of topics or sub-areas. The timing, exact wording, and time allocated to each question area are left to the interviewer's discretion.

This mode of interviewing is especially effective with busy executives and technical experts. Basic market intelligence, such as trends in technology, market demand, legislation, competitive activity, and similar information are amenable to such interviews. The open structure ensures that unexpected facts or attitudes can be pursued.

This type of interview is demanding, and much depends on the interviewer's skill. First, the interviewer must be sufficiently persuasive to get through the shield of secretaries and receptionists around many executives, to get an appointment. The challenge is to establish rapport and credibility in the early moments of the interview, and then maintain that atmosphere. For this, there is no substitute for an informed, authoritative person who can relate to respondents on their own terms. This can be achieved by asking the respondent to react to specific information provided by the interviewer. Care should be taken to avoid threatening questions. A good opener might be, "If you had to pick one critical problem affecting your industry, what would it be?" Co-operation sometimes can be improved by offering a *quid pro quo*, such as a summary of some of the study findings.

Keeping records is a problem with these interviews. Some executives dislike tape recorders, so it may be necessary to use a team of interviewers who alternate between asking questions and recording responses. To keep the interview as short as possible, it is usually best to leave behind a structured questionnaire for any specific data that are wanted, because this can be assigned to the interviewee's staff for answering. Finally, since the appropriate respondents for these studies are often difficult to identify, and may represent many parts of an organization, it is always advisable to ask for recommendations about which other people it might be useful to interview.

Individual in-depth interviews are also used in consumer markets to identify product benefits and trigger creative insight.

The interview is typically conducted by a trained field worker who is equipped with a list of topics or open-ended questions. The respondent is encouraged to respond in his or her own words, and the interviewer is trained in asking probing questions such as, "Why is that so?," "Can you elaborate on your point?," or "Would you give me some specific reasons?" These questions are not intended to tap subconscious motivations; rather, they

Table 5.1 Comparing in-depth interviews with focus groups

	Focus groups	*In-depth interviews*
Group interactions	Group interaction may stimulate thoughts from respondents	There is no group interaction. Therefore, stimulation for ideas from respondents is initiated by the interviewer
Group/peer pressure	Group pressure and stimulation may clarify and challenge thinking Peer pressure and role-playing may occur and may be confusing to interpret	In the absence of group pressure, the thinking of respondents is not challenged With one respondent, role-playing is minimized and there is no peer pressure
Respondent competition	Respondents compete with one another for time to talk. There is less time to obtain in-depth details from each participant	The individual is alone with the interviewer and can express thoughts in a non-competitive environment. There is time to obtain detailed information
Influence	Responses in a group may be "contaminated" by opinions of other group members	With one respondent, there is no potential for influence from other respondents
Subject sensitivity	If the subject is sensitive, respondents may be hesitant to talk freely in the presence of several other people	If the subject is sensitive, respondent may be more likely to speak to a single interviewer
Interviewer fatigue	One interviewer can easily conduct several group sessions on one topic without becoming fatigued or bored	Interviewer fatigue and boredom are problems when many individual interviews are needed
Amount of information	A relatively large amount of information can be obtained in a short time at relatively small cost	A large amount of information can be obtained, but it takes time to obtain it and to analyze the results. So costs are relatively high
Stimuli	The volume of stimulus materials that can be used is limited	A fairly large amount of stimulus material can be used
Interviewer schedule	It may be difficult to assemble respondents if they are a difficult type to recruit (such as busy executives)	Individual interviews are easier to schedule

Source: Qualitative Research Council of the Advertising Foundation (1985), Stokes and Birgin (2006)

simply ask about conscious reasons to help the researcher form a better picture of what is going on in the respondent's mind. In-depth interviews are versatile, but they require careful planning, training, and preparation.

The summary report will look similar to one written for a focus group study, as the analyst looks for common themes in the transcripts, and these are noted in the report.

Verbatim responses are included to support the analyst's conclusion, and any significant differences of opinion that are found in the respondents' comments are noted. Again, it is vital to use an analyst who is trained and experienced in interpreting such qualitative data.

There are no hard-and-fast rules for choosing focus groups rather than individual interviews for qualitative studies. The comparison in Table 5.1 may help make the choice.

The essence of these interviews is that people may be questioned and probed extensively about issues they rarely reflect upon. Therefore care must be taken not to upset or disturb respondents. Another methodological issue is the question of confidentiality. In quantitative research, the respondent identity is generally unimportant. The essence of sampling theory is that a sufficiently large and randomly chosen sample will represent the views. In qualitative research (and especially at in-depth interviews) the relationship between the individual respondents and their views is at the heart of analyses and interpretation. It is not possible to reach qualitative findings without having 'revealed' the individual as part of the research process. Because of this, respondents may be unwilling to take part in qualitative research or, if they do, are guarded with their responses. If respondents are to reveal deeply held feelings, perhaps in front of strangers, they have to be reassured of how the data captured will be used. Ethical problems also arise when videotaping interviews. How much to tell respondents and what information the clients should be allowed to access can be an issue. However, the researcher should always be sensitive to the questions and the comfort level of the respondents.

Marketing research in action

Kraft singles – cheese

The problem

Kraft Singles once dominated the dairy section for processed cheese slices in the US, but the product wasn't keeping up with market growth. While category sales inched up 1.6 percent between 1988 and 1998, the brand's share declined 0.2 percent. Advertising that had been shown since 1996 was losing its effect. How could Kraft reverse the trend?

Market research

First, Kraft had to figure out what women, particularly mothers, felt about Kraft Singles. It sent out a group of ethnographers from Strategic Frameworking to talk to women aged 25 to 64 in their homes while they were making sandwiches. They told researchers they knew what their children liked and disliked. They felt good giving Kraft Singles to their children because of its nutritional value. Mothers in focus groups repeated the same sentiments, but there was a hitch: while they knew Kraft Singles were a favourite, they could be persuaded to buy cheaper products.

Kraft needed to dissuade mothers from switching to a less-expensive brand, but how? A phone survey by Market Facts gave some clues. Among those polled who bought Kraft Singles, 78 percent considered the product to be a source of calcium. And 84 percent of women with children under 12 said they would be motivated to buy the brand because of that. Based on this research, Kraft researchers focused on two concepts that could stop mothers from defecting to competitors: show how much kids loved the taste of Kraft Singles, and emphasize that the brand provided the calcium they needed.

Problem-solving

The advertising agency J. Walter Thompson produced two commercials and showed them to women for feedback. Two problems emerged. First, the idea that kids love the taste of Kraft Singles didn't come across strongly enough. And simply stating that they were a valuable source of calcium didn't work. The campaign needed a creative element to grab the attention of its target audience.

So another commercial was developed with two kids eating gooey, grilled-cheese sandwiches while a male voiceover said: "Two out of five kids don't get enough calcium." The visual communicated the great taste of Kraft Singles, mothers in focus groups agreed. But some participants had issues with the "two out of five" statement, saying that it played too much on their guilt. To soften the message, Kraft switched to a female voiceover and used the Dairy Fairy, an animated character from a previous campaign, to lighten the tone. Copy testing by research agency Millward Brown showed that the commercial performed significantly above the norm on measures such as branding and persuasion.

The pay-off

In the fourth quarter of 1998, Kraft showed "The Calcium They Need" advert in five markets to evaluate its performance. The campaign led to a 10.6 percent sales increase in these markets. Based on this, the campaign went national in January 1999 and continued to boost revenue. Volume grew 14.5 percent and sales 11.8 percent. About two-thirds of the growth in sales was attributed to the campaign.

Source: Adapted from: www.kraft.com; American Demographics (2000); other public sources

5.3 Protocol analysis

Protocol analysis involves placing people in decision-making situations and asking them to talk about everything they consider when making a choice. It is a qualitative research technique that has been developed to gain insight into the consumer's decision-making processes. After several people have provided protocols, the researcher reviews them and looks for commonalities such as evaluative criteria used, number of brands considered, types and sources of information, and so forth. Protocol studies are useful in two situations. First, they are helpful for purchases involving a long time frame in which several decision factors must be considered, such as buying a house. By having people describe the steps they go through, a researcher can piece together the process. Second, when the decision process is very short, recall may be faulty and protocol analysis can be used to slow down the process.

5.4 Projective methods

Projective techniques involve situations in which participants are placed in simulated activities in the hopes that they will divulge things about themselves that they might not reveal under direct questioning. Respondents are asked to respond to stimuli and the hope is they will project aspects of their own thoughts or feelings via the use of stimuli (Boddy, 2005).

Projective methods were introduced by Mason Haire (1950), famous for his psychological study of buyers 'shopping lists' (Anderson, 1978), and developed by motivational researchers such as James M. Vicary (1955) and psychologist Ernest Dichter (1960, 1962, 1964, 1971). Dichter founded the Institute for Motivational Research and became "immortalized" in Vance Packard's bestseller *The Hidden Persuaders* (1957), a critical book about how psychological techniques were being used by companies for persuading consumers to buy products.

Projective techniques are appropriate in situations in which the researcher is convinced that respondents will hesitate to relate their true opinions. These situations may include

Marketing research in action
Use of projective techniques by Philips

Philips of the Netherlands is using projective techniques to find out how its shaver is perceived against competitive products. In face-to-face interviews Philips asked respondents to personalise three internationally known domestic appliance brands: "What would these brands look like if they would be human beings: age, gender, profession, appearance, clothes, personal interests?" Philips also used the "party-mapping" technique: "Suppose these brands would organize a party, who would be the 'bright spark' of the party, who would be the silent type, who would be talking to each other, etc." Although the process was lengthy, the results were valuable and interesting. Most respondents had no difficulty in answering the questions and enjoyed the game.

Another technique used by Philips was to let respondents personalize different brands as in this interview with an English woman:

Moderator: What image do you have of the "Braun man?"

Respondent: Blonde, probably tall, confident, tends to dress in suits, would have a German car – a Mercedes or BMW – probably the latter. He would probably have a physical hobby, anything in which he can show off his confidence, such as sports.

Moderator: Now about Philips, could you give me a picture of Philips?

Respondent: Well, this person is more likely to be dark-haired, medium height, again confident, but not overwhelming like his Braun colleague … umm, think he will have a top-of-the-range car that is not ostentatious and shouts money! I think this person is going to be more of a family person.

The outcomes show that respondents can associate not only on a product level but also on a brand/lifestyle level, shedding light on the deeper layers of brand imagery.

Source: Adapted from www.philips.com; Scholl et al. (2002)

behaviours such as tipping waitresses, socially undesirable behaviours such as smoking or alcohol consumption, questionable actions such as littering, or illegal practices.

There are five common projective techniques used by marketers. These are discussed below.

Word association test

The word association technique asks respondents to give the first word or phrase that comes to mind after the researcher says a word or phrase. The list of items used as stimuli should include a random mix of such neutral items as "chair," "sky," and "water," interspersed with the items of interest, such as "shopping downtown," "holiday in Greece," or "hamburger helper." The list is read quickly to avoid allowing time for defence mechanisms to come into play. Responses are analyzed by calculating:

- the frequency with which any word is given as a response;
- the time taken for a response; and
- the number of respondents who do not respond at all to a test word within a reasonable time.

The result of a word association task is often hundreds of words and ideas. To evaluate quantitatively the relative importance of each, a representative set of the target segment can be asked to rate, on a five-point scale, how well the word fits the brand, from "fits extremely well" to "fits not well at all." It is also useful to conduct the same associative research on competitive brands. When such a scaling task was performed for McDonald's on words generated from a word association task, the strongest associations were with the words Big Macs, Golden Arches, Ronald, Chicken McNuggets, Egg McMuffin, everywhere, familiar, greasy, clean, food, cheap, kids, well-known, French fries, fast, hamburgers, and fat (Baker, 2001, 392).

The word association technique has also been particularly useful for obtaining reactions to potential brand names. Consumers associate a brand with: product attributes; intangibles; customer benefits; relative price; use/application; user/customer; celebrity/person; lifestyle personality; product class; competitors; and country/geographic area. This technique is used extensively to explore these brand associations. Word association has also been used to obtain reactions to and opinions about advertising slogans.

Sentence completion test

With sentence completion, respondents are given incomplete sentences and asked to complete them in their own words. The researcher then inspects these sentences to identify themes or concepts. The notion here is that respondents will reveal something about themselves in their responses. For example, suppose that a make of tea was interested in expanding its market to teenagers. A researcher might recruit high-school students and instruct them to complete the following sentences:

Someone who drinks hot tea is…
A mother who serves tea to her family is…

The researcher would look at the responses and attempt to identify themes. For example, the theme identified for the first sentence might be "healthy," which would signify that tea was perceived as a drink for those who are health-conscious. Given this information, the company might deduce that there is room to capitalize on the hot tea market with teens.

Picture test

With a picture test, an image is shown to participants who are instructed to describe their reactions by writing a short story about the picture. The researcher analyzes the content of these stories to ascertain feelings, reaction, or concerns generated by the picture. Such tests are useful when testing pictures being considered for use in brochures, advertisements, and on product packaging. Reactions would be subjected to expert interpretation.

Cartoon or balloon test

With a **balloon test**, a cartoon with an empty "balloon" above the head of one of the characters is given to subjects who are instructed to write in the balloon what the character is saying or thinking. The researcher then inspects these thoughts to find out how subjects feel about the situation in the cartoon.

These frequently depict two people talking in a particular setting. The comments of one person are shown in a "speech balloon"; the other person's "balloon" is empty and the informant is asked to give a reply that fits the situation. Typical situations could cover conversations between husband and wife, mother and child, shop assistant and customer, garage mechanic and car owner, etc. This "third party" test is particularly useful because it allows people to be less inhibited than they might be if asked to describe their own reactions.

Third-person techniques

By asking how friends, neighbours, or the average person would think or react to a given situation, the researcher can observe, to some extent, the respondents projecting their own attitudes onto this third person, so revealing more of their own true feelings. Magazines use this technique to identify which articles to feature on the cover, to stimulate news stand sales. Direct questioning as to the articles of greatest interest to the respondent tends to be confounded by socially desirable responses. For example, articles on complex issues of foreign affairs are rated highly interesting to the respondent during direct questioning, but are not thought to be of interest to the neighbours.

Another variant of this technique provides a shopping list or a description of a person's activities, and asks respondents to describe the person. The respondents' attitudes towards the activities or items on the list will be reflected in their descriptions of the person. Usually, two lists are prepared and presented to matched sets of respondents; these could be grocery shopping lists, in which all items are identical except one. Differences in the descriptions attributed to the two lists can reveal the respondents' underlying attitudes toward the product or activity being studied.

A pioneer study involving third-person technique was connected with stereotyping of types of US housewives' grocery-buying habits. In 1949, a study was undertaken by Haire to determine the motivations of consumers towards instant coffee in general and the Nescafé product in particular (Haire, 1950).

When housewives were asked whether they liked instant coffee, most of those who rejected it blamed the taste. However, there was a suspicion that this was not the real reason. Two shopping lists were prepared, identical except that one had Nescafé instant coffee and the other Maxwell House (drip-grind) coffee. These shopping lists are given below:

Shopping list 1	Shopping list 2
1½ lb hamburger meat	1½ lb hamburger meat
2 loaves of Wonderbread	2 loaves of Wonderbread
Bunch of carrots	Bunch of carrots
1 can Rumford's baking power	1 can Rumford's baking power
1 lb Nescafé instant coffee	1 lb Maxwell House coffee (drip grind)
2 cans Del Monte peaches	2 cans Del Monte peaches
5 lb potatoes	5 lb potatoes

A hundred respondents were asked to project themselves into the buying situation and characterize the woman who bought the groceries. The two lists were distributed (only one list to each person), each respondent being unaware of the existence of an alternative list. The findings revealed that the buyer of instant coffee was seen as lazier, less well organized, more spendthrift, and not as good a wife as the housewife using the other coffee.

The research has been subject to considerable scrutiny over the years. Arndt undertook a similar survey among Norwegian housewives in 1971 with different products: the baking powder was changed to Freia, and Nescafé replaced by Friele coffee. Because pilot research revealed criticism of the Haire shopping list for alleged lack of proportion in the quantities specified for the various items, some modifications were also made to quantities, e.g. carrots were increased from one to two bunches. The results indicated that the "instant coffee" housewife may have become associated with "modernity and more intense involvement in the world around."

Role playing

With role playing, participants are asked to pretend they are a "third person," such as a friend or neighbour, and to describe how they would act in a certain situation or to a specific statement. By reviewing their comments, the researcher can spot latent reactions, positive or negative, conjured up by the situation. It is believed that some of the respondents' true feelings and beliefs will be revealed by this method because they can pretend to be another individual.

Another technique with similar expressive objectives is the **role rehearsal** procedure used as part of a focus group discussion. The participants in a focus group are encouraged, by offering them an incentive, to alter their behaviour pattern in some extreme way.

5.5 Grounded theory

Grounded theory is used to explore phenomena within their own terms of reference "grounded" in reality. A differentiating feature of grounded theory is the emphasis on a close examination of empirical data prior to focused reading of the literature.

In 1967, Glaser and Strauss (1967) developed a method of analyzing data that built its own ("grounded") theories while data was being collected, rather than testing hypotheses about theories that had been determined before the data collection began. The methodology has since been widely used in sociology and many other areas, such as psychology, nursing, education, social work and anthropology, and recently in management and business research.

Glaser and Strauss accepted that the study of people should be scientific, in the way understood by quantitative researchers. This means that it should seek to produce theoretical propositions that were testable and verifiable, produced by a clear set of replicable procedures. Glaser and Strauss defined theory as: "theory in sociology is a strategy for handling data in research, providing modes of conceptualisation for describing and explaining. The theory should provide clear enough categories and hypotheses so that crucial ones can be verified in present and future research; they must be clear enough to be readily operationalised in quantitative studies when these are appropriate."

The grounded theorist follows a set of systematic procedures for collecting and analyzing data.

The grounded theory process involves identifying theoretical categories that are derived from the data through the use of the constant comparative method. This requires the researcher to compare the contents of one interview or observation episode with another or with emerging theoretical concepts in an effort to identify underlying themes. Similarities and differences in the data are noted, leading to the derivation of theoretical categories that can help explain the phenomenon under investigation (Glaser and Strauss, 1967; Glaser, 1992). Not only is the intention to provide explanations of social phenomena, but also to provide insight to those engaged in the behaviour under investigation.

Data collection

A distinctive feature of this approach is that both the collection of data and the analysis take place simultaneously, with the aim of developing general concepts to organize data and to integrate the data into a more general, formal set of categories. The research process involves progressing through several stages.

The data collector should try not to impose a prior framework on the perceptions of meanings, definitions or interpretations that respondents provide, and not contaminate the meanings of the respondents. So interviews of individuals and groups will usually appear to be *conversations* where the interviewer operates at the same level as the respondent, usually in *the field* like "give and take" and empathetic understanding. A grounded theory researcher will not have an interview protocol, but may have a short list of probe issues that grows as the number of interviews increases. Analyses of these will unearth issues that need to be checked in later interviews. These issues may or may not come from prior knowledge or research.

Examination of data

This is usually completed in a group situation where different people focus on sections of interviews and are asked to interpret what they are seeing. These are written up on a flipchart to examine the range of perspectives, but also identify connections among the issues, problems or themes. At this stage the issues are implicit and not systematically worked out.

Coding

This procedure aims to organize data into themes or codes. This is done firstly by "open coding." Researchers are then encouraged to think about different dimensions of the open-coded categories, termed "dimensionalizing," and to find links between categories by "axial coding." Different events and situations are observed to build up a complete picture of the variations within a theoretical category through "theoretical sampling." Then, more data would be gathered in a direction driven by the concepts derived from the evolving theory and based on the concept of "making comparisons" – looking for further instances of the derived theory that present a contradictory view, to a point where there are no contradictory views. Eventually, categories are refined so that a theoretical framework emerges, termed "selective coding." Coding procedures help to:

- Build rather than test theory;
- Provide researchers with analytic tools for handling masses of raw data;
- Help analysts to consider different meanings of phenomenon;
- Be simultaneously systematic and creative;
- Identify, develop, and relate the concepts that are the building blocks of theory.

Using qualitative data analysis software

The process of coding described above would typically be conducted using proprietary software, helping the researcher to code data in a consistent manner, to search for themes and codes, and examine the context in which they emerge in a transcript of an interview or number of interviews. The connection of codes and themes help to establish the nature of grounded theory. The software allows codes and themes to be changed so they may be viewed from different perspectives. From this, the researcher develops further issues and individuals to investigate, and the interpretation and theory emerge. Software for analyzing qualitative data is discussed in Chapter 4.

Presenting diagrams

Grounded researchers use diagrams to represent the relationship of theoretical categories. This helps to focus on the individual categories and their inter-relationships. Many software packages help to build such diagrams, helping the researcher to visualize data as they are building a theory. The use of diagrams is therefore vital in developing theory as well as in the presentation of a theory when analysis is complete.

Attempting to gain an objective viewpoint

For the grounded theorist, data collection and analysis occur in alternating sequences. Analysis begins with the first interview and observation, which leads to the next interview or observation, followed by more analysis, more interviews or fieldwork, and so on. Analysis drives the data collection. Therefore, there is a constant interplay between researcher and the research act, and care must be taken to maintain a balance between objectivity and sensitivity. Objectivity is necessary to arrive at an impartial and accurate interpretation of events and increase confidence in the results. Sensitivity is required to perceive the nuances and meanings of data and to recognize the connections between concepts, enabling creativity and sensitivity.

During the analytic process, grounded researchers attempt to set aside their knowledge and experience to form new interpretations about phenomena. Most researchers have learned that complete objectivity is impossible and that in every piece of research, quantitative or qualitative, there is an element of subjectivity. What is important is to recognize that subjectivity is an issue and that researchers should take appropriate measures to minimize its effect.

In qualitative research, objectivity does not mean controlling the variables, it means openness, a willingness to listen and to "give voice" to respondents, be they individuals or organizations. It means hearing what others have to say, seeing what others do and representing them as accurately as possible.

Ultimately, grounded theory is expected to generate findings that are meaningful to decision-makers, and appropriate to tasks they face. As with other "interpretivist" forms of research, if it is found meaningful and used successfully, there is further evidence of the theory's validity.

Marketing research in action
Using grounded theory to analyze beer consumption in Australia

The aim was to explore a popular Australian activity to provide an insight into the consumption process in general, and the consumption of beer in particular.

Alcohol plays a symbolic role in Australian culture, with beer being closely associated with the country's lifestyle. Australians are the ninth largest per capita consumers of beer in the world. Most beer consumed in Australia is full-strength beer, with the average Australian drinking 70.8 litres a year.

Beer has long had particular relevance for the working man in societies with British origins (Barr, 1995). The relative consumption levels between the sexes indicated that beer played a much more important role in the lives of Australian men than in the lives of Australian women. The association of beer with masculinity has also been suggested although this association is common in other western countries.

The methodology

According to the requirements of grounded theory, a literature review was conducted mainly after data were collected, and the central themes were allowed to emerge from the data rather than being forced to fit a theoretical framework. Participant observations, non-participant observations, and interviews were used to gather data relating to beer consumption. More than 400 people were interviewed for the study, of whom 109 were interviewed and observed in 23 pubs and clubs in three states (Western Australia, New South Wales, and Victoria). Informants approached in public drinking contexts were asked to discuss their beer consumption behaviours in both public and private contexts.

In addition to beer consumer informants, five brewery representatives from two big brewers operating in Australia and nine bartenders from a range of drinking venues were used as informants. They develop profiles of the typical consumers of various brands. The bartenders were highly experienced observers of those consuming alcohol, particularly beer. They provided a degree of continuity to the study by describing the drinking habits of specific individuals over weeks, months, and, in some cases, years.

After the respondents were interviewed the transcripts and their observation notes were imported into the NUD*IST software (see Chapter 4) for coding.

The findings

The primary concern to the Australian beer drinkers was found to be "image management."

Image management in this context refers to the activities undertaken by drinkers that communicate their membership of specific groups that develop and reinforce their self-concepts, and maximize the outcomes of the stereotyping activities of others to enhance self-esteem. Beer drinkers try to communicate important aspects of themselves to others. It is an attempt to achieve their ideal self-images, enabling the satisfying

➤

relationships they desire. Males communicate their masculinity, and females can communicate their social equality through drinking beer, although females can also communicate their femininity through non-consumption.

Similarly, those belonging to higher social classes can demonstrate their separation from the working classes through non-consumption, or their choice of a select group of beer brands.

Drinkers engage in different stages of image management when drinking, including their brand choices, location choices, posturing while consuming, and discussions with others regarding beer as a product category.

Image management becomes more difficult as more brands are introduced to the market, as is the case in the Australian beer market, so consumers can become more uncertain in their decisions.

The elements of image management also include "image monitoring." This has two main components, self-monitoring and environmental monitoring. For drinkers to manage their images through beer consumption or non-consumption, they need to be aware of their own behaviours and the perceptions that others hold of these behaviours. The beer drinkers in the study demonstrated a need to monitor others' reactions to their choice of brand and the volume of beer consumed.

The "grounded theory analysis" of Australian beer consumption outlined above has implications for existing consumer behaviour theories. The assumption of an autonomous consumer involved in individual decision-making is challenged. To conclude, the "grounded theory" method has helped in identifying the purpose behind consumption behaviour and the process involved. These findings have both theoretical and practical implications for understanding beer consumption behaviour and giving breweries ideas for marketing.

Source: Adapted from Pettigrew (2002)

5.6   Action research

The social psychologist Kurt Lewin is generally thought to have coined the term "action research." He envisaged a process whereby one could construct a social experiment with the aim of achieving a certain goal. He set the stage for knowledge production based on solving real-life problems. From the outset, he changed the role of researchers from being a distant observer to being involved in solving problems.

Action research is composed of three elements, all of which have to be present.

■ *Research*. Research based on any quantitative or qualitative techniques, or combination of them, generates data, with subsequent analyses and interpretation and shared knowledge.

■ *Participation*. Trained researchers serve as facilitators and "teachers" to team members. All individuals set their action research agenda, generating the knowledge necessary to transform the situation and put the results to work. Action research is a participatory process in which everyone involved takes some responsibility.

■ *Action*. The research aims to alter the initial situation of the organization in the direction of a more self-managed and more rewarding state for all parties.

5.7   The Delphi method

Forecasting sales for a new product has long been a challenge. For companies producing and selling high-volume items, such as a national packaged foods manufacturer, this task has huge economic effects especially in the first few months. At the very least, under-forecasting may result in lost sales and market opportunities while over-forecasting may result in huge inventory and spoilage costs.

Classical forecasting techniques (e.g., time series) are difficult to apply to products that have no history, which means that a judgemental method must be used.

The method recognizes that using the estimates of many experienced and knowledgeable people is better than using the judgement of a few and provides a framework for doing this.

The technique was developed at the Rand Corporation in the 1950s. It is based on an independent survey of a group of experts. The results are fed back anonymously to the experts for subsequent rounds of projections, in which individuals may modify their views because of the consensus. The independence (i.e., not seeing who projected what but just the consensus average and range), avoids bias transfer and intimidation.

The name was coined by Kaplan (Woudenberg, 1991), who headed a research programme trying to improve the use of expert opinion in policy-making at the Rand Corporation following the Second World War. In Greek mythology, the oracle at Delphi was consulted to forecast the future so that correct and timely decisions could be made before embarking upon a course of action such as waging war. Kaplan had the notion that experts could be solicited for their opinions or expectations about the likelihood of events or scenarios of interest to the company.

The Delphi method has five characteristics:

■ The sample consists of a "panel" of carefully selected experts representing a broad spectrum of opinion on the topic or issue being examined.
■ Participants are usually anonymous.
■ The "moderator" (researcher) constructs a series of structured questionnaires and feedback reports for the panel over the course of the study.
■ It is an iterative process often involving three or four iterations or "rounds" of questionnaires and feedback reports.
■ There is an output typically in the form of a research report with the Delphi results, the forecasts, policy and options with their strengths and weaknesses, recommendations to senior management and, possibly, action plans for developing and implementing the programmes.

Marketing research in action
The Delphi method used for product development

For one project, Delphi research was used to develop a food product with a long shelf-life that did not require cooking or warming up. The research took the following steps:

1. Analysis of the Delphi results, mapping out the evolving consumption opportunities (and their relevant motives) pertaining to the company's business idea. Although food habits are very slow to change, the effect of the different working hours and types of jobs (less industry and more services), the population's ageing, and a greater attention to health-oriented food are causing changes that will occur within five to seven years.
2. Definition of possible product concepts, in line with the changes expected in the near future.
3. Identification of weak signals coming from present behaviours by analyzing research on food habits. Sociodemographic research showed that a few behavioural patterns, which the Delphi method expected to become widespread over ten years, were already spreading among people with less traditional lifestyles.
4. Confirmation of weak signals and identification of products (five product lines were found that shared a few basic elements such as recipes, ingredients, and service level) with the new product concept. Sales trends among the five products indicated they had small markets, but trends were favourable.
5. Defining the contents of the concept to convert it into a briefing for research and development. Elements were separated into: basic ingredients; their qualitative features; importance of organoleptic elements (smell, colour, taste); importance of aesthetic aspects; physical elements of packaging; packaging size; product service level; and emotional elements (naturalness, lightness, taste, health, etc.).

   Priorities were assigned to the elements because some of them caused technical or economic problems not in line with the product budget.
6. Identification of the positioning, which would influence both the recipe and advertising. Delphi research helped determine which food style would become dominant, and in identifying the value system it was based on so that a particular nutritional area could be chosen.

The next steps were: elaboration of the recipes, prototypes at experimental cooking level, and the product-concept test, which showed far more consensus on the concept than other research projects.

Source: Adapted from Bolongaro (1994)

The steps to be followed in generic Delphi sales forecasting are:

1. Select experts. The selection criteria are primarily intuitive. The panel should be made up of people experienced in some phases of the planning, execution or meas-

urement of the new product process. Varied representation is a desired feature and their biases are acceptable. Key internal managers and outside sources such as trusted customers, trade people and the like are desired. The panel size should be fifteen to twenty-five.

2. Contact the selected experts and ask them for their forecasts of the product you are interested in.
3. Compute the average and range of forecasts of the panel. The average is called the consensus forecast.
4. Contact the panel again and provide the consensus and range of forecasts, asking them if they wish to revise their forecasts.
5. Compute the average and range of the revised forecasts. Repeat steps four and five if more rounds are desired. Past studies show that improvement in forecast accuracy falls off sharply after two to three rounds. For typical new product forecasting, a well-developed system needs only two rounds, which is easier to manage and execute.

In the second and subsequent rounds, respondents with extreme projections tend to provide written reasons for their values. Their comments should be made available anonymously to all experts.

It will always be hard for experts to submit to other people's views. One should provide the experts with all relevant positive and negative information at the first round, and the consensus forecast at the second round with a comparison against their forecast. At this point they can re-evaluate their numbers with comfort. The goal is, of course, for the second round consensus to converge to a more accurate projection.

Advantages and limitations of the Delphi technique

The use of the Delphi technique generally offers the following advantages:

- It can help identify the questions critical to change in areas where conventional methodology is inadequate.
- Forecasting can be made relatively quickly and inexpensively.
- Different points of view, ranging from public policy-makers to industry executives, are elicited and weighed.
- If basic data are sparse or lacking, there may be no alternative to the Delphi technique.

The technique also has limitations or disadvantages:

- Expert opinions are generally less satisfactory than facts.
- Responsibility is dispersed, and good and bad estimates are given equal weight.
- The method is usually more reliable for aggregate forecasting than for developing reliable breakdowns by specific territory, customer groups.

Linstone and Simmonds (1977) contend that the main weakness in Delphi is that some questions are not asked – especially those that seem unimportant when beginning the study. Although the technique is generally considered worthy of continued use and development, it is nevertheless looked on as a rather special methodology for modelling. A further problem encountered in Delphi studies is a high drop-out rate, up to half in each round (Laczniak and Lusch, 1979).

A recent development is the "Delphi conference," in which a computer operates as a real-time accounting system of members' responses. This allows a set of individuals to communicate rapidly with one another in generating group forecasts and in making policy decisions.

5.8   Scenario planning

This section is based on Verity (2003). Scenario techniques can be applied to almost any business issue that contains degrees of uncertainty. They are best known for their corporate, high-level, global and long-term use, but scenarios can be used to answer very specific issues of competitive strategy, marketing and organizational capability. The paradox is that this very flexibility and widespread applicability seems to limit the technique's acceptance in everyday use. It is a difficult technique to define and describe. There are different schools of thought about what scenarios are for, how they should be built and when they should be used.

What is scenario planning?

Herman Khan and his associates at the Rand Corporation in the 1950s and 1960s first started building scenarios. Their objective was to explore how a nuclear war might erupt between the USA and the Soviet Union, by describing possible logical paths to different outcomes. Khan pioneered the technique of "future-now" thinking, aiming through the use of detailed analysis plus imagination, to be able to write a report in the present as if it were being written in the future.

Into the 1970s the technique was extended, by Khan at the Rand Corporation and later at the Hudson Institute (a think tank, which Khan set up) for corporate use and for application to thinking about societies in general. General Electric was one of the first companies to use the technique in the 1960s and 1970s, but it was Pierre Wack at Shell and Peter Schwartz (1991) at Stanford Research Institute at Stanford University during the 1970s and 1980s who really introduced scenario planning to management as a strategy tool.

Schwartz (1991) defined scenarios as: "alternative, plausible stories of how the world may develop." He emphasized that the outcome was not an accurate forecast of future events, but a deeper understanding of the forces that might push the future along different paths. Therefore, describing what scenario planning is and choosing a process is not straightforward. To quote Schoemaker (1993): "The term scenario has many meanings, ranging from movie scripts and loose projections to statistical combinations of uncertainties."

Scenarios have been developed for countries, for regions, for issues (the future of crime, the future of women) and for companies. Among those examples developed for organizations, there can be many levels of analysis, from global, external, environmental to focused, internal issues. The length of the time considered tends to correlate with the scale and scope of the exercise.

Macro/industry scenarios

Macro scenarios can provide insights into possible industry changes. They can expose possible shifts in macroeconomic, political, or social variables that are not foreseen in a more industry-centred view of the external environment. By macro scenario, Porter (1985) is referring to changes that might occur outside of his industry structure forces, i.e., those that are covered by the PEST model in other textbooks (Hollensen, 2004).

Micro-scenarios

Scenarios are diverging, but plausible, views of the future, differing from forecasts in that they explore possible futures rather than predict a single point future. Figure 5.1 shows two different scenarios – A and B – where the outcome, measured on two dimensions, is influenced by both convergent and diverging forces.

Figure 5.1 shows that diverging and converging factors have to be balanced. Time flows from the left to the right. The courses of the scenarios pass through a number of time windows, each made up of the key dimensions, which the scenario writers want to highlight. In Figure 5.1 two "time windows" are shown: one in two years from now and another one in five years from now. For a globally oriented company the two dimensions could be worldwide market share and worldwide market growth for a product. The convergent forces illustrated in Figure 5.1 would mean that Scenario A and B would come nearer to

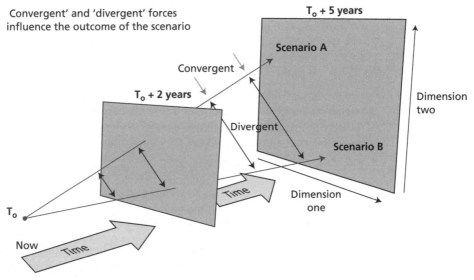

Figure 5.1 Development of scenarios A and B over time
Source: Hollensen (2004)

each other over time. Divergent forces would have the opposite effect. Examples of convergent forces would be:

- A high degree of macroeconomic stability in international markets.
- An increasing standardization of products across borders.

An example of a divergent force would be: 'High degree of cultural diversity among target international markets'.

Scenario planning enables the study of a range of alternative futures each of which is different from the other and from the current operating environment. Rather than rely on a single "most likely" forecast, it is possible to compare and contrast opinions on how an industry might evolve.

Since it is externally oriented, scenario planning is good at identifying growth strategies for the company as well as potential threats to the market positions, and also helping to identify external industry changes that are affecting market share or margins.

Application of scenario planning

Scenario techniques can be applied to almost any business issue. They are best known for their corporate, high-level, global and long-term use, but the method can be used to answer specific issues of competitive strategy, marketing problems or problems of organizational capability. Scenario thinking has led to a product launch. Millett (2003) describes how, in the mid-1990s, the US technology company Battelle worked with a company to think about cleaning products by exploring trends such as an ageing population, more households with two wage-earners, and growing concerns about health and welfare. From these trends emerged future consumer values of convenience, speed and thoroughness that led to the launch of a hygienic, disposable cloth for cleaning surfaces (Battelle, 1998).

A focused scenario technique was similarly used to investigate the next decade of the UK market for liquefied natural gas (LNG) as an environmentally friendly replacement for petrol, in the light of the development of cleaner petrol, inner-city pollution and the prospect of hydrogen-fuelled car engines. The outcomes were used to test how effectively the assets, capabilities and culture of the company conducting the research could deliver the fuel. Risks for the near-term future if contingencies were not urgently addressed were clear. For example, the fuels network could not cope with consumer expectations in two of the three scenarios. Given the time required to build this capability, it was seen as urgent to make plans for strategic investment in distribution. This was especially important since it was clear that the closest competitor was in a stronger position with a more flexible system already in place.

Guidelines for scenario planning

- *Establish a core planning team.* Analyzing the strategic implications of scenarios is best done in teams. The creative dynamics of an effective group are likely to provide the type of breakthroughs that will make the process worthwhile. A good rule of thumb is to have five to eight people in the planning group.

- *Get a cross-section of expertise*. Include the heads of all functional areas. Also, include individuals outside the top executives to bring new perspectives.
- *Include outside information and outside people*. Focus on injecting interesting and challenging perspectives into the discussion.

5.9 Summary

Qualitative research techniques aim to understand people's thinking. In-depth interviews have been adapted to probe into consumer motivations and hidden concerns. Protocol analysis induces participants to "think aloud" so researchers can map the decision-making process. Projective techniques, such as word association, sentence completion, and role playing, are also useful in unearthing motivations, beliefs, and attitudes that subjects may not be able to express well verbally.

Grounded theory is complex and time-consuming, and its potential to help understand some aspects of some social marketing processes has not been realized. Similarly, ethnographic studies are also complex and time-consuming. However, the benefits of closeness to a reality and the depth of understanding that can be achieved, which may also lead to new insights, far outweigh the disadvantages. Data collection largely precedes the review of the relevant literature to allow the emergent themes to most closely reflect the nature of the data as opposed to conclusions drawn from the existing literature.

The Delphi method has mainly been developed for forecasting developments in the environment. The method recognizes that the synergy of using the estimates of many experienced and knowledgeable people is better than using the judgement of a single person. This method uses an independent survey of a group of experts. Results, including comments, are fed back anonymously to the experts for subsequent rounds of their projections, which they may modify because of their view of the consensus.

Scenario planning techniques are best known for their corporate, high-level, global and long-term use, but they can also be used to answer specific issues of competitive strategy, marketing and organizational capability.

The Delphi method and scenario planning can also be used internally in compiling a SWOT analysis for a specific company. The moderator should try and circulate the views until consensus is reached.

Questions

1. Compare and contrast the unique characteristics and advantages/disadvantages of the in-depth and focus group interviewing techniques.

2. What are the requirements of a researcher undertaking in-depth interviews? Why are these requirements particularly important when conducting interviews with managers?

3. Why is the context of questioning particularly important when conducting in-depth interviews in international marketing research?

4. Which difficulties might be encountered when conducting qualitative in-depth interviews in an international context?

5. What is the purpose of projective techniques? Under what circumstances should projective techniques be used?

6. Describe a situation where an in-depth interview or a projective technique might upset potential respondents.

7. Describe the "word association technique" and the "story completion technique." Give examples of the types of respondents and the context in which such techniques would work.

8. Describe a projective technique that you feel would work particularly well by e-mail.

9. Consumer drawing tests may ask study participants to draw the kind of person that would be consuming a particular product. Draw a typical Citroën and VW car-owner. What do the drawings suggest about the participants' perceptions of Citroën and VW car-owners?

10. What stages are involved in the application of a grounded theory approach?

11. Explain the stages in using the Delphi method. In which circumstances is it relevant to conduct a Delphi study within a company?

References

American Demographics (2000) "Cheese please: Kraft Singles talk to moms about kids and calcium." March. 6.

Anderson, J. C. (1978) "The validity of Haire's shopping list projective technique." *Journal of Marketing Research*. Vol. 15, no. 4. 644.

Arndt, J. (1983) "Haire's shopping list revised." *Journal of Advertising Research*. Vol. 13, no. 5 (October). 57–61.

Baker, M. J. (2001) "Selecting a Research Methodology," *The Marketing Review*. Vol. 1, 3. 373–97.

Barr, A. (1995) *Drink*. Bantam Press, London.

Battelle (1998) "Battelle forecasts breakthroughs for future household products." February 25. (www.battelle.org/news/98/34topten.stm).

Boddy, C. (2005) "Projective techniques in market research: valueless subjectivity of insightful reality?" *International Journal of Market Research*. Vol 47, issue 3. 239–54.

Bolongaro, G. (1994) "Delphi technique can work for new product development." *Marketing News*, 6/6/94. Vol 28, issue 12. 32–4.

Dichter, E. (1960) *Strategy of Desire*. Doubleday, New York.

— (1962) "The world customer." *Harvard Business Review*, July–Aug. 113–22.

— (1964) *Handbook of Consumer Motivations. The psychology of the world of objects*. McGraw-Hill, New York.

— (1971) *Motivating Human Behaviour*, McGraw-Hill, New York.

Glaser, B. G. (1992) *Basics of grounded theory analysis: emergence vs. forcing*. Mill Valley, CA: Sociology Press.

Glaser, B. G. and Strauss, A. (1967) *The Discovery of Grounded Theory*. Aldine Publishing, Chicago, IL. 80–95.

Goldfisher, Ken (1993) "Modified delphi: A concept for new product forecasting." *Journal of Business Forecasting Methods and Systems*. Winter. 10–11.

Haire, M. (1950) "Projective techniques in marketing research." *Journal of Marketing*. Vol. 14, no. 5. 649–656.

Hollensen, S. (2004) *Global Marketing: A decision-oriented approach*. Financial Times/Prentice Hall, Harlow. 222.

Laczniak, G. R. and Lusch, R. F. (1979) "Future Research for Managers." *Business*. Vol. 29, no. 1. Jan–Feb. 41–9.

Lewin, K. (1946) "Action research and minority problems." *Journal of Social Issues*. Vol. 2, no. 4. 34–46.

Linstone, H. A. and Simmonds, W. H. C. (1977) *Future Research: New directions*. Addison-Wesley, London. 88–90.

Millett, S. (2003) "The future of scenarios: challenges and opportunities." *Strategy and Leadership*. 31(2). 16–25.

Packard, Vance, (1957). *The Hidden Persuaders*. Random House, New York.

Pettigrew, S. (2002) "A grounded theory of beer consumption in Australia." *Qualitative Market Research*. Vol. 5, no. 2. 112–122.

Porter, M. E. (1985) *Competitive Advantage*. Free Press, New York.

Qualitative Research Council of the Advertising Foundation (1985) *Focus Groups: Issues and approaches*, New York City. 78.

Schoemaker, P. J. H. (1993) "Multiple scenario development: its conceptual and behavioural foundation." *Strategic Management Journal*, 14. 193–213.

Schwartz, P. (1991) *The Art of the Long View*. Doubleday, New York.

Scholl, N., Mulden, S. and Drent, R. (2002) "On-line qualitative market research: interviewing the world at a fingertip." *Qualitative Market Research*. Vol. 5, no. 3. 210–223.

Stokes, D. and Birgin, R. (2006) "Methodology or methodolatry? An evaluation of focus groups and depth interviews." *Qualitative Market Research: An International Journal*. Vol 9, no 1. 26–37.

Verity, J. (2003) "Scenario planning as a strategy technique." *European Business Journal*. Vol. 15, no. 4. 185–195.

Vicary, James M. (1955) "Seasonal psychology." *Journal of Marketing*. Vol. 20. 394–7.

Woudenberg, F. (1991) "An evaluation of Delphi." *Technological Forecasting and Social Change*. Vol. 40. 132.

6 Measurement and scaling

Learning objectives

After studying this chapter you should be able to:

- Explain the concepts of measurement and scaling and show how the latter may be considered an extension of measurement.
- Discuss the primary scales of measurement and differentiate nominal, ordinal, interval and ratio scales.
- Introduce the different types of scales used for measuring attitudes.
- Give a description of each of the well-known scales that are used to measure attitudes.
- Discuss the considerations involved in transferring and implementing standard measurement scales across borders (in an international setting).
- Explain reliability and validity and distinguish between them.
- Discuss the main approaches to reliability and validity assessment.
- Identify ways to improve the reliability of measurement scales.
- Explain the relationship between reliability and validity.

6.1 Introduction

In this chapter the basic concepts of measurement and scaling are introduced and defined, distinguishing between the various types of measurement scales. Readers, who want to obtain a deeper insight should examine the more specialized books by Kerlinger and Lee (2000) or Nunnally and Bernstein (1994).

Once a marketing researcher has a clear understanding of what he or she wishes to understand in a group of target respondents, the concepts of scaling and measurement should be considered. These concepts are vital in developing questionnaires or instruments of measurement that will fulfil the research objectives in the most accurate manner.

The term **scaling** refers to procedures for attempting to determine quantitative measures of subjective and sometimes abstract concepts. For example, we assign a number scale to the various levels of heat and cold and call it a thermometer.

Accurate measurement of constructs is essential in making decisions, and this chapter addresses the importance of measuring customers' attitudes and behaviours, and other marketplace phenomena. The measurement process is described and the central decision rules needed for developing scale measurements. The focus is on basic measurement issues, construct development, and scale measurements. Note that construct development is not the same as construct measurement. For true construct measurement to take place, the researcher needs to understand scale measurements as well as the interrelationships between what is being measured and how to measure it.

This chapter discusses four scales of measurement: nominal, ordinal, interval and ratio, and describes both comparative and non-comparative scaling techniques in detail. The considerations involved in implementing scaling techniques when researching international markets are discussed.

Often, a researcher is interested in testing whether a construct developed in one country holds in another country, or examining similarities and differences in constructs across countries or geographic areas. Typically, an operational measure of the construct has already been developed in the base country and the task facing the researcher is to see whether the construct can be meaningfully measured in the same way elsewhere.

Procedures for developing a scale to measure an underlying construct in a single country are relatively straightforward. Developing a scale in a multi-country environment is considerably more complex and challenging, and presents the researcher with two intertwined issues. The fundamental question is whether the same construct exists in different countries. A particular construct identified in one country may not exist in another country or may not be expressed in the same terms.

This chapter examines the various issues in developing scales to be used in multi-country research. These issues include how items are developed, whether different scale items function the same, and assessing whether measures are reliable and equivalent in different countries are addressed. Some illustrations of how scales have been applied cross-culturally are discussed. The chapter concludes with a discussion of ethical issues that arise in scale construction.

6.2 The measurement process

Most questions in marketing research surveys are designed to measure attitudes. What management really wants to understand – and ultimately influence – is behaviour. For many reasons, however, they are likely to use attitude measures instead of behaviour measures. First, there is a widely held belief that attitudes are precursors of behaviour. If consumers like a brand, they are more likely to choose that brand over one they like less. Second, it is generally more feasible to ask attitude questions than to observe and interpret actual behaviour. Attitude measures offer a greater advantage over behaviour measures in their capacity for diagnosis or explanation.

Measurement is defined as the process of assigning numbers or other symbols to certain characteristics of the object of interest, according to some prespecified rules. How this is done is strongly influenced by the sort of information that is being sought.

Usually, numbers are assigned because of the ease of application in mathematical and statistical analyses. Certain rules should be followed when assigning numbers for measurement. There should be a one-to-one correspondence between the number and the characteristic, and this assignment should be constant over time. Scaling is the process of creating a continuum on which objects are located according to the amount of the measured characteristics they possess.

Critical to collecting primary data is the development of well-constructed measurement procedures. It is important to realize that measurement consists of two different development processes, which can be labelled **construct development** and **scale measurement**. To achieve the overall goal of obtaining high-quality data, researchers must understand what they are attempting to measure before developing the appropriate scale measurement. The goal of construct development is to identify and define what is to be measured, including any dimensionality traits. In turn, the goal of scale measurement is to determine how to measure each construct precisely.

Construct development

Precise definition of marketing constructs begins with defining the purpose of the study and providing clear expressions of the research problem. Without a clear initial understanding of the research problem before the study begins, the researcher can end up collecting irrelevant or low-quality data.

Construct development can be viewed as an integrative process in which researchers focus their efforts on identifying the subjective properties for which data should be collected for solving the defined research problem. Identification of which properties should be investigated requires knowledge and understanding of constructs and their dimensionality, validity and operationalization.

At the heart of construct development is the need to determine exactly what is to be measured. After the decision-maker and researcher establish what objects are relevant to the redefined research problems, the next step is to identify the pertinent objective and subjective properties of each object of concern.

In cases where data are needed for insight into the composition of an object, the research focus is limited to measuring the object's objective properties. In contrast, when data are needed to help understand an object's subjective properties, then the researcher must identify sets of measurable subcomponents that can be used to clarify the abstractness associated with the object's subjective properties.

In determining what is to be measured, researchers must keep in mind the need to acquire relevant, high-quality data, data structures, and information to support management's decisions.

As mentioned in Chapters 4 and 5, market researchers can use a variety of qualitative data collection methods (such as focus groups and in-depth interviews) among a few customers to develop preliminary insights into the set of identifiable and measurable components associated with an abstract construct.

Construct operationalization is a process whereby the researcher explains a construct's meaning in measurement terms by specifying the activities or operations necessary to measure it. The process focuses on the design and use of questions and scale measurements to gather the data structures needed. Since many constructs, such as customer satisfaction, preferences, emotions, quality images, and brand loyalty, cannot be directly observed or measured, the researcher attempts to indirectly measure them through operationalization of their components.

6.3 Basic scales of measurement

Scaling is the process of creating a continuum on which objects are located according to the amount of the measured characteristics they possess. An illustration of a scale that is often used in research is the dichotomous scale for sex. The object with male (or female) characteristics is assigned the number 1 and the object with the opposite characteristics is assigned the number 0. This scale meets the requirements of the measurement process in that the assignment is one to one and it does not vary with respect to time and object.

There are four basic scales: nominal, ordinal, interval and ratio (see Table 6.1).

Nominal scale

Marketing researchers use nominal scales to identify characteristics of their test subjects. These can be gender, social class, race, religion, habits, traits, and physical location. The categories created by nominal scales must include every test subject or product in only one category for a particular characteristic.

In international marketing research, nominal measures are the simplest type of measures and pose the least burden on the respondent. They are appropriate for illiterate respondents or those with low level of education. The respondent simply has to decide whether or not the characteristic or category applies. Such measures do, however, require that the definition of a category is unambiguous and familiar to the respondent.

Ordinal scale

An ordinal scale is obtained by ranking objects or by arranging them in order with regard to some common variable. The question is simply whether each object has more or less of this variable than some other object. The scale provides information as to how much difference there is between the objects.

Because the amount of difference between objects is not known, the permissible arithmetic operations are limited to statistics such as the median or mode (but not the mean).

Marketers use ordinal scales to gather a variety of information, such as consumer taste preferences and comparisons involving pricing, packaging, promotion, quality, and performance rankings.

In international marketing research, the most direct way to collect ordinal data is to ask respondents to order objects in relation to some attribute. For well-educated respondents this is a relatively simple and straightforward task, but when the research is conducted among less literate populations, physical stimuli may be needed.

Table 6.1 Types of scales and their characteristics

Scale	Basic characteristics	General example	Marketing example	Permissible statistics/tests
Nominal	Numbers identify and classify objects; objects are either identical or different	Numbering of soccer players	Brands in category No. of countries where company has agents	Percentages Mode[1] Chi-square Binomial[2] Contingency coefficient
Ordinal	Objects are greater or smaller Numbers indicate the relative positions of the objects but not the magnitude of differences between them Comparative, rank order, itemized category, paired comparison	Quality of wool Hardness of minerals Popularity ranking of actors Pleasantness of odours	Preference ranking of brands Image ranking of companies	Percentile Median Spearman's rank-order correlation Randomized block design ANOVA (Friedman Test) Sign test[2]
Interval	Differences between objects can be compared; zero point is arbitrary Likert, Thurstone, Stapel, associative, semantic-differential	Temperature Energy	Buying-probability scale satisfaction scale agreement (Likert) bipolar (semantic differential)	Mean Standard deviation Product moment correlations/t-tests[3] ANOVA Regression Multivariate analysis
Ratio	There is a meaningful zero, so comparison of absolute magnitudes is possible	Distance Weight Density Resistance Pitch scale Loudness	Sales Market share Advertising budget Sample size	Geometric mean[4] Harmonic mean Coefficient of variation[5] Multivariate tests
Logarithm	Items of extreme varying size can be directly compared	Richter/Mercalli scales (earthquakes) Hertzsprung–Russell diagram (astronomy)	Learning/experience scales Comparing performance data of firms of very different sizes	If transformed to ratio scale: all known multivariate tests

Interval scale

In an interval scale the numbers used to rank the objects also represent equal increments of the attribute being measured. This means that differences can be compared.

Interval scales have the same characteristics as ordinal scales except that they can show relative differences in rankings. For example, ordinal scales do not assume that the distance between one and two is equal to the distance between three and four. With interval scales, these distances are assumed to be the same. Furthermore, in interval scales the distance between one and three is assumed to be equal to the distance between two and four.

Temperature scales, such as thermostats and thermometers, are interval scales. Although interval scaling uses equal intervals between successive ranks, there either is no fixed zero point or the zero point is arbitrary (on a celsius scale 0 °C is where water freezes and 100 °C where it boils). Interval scale distances are sensitive to scale transformations. For example, 10 °C on a centigrade (or Fahrenheit scale) is not twice as hot as 5 °C. Also, the equation $10° = 2*5°$ does not make any sense. Even transforming from one temperature scale to another causes problems: the distance between 5 °C and 10 °C is 5 °C. However, once 5 °C and 10 °C are converted to Fahrenheit – 41 and 50 – the difference is 9 °F.

Ratio scale

A ratio scale is a special kind of interval scale that has a meaningful zero point. With such a scale of weight, market share, or euros in savings accounts for example, it is possible to say how many times greater or smaller one object is than another. This is the only type of scale that permits comparisons of absolute magnitude. For example, if a company's sales were €1 million in 2002 and €2 million in 2003, we can conclude that sales doubled in one year.

Without an absolute zero point, we cannot draw this conclusion. Ratio scales are the most commonly used scales in business.

6.4 Measuring attitudes

The **Thurstone scale** was the first formal technique for measuring an attitude. It was developed by L. L. Thurstone in 1928, as a means of measuring attitudes towards religion. It is made up of statements about a particular issue, and each statement has a numerical value indicating how favourable or unfavourable it is judged to be. People mark each of the statements to which they agree, and a mean score is computed, indicating their attitude.

Researchers use two categories to measure people's attitudes: comparative and non-comparative rating scales (see Figure 6.1). In comparative rating scales, respondents compare one characteristic or attribute against a specified standard, according to some pre-determined criterion. Since the standard of comparison is specified, researchers have a reference point. For example, a respondent might be required to compare one brand of cereal against the other brands that they consider when making a purchase in a super-market. Results have to be interpreted in relative terms and have ordinal or rank-order properties. The scores obtained indicate that one brand is preferred to another, but not by how much.

The main benefit of **comparative scaling** is that small differences between stimulus objects can be detected. As they compare the stimulus objects, respondents are forced to choose between them. In addition, respondents approach the task from the same known reference points. Consequently, comparative scales are easily understood and can be applied easily.

In **non-comparative** scales, also referred to as monadic or metric scales, each object is scaled independently of the others in the stimulus set. The resulting data are generally

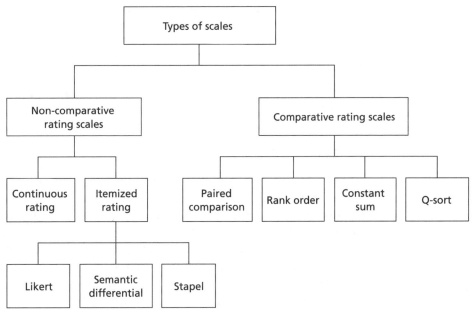

Figure 6.1 Types of scales

assumed to be interval or ratio-scaled. For example, respondents may be asked to evaluate Pepsi on a 1 to 6 preference scale (1 = not at all preferred, 6 = greatly preferred). Similar evaluations would be obtained for Coke and Virgin Cola. As can be seen in Figure 6.1, non-comparative scales can be continuous rating or itemized rating scales. The itemized rating scales can be further classified as Likert, semantic differential or Stapel scales. Non-comparative scaling is the most common scaling technique in marketing research.

Continuous rating

In continuous ratings (or graphic ratings) respondents indicate their responses on a continuum. Between the continuum's extreme points are responses that represent a gradual progression toward the extremes. Respondents place a mark at a location on the continuum that reflects their response to the question.

If a blank line is used (see Figure 6.2) the researcher applies a numerical scale after respondents complete the survey. Either way, the researcher segments all responses into a usable number of groups and then analyzes the information as interval data.

Although continuous rating scales are easy to apply, marketing researchers seldom use them because they are not very reliable. This is because there are usually no standard responses.

These scales also cause problems for international researchers. Less-educated respondents have difficulty conceptualizing a continuous scale with equally divided intervals. Hence, the researcher must allow considerable time to explain the scale.

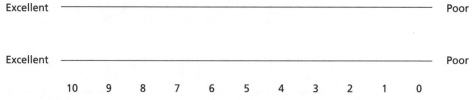

Figure 6.2 Examples of continuous rating scales

Itemized rating

Itemized rating scales resemble graphic ratings, except that respondents select from a finite number of choices rather than from the theoretically infinite number on a continuum. Each choice has a number or descriptor associated with it. For example, respondents may be asked to respond to the statement "When I visit Tesco, it is a pleasant experience" by selecting from the following choices: "strongly agree," "agree," "neutral," "disagree," and "strongly disagree." The strengths of these scales are that respondents can complete each question in a relatively short time and researchers can easily analyze the responses, because quantitative scores can be assigned to each response.

Likert scale

Named after Rensis Likert, this scale is a widely used rating scale that requires the respondents to indicate a degree of agreement or disagreement with each of a series of statements about the stimulus objects (Likert, 1932). Typically, each scale item has five response categories, ranging from "strongly disagree" to "strongly agree" (see Figure 6.3).

1. My bank provides excellent customer service

Strongly agree	Agree	Neither agree nor disagree	Disagree	Strongly disagree
+5	+4	+3	+2	+1
☐	☐	☐	☐	☐

2. My bank has convenient locations

Strongly agree	Agree	Neither agree nor disagree	Disagree	Strongly disagree
+5	+4	+3	+2	+1
☐	☐	☐	☐	☐

Figure 6.3 Examples of a Likert scale

Responses may be analyzed either individually or on a total ("summated") basis by adding across items. If the summated basis is used, the scoring must remain consistent throughout the survey. For example, all favourable responses would be represented by high scores, and all unfavourable responses would be represented by low scores. When negative statements are included, the scores must be adjusted to maintain the pattern of high scores representing favourable and low scores unfavourable responses.

A balanced scale has the same number of positive and negative categories; a non-balanced scale is weighted towards one end or the other. If the researcher expects a wider range of opinions, then a balanced scale probably is in order. If research has determined that most opinions are positive, then the scale should contain more positive gradients than negative. This would enable the researcher to ascertain the degree of positiveness toward the concept being researched.

For example, if the first statement in Figure 6.3 read "My bank does not provide excellent customer service," then the scale would be reversed so that a "strongly disagree" score was assigned "+5." "Strongly disagree" is a positive response in this case, so reversing the scale maintains the pattern of +5 representing the most favourable response.

The plus signs used in the responses show the direction (positive versus negative). Minus signs could have just as effectively been used, where "−2" indicated "strongly disagree," "0" indicated "neutrality," and "+2" indicates "strongly agree."

The semantic differential scale

The semantic differential scale is a specialized scaled-response question format that sprang from the problem of translating a person's qualitative judgements into quantitative estimates. Like the modified Likert scale, this one has been borrowed from another area of research, namely the work of Charles Osgood in semantics. This scale contains a series of bipolar adjectives for the various properties of the object under study, and respondents indicate their impressions of each property by indicating locations along its continuum. The focus of the semantic differential is on the measurement of the meaning of an object, concept, or person. Because many marketing stimuli have meaning, mental associations, or connotations, this type of scale works very well when the marketing researcher is attempting to determine brand, store or other images.

The construction of a semantic differential scale begins with the determination of a concept or object to be rated. The researcher then selects bipolar pairs of words or phrases

Sweet	___ ___ ___ ___ ___ ___ ___	Sour
Tasty	___ ___ ___ ___ ___ ___ ___	Tasteless
Satisfying	___ ___ ___ ___ ___ ___ ___	Unsatisfying
Expensive	___ ___ ___ ___ ___ ___ ___	Inexpensive

Figure 6.4 Example of a bipolar scale (semantic differential)

Our restaurant	
+5	+5
+4	+4
+3	+3
+2	+2
Expensive	Helpful
−1	−1
−2	−2
−3	−3
−4	−4
−5	−5

Select a plus number for words that you think describe the restaurant accurately. The more accurate you think the description is, the larger should be the plus number selected. Conversely, select a minus number for words which do not describe the restaurant. The less accurate you believe the description to be, the larger should be the minus number you select.

Figure 6.5 The Stapel scale, used in an example with a restaurant

that could be used to describe the object's salient properties. Depending on the object, some examples might be "friendly-unfriendly," "hot-cold," "convenient-inconvenient," "high quality-low quality" and "dependable-undependable."

Suppose a soft drinks maker wanted to find out what consumers thought about its products. Figure 6.4 shows a sample of pairs that respondents could use to evaluate a drink.

The opposites are positioned at the endpoints of a continuum of intensity, and it is customary, although not mandatory, to use seven separators between each point. The respondent then indicates their evaluation of the performance of the object, such as a brand, by marking the appropriate line. The closer the respondent marks to an endpoint on a line, the more intense is his or her evaluation of the object being measured.

Stapel scale

The Stapel scale mirrors the semantic differential scale, but instead of using two dichotomous descriptive words or phrases as choices, only one word or phrase is used. This makes the task easier for both the rating developer and the respondent to use. Furthermore, although points are not assigned numbers in a semantic differential scale, they are assigned numbers in a Stapel scale, typically using a ten-point scale. Categories may be assigned a range of +5 to −5 (see Figure 6.5). The downside of the Stapel scale is the potential biasing of the respondent by the word choice of the categories.

Comparative rating scales

Comparative rating scales allow respondents to make comparisons according to some predetermined criterion, such as importance of or preference for something. Four common comparative scales are paired comparisons, rank order, constant-sum and Q-sort.

Paired comparisons

The respondent is presented with two objects at a time and is required to indicate a preference for one of the two according to some stated criterion. The method yields ordinal scaled data, for example, brand A is better than brand B, or, brand A is cleaner than brand B. It is often applied in cases where the objects are physical products. One important point about data obtained through paired comparisons is that the ordinal data can be readily converted into interval-scaled data.

In Figure 6.6 the number of required comparisons is determined by applying the following formula:

$$\text{Number of required comparisons} = [n*(n-1)]/2$$

Where n indicates the number of individual items being compared. This requisite number demonstrates a shortcoming of the paired-comparison technique. When several comparisons are required, the technique becomes less effective and less accurate due to respondent fatigue. For example, with seven brands, twenty-one comparisons are necessary. Another concern among researchers is that when comparisons are made, the order of the items or questions can bias the outcome.

Paired-comparison data can be analyzed in several ways. The researcher can calculate the percentage of respondents who prefer one stimulus over another by summing the elements of Figure 6.6 for all the respondents, dividing the sum by the number of respondents, and multiplying by 100. Simultaneous evaluation of all the stimulus objects is also possible. Under the assumption of transitivity, it is possible to convert paired-comparison data to a rank order.

Instructions
We are going to present you with six pairs of bottled beers. For each pair, please indicate which of the two brands of beer in the pair you prefer.

Reading from

	Holsten	Stella Artois	Grolsch	Carlsberg
Holsten	–	0	0	1
Stella Artois	1	–	0	1
Grolsch	1	1	–	1
Carlsberg	0	0	0	–
Number of times preferred	2	1	0	3

Note: A 1 in a box means that the brand in that column was preferred over the brand in the corresponding row. A 0 means that the row brand was preferred over the column brand.

Figure 6.6 Using paired comparisons for bottled beer preferences

Please rank the following restaurants according to the friendliness of their personnel. Place the number 1 beside the restaurant that you feel has the most friendly personnel, 2 by the restaurant with the next most friendly personnel, and so on until all restaurants have been rated.

_____ McDonalds

_____ Burger King

_____ Taco Bell

_____ Arby's

_____ KFC

Figure 6.7 Rank-order scale for evaluating restaurants

To arrive at a rank order, the researcher determines the number of time each brand is preferred by summing the column entries in Figure 6.6. Therefore, this respondent's order of preference, from most to least preferred, is Carlsberg, Holsten, Stella Artois, and Grolsch.

Rank-order-scales

Rank-order scales require respondents to arrange a set of objects with regard to a common criterion: advertisements in terms of interest, product features in terms of importance, or new-product concepts with regard to willingness to buy in the future. The result is an ordinal scale with the inherent limitation of weak scale properties. Ranking is widely used in surveys, however, because it corresponds to the choice process occurring in a shopping environment where a buyer makes direct comparisons among competing products (brands, flavours, product variations, and so on). See Figure 6.7.

Rank-order scales are not without problems. Ranking scales are more difficult than rating scales because they involve comparisons, and hence require more attention and mental effort. The ranking technique may force respondents to make choices they might not otherwise make, which raises the issue of whether the researcher is measuring a real relationship or one that is artificially contrived.

Due to the difficulties of rating, respondents usually cannot meaningfully rank more than five or six objects. The problem is not with the ranking of the first and last objects but with those in the undifferentiated middle. When there are several objects, one solution is to break the ranking task into two stages. With nine objects, for example, the first stage would be to rank the objects into classes: top three, middle three, and bottom three. The next stage would be to rank the three objects within each class.

Constant-sum scales

Respondents are asked to allocate a number of points, say, 100, among objects according to some criterion, for example, preference or importance. They are instructed to allocate the points such that if they like brand A twice as much as brand B, they should assign twice as many points to brand A.

Divide 100 points among the following fast-food establishments to indicate your relative preference for each:

Restaurant	Points
McDonald's	_____
Burger King	_____
Taco Bell	_____
Arby's	_____
KFC	_____
Total	__100__

Figure 6.8 An example of constant-sum scales

To determine the relative preference of college students for different fast-food restaurants, a researcher could randomly sample 100 students and ask them to do the task indicated in Figure 6.8.

The advantages of this scaling technique are that it does not require a large number of individual comparisons, as paired comparisons can, and the point system indicates strengths of preferences.

However, as with previous techniques, the options should be limited to a manageable number. The total points must add up to 100 (or any other predetermined amount), so too many choices may cause problems, because some respondents will invariably assign points that add up to more or less than 100.

Another problem is the requirement that respondents allocate points in a way that indicates their relative preference among items. This requires that respondents understand proportion, which is not always a realistic expectation.

A final shortcoming is that it has not been definitely established that the data produced uses an interval scale. This form of scaling has not been thoroughly tested, so most marketers use it with caution.

Q-sort scaling

When the number of objects or characteristics that are to be rated is very large, it becomes tedious for the respondent to rank order or do a pairwise comparison, and problems and biases creep into the study. To deal with such a situation, the Q-sort scaling process is used. With this technique, respondents are asked to sort the various characteristics or objects that are being compared into groups, such that the distribution of the number of objects or characteristics in each group follows a normal distribution.

A relatively large number of groups or piles should be used to increase the reliability or precision of the results.

For example, respondents are given one hundred attitude statements on individual cards and asked to place them into eleven piles, ranging from "most highly agree with" to "least highly agree with." The number of objects to be sorted should neither be less than sixty nor more than one-hundred-and-forty; a reasonable range is sixty to ninety objects. The number of objects to be placed in each pile is pre-specified, often resulting in a roughly normal distribution of objects over the whole set.

6.5 Reliability and validity in measurement

Whenever items or individuals are measured, error is likely. Unintentional mistakes may occur when something under investigation is measured and the true response is sought but not revealed. This is common in research. Since virtually all research efforts are flawed, marketing researchers must routinely measure the accuracy of their information. Researchers must determine measurement error, which is the difference between the information sought and the information actually obtained in the measurement process. Every measurement includes true, accurate information plus some degree of error. We can summarize this idea as follows:

Measurement results = True measurement + Measurement error

Two potential sources of error exist in the measurement process: systematic error and random error. Therefore we can extend the equation as follows:

Measurement results = True measurement + (Systematic error + Random error)

Systematic error is caused by a constant bias in the design or implementation of the measurement situation. This type of error occurs in samples where the findings are either consistently higher or consistently lower than the actual value of the population parameter being measured. Systematic error is also referred to as non-sampling error, because it encompasses all types of errors except those brought about by random sampling.

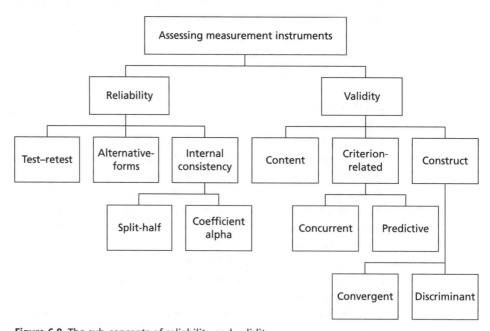

Figure 6.9 The sub-concepts of reliability and validity

In relation to assessing errors in the measurement instruments, reliability and validity are two central concepts. Figure 6.9 shows how the two concepts may be divided into sub-concepts.

Reliability

A reliable scale is a prerequisite to sound research. Reliability refers to the ability of a scale to produce a consistent result if repeated measurements are taken. If a professor gives a group of students two different (independent) tests to measure their knowledge of marketing research, and the students' scores from the two measures are very similar, then the measures can be said to be reliable since they replicated each other's scores. Reliability is the extent to which scales are free of random error and so produce consistent results. In general, the less random error detected, the more reliable the data will be. Systematic sources of error do not lessen reliability, because they consistently influence the measurement rather than create inconsistencies to it.

In **test–retest reliability**, respondents are given identical sets of scale items at two different times, under nearly equivalent conditions. The time interval between tests is typically two to four weeks. The degree of similarity between the two measurements is determined by computing a correlation coefficient. The higher the correlation coefficient, the greater the reliability.

That test–retest approach is subject to time constraints, which creates another potential problem for the researcher. The greater the time interval between the first and second tests, the less reliable the scale will be. Also, environmental and personal elements may change and alter the results of the second test.

Another issue is that it is often difficult to persuade the original respondents to take a second test. There may also be a carryover effect from the first measure. This is called the **halo effect**. Suppose respondents were initially asked to rate the service of a shop. Their response to a similar question asked two weeks later may be influenced by their initial response. A third problem with test-retest reliability is that some situations can be measured only once. If Procter & Gamble wants to examine consumers' initial reaction to an advertising campaign for Tide, it can be measured only once.

Alternative-forms reliability (sometimes called "equivalent-forms reliability") is the ability of two "equivalent" scales to obtain consistent results. To carry out this test, researchers administer one scale to respondents and, about two weeks later, administer the second equivalent scale to the same respondents. In theory, there should be no carryover effect, because the items are different, so scores from the first scale should not affect scores on the second. A similar number of questions should be used on each scale to measure the topic under investigation. After the respondents have completed the two scales, researchers compare the measurement instruments item-by-item to determine how similar they are. The problem with alternative-forms reliability lies in constructing two scales that appear different yet have similar content. The alternative-forms test is similar to the test-retest method except that the test-retest method uses the same measurement instrument both times, not two different instruments.

In **internal-consistency reliability**, two or more measurements of the same concept are taken at the same time and then compared to see whether they agree. Suppose the following four statements using a Likert scale (choices range from "strongly agree" to "strongly disagree") are used to determine consumers' attitudes towards My Bank's customer service: "I always enjoy visiting My Bank," "I like the people who work at My Bank," "My Bank satisfies my banking needs," "The services I receive at My Bank are excellent." The extent to which the four measures correlate across a sample of respondents indicates the reliability of the measures. As the correlation increases, the reliability of the measures increases.

The easiest way to test for internal consistency is to use the **split-half** technique. This method assumes that these items can be divided into two equivalent subsets that can be compared. Several methods have been devised to divide the items randomly into halves and compute a measure of similarity of the total scores of the two halves across the sample. An average split-half measure of similarity, coefficient alpha, can be obtained from a procedure that has the effect of comparing every item with every other item.

Coefficient alpha (or Cronbach's alpha) is a technique for judging internal consistency of a measurement instrument by averaging all possible ways of splitting test items and examining their degree of correlation (Cronbach, 1951). The greater the correlation is to a score of 1, the higher the internal consistency (Cronbach, 1990). A score of 0.60 or less indicates that the items measure different characteristics.

How can reliability be improved?
Here are some ways to improve reliability:

- Increase the number of measurements. Instead of using the scores from one test, sum or average the scores on several equivalent forms of the test. To do this, increase the number of test items, checking to make sure that the new items examine similar concepts.
- Use good experimental controls. To minimize non-systematic or random factors, the testing situation must be conducive to achieving consistent responses. Therefore, make sure that lighting is comfortable and consistent, measuring devices such as stopwatches work properly, the measurement scale is reliable and consistent, and test administrators know how to avoid creating bias in respondents.
- Be careful to select only items relevant to the topic for measurement. Define the study topic carefully and correctly and then write test items that will accurately reveal information about that topic.

Validity

Just because a measurement scale produces consistent results doesn't mean it measures the right concept. Validity is the degree to which a test measures what it is supposed to measure: "Are we measuring what we think we are measuring?"

All too often researchers think they are measuring one thing when they are actually measuring something else. There are several ways to assess the validity of measurement instruments: content validity, criterion-related validity, construct validity, convergent validity, and discriminant validity.

One way to judge the **content validity** of a scale is to ask experts on the test topic to assess the scale. Scales that pass this test are said to have content validity. This test is subjective because the personal experiences and beliefs of the experts inevitably come into play. Content validity is the most often used validation technique, because it is not time-consuming and is easy to do.

Criterion-related validity is the ability of a scale to perform as predicted in relation to a specified criterion. The criterion is the attribute of interest. The predictor is the respondent's score. Suppose that a post graduate business school tries to determine applicants' potential by asking them all to take an admissions test. The criterion is each applicant's potential to succeed on the course. The predictor is the applicant's test score. What is important is how well the predictor determines the applicant's potential for success in the course.

There are two types of criterion-related validity: concurrent validity and predictive validity.

Concurrent validity evaluates how well the results from one scale correspond with the result from another when the scales measure the same phenomenon at the same time. Validity is determined by how closely the results correlate with each other. Concurrent validity also assesses how well a set of independent variables can predict the dependent variable in the light of new information. Assume that respondents have filled in a questionnaire and that a model has been built based on relationships between variables. For example, a discriminant model (see Section 10.1) has been established to differentiate between customers and non-customers or, say, between owners of local cars and foreign cars. If the model possesses good concurrent validity then it should be able to classify a fresh sample of customers (sometimes called a hold-out sample) into customers and non-customers based on the previously established model. And the percentage of correctly classified cases should clearly outperform any chance-based criterion.

Predictive validity is the ability of a scale to predict a future occurrence or phenomenon. What differentiates this form of validity from concurrent validity is the time period when the tests are administered. If a brand's market share one year after the launch is 17 percent and the agency's market research prior to the launch predicted a share of 16 to 19 percent with a 95 percent probability, this is an example of good predictive validity.

Construct validity concerns an abstract, unobservable, hypothesized concept. Constructs can be characteristics such as intelligence, aptitude, strength, love, and creativeness. In marketing, constructs that researchers often want to measure include service quality, customer satisfaction, and brand loyalty.

Because of their abstract nature, there is no direct way to measure constructs, so researchers measure observable phenomena that theoretically demonstrate the presence of the construct. Suppose a researcher wants to measure the quality of a company's service. Theory states that the amount of repeat business, an observable phenomenon, reflects service quality, an unobservable phenomenon. If this theory is valid, an instrument can be created that measures repeat business and uses the results as a measurement of service quality. A scale has construct validity if it measures an observable phenomenon that an underlying theory correlates with the construct of interest. Stated another way, construct validity assesses how well ideas or theories are translated into real measures. In this case, a scale has construct validity if it can show that repeat business demonstrates service quality. The validity of the underlying theory, that repeat business demonstrates service quality, is key to the validity of the scale. If the theory is wrong and there is no association between the two, then the scale is not valid; that is, it won't measure service quality even if it does measure repeat business well.

When construct validity is not found, it may be due to either a lack of construct validity or a flaw in the theory. To avoid these problems, researchers try to establish the construct validity of a measure by relating it to many constructs rather than just one. Researchers also try to use proven theories.

Construct validity exists if both convergent and discriminant validity are present. **Convergent validity** is the ability of a scale to correlate with other scales that purport to measure the same concept, the logic being that two or more measurements of the same concept using different scales should agree if they are valid measures of the concept. If the results from different scales that claim to measure the same construct are highly correlated, then convergent validity is established.

EXHIBIT 6.1 LOW CONSTRUCT VALIDITY IN AN EMPIRICAL STUDY BASED ON SELF-REPORTS

In a study of consumer use of coupons, the authors raised doubts about the criterion or construct validity of the self-reported approach:

"The use of retrospective self-reports rather than actual ... usage behaviour is a notable research limitation. The extent to which self-report data mirror actual ... usage is problematic. A field study was performed to validate the accuracy of self-reported data. Research assistants were positioned in two grocery stores to observe unobtrusively actual coupon usage behaviour. A sample of 205 shoppers, who were ignorant that their behaviour had been observed, later received a mailed questionnaire, which included questions regarding self-reported coupon usage. Self-report data from the 146 responding households were correlated with their previously observed coupon redemption behaviour. A statistically significant though modest correlation was obtained ($r = 0.32$, $p < 0.001$). The absence of a stronger relationship is due, on the one hand, to the inherent fallibility of self-reported data, on the other hand, to imperfections in the validation procedure."

Source: Adapted from Shimp and Kavas (1984) and other public sources

---

Discriminant validity has nothing to do with discriminant analysis, rather, it is the opposite of convergent validity. Discriminant validity is a scale's lack of correlation with another scale that purports to measure different concepts. In other words, the results of two scales measuring unrelated concepts should display no correlation.

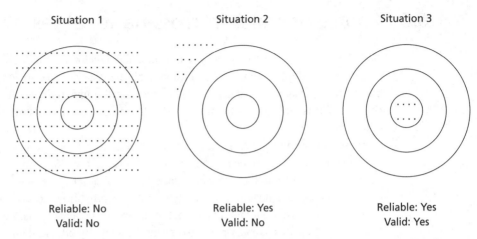

Figure 6.10 Illustration of reliability and validity. *Source*: Adapted from Hollensen (2004)

Relationship between reliability and validity

Ideally, a measurement used by a market researcher should be reliable and valid. Figure 6.10 shows various types of reliability and validity measures. Although this figure treats validity and reliability as being independent of each other, there is actually a one-way relationship between them. A scale must be reliable to be valid; but it does not have to be valid to be reliable. Further, reliability is a necessary but not sufficient condition for validity, because validity also requires other factors to be satisfied (that is, supported from theory and observation).

Validity is *not* a necessary condition for reliability. For deeper coverage of validity and reliability see Carmines and Zeller (1979).

Generalizability refers to the extent to which it is possible to generalize from the present sample data to the universe. Usually, a poll that is based on a nationally representative sample of a thousand or more voters is believed to possess generalizability. In contrast comprehensive quantitative models of consumer behaviour like the LISREL model sometimes are criticized due to low generalizability. This happens because the model's parameters cannot be applied to a universe or market environment outside the one (the specific sample) that was used for building the model. A study finding or a model may possess good validity and be reliable while its findings are not generalizable.

Everything else being equal (i) the bigger the sample, (ii) the simpler and less ambiguous the questions used and (iii) the smaller the number of questions – the higher the generalizability. Conversely, (i) the smaller the sample, (ii) the more complex the questions and (iii) the bigger the number of questions, the lower the generalizability. Readers interested in generalizability should see Rentz (1987) and Shavelson and Webb (1991).

6.6 Choice of scales in cross-national research

A challenge facing cross-cultural researchers is the development of scales that measure a construct in multiple countries. In addition to all the issues related to achieving comparability and equivalence in the instrument, there is the underlying issue of whether the construct exists and can be measured using the same or similar instrument in more than one culture.

Most published research dealing with cross-cultural scales reports the results where a scale that has been developed in one country, typically the US, is applied in other countries. Few, if any, modifications are made to the original scale, with the exception of dropping items that do not exhibit high levels of reliability. In taking this approach, researchers are assuming that a construct found in one country is manifested in the same form in another. Researchers may also adapt the scale by adding items to enhance their ability to identify culture-specific constructs.

Scale development can take place at the levels of an individual or the country. Most of the scaling literature deals with individual level scales or scales that are based on individuals' data but ascribed to the country. Scales can also be developed using macro-country data, in which case they would reflect country characteristics. Scales may also be based on individuals' responses as members of an organization. In this case inferences would be made about the organization.

In general, verbal scales are more effective among less-educated respondents, but a more appropriate procedure for illiterate respondents would be scales with pictorial stimuli. For example, in the case of lifestyle, pictures of different lifestyle segments may be shown to the respondents and they may be asked to indicate how similar they perceive themselves to be to the one in the picture. Other devices such as smiling faces (Figure 6.11) and a thermometer scale are also used among less-educated respondents.

Moreover, culture can affect the responses and may induce bias. The Likert scale is culture-bound and should be treated as a culture-specific instrument. Research has been conducted to find out whether there is a pan-cultural scale. Bearing in mind the drawbacks of administering scales to respondents in different countries, the one scale that has consistently provided accurate results is the semantic differential scale. Because the adjectives on the polar ends of the scale are opposite in meaning, it is easier for the respondent to understand and answer questions in a manner that is useful to the researcher (Kumar, 2000).

Smiling face descriptors

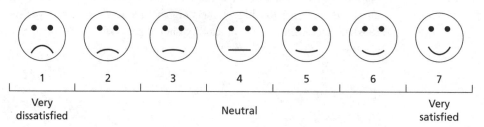

Figure 6.11 Smiling face descriptors

Designing scales for international marketing research calls for a great deal of adaptation on the researcher's part. It has to be decided whether a single scale can be used in all of the countries or whether it should be customized for each country. In the US, a five or a seven-point scale is used, but people in other countries, such as France, are familiar with a twenty-point scale. Semantics plays an important role in the accuracy with which a scale measures any given attribute. Many cultures tend to overstate their feelings, while others are more modest. The word "excellent" may connote very different levels of perfection to Japanese and Scandinavians. Adjustments for such linguistic differences have to be made. It has been observed that verbal rating scales work the best in the international context. All respondents are accustomed to talking about their feelings, irrespective of their country or culture. In international marketing research we will often find some degree of construct bias in the research process. Construct bias is likely to be present if the construct being studied differs across countries, or if the operationalization does not fit cultural understanding. Construct bias can, for example, be induced if behaviours are sampled that are not associated with the construct studied. The use of butter for baking in one country cannot be compared with the use of butter for spreading in another country and, as a consequence, attitudes towards butter will reflect quite different notions about the use of butter (Herk et al., 2005).

6.7 Summary

Measurement is the assignment of numbers or other symbols to characteristics of objects according to set rules. Scaling involves the generation of a continuum upon which measured objects are located. The four primary scales of measurement are nominal, ordinal, interval and ratio. Of these, the nominal scale is the most basic in that the numbers are used only for identifying or classifying objects. In the ordinal scale, the numbers indicate the relative position of the objects but not the magnitude of difference between them. The interval scale permits a comparison of the differences between the objects.

Attitudes are tendencies to respond in a consistently favourable or unfavourable manner towards something. They are learned and can change.

Methods to assess attitude can be classified as comparative or non-comparative rating scales. Comparative rating scales specify a standard of comparison and ask respondents to compare the test stimulus against this standard. The most popular types of comparative rating scales are paired comparisons, rank order, constant-sum, and Q-sort scales. In non-comparative rating scales, a standard of comparison is not specified, so researchers do not know the standard against which respondents are comparing the test stimulus. Common non-comparative rating scales include graphic rating and itemized rating (Likert, semantic differential, and Stapel).

Researchers must measure the extent to which error exists in their measuring instruments, by assessing the reliability and validity of measurement.

Reliability refers to the extent to which a scale produces consistent results if measurements are repeated. An attitude measure has validity if it measures what it is supposed to measure. A reliable measure is one in which a respondent responds in the same or in a very similar manner to identical or nearly identical questions.

It is possible to have reliable measurements that are invalid. Validity is defined as the accuracy of the measurement. It is an assessment of the exactness of the measurement relative to what actually exists. So, a valid measure is one that is truthful. Generalizability refers to the extent to which it is possible to generalize from sample data to the universe. A study finding or a model may have good validity and be reliable while its findings are not generalizable.

Critical issues in multi-country scale development are the types of measurement techniques used to gather the data as well as the underlying reliability of the data. As scale construction begins, the researcher must assess whether individual scale items function in the same way in each context or culture. Further, an assessment must be made as to whether the measures are in fact equivalent.

Questions

1. What is "measurement"?

2. What is the difference between ordinal and interval scales? How are they similar?

3. What is the difference between interval and ratio scales? How are they similar?

4. Describe the constant-sum scale. How is it different from other comparative rating scales?

5. What is the difference between a semantic differential scale and a Stapel scale? How are they similar?

6. What factors do researchers consider when deciding whether to use an even or an odd number of choices on a measurement scale?

7. Create a measurement instrument that measures college students' degree of satisfaction with the computers they use.

8. A marketing researcher wants to know which brand of shoe female consumers prefer from a choice of eighteen brands. Using a paired-comparison scale, how many comparisons are necessary?

9. What are the arguments for and against the inclusion of a neutral response position in a symmetric scale?

10. Can random error be avoided? If so, how? If not, why not?

11. How does reliability differ from validity? In your answer, define each term.

12. What are the differences between test–retest and other forms of reliability? What is criterion validity? How is it assessed?

13. When assessing a measurement instrument's construct validity, why is it necessary for the instrument to have a theoretical foundation?

14. What is the halo effect, and how does a researcher allow for it?

15. What are the necessary conditions for a study's generalizability?

References

Carmines, E. G. and Zeller, R. A. (1979) *Reliability and Validity Assessment*. Sage, Beverly Hills, CAL.

Cronbach, L. J. (1951) "Coefficient alpha and the internal structure of tests." *Psychometrika*. 16. 297–335.

Cronbach, L. J. (1990) *Essentials of Psychological Testing*. Addison-Wesley.

Herk, Hester van, Poortinga, Y. H., Verhallen, T. M. M. (2005) "Equivalence of survey data: relevance for international marketing." *European Journal of Marketing*. Vol 39. no 3/4. 352–64.

Hollensen, S. (2004) *Global Marketing: A decision-making approach*. Financial Times/Prentice Hall, Harlow. 154.

Kerlinger, N. and Lee, H. B. (2000). *Foundations of Behavioural Research*. Harcourt, New York.

Kumar, V. (2000) *International Marketing Research*. Prentice Hall, NJ. 193.

Likert, R. (1932) *A Technique for the Measurement of Attitudes*. McGraw-Hill, New York.

Nunnally, J. C. and Bernstein, I. H. (1994) *Psychometric Theory*. McGraw-Hill, New York.

Rentz, J. O. (1987) "Generalizability theory: a comprehensive method for assessing and improving the dependability of marketing measures." *Journal of Marketing Research*. Vol. 24 (February). 19–28.

Shavelson, R. J. and Webb, N. M. (1991) *Generalization Theory – A primer*. Sage, Beverly Hills, CAL.

Shrimp, T. A. and Kavas, A. (1984) "The theory of reasoned action applied to coupon usage." *Journal of Consumer Research*. No. 11 (December). 785–809.

End notes

[1] The mode is the most common (frequent) value.

[2] Use the binomial test when there are two possible outcomes. You know how many of each kind of outcome (traditionally called "success" and "failure") occurred in your experiment. You also have a hypothesis for what the true overall probability of "success" is. The binomial test answers this question: if the true probability of "success" is what your theory predicts, then how likely is it to find results that deviate as far, or further, from the prediction? The sign test is a special case of the binomial case where your theory is that the two outcomes have equal probabilities.

[3] *t-tests* are a special case of ANOVA: if you analyze the means of two groups by ANOVA, you get the same results as doing it with a t-test.

[4] The geometric mean of a sequence:

$$\{a_i\}_i^n = i$$

$$G(a_1, \ldots, a_n) \equiv \left(\prod_{i=1}^{n} \right)^{1/n}$$

is defined by:

Thus,

$$G(a_1, a_2) = \sqrt{a_1 a_2}$$

$$G(a_1, a_2, a_3) = (a_1 a_2 a_3)^{1/3},$$

and so on.

For example, suppose you have an investment that earns 10 percent the first year, 60 percent the second year, and 20 percent the third year. What is its average rate of return? It is *not* the arithmetic mean, because what these numbers mean is that on the first year your investment was *multiplied* (not added to) by 1.10, on the second year it was multiplied by 1.60, and the third year it was multiplied by 1.20. The relevant quantity is the geometric mean of these three numbers.

The question about finding the average rate of return can be rephrased as: "by what constant factor would your investment need to be multiplied by each year in order to achieve the same effect as multiplying by 1.10 one year, 1.60 the next, and 1.20 the third?" The answer is the *geometric mean*:

$$(1.10 \times 1.60 \times 1.20)^{1/3}$$

If you calculate this geometric mean you get approximately 1.283, so the average rate of return is about 28 percent (not 30 percent, which is what the arithmetic mean of 10 percent, 60 percent, and 20 percent would give you).

Any time you have a number of factors contributing to a product, and you want to find the "average" factor, the answer is the geometric mean.

[5] The coefficient of variation (%) of a set of values is calculated as:

100*(standard deviation)/(mean value of set)

Example: in a series of wage distributions over time, the standard deviation may rise over time with inflation, but the coefficient of variation may not, and thus the fundamental inequality may not.

7 Survey and questionnaire design

Learning objectives

After studying this chapter you should be able to:

- Understand the definition and purpose of research design.
- Recognize the role of the questionnaire in the data collection process.
- Identify the main considerations when selecting a survey method.
- Specify an appropriate data collection method for a given research design.
- Discuss the advantages and disadvantages of personal surveys, telephone surveys, and online surveys.
- Explain the issues in international marketing research design.
- Define the purpose of a questionnaire.
- Describe the process of designing a questionnaire, the steps involved and guidelines that must be followed at each step.
- Discuss the considerations involved in designing questionnaires for international marketing research.
- Understand the concept of sampling.
- Explain the steps in developing a sampling plan.

7.1 Introduction

This chapter discusses issues that arise in conducting surveys. A survey design is the detailed blueprint used to guide a research study towards its objectives. The process of designing a survey involves many interrelated decisions. The most significant decision is the choice of research approach, because it determines how the information will be obtained, ensuring that the pieces fit together. The achievement of this fit among objectives, research approach, and research tactics is an iterative process in which decisions are constantly reconsidered in light of subsequent decisions. The importance of questionnaires is discussed and how researchers must put themselves in the shoes of target respondents to design an effective questionnaire. This forms the basis for gathering the necessary information from the respondents. To obtain information from every person in a market is usually impossible and obviously impractical. For these reasons, marketing researchers make use of a sample.

7.2 Survey design

Every research problem is unique in some way, and care must be taken to select the most appropriate set of approaches for the problem at hand. However, although every research problem may seem unique, there are usually enough similarities among such problems to allow decisions to be made in advance, as to the best plan to use to resolve the problem, and there are some basic survey designs that can be matched to given problems.

There are three basic ways of obtaining primary data in marketing research: survey, observation, and experiment. Surveys are the most widely used method of data collection in commercial marketing research.

Compared with observation or other qualitative methods, survey methods allow the collection of significant amounts of data in an economical and efficient manner, and they typically allow for much larger sample sizes. There are five advantages of using survey methods.

- Standardization. Questions are preset and organized in a particular arrangement on a questionnaire, and survey methods ensure that all respondents are asked the same questions and are exposed to the same response options. Thus, the researcher is assured that every respondent will be confronted with questions that address all the information objectives driving the research project.
- Ease of administration. Sometimes an interviewer is used, and survey modes are easily geared to such administration. On the other hand, the respondent may fill out the questionnaire unattended (sometimes this approach is referred to as a **self-explicated interview**). In either case, the administration aspects are much simpler than, for example, conducting a focus group or interviewing. The simplest method is a postal survey in which questionnaires are sent to prospective respondents.
- Ability to tap the "unseen." The four questions of what, why, how, and who help uncover "unseen" data. For example, a working parent may be asked to explain how important the location of a school was in his or her selection of the child's school. A researcher can inquire as to how many different schools the parent seriously considered before deciding on one, and go on to gain an understanding of the person's financial or work circumstances with a few questions on income, occupation, and family size. Much information is unobservable and requires direct questions.
- Suitability to tabulation and statistical analysis. The marketing researcher ultimately must interpret the patterns or themes sometimes hidden in the raw data collected. Statistical analysis, both simple and complex, is the preferred means of achieving this goal, and large cross-sectional surveys perfectly complement these procedures. Qualitative methods, in contrast, prove much more frustrating in this respect because of their necessarily small samples, need for interpretation, and general approach to answering marketing managers' questions. Increasingly, questionnaire design software

includes the ability to perform simple statistical analyses, such as tabulations of the answers to each question, as well as the ability to create graphs summarizing these tabulations.

■ Sensitivity to subgroup differences. Because surveys involve large numbers of respondents, it is relatively easy to "slice" up the sample into demographic groups or other subgroups and then to compare them for market segmentation implications. The large sample sizes that characterize surveys facilitate subgroup analyses and comparisons of various groups in the sample.

Forms of market research

Market research surveys typically take one of five forms:

■ Personal surveys, in which face-to-face interviews are conducted at respondents' homes or offices.
■ Intercept surveys, in which face-to-face interviews are conducted with people who are stopped at a public location such as a shopping centre.
■ Telephone surveys, in which people are interviewed over the telephone.
■ Postal surveys, in which people complete self-administered questionnaires that are sent to them.
■ Online surveys, in which people fill out a questionnaire that is sent by e-mail.

Personal surveys

The oldest form of survey research is personal interviews conducted at a respondent's home or workplace. This method allows control over who answers the questions and maximum flexibility in the questionnaire design. However, the fact that interviewers must travel to meet respondents makes personal interviewing costly compard with other methods.

Because of the high cost, personal interviewing is rarely used in consumer research. It is mostly used for consumer research in countries where telephone surveys are not culturally accepted, and for surveys of business executives. Business surveys are often done with respondents who control large budgets and often use open questions that require probing and elaboration. The individual value of these respondents and the complexity of the interviews justify the expense of personal interviewing.

The flexibility of personal surveys in terms of questionnaire design is unrivalled among the possible methods of data collection. This is because the interviewer can:

■ control the order of the questions;
■ probe unclear answers and ask complex questions;
■ implement branching instructions, which means asking or not asking certain questions depending on the answers to previous questions;
■ show the respondent lists of responses to help with questions that have many categories;
■ explore unstructured, "conversational" topics;
■ conduct a lengthy interview; in fact, interviews lasting an hour or more are not uncommon.

Such flexibility makes personal surveys a preferred method when their cost is not prohibitive. Cost is the big disadvantage of personal surveys, though sample quality is excellent.

Intercept surveys

Because of the high cost of personal surveys, most consumer surveys that use face-to-face interviewing are done by interviewing at a much lower cost than in-home surveys because travel costs are eliminated.

The most popular location for "intercept" surveys is in a high street or shopping centre, because they provide access to a general population that is appropriate for most research. In most intercept surveys, interviewers are sent out to recruit anyone who looks as if she or he might qualify for the survey. People are approached and asked to participate in interviews on the spot. If they agree, the interview is administered and the respondent is thanked and paid (in some cases). If they refuse, the interviewer picks another person.

Because intercept surveys are done face-to-face, they offer the same flexibility as a personal survey. The difference is that intercept surveys are conducted under greater time pressure. In most cases, the interview should not take more than a few minutes unless respondents are paid, because people won't accept a prolonged interruption of their activities.

Sample quality is a weak point of such surveys. This method is not used for surveys of business executives, except for occasional studies at trade shows, because executives are not easy to identify in the street. Even for consumer studies, it can be difficult to find good intercept sites. Most marketing research intercepts are done in shopping centres, but many refuse access even when offered rental payments. This limits the extent to which respondents will represent a general population.

Even with access to a mall, low co-operation rates impair the quality of the sample. This is not surprising since many shoppers have limited time.

Telephone surveys

Telephone surveys are widely used, especially in consumer research. They offer better population coverage than intercept surveys but are limited by the fact that interviewers cannot show things to respondents.

In surveys of organizations, companies are selected and phone numbers are found for those companies. In consumer surveys, the telephone numbers are drawn directly from a directory or with a technique called random digit dialling.

Once the sample is drawn, interviewers call the selected people (or selected numbers) and seek co-operation with the survey. If the desired respondent isn't in, the interviewer asks for a good time to call back and tries later. Call-backs should continue until:

- the interview is completed;
- the interview is refused;
- the potential respondent is found to be ineligible; or
- a limit on the number of call-backs is reached.

Telephone interviewers generally work from central offices and most big research companies use computer-assisted telephone interviewing (CATI) systems. In a CATI system, the interviewer sits in front of a screen on which the questions appear and enters the answers directly into the computer.

Telephone surveys are administered by interviewers, so they offer control of the question sequence, the ability to implement branching instructions, and the opportunity to probe unclear answers.

Since telephone interviews are not conducted face-to-face, it is not possible to show products, packages, or advertisements to the respondent unless they have been sent in advance. Also, it is not possible to provide respondents with printed lists of responses for questions with many options. Because of this, and because respondents must be able to keep the question and the responses in their heads, questions should be simple and the number of responses limited.

Sometimes these shortcomings are circumvented by using the TMT approach (telephone–mail–telephone). According to this method, a respondent is phoned and asked whether the agency may post an information pack containing a sample product, a questionnaire with some pictures, and so on. The respondent is asked for a date and time when the agency is allowed to call back for a follow-up interview. The interview can be carried out with the respondent having the necessary items to hand.

Interviews up to twenty minutes long are common and do not cause problems. However, it is possible that a survey call will come at a time that is inconvenient for the respondent. Since the interviewer cannot see this, it is polite to ask if the respondent is free to talk. If not, an appointment should be made for another time.

The sample quality of telephone surveys depends on:

- whether the potential respondents have telephones;
- whether those phones are identified in lists such as the telephone directory; and
- whether the potential respondents are willing to participate.

The main sampling problems with telephone surveys are non-availability and lack of co-operation. The people who are contacted on the first call are likely to be housewives or retired people. This creates a bias toward less active people unless the survey organization calls back until designated respondents are reached. Non-co-operation is difficult to solve.

One way to reduce both refusals and non-contacts is to broaden the definition of who is eligible to respond. Surveys that accept information from any member of a household usually get higher co-operation rates than surveys directed at specific individuals. An intermediate approach is to ask for a specific individual. If that person refuses or is unavailable, to ask whether any other member of the household is knowledgeable about the survey topic and interview that person instead, as long as the substitute respondent fits the required profile.

One factor that may significantly reduce co-operation rates is significant consumer dissatisfaction with telemarketing.

Telephone surveys of business populations present different issues from those posed by consumer surveys. The problem in industrial surveys, apart from obtaining co-operation, is locating the right person within the organization to interview. Usually, this is done by starting with a job title and then getting referred from one person to another until the right person is reached. The telephone is ideal for this. In fact, industrial postal surveys generally require advance telephone calls to identify names, titles, and exact addresses of people to whom questionnaires should be sent.

Once the proper respondents are identified, reaching them may still be a problem. A secretary or other "gatekeeper" may limit access to them.

Postal surveys

In a postal survey, a sample of addresses and names are drawn from a list, and the questionnaire is sent out with a cover letter. (Some studies begin with an advance postcard to explain the survey and alert potential respondents that it is coming.)

Approximately two weeks after the first questonnaire, a follow-up questionnaire and letter are sent to non-respondents. Two weeks later, a second follow-up is sent. If total response is not satisfactory after this second follow-up, it is possible to use telephone interviews to survey a sample of the non-respondents and measure whether they are different in some way from respondents.

A limitation of postal surveys is that they can be used only for short surveys with mainly closed questions. Response rates drop sharply if the questionnaire is longer than four pages.

The questionnaire should offer response categories or at least not require substantial amounts of writing. This reluctance to answer open questions stems not only from the time and effort required but also from the fact that many respondents are uncertain of their spelling and grammar and do not want to be embarrassed. Open questions in such surveys usually reduce the co-operation rate substantially while yielding little information.

Another complication is that question order cannot be controlled, as it is in personal interviews. You have to assume that respondents will read all the questions before answering any of them. This makes it possible for questions at the end of the questionnaire to influence questions at the beginning, which may sometimes be undesirable. Questions intended to measure respondents' level of knowledge about a product, service, or issue don't work well because respondents are free to look up the answers or ask someone else.

Low response rates create a risk of high non-response bias (i.e. risk of large differences between data for the overall population of interest and data for those who responded).

There are two main sources of non-response bias in postal surveys with low co-operation rates. First, because surveys of the general population require respondents to have reasonable reading skills, co-operation rates are generally higher for people with higher levels of education. A second, and more serious, issue is that co-operation on such surveys is influenced by respondents' interest in the topic. In attitude surveys, those who feel strongly about something are more likely to respond than are those who don't care. For new products or services, those who are interested are more likely to respond, producing overestimates of market interest.

These biases become smaller as sample co-operation increases, but they never vanish from postal surveys. Unlike telephone and face-to-face surveys, in which people refuse before they really know anything about the topic, you must assume that non-respondents to a postal survey looked at the questionnaire and decided they weren't interested.

Another sampling problem is that you can't be certain who the respondent is, especially respondents in B2B mail surveys, and some estimates suggest that one-third of consumer postal surveys are filled out by someone other than the designated respondent (Loosveldt et al., 2004).

Non-response rates and wrong-respondent identity problems in B2B studies are especially severe when researchers fail to make phone calls to identify the right person for mailing purposes.

In both industrial and consumer research some companies offer postal panels for survey purposes. These panels are households that have agreed, often for incentives, to answer surveys. These panels are usually balanced by education and other demographic variables to reduce sample bias. They offer a good way to get relatively quick, relatively high response rates at low cost. However, they cannot be viewed as random samples. Response rates in male panels may approach 80 percent if the topic is interesting to respondents (political issues) or if good incentives are provided. But typical panels of, 1,000 or 2,000 respondents cause other methodological problems to the analyst. From a technical perspective, measurements obtained over time from a panel are times series or multiple measures of the same units and are therefore not independent measures. Since statistical formulas and experimental designs often assume independence, a panel violates these assumptions. For example, a panel is inappropriate for measuring brand awareness before and after a campaign. Why? Assume that we ask members of the panel whether they know a brand before the campaign, and ask them the same question again after the campaign. If their knowledge has increased, what has caused the increased awareness? The campaign or the fact that panellists remember the brand because it appeared in the questionnaire received before the campaign? Remedies for adjusting data, computations and formulas when panel data are involved are discussed in Finkel (1995) and Hsiao (2002).

Online surveys

The popularity of e-mail/internet surveys has surged. There are several reasons for this:

- The speed with which a questionnaire can be created, distributed to respondents, and the data returned. Since printing, mailing, and data keying delays are eliminated, data can be available within hours of writing a questionnaire. Responses are in electronic form, so statistical analysis software can be programmed to process standard questionnaires and return statistical summaries and charts automatically.
- Low cost. Printing, mailing, keying, and interviewer costs are eliminated, and the incremental costs of each respondent are typically low, so studies with large numbers of respondents can be done at substantial savings compared with postal or telephone surveys (Ilieva et al., 2002). Roster et al. (2004) found that the cost for a web survey was 53 percent lower than for a similar telephone survey. The web garnered a lower response rate, but the findings lend support to the notion that web surveys may be equally, if not more, accurate than telephone surveys in predicting behaviours. This result is also confirmed by Coderre et al. (2004), whose results show that the quality of qualitative data obtained through a web survey was comparable with that of information obtained through telephone and postal surveys.
- With the creation of respondent panels on the internet, the researcher can create longitudinal studies by tracking attitudes, behaviour, and perceptions over time.

Sophisticated panel tracking software can tailor follow-up questions in the next survey, based upon responses from a previous survey. Also, missing answers can be filled in.

- Typically, it isn't worthwhile to conduct a phone survey to ask two or three questions. But on the web, a survey component can be included within a general site that is used for marketing or business transactions.
- The ability to reach large numbers of people. The internet is an international arena where many barriers to communication have been erased (Wilson and Laskey, 2003).
- Questionnaires delivered on the web have some unique advantages. They can be made visually pleasing with attractive fonts and graphics. The graphical and hypertext features of the web can be used to present products for reaction or to explain service offerings. This multimedia ability of web-based questionnaires is unique.

Despite the advantages of online surveys there are still drawbacks. Perhaps the largest problem is that internet users are not representative of the population as a whole.

- Users tend to be male, well educated, technically oriented, relatively young, and have above-average incomes (Schillewaert and Meulemeester, 2005). This is changing, however, as more people access the internet.
- Security. Users are worried about privacy issues. However, given the commercial incentives for insuring that information such as credit card numbers can be transmitted safely, encryption methodology will be at the forefront of internet developments.
- When an unrestricted sample is set up on the internet, anyone who desires can complete the questionnaire. It is fully self-selecting and probably representative of nothing except web surfers. The problem gets worse if the same person can access the questionnaire over and over.

Recruited internet samples are used for targeted populations in surveys that require more control over the sample. Respondents are recruited by telephone, post, e-mail, or in person. After qualification, they are sent the questionnaire by e-mail, or are directed to a website that contains a link to the questionnaire. At websites, passwords are used to restrict access to the questionnaire. Since the make-up of the sample is known, completions can be monitored and follow-up messages can be sent to those who do not complete the questionnaire to improve the participation rate.

Screened-sample questionnaires typically use a branching or skip pattern for asking screening questions to determine whether or not the full questionnaire should be presented to a respondent. Some web survey systems can make immediate market segment calculations that assign a respondent to a particular segment based on screening questions, and then select the appropriated questionnaire to match the respondent's segment.

A number of factors or considerations may affect the choice of a survey method in a given situation. The researcher should choose the survey method that will provide data of the desired types, quality, and quantity at the lowest cost.

Various survey methods each have certain inherent strengths and weaknesses with regard to producing quality data (Table 7.1).

In some cases, online surveys may be the only way for consumers to respond. In researching the mobility-disabled market, Ray and Tabor (2003) found that these

Table 7.1 Advantages and disadvantages of different survey methods

Survey method	Advantages	Disadvantages
Personal surveys	■ Respondent is at ease and secure at home; face-to-face contact; can observe respondent's home or working place; interviewer can show, explain, probe, etc. ■ Often much in-depth information per interview is gathered ■ Multimethod data collection, including observation, visual clues, and self-administered sections, are feasible ■ Rapport and confidence-building are possible (including any written reassurances that may be needed for reporting sensitive material)	■ Greater chance of interviewer bias; potential sampling problems ■ Field staff required ■ Cost per interview can be high; interviewer must travel to respondent's place ■ The data collection period is likely to be longer than for most procedures
Intercept surveys	■ Interviewer can show, explain, probe as in door-to-door ■ Fast and convenient data collection ■ Same as personal surveys	■ There may be many distractions in a street environment; respondent may be in a hurry or not in a proper frame of mind; more chance for interviewer bias; non-probability sampling problems ■ Intercept company often has exclusive interview rights for a shopping mall (especially in the US)
Telephone surveys	■ Lower costs per interview than personal surveys ■ Interviewer starting and management easier than personal interviews; ■ Random-digit-dialling sampling of general population ■ Likely better response rate from a list sample than from mail	■ Sampling limitations, especially as a result of omitting those without telephone ■ Non-response associated with random dialling sampling is higher than with interviews ■ Possibly less appropriate for personal or sensitive questions if no prior contact ■ Questionnaires or measurement constraints, including limits on response alternatives, use of visual aids, and interviewer observations
Postal surveys	■ Elimination of interviewer and associated biases; respondent can complete the questionnaire when convenient; respondent also can look up information and work at own pace ■ Respondents have time to give thoughtful answers, look up records, or consult with others ■ Ease of presenting questions requiring visual aids (in contrast to telephone interviews) ■ Cost of interviewer eliminated	■ Especially careful questionnaire design needed ■ Low response rates ■ Open questions usually are not useful ■ The interviewer is not present to exercise quality control with respect to answering all questions, meeting questions objectives, or the quality of answers provided
Online surveys	■ Ease of creating and posting ■ Inexpensive to administer; respondent can be shown stimuli and possible rewards ■ Data can be quickly gathered ■ Low costs per respondent ■ Very flexible and fast online statistical analysis available	■ Respondents must have access to the internet ■ Population skewed toward young, educated, above-average income respondents ■ Unrestricted sample is a simple convenience sample ■ Buying an e-mail list can be expensive and not up-to-date. People change e-mail addresses more often than they change phone numbers (Ray and Tabor, 2003) ■ Loss of anonymity

respondents could type and click more easily than write on paper. While many computer users with disabilities have an internet connection, mainstream advertising to the disabled community has not been well-explored.

International market surveys

The survey methods should be adapted to the specific cultural environment and should not be biased in terms of any one culture. This requires careful attention at each step of the questionnaire design process. The information needed should be clearly specified. It is important to take into account any differences in underlying consumer behaviour, decision-making processes, psychographics, lifestyles and demographic variables (Frevert, 2000).

Also, the comparability of data from different countries and cultural contexts has to be assessed. Comparability in this sense is defined as data that have the same meaning or interpretation and the same level of accuracy, precision of measurement, or reliability. If data and research design are not comparable from country to country, mistaken inferences may be made about differences or similarities between countries.

In the context of demographic characteristics, information on marital status, education, household size, occupation, income and dwelling unit may have to be specified differently because these variables may not be comparable across countries. For example, household definition and size varies greatly, given the extended family structure in some countries and the practice of two or more families living under the same roof.

Although personal interviewing may dominate as a survey method in many western countries, different survey methods may be favoured in other countries. Hence, the questionnaire may have to be suitable for administration by more than one method. For ease of comprehension and translation, it is better to have two or more simple questions rather than a single complex question. In overcoming the inability to answer, the variability in the extent to which respondents in different cultures are informed about the subject matter of the survey should be taken into account. Respondents in some parts of the world may not be as well informed on many issues as people in other parts.

The use of unstructured or open-ended questions may be desirable if the researcher lacks knowledge about the determinants of response in other countries.

Marketing research in action
The difficulty of obtaining comparable cross-national samples

The difficulty of obtaining proper samples that can be compared on a cross-cultural basis is illustrated by the early efforts of marketing researchers to conduct international studies. In the 1960s, Lorimor and Dunn carried out a study that aimed to compare the use of mass media in France and Egypt.

According to the findings, 56 percent of respondents in the French subsample had a TV in the household, compared with 96 percent of Egyptian households. This conflicted with statistics from the United Nations according to which there existed 274 TV licences per 1,000 people in France compared with only 17 in Egypt. The average household size in Egypt is about five, twice that of France, and generally it appears that more people sit in front of an Egyptian TV, but such a difference should not alter the number of households with a TV (unless there has been a bias towards interviewing several persons in households with TV). Theoretically, the difference might be caused by a higher number of unlicensed TVs in Egypt. While this presumption may be true, it was not the cause of the findings by Lorimor and Dunn. The difference appears to have been of a technical nature:

- Sampling of Egyptian respondents was based on a listing of households in Cairo that had installed power cables for appliances.
- French respondents were drawn from middle/upper class districts of Paris. The selection of units was done by cluster sampling n street blocks out of N blocks with subsequent random selection of m households within each of the n blocks chosen. Simultaneously respondents were stratified with regard to age, gender and employment.

It appears that the Egyptian sample was only representative for a tiny upper-upper class of the country's population. Note also that both samples consisted of urban residents only.

The researchers were well aware of the problems caused by differences in samples obtained. However, there was little they could do about it. See Lorimor and Dunn (1967, 1968a, 1968b).

7.3 Questionnaire design

Questionnaire design is key to both qualitative and quantitative research. In the former, even small samples can be investigated using semi-structured (or in other cases, unstructured) questionnaires to elicit answers and to probe interviewees' responses. The questionnaire in quantitative research is used as a survey instrument with larger samples, normally containing structured questions for ease of coding and analysis.

A questionnaire is a data collection instrument, formally setting out the way in which research questions should be asked. Even simple questions need proper wording and organization to produce accurate information. Consideration needs to be given to how questions should be worded, in the light of the objectives of the research, and the target group of respondents. Attention also needs to be given to the organization of the questionnaire and to testing.

There are limitations to what a questionnaire can measure, especially when it comes to product recalls because people can only accurately report upon the item they have bought for a limited time after the actual purchase.

A questionnaire has specific objectives:

- To translate the information needed into questions that the respondents can and will answer. Developing questions that will yield the desired information is difficult. Two

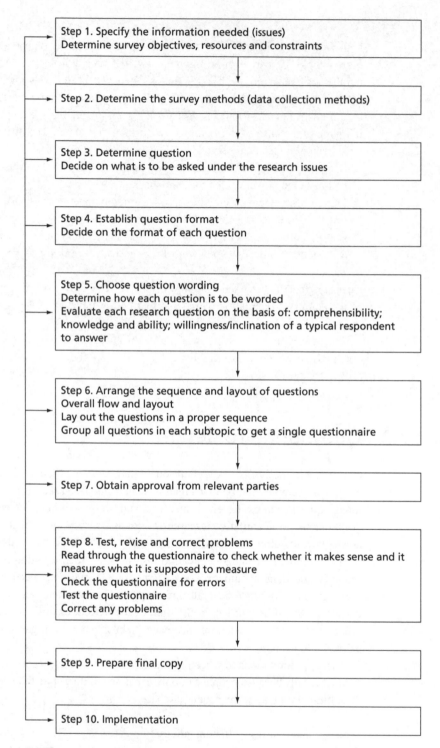

Figure 7.1 The questionnaire design process

apparently similar ways of posing a question may result in different information. Hence, this objective is a challenge.

- A questionnaire must motivate the respondent to become involved in the interview, to co-operate, and to complete the interview. Before designing a questionnaire, the researcher must evaluate "what is the respondent going to get out of this" and appreciate what respondents go through when approached and questioned. Not all respondents are the same in what they seek from a questionnaire or interview process.

- A questionnaire should minimize response error. Such errors arise when respondents give inaccurate answers or when their answers are mis-recorded or mis-analyzed. A questionnaire can be a significant source of response error and minimizing this error is an important objective of questionnaire design.

To develop a further understanding of questionnaire design, the process can be presented as a series of steps (Figure 7.1). The process outlined in Figure 7.1 shows that the ten steps are interrelated and the development of a questionnaire involves much iteration and interconnection between stages.

Step 1: specify the information needed

The research process often begins when the international marketing manager, brand manager, or product development specialist has a need for decision-making information that is not available.

Five classes of information, generally useful for marketing decisions have been identified:

- Facts and knowledge: what are the beliefs, perceptions, and depth of knowledge of the survey respondents about, for example, specific products, services, industries, or organizations?

- Opinions: what are the existing attitudes towards products, etc., including an assessment of the strength with which these attitudes are held?

- Motives: what motivates buyers of various kinds of products or services?

- Past behaviour: what are the patterns of consumption over specified time periods? Insight will be given into factors such as brand loyalty. Observational techniques, such as home audits, will help in verifying reported consumption behaviour.

- Future behaviour: indications of possible behaviour may be gleaned from sensitive questioning.

Included in this approach, of course, would be an evaluation of the nature of buying behaviour, which may be complex, and making a list of research objectives.

The first step in questionnaire design is to specify the information needed. It is helpful to review the components of the problem and the approach, particularly the research question, hypotheses and characteristics that influence the research design. To further ensure that the information obtained fully addresses all the components of the problem, the researcher should prepare a set of variables, which would influence the decision-making problem.

The project's research objectives should then be translated into information goals that are specific enough to guide question formulation, thinking ahead to the types of tables and graphs that can be used in the final report.

Clearly define the target respondents. The characteristics of the respondent group have a great influence on questionnaire design. The wording and style of questions that may be appropriate for finance directors being surveyed about their IT needs may not be appropriate for retired persons being asked about their holidays. The more diversified the respondent group, the more difficult it is to design a single questionnaire appropriate for all.

Step 2: determine the survey methods

Section 7.1 discussed ways of collecting survey data. Each method will influence questionnaire design. For example, a telephone interview often requires a rich verbal description of a concept to make certain the respondent understands the idea being discussed. In contrast, in an interview, the researcher can show the respondent a picture or demonstrate the concept.

If you want respondents to react to physical stimuli, face-to-face interviews are best. Telephone surveys are very limited in this regard, though it may be possible to send materials to respondents in advance of a phone interview.

Step 3: determine question type and content

Two main types of question response formats are used in marketing research. **Open-ended questions** are those in which respondents can reply in their own words. In other words, the researcher does not limit the response choices. The advantage of such responses is that they can provide the researcher with a rich array of information. The respondent is answering from his own frame of reference. Advantages are described in "real world" terminology rather than marketing jargon. Often this is helpful in designing promotional themes and campaigns. It enables copywriters to use the consumer's language. This rich array of information can now be captured even in computer-assisted interviews.

Open-ended questions are not without their problems. Editing and interpretation of responses are problematic. If too many categories are used, data patterns and response frequencies may be difficult for the researcher to interpret. If the categories are too broad, the data are too general and meaning may be lost. Even if a proper number of categories is used, editors may have to interpret what the interviewer has recorded and force data into a category.

A related problem of open-ended questions is interviewer bias. Although training stresses the importance of verbatim recording of open-ended questions, it is often not practised in the field. Also, slow writers may miss important comments.

Open-ended questions also may be biased towards the articulate interviewee. A person with elaborate opinions and the ability to express them may have much greater input than a shy, inarticulate, or withdrawn respondent. Yet they could be equally likely prospects for a product.

So, a basic problem with open-ended questions lies in interpreting and processing data. In fact, a two-phase judgement must be made. First, the researcher must decide on the proper set of categories and then each response must be evaluated as to which category it falls into.

In general, open-ended questions are useful in exploratory research and as opening or closing questions. They should be chosen with care as their disadvantages can outweigh their advantages in a large survey.

Closed questions require the respondent to make a selection from a list of responses. The primary advantage of a closed question is simply the avoidance of many of the problems of open-ended questions. Interviewer and coder bias are removed because the interviewer is simply checking a box, circling a category, recording a number, or punching a key.

The simplest form of a closed-ended question is the dichotomous choice. An example is:

Do you think that this year's inflation will be greater or less than last year?
- Greater than last year
- Less than last year

Note that the respondent is limited to two answers. It is easy to administer and usually evokes rapid response. Often a neutral or no opinion/don't know is added to dichotomous questions to take care of those situations. Dichotomous questions are prone to measurement error. Because alternatives are polarized, possible choices between the poles are omitted. Thus, question wording is critical to obtain accurate responses.

In the above question, response may vary depending upon whether greater than or less than is listed first. These problems can be overcome using a split ballot technique. One-half of the questionnaires are worded with greater than listed first and the other half with less than first. This procedure will aid in the reduction of potential bias.

As well as open-ended and closed questions, there are **multiple-choice** questions. These overcome many of the disadvantages of open-ended questions because interviewer bias is reduced and the questions are administered quickly. Also, coding and processing of data is much less costly and time-consuming. In self-administered questionnaires, respondent co-operation is improved if the questions are structured.

In multiple-choice questions, the researcher provides a choice of answers and respondents are asked to select one or more of the options given. Sometimes the respondent is asked to only select one item. For instance, a question might ask the respondent "What is your preferred brand? Alternatively, it could ask the respondent to indicate, say, three favourite brands. A third way would be to simply let the person make the choices that are regarded as relevant or that apply. Consider the following example:

Please indicate all the brands of soft drinks that you have consumed in the past week.
Please check all that apply.

1   Coca-Cola   __
2   Pepsi-Cola   __
3   Fanta   __

4   Seven Up   __

.

.

.

14   Dr Pepper   __
15   Other
    (please specify)   __

Of concern in designing multiple-choice questions is the number of options and the order of potential responses, known as position bias. The response options should include all possible choices. The general guideline is to list the important options and to include another labelled "Other (please specify)," as shown above. The responses should be mutually exclusive.

Multiple-choice questions are not without disadvantages. Considerable effort is required to design effective multiple-choice questions and qualitative techniques may be required to determine the appropriate response options. It is difficult to obtain information on items not listed. Even if an "Other (please specify)" category is included, respondents tend to choose from the list. In addition, showing respondents the list of answers produces biased responses. There is also the potential for order bias.

The choice between open- and closed-response questions is not necessarily an either/or distinction. Open-response questions can be used with closed-response questions to seek additional information. Using an open-response question to follow up a closed question is called a probe. **Probes** can combine some advantages of both open and closed questions. They can be used for specific pre-chosen questions or to obtain additional information from only a subset of people who respond to previous questions in a certain way. A common example of the latter is to ask respondents who choose "none of the above" a follow-up question to expand on their answer. There are two general purposes for the use of probes in a questionnaire. The first is to pinpoint questions that were difficult for respondents. Adequate testing of questions reduces the need for probes. The second purpose is to aid researcher interpretation of respondent answers. Answers to open-response follow-ups can provide valuable guidance in the analysis of closed-response questions.

Step 4: establish question format

Every question in a questionnaire should contribute to the information needed or serve some specific purpose. It is useful to ask some neutral questions at the start to establish involvement and rapport, particularly when the topic of the questionnaire is sensitive or controversial. Sometimes filter questions are asked to disguise the purpose or sponsorship of the project. For example, rather than limiting the questions to the brand of interest, questions about competing brands may be included. At times, certain questions may be duplicated to assess reliability or validity.

Once a question is deemed necessary, the researcher must make sure that it is sufficient to get the desired information. Sometimes several questions are needed to obtain the required information in an unambiguous manner.

A **double-barrelled question** is really two different questions posed in one question. With two questions posed together, it is difficult for a respondent to answer either directly. Consider a question asked of patrons at a restaurant "Were you satisfied with the food and service?" How does the respondent answer? If they say "yes" does that mean they were satisfied with the food? The service? A combination? The question would be much improved by asking about a single item: one question for food and another question for service.

Step 5: choose question wording

The wording of specific questions always take a significant amount of time. It is a skill developed over time and subject to constant improvement.

Questions are the raw material of questionnaires and vital to the quality of the research. Question wording is the translation of the desired question content and structure into words that respondents can clearly and easily understand. Deciding on the wording is perhaps the most critical task in developing a questionnaire. If a question is worded poorly, respondents may refuse to answer it or answer incorrectly. Even small changes in wording can shift respondent answers, but it is difficult to know whether or not a wording change will have such an effect.

Question phrasing depends on such factors as the information being sought, the characteristics of target respondents, and where the survey is administered. Good questionnaire writing requires that researchers follow these guidelines:

- The questions should be easy to understand. Ordinary words should be used in a questionnaire, and they should match the vocabulary and intellectual level of the respondents. The most common pitfall is to use technical jargon or specialized terms. Special care must be taken to avoid words that have different meanings for different groups. This can be readily appreciated in cross-cultural studies, where translation problems are profound. One socio-economic group may refer to the evening meal as dinner, while others call this meal supper and have their dinner at noon. Most respondents do not understand technical marketing words. Never forget that you are imposing your language upon respondents in the form of a questionnaire. Your language communicates and puts respondents in a particular frame of mind as they answer the questions you pose. Unless that language is meaningful to respondents, they will be put in a frame of mind that you may not intend, and be answering different questions from those you set.
- Questions should be focused on a single issue or topic. The researcher must stay focused on the specific issue or topic. The question "What type of hotel do you usually stay in when on a trip?" is too vague. A more focused version is "When you are on a family holiday and stay in a hotel at your destination, what type of hotel do you typically choose?"
- The question should be a grammatically simple sentence. A simple sentence is preferred over compound and complex sentences. The more complex the sentence, the greater the potential for respondent error. To avoid these problems, the researcher should strive to use a simple sentence structure, even if two separate sentences are

necessary for the question. What is an appropriate length of a question? A common rule of thumb is to limit the number of words in any question to under 20. Under certain circumstances, a question may have to be long in order to avoid ambiguity, but this should be the exception. A questionnaire filled with long questions is tiring to answer and more difficult to understand. Brevity will help respondents to comprehend the central question and reduce the distraction of wordiness.

■ Avoid leading questions. A leading question is one that suggests the answer or reveals the researcher's (or interviewer's) opinion. This can be done easily by adding "don't you agree?" or "wouldn't you say?" to a desired statement. A loaded question introduces a more subtle bias. A common type of loading of possible responses is through failure to provide a full range of options, for example, by asking, "How do you generally spend your free time – watching television, or what?" Simply adding "I'm sure you agree" or "Don't you think?" to a statement can bias responses. Researchers have also found that respondents tend to agree with plausible propositions unless they have a strong opinion or choices are provided. Even when options are offered, respondents tend to agree rather than disagree with plausible statements. Given this tendency, questions should be worded neutrally.

■ Consider the ability of the respondent to answer the question. Asking respondents about a brand or store that they have never encountered creates a problem. When a question is worded in such a manner that it implies that the respondent should be able to answer it, then often a reply will be forthcoming, but it will be nothing more than a guess. This creates measurement error, since uninformed opinions are being recorded. A second problem is forgetfulness. For example, "What was the name of the last film you saw on TV?" "Who were the stars?" To avoid the problem of a respondent's inability to remember, time periods should be kept relatively short.

■ Consider the willingness of the respondent to answer the question. Reporting of an event is likely to be distorted in a socially desirable direction. If the event is perceived as embarrassing, sensitive in nature, threatening, or divergent from one's self-image, it is likely either not to be reported or to be distorted. Embarrassing topics that deal with things such as borrowing money, personal hygiene, sexual activities, and criminal records must be phrased in a careful manner to minimize measurement error (Wrobel, 2002). One technique is to ask the question in the third person. For example, "Do you think that most people spend more using their credit cards than they should?" By asking about "most people" rather than about the respondents themselves, researchers may be able to learn more about the respondents' attitude to credit and debt. A third method for soliciting embarrassing information is to state that the behaviour or attitude is not unusual before asking the question. For example, "Millions of people suffer from hemorrhoids; do you or any member of your family suffer from this problem?" This technique is called "using counter-biasing statements," and makes embarrassing topics less intimidating for respondents to discuss.

Step 6: arrange the sequence and layout of questions

After questions have been formulated, the next step is to order them and develop a layout for the questionnaire.

Questions should be asked in a logical order. All questions that deal with a particular topic should be asked before beginning another topic. When switching topics, brief transitional phrases should be used to help respondents switch their train of thought.

"Branching" or "skipping," a procedure in which certain questions are not asked if they do not apply to a respondent, should be designed carefully. Branching questions direct respondents to different places in the questionnaire based on how they respond to the question at hand. These questions ensure that all possible contingencies are covered. A simple way to account for all contingencies is to prepare a flowchart of the logical possibilities and then develop branching questions and instructions based on it.

Branching is most easily done in computer-assisted telephone interviews or online surveys, where software can perform the branching. The logical order of a questionnaire could be:

- Use screener questions to identify qualified respondents. Most market research employs some variation of quota sampling. Only qualified respondents are interviewed, and specific minimum numbers (quotas) of various types of qualified respondents may be desired. A study on food products generally has quotas of users of specific brands, a magazine study screens for readers, a cosmetic study screens for brand awareness and so forth. Thus, any demographics obtained provide a basis for comparison against persons who qualify for the study. A long screener can significantly increase the cost of the study. It means that you are obtaining more information from every contact with a respondent. Short screeners quickly eliminate unqualified persons and enable the interviewer to move to the next potential respondent. Yet a long screener can provide important information on the nature of non-users, or persons unaware of the product or service being researched.
- After introductory comments and screens to find a qualified respondent, the initial questions should be simple, interesting, and non-threatening. Income or age questions might be disastrous. These are often considered threatening. The initial question should be easy to answer without much forethought.
- Ask general questions first. Once the interview proceeds beyond the opening "warm-up" questions, the questionnaire should proceed in a logical fashion. General questions are covered first to get the person thinking about a concept, company, or type of product, and then the questionnaire moves to the specifics.
- Ask questions that require effort in the middle of the questionnaire. Initially, the respondent is only vaguely interested and understanding of the nature of the survey, until the process builds momentum and commitment to the interview. When the interviewer shifts to questions with scaled-response formats, the respondent must be motivated to understand the response categories and options. Build interest and commitment early to motivate the respondent to finish the questionnaire.
- Put sensitive, threatening, and demographic questions at the end. Sensitive topics include money, personal hygiene, family life, political and religious beliefs, and involvement in accidents or crimes. In industrial surveys, sensitive questions may encompass much of what a company does, especially if it reveals strategy and plans. Placing these questions at the end ensures that most of the questions will be answered before respondents become defensive or break off the interview. Moreover, rapport has

been established between the respondent and the interviewer by this time, increasing the likelihood of an answer.

Conclude the survey by thanking respondents for their time. You may also want to inform respondents how they can obtain the results of the survey.

The format, spacing and positioning of questions can have a significant effect on the results, particularly in self-administered questionnaires. It is good practice to divide the form into parts. Several parts may be needed for questions pertaining to the basic information.

Each questionnaire should be numbered. This helps the control questionnaires in the field as well in coding and analysis. Numbering makes it easy to account for the questionnaires and to determine whether any have been lost.

Finally, don't make the questionnaire too long. Long questionnaires are tiring and overwhelm respondents. As respondents exceed the time they have mentally set aside to complete the survey, their responses are no longer accurate. Furthermore, long questionnaires tend to have high non-response rates.

Step 7: obtain approval from relevant parties

Copies of the draft questionnaire should be distributed to all parties that have direct authority over the project. The client is given the opportunity to comment during the client approval stage, in which the client reviews the questionnaire and assesses whether it covers all of the appropriate issues. If questions are either inappropriate or perhaps can be improved, it is necessary for the client to convey these changes to the researcher. This may cause changes, but it is important for the client to approve the questionnaire that will be used.

Client approval ensures that the client is aware of the survey's progress, and the initialled questionnaire ensures that the researcher is protected against any later claims that the questions were incomplete or done incorrectly.

Step 8: test, revise and correct problems

Once approval has been obtained, the questionnaire should be tested to identify and eliminate problems. The most basic test is to have as many people as possible look at drafts of the questionnaire as a sounding board. The worst problems will be uncovered by these reviews.

Ideally, a pilot test is done by the best interviewers who will ultimately be working on the job and is administered to target respondents for the study. They are told to look for misinterpretations by respondents, lack of continuity, poor skip patterns, additional choices for pre-coded and closed questions, and general respondent reaction.

Testing could also involve a trial run of the questionnaire using a small sample of respondents, say five to ten, from the target population. While the sample may be small, it should cover all subgroups of the target respondents. The goal of testing is to check that the questionnaire will capture the information sought by the researcher. Testing helps refine the instrument and identifies errors that may be apparent only to the target

Marketing research in action

Example of pre-codes in a questionnaire and the resulting computer data file

Variables	Questions
1	1 Have you purchased a Pizzazza pizza in the last month?

✗ Yes (1) ___ No (2) ___ Unsure (3)

2 The last time you bought a Pizzazza pizza did you (cross only one):

Variables		
2	___ Have it delivered to your house?	(1)
	___ Have it delivered to your place of work?	(2)
	___ Pick it up yourself?	(3)
	✗ Eat it at the Pizzazza pizza restaurant	(4)
	___ Purchase it some other way?	(5)

3 In your opinion, the taste of a Pizzazza pizza is (tick only one):

Variables		
3	___ Poor	(1)
	___ Fair	(2)
	✗ Good	(3)
	___ Excellent	(4)

4 Which of the following toppings do you typically have on your pizza? (Cross all that apply.)

Variables		
4	___ Green pepper	(0;1)
5	___ Onion	(0;1)
6	**✗** Mushroom	(0;1)
7	___ Sausage	(0;1)
8	**✗** Pepperoni	(0;1)
9	___ Hot peppers	(0;1)
10	**✗** Black olives	(0;1)
11	___ Anchovies	(0;1)
12	___ Pineapple	(0;1)
13	___ Shrimps	(0;1)

5 How do you rate the speediness of Pizzazzas restaurant servi ce once you have ordered? (Circle the appropriate number if a 1 means very slow and a 7 means very fast.)

Variables	
14	Very slow 1 2 3 4 5 ⑥ 7 very fast

6 Please indicate your age:

Variables		
15	___ 0–15 years	(1)
	___ 15–25 years	(2)
	✗ 26–40 years	(3)
	___ 41–60 years	(4)
	___ Over 60 years	(5)

7 Please indicate your gender:

Variables		
16	**✗** Male	(1)
	___ Female	(2)

8 Please indicate which country you are from (cross only one):

Variables		
17	___ US	(1)
	___ Canada	(2)
	✗ UK	(3)
	___ Germany	(4)
	___ France	(5)
	___ Italy	(6)
	___ Russia	(7)
	___ China	(8)
	___ Other country	(9)

Note: the 0;1 indicates the coding system that will be used. Each response category must be defined as a separate question = variable, 0=No, 1=Yes

Figure 7.2 Standardized questionnaire   ➤

A pizza company, Pizzazza, wants to carry out a consumer survey with a standardized (but translated) questionnaire in the US, Canada, UK, Germany, France, Italy, Russia and China. The questionnaire is shown in Figure 7.2.

		Variables															
	1	2	3	4	5	6	7	8	9	10	11	12	13	14	15	16	17
1																	
2																	
3																	
.																	
.																	
.																	
.																	
10	1	4	3	0	0	1	0	1	0	1	0	0	0	6	3	1	3
.																	
.																	
n																	

(Respondent number shown along the left axis.)

Figure 7.3 Data file (only results for respondent number 10 are shown)

The results of respondent number ten are shown in the data file of Figure 7.3.

In the questionnaire there are eight questions and seventeen variables. Once the data matrix is complete, quantitative data analysis may be undertaken using a statistical software package such as SPSS or SAS.

population. More specifically, its value comes from determining whether questions make sense, are in logical order, contain biased wording, or will provide the researcher with the desired information.

Testing is usually done in two stages. The first stage is personal interviews, regardless of the way the questionnaire will later be administered, because researchers need to observe the behaviours of both the interviewers and the respondents. Respondents' reactions to the questions are the primary interest. The interviews can be carried out through protocol analysis or debriefing. Protocol analysis is an interviewing technique in which respondents think aloud while responding to each question. Debriefing is an interview conducted after respondents have completed the questionnaire. The respondents are then informed that the exercise was a test and are asked to share with the researcher their thoughts about the question, their answers, and any shortcomings of the survey.

The second testing stage involves administering the survey to a small sample in an environment as similar as possible to the one in which the questionnaire will ultimately be administered. This stage often reveals problems that cannot be detected in personal interviews. In either phase, researchers should attempt to eliminate any problems and revise the questionnaire.

After the questions have been checked, a numerical code is allocated to each type of response to aid data processing. All possible answers may be listed and coded in advance of the interview and, in surveys of any size, this is done wherever possible. If responses cannot be allocated to a range of possible answers, coding can take place after the interview. Especially, pre-coding is relevant in quantitative surveys with closed questions.

Step 9: prepare final copy

Even the final copy phase does not allow the researcher to relax. Precise typing instructions, spacing, numbering, and pre-coding must be set up, monitored, and proof-read. In general, the quality of copying and the paper used is a function of who will see the questionnaire.

Step 10: implementation

Most research interviewing is conducted by a field services department. It is their duty to complete the interviews and send them back to the researcher. In essence, field services are the production line of marketing research.

Supervisor's instructions inform interviewers of the nature of the study, start and completion dates, quotas, reporting times, equipment and facility requirement, sampling instructions, number of interviewers required, and validation procedures. Detailed instructions are required for any taste test that involves food preparation.

The supervisor's instructions are vitally important. Without clear instructions, the interview may be conducted in ten different ways in ten different countries.

Call record sheets are used to measure the efficiency of the interviewers. A form normally indicates the number of contacts and the results of the contact. A supervisor can examine calls per hour, contacts per completed interview, average time per interview, and similar measures to analyze an interviewer's efficiency. If, for example, contacts per completed interview are high, the field supervisor should examine the reasons behind it. Perhaps the interviewer is not using a proper approach or the area may be difficult to cover.

7.4 Sampling

Once the researcher has decided how primary data is to be collected, the next task is to obtain a sample of respondents that is representative of the target population. The main sampling techniques can be divided into probability and non-probability methods. In **probability sampling** each element of the population has a chance of being selected. In such cases it is possible to compute sampling variation and project the results to the entire population. In the case of **non-probability sampling**, the chance of selection of a particular population element is known and, strictly speaking, results cannot be projected to the entire population. Although sampling can be technically rigorous, the need to be so does depend on the particular application.

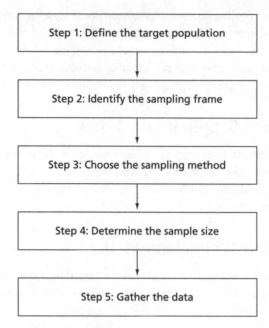

Figure 7.4 The five-step sampling process

There are two general reasons why a sample is more desirable than a census. First, there are practical considerations such as cost and population size that make a sample preferable. Taking a census is expensive as consumer populations may number in the millions. Second, typical research firms or the typical researcher cannot analyze the huge amounts of data generated by a census. Although statistical software can handle thousands of observations with ease, programs slow down appreciably with tens of thousands, and most are unable to accommodate hundreds of thousands of observations. In fact, even before a researcher considers the size of the computer or tabulation equipment to be used, he or she must consider the various data preparation procedures involved in just handling the questionnaires or responses and transferring these into computer files. The sheer physical volume places limitations on the researcher's staff and equipment.

The sampling process (Figure 7.4) can make the sampling experience less complex.

Step 1: determine the target population

The population is the total group to be studied, the **target population** (universe). It is the grand total of what is being measured: consumers, stores, households or whatever. If the purpose of the study has been well-defined, the population is also well-delineated. This is crucial if the study is to be significant and practical for the guidance of marketing management.

"Target" refers to the conditions that separate those who are of interest to a research project from those who are not. For example, common boundary conditions in marketing research could include:

- whether a person has bought the product in question within some qualifying time frame;
- whether that person intends to buy within some time frame;
- whether that person is in the geographic market; and
- whether that person is an adult.

Finally, population boundaries may be set by cost. For example, a telephone survey to measure opinions about a supermarket might be limited to certain area codes that are expected to account for most customers, even though customers who come from outside the area will be missed by this definition.

Step 2: identify the sampling frame

After defining the target population, a frame of the population must be obtained before sampling can begin. A **sampling frame** is a list or system that identifies every member of the target population so that a sample can be drawn without the necessity of physically contacting every member of the population. It can be a list of names and telephone numbers, as in telephone surveys, an area map of housing or a list of addresses purchased from a mailing list supplier. It could also be a database. The frame defines the sampling unit, the unit used in the design of the sample. The frame, and therefore the sampling unit, may take the form of households, students, retail stores of a particular defined type (nature and size, for instance), businesses or transactions. However, lists are not always available. In such a situation, some sort of counting system must be used to keep track of population members and identify the selections; for example every fourth shopper could be selected.

Step 3: choose the sampling method

As indicated in Figure 7.5 (on page 164), there are two main types of sampling methods: probability sampling and non-probability sampling.

Probability samples comprise samples in which the elements being included have a known chance of being selected. A probability sample enables sampling error to be estimated. This, in simple terms, is the difference between the sample value and the true value of the population being surveyed. A sampling error can be stated in mathematical terms: usually plus or minus a certain percentage. A larger sample usually implies a smaller sampling error.

Non-probability samples are ones in which participants are selected in a purposeful way. The selection may require certain percentages of the sample to be women or men, housewives under thirty or a similar criterion. This type of selection is an effort to reach a cross-section of the elements being sampled. However, because the sample is not rigorously chosen it is statistically impossible to state a true sampling error. The box overleaf shows how an entertainment company used non-probability samples prior to launching a new product line of videocassettes.

Marketing research in action

An entertainment company uses non-probability samples

Scandinavia's biggest entertainment and media companies asked a research agency to suggest an experimental research design that could be used for a systematic assessment of several critical aspects in connection with a forthcoming market launch in Sweden, Norway, Finland and Denmark.

The company was about to launch a series of prerecorded VHS videocassettes. At the time of the launch (1988) the market for prerecorded videocassettes was almost nonexistent in Scandinavia. Videocassettes of films could be rented for twenty-four hours at specialized stores, gasoline stations, etc. Some pornographic videos could be bought in sex shops, but an established market for the sale of normal prerecorded videos did not exist.

Four videos were selected for the experiment, a Disney film and three other films aimed at families (parents and especially at teenagers).

Several research questions were of interest to the companies:

- Managers had almost no idea about what would comprise a realistic market price. Prices ranging from €10 to €100 at today's prices were being mentioned.
- No-one knew about price elasticity in this emerging market.
- Moreover it was unknown whether the prices in the four markets should be the same or if a price discrimination strategy should be pursued.
- The four videos represented different kinds of films. Could they be targeted at the same segment or segments?

According to managers the consumption unit of a videocassette was the household. Moreover, three characteristics of a household were regarded as being essential:

- Presence of at least one child (whether pre-teen or teenager) living in the household.
- Presence of a video machine.
- A respondent needed to be a parent and also willing to participate in a Hall test.

First, a brief screening interview was carried out by interviewers placed on streets and public places in the capitals of the four countries. By definition, "every tenth adult-looking person" passing an imagined line on selected test days and time intervals, was approached by the interviewers. Only if the answer to all three of the above factors was "yes," could the person be guided to a nearby venue to answer a questionnaire (the Hall test).

Obviously, a systematic sample ("every tenth person") of persons walking on a street, say, in the centre of Copenhagen, does not constitute a representative sample of the Danish population. The sample's urbanization will be far too high and there will be an over-representation of non-residents, such as tourists. But for a moment, assume that the sample was representative: on average, how many persons should be screened for every one that fulfilled the three screening criteria above?

- About 38 percent of Denmark's 2.3 million households had a child/children living at home.
- At the time of the study, 37 percent of Danish households with children living at home possessed a video (only 27 percent of all households overall owned a video. So the penetration among households with children was definitely higher). Since

0.38 * 0.37 = 0.14, only 14 percent of the population fulfilled the first two criteria listed above.

- A person may fulfil the first two criteria but not the third. Someone regarded as "an adult-looking person" by an interviewer might be a nineteen-year-old boy living at home. He is not a parent yet.
- Many people approached on the street in Copenhagen are not residents, but foreign tourists. So they are not part of the universe of Danish households.
- The screening was conducted in the run-up to Christmas and it was cold, so many people approached by interviewers refused to take part in the screening interview.
- A lot of people who agreed to take part in the screening interview passed the three criteria, were Danish residents and, nevertheless, declined to take part in the more time-consuming Hall test.

To sum up, less than one person out of every twenty approached by an interviewer ended up completing the Hall interview. Stated differently, 200 interviews conducted in Denmark necessitated more than 4,000 initial contacts by interviewers.

The total study involved 200 completed interviews in each of the four capital cities.

The study also addressed another problem: how do you ask people how much they are willing to pay for a product that is part of a new category, and, where people have difficulties making price inferences, how do you compare prices of one product with that of competing ones? This problem was addressed by using two versions of the price question. In each country 100 respondents were exposed to these versions:

- (Indirect) What do you think this videocassette (person was handed over the cassette for inspection) would cost if it were on sale in a store tomorrow?
- (Direct) What would be the highest price that you would be willing to pay for this videocassette (handed over)?

In both cases a detailed scaling was provided to the respondent.

Not surprisingly, respondents on average expected prices to be significantly higher than they personally claimed to be willing to pay (no respondent was exposed to both versions of the questions).

The company decided to set the market price approximately as an average of A and B but somewhat closer to B.

Another interesting finding was that price expectations, independent of version, were regarded to be clearly higher in Norway than in the other countries. It appeared that the price elasticity was lower in Norway. This seemed to fit nicely with the fact that the general price level in Norway was higher than in the other countries (inflation in Norway was high because of overheated demand caused by the country's big revenues from oil exports). Price expectations were regarded to be lowest in Finland. These findings provided managers with important clues with regard to differentiating prices across Scandinavian markets.

During the interviewing phase, the research agency had been asked to include a quota sampling in the design. Respondents in the Hall test should be about equal by sex. After the interviewing phase was finished it turned out that this criteria was clearly violated with regard to the Finnish sample. Some 87 percent of those interviewed in Helsinki were females, most probably from households with above-average income. Why? It turned out that the agency conducting the interviews in Helsinki had placed the interviewers outside shops that sold expensive products for women.

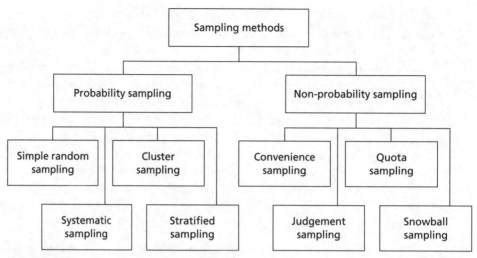

Figure 7.5 Types of sampling method

Most samples chosen for applied research are non-probability samples (Figure 7.5). A true probability sample, because of the stringent requirements, is likely to be far too expensive and too time-consuming for most uses. The sampling method chosen for any particular study, therefore, must be explained carefully, with the reasons for its acceptability and likelihood of supplying accurate data.

The research plan may not require that a whole country be sampled. Cost and time factors may lead to the decision to cover only part of a country.

Probability sampling

Simple random sampling is a technique in which each element of the population has an equal chance of being selected. Simple random sampling is carried out by assigning each element of the sampling frame a number. Then a series of random numbers is generated, using either a computer or random number table. The sample becomes the elements whose numbers appear on the list of random numbers. This method is appealing because it produces an unbiased estimate of the population's characteristics. It guarantees that every member of the population has a known and equal chance of being selected; therefore, the resulting sample, no matter what the size, will be a valid representation of the population.

However, there are some disadvantages.

To obtain a simple random sample is not easy or practical in many circumstances. It may be time-consuming or costly and sometimes is theoretically impossible. For example, if we wish to take a simple random sample from a large finite population of one million families, although it is possible, it is not a simple task to assign a number to each of the families and then draw a sample at random from the numbers. When a population is infinite, numbering each element is impossible. Therefore, simple random sampling needs modifications. The most common types of modified probability samples are systematic, stratified, and cluster samples.

Systematic sampling is a technique in which a sample is drawn by choosing a beginning point in a list and then sequentially selecting every k^{th} element from the list. For a systematic sample, the items in the population must be ordered. The selection procedure depends on the number of items in the population and the size of the sample. The number of items in the population is first divided by the number desired in the sample. The quotient is k, indicating whether every tenth, eleventh, or perhaps hundredth element in the population is to be selected. The first item of the sample is selected at random. The rest of the sample is chosen by selecting every k^{th} element from the ordered list until the sample size is reached.

The popularity of systematic sampling has fallen because computerized databases now have a random number selection capability. However, in the special case of a physical listing of the population, such as a membership directory or a telephone book, systematic sampling is often chosen over random sampling because of its economic efficiency. In this instance, systematic sampling can be applied with less difficulty and accomplished in a shorter time period than can simple random sampling. Furthermore, systematic sampling has the potential to create a sample that is almost identical in quality to samples created from simple random sampling.

The essential difference between systematic sampling and simple random sampling is apparent in the use of the words "systematic" and "random." The system used in systematic sampling is the skip interval, whereas the randomness in simple random sampling is determined through the use of successive random draws.

In **cluster sampling**, a random sample of subgroups is chosen and all members of the subgroups become part of the sample. It is done by first dividing the population into subgroups. Then a random sample of subgroups is chosen, and all members of the chosen subgroups are included in the study. Notice here that not all subgroups are selected, but those that are selected compose the sample. If the researcher samples all of the members of the selected subgroups, it is a one-stage cluster sample. If a sample of members of the selected subgroups is randomly selected, it is a two-stage cluster sample.[1] One of the most popular ways of forming a cluster is by geographic areas. For the first step, the researcher could select a random sample of areas, and then for the second step pick a probability method to sample individuals within the chosen areas. The two-step area sample approach is preferable to the one-step approach because there is always the possibility that a single cluster may be less representative than the researcher believes. But the two-step method is more costly because more areas and time are involved.

The greatest danger in one-stage cluster sampling is cluster specification error that occurs when the clusters are not homogeneous.

In **stratified sampling**, the researcher first divides the population into natural subgroups that are more homogeneous than the population as a whole. Then items are selected for the sample at random or by a systematic method from each subgroup. This method is usually used when a large variation exists within a population and the researcher has some prior knowledge about natural subgroups within the population. Estimates of the population based on the stratified sample usually have greater precision (or smaller sampling error) than if the whole population were sampled by simple random sampling.

The number of items selected from each stratum may be proportionate or disproportionate to the size of the stratum in relation to the population. Under the proportionate method, for example, if the size of stratum A is 30 percent of the population, then 30 percent of the sample will come from stratum A. So, if the sample has 300 items,

Table 7.2 Examples of proportionate and disproportionate stratified sampling

Strata (size of companies)	Target population in country x (number of companies)	Proportionate stratified sample (1% of strata) (number of companies)	Disproportionate stratified sample (number of companies)
Large companies	100	1% = 1	21% = 21
Medium companies	1,000	1% = 10	3% = 30
Small companies	10,000	1% = 100	0.6% = 60
Total	11,100	1% = 111	1% = 111

30 percent of the sample size, or 90 items, are to be selected from stratum A. When the selection is disproportionate, it is relatively difficult to weigh the results from individual strata properly.

The main benefit of stratified sampling is that the sample will include items from each stratum. Table 7.2 shows that if the stratified sample of companies is proportionate, the large companies are only represented with one company in the sample of 111 companies. Taking the importance of the large companies into consideration, the proportion of large companies should be higher. Therefore, in this case represented in Table 7.2 we would prefer a disproportionate sample.

There are times when stratified sampling is used in marketing research because skewed populations are encountered. Prior knowledge of populations under study, augmented by research objectives sensitive to subgroupings, sometimes reveals that the population is not normally distributed. Under these circumstances, it is advantageous to apply stratified sampling to preserve the diversity of the subgroups. Usually, a surrogate measure, which is some observable or easily determined characteristic of each population member, is used to help partition or separate the population members into their various subgroups. In Table 7.2 the surrogate measure is the size of the companies (could be sales or number of employees).

Non-probability sampling methods

All of the sampling methods described so far embody probability sampling assumptions. In each case, the probability of any unit being selected from the population into the sample is known, even though it cannot be calculated precisely.

Convenience samples are samples drawn at the convenience of the interviewer. The selection of place and, consequently, prospective respondents, is subjective rather than objective. Certain members of the population are automatically eliminated from the sampling process.

When researchers have little time or money available for an elaborate study, they may do convenience sampling, selecting sample items that are easy to obtain. In fact, there may be no other way to gather data in some cases than to sample a group of individuals who are available. Often, for example, college professors will use their students as a sample, because students are a captive audience and are convenient for the study. The problem here lies with the subjective selection of the sample and the lack of generalizability of the results (Wansink, 2002). What follows shows how using a convenient sample led a marketer to reposition a product so that it no longer met the needs of the market it was aimed at.

Marketing research in action

The danger of using convenient samples for new product testing

While a convenient sample represents a quick way of obtaining relevant marketing input, it may lead to inappropriate decisions and even result in "mis-marketing." Some decades ago, a soft-drink company wanted to launch a drink in a foreign market. The local distributor in charge of the campaign wanted to carry out "some kind of marketing research" before the launch. But since the time was critical and the money short, it was decided to ask teachers in a nearby school to distribute several hundred questionnaires among teenagers at the school. The prospects were asked to taste the drink – provided by the distributor – and to answer a few questions about the drink's taste. According to the test, the drink was too sweet. Consequently, some of the sugar was removed before the drink was launched. This was done because the local distributor wanted to tailor the product for the local market. However, the promotional campaign for the product was not aimed at teenagers, but at pre-teens. For example, advertisements were placed in Donald Duck comics but not in, say, magazines for teenagers on popular music, love, pop stars, etc.

So, based on information obtained from the convenient sample, the product had been repositioned for a teenager market while the promotional strategy was for pre-teens. Pre-teenagers, it turns out have a much stronger preference for a sweet and sugared taste.

After a year or so of disappointing sales the product was withdrawn.

Source: Adapted from Hegedahl and Thygesen Poulsen (1980)

Judgement samples differ from convenience samples because they require a judgement or an "educated guess" as to who should represent the population. Often the researcher or some individual helping the researcher who has considerable knowledge about the population will choose those individuals whom they feel constitute the sample. It should be apparent that such samples are highly subjective and, therefore, prone to error. Focus group studies often use judgement sampling rather than probability sampling.

Quota samples establish a special quota for various types of individuals to be interviewed.

Researchers may want to ensure that their sample includes a sufficient number of individuals with a particular characteristic that affects the study. In these cases the researchers determine the percentage of the target population that possesses the characteristics of interest and specify the number of these individuals to be included in the sample to reflect their proportion in the population.

Quota samples are often used by companies that have a firm grasp on the features characterizing the individuals they wish to study. A large bank, for example, might stipulate that the final sample have an equal number of males and females because in the bank's understanding of its market, the customer base is equally divided between the two sexes.

When done conscientiously and with a firm understanding of quota characteristics, such sampling can rival probability sampling in the minds of researchers.

Snowball samples require respondents to provide the names of additional respondents. Such lists begin when the researcher compiles a short list of sample units that is smaller than the total sample for study. After each respondent is interviewed, they are asked to name other possible respondents. In this manner, additional respondents are referred by previous respondents. Or, as the name implies, the sample grows just as a snowball grows when it is rolled downhill.

Snowball samples are most appropriate when there is a limited and disappointingly short sample frame and when respondents can provide the names of others who would qualify for the survey. The non-probability aspects of snowball sampling come from the selectivity used throughout. The initial list may also be special in some way, and the primary means of adding people to the sample is by tapping the memories of those on the original list. Referral samples are often useful in industrial marketing research situations.

Step 4: determine the sample size

Having chosen the sampling method, the next step is to determine the appropriate sample size. If the sample size is too large, more money and time will be spent than is necessary, but the result obtained from the large sample may not be more accurate than that from a smaller sample. On the other hand, if the sample size is too small, the study may not reach a valid conclusion. It is important to realize that the more elements that are properly sampled from the population, the less the sampling error. This error exists because the whole population is not examined, ultimately leaving something out of the investigation.

The most correct method of determining sample size is the confidence interval approach, which applies the concepts of accuracy (sample error), variability, and confidence interval to create a "correct" sample size. Because it is, theoretically, the most correct method, it is the one used by national opinion polling companies. To describe the confidence interval approach to sample size determination, we first describe an underlying concept.

The larger a probability sample is, the more accurate it is (less sample error), indicating that there is a relationship between sample size and the accuracy of that sample. However, the relationship between sample size and accuracy is not linear – doubling the sample size

Table 7.3 95% confidence intervals (= sample error = E) obtained around estimates of proportions, given various sample sizes

Prestudy estimate of the proportion (p)	Given sample size (n) needed to be 95 percent confident the after-study estimate is within ±E of the true proportion						
	n = 50	100	200	300	500	1,000	5,000
1% or 99%	2.8%	2.0%	1.4%	1.1%	0.9%	0.7%	0.3%
2% or 98%	3.9	2.8	2.0	1.5	1.3	0.9	0.4
5% or 95%	6.1	4.3	3.0	2.5	2.0	1.5	0.6
10% or 90%	8.4	5.9	4.2	3.4	2.7	1.9	0.9
20% or 80%	11.1	7.9	5.6	4.6	3.5	2.5	1.1
30% or 70%	12.7	9.0	6.4	5.2	4.0	2.9	1.3
40% or 60%	13.6	9.6	6.8	5.6	4.3	3.1	1.4
50%	13.9	9.8	7.0	5.7	4.4	3.1	1.4

does not halve the sample error. In fact, the sampling error diminishes in accordance with the square root of the growth in sample size. So if the sample doubles, the sampling error decreases by a little more than 40 percent. Because of this statistical relationship you have to quadruple a sample in order to halve the sample error. Table 7.3 also shows this principle.

Results that are not shown in Table 7.3 can be determined by applying this formula:

$$E = z_{\alpha/2} \sqrt{\frac{p(1-p)}{n}}$$

(1)

(For a crash course in such statistics, see www.pearsoned.co.uk/schmidt, appendices B, C and D.)

This example shows the use of Table 7.3. A sample of 50 European companies has shown that 60 percent of these have a website. From Table 7.3, there is a sample error of ± 13.6 percent connected to this measure, meaning that the "true" measure (with 95 percent probability) would be between 60 − 13.6 = 46.4 percent and 60 + 13.6 = 73.6 percent.

Applying the above formula yields:

$$E = 1.96 \sqrt{\frac{0.60\,(0.40)}{50}} = 0.1358, \text{ which corresponds with} \pm 13.6\%.$$

If the researcher would like to halve the sample error from 13.6 percent to 6.8 percent they would have to quadruple the sample size from fifty to two-hundred. Therefore, determining the sample size mainly depends on the acceptable sample error.

If we solve equation (1) with respect to n, we obtain the sample size directly based on the proportion and the error:

$$n = \frac{(z_{\alpha/2})^2\, p(1-p)}{E^2}$$

(2)

Using the same numerical data we have:

$$n = \frac{(1.96)^2 \times (0.60) \times (0.40)}{(0.1358)^2} = 50$$

Note that as the acceptable level, or E, decreases (precision increases), the sample sizes grow. If in the above example we use an E of 0.05, the required sample size grows to 369:

$$n = \frac{(1.96)^2 \times (0.60) \times (0.40)}{(0.05)^2} = 369$$

It is clear that costs have to be considered because if you quadruple the sample size you typically also quadruple sample data collection costs.

In situations where the calculated sample size represents more than 10 percent of the population, one needs to adjust the sample size for the **finite population correction** factor. Assume the survey is confined to companies within a specific industry where only 800 companies are registered. How does this affect the necessary sample size?

This can be computed using the correction factor (referring to the previous example with an E of 0.05):

$$n_{finite} = \frac{nN}{N + n - 1} = \frac{(369) \times (800)}{800 + 369 - 1} \approx 253$$

In the present case it is not necessary to sample 369 companies but only 253.

Step 5: gather the data

Gathering data is a two-stage process. First, the sample unit must be selected. Second, information must be gained from that unit. Simply put, you need to choose a person and ask him or her some questions. However, not everyone will agree to answer. So there comes the question of substitutions. Substitutions occur whenever an individual who was qualified to be in the sample proves to be unavailable, unwilling to respond, or unsuitable.

The final activity in the sampling process is the assessment stage. Sample assessment can take a number of forms, one of which is to compare the sample's demographic profile with a known profile such as the census. With quota sample validation, the researcher must use a demographic characteristic other than those used to set up the quota system. The essence of sample validation is to assure the client that the sample is, in fact, a representative sample of the population about which someone wishes to make decisions.

7.5 Summary

Surveys provide the important advantages of standardization, easy administration, discovering motives for behaviours, simple tabulation, and ability to investigate subgroupings of respondents. Personal interviews are advantageous because they allow feedback, permit rapport building, facilitate certain quality controls, and capitalize on the adaptability of a human interviewer. However, they are slow, prone to human errors and expensive.

After defining a questionnaire and explaining its role in the data collection process, the criteria for good questionnaire construct was established. Questionnaire development is addressed in a sequential format beginning with survey objectives, resources, and constraints. The process contains ten steps (Figure 7.1).

Information about the characteristics of a population may be obtained by drawing samples from the target population. Budget and time limits, large population size, and small variance in the characteristic of interest favour the use of a sample. Sampling is preferred when the cost of any sampling error is low. The opposite set of conditions favours asking everyone in the population.

Sampling design begins by defining the target population in terms of elements, sampling units, extent and time. Then the sampling frame should be determined. A sampling frame is a representation of the elements of the target population. At this stage, it is important to recognize any sampling frame errors. The next step involves selecting a sampling technique and determining the sample size. In addition to quantitative analysis, several qualitative considerations should be taken into account in determining the sample size. Execution of the sampling process requires detailed specifications for each step. Finally, the selected sample should be validated by comparing characteristics of the sample with known characteristics of the target population.

Sampling techniques may be classified as either non-probability or probability techniques.

When conducting international marketing research it is desirable to achieve comparability in sample composition and representativeness even though this may require the use of different sampling techniques in different countries.

Non-probability sampling is based on researchers' subjective judgement rather than on scientific principles. However, this does not mean the results are useless. On the contrary, a researcher may do a good job in portraying the target population, but without scientifically determined samples, there is no way to determine how precise the results are. But the ease of obtaining the sample and the low cost associated with drawing non-probability samples often compensate for their lack of statistical support. Judgement sampling, convenience sampling, quota sampling, and snowball sampling are popular non-probability sampling methods.

Probability sampling is any sampling plan in which the chance of being selected is known and equal for every sampling unit in the population. Statisticians prefer these methods since sampling selection is objective and the sampling error may be measured. Simple random sampling, systematic sampling, stratified sampling, and cluster sampling are types of probability sampling methods.

For a sample to be statistically useful, it must be representative of the target population. While industry rules of thumb, affordability, and statistical methods can all be used to determine sample size, the statistical method is preferred, because it is supported by scientific principles. Using this method, researchers need three pieces of information: desired precision, desired confidence level, and an estimation of the population standard deviation or parameter.

Questions

1. What is the purpose of a questionnaire?

2. How would you determine whether a specific question should be included in a questionnaire?

3. What kind of survey method would you recommend to research the question of why female shoppers choose a particular shop at which to buy clothing?

4. Discuss the advantages and disadvantages of open-ended questions and closed questions.

5. What are the issues involved in designing multiple-choice questions?

6. What are the guidelines available for deciding on question wording?

7. What is a leading question? Give an example.

8. Outline the procedure for developing a questionnaire. Assume that you are developing a questionnaire for a new sandwich for a fast-food chain in several countries. Use this situation to discuss the questionnaire development.

9. Design three open-ended and three closed questions to measure consumers' attitudes towards a make of car.

10. Once a questionnaire is developed, what other factors need to be considered before giving it to interviewers?

11. Why is testing a questionnaire important?

12. What are the advantages and disadvantages of online surveys?

13. What problems might be encountered by a domestic research company in conducting an international research study?

14. What problems are faced by researchers conducting research in developing countries?

15. Describe the sampling design process.

16. Distinguish between probability and non-probability samples. What are the advantages and disadvantages of each? Why are non-probability samples popular in marketing research?

17. Describe snowball sampling. Give an example of a situation in which you might use this type of sample. What are the dangers associated with this type of sample?

18. What are the differences between proportionate and disproportionate stratified sampling?

19. What is the least expensive and least time-consuming of all sampling techniques?

20. What is meant by a "skewed" population? Illustrate what you think is a skewed population distribution variable and what it looks like.

21. Differentiate one-step from two-step area sampling, and indicate when each one is preferred.

22. Discuss the factors that determine sample size.

23. Suggest a research design that could have prevented the case of mis-marketing described in the Marketing research in action box on page 167. Use a reliable, yet affordable research design. Face-to-face interviews with a nationally representative sample of, say, 2,000 children aged from six to twelve years would be too expensive. Discuss ways of using a convenient sample but to use it in a better way than was done in the case.

References

Coderre, F., Mathieu, A. and St-Laurent, N. (2004) "Comparison of the quality of qualitative data obtained through telephone and postal email surveys." *International Journal of Market Research*. Vol 46, no. 3. 347–57.

Finkel, S. E. (1995) *Causal Analysis with Panel Data*. Sage, Beverly Hills, CA.

Frevert, B. (2000) "Is global research different?" *Marketing Research*. Spring. 49–51.

Hegedahl, P. and Thygesen Poulsen, P. (1980) *Mismarketing*. Børsens Forlag, Copenhagen.

Hsiao, C. (2002) *Analysis of Panel Data*. Cambridge University Press, Cambridge.

Ilieva, J., Baron S. and Healey, N. M. (2002) "Online surveys in marketing research: pros and cons." *International Journal of Market Research*. Vol. 44, quarter 3. 361–382.

Lorimor, E. S. and Dunn, S. W. (1967) "Four measures of cross-cultural advertising effectiveness." *Journal of Advertising Research*. Vol. 7, no. 4 (December). 11–13.

—- (1968a) "Use of mass media in France and Egypt." *Public Opinion Quarterly*. Vol. 32 (spring). 680–87.

—- (1968b) "Reference groups, congruency theory and cross-cultural persuasion". *Journal of Communication*. Vol. 18 (December). 354–368.

Loosveldt, G., Carton, A. and Billiet, J. (2004) "Assessment of survey data quality: a pragmatic approach focused on interviewer tasks." *International Journal of Market Research*. Vol. 46, no. 1. 65–82.

Ray, N. M. and Tabor, S. W. (2003) "Cyber-surveys come of age." *Marketing Research*. Spring. 32–37.

Roster, C. A., Rogers, R. D., Albaum, G. and Klein, D. (2004) "A comparison of response characteristics from web and telephone surveys." *International Journal of Market Research*. Vol. 46, quarter 3. 359–373.

Schillewaert, N. and Meulemeerster, P. (2005) "Comparing response distribution of offline and online data collection methods." *International Journal of Market Research*. Vol. 47, no. 2. 163–78.

Wansink, B. (2002) "Building a successful convenience panel." *Marketing Research*. Fall. 23–27.

Wilson, A. and Laskey, N. (2003) "Internet-based marketing research: a serious alternative to traditional research methods?" *Marketing Intelligence & Planning*. 21/2. 79–84.

Wrobel, V. (2002) "Not in front of your mother!" *Qualitative Market Research*. Vol. 5, no. 1. 19–27.

End note

[1] Calculating probability of being chosen to be a sample in a two-stage model is based on the Bayesian probability. This view of probability was proposed in the eighteenth century by Thomas Bayes, an English clergyman who died in 1760. Bayes wrote a paper (published posthumously in 1763) in which he proposed a rule for accounting for uncertainty that has become known as Bayes' theorem. This became the foundation for Bayesian statistical inference. In Bayesian statistics, probabilities reflect a belief about the sample of data under study rather than about the frequency of events across hypothetical samples. Bayes' Theorem exploits the fact that the joint probability of two events, A and B, can be written as the product of the probability of one event and the conditional probability of the second event, given the occurrence of the first event. If we consider "A" to be our "hypothesis" (H) in the absence of any observations "B" (or "D" for data), we can express the rule as follows:

$$Pr(H|D) = Pr(D|H) \times Pr(H)/Pr(D)$$

The probability of the hypothesis given (or "conditional" on, the meaning of the "|" symbol) the data is equal to the probability of the data given the hypothesis times the probability of the hypothesis divided by the probability of the data. We refer to the Pr(H) as the prior probability and Pr(H|D) as the posterior probability.

8 Quantitative models in marketing

Learning objectives

After studying this chapter you should be able to:

- Explain the purpose of model construction.
- Determine the characteristics of a successful model.
- Be able to distinguish between categories of models.
- Assess the value of additional information.
- Evaluate how model parameters affect product penetration.
- Discuss the applicability of generic models on international marketing problems.

8.1 Properties of a good model

According to one of the pioneers of marketing models, John Little (1970):

- good models are hard to find;
- good parameterization is even harder;
- managers do not understand models;
- most models are incomplete.

There can be little doubt that Little's statement is of even greater relevance if we deal with models that aim to describe and analyze international or cross-cultural marketing problems.

Marketing research in action
Types of marketing models and their purpose

Models of consumer behaviour and media planning usually assume that consumers are exposed to advertising in a variety of print media, broadcast programming and TV channels. While this applies in countries such as the US, France and Japan, it may not apply to consumers in Africa and the Middle East, either because the consumers are not literate, they cannot afford to approach such media, the media do not exist, or the government controls advertising in the media.

Models of product innovation or product launches are of little value if the market deems the product unacceptable. An alcoholic beverage cannot be launched in Muslim countries, chewing gum has been prohibited in Singapore and there are increasing global restrictions on cigarette smoking.

Pricing models may apply to markets without government regulation of prices. But they are probably invalid or of limited validity when analyzing markets where the authorities have established minimum or maximum prices for goods and services. Moreover: can the same model be used for describing the German beer market, where more than 1,000 producers compete and the biggest competitor has a national share of 8 percent, and the Danish market, where one company, Carlsberg/Tuborg, has more than 70 percent of the market?

Distribution models assume that the appropriate vertical and horizontal channels are available, though there are variations, "home parties" (the key to Tupperware's success) and "snowball systems" are legal ways of distributing goods in some countries, but forbidden or strictly regulated in other countries.

Availability of valid measurements constitutes a necessary but not sufficient condition of a good model. As Table 8.1 shows, many other factors are also of importance.

- A model should be comprehensive and not omit any critical relationships, and yet be as simple as possible.
- All relationships that do not facilitate the understanding of the phenomenon in a significant way should be excluded.
- The model should be without error. This implies that external constructs or variables should not retard an understanding of internal causal links. Likewise, spurious effects should not be confounded with true relationships.

Table 8.1 Properties of a good model

1 Comprehensive	8 Operational
2 Simple	9 Generalizable
3 Little "noise" or error	10 Communicable
4 Measurable	11 Has implications for managers
5 Valid and reliable	12 Successful
6 Robust	13 True
7 Logically consistent	

■ The variables of the model ought to be quantitatively measurable. While verbal, or qualitative, models may make sense, they are beyond the scope of this text.

■ The overall model as well as the involved measurements must be both valid and reliable. Scales must work well and estimates make sense.

■ It must be robust (stable and insensitive to minor changes in the environment). A model is said to possess robustness if it is difficult for a user to obtain incorrect answers.

■ Consistency is needed. For example, since negative sales and prices make little sense in the real world, the model counterpart should satisfy the same constraints.

■ Operational properties are important. While game theory and linear programming possess excellent theoretical properties they often lack everyday applicability.

■ Hypothesized patterns and estimates ought to be generalizable. They should work properly in different settings. However, a model of individual buying behaviour may work well in North America while it performs poorly in developing countries where many of the household's purchases are physically carried out by the grandmother. If this is the case, a refined model of family or household buying behaviour might better fit the data.

■ Findings must be communicable. This implies that findings must facilitate an understanding of the problem to managers. It must make sense.

■ Management must be able to transform the insight gained to tactical and/or strategic decisions with regard to a product launch, pricing, advertising, distribution and so on.

■ The model must be successful. Unfortunately, a model's long-term successfulness can only be assessed properly by posterity's observers.

■ A model has to be true as demonstrated by it agreeing with known facts.

EXHIBIT 8.1 GROWING SALES MAY CONCEAL A COMING SALES DECLINE

The market for chewing gum in an industrialized country has been growing for decades and appears to keep expanding, but the population is growing slowly. Closer inspection of the country's population pyramid might raise concern about future sales. Assume that birth rates have been declining for years and that the average age of the population is going up. Why should this make us worry? Well, because the consumption of chewing gum is inversely related to age. So within a few years, sales will probably start declining since the number of heavy users (teenagers) is declining while the number of elderly non-users is increasing.

8.2 Different categories of models

It is useful to distinguish between five types of models:

■ verbal;
■ conceptual;
■ graphical;
■ statistical;
■ mathematical.

The first three types will be briefly explained, whereas the statistical and mathematical models will be dealt with in some detail.

An introduction to game theory (a mathematical model) can be found at www.pearsoned.co.uk/schmidt (Appendix 8-A).

Verbal model: description of a market launch

The word-of-mouth spread of knowledge about a product is an example of a simple verbal model. When a product or service is launched, sales often start slowly until some people (early adopters) become aware of the product. They buy it and start using it. If they are satisfied with the product, they recommend it to family members and to friends via word-of-mouth communication. This leads to an acceleration of sales growth, and the producer (importer) is encouraged to place advertisements in various media. At some point, the market potential is approached and growth slows down.

Conceptual model: a test-marketing simulator

Figure 8.1 provides an example of a conceptual model. It shows how different types of research data are used as input by subsequent models of purchase behaviour to forecast the market share of a product that has not yet been launched. The model states that management planning data and behavioural data are inputs to a penetration model, while the same two types of data, supplemented with psychometric data, are inputs to a brand choice

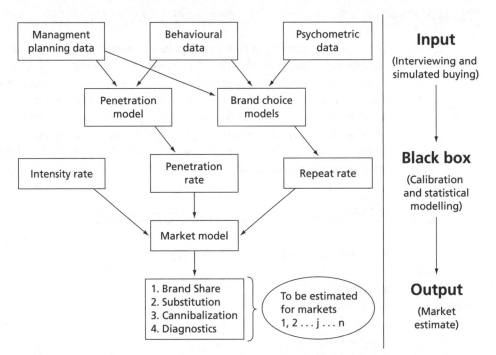

Figure 8.1 A conceptual model: the GfK TESI® market penetraton simulator
Source: Erichson (1987)

model. The first model is used to estimate a penetration rate while the latter is used to establish a rate of repeat buying behaviour. Both estimated rates are then supplemented by an approximated intensity rate and subsequently the three measures are input to the marketing model.

Finally, the market model provides an estimate of:

- the new product's market share,
- which competitor's products the product will substitute and to what degree;
- which of the company's own brands it is thought to cannibalize and by how much;
- some diagnostics are provided, such as how sensitive the estimates are to changes in the marketing strategy parameters of competitors (triggered by the product). Note that the modelling (including the sampling and interviewing) has to be carried out for each product and market.

The GfK Group has done hundreds of such studies for its clients in countries such as Germany, Italy and Denmark. Note, that this type of conceptual model is limited to branded products with high repeat purchase rates such as food products and detergents. Other market simulation models are Assessor (Silk and Urban, 1975), Comp (Burger et al., 1981), and Litmus (Blackburn and Clancy, 1982). Most international marketing research agencies supply at least one pre-test model.

Graphical model: a perceptual space

A graphical model displays distinct features of a phenomenon in space, such models will not be discussed further here, since perceptual space is covered separately in Chapter 13. (Figure 13.1 on page 379 is an example of perceptual space.) There we provide technical details on how a perceptual space is established using software, and how input data must be formatted.

Statistical model: Bayesian decision theory

A statistical model uses systematic statistical reasoning. A numerical example may help to clarify this (Green et al., 1988). Assume that a company wants to launch a new product. Before the launch, managers want to assess three scenarios, as in Table 8.2.

Based on experience, managers estimate that there is a 30 percent chance of a best possible outcome, 50 percent chance of the modest scenario, and a 20 percent probability of failure. So, should the product be introduced, assumed that the above figures apply? See Table 8.3.

Table 8.2 Three scenarios to be assessed

Scenarios	Market share (%)	Profit
1 A best possible case	15	€20 million
2 A modest or "realistic" scenario	5	€5 million
3 A disaster scenario	1	−€10 million

Table 8.3 Assessing a launch under different scenarios

				Scenarios		
	S_1		S_2		S_3	
Decision	$P(S_1)$	15% share	$P(S_2)$	5% share	$P(S_3)$	1% share
Introduce	0.3	€20m	0.5	€5m	0.2	−€10m
Don't Introduce	0.3	0	0.5	0	0.2	0

If we do not introduce the product, the expected income is zero. The expected payoff of introducing product is calculated as €6.5 million:

$$[0.3 \times (20) + 0.5 \times (5) + 0.2 \times (-10)]$$

Assume, for a moment, that the company could consult an infallible soothsayer with a crystal ball. Moreover, presume that the product needs to move along one of a hundred available paths that leads to the future market reality. Thirty of these paths will provide us a profit of €20 million, fifty paths yield a profit of €5 million while the remaining twenty paths will lead us to a disastrous loss of €10 million.

The problem is that we usually have no idea concerning which of the hundred paths lead us to the profit, and which twenty make us, unknowingly, head for disaster. To make things worse, we only have one shot. However, the soothsayer is able to identify or label them for us ("Path 1 ⇒ profit of 5, Path 2 ⇒ loss of 10, Path three ⇒ profit of 5, etc."). It is easy to see that, possessing this window to the future, we would decide *not* to launch the product, if we knew that the third scenario (S_3) would prevail. By acting thus, we would at least prevent losing money. Consequently, our soothsayer-assisted expected profit would be €8.5 million [$0.3 \times (20) + 0.5 \times (5) + 0.2 \times (0)$]. Everything else being equal, we would be better off in the long run by paying the soothsayer up to €2 million for the service [8.5 − 6.5]. This net value is called **the expected value of perfect information**.

Unfortunately, perfect knowledge of the future does not exist. However, we might be able to approach perfect knowledge by using market tests. Assume that we work with a research agency that operates on a global scale, such as A.C. Nielsen, GfK, Burke or Sofres. Based on an inspection of the agency's track record, we can establish the data shown in Table 8.4.

The table is to be understood in the following way. In six out of ten situations where a market share of 15 percent turned out once the market conditions became stable, the

Table 8.4 Possible outcomes of market test by the agency

	Probability of forecasting outcome		
Scenario	Z_1 (share > 10%)	Z_2 (3% < share <10%)	Z_3 (share < 3%)
S_1 (15% share)	0.6	0.3	0.1
S_2 (5% share)	0.3	0.5	0.2
S_3 (1% share)	0.1	0.2	0.7

research agency has, based on a test, forecast a market share of more than 10 percent (cell S_1Z_1). However, in three out of ten cases, the agency underestimated the outcome and forecast a moderate scenario with a share of between 3 percent and 10 percent (cell S_1Z_2). Finally, in one out of ten cases the agency failed: it forecast a market share less than 3 percent while the market share turned out to be 15 percent (cell S_1Z_3).

Usually, a test pitfall of category S_3Z_1 (a "progressive" or "over-optimistic" estimation of market potential) is regarded as worse than S_1Z_3 (a conservative underestimation). Some researchers recommend establishing different weights that adjust for different consequences of alternate outcomes. A performance score, not unlike the one shown in Table 8.4 or even better has been reported by researchers and agencies that work with and use test marketing simulators such as TESI (Erichson, 1987) and Assessor (Urban and Hauser, 1993).

Assuming that the data in Tables 8.3 and 8.4 are true, it is possible to compute the value of market research, perceived as an upper limit that should not be exceeded (it cannot be justified to pay more for the research). This amount is called **the expected value of additional information**. How do we compute this value? Simply by carrying out a **pre-posterior analysis** in accordance with Bayes' theorem.[1]

First, we compute the **marginal probabilities** by multiplying the probabilities of the different scenarios by the probabilities of a given test result's (in)capability to "hit the truth" and add the numbers (Z_{11} refers to the first cell in Table 8.4):

$$S_1 \times Z_{11} = (0.3 \times 0.6) = 0.18$$
$$S_2 \times Z_{12} = (0.5 \times 0.3) = 0.15$$
$$S_3 \times Z_{13} = (0.2 \times 0.1) = 0.02$$
$$\Sigma = 0.35$$

Next, we compute the corresponding **posterior probabilities** $(PS_i|Z_1)$:

$$0.18/0.35 = 0.5143$$
$$0.15/0.35 = 0.4286$$
$$0.02/0.35 = 0.0571$$
$$\Sigma = 1.0000$$

We repeat the calculations with the numbers in the remaining columns. Once we have done this, we are able to establish the Bayesian decision tree and put in the appropriate profits accompanying the different states of nature as well as the corresponding posterior probabilities (reflecting the uncertainty of the market test). This has been done in Figure 8.2.

Looking at the far right of the upper branch we see the three posterior probabilities and the accompanying profits. We now simply multiply these three profit figures by the corresponding probabilities and add the numbers:

$$(0.5143 \times 20) + (0.4286 \times 5) + (0.0571 \times -10) = 11.858$$

That is the expected outcome of option A_1 (to launch). Not launching would give zero profit (option A_2). But since the expected value of A_1 is better than A_2, we chose A_1. These

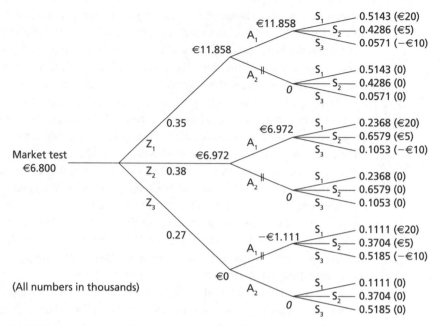

Figure 8.2 Bayesian decision tree
Source: Adapted from Green and Tull (1978)

computations have to be repeated for the middle and the lower of the three main branches. Finally, we multiply the expected values by the marginal probabilities of the test's outcome:

$$(11.858 \times 0.35) + (6.972 \times 0.38) \text{ and } (0 \times 0.27) = €6.800 \ (\times 1,000)$$

This figure is called **the expected payoff after research**. The expected **payoff without research** was €6.500. The difference between the two estimates is €300,000. This number is called the **expected value of additional information**.

Finally, detracting the cost of the test, say, €100,000, from the €300,000 gives the **net expected payoff of research**. In this case, the estimate would be €200,000. So, based on the above assumptions, it is better to carry out the market test, and, based on the test, the company should launch the product. However, this need not be the case universally. Due to differences with regard to the business cycle, consumer expectations, the overall robustness of the economy, etc., the optimal decision may be to launch the product in some markets but not in others. In some countries it may be recommended to carry out additional research, while in other countries conducting separate research seems not worth the effort (the net expected payoff of research is negative).

Basically, the Bayesian approach has four critical inputs:

■ the number of scenarios to be assessed;
■ the size of the profit, given the actual level;
■ the probability of the given state of nature;
■ the historic "performance matrix" of the research agency (Table 8.4).

Table 8.5 Possible outcomes of market test by a "miserable" agency

State of nature	Probability of forecasting outcome		
	Z_1 (share > 10%)	Z_2 (3% < share < 10%)	Z_3 (share < 3%)
S_1 (15% share)	0.1	0.8	0.1
S_2 (5% share)	0.1	0.1	0.8
S_3 (1% share)	0.8	0.1	0.1

It is easy to see that a change in any of these inputs will change the expected profit. Assume that the probabilities of the expected scenarios is changed because the company is less optimistic. With new scenario probabilities of $S_1 = 0.2$, $S_2 = 0.3$ and $S_3 = 0.5$ (and leaving everything else unchanged), the expected value of the upper branch is reduced from €11,858 to €9,034. The probability of Z_1 is reduced from 0.35 to 0.26 and the expected value after research becomes €3.298 (formerly €6,800).

Assume that the expected payoffs in Table 8.3 change to $S_1 = 10m$, $S_2 = 5m$ and $S_3 = -20m$. Also, let the probabilities of the three scenarios be those of Table 8.3 and let the possible outcome of the market test be the ones of Table 8.4. In this case a launch is only profitable given that research is carried out. Why? Because the expected profit without research now is negative $(0.3*10) + (0.5*5) + (0.2*-20) = -1.5$. The reader should check if it is correct that in this situation the expected payoff after research is €3.5m implying that the expected value of additional information is €5m (the range from -1.5 to 3.5).

Although highly unlikely, situations may appear where the expected payoff after research becomes even *lower* than the expected payoff without research, implying that the expected value of additional information becomes negative. In the above example, 3.298 was lower than 6.500, but let us look at another example and assume a research agency has a miserable performance matrix, as in Table 8.5.

The reader is encouraged to compute the expected value of additional information given that the performance matrix has changed to the one shown in Table 8.5 and assuming that the probabilities of the states of nature and the attached profits are the same as in the previous example ($S_1 = 0.2$, $S_2 = 0.3$ and $S_3 = 0.5$). The expected payoff after research is €3,950,000, so the expected value of additional information is €3,950,000 − €6,500,000 = −€2,550,000. Clearly, in this case the company is better off *not* carrying out the research.

It is very easy to perform a Bayesian sensitivity analysis by using the formula editor in spreadsheet software such as Presentations, Excel or Lotus. After having done the simple coding, one can change *either* the scenario probabilities, *or* the related profits *or* the figures of the research–performance matrix. Do not change more than one of the parameters at a time (and remember that the rows as well as the columns of the quality matrix must add up to 1.00). Comprehensive texts on Bayesian decision theory are Schlaifer (1959), Chernoff and Moses (1987), Viertl (1987) and Carlin and Louis (2000).

Mathematical model: the Bass new product growth model

A mathematical model tries to mimic the market characteristics by using mathematical relationships. One of the best-known mathematical marketing models is the

Table 8.6 Parameters for penetration model

Description of model parameter	Notation
1 The cumulative number of adopters *to date*: the number of consumers who have purchased the product so far	$\sum_{1}^{t-1} Q$
2 The *final* cumulative number of adopters: the ultimate number of buyers, at the point of market saturation. Cumulative number of buyers once the market is saturated (the potential is reached)	$\sum_{1}^{\infty} Q$
3 The effect of *innovation*: relative importance of first buyers and early adopters	p
4 The effect of *imitation*: relative importance of imitators and laggards	r

product innovation or market penetration model developed by Bass (1969). It is typically used for analyzing products with a life cycle of several years (or decades), notably popular consumer durables. According to Bass, the typical product life cycle can be properly modelled using a functional relationship. The penetration model assumes that four parameters can be assessed, as in Table 8.6.

Formally, the Bass model states that:

$$Q_t = p\left(\sum_{1}^{\infty} Q - \sum_{1}^{t-1} Q\right) + r\left(\frac{\sum_{1}^{t-1} Q}{\sum_{1}^{\infty} Q}\right) \times \left(\sum_{1}^{\infty} Q - \sum_{1}^{t-1} Q\right)$$

Where Q_t is the number of adopters at time t (consumers expected to buy the product during next year).

A numerical example may help to understand how the model works. Assume that a prestigious sports car is about to be launched on the Portuguese market. Since the car is very expensive, the management knows that only a few cars can be sold during the first year. Furthermore, it is improbable that the company will ever sell more than one-hundred cars. To be realistic, it estimates the size of the total market for this luxury item at eighty cars. The planning horizon is set to ten years (starting with 1998).

Based on the experience of earlier launches, it is guessed that four cars can be sold in the first year. A few prestigious dealers are usually eager to buy such an expensive car and sell it to one of their wealthy customers. The Bass model has been applied to thousands of historic datasets of product launches. An inspection of some of these data show that the model fits the data for expensive sports cars well when the constant of innovation (p) is fixed at 0.05 and the constant of imitation (r) is fixed at 0.33.

Figure 8.3 provides the computational details. Note, that sales at period t (i.e., 7 at 2001) is added to the accumulated sales at $t-1$ (15 at 2000) to form the accumulated sales at t (22 at 2001). In the year 2008 a total of 72 cars have been sold. While a few cars will still be sold after 2008, sales have started to level off years earlier. Note that sales increase during the first three years (from 5 in 1999 to 7 in 2001) but have declined toward the end

$$Q^t = p\left(\sum_1^\infty Q - \sum_1^{t-1} Q\right) + r\left(\frac{\sum_1^{t-1} Q}{\sum_1^\infty Q}\right) \times \left(\sum_1^\infty Q - \sum_1^{t-1} Q\right)$$

Q_t	$=$	Number of adopters at time t (1999)
Q_∞	$= 80$	Ultimate number of adopters
Q_{t-1}	$= 4$	Cumulative of adopters to date (1998)
p	$= 0.05$	Innovation constant
r	$= 0.33$	Imitation constant

Sale in given period

Accumulated sales
(4 in 1998 +
5 in 1999 = 9)

Q_{1999}	$=$	$0.05(80\text{-}04) + 0.33(04/80)(80\text{–}4) = 5.05 = 5/9$
Q_{2000}	$=$	$0.05(80\text{-}09) + 0.33(09/80)(80\text{–}9) = 6.19 = 6/15$
Q_{2001}	$=$	$0.05(80\text{-}15) + 0.33(15/80)(80\text{–}15) = 7.27 = 7/22$
...		... ...
Q_{2008}	$=$	$0.05(80\text{-}68) + 0.33(68/80)(80\text{-}68) = 3.97 = 4/72$

Figure 8.3 Launch of a luxury car in Portugal

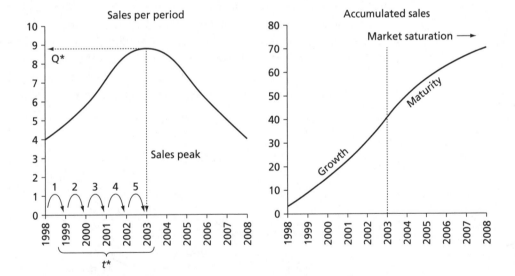

The number of periods
elapsing until the sales peak
is defined and computed thus:

$$t^* = \left[\frac{1}{(p + r)}\right] \times \ln\left(\frac{r}{p}\right) = \left[\frac{1}{(0.05 + 0.33)}\right] \times \ln\left(\frac{0.33}{0.05}\right) = 4.97 \approx 5$$

The sale during the period
of peak sale is defined and
computed thus:

$$Q_t^* = \frac{\left[\left(\sum_1^\infty Q\right) \times (p + r)^2\right]}{(4r)} = \frac{\left[(80) \times (0.33 + 0.05)^2\right]}{(4 \times 0.33)} = 8.75 \approx 9$$

Figure 8.4 Penetration of new luxury car in Portugal

Table 8.7 Effect of innovators and imitators

	Innovation effect		Imitation effect		Total
Q_{1998}	0.05(80–04) =	3.80	0.33(04/80)(80–04) =	1.25	5.05
Q_{2008}	0.05(80–68) =	0.60	0.33(68/80)(80–68) =	3.37	3.97

of the period (4 in 2008). But when precisely do the sales peak, and how many cars are sold during the peak period?

Figure 8.4 displays the appropriate functional relationships concerning the sales per period as well as the accumulated sales. The first of the two small formulas at the bottom of the figure helps us to estimate how many periods will pass before the annual sales peak and subsequently level-off. The second formula calculates how many units will be selling once t is at a peak. Both the Bass formula and the small optimization formulas of Figure 8.4 are easy to calculate using a spreadsheet formula editor. Note that the model mimics the assumption that, relatively, most sales during the early period go to the innovators, while during the end of the period most are sold to the imitators (Table 8.7).

Figure 8.5 shows a forecast study by the authors concerning the market for pagers and car-based global positioning systems (GPS) in Germany. The forecast is based on initial sales figures (Q_T), valid for 1998 and on estimates provided by experts concerning the expected market size within a ten-year planning horizon. Based on hundreds of product launches that have been Bass-modelled, the size of the parameter p and imitation r have been estimated. With regard to GPS units, two scenarios, an optimistic ($p = 0.05$) and a moderate (0.025) are provided. Note that the optimistic estimate accelerates market growth. While a mathematical forecasting model like the Bass penetration model can be very useful if available data are limited, the approach must be treated with caution. The following example of a Philips hair clipper may help in clarifying this.

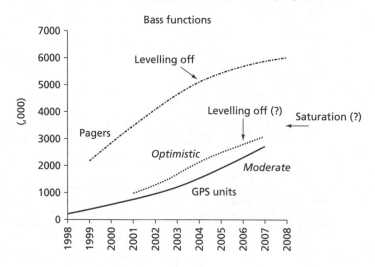

ΣQ = 4.0m units, $p_{moderate}$ = 0.025, $p_{optimistic}$ = 0.05, r = 0.33 for GPS

ΣQ = 6.4m units, p = 0.05, r = 0.33 for pagers

Figure 8.5 Market for pagers and for car-based GPS units in Germany 1998–2008

Marketing research in action
Philips hair clipper in Denmark

In 1976, Philips launched a hair clipper in Denmark. A hair clipper is a combination of a electric scissor and a comb. The product was for children (unlike today, where the clipper is usually aimed at men). In the mid-1970s, most European economies were compromised by an energy crisis, and so was the budget of the typical household. Especially affected were families with children, who had to cut spending, wherever possible.

A child's hair grows fast and needs to be cut every five or six weeks. If a couple has three pre-teen children, and each needs to have his/her hair cut about ten times a year this approximates to $30 \times €20 = €600$ (at 2005 prices). This equates to 3–5 percent of a middle-class household's disposable income. Since a clipper can be bought for less than €100 (2005 prices), the payback time would be only a few months. This was the underlying rationale behind the launch.

The product had sold fairly well in several European markets. Rooted in its experience from compatible European markets, Philips managers estimated the market potential of the clipper in Denmark to be 25 to 30 percent of households or about $600,000 \ (= \Sigma Q_{(1976-)})$. The sale in the year of the launch was set at 10,000 units

$$Q_t = p \left(\sum_1^\infty Q - \sum_1^{t-1} Q \right) + r \left(\frac{\sum_1^{t-1} Q}{\sum_1^\infty Q} \right) \times \left(\sum_1^\infty Q - \sum_1^{t-1} Q \right)$$

$\Sigma Q_{1-\infty}$	= 600.000	Q_{1976}	= 10.000 $\Sigma Q_{1976-1979}$ = 60.000
p	= 0.017	r	= 0.285

Q_{1977}	= 0.017(600,000–10,000)+0.285(10,000/600,000) (600,000–10,000) = 12,833
Q_{1978}	= 0.017(600,000–22,833)+0.285(22,833/600,000) (600,000–22,833) = 16,072
Q_{1979}	= 0.017(600,000–38,905)+0.285(38,905/600,000) (600,000–38,905) = 19,908

$\Sigma Q_{1976-79}$ = 10,000 + 12,833 + 16,072 + 19,908 = 58,813 (~ 60,000)

$$t^* = \left[\frac{1}{(p+r)} \right] \times \ln\left(\frac{r}{p} \right) = \left[\frac{1}{(0.017+0.285)} \right] \times \ln\left(\frac{0.285}{0.017} \right) = 9.34 \approx 9$$

$$Q_t^* = \frac{\left[\left(\sum_1^\infty Q \right) \times (p+r)^2 \right]}{(4r)} = \frac{[(600,000) \times (0.285+0.017)^2]}{(4 \times 0.285)} \approx 48,000$$

Figure 8.6 Philips' launch of a children's clipper in Denmark

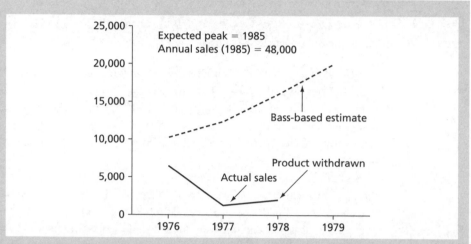

Figure 8.7 Bass-based market estimate and reality for Philips' clipper launch

($= Q_{1976}$). Moreover, managers estimated that 10 percent of the market potential would be sold after four years ($\Sigma Q_{(1976-1980)}$). Based on these estimates, we can compute the appropriate values of p and r by way of interpolation (Figure 8.6). When setting the rate of innovation, p, to 0.017 and the rate of imitation, r, to 0.285, we note that the accumulated sale after four years is about 60,000.

This example gives all the necessary parameters of the Bass function that the management was using. Once more, it is an easy task to compute when sales were expected to peak (after nine periods, in 1985) and what the expected annual sales would be during that year (48,000 units). Figure 8.7 compares the estimate with the realized sales.

What went wrong? No one knows. But it is guessed that an important reason for the failure was the absence of TV advertising (before 1989 television was not available to marketers in Denmark). Very few households had satellite dishes or cable at the time. Therefore, Philips could not use its preferred medium when launching the clipper. Instead of using TV, the company was forced to use static print ads – a medium poorly suited to selling a dynamic product like the clipper: indeed, it turned out that the clipper had sold relatively well in markets where TV advertising was available. Based on the Danish experience, the company learned that for a product like the clipper to succeed it is necessary to expose the target group (mothers) to detailed advertising that vividly demonstrates its ease of use. That is impossible in a print advert.
Source: Adapted from Hegedahl and Poulsen, 1980 (in Danish)

The example underlines the importance of being cautious when using abstract approaches such as the Bass model. It is a crude, non-linear mathematical composite that has been constructed to fit an array of historical US data. It assumes that the forecast is *completely* determined by:

- ultimate market size;

- sale during period of launch;
- the relative effect of innovators and imitators.

However, the model ignores the effects of:

- advertising;
- price;
- promotion;
- distribution;
- product development;
- repeat purchase;
- competition.

Considering all these weaknesses, why bother with the Bass model? Answer: it is simple to use and models that are much more advanced often do not perform better. Moreover, in many situations the model is found to perform well (Bass et al., 1994).

Much empirical research has been triggered by the Bass model (Bulte, 2000 and 2001). The purpose of most studies has been to assess the model's predictive validity. Sultan et al. (1990) conducted a meta-analysis of innovation diffusion based on 161 applications of the Bass model across fifteen academic publications. The grand mean of p was reported as 0.03 (0.04 after correcting for various factors) while the mean for r was 0.38 (0.30).

It should be noted that extensions of the Bass model are available. Fisher and Pry (1971) modify the penetration model so that a product launch is corrected by the penetration rate of the old product that it is assumed to replace. Horsky and Simon (1983) incorporate the effect of advertising in the innovation coefficient. Kalish (1985) covers the effects of pricing, advertising and uncertainty. The approach of Easingwood et al. (1983) allows for asymmetric diffusion curves and for the fact that word-of-mouth may vary over time. Gatignon et al. (1989) deal with differences in diffusion rates across countries.

In applied settings it is not uncommon to use hybrid models. For example, a test market simulator like GfK's TESI is itself a conceptual model from a holistic perspective, while the elements or building blocks of the model contain several "nested" mathematical models like a market penetration model, a repeat buying model, a brand choice model, etc.

8.3 Building models

Leeflang and Wittink (2000) provide a checklist of topics that a researcher should consider prior to building a model. See Figure 8.8:

- Every model builder must evaluate whether the use of a model can improve managerial decision-making.
- The builder should define the intended use of the model (what is it good for?).
- The complexity, completeness and integration ought to be assessed.

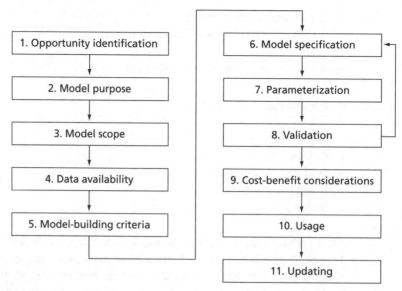

Figure 8.8 Building a model
Source: Leeflang and Wittink, 2000

- How can the necessary data be obtained? Are they accessible and available in the appropriate level of aggregation?
- The structure of the model must be easy to understand and appear straightforward to implement.
- A specification of the level of analysis ought to be clear: does one focus on generic product categories or selected brands?
- Can the model parameters of interest be estimated?
- Does the model have diagnostic predictive properties?
- Can cost and benefit figures be assessed?
- Is the model useable?
- Can it be improved and updated?

Needless to say, few, if any, models meet all of the above expectations. Finally, we might add one more quality merit. Does the model possess global properties: is it "globalizable"?

A comprehensive source on marketing models is Lilien et al. (1992) as well as the special issue of the *International Journal of Research in Marketing* (Various, 2000).

8.4 Summary

Models help structure, display, and comprehend complex phenomena. A good model is comprehensive yet simple, can be measured without error, is valid and reliable, robust and logically consistent, operational, generalizable, communicable, possesses managerial implications and is successful and true.

The advantage of a good model is its ability to simplify a complex and diffuse reality. An appropriate theoretical or symbolic algorithm may extract the crucial characteristics of a phenomenon. The disadvantage of using a model is the risk of oversimplifying the problem.

The five types of models are:

- A verbal model (a textual description).
- A conceptual model (a flow chart with "boxes and arrows" indicating hypothesized causal relationships).
- A graphical model (a perceptual space).
- A statistical model (a decision tree based on probabilistic inferences).
- A mathematical model (e.g., a formula predicting the market penetration of a product).

Building a model starts with identifying the opportunities. Next, the model's purpose and scope must be defined and the availability of data assessed. The model-building criteria are established and the model and its parameters specified. Every model is subject to valida-tion and to cost-benefit considerations. A dynamic model is characterized by continuous updating.

Questions

1. Could the GfK TESI test market simulator be used for forecasting the following product launches?
    - Detergents in India.
    - Chocolate in Luxembourg.
    - Insurances in Poland.
    - Cars in Germany.

2. The forecast shown in Figure 8.5 (pagers and GPS units in Germany) was made in 1997. Update the sales from online sources and market estimates. How did the Bass forecast perform?

3. Hypothesis: "If a product has proven to be successful in the home market, then the product's diffusion rate in foreign markets is likely to be much faster than in the home market." Debate on the pros and cons of this statement.

4. Do you think the parameters of the Bass model (coefficient of imitation and inno-vation) differ on a cross-cultural basis? Everything else being equal, where do you believe the coefficient of innovation to be higher in each of these four pairs of coun-tries (please substantiate):
    - France or Slovenia.
    - Mexico or Germany.
    - China or USA.
    - Saudi Arabia or the Czech Republic.

References

Bass, F. M. (1969) "A New product growth model for consumer durables." *Management Science*. 15 (Jan). 215–27.

Bass, F. M., Krishan T. V. and Jain, D. J. (1994) "Why the Bass model fits without decision variables." *Marketing Science*. 13 (3). 203–24.

Blackburn, J. D. and Clancy, K. J. (1982) "Litmus: A new product planning model." *TIMS/Studies in Management Science*. 18. 43–61.

Bulte, C. V. d. (2000) "New product diffusion acceleration: measurement and analysis." *Marketing Science*. 19 (4). 366––80.

Bulte, C. V. d. (2001) "A meta-analysis of applications of the bass diffusion model." *EMAC Proceedings*, Bergen. session 2.5.2.

Burger, P. C., Gundee, H. and Lavidge R. (1981) "A comprehensive system for the evaluation of new products" in Wind, Y., Mahajan, V. and Cardozo, R. N. (eds) *New Product Forecasting: Models and applications*. Lexington. 269–83.

Carlin, B. P. and Louis, T. A. (2000) *Bayes and Empirical Bayes Methods for Data Analysis*. CRC Press, NY.

Chernoff, H. and Moses, L. E. (1987) *Elementary Decision Theory*. Dover, NY.

Easingwood, C., Mahajan, V. and Muller, E. (1983) "A non-uniform influence innovation diffusion model of new product acceptance." *Marketing Science*. 2 (summer). 273–96.

Erichson, B. (1987) "TESI: The G&I testmarket simulator" in *Micro and Macro Modelling: Research on prices, consumer behaviour, and forecasting. EMAC/ESOMAR Symposium*. Amsterdam. 201–8.

Fisher, J. C. and Pry, R. H. (1971) "A simple substitution model of technological change." *Technological Forecasting and Social Change*. 3. 75–88.

Gatignon, H., Eliashberg, J. and Robertson T. S. (1989) "Modelling multinational diffusion patterns: an efficient methodology." Working paper. Wharton Business School, University of Pennsylvania.

Green, P. E. and Tull, D. S. (1978) *Research for Marketing Decisions*. Prentice-Hall, Englewood Cliffs, NJ. 43–49.

Hegedahl, P. and Poulsen, P. T. (1980) *Mismarketing*. Børsen Bøger, Copenhagen (in Danish). 132–144.

Horsky, D. and Simon, L. S. (1983) "Advertising and the diffusion of new products." *Marketing Science*. 2 (winter). 1–10.

Kalish, S. (1985) "A new product adoption model with price, advertising, and uncertainty." *Management Science*. 31, (Dec). 1569–1585.

Leeflang, P. S. H. and Wittink, D. R. (2000) "Building Models of Marketing Decisions: Past, Present and Future." *International Journal of Research in Marketing*. 17 (2–3). 105–126.

Lilien, G., Kotler, P. and Moorthy, K. S. (1992) *Marketing Models*. Prentice-Hall, New York.

Little, J. D. C. (1970) "Models and Managers: The concept of a decision calculus." *Management Science*. 16. B466–B485.

Schlaifer, R. (1959) *Probability and Statistics for Business Decisions*. McGraw-Hill, NY.

Silk, A. J. and Urban, G. L. (1975) "Pre-test-market evaluation of new packaged goods: a model and measurement methodology." *Journal of Marketing Research*, 15. 171–191.

Sultan, F., Farley, J. U. and Lehmann, D. R. (1990) "A meta-analysis of applications of diffusion models." *Journal of Marketing Research*. 27 (Feb). 70–77.

—— (1996) "Reflections on a meta-analysis of applications of diffusion models." *Journal of Marketing Research*. 33 (May). 247–249.

Takada, H. and Jain, D. (1991) "Cross-national analysis of diffusion on consumer durable goods in Pacific Rim countries." *Journal of Marketing*. 55 (Apr). 48–54.

Urban, G. L. and Hauser, J. R. (1993) *Design and Marketing of New Products*. Prentice-Hall, NJ. 468–474.

Various (2000) "Marketing modelling on the threshold of the 21st century." *International Journal of Research in Marketing*. Vol. 17, no. 2–3.

Viertl R. (ed.) (1987) *Probability and Bayesian Statistic*. Plenum, NY.

End note

[1] According to Bayes' theorem:

$$P(S_j|Z) = \frac{P(Z|S_j) \times P(S_j)}{\sum\limits_{i=1}^{n} P(Z|S_j) \times P(S_j)}$$

where:

$P(S_j|Z)$ = Conditional probability of a particular state of nature S_j being true, given some observed sample event, Z. $P(S_j)$ = Prior probability of state of nature, S_j. $P(Z|S_j)$ = *Conditional probability* of observing event Z, given that S_j is true. The term $P(Z|S_j)$ $P(S_j)$ expresses the *joint probability* of observing Z under state of nature S_j.

9 Analysis of variance and multiple regression

Learning objectives

After studying this chapter you should be able to:

- Explain the types of market research challenges facing a company.
- Give an overview of methodological and practical problems involved in gathering and analyzing data from foreign markets.
- Explain the difference between independent and dependent measures and distinguish between different types of measurement scales.
- Define when and how analysis of variance and covariance can be used for studying problems related to cause and effect in international marketing.
- Explain when and how multiple regression can help study dependence relationships between sets of international data.
- Give a basic overview of methodological problems arising from the interaction of factor levels.

9.1 Introduction

The decision to internationalize a company's operations might be triggered by two opposing causes:

- Sales on the home market are declining and/or competition is fierce.
- Sales at home are doing very well.

While falling sales at home may force the company to export itself out of the problems, flourishing sales may make managers feel that the sky is the limit. Usually, in neither case will the company do much about market research before or during the launch of international operations. However, most companies sooner or later will experience problems with their international operations. If things do not develop quite as they expected, the following causes might be involved:

- Sales are going down in important markets.
- Business is thriving in some markets, while developing disappointingly in others.
- Increasingly, customers in basic markets prefer to buy competitors' products.
- While the flagship (cash cow) does relatively well, the new product does not meet targets.
- Primary customers are elderly, light users, while heavy-using youngsters tend to prefer the competitors' brands or substitute products.

Dissatisfying sales should make managers scrutinize things carefully. First, they should figure out which data are needed for a detailed analysis of the problem:

- Is the necessary data available?
  - Does it exist somewhere (secondary sources)?
  - If it does not exist, is it obtainable (by primary means)?
- How can managers access the necessary data?
- If data can be acquired for an affordable price . . .
  - Is it reliable?
  - Is it valid?
  - Can it be generalized?
  - Can the company handle the data format?
  - Are formats, scales, etc. comparable across markets (countries)?
  - Does missing data comprise a problem?
  - Does data for some countries look strange vis-à-vis local data?

According to textbooks on quantitative data analysis, managers should be very concerned about data quality. For example, missing data detected in responses from self-administered questionnaires might be caused because respondents:

- do not want to answer;
- do not dare to answer (sensitive topics are involved);
- have a low level of involvement (topics do not cause proper interest);
- do not understand the question;
- do not know how to answer.

Also, missing data in a foreign market can be caused by reasons we do not experience in the home market.

9.2 Variance as a tool for analyzing sales

Sometimes, managers will want to scrutinize a company's performance with regard to revenues, costs, profits, customer satisfaction, employee motivation, etc. Fortunately, many powerful analytical tools can help conduct in-depth analysis of a company's performance according to key criteria. In the remainder of this chapter we show how an international

Marketing research in action
Problems when gathering data abroad

It is a well established fact that some respondents do not answer properly on sensitive topics. While it is common for a Scandinavian citizen to provide answers on his or her sexual habits, posing this type of question would cause problems in countries with a predominantly Catholic or Muslim population. Moreover, while most European and North American respondents have no problems providing responses to public authorities, this may not hold true in a country where citizens are frequently intimidated by authoritarian institutions. And even French and Danes may not like to tell the public authorities about their income, alcohol consumption, etc. It is obvious that you cannot ask meaningful questions of people if they do not know how to answer or if they do not respond in an appropriate way. It does not make sense to ask about alcohol consumption in a country where the citizens do not drink alcohol (or are prohibited from doing so). Likewise, we cannot ask a sample of villagers in a developing country which handheld computer they prefer.

Sometimes, missing data are explainable. It is known that in some countries, males tend to answer questions on behalf of the female. In Muslim countries it makes little sense to approach women at all unless a male household member is present. In other countries, it might be possible to contact a female audience, but females' response rates are significantly lower when compared with males. Or vice versa: for example, women may provide better responses on household products that they typically buy. Since men usually do not buy detergents, their responses will contain significantly more missing data with regard to "preferred brand" when compared with women's responses. In such cases, missing values on one variable (detergents) depends on another variable (gender). The analyst should be careful with regard to missing responses that appear in data emanating from foreign markets. Specifically, one should look for patterns in the structure of the missing data: do they correlate with gender, age, income, education, region, urbanization, etc.?

marketing manager can use the analysis of variance and covariance and multiple regression. Later chapters cover other advanced techniques.

Analysis of variance (ANOVA) is undoubtedly one of the most elegant, powerful and useful techniques in modern statistics. The only requirement for performing ANOVA is that the data to be analyzed can be separated into a few groups based on a discrete variable.

The underlying rationale of ANOVA is to split the total variance into two components: the variance *between* the groups; and the variance *within* the groups. Technically speaking, the former variance is called the **treatment effect** while the latter is called the **random variance** or **error**. The discrete grouping variable (also called predictor or independent variable) may refer to, say, different foreign subsidiaries, export managers in different countries, customers in selected markets and so on. The dependent measure (sometimes called **criterion variable**) could relate to sales, costs, profits, number of customer visits or orders gained, satisfaction among customers or employees. The dependent variable must be either metric or interval-scaled. In Chapter 6 we used the term "ratio scale" when referring to a "hard" scale. In this chapter we wish to emphasize the difference between the analytical properties of a metric and a non-metric scaled variable. It is important to understand this duality as it has significant implications for selecting the appropriate statistical model for analyzing our data.

Assume an analysis is to be made of the number (frequency) of customer visits made by the company's export managers in three compatible countries over twelve successive months. If the variance between the groups (countries) with regard to number of visits is *significantly* greater than the variance within, then differences are said to exist, and vice versa. The variance between groups will be greater than the variance within, *provided that differences among means exist*.

A small numerical example may help in clarifying the basics of ANOVA. Before proceeding, the reader should study Table 9.1. This will help avoid some confusion with regard to methodological terms. Because of variations in style, authors often use synonyms. For example, independent variables are sometimes called predictors in regression, while they are often named treatment variables in ANOVA and so on. This can be bewildering.

Later in this chapter we will refer to the statistical software tool SPSS. Here we will discover that there are many names for such things. Some examples from SPSS program dialogue boxes: in linear regression the independent variable is called "independent." In one-way ANOVA, it is called "factor" and in a related method, general linear model, it is named "fixed factor." In logistic regression, the independent is termed "covariate" which is really misleading, compared with how the expression is normally used. Such confusion is common in statistical software tools, and SPSS terminology is no more confusing than any other program.

Simple ANOVA[1]

The managers of Luxwell, a German producer of luxurious sports vehicles, are assessing sales at three of the company's showrooms. They are comparable with regard to size and

Table 9.1 Terms and synonyms used in this chapter and elsewhere

Model	$Y = a + bX_1 + cX_2 + \ldots + iX_n$
Variable notation	X: Independent; explaining; explanatory; predictor; regressor; treatment; fixed; grouping; (covariate, categorical covariate) Y: Dependent; criterion; response; target (grouping, category)
Scales	Interval: metric; ratio Nominal: categorical, non-metric, dummy, binary, dichotomous
Coefficients	b, c, etc.: Regression coefficient; regression estimate; parameter estimate; path (LISREL); part worth utility (conjoint analysis)

Note: some of these terms are not synonyms. For example, a ratio scale differs from an interval scale in that it has a natural zero point. A relative change in temperature measured in Celsius transforms to a different change when expressed in Fahrenheit (interval). But a relative change when measured in meters transforms to the same change expressed in yards or feet (metric). However, it is our experience that the term interval is often used such that it is meant to include variables that are metric-scaled.

interior design. Each unit consists of an area where the cars are displayed and sales offices. The purpose of the project is to evaluate the need for extra marketing to gain sales. The showrooms are in France (Paris), Germany (Berlin) and Italy (Rome). Concerning each unit the following holds: 50,000 households with an annual income of at least €300,000 are less than two hours' travelling time away.

Table 9.2 displays the quarterly sales figures in units for 1999 and 2000 across the three outlets. For example, seventy-seven of the 811 Series were sold in the Paris showroom during the first quarter of 1999. Table 9.2 also shows total sales over two years, the average sales as well as the variance in sales for each outlet.

Before running ANOVA it is recommended to test whether the involved variances belong to the same universe. This is done by testing for homogeneity of variances. If the outcome of this test is significant (a probability of less than 5 percent), then the hypothesis of homogeneity (or equality) of variances is rejected. Such an outcome would imply that, due to methodological considerations, running an ANOVA cannot be justified because the empirical data is too heterogeneous. If we want to compare subsets of data, i.e. columns of observations, by looking at the means, the inspected subsets must at least roughly share one crucial characteristic, namely the dispersion around the mean.

It is easy to test for equality of variances because the test is available in many software packages. In Excel one just needs to tap *[Tools]* on the tools-bar, then tap *[Data Analysis]*, which is part of the Analysis Toolpak, and finally highlight *[F-Test Two-Samples for Variances]* from the list of options and click OK. If you do this, a pop-up appears and asks you to select the range (columns) for variable 1 and subsequently for variable 2. Data need to be organized as in Table 9.2, that is, one column for each country. Figure 9.1 displays the input data, the data analysis main dialogue box with the appropriate procedure highlighted, and the outcome of each of the three tests.

Note that the third comparison is marginally significant: $P(F< = f)$ one tail $= 0.08$. This happens because the variance of the Italian data is about three times that of the German (however, the sample size is small). Since none of the three test values is less than

Table 9.2 Luxwell's sales of the 811 series at the company's capital exhibition centre in three countries[1]

Period	France		Germany		Italy	
1999_1	X_{11}	77	X_{12}	88	X_{13}	85
1999_2	X_{21}	82	X_{22}	94	X_{23}	85
1999_3	X_{31}	86	X_{32}	93	X_{33}	87
1999_4	X_{41}	78	X_{42}	90	X_{43}	81
2000_1	X_{51}	81	X_{52}	91	X_{53}	80
2000_2	X_{61}	86	X_{62}	94	X_{63}	79
2000_3	X_{71}	77	X_{72}	90	X_{73}	87
2000_4	X_{81}	81	X_{82}	87	X_{83}	93
	X_{T1}	648	X_{T2}	727	X_{T3}	677
	X_1 (mean)	81.0	X_2 (mean)	90.9	X_3 (mean)	84.6
	X_1 (var)	13.1	X_2 (var)	7.0	X_3 (var)	21.1
		$X_{TT} = 2,052$		X_{TT} (mean) $= 85.5$		

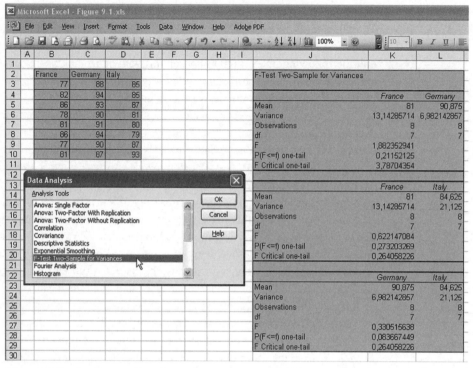

Figure 9.1 Testing for equality of sample variances in Excel

0.05, the test of homogeneity of variances is taken as true. This implies it is feasible to pool the variances and to assume that the sales data with regard to variance belong to the same "universe of variation phenomena."[2] Having accepted the homogeneity of group variances, it is possible to proceed to ordinary ANOVA. Table 9.3 provides all the necessary calculations. The reader is encouraged to check them with a calculator.

To run the example in Excel tap *[Tools]* at the toolbar, then *[Data Analysis]* and *[Anova: Single-Factor]*. Figure 9.2 displays the raw data, the ANOVA dialogue box with

Table 9.3 Analysis of variance – Luxwell 811 quarterly sales 1999–2000 in three compatible outlets

Source of variation	Degrees of freedom	Sum of squares	Mean square	F-ratio
Among	$t - 1 = 2$	399.25	199.6	14.5
Within	$n - t = 21$	288.25	13.8	$(p < 0.01)$
Total	$n - 1 = 23$	688.0		
Correction	$(X_{TT})^2/n = C$	$(2052)^2/24 = 175446$		
Total SS	$\Sigma X^2_{ij} - C$	$(77)^2 + (82)^2 + \ldots + (87)^2 + (93)^2 - 175446 = 688.0$		
Among SS (treatment) $\Sigma X^2_{Tj}/n_j - C$		$[(648)^2 + (727)^2 + (677)^2]/8 - 175446 = 399.3$		
Within SS (error)	$\Sigma X^2_{ij} - (\Sigma X^2_{Tj})/n_j$	$(77)^2 + (82)^2 + \ldots + (87)^2 + (93)^2 - [(648)^2 + (727)^2 + (677)^2]/8 = 288.25$		

Note: C is also called intercept. $R^2 = 0.58$ (=399.3/688.0)

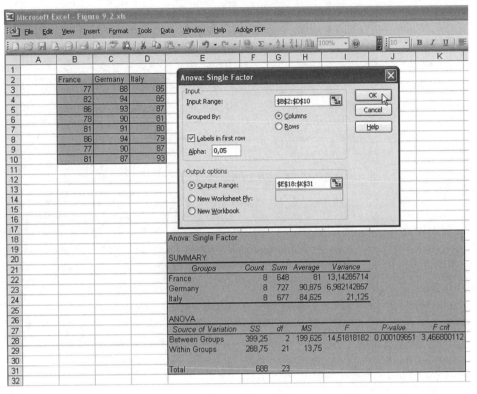

Figure 9.2 ANOVA of Luxwell sales across countries (Excel)

appropriate settings and the output. As can be easily checked, most of the values in Table 9.2 appear in the Figure 9.2.

The F-value (14.5) is extreme and shows that average sales of the Luxwell 811 differ across the three outlets. While ANOVA shows the difference, it is not specific concerning significant differences in sales between, say, two outlets. For a fuller answer to this question, three identical tests are needed each checking whether the sales-means between two outlets are equal. The appropriate test is a student's t-test. It can be run using Excel *[Data Analysis, t-Test: Paired Two Sample for Means]*.[3]

Figure 9.3 displays the, slightly edited, output. Two rows are of primary interest, the rows *[Mean]* and *[P(T< = t) two-tail]*. Consider the third comparison. The average or mean sales are 90.88 in Germany and 84.63 in Italy. According to the t-test, the probability that this difference in means is caused by randomness is 0.03 or 3 percent. This is less than 0.05 or 5 percent, that usually represents the cut-off line between significance and non-significance.[4] The observed t-stat value of the third comparison is 2.77, somewhat beyond the threshold level *[t-Critical two-tail]* of 2.36. From a theoretical perspective, sales in one country can be both significantly higher and lower than in the other country and therefore, the appropriate t-test has two tails instead of one. If the sales in one country had been 0, the appropriate test would have been a one-tailed test (since sales cannot be negative).

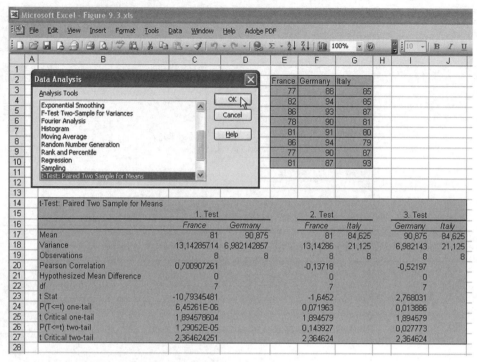

Figure 9.3 Luxwell sales – differences in means (Excel)

The conclusions are that:

- Sales in Germany are higher than in France. The difference is highly significant (on the 0.001 level).
- Sales seem to be higher in Italy than in France, but the difference in means is not statistically significant.
- Sales in Germany are higher than in Italy. The difference is significant (on the 0.05 level).

Simple ANOVA using SPSS

Note, that when running SPSS, the input file must be organized so that there are two variables (columns of data), one containing the country variable and the other one containing the corresponding sales data. See Figure 9.4.

There is one thing more you need to know before putting data into the SPSS data editor. In the lower left corner of the SPSS editor screen, you can change between *[Data View]* and *[Variable View]*. Normally, when SPSS is opened, the spreadsheet-like view is seen *[Data View]*. To change this, tap the *[Variable View]* tag. Then the screen changes to the one shown in Figure 9.5 (you must plug in at least one number for each variable first, while being in data-view).

Now you can enter variable names (if your variable name exceeds 8 characters, you must adjust the default width of 8, to say, 12). In this example, make the following changes: change *[var00001]* to *[country]* and *[var00002]* to *[sales]*. In the *[Type]* column,

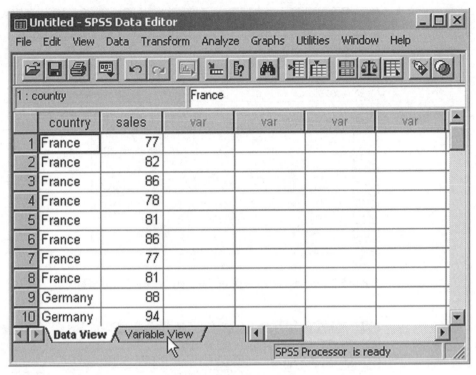

Figure 9.4 Luxwell case – running SPSS ANOVA

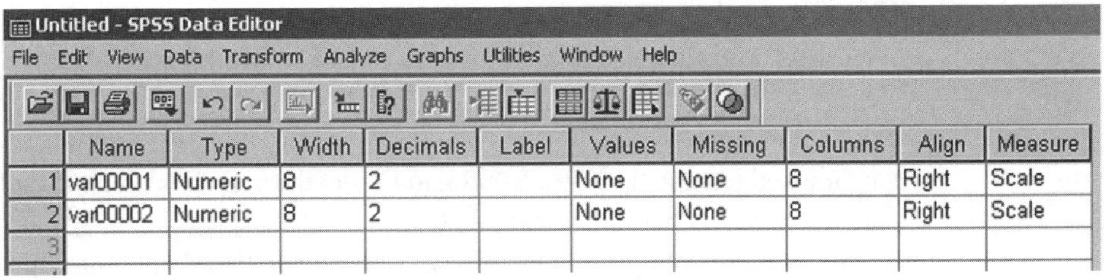

Figure 9.5 Default appearance of the variable view screen

tap the right corner of the *[Numeric]* cell or field in the first row. If you do this, a pop-up appears that looks like Figure 9.6.

Since the *[country]* variable, formerly *[var00001]*, does not contain numeric information but the name (text) of one of the three countries, the button for *[string]* must be selected. String is SPSS terminology for text. Note that if string format is selected, and if you then enter text (or anything else) into the cells of this variable, it will, by default, be centred left. Also, set the decimal places to 0 (since the data set has none). Click *[OK]*.

By now the *[Variable View]* should look like Figure 9.7. For *[country]* the *[Type]* is now *[String]*, and *[Decimals]* is *[0]*. Note that the *[Align]* column has changed to *[Left]* and that the *[Measure]* is now *[Nominal]*. The last two changes are consequences of changing the *[Type]* column from *[Numeric]* to *[String]*. The data in the country column

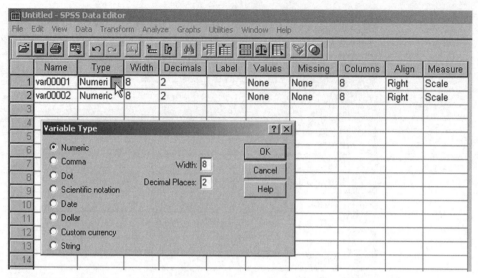

Figure 9.6 Default appearance of the *[Variable Type]* pop-up box

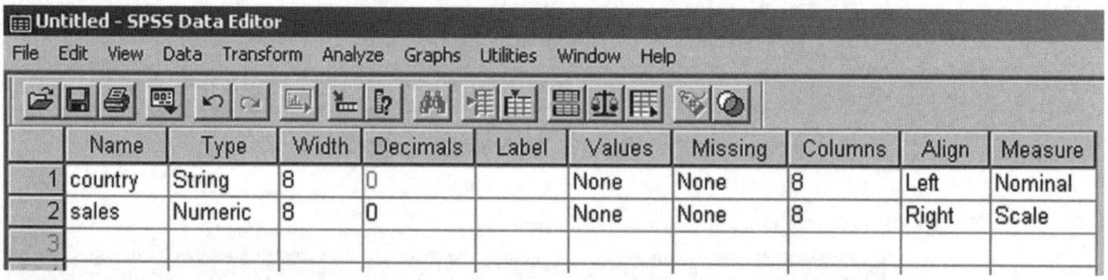

Figure 9.7 Correct appearance of the SPSS variable view screen for ANOVA

are aligned left and therefore SPSS knows that the variate is nominal and that observations are not numbers but rather text/signs.

After these set-up changes, flip back to *[Data View]* and enter the data as shown in Figure 9.4. Next, tap *[Analysis]* at the main menu-bar and a drop-down list appears. SPSS usually contains somewhere between eighteen and twenty options, depending on the add-on licences bought.[5] See Figure 9.8. Now scroll down to *[Generalized Linear Model]*, so that it is highlighted and then select *[Univariate]* from the list of sub-options.[6] When doing so, the *[Univariate]* pop-up screen appears. It looks like Figure 9.9.

We notice that two variable names appear in the white box on the left. The prefix of "country" indicates that it is a string variable. In SPSS 14 the scaling of a variable is indicated by a tiny icon appearing as a suffix to the variable in the variable fields: 1. A string variable (text): blue/red ball and letter "a" (yellow); A nominal variable: blue/red/green ball; An ordinal variable: blue/yellow/red historgram; A ratio/metric variable: yellow ruler. The icons differ from earlier versions. Moreover, SPSS' data mining program Clementine (see Chapter 17) uses a different terminology.

Since ANOVA assumes the dependent variate to be metric, you cannot click "country" into the *[Dependent]* box (if you highlight "country" the button to the left of the

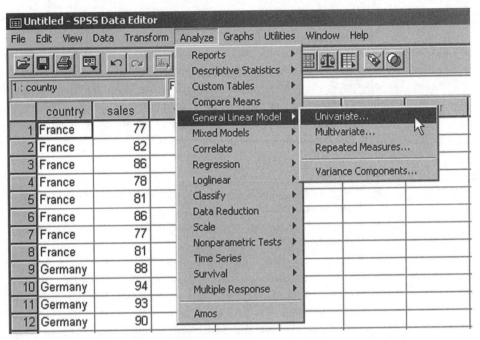

Figure 9.8 Appearance of SPSS data screen

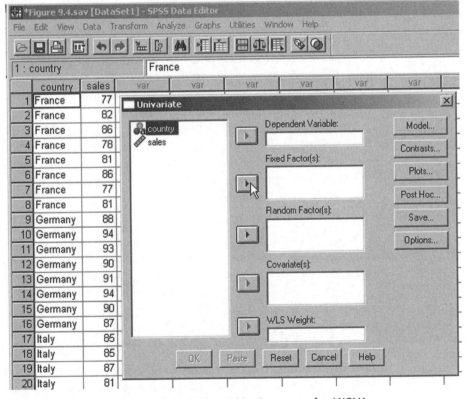

Figure 9.9 Correct appearance of the SPSS variable view screen for ANOVA

[Dependent Variable] box is non-clickable). However, if you highlight "sales," the button becomes clickable. That is because the "sales" variate is metric.

So, click "sales" into the *[Dependent Variable]* box and then "country" into the *[Fixed Factor(s)]* box.[7] Note that the *[OK]* button has become clickable, implying that the set-up choices for the job have been made.[8] However, when working with SPSS, we might quite often want to change some default settings that manoeuvre the program and control its output. This can be done by tagging one of the buttons that appear in a procedure's main dialogue box. In the *[General Linear Model, Univariate]* screen the following buttons are available:

- Model: a custom model can be built and one can change between different types of sum of squares matrices.
- Contrasts: tests for differences among levels of a factor. A drop-down list provides six tests (default is "none").
- Plots: one can request plots of main (treatment) effects and interaction effects.
- Post Hoc: specified tests that can be used, assuming one has determined that differences exist among means. Eighteen tests are available (four do *not* assume equal variances).
- Save: it is possible to save certain output figures (residuals, predicted values, etc.) for further analysis. Note that these values usually appear in the working datascreen as new variable columns.
- Options: in this dialogue box, the analyst may request some output statistics that otherwise would be suppressed in the printout. Statistics include descriptives, parameter estimates, a homogeneity test, etc.

In the present case, click *[Options]* and flag *[Descriptive statistics]* and *[Homogeneity tests]*. Having done this, the screen should look like Figure 9.10. That is all we want to do for now, so click *[OK]*, and Table 9.4 appears. Compare this with manual calculations in Table 9.3 and with Figure 9.2 (the Excel run).

The homogeneity statistics in Table 9.4 differ from those of Figure 9.1. That is because the underlying tests are not the same: while the test conducted in Figure 9.1 performs pairwise tests, SPSS's version uses a simultaneous test of all three groups. However, both tests lead to the same conclusion, namely that the hypothesis of homogeneity of variances is accepted on the 0.05 alpha level.

In SPSS output the test is called "Levene's Test of Equality of Error Variances." In Appendix D (on the website www.pearsoned.co.uk/schmidt), Question 2.3, we show in detail how the Levene Test is computed, using a different numeric example.

We notice that the F-value 14,518 fits with the corresponding value of both mutual calculations of Table 9.3 and the Excel run of Figure 9.2.

A factorial design: analysis of interaction

Basically, Luxwell produces two models of cars, 811, "the mother of all sports cars" and Coxtan – the cabriolet version. Luxwell's management wants to assess whether sales across the three outlets vary by model type. Therefore, it has obtained data specified by

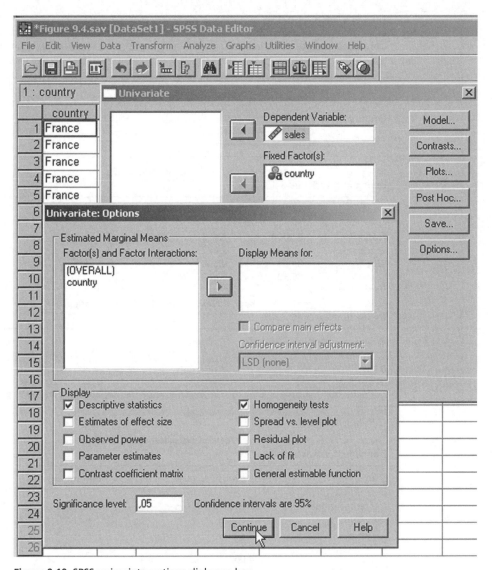

Figure 9.10 SPSS univariate options dialogue box

model concerning the first three quarters of 2001 (the fourth quarter was excluded from the analysis since it was deemed atypical). See Table 9.5.

From Table 9.5, note that 811 outsells Coxtan across all three outlets. Once again, total sales in Germany exceed sales in Italy and France. Luxwell's management wants to explore whether the differences in sales across countries as well as across models are significant. The task has to be done simultaneously so that possible interaction effects can be assessed. Why is interaction important? The managers know that sometimes it is not appropriate to assess two effects in isolation. It cannot be assumed beforehand that a specific "treatment effect" of one variable (i.e. the cabriolet level) works better with a specific treatment effect of another variable. In southern Europe the climate is more suited

Table 9.4 SPSS ANOVA output (simple ANOVA)

Univariate analysis of variance

Between-subjects factors

		N
Country	France	8
	Germany	8
	Italy	8

Descriptive statistics

Dependent variable: Sales

Country	Mean	Std deviation	N
France	81.000	3.625	8
Germany	90.88	2.642	8
Italy	84.63	4.596	8
Total	85.50	5.469	24

Levene's test of equality of error variances[a]

Dependent variable: Sales

F	df1	df2	Sig.
0.792	2	21	0.466

Tests the null hypothesis that the error variance of the dependent variable is equal across groups.

[a] Design: Intercept + Country

Tests of between-subjects effects

Dependent variable: Sales

Source	Type III sum of squares	df	Mean square	F-ratio	Sig.
Corrected model	399.250[b]	2	199.625	14.518	0.000
Intercept	175446.000	1	175446.000	12759.709	0.000
COUNTRY	399.250	2	199.625	14.518	0.000
Error	288.750	21	13.750		
Total	176134.000	24			
Corrected Total	688.000	23			

[b] R-square = 0.580 (adjusted R-square = 0.540)

Table 9.5 Crosstab of Luxwell sales: model type by country (first three quarters of 2001)

Model type	Country			
	France	Germany	Italy	Total
Coxtan	70, 75, 79	85, 88, 93	77, 81, 78	
Sum	224	266	236	726
811	91, 90, 87	94, 97, 93	87, 90, 90	
Sum	268	284	267	819
Total	492	550	503	1545

to an open sports car. Therefore, the Coxtan model might sell better when combined with the country level Italy (as compared with Germany). The present data set does not lend support to this hypothesis, though (but the data set is artificial).

This example with two factors can be analyzed using SPSS in the following way:

1. As before, begin with tabbing [*Analyze*] and [*General Linear Model, Univariate*].
2. In the [*Univariate*] dialogue box click "sales" into the [*Dependent Variable*] field and subsequently both "model" and "country" into the [*Fixed Factors*] field. From a methods perspective, the two car models and the three countries are the fixed/treatment or independent variables, while sales is the dependent variable.
3. Although the above set-ups are sufficient for running the analysis, request a graphic that is not part of the default output: click [*Plots*] and a dialogue box appears. In this box, click "country" into [*Horizontal Axis*] field and "model" into the [*Separate Lines*] field.
4. Having done this, the screen looks like Figure 9.11. Note that Figure 9.11 also shows how the data screen has to look. Both predictor variables are nominal scaled ("string type" in SPSS language).
5. When clicking [*Add*], the text "country*model" appears below in the [*Plots*] field while the two earlier fields have become empty; "country*model" indicates that you have requested a plot of interaction between the treatment factors "model" and "country".
6. Click [*Continue*] and [*OK*].

The output is displayed in Table 9.6 and Figure 9.12.

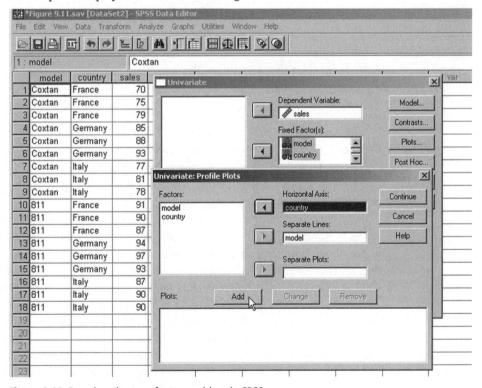

Figure 9.11 Running the two-factor problem in SPSS

Appendix 9-A shows how the numbers displayed in Table 9.6 – main and interaction effects – are computed using multiple regression with dummy coding. This can be found at www.pearsoned.co.uk/schmidt.

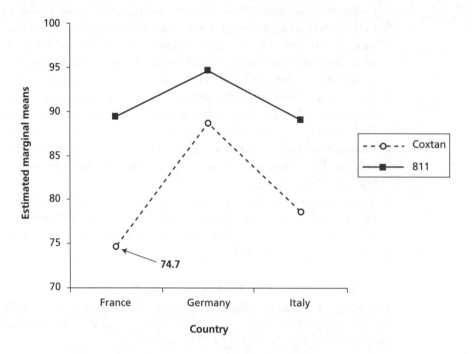

Note: 74.7 = (70 + 75 + 99)/3 (from Table 9.5)

Figure 9.12 Plot of interaction: model by country

The two-factor problem can be run in Excel as well. Click *[Data Analysis]*, *[Anova: Two Factor with Replication]*. Figure 9.13 displays the input form of the sample problem, the necessary settings and the resulting output. Once more, notice that the input in Excel (cells B2–E8) looks different from the SPSS format of Figure 9.11. However, critical output figures are the same.

Returning to the output generated by SPSS, Table 9.6 displays the results of a two-factor ANOVA of model series by country (the design is also known as a 2×3 factorial experiment). According to Table 9.6, the model-type effect is bigger (more important) than the country-effect: the F-value for the model component is 54.7 (1,12 df) versus 18.0 (2,12 df) for the country component. However, both values are highly significant.

An inspection of Figure 9.12 shows that some kind of linear interaction is involved. While the difference between the models is modest in Germany, it is sizeable in Italy and even more so in France. Also, note from Table 9.6 that the F-ratio (2,12 df) of the interaction between model and country – 3.209 – is marginally significant (one-tailed test).

Virtually all products have multiple features. Moreover, many products are sold in a lot of international markets simultaneously. Some of them can be consumed and enjoyed

Table 9.6 Two-factor ANOVA: model series by country (Luxwell case)

Univariate analysis of variance

Between-subject factors

		N
Model	811	9
	Coxtan	9
Country	France	6
	Germany	6
	Italy	6

Test of between-subjects effects

Dependent variable: Sales

Source	Type III sum of squares	df	Mean square	F-ratio	Sig.
Corrected model	853.167[a]	5	170.633	19.439	0.000
Intercept	132612.500	1	132612.500	15107.753	0.000
MODEL	480.000	1	480.500	54.741	0.000
COUNTRY	316.333	2	158.167	18.019	0.000
MODEL*COUNTRY	56.333	2	28.167	3.209	0.077
Error	105.333	12	8.778		
Total	133571.000	18			
Corrected total	958.500	17			

[a] R-square = 0.890 (adjusted R-square = 0.844)

almost everywhere and there is no guarantee that customers in, say, Germany, Argentina, Zaire, or Malaysia evaluate the same aspects of the product in the same way. The majority of consumers in one country may prefer the sweet taste in combination with the picturesque packaging, while most consumers in another country prefer a different flavour and a package with detailed labelling. Needless to say, therefore, an analysis of the interaction of marketing variables can be extremely useful for the marketer when comparing performance in international markets. (Indeed, a systematic design and analysis of interactions is the underlying rationale of conjoint analysis, a product development method to be covered in Chapter 14.) In the present context, a systematic analysis of interactions yields five different cases. See Figures 9.14 and 9.15.

Consider panel 1 in Figure 9.14: regardless of which country we are looking at, the 811 sells about twenty units more than the Coxtan. The lines are parallel, and so there is no interaction. While the issue of linearity is not important here (in the present case countries appear as different levels of a nominally scaled variable), the horizontal axis could refer to, say, differently sized advertising campaigns, i.e. €5 million in France, €10 million in Germany and €15 million in Italy during a three-month launch campaign (and assuming that 60 percent of the budget was used on the 811). So, if quantitative factors are involved, linearity and deviations from linearity can be of importance to the analyst.[9]

In panel 2, while the lines are not parallel, there is still no interaction. Sales of both sports car models are low in France, while sales are almost equally good in Italy and Germany. Across all markets the 811 sells ten units more.

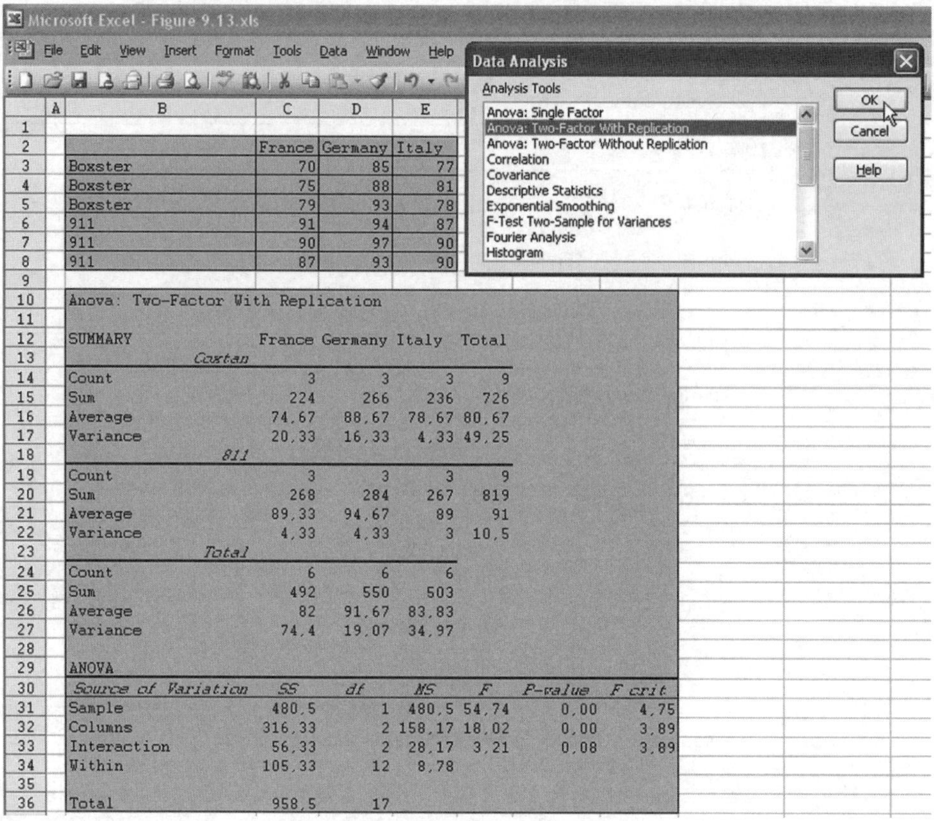

Figure 9.13 Running the two-factor problem in Excel

In panel 3, for France, both models sell almost equally well (10 percent difference), while in Italy sales of the 811 are almost fifty higher than the Coxtan. Since the lines are not parallel, interaction is present. However, the order is not violated: across all three countries the 811 sells better than the Coxtan. Therefore, the interaction is said to be ordinal.

In panel 4, sales of 811 are best in Italy and worst in France. Concerning the Coxtan, the relationship is reversed: sales are best in France and worst in Italy. So, the "cross-cultural sales rank" is not independent of model. If we had been looking at data that were pooled across models, we would conclude that Luxwell was selling 130–135 cars in each country. Thereby we would miss the important point that in Italy seven out of ten Luxwell sold are 811s, while both models sell equally well in France. Because the "sales-rank" order is reversed, we call this type of interaction a **disordinal interaction**. Since the sales volume in units is higher for the 811 than for the Coxtan in all markets, there is no crossover.

Figure 9.15 displays an example of **disordinal interaction with crossover**. In France, the Coxtan clearly is the flagship while the 811 sells badly whereas in Italy the situation is reversed: the 811 is the star and the Coxtan is the dog. Using pooled data would only tell

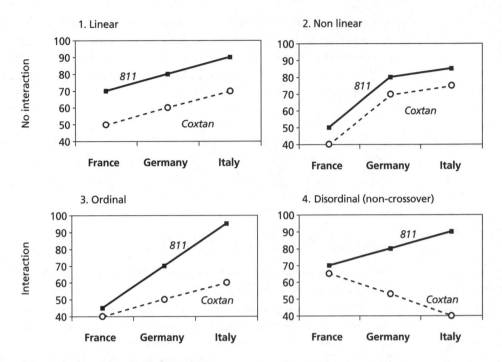

Figure 9.14 Patterns of interaction

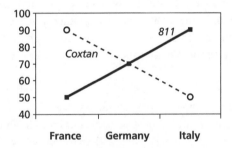

Figure 9.15 Disordinal nonlinear interaction with crossover

us that we are selling 140 units on each market (or, say, seventy units of each model), which would indeed be misleading.

This discussion is based on artificial data, oversimplified, and serves a pedagogical purpose. But imagine a globalized multi-product company such as Procter and Gamble, Colgate, Lever or Cadbury Schweppes. The reader should note that many multi-product companies do not engage in very detailed breakdowns of their product lines. A company like the Danish Carlsberg Brewery markets almost a thousand different brand sizes. How can the company's management know if interaction with regard to price, package design, flavour, alcoholic content, etc., is present across markets? There can be no question that all kinds of interaction can be found.

What should make us worry is disordinal interaction, as seen in Figure 9.15. Unfortunately, this is a type of interaction that is very widespread in applied cross-cultural marketing settings:

- Brand names are better received by consumers in some countries than in others.
- Some package formats or sizes sell much better in some markets than in others.
- Distribution patterns that fit some countries are inappropriate in others.
- Price expectations that are accepted in some places are less accepted elsewhere (price elasticities vary across markets).

Appendix 9-A shows how the interaction-term as well as most figures appearing in Table 9.6 can be computed by way of multiple regression. Visit www.pearsoned.co.uk/schmidt.

Analysis of covariance (ANCOVA)

Recently, Luxwell's management received sales data from its three capital exhibition centres covering 2002 and 2003 (Table 9.7).

Table 9.8 displays the result of an ANOVA based on the data in Table 9.7. According to the fresh data, differences in sales across countries are *not* statistically significant. While some minor differences are detected – sales in France turned out to be lower – the F-ratio for COUNTRY is only 1.480 corresponding to a probability of 0.250. Thus we accept hypothesis H_0 stating that there is no difference.

However, a clever manager presumes that the figures may be confounded by other data: it cannot be ruled out that an exogenous variate distorts the picture. To investigate this supposition he obtains a measure of the number of persons visiting the exhibition centres ("store traffic") during the involved quarters (visitors in thousands, rounded). See Table 9.9.

While sales in Germany and Italy were similar, the number of visitors in the Italian outlet was about 85 percent higher. Stated differently, the probability of a German visitor buying a car was almost twice that of an Italian visitor. The German outlet sold nearly the same number of cars as the Italian outlet with only half as many visitors. This difference

Table 9.7 Luxwell sales of series 811 at capital exhibition centre

Period	France	Germany	Italy
2002_1	87	92	92
2002_2	94	96	103
2002_3	92	99	111
2002_4	82	98	85
2003_1	95	105	86
2003_2	102	106	83
2003_3	87	98	107
2003_4	93	91	109
X_T	732	785	777
$X_{(mean)}$	91.50	98.13	97.13

Table 9.8 SPSS ANOVA output (simple ANOVA)

Univariate analysis of variance

Tests of between-subjects effects

Dependent variable: SALES

Source	Type III sum of squares	df	Mean square	F-ratio	Sig.
Corrected model	201.083[a]	2	100.542	1.480	0.250
Intercept	219077.042	1	219077.042	3224.261	0.000
COUNTRY	201.083	2	100.542	1.480	0.250
Error	1426.875	21	67.946		
Total	220705.000	24			
Corrected total	1627.958	23			

[a] R-square = 0.124 (adjusted R-square = 0.040)

Table 9.9 Luxwell series 811 – using number of visitors ("store traffic") as a covariate

Period	France		Germany		Italy	
	Sales	Visitors (000)	Sales	Visitors (000)	Sales	Visitors (000)
2001_1	87	5	92	2	92	4
2001_2	94	6	96	1	103	9
2001_3	92	3	99	3	111	12
2001_4	82	2	98	4	85	2
2002_1	95	7	105	7	86	3
2002_2	102	8	106	6	83	6
2002_3	87	5	98	4	107	10
2002_4	93	6	91	2	109	8
X_T	732	42	785	29	776	54
$X_{(mean)}$	91.50	5.25	98.13	3.63	97.13	6.75
		Total sales: 2,293		Total traffic: 125		

is properly appreciated in a covariance analysis where store traffic is used as a covariate to adjust the sales figures. Once more, let us see how the problem is solved using SPSS.

1. As usual, start by requesting the *[Univariate]* version of the *[Generalized Linear Model]*.
2. In the white box on the left of the main dialogue box there are three variables, "[A] country," "[#] sales" and "[#] traffic." Note that the independent covariate "traffic" – like the dependent variable "sales" – is a metric variable.
3. Similarly to simple ANOVA shown earlier we put "sales" into the *[Dependent Variable]* field and "country" into the *[Fixed Factor]* field.
4. Finally, we tap the "traffic" variable into the *[Covariate]* field. Assuming that the screen looks like the one in Figure 9.16, tap *[OK]*. The corresponding SPSS output is shown in Table 9.10.

Note: To obtain precisely the figures displayed in Table 9.10, click *[Model]* and in the univariate dialogue box change the sum of squares type from III (default) to I (otherwise, the values in the rows concerning "Intercept" and "Traffic" will look different).[10]

While a preliminary analysis showed no difference in sales, a significant difference is detected once the raw sales figures are adjusted for the effect of the covariate. Note that

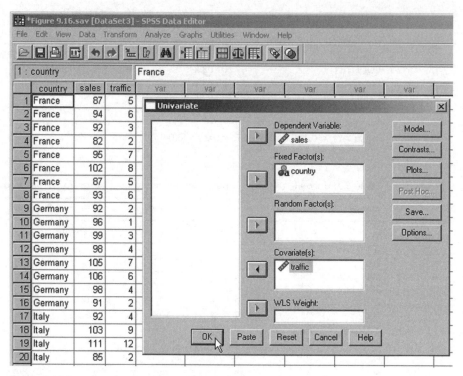

Figure 9.16 Running the ANCOVA problem in SPSS

Table 9.10 SPSS ANCOVA output

Univariate analysis of variance

Tests of between-subjects effects

Dependent variable: SALES

Source	Type I sum of squares	df	Mean square	F-ratio	Sig.
Corrected model	1265.399[a]	3	421.800	23.268	0.000
Intercept	219077.042	1	219077.042	12085.037	0.000
TRAFFIC	773.626	1	773.626	42.676	0.000
COUNTRY	491.773	2	245.887	13.564	0.000
Error	362.559	20[b]	18.128		
Total	220705.000	24			
Corrected total	1627.958	23			

[a] R-square = 0.777 (adjusted R-square = 0.744); [b] One degree of freedom is lost within treatments by computing the pooled within-treatments regression between response and covariate.

the F-ratio for COUNTRY, now that it has been corrected for the disturbing influence of the covariate, is highly significant (13.564). Therefore, considering the new data, which helped us to form a better model, our conclusion changes: sales across three outlets are different, but the "true" sales data was confounded by the differences of customers visiting the outlet.

Appendix 9-B shows how the critical value (13.564) as well as other critical figures of Table 9.10 are computed by using multiple regression with dummy coding. Visit www.pearsoned.co.uk/schmidt.

Notice that visits in the German outlet were much more successful with regard to generating sales (see Table 9.11).

Could this finding be of interest to the international marketing manager? It tells the manager that the German outlet is somehow better at selling Luxwell. Now this may be for an obvious reason – Germany is the home market of Luxwell. Moreover, Italy itself has several other producers of sports cars – Ferrari, Maserati and Lamborghini. However, the relative efficiency of the German outlet might be caused by marketing variables:

- Sales staff at the German outlet may be more qualified and better trained.
- There may be more sales personnel per square metre in Germany.
- The German outlet perhaps has a more impressive showroom.

It should be relatively easy to obtain data on the second point. If so, one could use the "sales personnel per square metre" as a separate covariate. Note that the Italian outlet has been successful at persuading visitors to visit the showrooms, so the difference in performance cannot be explained by more efficient advertising in Germany. But it might be worth investigating the effect of other marketing variables so the manager can figure out whether, say, the Italians need better sales training, if more staff are needed, or whether the design of the Italian showroom needs to be improved.

When should a covariance analysis be carried out?

Covariance analysis offers a partial substitute for control in cases where it is suspected that some variable(s) not under control is affecting the response variable. The effect of the covariate is removed separately (by regression) from both the among-groups and the within-groups sum of squares. In this way the residuals (following the regression part) are

Table 9.11 Visits to the German showroom resulted in more sales

[a] (732/42,000)*100%, [b] 42,000/732	France	Germany	Italy
Percentage of visitors who bought a car	[a]1.74%	2.71%	1.44%
Average number of visitors needed to generate a sale	[b]57.4	36.9	69.5

net of the covariate. The influence of the covariate is no longer buried in the error variance and the effect is to increase the sensitivity of the F-test.

Ideally, covariance analysis should be employed in cases where the covariate is, first, highly correlated with the response variable(s); and, second, not correlated with the treatment variable(s). If correlation with the response variable is low, the sensitivity of the experiment is not appreciably increased. If the covariate is correlated with the treatment variable, removal of its effect also removes some of the variance the response variable shares with the treatment variable (Green et al., 1988).

As the reader may check on the website (www.pearsoned.co.uk/schmidt), the above assumptions are roughly fulfilled with regard to the data example of Table 9.9:

- R between Sales (response variable) and Traffic (covariate) is 0.69 or $\sqrt{0.475}$ (see Appendix 9-B); while
- R between the Traffic (covariate) and – dummy coded – treatment variable Country is 0.46 or $\sqrt{0.210}$ (see Appendix 9-B).

The above sections only deal with simple ANOVA and analysis of covariance (ANCOVA). If several predictors, several dependents and one or more covariates are involved, the appropriate multivariate techniques are MANOVA and MANCOVA (where the M stands for "multivariate"). For instance, Luxwell's management might use several dependents, predictors and covariates, as in Table 9.12.

While SPSS *[General Linear Model, Univariate]* can easily handle such problems, it is beyond the scope of the present text. The interested reader is encouraged to inspect texts such as Hair et al. (1998), Green (1978), and Snedecor and Cochran (1989). Good treatises on ANOVA and ANCOVA can be found in Moroney (1951), Iversen and Norpoth (1987), Girden (1992), Brashers and Jackson (1994), and Wildt and Ahtola (1979).

9.3 Using multiple regression for analyzing exports

In ANOVA it is assumed that you have a metric dependent variable (e.g. sales) and one or several non-metric predictors (e.g. country of origin, car-model). In multiple regression there is also a metric dependent variate. But unlike in ANOVA, the predictors are metric

Table 9.12 Options for analysis

Dependents	Y_1	Quarterly sales		
	Y_2	A customer satisfaction score		
	Y_3	Average income among households in region (possible covariate)		
Predictors	X_1	Country	X_5	Customer segments
	X_2	Model type	X_6	Marital status
	X_3	Terms of payment	X_7	Home ownership
	X_4	Features	X_8	Occupation
Covariates	Z_1	Store traffic		
	Z_2	A weighted weather index based on temperature and hours of sunshine		

as well. In "ideal" regression settings, measurements are ratio-scaled (e.g. revenues, costs, price, number of customers, etc.), but they must be at least interval-scaled (e.g. satisfaction scores, buying probabilities, scales of beliefs and attitudes, grading scores, etc.).[11]

Textbooks on statistics and marketing research tend to have chapters on simple and multiple regression. An excellent, though matrix-oriented introduction, is provided in Green (1978); less technical coverage can be found in Hair et al. (1998). Good textbooks on the regression technique are Kleinbaum, Kupper and Muller (1988), Cohen and Cohen (1984), Kutner et al. (1996), and Weisberg (1985), for students with a firm grasp on statistics).

Most pedagogical and numerical examples on regression found in textbooks involve intra-country problems where the dependent measure is brand sales, while predictors are price, advertising expenditures, distribution-cost, and product development expenditures. Sometimes, data on the predictors are regressed with the dependent using a time lag of one or more periods (temporal asymmetry with X_1–X_n happening before Y).[12]

Multiple regression is also suitable for the analysis of international and export-related marketing problems.

A numerical example

Once more, a small numerical example may serve to clarify the method. The following discussion only assumes a modest knowledge of regression analysis.

Ten export managers from small companies have been interviewed and asked a few questions on their company's performance and on management's actual attitude towards exporting.

Three of the items/questions used are shown in Table 9.13.[13]

The managers' answers are provided in Table 9.14. Columns b to d display the raw data. Since an estimate is needed of the linear regression function, calculations have been made of the necessary squares (e to g), cross products (h to j), column totals and mean plus standard deviation of the raw data.

Table 9.15 shows how to calculate the regression coefficients and the coefficient of multiple determination.[14]

1. Take the variable-means and column totals of Table 9.14 and place them in the appropriate rows of Table 9.15 to obtain the mean corrected values.
2. There are two coefficients (b_2 and b_3) of predictors (X_2 and X_3), to estimate. To do this, establish a small system of two equations with unknowns (i). Since the values of six of

Table 9.13 Questions asked of export managers

	Variable description	Scaling
Y_1	Willingness to export	1 (definitely *not* interested) to 5 (definitely interested)
X_2	Company revenue	In millions of euros
X_3	Years of operation in the domestic market	Number of years

Table 9.14 Willingness to export (Y_1), revenue (X_2) and years of domestic operation (X_3) of ten companies. Computation of sums of squares and cross products

a	b	c	d	e	f	g	h	i	j
obs	Y_1	X_2	X_3	Y_1^2	X_2^2	X_3^2	Y_1X_2	Y_1X_3	X_2X_3
1	5	4.0	6.5	25	16.00	42.25	20.0	32.5	26.0
2	3	2.0	6.0	9	4.00	36.00	6.0	18.0	12.0
3	2	2.0	5.8	4	4.00	33.64	4.0	11.6	11.6
4	4	1.0	7.0	16	1.00	49.00	4.0	28.0	7.0
5	5	3.0	6.5	25	9.00	42.25	15.0	32.5	19.5
6	1	0.9	5.0	1	0.81	25.00	0.9	5.0	4.5
7	2	0.9	5.0	4	0.81	25.00	1.8	10.0	4.5
8	3	3.6	6.5	9	12.96	42.25	10.8	19.5	23.4
9	3	0.9	6.0	9	0.81	36.00	2.7	18.0	5.4
10	2	0.9	6.0	4	0.81	36.00	1.8	12.0	5.4
Totals	30	19.2	60.3	106	50.20	367.39	67.0	187.1	119.3
Mean	3.00	1.92	6.03						
SD	1.333	1.217	0.65						

Table 9.15 Computation of partial regression coefficients and the coefficient of multiple determination

A. *Mean corrected sums of squares and cross products (from Table 9.14):*

Σy_1^2	=	ΣY_1^2	−	ny_1^2	=	106.00	−	10(3.0)²	=	16.000
Σx_2^2	=	ΣX_2^2	−	nx_2^2	=	50.20	−	10(1.92)²	=	13.336
Σx_3^2	=	ΣX_3^2	−	nx_3^2	=	367.39	−	10(6.03)²	=	3.781
Σy_1x_2	=	ΣY_1X_2	−	ny_1x_2	=	67.00	−	10(3.0)(1.92)	=	9.400
Σy_1x_3	=	ΣY_1X_3	−	ny_1x_3	=	187.10	−	10(3.0)(6.03)	=	6.200
Σx_2x_3	=	ΣX_2X_3	−	nx_2x_3	=	119.30	−	10(1.92)(6.03)	=	3.524

B. *Solving for the regression equation:*

(i) Σy_1x_2 = $\Sigma x_2^2 b_2$ + $\Sigma x_2x_3 b_3$
    Σy_1x_3 = $\Sigma x_2x_3 b_2$ + $\Sigma x_3^2 b_3$

(ii) 9.400 = $13.336b_2$ + $3.524b_3$
     6.200 = $3.524b_2$ + $3.781b_3$

(iii) b_2 = 0.3603 = b_3 = 1.3040

(iiii) a = $y_1 − b_1x_1 − b_2x_2$
      a = 3.0 − 0.3603(1.92) − 1.3040(6.03) = −5.5545

C. *Computing the coefficient of multiple determination:*

$R^2y_1.x_2.x_3$ = $[b_2\Sigma y_1x_2 + b_3 \Sigma y_1x_3]/\Sigma y_1^2$
= [0.3603(9.4) + 1.3040(6.2)]/16 = 0.7170 (r = 0.8468)

Note: Capital letters imply sum of squares and cross products. Small italics imply mean corrected or deviation sum of squares and cross products. Small bold letters imply means. Small, italicized bold letters imply regression parameters to be estimated.

the 'building blocks' are known, the values just computed can be substituted into the formulas (ii). That results in two equations with two unknowns which can be solved easily (iii). Once the two regression coefficients b_2 and b_3 are known, the constant (a) can be computed (iiii).
3. Now the coefficient of multiple determination can be computed. This figure shows how good the model is ($R^2 = 0.7170$).

The linear equation is thus determined: $Y_1 = 0.3603X_2 + 1.3040X_3 - 5.5545$

- For every million euro a company's revenue (X_2) increases, the willingness to export (Y_1) grows with 0.3603 units (on the 1–5 scale).
- With every year of domestic operation (X_3), the export-willingness increases with 1.3604 units.

The reader should keep in mind that this interpretation is based on a strict assumption of *ceteris paribus* (everything else being equal). Moreover, it only holds within the defined range of the observed values, because, for example, we might have received data on X_2 and X_3 from one more company. Assume this is the case, though, but we were unable to interview the company's export manager. Then, the regression equation can be used to forecast the manager's export willingness. The new company has revenues of €4 million and has been active on the domestic market for ten years. Thus, the estimate of Y_1 becomes:

$$Y_1 = 0.3603(4) + 1.3040(10) - 5.5545 = 8.9267$$

This value falls far outside the allowable range, since the measurement instrument concerning Y_1 has a defined range spanning between one and five.

In our small numerical example, the predictors are ratio-scaled while the dependent is interval scaled. This implies that the scale of the dependent variate is weaker than that of the predictors. In theory, the dependent should be at least as strongly scaled as the independents.

However, as long as precautions are taken in implying literally from data to forecast, the results can help understand the problem. A matrix of simple correlations (computations not shown) shows that X_3 is better at predicting Y_1 than X_2, and that the correlations between X_2 and X_3 (the intercorrelation of predictors) is less than 0.5 (from Table 9.15 the correlation of the total model was 0.8468):

R	Y_1	X_2
X_2	0.644	
X_3	0.797	0.496

The numerical example involved a lot of computations. While it makes intellectual sense to have at least once in a lifetime worked one's way through the manual calculations, it is usual to let the computer do the tedious computations.

Multiple regression using SPSS and Excel

For a researcher, few things in life are easier than running a regression analysis on SPSS:

1. First, plug in the data.
2. Tap *[Analyze]* from the main toolbar, scroll down.
3. Request *[Regression – Linear]*. The SPSS "Linear Regression" screen appears (Figure 9.17).
4. Highlight *Y*1 and click it into the *[Dependent]* box.
5. Highlight *X*2 and *X*3 and click them into the *[Independent(s)]* box.
6. Click *[OK]*.

After a second the output, Table 9.16, appears. Even if there are hundreds of variables and thousands of observations, it still only takes this simple process to produce an output. To tailor the analysis and the output, just requires using the dialogue boxes of the regression method. SPSS has made the life of a "number cruncher" very easy.

Table 9.16 displays the output from SPSS. While some of the figures appear in the manual calculations, several do not. So Table 9.17 (on page 224) explains how every figure in Table 9.16 is computed. Such detailed explanation is not provided for the remaining chapters of the book. However, most of the calculations can be checked by consulting textbooks on multivariate analysis, such as Green (1978).

Table 9.16 Output from SPSS linear regression

		Variables entered/removed		
Model	*Variables entered*	*Variables removed*	*Method*	
1	X3, X2	.	Enter	

		Model summary		
Model	R^1	*R-square*[2]	*Adjusted R-square*[3]	*Std error of the estimate*[4]
1	0.847	0.717	0.636	0.804

		ANOVA				
Model		*Sum of squares*[5]	*df*[6]	*Mean square*[7]	*F*[7]	*Sig.*[7]
1	Regression	11,471	2	5.736	8,866	0.012
	Residual	4,529	7	0.647		
	Total	16,000	9			

		Coefficients				
		Unstandardized coefficients		*Standardized coefficients*		
Model		B^8	*Std Error*[9]	*Beta*[10]	*t*[11]	*Sig.*[11]
1	(Constant)	−5.555	2.677		−2.075	0.077
	X2	0.360	0.254	0.329	1.420	0.199
	X3	1.304	0.476	0.634	2.737	0.029

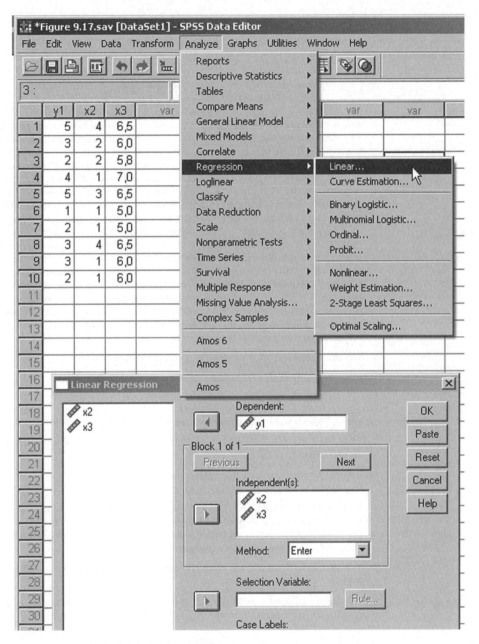

Figure 9.17 Multiple regression using SPSS

Running multiple regression in Excel is also easy but it works differently:

1. In Excel's standard toolbar tab *[Tools]*, *[Data Analysis]*, *[Regression]*.
2. The regression dialogue box of Figure 9.18 appears with blank fields and checkboxes.

Table 9.17 Detailed explanation of estimates in SPSS output (Table 9.16)

1, 2 **R** and **R-square** can be found in part C of Table 9.15

3   The **adjusted R-square** is computed thus:

$$R^2_{Adj} = 1 - \left[(1-R^2) \left\{ \frac{(m-1)}{(m-n-1)} \right\} \right] = 1 - \left[(1-0.717) \left(\frac{9}{7} \right) \right] = 0.636$$

where m = number of observations (10), n = number of predictors (2). The formula implies – holding sample size constant – that the downward adjustment of R^2 becomes greater, as the number of predictors increases. Adjusted R^2 intends to correct for the tendency of uncorrected (ordinary) R^2 to capitalize on chance variation in the specific data set under analysis. Adjusted R^2 is sometimes called *correction for shrinkage*. By definition, the figure becomes smaller as we have fewer observations per variable. Adjusted R-square is particularly useful in comparing across regression equations involving different numbers of independent variables or different sample sizes, because it allows for the specific number of independent variables and the sample sizes on which it is based. Note that adjusted R-square is an approximately unbiased estimator of the true R-square. Like most unbiased estimators of positive parameters, adjusted R-square can be negative! For instance, if in the above formula n exceeds 8, adjusted R-square becomes negative (for n=8, R^2 has no solution). Example: if you regress X_4 on X_3 (Table 9-D.1 in Appendix 9-D) the adjusted R^2 becomes: 1 – [(1 – 0.058)* (9/8)] = –0.06. Note also that, while ordinary R^2 can never decrease when a new predictor is added, adjusted R^2 may actually decrease. This is because the increase in accounted for sum of squares may be more than counter balanced by the loss of degree of freedom ($m - n - 1$).

4   The standard error of the estimate is computed thus:

$$SE = \sqrt{\frac{(1-R^2)(\sum y_1^2)}{(m-n-1)}} = \sqrt{\frac{(0.283)(16.00)}{7}} = 0.8043$$

where 16.00 is the mean corrected sum of squares of Y_1 (see A in Table 9.15)

5   11,471 = 0.717 * 16.000; 4,529 = 0.283*16,000 (explained and unexplained variance, respectively)

6   Degrees of freedom: m (observations) = 10, n (variables) = 3
Regression = $n-1$ = 2, Residual = $m-n$ = 7, Total = $m-1$ = 9

7   5.736 = 11.471/2; 0.647 = 4.529/7; 8.866 = 5.736/0.647; 0.012 = 8.866 ($F_{2,7}$) – In the F-distribution with two degrees of freedom in the denominator and seven in the numerator, the value 8,866 corresponds to an alpha value of 0.012 – stated differently, there is 98.8% probability that the model is significant.

8   The unstandardized regression coefficients, b_2, b_3, and a appear in (iii) and (iiii) of Table 9.15

9   The unstandardized standard error of a regression coefficient, say, of X_2 is computed thus:
(i)   The correlation, R, between X_2 and the remaining predictors (here: only X_3) = 0.496
(R^2=0.246)
(ii)   Now, $Z = 1/(1 - R^2_{X2'X3}) = 1/(1 - 0.246) = 1.3263$
Finally,

(iii) $SE(b_2) = \left(\frac{SDY_1}{SDX_2} \right) \sqrt{\frac{Z(1-R^2)}{(m-n-1)}} = \frac{1.333}{1.217} \sqrt{\frac{1.3263(0.283)}{7}} = 0.254$

SDY_1 (1.333) SDX_2 (1.217) are found in the bottom of Table 9.14. Note that the latter result can also be found by use of matrix algebra[15]

10   The standardized beta coefficient, say of X_2, 0.329 = (1.217/1.333)(0.360)

11   The corresponding t-value 1.420 = 0.360/0.254; according to the t-distribution (two-tailed test) with $m - n - 1$ = seven degrees of freedom, 1.420 transforms to a probability value of 0.199.

For details and specifics on computational formulas and their rationale, see Green (1978)

3. Click the button at the right of the *[Input Y Range]* field. Use the pointer to select columns A1 to A11. Click the button again.

4. Next, click the button at the right of the *[Input X Range]* field. Use the pointer for selecting the columns B1 to C11. Click the button again.

5. Flag *[Labels]*. Also flag *[Confidence Level]* and select, say, 90 (percent). You will get the 95 percent level anyway and when you do nothing here you get the 95 percent intervals printed twice!

6. Do *not* flag the *[Constant is Zero]* checkbox. In Excel 2002 and earlier versions this option contains a serious flaw. So do *not* use it![16]

7. We will not discuss the different plots that Excel can produce. So do not flag them.

8. Select an appropriate *[Output Range]* and finally click *[OK]*.

The output of Table 9.18 appears. As the reader may check, most of the output figures of Table 9.18 also are found in the SPSS output of Table 9.16. Excel by default reports the confidence interval of the regression estimates ($X2$ and $X3$). While confidence intervals are not part of SPSS's default output, the 95 percent interval can be requested by flagging *[Confidence intervals]* in the *[Statistics]* dialogue box. See the bottom of Figure 9.17.

Compare the 95 percent and the 90 percent level confidence intervals in the Excel output and note that *narrowing* the confidence *level* (going from 90 percent to 95 percent) *increases the width* of the interval. And vice versa. This is the classical dilemma of inferential statistics.

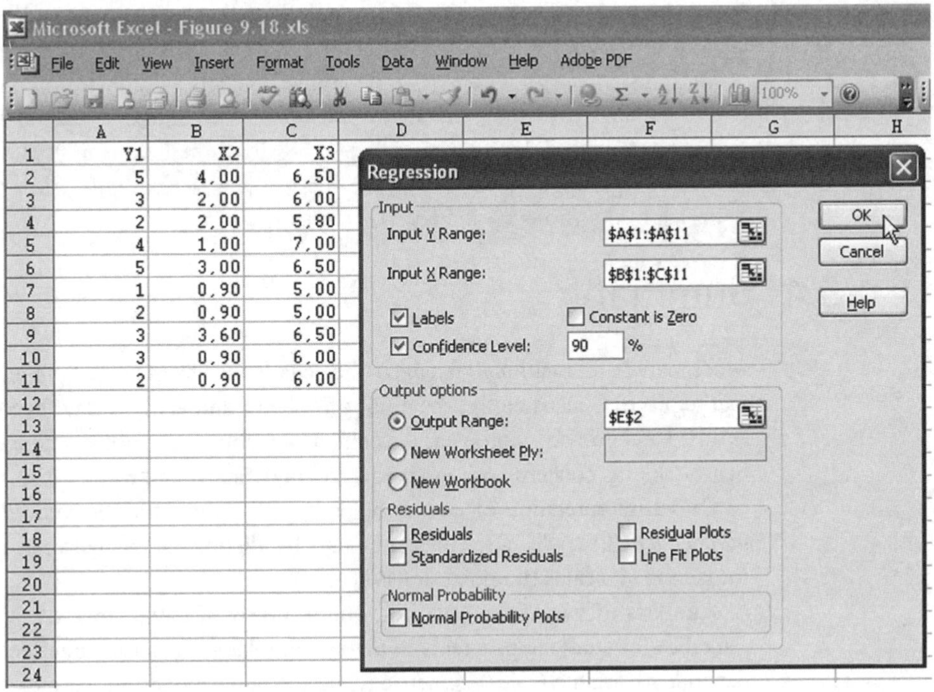

Figure 9.18 Multiple regression using Excel

Table 9.18 Output from Excel linear regression (compare with Table 9.16)

Regression statistics

Multiple R	0.847
R-square	0.717
Adj. R-square	0.636
Standard error	0.804
Observations	10

ANOVA

	df	SS	MS	F	Significance F
Regression	2	11.471	5.736	8.866	0.012
Residual	7	4.529	0.647		
Total	9	16			

	Coefficients	SE	t-stat	P-value	Lower 95%	Upper 95%	Lower 90.0%	Upper 90.0%
Intercept	−5.555	2.677	−2.075	0.077	−11.885	0.776	−10.627	−0.483
X2	0.360	0.254	1.420	0.199	−0.240	0.960	−0.120	0.841
X3	1.304	0.476	2.737	0.029	0.177	2.431	0.401	2.207

■ Two appendices for this chapter at www.pearsoned.co.uk/schmidt cover two important topics in multiple regression: Appendix 9-C shows how to adjust data for autoregression while Appendix 9-D provides an introduction to stepwise regression.

■ Appendix A introduces several real-life sample data sets. One of them is called "export manager survey." The respondents of this survey are 456 export managers. The questionnaire contains several variables that are suitable for running the analyses introduced in this chapter and in the next. The raw data file *Export_Manager_Survey.sav* is in a SPSS file format and can be downloaded from the above site. Note that saving the file in Excel format will delete the labels connected to the variables and levels.

9.4 Summary

A company's international managers face challenges from fierce competition in the global marketplace. Consequently, the ability to obtain and analyze data becomes essential for survival and growth. Moreover, the company encounters serious methodological and practical problems concerning how to analyze, understand and react, given the data at hand.

Often, interpretation of data is helped by differentiating between *dependent* (Y) and *independent* ($X1$, $X2$, etc.) measures and by distinguishing between different types of measurement scales (nominal, interval, etc.).

Analysis of variance (ANOVA) and **analysis of covariance** (ANCOVA) are useful remedies for studying problems in marketing related to cause and effect. In ANOVA, the dependent variable (sales) is metric while the independent measure (e.g. preferred brand, marital status, e.g. country of origin, etc.) is nominal or categorically scaled. The purpose

of ANOVA is to assess whether the means of the different treatment groups are significantly different. The null-hypothesis is that all means – apart from measurement error –
are equal. Technically, the total variance is split into one part (called treatment) that can
be explained by the statistical model, and another part (error) that cannot be explained. The
ratio of the treatment part and the error part (adjusted by the degrees of freedom) is
assessed by use of an F-test. If the test shows significance, it can be concluded that there
is a statistical difference between, say, income (dependent) and preferred brand (predictor). While significance in an ANOVA test shows that differences between levels of the
independent variables transform to differences in mean on the dependent variable, the test
says nothing specifically about the significance of individual differences between means.
The significance of pairwise differences can be computed by using either a paired t-test
(when both samples have the same number of observations) or by way of a z-test (in Excel:
Tools, Data Analysis, z-Test: Two sample for Means).

According to theory, an ANOVA cannot be justified if there is no homogeneity
amongst variances of the subsamples. For example, if the variance of the dependent
income variable varies markedly across different levels of the predictor preferred brand,
and if this variation is statistically significant, then ANOVA is not an option. An appropriate test in that regard is an F-test for homogeneity of variances. An alternative is
Levene's test. Provided such a test shows significance, one should drop ANOVA and carry
out a Kruskal-Wallis test instead. This test does not necessitate homogeneity of variances.
However, it is a non-parametric test that is based on a chi-square distribution and therefore it is a weaker test.

In ANOVA it is possible to assess the influence of several predictors simultaneously. If
two predictors are involved, for example brand name and country of origin, the analysis is
called a **two-factor ANOVA**. While the two-factor model provides a more complex
insight into the problem, one should be concerned about a statistically significant interaction between the factors. Maybe the brand "Napoleon" sells better if the brand is French
rather than German. Likewise, a sports car perhaps sells better when the colour is red
rather than grey. Appendix 9-A gives a technical introduction to two-factor ANOVA (see
www.pearsoned.co.uk/schmidt).

An analysis of variance may have several dependent variables (i.e. $Y1$ = sales per
employee and $Y2$ = sales per square metre). In such a case, the analysis is called
MANOVA (multivariate analysis of variance).

In some situations, an ordinary (M)ANOVA test leads to invalid results because the
true effect of the predictor variable (e.g. marital status) is underestimated. This happens
because the dependent variable (e.g. sales) correlates highly with or "is buried in" another
variable (e.g. household income). With ANCOVA the endogenous dependent measure
(sales) is corrected by the influence of an exogenous variable (e.g. household income).
Appendix 9-B shows in detail how ANCOVA can be used for computing ANOVA estimates that are net of the influence of the covariate (see www.pearsoned.co.uk/schmidt).

Like ANOVA, **multiple regression** facilitates the understanding of dependence
relationships between sets of data. In both ANOVA and regression the dependent variable
(e.g. sales) is metric/interval-scaled. But while the independent variable is categorical/
nominal-scaled in ANOVA (e.g. marital status) it is *also* metric/interval-scaled in
regression (e.g. household income).

A typical multiple regression analysis consists of a dependent variable (e.g. sales) and a lot of independent variables (price, advertising expenditures, etc.). The relationship between dependent and independent variables can be modelled as a regression equation of the form $Y = X1 + X2 + ...Xm$. The relationship between two variables, for instance the dependent variable (sales) and the independent variable can be either positive (advertising expenditures) or negative (price). The relationship is called a correlation, r, a figure that varies between $+1,0$ (perfect positive correlation) and $-1,0$ (perfect negative correlation).

The overall model's success is expressed by a coefficient of determination, R^2. The coefficient of determination is the relation between the explained and the unexplained variance. The explained variance is the amount of variability in Y that can be accounted for by $X1 + X2 + ...Xm$. Like in ANOVA, the appropriate test is an F-test. The R^2 statistic varies between 0 and 1.0. The 0 indicates a situation where there is no relationship at all between the dependent and the independent variable while 1.0 implies that the independent variables in unison are able to explain perfectly the dependent variable.

The relation between a specific independent variable and the dependent is called a parameter or regression coefficient. If unstandardized, this value has no upper or lower bound. The parameter coefficient indicates to how much (magnitude or intensity) and in which way (direction) the independent variable influences the dependent. It denotes how a change in the independent variable transforms to a change in the value of the dependent measure (e.g. an increase in $X1$ by 1 unit transforms to a $+0.4$ unit change in Y).

In empirical settings it is common to use many predictors. However, several or perhaps the majority of these predictors will have no measurable effect on the dependent variable. Stepwise regression can be used for identifying or filtering out those k of m independent variables that have a statistically significant influence on Y. According to stepwise regression theory, the m-k non-significant variables are excluded from the regression model. In Appendix 9-D we show how stepwise regression works (see www.pearsoned. co.uk/schmidt).

Traditional regression is formally called OLS (ordinary least squares). This algorithm assumes that the observations are independent. If they are not, the model's parameters are biased. Since some data, such as times series data and observations obtained from survey panels, are repetitive and dependent measures, OLS does not apply, unless the observations are adjusted. Normally one would need to employ other regression algorithms, such as GLS (generalized least squares). Appendix 9-C shows how times series data (often) can be adjusted such that the regression parameters become valid (see www.pearsoned.co.uk/schmidt).

Questions

1. The propensity of an average German visitor to buy a Luxwell is about twice that of an Italian visitor (Table 9.11). How could this information be of use to Luxwell's marketing managers?

2. Figure 9.12 displays a plot of interaction (based on Table 9.5). Compare this plot with

the five cases of interaction shown in Figures 9.14 and 9.15. When commenting on the numerical example of Tables 9.5 and 9.6 and Figure 9.12 (only the context differs), the authors of a classic textbook on marketing research stated: "Technically, what is shown [in Figure 9.12] is an *ordinal* interaction. By this is meant that sales in Germany are still higher than sales in France, independent of car model type – it is the *incremental* difference that varies. If the average sales response to the combination of Germany and 811 had been, only 72 units, then *disordinal* interaction would have been involved." See Green, Tull and Albaum (1988), page 479. Do you agree?

3. In the numerical example on multiple regression (Tables 9.14–9.15) it turns out that the simple correlation among the predictors $X2$ and $X3$ is less than 0.5 (less than each of their respective simple correlation with the dependent variable). Is this a good or a bad sign from an overall model perspective?

References

Aaker, D. A., Kumar V. and Day, G. S. (2001) *Marketing Research*. Wiley, New York. 515–517.

Anderson, D. R., Sweeney, D. J. and Williams, T. A. (2002) *Statistics for Business and Economics*. South-Western Publishing/Thomson Learning, Mason (OH).

Brashers, D. E. and Jackson S. E. (1994) *Random Factors in ANOVA*. Sage, Beverly Hills, CA.

Cohen, J. and Cohen, P. (1984) *Applied Multiple Regression/Correlation Analysis for the Behavioral Sciences*. Lawrence Erlbaum, Hillsdale, NJ.

Edwards, A. L. (1979) *Multiple Regression and the Analysis of Variance and Covariance*. W. H. Freeman, San Francisco.

Girden, El. R. (1992) *ANOVA: Repeated Measures*. Sage, Beverly Hills, CA.

Green, P. E. (1978) *Analyzing Multivariate Data*. Dryden Press, Hinsdale (IL). 107–24.

Green, P. E., Tull, D. S. and Albaum G. (1988) *Research for Marketing Decisions*. Prentice-Hall, Englewood-Cliffs (NJ). 471–484.

Hair, J. F., Anderson, F. E., Tatham, R, L. and Black, W. C. (1998) *Multivariate Data Analysis*. Prentice-Hall, Upper Saddle River (NJ). 326–86.

Iversen, G. R. and Norpoth, H. (1987) *Analysis of Variance*. Sage, Beverly Hills, CA.

Johnston, J. and Dinardo, J. (1997) *Econometric Methods*. McGraw-Hill, New York. 162–243; 388–411.

Kerlinger, N. and Lee, H. B. (2000) *Foundations of Behavioural Research*, Harcourt, Fort Worth, TX.

Kleinbaum, D. G., Kupper L. L. K. and Muller K. E. (1988) *Applied Regression Analysis and Other Multivariable Methods*. PWS-Kent, Boston, MA. 260–96.

Knüsel, L. (1998) "On the Accuracy of statistical distributions in Microsoft Excel 97." *Computational Statistics and Data Analysis*. Vol. 26. 375–77.

Knüsel, L. (2002) "On the Reliability of Microsoft Excel XP for statistical purposes." *Computational Statistics and Data Analysis*. Vol. 39. 109–10.

Kutner, M. H., Nachtschiem, C. J., Wassermann, W. and Neter, J. (1996) *Applied Linear Statistical Models*. Irwin/McGraw-Hill, Homewood, IL.

McCullough, B. D. and Wilson, B. (1999) "On the accuracy of statistical procedures in Microsoft Excel 97." *Computational Statistics and Data Analysis*. Vol. 31. 27–37.

McCullough, B. D. and Wilson, B. (2002) "On the accuracy of statistical procedures in Microsoft Excel 2000 and Excel XP." *Computational Statistics and Data Analysis*. Vol. 40. 713–21.

Moroney, M. J. (1951) *Facts from Figures*, Penguin Books, Harmondsworth, Middlesex (UK).

Morris, D. (2001) *The Naked Ape*, Trafalgar Square (VT). 371–457.

Newbold, P., Carson, W. L. and Thorne, B. (2003) *Statistics for Business and Economics*. Prentice Hall/Pearson Education, Upper Saddle River (NJ).

Pindyk, R. S. and Rubinfield, D.L. (1998) *Econometric Models and Economic Forecasts*. McGraw-Hill, Boston, MA. 463–601.

Rutherford, A. (2001) *Introducing Anova and Ancova: A GLM Approach*. Sage, Beverly Hills (CAL).

SAS/STAT Version 6, 4th edn (1989) SAS Institute, Cary, NC. 115–124.

Snedecor, G. W. and Cochran, W. G. (1989a) *Statistical Methods*. Iowa State University Press, Ames (IA). 251–253.

Snedecor, G. W. and Cochran, W. G. (1989b) *Idem*. 219–222; 237–253.

SPSS Advanced Statistics 7.5 (1997) SPSS, Chicago, IL. 17–18.

Weisberg, S. (1985) *Applied Linear Regression*. Wiley, New York.

Wildt, A. R. and Ahtola, O. (1979) *Analysis of Covariance*. Sage, Beverly Hills, CA.

End notes

[1] This example can be compared directly with the ones used by Green et al. (1988) by making the following substitutions: country = shelf height with levels, France = knee level, Germany = waist level, Italy = eye level; model-type = shelf facing with levels, 811 = full width, Coxtan = half width. Once you have performed these substitutions, you have access to a much more detailed discussion of simple ANOVA, two-factor ANOVA and ANCOVA.

[2] SPSS's homogeneity of variance test is based on Levene's Statistic (it tests all treatment levels simultaneously, not on a pairwise basis). See Snedecor and Cochran (1989a) for a discussion of such tests.

[3] The compatible test in SPSS is found by tabbing *[Analyze, Compare Means, Paired-Samples t-Test]*.

[4] As long as the mean value of the second group in the comparison (i.e. Germany) exceeds the first group, the t-stat value will be negative, implying that the empirical test value is found on the left side of the bell-shaped t-distribution.

5 For instance, *[Time Series]* assumes a Trends licence while *[Data Reduction, Correspondence Analysis]* presumes a Categories licence.

6 Another way of running the analysis is by selecting *[Analyze]*, *[Compare Means]* and *[One-Way ANOVA]*. But first change the levels of the country-variable to numeric figures, say, France = 1, Germany = 2 and Italy = 3. Next, in *[Variable View]* change the *[Type]* of the *[Country]* variable back from *[String]* to *[Numeric]*. In the One-Way ANOVA dialogue box, click "Sales" into *[Dependent list]* and "Country" into *[Factor]*. In the *[Options]* dialogue box flag *[Descriptive]* and *[Homogeneity of variance test]*. Click *[Continue]* and *[OK]*. The output is similar to the one of Table 9.4 and the main statistical figures of the output are the same. However, this more simple ANOVA approach was not used because it can only handle simple problems. It cannot manage simultaneous analysis of several factors, interaction effects, analysis of covariance, fixed versus random effects, etc.

7 ANOVA differentiates between *fixed* and *random* factors/explaining variables. In the example the factors are fixed. This implies that all available observation are used in doing the calculations. The universe comprises only eight observations across three countries. In real life, there would be records on, say, eighty monthly observations. However, we might only wish to analyze a portion of it. Thus, we might sample 10 percent ($N = 80$ and $n = 8$). In such a case, the appropriate ANOVA is a *random* model. In some situations, the researcher will want to use all available data on one factor/variable but only a subsample on another. If this is the case, the appropriate model would be a *mixed* model (see Snedecor and Chochran, 1989b).

8 While this does *not* ensure the "correct" setup settings, SPSS has sufficient information to produce "some kind of" output, though it may appear strange. Having run an analysis, we often experiment with settings between runs.

9 In the present case, linearity is misleading. If we arbitrarily change the order in which the countries appear in panel 1 from France–Germany–Italy to France–Italy–Germany, the functional relation would be non linear. But there would still be no interaction.

10 For details of the four different algorithmic approaches to computing the sum of squares, see SAS/STAT (1990) and SPSS Advanced Statistics (1997). Using type I makes it easier to compare the example with the ANCOVA-regression approach in Appendix 9-B. Also, using Type I makes it easier to compare findings with Green (1978) and Green, Tull and Albaum (1988). Applying type III implies that treatment and error variances do not add up to the total variance in the output table.

11 Predictors can be dummy coded. This is the case in conjoint analysis where predictors are nominal-scaled. Dummy coding is covered in Kerlinger and Lee (2000), 792–5 and in Kleinbaum, Kupper and Muller (1988).

12 Note that one cannot uncritically use multiple regression when analyzing times series data. Appendix 9-A.3 on the website www.pearsoned.co.uk/schmidt provides an introduction to the analysis of times series data. For an in-depth discussion on the topic, see Johnston and Dinardo (1997) or Pindyk and Rubinfeld (1998).

13 Abridged from Aaker, Kumar and Day (2001).

14 The raw data involves calculations in part A of Table 9.15 with four digits. To prevent rounding errors when comparing with a computer run, manual calculations should involve six digits after the decimal point.

15 The inverse of a 2×2 matrix A is always found in the following way (the inverse is denoted A^{-1} and the determinant |A|):

$$A = \begin{vmatrix} 1 & 2 \\ 3 & 4 \end{vmatrix}; |A| = (1)(4) - (2)(3) = -2; A^{-1} = \left(\frac{1}{-2}\right) \begin{vmatrix} 4 & -2 \\ -3 & 1 \end{vmatrix} = \begin{vmatrix} -2 & 1 \\ 1.5 & -0.5 \end{vmatrix}$$

The product of the matrix and its inverse always results in the identity matrix (a matrix with unities along the main diagonal and zeros off-diagonal).

$$Test: AA^{-1} = I; \begin{vmatrix} 1 & 2 \\ 3 & 4 \end{vmatrix} * \begin{vmatrix} -2 & 1 \\ 1.5 & -0.5 \end{vmatrix} = \begin{vmatrix} 1 & 0 \\ 0 & 1 \end{vmatrix}$$

$(1)(-2)+(2)(1.5) = 1, (3)(-2)+(4)(1.5) = 0, (1)(1)+(2)(-0.5) = 0, (3)(1)+(4)(-.5) = 1$

In our example the computations become:

$$R_{x2x3} = \begin{vmatrix} 1 & 0.496 \\ 0.496 & 1 \end{vmatrix}; |R| = (1)^2 - (0.496)^2 = 0.754; R^{-1} = \left(\frac{1}{0.754}\right) \begin{vmatrix} 1 & -0.496 \\ -0.496 & 1 \end{vmatrix} = \begin{vmatrix} 1.3263 & -0.6578 \\ -0.6578 & 1.3263 \end{vmatrix}$$

$$Test: RR^{-1} = I; \begin{vmatrix} 1 & 0.496 \\ 0.496 & 1 \end{vmatrix} * \begin{vmatrix} 1.3263 & -0.6578 \\ -0.6578 & 1.3263 \end{vmatrix} = \begin{vmatrix} 1 & 0 \\ 0 & 1 \end{vmatrix}$$

$(1)(1.3263)+(.496)(-.6578) = 1. (.496)(1.3263)+(1)(-.6578) = 0.$
$(1)(-.6578)+(.496)(1.3263) = 0. (.496)(-.6578)+(1)(1.3263) = 1$

[16] According to Microsoft, one should "... avoid the regression tool when you have to click to check the *[Constant is Zero]* checkbox. This has been corrected in Excel 2003 ... If you use Excel 2002 or earlier ... regression sum of squares, r-squared, and F-statistic values *are always incorrect* for the case where the regression is forced through the origin."

For a discussion of flaws in Excel's data analysis toolpack, see Knüsel (1998, 2002) and McCullough and Wilson (1999, 2002).

10 Discriminant analysis and logistic regression

Learning objectives

After studying this chapter you should be able to:

- Define the circumstances when a discriminant analysis can be used for profiling categories.
- Clarify the difference between regression analysis and discriminant analysis.
- Explain the underlying rationale of a discriminant function and how it can be employed for prediction purposes.
- Understand a classification table and misclassifications.
- Clarify when a logistic regression analysis is appropriate and explain the difference between discriminant analysis and logit models.
- Show how a logistic regression must be interpreted – compared with an ordinary regression analysis.

10.1 Discriminant analysis

Introduction

This chapter is dedicated to two methodological cousins of regression analysis. This section covers a type of analysis that has grown in popularity during recent decades. Half a century ago M. J. Moroney in his book on statistical methods, *Facts from Figures*, commented upon the rare use of discriminant analysis: "There seems to be very little application in industry of Discriminatory Analysis; yet one would imagine that it should prove extremely useful in many situations" (Moroney, 1951).

Even today, only some textbooks in business statistics and primers in marketing research cover the technique, and most of those that do only dedicate a few pages to the technique as part of an overview chapter on multivariate techniques. However, many advanced texts in marketing research have a separate chapter on the method. Sometimes, it shares a chapter with a related method, such as CHAID (Chi-Square Automated Interaction Detection), logistic regression or canonical correlation. But what is discriminant analysis and why should it interest the international marketer? A simple numerical example may help explain the method. Look at Table 10.1.

Table 10.1 Methodological differences between ANOVA, regression analysis and discriminant analysis illustrated by types of scales and examples of variables

	Scaling of dependent variable	*Scaling of independent variables*
ANOVA	*Ratio/Interval:* Age, income, turnover, cost, agreement scale	*Nominal/Categorical:* Gender, occupation, brand-choice, country of origin [*ANCOVA:* covariate ratio scaled]
Regression	*Ratio/Interval:* Age, income, turnover, cost, agreement scale	*Ratio/Interval:* Age, income, turnover, cost, agreement scale
Discriminant and logistic regression	*Nominal/Categorical:* Gender, occupation, brand-choice	*Ratio/Interval (Logistic: also categorical):* Age, income, turnover, cost, agreement scale, citizenship (dummy coded)
Analysis of crosstabs	*Nominal/Categorical:* Gender, occupation	*Nominal/Categorical:* Education, brand-choice

If one has a rudimentary knowledge about ANOVA and multiple regression, understanding discriminant analysis should not be difficult.

First, Table 10.1 shows that the scaling-type of the dependent (criterion) and the independent (predicting/explaining) variables is reversed if we compare ANOVA with discriminant analysis (DA):

■ ANOVA: differences in the choice of brands "imply" or "produce" differences in age/income profiles. So, differences in age are traced back to or transform to differences in brand preferences. Stated otherwise, preferences for different brands amongst customer groups *explain* differences in age or income. According to the ANOVA model, the data are controlled for mean differences in age or income along different levels of a category variable, such as brand preference or occupation. From a models perspective, brand-choice serves as treatment, and income or age depends on the specific level of the treatment variable. At a risk of oversimplifying, one could say that in ANOVA, the researchers' interest centres more on age or income of the consumer than on brand choice.

■ Discriminant analysis: differences in age/income profiles imply differences in brand preferences. So, differences in age or income explain why customers prefer different brands. In discriminant analysis the interest centres on brand choice or, say, occupation of customers (more than on age or income). Stated popularly: according to ANOVA, the brand "makes" (determines/forms) the age while according to discriminant analysis, the age "makes" (determines/forms) the brand choice. If the basic assumption of DA (normality) is violated, if some of the independent variables are categorical, or if the analyst prefers to run a "regression-like" analysis on a nominally scaled dependent variable, then a binary or multinomial logistic regression may be an option.

■ Regression analysis: in regression, both dependent and independents are ratio- or interval-scaled. So, in regression, the scalings of ANOVA (dependent) and DA (independent) are confounded.

From a formal perspective, discriminant analysis is a special case of regression where the dependent variate only has a small number of different (non-equal) discrete values. Another "hybrid" method is regression analysis with dummy coding of predictors. Basically, this is the same as ANOVA. And when both dependent and independent are categorically scaled, the result is either a crosstab analysis or a correspondence analysis. The latter analysis is covered in Chapter 13 (section 13.3).

A numerical example in discriminant analysis

Assume that the Goodbeer Brewing Company – a Scandinavian brewer of beers – considers launching a beer on the British and Danish markets. Moreover, presume that Goodbeer's international advertising agency has suggested that the accompanying advertising campaign addresses two topics or, maybe better, uses two societal values or themes. First, is the status of the country as a kingdom (headed by a royal family). Goodbeer is known for using the statement "By Appointment to the Royal Danish Court" in its advertisements and on the bottle labels. Second, in a modern liberal democracy, it is regarded as socially acceptable to engage in or sympathize with consumption of beer, at least as long as the consumption is kept at a moderate level.

- It is impossible to have a member of the royal family promote a beer from Goodbeer. Nor is that what Goodbeer's managers want. First of all, they want to know if a royal undertone is at all advantageous. Imagine an advertisement mentioning the "kingdom" combined with pictures of The Royal Guard, a well-known castle, etc. However, if too many people have negative impressions of, or apathetic feelings towards, the monarchy, then it is not recommended to use royal symbols in a broad marketing strategy.
- What constitutes a moderate or tolerable level of alcoholic consumption? The amount of alcohol that someone can drink without experiencing the symptoms of drunkenness varies from person to person. But according to the Danish National Board of Health, the "recommended limit" is set to three drinks a day for men and two for non-pregnant women. Note that a "drink" is either 0.33 litres of beer (4.6 percent alcohol), 0.2 litres of wine (11 percent alcohol) or 0.2 centilitres of spirit (40 percent alcohol). Goodbeer's management is very aware of the link between crimes such as drunk-driving, violence, rape, and hooliganism, and over-consumption of alcoholic beverages such as beer. The managers also know there is sound scientific evidence of a link between drinking disorders and physical and psychological problems, such as headaches, kidney failure, impotence, depression and aggression.

Goodbeer's core business is selling beer. Therefore, management is interested in keeping up to date with the level of beer consumption that the public deems is within a socially acceptable range.

Before conducting a big quantitative survey concerning the appropriateness of the two campaign issues, Goodbeer decides to carry out a small pilot study. The test is conducted at the end of a focus group interview with respondents in Britain and Denmark. In both countries, five respondents are asked to express their degree of consent to two statements on a twelve-point magnitude scale, stretching from 1 = definitely disagree, to 12 = definitely agree. The statements are:

Table 10.2 Responses from beer focus groups

Obs.	Y	X_1	X_2	X_1^2	X_2^2	$X_1 X_2$	
1	British	2	4	4	16	8	
2	British	3	2	9	4	6	
3	British	4	5	16	25	20	
4	British	5	4	25	16	20	
5	British	6	7	36	49	42	
British average:		4.0	4.4	90	110	96	(Σ)
6	Danish	7	6	49	36	42	
7	Danish	8	4	64	16	32	
8	Danish	9	7	81	49	63	
9	Danish	10	6	100	36	60	
10	Danish	11	9	121	81	99	
Danish average:		9.0	6.4	415	218	296	(Σ)
Grand mean		6.5	5.4				
Grand SD		3.028	2.011				

- (X_1) The royal family of my home country is doing a good job. Abbreviated: "RoyalsOK".
- (X_2) It is OK to drink up to three beers a day: "BeerOK".

The country of origin of the respondents (Y) is coded 1 to indicate a British respondent and 2 to identify a Danish respondent.

The outcome is shown in Table 10.2. The table also displays the squared values and the cross-product of the dependent measurements, as well as the summed values (the latter columns are used for the computations in Table 10.3).

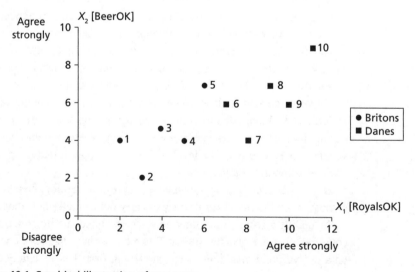

Figure 10.1 Graphical illustration of responses

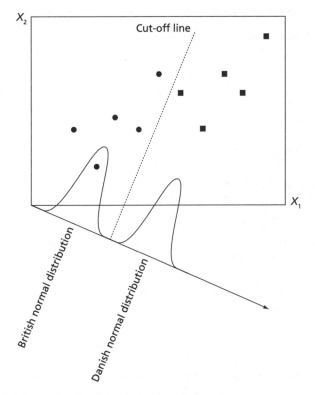

Figure 10.2 Underlying rationale of discriminant analysis

It seems that variable X_1 ("RoyalsOK") is best at discriminating between Britons and Danes. The difference on average is 5.0 (9.0–4.0) on X_1 but only 2 (6.4–4.4) on X_2. The Danes on average like their royals better than do the Britons. Figure 10.1 displays the sample data in a two dimensional space.[1]

Figure 10.2 illustrates the underlying rationale of the discriminant model. Danes and Britons are regarded not as one sample but are treated as two sub-samples, each of which is normally distributed. Next, a discriminant axis is established and the respondents' co-ordinates in two-dimensional X_1, X_2 space are projected on to the axis. It is assumed that the cases will distribute such that the density of observations is highest at the peak of the two normal distributions and that the density declines as observations divert from the peak.

Let the above theoretical considerations suffice for the moment. Turning back to the sample data set, Table 10.3 shows how the discriminant function is estimated, based on the data of Table 10.2.

Readers interested in an in-depth discussion of the computational details here are encouraged to turn to specialized texts like Green, Tull and Albaum (1988) or Green (1978). Note that the same numerical example (artificial data set) is used here as in these texts (only the context or case environment varies).

From a practical perspective, the discriminant function can be used for prognostic purposes. However, discriminant analysis is used differently from the usual forecasting methods based on either regression or on specialized models (smoothing, moving average,

Table 10.3 Computations involved in estimating the discriminant function

From Table 10.2: Mean corrected sums of squares and cross products

Formulae			British		Danish			Totals
Σx_1^2	$=$	$\Sigma X_1^2 - nX_{1av}^2$	$90 - 5(4)^2$	$= \quad 10.0$	$415 - 5(9.0)^2$	$=$	10.0	20.0
Σx_2^2	$=$	$\Sigma X_2^2 - nX_{2av}^2$	$110 - 5(4.4)^2$	$= \quad 13.2$	$218 - 5(6.4)^2$	$=$	13.2	26.4
$\Sigma x_1 x_2$	$=$	$\Sigma X_1 X_2 - nX_{1av} X_{2av}$	$96 - 5(4)(4.4)$	$= \quad 8.0$	$296 - 5(9)(6.4)$	$=$	8.0	16.0

Solving for the discriminant weights (k_1 and k_2):
To find k_1 and k_2, we solve the simultaneous equations...

1. $\Sigma x_1^2 k_1 + \Sigma x_1 x_2 k_2 = X_{1av}$ (Danish) $- X_{1av}$ (British) and
2. $\Sigma x_1 x_2 k_1 + \Sigma x_2^2 k_2 = X_{2av}$ (Danish) $- X_{2av}$ (British) $\Rightarrow$
1. $20.0 k_1 + 16.0 k_2 = 5$ and
2. $16.0 k_1 + 26.4 k_2 = 2$

That's two equations with two unknowns. Solving these gives $k_1 = 0.368$ and $k_2 = -0.147$.
Thus, the discriminant function is obtained: $Z = 0.368X_1 - 0.147X_2$

seasonal decomposition, ARIMA, etc.).[2] While forecasting methods predict events based on historic times series data, discriminant analysis predicts concurrent events based on present (cross-section) data.

Technically, use of the discrimination function corresponds to the way that the regression line is used in regression analysis. Therefore, recalling some aspects of regression analysis from an earlier chapter may help our understanding. In Section 9.3 of Chapter 9, a numerical example was used to illustrate multiple regression. Table 9.15 displayed the computations. The regression line estimated was:

$$Y_1 = 0.3603X_2 + 1.3040X_3 - 5.5545$$

where

Y_1 = willingness to export (1 = definitely *not* interested to 5 = definitely interested)
X_2 = Company's revenue in millions of euros
X_3 = years of operation in domestic market

Assume that the data on X_2 and X_3 came from one more company. However, in this case the interviewers have not been able to talk to the company's export manager. Instead, the regression equation is to be used to give a best estimate with regard to the manager's attitude to exports. The new company has revenues of €5 million and has been operating at home for six years. The estimate of Y_1 becomes:

$$Y_1 = 5 (0.3603) + 6 (1.3040) - 5.5545 = 4.0710 (\approx 4)$$

So, in considering the extra company's revenue and years of operation, and assuming that the model holds, the manager would be expected to be quite willing to export (4 is above middle on a 1–5 scale).

The basic difference between the regression line and the discriminant line concerns the dependent variable. Based on the X-values, we want to come up with an estimate of Y.

- A regression line helps approximate a value on *a continuous scale* – "4.0710" is a value on the continuous 1–5 export-willingness interval scale.
- A discriminant line helps to estimate whether the dependent value possesses *one or another non-metric characteristic* (i.e. 1= British *or* 2=Danish). Here, a metric figure such as 1.4260 makes no sense.

Corresponding to the regression case above, presume that survey-based data is available on a person concerning variables X_1 ("royalsOK") = 7 and X_2 ("beerOK") = 5. However, data is missing on one dependent measure, here: the person's nationality, Danish or English. Which nationality does the discriminant model suggest? The answer can be found by substituting the independent measures (7 and 5) into the discriminant function in Table 10.3 (bottom): $Z = 0.368X_1 - 0.147X_2$. Insert the empirical values for X_1 and X_2: 0.368(7) − 0.147(5) = 1.841.

Since this value is above the cut-off line arising perpendicular from the threshold-value of 1.598 in Figure 10.3, the best guess is that the respondent is Danish. The value 1.596 results from submitting the grand mean (6.5, 5.4) into the function. Note that the (numeric) ratio of the two estimated parameters (0.147/0.368) = 0.3995. The Arcsin of 0.3995 equals 23.5°. This corresponds to the angle between the discriminant axis and the X_1-axis.

In the numerical example, it is possible to discriminate between the two categories, Danes and Britons. In real-life situations this will never be the case. A proportion of cases will always be misclassified. In Figure 10.4, the nationality of one person in each group

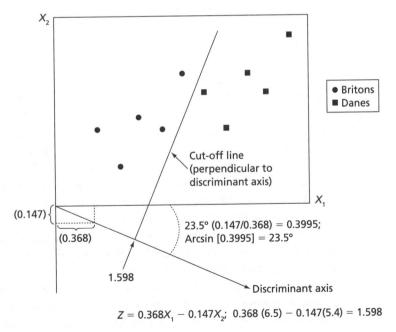

$$Z = 0.368X_1 - 0.147X_2; \; 0.368\,(6.5) - 0.147(5.4) = 1.598$$

Figure 10.3 Plotting the discriminant function

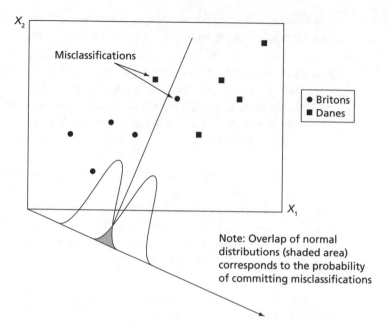

Figure 10.4 Discriminant analysis with misclassifications

has been changed. As a consequence, it is impossible to discriminate perfectly between the two groups. Misclassifications cannot be avoided (unless the linearity assumption is relaxed). When classifying in discriminant analysis, two kinds of error occur: falsely accepting a Briton as being a Dane; and erroneously presuming a Dane to be a Briton (readers may recall type 1 and type 2 errors, known from testing of hypotheses in basic statistics).

Usually, discriminant analysis would not be used for determining the nationality of a person, at least not when analyzing international marketing data. In cross-cultural marketing research the nationality of respondents is usually known. What causes interest then is to identify a subset of m predictor variables amongst the entire set of p predictors that are especially effective at explaining the differences between the categories of the dependent variable. In a real-life study there will be many predictors (say, 100 statements on lifestyle, attitudes, beliefs and interests) and not just five respondents from Britain and Denmark respectively, but, say, 600 respondents from each of the countries.

Technically, the numerical example is called a two-group discriminant analysis. However, in Figure 10.5 the example is expanded to three groups. Moreover, note that the dispersion of the normal distributions differs.[3]

In the numerical example of Tables 10.2 and 10.3, only one discriminant function or axis had to be computed (Figure 10.3). But, assume that the dependent variable has g levels and that there are m predictors. In such a case, one can find up to min $(g-1, m)$ discriminant axes – usually there are many more predictors than there are levels of the dependent variable. An example: if one has, say, 20 predictors and a dependent variable that has five levels, then it is possible to estimate up to four discriminant functions. Normally, not all of them will be significant, though. However, corresponding to Figure

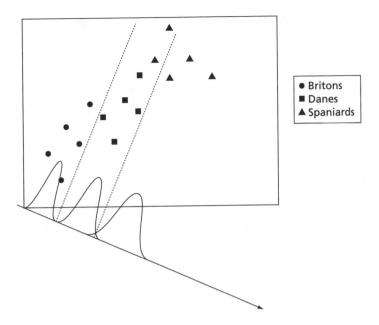

Figure 10.5 Multiple discriminant analysis

10.3, one could project two discriminant axes into Figure 10.5. Note that they would *not* be orthogonal to each other, although projection of observations on them would be uncorrelated. Sometimes the first discriminant axis is better at separating, say, groups 1 and 2, while the second discriminant axis is better at separating groups 1 and 2 from group 3. Readers interested in multiple discriminant analysis are encouraged to consult some of the advanced textbooks on the topic in the References.

There is a good chance that discriminant analysis can help to focus on ten to twenty variables where the cross-country differences are both operationally and statistically significant. If this is the case, the remaining 80–90 variables may be discarded since the differences between groups are not significant and so based on chance. When working with bigger data sets, it is usual in SPSS to employ *[Use stepwise method]*, see Figure 10.6, discriminant analysis main dialogue box. Stepwise discriminant analysis is not discussed here (the approach resembles the *Stepwise regression method* covered in Appendix 9-D at www.pearsoned.co.uk/schmidt). Instead, this section shows how to run the analysis using SPSS discriminant.

Running discriminant analysis in SPSS

Figure 10.6 displays the SPSS data screen with the data set from Table 10.2. Note that British respondents are coded as "1" and the Danish respondents as "2."[4] Then we use labels to re-establish a link between codes and category levels.[5]

SPSS treats discriminant analysis as a method for classifying data and has put it into a subset of methods that also includes clustering methods (see Chapter 12). While this is formally correct, one usually regards discriminant analysis as an *a priori* categorization (the categories are known before running the analysis). In cluster analysis, on the other hand, the categories are formed as a result of the analysis.

Figure 10.6 displays most of the set-up choices that are necessary to run a discriminant analysis.

1. Clicking *[Classify, Discriminant]* provokes the main dialogue box. Highlight *[country]* and tab the upper button.
2. The "country" variable appears in the *[Grouping Variable]* field with a (??) suffix attached. Click the *[Define Range]* button. And tab 1 for Minimum, 2 for Maximum and *[Continue]*. [6]
3. Highlight "royalsok" and "beerok"; then click the lower button. The two variables appear in the *[Independents]* field. Note that the *[OK]* button now has become clickable, indicating that SPSS has enough information to run the analysis. However, the analysis needs refining before the run is made.
4. Click the *[Statistics]* button and the statistics dialogue box appears. See the lower left panel of Figure 10.6. To include *[Means]*, *[Univariate ANOVA]* and *[Function Coefficients, Unstandardized]* in the output, request these options by flagging them. Click *[Continue]*.
5. In the main dialogue box, click *[Classify]*. The classify box appears. See the lower right panel of Figure 10.6. In this example, both groups, Britons and Danes, contain

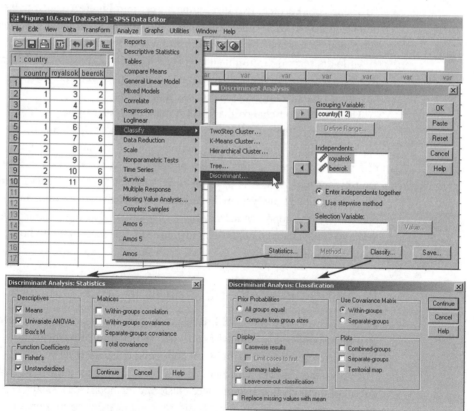

Figure 10.6 Discriminant analysis using SPSS

Table 10.4 SPSS discriminant analysis output (abridged)

Group statistics

Country (Y)		Mean	Std Deviation	Valid N (Listwise)	
				Unweighted	Weighted
British	royalsok	4.00	1.581	5	5.000
	beerok	4.40	1.817	5	5.000
Danish	royalsok	9.00	1.581	10	5.000
	beerok	6.40	1.817	10	5.000
Total	royalsok	6.50	3.028	10	10.000
	beerok	5.40	2.011	10	10.000

Test of equality of group means

	Wilks' Lambda	F	df1	df2	Sig.
Royalsok (X_1)	0.242	25.000	1	8	0.001
Beerok (X_2)	0.725	3.030	1	8	0.120

Canonical discriminant function coefficients

	Function 1
royalsok	0.837
beerok	−0.335
(Constant)	−3.632

Classification results[a]

		Country	Predicted group membership		Total
			British	Danish	
Original	Count	British	5	0	5
		Danish	0	5	5
	%	British	100.0	0.0	100.0
		Danish	0.0	100.0	100.0

[a] 100.0% of original group cases correctly classified

five subjects and are equal in numbers. But this will normally not be the case. Therefore the program must be told to base statistical computations concerning model fit on the number of cases appearing in the respective groups. This is done by changing the default-radio button of *[Prior Probabilities]* to *[Compute from group sizes]*. Finally, request a *[Summary table]*. Click *[Continue]* and *[OK]*.

6. A two-page output appears with twelve tables. The four tables to be discussed are displayed in Table 10.4.

We now discuss the output of the analysis and compare it with the manual computations in Tables 10.2 and 10.3. (See Table 10.4.)

Table 10.5 Weightings requested in Figure 10.6

	I	II	(I*II)
	Canonical discriminant function coefficients (from Table 10.4)	Standard deviation of individual discriminant scores (from Table 10.6)	Weights or parameters of the discriminant function (from Table 10.3)
X_1 (royalsok)	0.837	0.400	0.368
X_2 (beerok)	−0.335	0.400	−0.147

- Group statistics: several of these values also appear in Table 10.2.
- Test of equality of group means: contains results from two simple ANOVAs, one with X_1 as dependent and Y as predictor and the other with X_2 as dependent and Y as predictor.[7] Note that, while predictor royalsok is significant, beerok is not. *Wilks' Lambda* indicates how well the categories are separated.[8] The smaller the statistics, the better the separation. For X_1 we have:

$$\Lambda_{m=1} = \cfrac{1}{1 + \cfrac{(g-1)}{(n-g)} \times F} = \cfrac{1}{1 + \cfrac{(2-1)}{(10-2)} \times 25,00} = 0.242$$

Where g = number of groups/categories, m is the number of independent variables, n is the number of observations and F, as always the ratio of variation *between* groups and *within* groups.[9]

- *Canonical discriminant function coefficients* are just the discriminant weights, requested in Figure 10.6 *[Function Coefficients, Unstandardized]*. The estimated parameters of the linear discriminant function that appear in Table 10.3 are *standardized* (constant = 0). The standardized weights equal the unstandardized weights, multiplied by the standard deviation of the individual discriminant scores in Table 10.6 (see Table 10.5). Canonical analysis is covered in Chapter 16.
- Classification results: this table tells us how successful the analysis is at correctly classifying the responses. The respondents' nationalities are known before the analysis. Then, based on the data, the program estimates the linear discriminant function. Finally, the model-fit is validated by comparing the original category of the groups with the group-category of the same subject, estimated by the discriminant function. If the subject's category predicted by the model equals the original category, the classification is correct. If not, a misclassification has been conducted.[10]

In Table 10.6 the discriminant scores of all ten respondents have been computed. When the values in the far right column are compared with Figure 10.3, all British respondents have values lower than the cut-off line (1.598) while all Danish respondents' values are beyond the line.

On a general level, the analytical merits of a classification table should not be overestimated. Indeed, excellent percentages of correct classifications often are caused by pure

Table 10.6 Computing discriminant scores of individual respondents

		I	II	III	IV	(I*II)+(III*IV)
Obs.	Y	X_1	$Weight_1$	X_2	$Weight_2$	Discriminant scores
1	British	2	0.368	4	−0.147	0.148
2	British	3	0.368	2	−0.147	0.810
3	British	4	0.368	5	−0.147	0.737
4	British	5	0.368	4	−0.147	1.252
5	British	6	0.368	7	−0.147	1.179
			British average:			0.825
			British standard deviation:			0.400
6	Danish	7	0.368	6	−0.147	1.694
7	Danish	8	0.368	4	−0.147	2.356
8	Danish	9	0.368	7	−0.147	2.283
9	Danish	10	0.368	6	−0.147	2.798
10	Danish	11	0.368	9	−0.147	2.725
			Danish average:			2.371
			Danish standard deviation:			0.400

technical factors – the classification algorithm operates without a validation sample and consequently, *the test of the model is performed on the very same data that were the basis for establishing the model*. Thus, the model is validated on itself. This corresponds to the German "Baron of Lies" von Münchausen, who once claimed to have pulled himself out of the mud by pulling his own hair. A model's "ordeal" implies a test on data that have had nothing to do with the construction of the model. Only a model that can successfully handle and predict new information possesses true generalizability. Thus, in the present case, the discriminant model should be able to classify correctly a new sample of, say, ten persons as being either British or Danish solely based on their measurements on X_1 and X_2.

The SPSS discriminant classify dialogue box supplies a *[Leave-one out classification]* cross-validation option. While cross validation is done only for those cases in the analysis, each case is classified by the function derived *from all cases other than that case*. When doing this on a systematic level the procedure approaches the so-called "Jackknife statistics" (Fenwick, 1979). Formal methods for minimizing misclassifications are available (Koehler and Erenguc, 1990).

To sum up (assuming the pilot test was replicated on a big random sample): the royal family as a promotional theme seems better suited for Denmark than for Britain. The Danes have a more positive perception of their court than the Britons. With regard to the attitudes on moderate beer consumption, this also is regarded more favourably in Denmark. However, here the perceptual differences between Danes and Britons are insignificant. The present data might encourage Goodbeer's managers to move ahead with the intended promotional campaign theme in Denmark. In Britain it seems risky or even counter-productive to base a campaign on the royal crown. Therefore, Goodbeer might be best advised to have its British advertising and marketing research agencies develop different campaign themes.

10.2 Logit choice models: when discriminant analysis (and ordinary regression) does not apply

Sometimes, neither discriminant analysis nor ordinary regression applies. Once more, a small numerical example may help understand the problem. Table 10.7 repeats some of the data from Table 10.2. But the X_2 column has been substituted by a new data column, X_{2new} (for comparison, the old X_2 data column is displayed on the far right). In this new example, the dependent measure, Y, refers to "Most recent brand purchase." "British" denotes a British beer (Britbrew's Silver Rush) while "Danish" stands for a Danish beer (Goodbeer's Hans). For simplicity, assume that the respondents used in the survey are ten randomly selected tourists on holiday in the Shetland Islands (for now the nationality of the tourists does not interest us, only the nationality of the brand they have bought). All respondents are staying in a town where there is only one small shop, which stocks two brands of beer, Silver Rush and Hans. As in the previous case, the two dependent measures refer to attitudes towards the royals, X_1, and towards beer drinking, X_2. (Let the wording of X_1 now be: "In general, the royals families in Europe are doing a good job." Let the X_{2new} wording be the same as X_1 used earlier).

Now assume that the data obtained from this small brand choice survey are the ones displayed in Table 10.7 (for the moment, ignore the old X_2 column).

Since the problem resembles the type encountered in section 10.1, discriminant analysis is used. Therefore, the approach is as in Figure 10.6. The only difference is that the original data column on X_2 is substituted by the X_{2new} column of Table 10.7. Furthermore, in the statistics dialogue box (lower-left panel of Figure 10.6) this time we flag *[Box's M]*,

Table 10.7 Ten consumers' brand choice

Obs.	Y	X_1	X_{2new}	X_{2old}
1	British	2	2	4
2	British	3	11	2
3	British	4	3	5
4	British	5	10	4
5	British	6	2	7
British average:		4.0	5.6	4.4
British SD:		1.581	4.506	1.817
6	Danish	7	5	6
7	Danish	8	6	4
8	Danish	9	5	7
9	Danish	10	6	6
10	Danish	11	7	9
Danish average:		9.0	5.8	6.4
Danish SD:		1.581	0.837	1.817
Grand Mean		6.5	5.7	5.4
Grand SD		3.028	3.057	2.011

Table 10.8 SPSS discriminant analysis output (abridged)

Pooled within-groups matrices[a]		X_1	X_2
Covariance	X_1	2.500	0.375
	X_2	0.375	10.500

[a] The covariance matrix has eight degrees of freedom

Covariance matrices[a]			
Y		X_1	X_{2new}
British	X_1	2.500	−0.25
	X_{2new}	−0.250	20.300
Danish	X_1	2.500	1.000
	X_{2new}	1.000	0.700
Total	X_1	9.167	0.611
	X_{2new}	0.611	9.344

[a] The total variance matrix has nine degrees of freedom

Box's test of equality of covariance matrices

Log determinants

Y	Rank	Log determinant
British	2	3.926
Danish	2	−0.288
Pooled within groups	2	3.262

The ranks of natural logarithms of determinant printed are those of the group covariance matrices

Test results		
Box's M		11.546
F	Approx.	2.809
	df1	3
	df2	11520.000
	Sig.	0.038

pooled *[Within-groups Covariance]*, *[Separate-groups covariance]* and *[Total covariance]*. These four statistics help assess whether the assumptions of a discriminant analysis are met. Now click *[Continue]* and *[OK]*. The resulting new and edited output is displayed in Table 10.8.

One of the basic assumptions of a discriminant analysis is that the *covariance matrices must be equal*, implying that observed differences between groups are attributable to random chance.[11] If this precondition of equality is not fulfilled, that is, if the null hypothesis of covariance matrix equality is rejected, then, strictly speaking, a linear discriminant function is not appropriate. If the covariances are unequal, a bias occurs in the test for equality of centroids. In the two groups case it turns out that the null hypothesis in the T^2 test (known as Hotellings T^2) is accepted more frequently, when the covariance matrices are unequal. Moreover, unequal covariances tend to boost classification errors, since the linear discriminant function assigns too many observations to the group with the larger covariance. With an increasing number of variables or when samples are disproportionate in size, the null hypothesis will be *rejected* more often when the means are in fact equal (Green, 1978, 170; Dillon and Goldstein, 1984).

A proper significance test for assessing the equality of covariance matrices is Bartlett's chi-square approximation. Table 10.8 contains the matrices that are necessary for computing Bartlett's approximation. Specifics on how to compute the chi-square test can be found in Green (1978, 169–71). The test is easy to perform. SPSS supplies a more sophisticated and complex test, called Box's M. It is an F-test, assessing for the equivalence of the covariance matrices for multivariate samples.[12]

Now, look again at Table 10.7. Obviously, the new data on X_2 differ in nature from the old ones. While the standard deviation of the two groups in X_{2old}, British and Danish, were the same, 1.817, there now is a notable difference: the British SD in X_{2new} exceeds the Danish SD by a factor five, 4.506 to 0.837 (while the corresponding means are almost the same, 5.6 and 5.8). Concern increases when studying Table 10.8: the covariance matrices appear to be highly different. Note there are two extreme observations (sometimes called "outliers" or "influential observations") on X_{2new} – observations 2 (11) and 4 (10) – both among people who recently bought the British Golden Bride beer. Due to these outliers, the corresponding cell entry on the British beer becomes 20.3 – many times the equivalent cell entry of the Danish beer (0.7).

The obvious inequality within group covariances is appropriately appreciated by the size of the Box's M value and the corresponding significance value (0.038). This value is significant on an alpha level of 0.05, and therefore one may question whether a discriminant analysis is at all justifiable.

Box's M is a rather complex statistic. Table 10.9 provides the theoretical formulae that are used for computing the figure as well as the involved degrees of freedom. While Box's M is a chi-square statistic, it transforms to an F-statistic. (For a detailed discussion of Box's M test, see Lattin et al., 2003.)

Box's M necessitates that one computes the so-called determinant of the pooled within group matrix as well as the separate groups matrices. For the pooled within group matrix (see top of Table 10.8) of a 2 × 2 this becomes:

$$\begin{vmatrix} a_{11} & a_{12} \\ a_{21} & a_{22} \end{vmatrix} = a_{11}a_{22} - a_{21}a_{12}; \begin{vmatrix} 2.500 & 0.375 \\ 0.375 & 10.50 \end{vmatrix} = (2.500)(10.50) - (0.375)(0.375) = 26.109375$$

$$ln(26.109375) = 3.262294 = ln|C_w|$$

This figure, 3.262, appears in the log determinant column of Table 10.8. The determinants of the two separate group covariances are computed correspondingly. Table 10.9 shows how the values appearing in the "log-determinant" and "test results" part of Table 10.8 are computed manually.[13]

To sum up, people who most recently bought a British beer disagree more on the performance of the royal family than do the buyers of a Danish beer. From a model

Table 10.9 Formulae for computing Box's M – small example (unequal covariances)

$$\rho = 1 - \frac{(2s^2 + 3s - 1)}{[6(s+1)(g-1)]} \left(\sum_{i=1}^{g} \frac{1}{(n_i - 1)} - \frac{1}{(n-g)} \right)$$

$$\tau = \frac{[(s-1)(s+2)]}{[6(g-1)]} \left(\sum_{i=1}^{g} \frac{1}{(n_i - 1)^2} - \frac{1}{(n-g)^2} \right)$$

$$f_1 = [(g-1)s(s+1)]/2$$

$$f_2 = \frac{(f_1 + 2)}{\left| \tau - (1-\rho)^2 \right|}$$

$$\gamma = \frac{(\rho - f_1 / f_2)}{f_1},$$

$$M = \rho \left[(n-s)\ln|C_w| - (n_1 - 1)\ln|C_{w1}| - (n_2 - 1)|C_{w2}| \right]$$

$$F_{f1,f2} = M\gamma$$

Where: g = number of groups   s = number of independent variables
         n_i = size of group i   n = total number of observations
         f_1 = df in numerator, f_2 = df in denominator

$$\rho = 1 - \left\{ \frac{[2(2)^2 + 3(2) - 1]}{[6(2+1)(2-1)]} \right\} \left\{ \left(\frac{1}{4} + \frac{1}{4} \right) - \left(\frac{1}{(10-2)} \right) \right\} = 0.72916667$$

$$\tau = \left\{ \frac{[(2-1)(2+2)]}{[6(2-1)]} \right\} \left\{ \left[\frac{1}{4^2} + \frac{1}{4^2} \right] - \frac{1}{8^2} \right\} = 0.07291667$$

$$f_1 = [(2-1)2(2+1)]/2 = 3$$

$$f_2 = \frac{(3+2)}{\left| 0.07291667 - (1 - 0.72916667)^2 \right|} = 11520$$

$$\gamma = \frac{(0.72916667 - 3/11520)}{3} = 0.24296875$$

$$M = [(10-2)(3.2623) - (4)(3.9257) - (4)(-0.2877] = 11.546$$

$$F_{3,11520} = (11.5464)(0.24296875) = 2.805; \ p-value = 0.03822$$

perspective, the significant difference implies that discriminant analysis should not be used.

Fortunately, skipping the discriminant analysis due to a violation in the assumptions does not rule out further analysis of our data. However, another model is needed. It turns out, that a binary logistic regression (also known as logit) is a proper modelling substitute when discriminant analysis cannot be used.

The logit model

Discriminant analysis centres on the question "Which group is the observation most likely to belong to?" Common applications of logit models focus more on estimating "How likely is the observation to belong to each group?" Thus, while logit models fall somewhere between regression and discriminant analysis in application, both logit and discriminant analysis make quantitative predictions about categorical variables (Lehmann, Gupta and Steckel, 1998).

The term "logit models" occasionally causes confusion. In the present context, we refer to what is known as **binary logistic regression**. A binary logistic regression model implies that the dependent variable has only two categories (corresponding to the two-group discriminant analysis). Sometimes, reference to logit models also is meant to include **multinomial logistic regression** and **(multinomial) probit models**. "Multinomial" denotes a case where the dependent variable has more than two categories. Sometimes a distinction is made between **multinomial** and **conditional** models, the latter referring to models were the independent variables focus on characteristics of a specific choice situation. In practice, the distinction is meaningless.[14] In this chapter, the terms binary logistic regression and logit models are used interchangeably, but the former is preferred when addressing technical topics and the latter when dealing with general issues.

Whereas ordinary regression uses a method known as ordinary least squares (OLS) for fitting the model, logit models employ what is known as the maximum likelihood (ML) estimation. The OLS approach minimizes the sum of squared linear differences between the actual and predicted values of the dependent variable. The approach assumes that the dependent variable is *linear* (scaled according to an interval or a ratio scale) and that measurements range from "little" to "much", or, more formally, that the interval covers the distance from $-\infty$ to $+\infty$ (or 0 to $+\infty$). However, when facing problems within economics and business, this assumption is often not fulfilled. In marketing research, measurements of purchase or related types of choice data are often encountered. In such situations the dependent variable is not linear but dichotomous or categorical. Either the customer has bought brand A (coded as "1") or not done so (coded as "0").

Consequently, when facing situations where the dependent variable assumes a nonlinear nature, a model is needed that can handle nonlinear dependency relationships. It appears that the logarithmic transformation of the dependent variable, employed by the ML approach, is appropriate for problems of this kind. The ML method can be used in an iterative manner to find "most likely" or "most probable" estimates of coefficients. OLS regression is covered in most undergraduate textbooks in business statistics and therefore it is assumed that students are familiar with this method. Specifics about the ML estimation procedure are beyond the scope of this text.[15]

The remainder of this chapter provides an introduction to logistic regression.[16]

Discriminant analysis is popular in situations where the researcher wants to assess differences between groups of respondents, and where these groups can be specified before running the analysis. Examples include customers versus non-customers, males versus females, Danish respondents versus British respondents, etc. A logit model usually is an option when the measure of the dependent variable involves an *act* or a *physical decision*, e.g. a choice between purchasing one of two brands of beer like Silver Rush and Hans, or a choice between entering one of two potential export markets. Often, the act (past behaviour) happened recently and the logit model is then used for estimating a probability of the same event appearing again either at a future point of time ('next purchase') or once a new person with known characteristics is modelled by the logit algorithm.

Advantages of logit models are:

- Logit models are less affected than discriminant analysis when the basic assumptions, particularly normality of variables, are not met (i.e. if covariances are not equal, see above). In practice, these suppositions are often not fulfilled. Logistic regression is much more robust when assumptions are violated, so its application is appropriate in many more situations.
- Even in situations where the prerequisites of a discriminant analysis are met, many researchers prefer logistic regression because it is similar to regression.
- A thorough understanding of discriminant analysis necessitates knowledge of matrix algebra and matrix eigenstructures because such terms usually appear in the software's unsuppressable default output. Logit output on the other hand can be understood without knowledge of matrix algebra.

Marketing research in action
Some technical issues with differences in logit algorithms

In ordinary regression, the error term follows a continuous scale. The error is free to assume any value from minus infinity to plus infinity; it has an expected value of *0* and a variance of σ. In logistic regression, the error term can only assume two states, either "1" or "0" – either "right" or "wrong" (so ordinary mean and variance of errors are invalid in a logit model). However, if one assumes a normally distributed error term for a probability model, which is possible, then the appropriate functional form is known as a **probit model**. Thus, the difference between a logit and a probit model simply concerns the scaling of the error term. According to Lattin, Carroll and Green (2003), 486, the differences between the binary logit and binary probit model are often not substantial.

The following section is confined to run and analyze one of SPSS's approaches to logit (binary logistic regression). Note though that SPSS also supplies a probit analysis: *[Analyze, Regression, Probit]*. The binary probit model as well as the multinominal logit and probit models are beyond the scope of the present text. Aldrich and Nelson (1985) and Borooah (2001) have more details on these extensions of the logit model.

- Like regression, logit models can handle independent categorical variables through dummy variable coding whereas in discriminant analysis use of dummy coded predictors creates problems with the equality of the covariance matrices.

While the logistic distribution has a shape that resembles the normal distribution, it differs slightly in not being completely bell-shaped and having fatter tails. Binary logistic only applies when the dependent variable has two categories. If more categories are involved, the analyst needs to either use the more complex multinomial logistic regression or the less robust multiple discriminant analysis. The box on page 251 has some technical details on logit models.

Logistic regression using SPSS[17]

In the previous section, the data in Tables 10.7 and 10.8 were not suited for discriminant analysis because the group covariance matrices were different. However, if a logit model is used for analyzing the data, there is no need to worry about group covariance equality. In the logit model:

1. Tap *[Analyze, Regression, Binary Logistic]*. Figure 10.7 displays the appearing dialogue box and data. To ease interpretation, we have recoded the levels of the dependent variable compared with Figure 10.6.
2. Now, '0' indicates purchase of a British beer while '1' refers to purchasing a Danish beer. This way of coding will facilitate our understanding, since it allows us to use one of the levels of the dependent variable (British) as a baseline level for assessing what happens when "moving from" British beer purchase to Danish beer purchase. In a real case setting, instead of British and Danish beer, we might have "our brand = 1" versus "other brand = 0," or "user=1" versus "nonuser = 0." In such a situation, it makes sense to treat the group of other brands, non-customers or non-users as a baseline. We can then explore in detail how the estimated coefficients change, assuming that we move from the level non-customer/non-user (0) to customer/user (1). In other words: which parameters facilitate a conversion from 0 ("them") to 1 ("us")? Note that the binary logistic procedure in SPSS accepts string variables (text) as input. Therefore, the 0/1 coding is not necessary. For obvious reasons the dependent variable must have exactly two levels.
3. It is very easy to do the necessary setups for running a Logistic Regression. Just click the "country" variable into the *[Dependent]* field and then "royalsok" and "beerok" into the *[Covariate]* field.[18]
4. A few words about the other options (not used here). If some of the "covariates" (= Independents, SPSS's name is confusing here) are categorical/nominal-scaled, then click the *[Categorical]* button, select the variables that are categorical-scaled, and click them into the "Categorical Covariates" field of that sub-box. It is also possible to tab a variable into a "Selection Variable" field and then use the *[Rule]* tag for defining certain logical criteria that a case must fulfil for being selected. The facility resembles *[Data, Select Cases, If condition is satisfied]* on SPSS's main menu bar. In *[Save]* it is possible to save "group membership" as predicted by the logit model, some statistics on

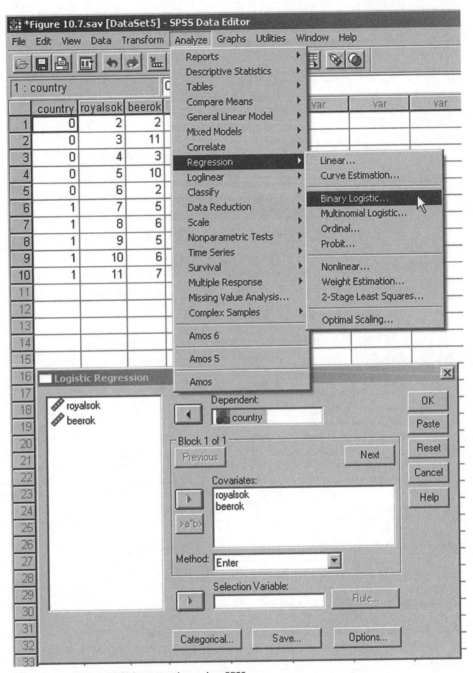

Figure 10.7 Binary logistic regression using SPSS

influencial observations (outliers) and residual values that are scaled in different ways. *[Options]* offers some appropriate test statistics and one can change pre-specified values for the stepwise procedure. The *[Previous/Next]* buttons are only of interest with an experimental design.

5. Now, click *[OK]* and the output of Table 10.10 appears (it has been abridged).

Table 10.10 SPSS binary logistic regression output (abridged)

Dependent variable encoding

Original value	Internal value
0	0
1	1

Block 0: Beginning block

Classification table [a,b]

			Predicted		
			Country		
	Observed		0	1	Percentage correct
Step 0	Country	0	0	5	0.0
		1	0	5	100.0
	Overall Percentage				50.0

[a] Constant is included in model   [b] The cut value is 0.500

Block 1: Method = Enter

Omnibus test of model coefficients

		Chi-square	df	Sig.
Step 1	Step	13.863	2	0.001
	Block	13.863	2	0.001
	Model	13.863	2	0.001

Model summary

Step	−2 Log likelihood	Cox & Snell R-square	Nagelkerke R-square
1	0.000	0.750	1,000

Classification Table [a]

			Predicted		
			Country		
	Observed		0	1	Percentage correct
Step 1	Country	0	5	0	100.0
		1	0	5	100.0
	Overall percentage				100.0

Variables in the equation

		B	S.E.	Wald	df	Sig.	Exp(B)
Step 1[a]	Royalsok	25.923	6470.659	0.000	1	0.997	1.71E+11
	Beerok	3.164	1850.869	0.000	1	0.999	23.674
	Constant	−179.853	45845.005	0.000	1	0.997	0.000

[a] Variables entered on step 1: Royalsok, Beerok

The 0/1 recoding of the example implies that there is no difference between the values of the 'original value' and the 'internal value' in the output (if the two levels do not agree, interpretation may be difficult). In the first step (Block 0, Step 0), only the constant is included in the model. The 'outlier ridden' observations of the English beer buyers (Country 0) are all incorrectly classified. On average, five out of ten of all buyers (including all buyers of Danish beer) are correctly classified – assuming that the attitude variables are not included in the analysis. Then, in block 1, the variables royalsok (X_1) and beerok (X_{2new}) are entered. As can be seen in the table 'omnibus test of model coefficients', introducing the independent variables results in a significant improvement of the model.

The Chi-Square-value of 13.863 corresponds to an alpha or significance level of less than 0.001. Moreover, as follows from the second classification matrix in Table 10.10, all ten cases are now correctly grouped. So the final model has a perfect fit (more about this below).

Model fit

Unlike in ordinary least-square regression, a regular R-square value does not exist in logistic regression. The most important statistic is an obscure figure called *–2 Log likelihood* (abbreviated −2LL). This chi-square goodness of fit statistic is produced as part of the maximum likelihood estimation process, and is an overall measure of the model fit. In a way it resembles the residual error sum of square in ordinary regression. A successful model should have a small value for –2LL. It is a relative figure that has no upper bound, while its minimum value is 0, indicating a perfect fit. Indeed, it would be more correct to characterize –2LL as a *badness of fit* measure since higher values imply worse fit. The –2LL value can also be used when comparing equations, with the difference representing the change in predictive fit from one equation to another.

The chi-square value of 13.863 in Table 10.10 simply equals the difference in –2LL of **the restricted model** (here the version that only includes the constant, also called the null-model) and **the full model** (version that includes the independent variables, X_1 and X_{2new}, sometimes called the saturated model). Since the net reduction in –2LL value – a drop from 13.863 to 0 – is significant, introducing the two marketing variables significantly improves model fit. Therefore, data on the respondents' opinion about the royal family and beer drinking in general appear to make an important difference in determining the likelihood of buying a British versus a Danish beer. But –2LL only gives us a tentative impression about our model's overall qualities. Since –2LL is an absolute measure, it cannot be used for assessing model fit across studies (when sample size, variables, market environments, etc., differ). Since an absolute measure possesses no generalizability, a relative measure is needed.

When using ordinary regression, the researcher has easy access to a valid measure of overall model fit, the coefficient of multiple determination, R^2. R^2 is confined to a $0-1$ interval, while the correlation coefficient is confined to the $[-1, +1]$ interval, where the ends indicate perfect negative and positive correlation, while 0 indicates that variables are uncorrelated. In logistic regression, a corresponding strict statistic is not available. Because $-2LL$ is an absolute measure it can only be used for determining the overall significance of the model and for assessing the model's properties as compared with models of a more or less parsimonious nature ("nested" models), when fitted on the same data.

Take a closer look at −2LL and two other fit statistics appearing in the output of Table 10.10. As recalled, −2LL of the final model is 0.000. However, it turns out that this perfect fit happens simply because the data being used (Figure 10.8) can be completely linearly separated.[19] If the fit had been incomplete and if the final classification table had contained misclassifications, then −2LL would have been a positive figure. Introducing the two independents decreases the −2LL by 13.863 (recall that if −2LL *decreases*, the fit *increases*). Stated otherwise, −2LL of the so-called null-model (including only the intercept) and of the final or full model are 13.863 and 0.000 respectively. We shall be using these two numbers shortly.

The relative model fit statistics that are available when dealing with logit models, Cox and Snell, and Nagelkerke attempt to approximate the percentage of variance explained in linear regression (both appear in Table 10.10). They do not have a sampling distribution and are therefore not amenable to testing. Being pseudo versions of R^2, they are only descriptive measures of fit. Below is the Cox and Snell formula to show how the statistic is computed.

$$R^2_{CS} = 1 - e^{\left\{-(\frac{2}{n})[LL(\beta) - LL(Null)]\right\}}$$

$$R^2_{CS} = 1 - e^{\left\{-(\frac{2}{10})[0 - (-6.9315)]\right\}} = 0.75$$

The above formula uses "LL," while the output literally contains the term "−2LL". β and *Null* refer to the final model and the null/baseline-model, respectively (so *LL(Null)* does not refer to the number zero). Table 10.10 found −2LL of the final model (Block 1, Model summary) to be 0.000, and so LL is also 0.000. −2LL of the Null-model was 13.863, implying that LL is −½(13.863) = −6.9315.[20] Nagelkerke's R^2 differs from Cox and Snell in that according to the Nagelkerke statistic the Cox and Snell R^2 of the most successful simple logit model is divided by the R^2 of the full model.

Here the simple models, $Y=X_1$ and $Y=X_{2new}$ yield Cox & Snell R^2 of 0.750 and 0.001, respectively (to check this, re-run the analysis of Figure 10.8 with one "covariate" at a time, first *royalsok/X₁* and then *beerok/X₂new*). From this, the R^2_{CS} of the logistic regression $Y = X_1$ is 0.75, which is the most successful simple model implying that $R^2_N = (0.750/0.750) = 1,000$ (see Table 10.8). In real life applications it is unusual to see Nagelkerke's R^2 or Cox and Snell's R^2 near 1.0. Values in the range of 0.3–0.5 are often described as excellent fits (Lattin et al., 2003, 486).

The Hosmer–Lemeshow goodness of fit statistic (not shown in Table 10.10) tests the assumption that data was originally generated by the estimated model. The direction of this test is contrary to what we are used to: a large chi-square value implies that the model does not fit the data. While Hosmer–Lemeshow is not part of the default output of SPSS, it can be requested in *[Regression, Binary Logistic, Options]*. Since the small example fits the data perfectly, the Hosmer and Lemeshow statistic is 0.000. Specifics of the procedure are discussed in Hosmer and Lemeshow (2000).

Interpreting coefficients

In ordinary linear regression, interpretation of the coefficients is straightforward. The coefficient is equal to the change in the expected value of the dependent variable per unit change in the corresponding independent variable. An example: in section 9.3, the equation $Y_1 = 0.3603X_2 + 1.3040X_3 - 5.5545$ was estimated. As recalled, the explanation was this: For every million euro a company's revenue (X_2) increases, the willingness to export (Y_1) grows with 0.3603 units (on a 1–5 scale) and with every year of domestic operation (X_3), the export-willingness increases with 1.3604 units. Unfortunately, the same approach is not applicable when dealing with a logit-type model, because this is not based on linear relations but probabilities. Therefore, the independent variable's effect on the dependent is modelled by way of a *logarithmic transformation*.

Some researchers regard logit coefficients as *elasticities*: the percent change in one variable that is associated with another variable. In Table 10.10 (bottom) the coefficients are 25.923 for X_1 (royalsok) and 3.164 for X_{2new} (beerok). Both independent variables used the same 1–12 interval scale, making a comparison between them easier. Note that the coefficient of X_1 is 8.2 times bigger than that of X_{2new}, implying that Y's sensitivity towards changes in X_1 is much greater when compared to changes in X_{2new}. Stated otherwise, the elasticity of X_1 is much greater than that of X_{2new} with regard to causing changes in Y. Since both estimates have a positive sign (positive elasticity), they both tend to increase the probability of purchasing Danish beer (instead of English). In other words, the higher the numeric values on the independent variables (especially on X_1, slightly on X_{2new}), the higher the probability of purchasing a Danish beer (moving from 0 to 1 on Y country).

Another way of interpreting a logit model involves the concept of odds. *Marginal odds* are the odds of being in one category rather than another of a variable (i.e. the odds of buying Danish beer instead of English beer). *Conditional odds* are the odds of being in one category rather than in another of a variable, given a specific value of a second variable (e.g. the odds of buying English beer, given that your gender is male).

Based on the concept of odds, a logistic regression coefficient is treated as an *odds ratio* (OR). The OR is a measure of association between an independent (X) and the dependent variable (Y). An OR > 1 implies that the odds of an event occurring (Y=1 instead of Y=0) *increase* when increasing the value or "magnitude" of the independent variable (respectively changing the level when the independent is categorical). If OR < 1 then the odds of the event occurring are *decreased*, while an OR=1 implies that there is no directional association and that odds are equal.

By definition, the OR is an asymmetric non-negative figure, and therefore, due to estimation considerations, the value is transformed to the natural logarithm. The transformed figure is called the logarithmic likelihood, better known as *log odds* of the number. The effect of the transformation is that a small OR, say 0.01, transforms to a negative log odds value, −4.61, while an OR of 1 corresponds to a log odds value of 0. An OR bigger than 1 translates to positive log odds. The effect of the logarithmic transformation is that the interpretation becomes: negative sign = decreased odds, positive sign=increased odds. The scale now has a natural zero-point, implying no association. The disadvantage is that it is hard to think in terms of "the natural logarithm of the odds ratio."

While both the direction and the significance of the effect can be obtained from the logarithmic coefficients (called B in SPSS output), we usually want to transform the coefficients back into the original OR by taking the antilog. SPSS does this automatically and labels the appropriate column Exp(B). See the far right bottom of Table 10.10.

Table 10.11 Exporting and company profit

Firm	Exporting activities/Y (1= Y, 0 = N)	Company growth/X (1=low to 3=high)
1	0	1
2	1	1
3	1	1
4	1	2
5	1	2
6	0	2
7	1	2
8	1	2
9	1	3
10	1	3
11	1	3
12	1	3
13	1	3
14	0	3
15	1	3
16	1	3
17	1	3

Table 10.12 Odds of exporting

Company growth	Exporting (1)	Not exporting (0)	Total	Odds of exporting
1 (Low)	2	1	3	2/1 = 2
2 (Medium)	4	1	5	4/1 = 4
3 (High)	8	1	9	8/1 = 8
Total	14	3	17	

Unfortunately, the output of Table 10.10 is not useful for illustrating the "log odds." However, Table 10.11 below may be used instead: A small sample of companies has been interrogated. The dependent variable (Y) indicates whether the company is exporting (1=yes, 0 = no), while the independent variable measures the sales growth of the company (1=low, 2 = medium and 3 = high – "low" could refer to an annual growth ranging between zero and five percent, and so on). For matters of convenience the companies have been sorted (ascending) according to growth. Table 10.11 lists export activities and growth level. See also Table 10.12. In the far right column of Table 10.12 the odds ratios of exporting across the three levels of company growth are computed.

Note that each time company growth goes up by one level, the odds of exporting doubles or increases by a factor of 2. Consequently, OR is 2.0. Another way to compute odds is by using probabilities. Three firms have low growth, and of these two are exporting, which corresponds to 0.667. For the medium level the probability is 0.8 and for high growth the probability is 0.888. In other words, the higher the company growth the higher the probability is that the company is exporting. Finally, the log odds are found as $\ln(2.0) = 0.693$. The number is positive, which indicates a positive functional relationship between company growth and the tendency to be engaged in exporting.

Table 10.13 Parameter statistics of exporting and company profit example

				Variables in the equation			
		B	S.E.	Wald	df	Sig.	Exp(B)
Step 1	Growth	0.693	0.807	0.737	1	0.391	2.000
	Constant	0.000	1.812	0.000	1	1.000	1.000

[a] Variable entered on step 1: Growth

Another statistic used when assessing logit coefficients is Wald. The Wald statistic is calculated for variables in the model to determine if a variable should be removed. It is analogous to testing the significance of a coefficient in linear regression.[21]

Table 10.13 shows the relevant output from SPSS binary logistic regression based on the data of Table 10.11 (bottom of the output). Again, the reader should check the results.

The odds ratio of 2.0 appears in the far right column entitled Exp(B). The corresponding log odds parameter (0.693) is shown in the first data column. In the present case where the independent variable is interval-scaled, the Wald statistic is found as $B^2/(S.E.)^2$ = $(0.693)^2/(0.807)^2$ = 0.737.[22] Due to the small number of observations used in the numeric example of Table 10.11, the parameter estimate B is not significant (0.391). Moreover, B and Wald of the constant are 0 whereas both the significance level and OR equal unity. This is a coincidence and will not be the case in applied studies.

While statistics on goodness of fit and coefficient significance help us to assess the properties of the model, care must be taken when interpreting the results. As recalled, the final model of Table 10.10 (numeric beer example) provides an excellent overall fit: $-2LL$ is 0.000 and Nagelkerke's R^2 is 1.000 (see the Model summary of Table 10.10). But while the model perfectly fits the data, none of the coefficients (variables in the equation) comes even close to significance. Table 10.10 shows that an excellent model fit is a *necessary but not at all sufficient precondition* of a successful model.

Stepwise approaches to logistic regression are available. They correspond to the stepwise methods discussed earlier in the context of regression and discriminant analysis. SPSS supplies no less than six different algorithms, conditional, Wald, and likelihood ratio, each in a forwards and a backwards version. They will not be discussed in this text, but the underlying rationale resembles that of ordinary stepwise regression (see Appendix 9-D at www.pearsoned.co.uk/schmidt).

In some situations a logit model can be used for an improved targeting of customers in database marketing.[23] Assume that a representative sample of 2,000 respondents have been asked whether they are interested in subscribing to a magazine about fishing. The study reveals some significant differences between non-prospects ($Y=0$) and prospects ($Y=1$). For example, prospects on average live in smaller households, are older, less educated, have lower income, live in rural districts, and 75 percent of them are males. Let us presume that the logit model is able to correctly classify 90 percent of respondents into prospects/non-prospects. Based on the parameters of the logit model the database-marketing firm can define threshold levels concerning the independent or predictor variables and use these levels in a marketing campaign.

Without the logit model, the firm would need to launch a promotional campaign, say, by direct mail, offering a couple of free issues of the magazine by way of a shotgun approach. If no selection criteria are available, all of the 1,600,000 people in the database would receive the marketing letter. If all these potential customers were contacted by mail, the cost of the campaign would be about 1,600,000 customers by €1. This cost must then be compared with the 1.5 percent, or 24,000, of those mailed who typically end up becoming subscribers. In this case, the cost of obtaining one subscriber would be 1,600,000/24,000 = €66.67.

Alternatively, the campaign could be mailed to, say, 320,000 of the database firm's 1,600,000 addresses that satisfy some specified characteristics on household size, age, education, income, residence, gender, etc., as revealed by the logit model.

In this case the logit model may help targeting customers so that only a fifth or 320,000 of the list are mailed, rooted on the findings of the logit model. Based on the model, say, 15 percent of the 320,000 end up as subscribers. In this hypothetical case the campaign would yield 48,000 subscribers based on 320,000 mails, at a cost of €6.67 per subscriber – a much more efficient way of targeting than the shotgun approach. Of course, targeting of the message to prospects necessitates that the database-marketing firm possesses usable background information on all prospects. In many countries, a company's storage and use of detailed databases on individuals is restricted by laws protecting the privacy of the citizen.

Computations that combine estimated logit parameters with background data from a representative sample are beyond the scope of the present text. The interested reader may inspect sources such as Lehmann, Gupta and Steckel (1998, 699–706), and Lattin, Carroll and Green (2003, 487–9).

The present section only covered binary logit, that is, cases were the dependent variable has two levels (like two-group discriminant analysis). However, the problem is extendable to situations were the dependent variable has more than two levels, for instance, were the dependent variable measures which of three or more brands the customer has purchased at subsequent occasions. Or which of selected export markets are best suited for launching or pilot-testing a product. As noted, SPSS has several procedures for handling such problems, such as *[Regression, Multinomial Logistic]*. As often is the case when extending the coverage of a rather comprehensive topic, running the analysis and understanding the output necessitate considerable skills. The student is encouraged to inspect the texts introduced earlier in this section (they all appear in the reference list).

Appendix A on the website introduces several real life sample data sets. One of them is called Export Manager Survey. The respondents of this survey are 456 export managers. The questionnaire contains a lot of variables that are suitable for running the analyses introduced in this chapter. It can also be used for analyses in the next chapter.

The raw data file Export_Manager_Surey.sav is in a SPSS file format and can be downloaded from www.pearsoned.co.uk/schmidt. The reader should note that saving the file in Excel format will delete the explaining labels connected to the variables and levels.

10.3 Summary

In many empirical settings, the dependent variable is not metric or interval-scaled but is instead nominal/categorical-scaled. When the dependent measure is, say, preferred brand, country of origin, or marital status then neither ANOVA nor regression analysis apply. In such a situation discriminant analysis might be an option. According to this method the dependent variable is assumed to be nominal-scaled – typically consisting of a few groups, categories or classes – whilst the independent measures (e.g. income, age) are metric/interval scaled – just like in regression. If the dependent variable is binary (e.g. female/male or customer/non-customer) the analysis is called two-groups discriminant analysis. When the dependent variable has several levels (e.g. marital status, country of origin, brands A/B/C/D) the analysis is called multiple discriminant analysis (MDA).

A discriminant analysis model aims to separate the groups by way of the independent variables. The successfulness of the discriminant model can be evaluated when inspecting the classification table. This table, which can be deducted from the model or be requested as part of the program output in SPSS, SAS, etc., shows how big a percentage of cases the estimated linear discriminant model is able to classify correctly, given the specific dataset and the frequency distribution of the nominal response variable. Correct classifications appear along the main diagonal while all other cells represent misclassifications.

The number of correct classifications must then be compared with the number of correct classifications that one would expect, provided that the data set had been generated by a random number generator. In any case, the performance of a classification table tends to be inflated. This is because the model is based solely on the data set under scrutiny. A generalizable discriminant model must be able to perform clearly better than chance when used for classifying a sample of cases that has not been used for establishing the model. This new sample is called holdout sample if it was part of the study but was ignored when estimating the model whereas a validating sample assumes that the data emanate from a separate sample.

A stepwise discriminant analysis is similar to stepwise regression and it helps the analyst to focus only on those independent variables that have statistically significant influence on the dependent variable.

Like other models, the discriminant model is based on certain algorithmic assumptions. For instance, the covariances of the categories must be equal across all dependent variables. If the distributional characteristics (i.e. the variances) vary noticeably between, say customers of brand A, B, and C – then discriminant analysis is not an option. Separate measures for testing for equality of covariances (e.g. Box's M) are available.

A discriminant analysis is suited to situations where the dependent variable is nominal/categorical-scaled while the independents are metric/interval-scaled. But sometimes the dependent variable is nominal-scaled while one or several independent measures are also nominal-scaled. For instance, when the dependent measure is country of origin and when the list of predictors contains variables such as gender, marital status or occupational status.

In situations where the discriminant models is not applicable because assumptions are violated, the analyst should use a logistic regression. As long as the dependent variable has only two levels (e.g. customers/non-customers, native/foreign) the model is called a binary logistic regression (logit). If more levels of the dependent are involved, it is called multi-nominal logit. A related method with slightly different modelling assumptions concerning the error term is called binary or (multinominal) probit.

The advantage of logit models is that they are quite robust with regard to the scaling of the independent variables and therefore they can be employed in situations where discriminant analysis is not applicable. The disadvantage is that a logistic regression is based not on the usual ordinary least squares regression (OLS) but on a maximum likelihood regression (ML), which performs a logarithmic transformation of the dependent variable. This implies some complications. For instance, model fit statistics such as R-square are not available. Some pseudo statistics such as $-2LL$, Cox and Snell and Nagelkerke do exist though. In logistic regression, estimates are not as straightforward to understand as they are in OLS regression ("a unit change in $X1$ transforms to a 0.35 unit change in the scale of Y"). Instead, one must perceive the parameters rather as tendencies, elasticities or probabilities.

One way of interpreting logit coefficients concerns the odds ratio (OR). An $OR > 1$ implies that the odds of an event occurring ($Y=1$ instead of $Y=0$) *increase* when increasing the value or "magnitude" of the independent variable (X). If $OR < 1$ then the odds of the event occurring are *decreased*. The natural logarithm of the OR is called log odds. An OR value less than 1 transforms into a negative log-odds value, an OR of 1.0 becomes a log-odds figure of 0.0 and an OR greater than 1 turns into a positive log-odds value.

Questions

1. The table below once more displays the small numerical example data set used for regression analysis (Table 9.14). In the same table we have twice been recoding values of the dependent variable Y_1. In column IIa, values of Y_1/II have been recoded so that 3, 4, and 5 are transformed to 1 while 1 and 2 are transformed to 0. In IIb, 4 and 5 from II are recoded as 1, while 1, 2 and 3 are recoded as 0. Columns IIa and IIb are coded so that they can serve as dependent or class variable in a two-group discriminant analysis. As before, X_2 (Revenue) and X_3 (Years of domestic operation) are treated as predictor variables. But $Y_{1\text{-liberal}}$ is now a dependent measure with two levels or categories $0 =$ unwilling and $1 =$ willing to export (the same with $Y_{1\text{-conservative}}$). The only difference between $Y_{1\text{-liberal}}$ and $Y_{1\text{-conservative}}$ is that the latter measure has a higher threshold level, 3 versus 2, with regard to when willingness on a five-point scale transforms to willingness on a 0/1 scale. Now, run a discriminant analysis using SPSS. Use the same options as shown in Section 10.1. Use data from column IIa and IIb respectively, as dependent measures. Compare the two outputs with regard to (i) predictor variable importance and (ii) classification properties. Which run is most successful? Assume that the sample was big and representative: which of the two recoding principles would you recommend and why? Would your recommendations always be the same, regardless of other exogenous variables?

2. Using the same data, now run two binary logistic regressions. Compare the two logistic regression models with regard to overall model fit and coefficient significance. Which run would you regard most successful and why?

3. Finally, compare all four outputs obtained (two discriminant and two logistic regressions) with the original regression analysis output (Table 9.12). Which comparisons can be made between the regression output and the output from the discriminant analysis and from logistic regression?

I	II	IIa	IIb	III	IV
Obs	Y_1	$Y_{1\text{-liberal}}$	$Y_{1\text{-conservative}}$	X_2	X_3
1	5	1	1	4.0	6.5
2	3	1	0	2.0	6.0
3	2	0	0	2.0	5.8
4	4	1	1	1.0	7.0
5	5	1	1	3.0	6.5
6	1	0	0	0.9	5.0
7	2	0	0	0.9	5.0
8	3	1	0	3.6	6.5
9	3	1	0	0.9	6.0
10	2	0	0	0.9	6.0

References

Aldrich, J. H. and Nelson, F. D. (1985) *Linear Probability, Logit, and Probit Models*, Sage: Beverly Hills, CA.

Borooah, V. K. (2001) *Logit and Probit: Ordered and multinomial models*. Sage: Beverly Hills, CA.

Costanza, M. C. and Afifi, A. A. (1979) "Comparison of stopping rules in forward stepwise Discriminant Analysis," *Journal of the American Statistical Association*. Vol. 74, 777–85.

Cox, D. R. and Snell, E. J. (1989) *The Analysis of Binary Data*, Chapman and Hall, London.

DeMaris, A. (1992) *Logit Modeling: practical applications*. Sage: Beverly Hills, CA.

Dillon, W. R. and Goldstein, M. (1984) *Multivariate Analysis: Methods and applications*. John Wiley, New York. 380.

Fenwick, I. (1979) "Techniques in market measurement: the jackknife." *Journal of Marketing Research*. Vol. 16, August. 110–14.

Goldstein, M. (1978) *Discrete Discriminant Analysis*, Wiley, New York.

Green, P. E. (1978) *Analyzing Multivariate Data*. Dryden Press, Hinsdale, IL. (142–89 and 290–317).

Green, P. E., Tull, D. S. and Albaum, G. (1988) *Research for Marketing Decisions.* Prentice-Hall, Englewood-Cliffs, NJ. 512–26.

Hair, J. F., Anderson, F. E., Tatham, R. L. and Black, W. C. (1998) *Multivariate Data Analysis.* Prentice-Hall, Upper Saddle River, NJ.

Hosmer, D. W. and Lemeshow, S. (2000) *Applied Logistic Regression.* John Wiley, NY.

Johnston, J. and Dinardo, J. (1997) *Econometric Methods.* McGraw-Hill, New York. Chapter 5.

Klecka, W. R. (1980) *Discriminant Analysis.* Sage, Beverly Hills, CAL.

Koehler, G. J. and Erenguc, S. S. (1990) "Minimizing misclassifications in linear Discriminant Analysis," *Decision Sciences.* Vol. 21, no. 1. 63–85.

Lachenbruch, P. A. (1975) *Discriminant Analysis*, Macmillan, London.

Lattin, J., Carroll, J. D. and Green, P. E. (2003) *Analyzing Multivariate Data.* Thomson, London. 442–46.

Lehmann, D. R. (1985) *Marketing Research and Analysis.* Irwin, Homewood, IL. 682–85.

Lehmann, D. R., Gupta, S. and Steckel, J. H. (1998) *Marketing Research.* Addison Wesley, Reading, MA. 691.

Menard, S. (2001) *Applied Logistic Regression Analysis.* Sage, Beverly Hills, CA.

Moroney, M. J. (1951) *Facts from Figures.* Penguin, Harmondsworth, Middlesex (UK). 319.

Morris, D. (2001) *The Naked Ape.* Trafalgar Square (VT).

Morrison, D. G. (1969) "On the interpretation of discriminant analysis." *Journal of Marketing Research.* Vol. 6. 156–63.

Mosteller, F. M. and Bush, R. R. (1954) "Selected quantitative techniques," in Lindzey, G. (ed.) *Handbook of Social Psychology*, Addison-Wesley, Reading, MA. 289–334.

Nagelkerke, N. J. D. (1991) "A note on a general definition of the coefficient of determination," *Biometrika.* Vol. 78, no. 3. 691–2.

Pampel, F. C. (2000) *Logistic Regression – A primer.* Sage, Beverly Hills, CA.

Pindyck, R. S. and Rubinfeld, D. L. (1998) *Econometric Models and Economic Forecasts.* McGraw-Hill, Boston, MA.

SAS/STAT Version 6, 4th edn, (1989). SAS Institute, Cary (NC).

SPSS Advanced Statistics 7.5. (1997). SPSS Inc., Chicago (IL).

End notes

[1] The two groups' variances on both X_1 (10.0) and X_2 (13.2) as well as their covariance (8.0) are identical (the covariance matrices are the same). This is a coincidence and represents a very unusual case. However, according to theory, pooling of the two groups' covariance matrices is only allowable if they are equal! More on this critical assumption in Section 10.2.

[2] Assumed that one has licensed SPSS's *Trends*, the main analysis toolbar contains a *[Time Series]* facility. Moreover, SPSS supplies advanced specialized modules for forecasting like *[Decision Time]* and *[What If]*.

[3] If the dependent variable does *not* exhibit equal levels of variance across the range of predictor variables, heteroscedasticity is said to exit. Such a situation is undesirable because the variance of the dependent variable being explained in the dependence relationship appears to be concentrated in only a limited range of independent values. Tests for homoscedasticity are available in most statistical software. Usually, such tests assume that the dependent measure is metric scaled, which is not the case in discriminant analysis. However, specific tests like Bartlett's and Box's M are available. They are briefly discussed in Section 10.2.

[4] Unlike in procedures like ANOVA, SPSS will not accept that the category or grouping variable is in string mode (text). This is because the grouping variable is assumed to have a defined range.

[5] In SPSS's data screen window, change from *[Data-View]* to *[Variable-View]* in the lower, left corner. Next, click the right part of the cell, where the row of the appropriate variable (i.e. country) crosses the *[Values]* column. Clicking it provokes a *[Value Labels]* dialogue box. Here you tap *1* for *[Value]* and 'British' for *[Value Label]*, then [Add]. This procedure has to be repeated for all levels. Finally, click *[OK]*. You can also connect labels to variables. This can be done by plugging in text in the appropriate cell in the *[Label]* column just left of the *[Values]* column. Label-text appears in the output but not in the input. Using labels can refine output and facilitate understanding, provided you want to export (i.e. using copy/paste) SPSS output to a word-processor, a spreadsheet, or to presentation software. *Warning:* Excel does *not* support SPPS labels and values. So, if you work in SPSS, while using labels and values to refine your data, saving your work in .xls format is *not* possible. If you do it and reload the file into SPSS, your values and labels are gone forever. You can, however, cut and paste the label column from SPSS to Excel.

[6] The program wants to know which levels you wish to analyze. Sometimes one may not be interested in analyzing all levels simultaneously. For instance, if your grouping variable contains eight countries or twelve brands, you might want to only analyze the countries you find most promising, or the brands you regard as your primary competitors. If this is the case, you want to select only the appropriate levels for scrutiny. Note, that the analyzed categories must go from minimum to maximum (the two ends of a continuum). If you want to analyze levels 1, 2, and 4, but not 3, then you must remove level 3 before running the analysis. This can be accomplished by clicking *[Data]* on SPSS's main menu bar. Then click *[Select Cases ...]*, change the radio button to *[If condition is satisfied]*. Click the *[If]* button. A "calculator-like" dialogue box or display appears. Here you can easily remove unwanted levels. In the present case the simple operator syntax "y<3 or y>3" keeps levels 1, 2 and 4 while 3 is excluded. Note that the data editor now contains a new dummy-scaled filter-variable (filter_$) that keeps track of your selection. The *[Select Cases]* option is a powerful tool, but should be treated with caution. Do not forget to tab *[Select Cases, Select All Cases]* as soon as you have finished analyzing the subset. Otherwise SPSS assumes that you want to perform subsequent analyses using the same subset of data.

[7] The reader can easily check this. Click *[Analyze]*, *[General Linear Model, Univariate]*, then drag X1 into the *[Dependent variable field]*, and drag Y into the *[Fixed Factors]* field. *[OK]*. The output table contains the F-value of 25,000. Repeating the operation, this time with X2 as dependent measure, provides an F-value of 3.030.

[8] Wilks' Lambda is the multivariate analogue to the K-samples test. Generally, the measure is the determinant of the pooled within-groups sum-of-squares and cross products matrix (SSCP) divided by the determinant of the total sample SSCP matrix. Statistics such as *Hotelling's T^2* and *Mahalanobis D^2* can be perceived as special cases of Wilks' Lambda. Details in Green (1978), 259–60 and 291–94.

[9] Here $F(X_1)$ is computed as (all numbers from Table 10.2):

Among groups sum of squares:

$$\left[\frac{(2+3+4+5+6)^2+(7+8+9+10+11)^2}{5}-\left(\frac{(2+3+4+5+6+7+8+9+10+11)^2}{10}\right)\right]=62.5$$

Within groups sum of squares:

$$\left(2^2+3^2+4^2+5^2+6^2+7^2+8^2+9^2+10^2+11^2\right)-\left(\frac{(2+3+4+5+6)^2+(7+8+9+10+11)^2}{5}\right)=20.0$$

Now $F_{1,8}=[(62.5/1)/(20/8)]=25.0$ where "1" refers to $g-1$ and "8" refers to $n-g$ and there are two groups and ten observations.

[10] The reader may recall that, when encountering the *[Classify]* dialogue box, the default option on *[Prior Probabilities]* was changed from *[All groups equal]* to *[Compute from group sizes]*. As mentioned, this is because the program must be told to adjust the discriminant function for differences in previous probabilities. Assume that in Table 10.2 observations 1, 2, and 10 had been Danish, while 3–9 had been British (leaving X_1 and X_2 values unchanged). In this case the group sizes are not equal: 70 percent are British and only 30 percent Danish. Performing the run in SPSS with *[All groups equal]* provides 60 percent correct classifications. Changing option to *[Compute from group sizes]* raises the percentage of correct classifications to 70 percent. Another approach would be to use the proportional chance criterion (Morrison, 1969): $p^2+(1-p)^2$, here $0.7^2+0.3^2$ $=0.58(\%)$. However, presuming that everyone belongs to the largest group (that is, everyone is assumed to be British) yields 70 percent correct classifications (!) – a percentage equalling SPSS's performance when choosing *[Compute from group sizes]*. Note once more that the example is small and artificial. However, if correct classification is more important than variable/dimension reduction, it is recommended to use group sizes that are *approximately* equal (merging subgroups before analysis could help). Statistics for testing the significance between obtained classification and chance-based criteria have been developed (Lehmann, 1985, 682–5). But their methodological justification is questionable when group sizes are not equal. For a brief and concise discussion on classification issues, see Green (1978), 183–85. It should be stressed that one may find differences between group means that are highly significant according to the so-called Mahalanobis distance *[Analyze, Classify, Discriminant, Use Stepwise Method, Method]* and yet find that the discriminant function is unsuccessful at classifying objects. What has been said up to now on classification *only applies to two-group classifications*. If more than two groups are involved then one will need to consult advanced texts (see the References list). SPSS easily handles more than two group classifications, but a numerical demonstration of the formulas, is beyond the scope of this book.

[11] In the numerical example of Tables 10.2 and 10.3 this condition was perfectly met. The covariances of the two groups were in fact identical:

Y		X_1	X_2
1	X_1	2.5	2.0
	X_2	2.0	3.3
2	X_1	2.5	2.0
	X_2	2.0	3.0

[12] The Box's M test assumes multivariate normality and is supposedly very sensitive. This means that a high p value will be a good, although informal, indicator of equality, while a highly significant result (low p value) may in practical terms be a too-sensitive indicator of inequality.

[13] In the present example, computing the simpler Bartlett's chi-square yields the same value, 11.546 (it has 3 degrees of freedom). Therefore, what SPSS actually does, is compute Bartlett's chi square and then transforms it to a value in the F-distribution (2.805). The net difference between Bartlett's statistics and Box's M, also known as the gamma-correction factor (confusing because ρ is the Greek character rho) – the value 0.72916667 in Table 10.9 – is not included in the computation of Box's M by SPSS. Including the correction factor in the numerical example gives a Box's M of $(0.72916667)(11.546) = 8.42$. For large samples with more than, say a hundred observations, the practical effect of the correction term will be negligible, since the uncorrected term will have to be multiplied with 0.99 or so. As can be seen from the ρ-formula in Table 10.9: (1) everything else being equal, if n approaches infinity, the correction term approaches unity; (2) likewise, if the number of groups increases, the correction term moves toward unity – in both cases the correction term has no effect on the outcome; (3) however, if the number of predictor variables increases, everything else being equal, the correction term becomes negative. Since negative values do not make sense in an F-distribution, the corrected Box's M cannot be computed.

[14] Note though, that SPSS's *[Analyze, Regression, Binary Logistic]* provides two stepwise 'conditional' procedures, one backward and one forward.

[15] See advanced econometric texts such as Johnston and Dinardo (1997, Chapter 5) and Pindyck and Rubinfeld (1997, Appendix 2.2. for General ML and Appendix 11.1 for applying ML to logit and probit models).

[16] For more on logit choice models, Lehmann et al. (1998) 691–715; Hair, Anderson, Tatham and Black (1998) 239–325; Lattin, Carol and Green (2003) 474–525, These texts have a broad perspective, such as marketing research (Lehmann et al.) or multivariate analysis (Lattin et al. and Hair et al.) and coverage of logit models is limited. For an in-depth treatment, see: Aldrich and Nelson (1985), DeMaris (1992), Hosmer and Lemeshow (2000), Pampel (2000), Borooah (2001), and Menard (2001).

[17] SPSS supplies than six procedures for logit problems: binary logistic; multinomial logistic regression; probit analysis; general loglinear analysis; logit loglinear analysis; and model selection loglinear analysis.

[18] What in most other SPSS procedures is called a metric scaled 'independent' variable is called a 'covariate' here. To make things even more confusing, what we would usually label a categorical or dummy coded independent variable, is named a 'factor' in *[Multinomial Logistic]* while it is entitled a 'categorical covariate' in *[Binary Logistic]*. SPSS supplies a 'patchwork' of procedures that handle logit choice problems: apart from the two just mentioned, there is a *[Probit]* procedure amongst the *[Regression]* subgroup of procedures. In the *[Probit]* dialogue box, one can request a *[Logit]* model! Moreover, in the *[Loglinear]* subgroup, there is a *[Logit]* model. In its dialogue box, one also has to bother with defining a 'contrast variable' – a categorical variable whose three or more levels are recoded as several 0/1 scaled variables (in a way a binary coded covariate). Furthermore, in *[Loglinear, General]* one can request *[Multinomial]*!

[19] The 'non-appropriate' discriminant analysis also manages to classify all ten observations correctly – as does the naked eye. If X_1 is the abscissa and X_{2new} the ordinate axis, then a perpendicular line between 6 and 7 on the X_1 axis correctly separates the 10 observations into the two groups.

[20] Note that $LL(0) = n \times \ln(2_1) = 10 \times (0.69315) = 6.9315$.

[21] However, Wald is biased when the coefficient "B" is large and has a tendency to accept a false null hypothesis, that is, sometimes the test fails to identify "truly" significant coefficients (see Pindyck and Rubinfeld (1997) 283–4.

[22] If the independent variable is categorical-scaled the computation is a bit more complex. The interested reader will need to inspect advanced and specialized texts that are mentioned in the References like Hosmer and Leneshow (2000), Pampel (2000) or Menard (2001).

[23] The same can be done by way of a Discriminant Analysis, provided that hypothesis of equality of covariance matrices is accepted. However, if the study is based on several hundred observations or more, the test will often result in a rejection of H-0 (Green, 1978, 170).

11 Profiling customers: factor analysis

Learning objectives

After studying this chapter you should be able to:

- Explain similarities between factor analysis and cluster analysis.
- Describe the purpose of conducting a factor analysis.
- Differentiate between a factor and a variable.
- Explain principles for deciding on the number of factors to extract.
- Understand why a rotation of factors often facilitates an interpretation.
- Outline how factor analysis can be used as input for an advertising strategy.
- Show how to run a factor analysis in SPSS.

11.1 Introduction: common aspects of factor and cluster analysis

This chapter covers factor analysis and Chapter 12 deals with its "inverse cousin," cluster analysis. What the two methods have in common is that they both perform categorizing or summarization of the data matrix: factor analysis categorizes the columns or variables (objects) of the data matrix while cluster analysis categorizes the rows or observations (subjects). See panels (a) and (c) in Figure 11.1.

Another important methodological characteristic uniting factor analysis and cluster analysis is that there is no assumption about a dependent-independent variable relationship. Recall that all methods discussed in Chapters 9 and 10 hypothesized a kind of relationship between a set of predictors ($X1, X2 \ldots Xn$) and a dependent variable (Y). The difference between the methods was related to how the variables were scaled (interval, nominal, etc.) and how well the data fitted or matched the underlying assumptions of the model's algorithm (deviations from normality, homogeneity of variances, heteroscedasticity, etc.).

In factor analysis and cluster analysis we have no pre-specified conjecture or theory about how to partition the data matrix into subsets of predictor and criterion variables. Instead, research interest centres on the whole set of interdependence relationships.

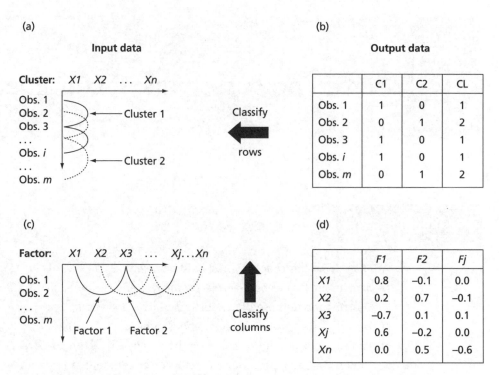

Figure 11.1 Relatedness of multivariate methods: cluster analysis and factor analysis

Many textbooks use the terms independence methods and dependence methods for distinguishing between different multivariate methods (some use the term interdependence instead of independence). In dependence methods such as ANOVA and regression, the involved algorithm assumes that there is one (or several) dependent variable(s) and one or several independent variables, whereas in independence methods such as factor and cluster analysis such assumptions are not made.

In factor and cluster analysis the data are "allowed to speak for themselves:" the establishment of the model is based on the specific data set under scrutiny. While this analytical strategy has definite merits, especially in the early phases of a research effort (say, when managers knows very little about consumers' attitudes towards a new product), it has one disadvantage: the generalizability of results may be a cause of concern. Whenever a specific data set is the sole feeder for a general model (without a pre-specified theory on relationships amongst variables), then this model's parameters (coefficients) are *completely* determined by the characteristics of this data set. If this data set is somehow atypical for the population, the estimated model most probably will be corrupt and its predictive properties will be invalidated.

Due to the above methodological differences compared with other multivariate methods, factor analysis and cluster analysis belong to the class of **independence methods**, while the methods covered in the two previous chapters (ANOVA, ordinary regression, discriminant analysis and logistic regression) are **dependence methods**.

In both factor analysis and cluster analysis the data matrix has n variables and m columns. Usually, the data will be interval-scaled. However, algorithms and software exist for handling data that are not interval-scaled. For example, if data are nominal or categorical-scaled and the researcher wants to analyze independence relationships among variables, the appropriate technique is a **latent structure analysis** (Lazarsfeld and Henry, 1968), if the data are ordinal-scaled, a suitable method is **non-metric factor analysis** (Lingoes and Guttmann, 1967; Kruskal and Shepard, 1974). There is more about **latent class analysis** in Chapter 15.

The SAS/STAT package has a procedure called Prinqual that is dedicated to factor analysis of non-metric data. These qualitative extensions of ordinary factor analysis will not be discussed in the present text. Readers interested in learning more about such problems should inspect the reference list at the end of this chapter.

The input variables to factor analysis or cluster analysis could be, say, 100 lifestyle statements (e.g. 'I prefer native brands to foreign brands' and scaled from 1 = totally agree to 5 = totally disagree) and then there could be 1,000 observations (e.g. filled in questionnaires gathered from survey respondents).

While the purpose of factor analysis is to categorize variables into subgroups or 'clusters' of variables sharing common characteristics, cluster analysis aims at categorizing observations into subsets of observations with common or similar response profiles. In factor analysis, a subgroup is called a **factor**, a **dimension** or a **principal component** while in cluster analysis a subgroup is just called a **cluster**.

The output of factor analysis is a matrix or table where the columns are the so-called factors while the rows are the variables (cell entries are confined to the interval from -1.0 to $+1.0$). The output of cluster analysis can be regarded or structured as a matrix where the columns are clusters while the rows are observations (cell entries can take on two states, *either* 0, non-member, *or* 1, member). See the first two data columns in panel (b), in Figure 11.1. Therefore, cluster analysis is a laterally reversed or inversed factor analysis. Indeed, methods exist that can cluster-analyze the variables (SAS's Proc Varclus works that way), and factor analyze the observations (a Q-type factor analysis).

In practice, the output of cluster analysis often appears as an extra column or data vector (sometimes called **cluster variable**) that is added to the input data at the far right end (or as the nth$+1$ variable). Thus, each observation is assigned a cluster number. This is illustrated in the far right column of panel (b) in Figure 11.1. Note that column CL has a value of 1 where C1 has a value of 1 while CL has a value of 2 when C2 has a value of 0.

Factor and cluster analysis are both statistical methods. Within a marketing setting the term "market segments" is often used instead of "clusters", and the terms are interchangeable. Simultaneously, there is a tendency to deduce or imply from "factors" to "most important issues" or "critical phenomena". While factor and cluster analysis are statistical techniques, the analyst is usually more interested in learning about the nature of the data and in uncovering hidden patterns than in statistical inference (while methods for statistical inference exist, however, they are seldom used due to lack of operational relevance).

Basically, the two techniques originate from different methodological algorithms and usually they serve unlike aims. From panels (c) and (d) of Figure 11.1 differences can be seen. First, the cell values concerning columns F1 and F2 in panel (d) are metric and all values fall within the range of -1 and 1, while cell values in columns C1 and C2 of panel (b) are dichotomous-scaled (dummy-coded) and restricted to two states, 0 and 1. Note also, that the far right columns in panels (b) and (d) differ. Values in column Fj of panel (d) resembles columns F1 and F2, while column CL of panel (b) is just a recoding or summarization of columns C1 and C2. As will be shown later, the cell value 0.8 concerning *X1* in column F1 of panel (d) is the simple correlation of the variable *X1* with the principal component, or most important dimension, F1 (since correlations can be negative, some cells in panel (d) are also negative). Using the notation of factor analysis, these correlations are called 'factor loading' (more on that later).

The difference between factor and cluster analysis in the way they are treated here may be summarized as follows:

1. In cluster analysis a subject (typically a respondent) can only be member of one subset (cluster) at a time. Thus mutual exclusivity amongst clusters is assumed. Note that observations that have the value '1' on C1 have a '0' on C2 (and vice versa). Indeed, since most cluster analysis methods are exclusive or non-overlapping, the observations of panel (b) can only possess the state '1' on a single cluster, and then by definition they assume the state '0' on all other cluster variables.
2. In factor analysis an object (typically a variable) is represented in different subsets (factors) by a weight (correlation or factor loading). Thus exclusivity among factors is not a necessity. It also holds that the data in each row when squared add to unity, thus $(0.8)^2 + (-0.1)^2 + \ldots + (0.2)^2 = 1.0$.

This chapter is dedicated to factor analysis. Appendix 11-A and Appendix 11-B (see www.pearsoned.co.uk/schmidt) address selected technical issues related to the method. Chapter 12 deals with cluster analysis.

11.2 Introductory aspects of factor analysis

Assume that the managers of a middle-sized bank are interested in learning more about how customers perceive different aspects of the bank's image and the service it offers. How important are different issues and is it possible to rank or order groups of issues based on the respondents' responses? Perhaps, several issues (variables) may be regarded as referring to or to be reflections of the same underlying dimension or 'super-variable'.

Since the managers are eager to shed light on the problem, they produce a questionnaire of 15 statements or image issues. All statements or items are arranged as in Table 11.1. Technically the scaling used is called a seven-point semantic differential. Moreover, it is bipolar, which means that respondents must choose a number, indicating different states of intensity in opinion between the two extremes. Below we show a sample of three items or variables that are used in the bank image case (we will use this example several times

Table 11.1 A response to the questionnaire

My bank is (has)...	1	2	3	4	5	6	7	
X1 Modern				X				Old-fashioned bank
X4 Interesting window displays	X							Uninteresting window displays
X8 Stagnant bank						X		Dynamic bank

Table 11.2 Selected bivariate correlations

	Variable	Correlation with X2 (friendly)
X1	Modern	0.65
X6	Successful	0.57
X7	Providing good advice	0.64
X8	Stagnant	−0.51
X9	Kind	0.72
X14	A bank for me	0.62

in this chapter). The response in Table 11.1 indicates that the respondent thinks her/his bank is quite modern (2), that its window displays are very interesting (1) and that the bank is quite dynamic and not stagnant (6).

The questionnaire is sent to a small random sample of respondents (all of them customers) and the day after they are phoned by an employee, who encourages them to participate in this customer survey. As an incentive, respondents are credited €5 in their account, provided that she or he returns a completed questionnaire. Within a week, the bank receives 114 responses.

First, a correlation analysis is done based on the data file containing the responses. Unfortunately, the analysis of correlations becomes cumbersome as the number of variables included grows. With 15 variables, a matrix that includes all pairwise correlations has 105 cells. And if the study contains 200 variables (which is not uncommon), then a full correlation matrix has 19,900 cells. Generally, if we have n items in a list, the number of pairwise comparisons equals $[n(n-1)]/2$.

Table 11.2 shows a small number of the 105 correlations in the banking case. From now on a variable is denoted by only referring to the left side of the semantic scale (so, variable 1 becomes just "modern").

Note that all six variables correlate highly with $X2$ (friendly). For the moment, let a correlation of 0.5 or more be regarded as "high". Basically, any correlation between variables is an indication of redundancy or "double counting." Only when variables are completely uncorrelated (when $r_{xy} = 0$) is there no "double counting" of information or shared variance at all. In the bank case, the correlation between $X1$/modern and $X2$/friendly is 0.65 implying that the two variables have almost two-thirds of the variance in common. In other words, there is a 65 percent "overlap" or tendency to tab in similar numbers on the 1–7 scale when answering $X1$ and $X2$.

Due to the double counting of variance there is a serious disadvantage linked to ordinary pairwise or bivariate correlation analysis. According to Table 11.2, $X1$ correlates 0.65 with $X2$ while $X6$ correlates 0.57 with $X2$. However, to discover how $X1$ correlates with $X6$, the full correlations table will have to be inspected with all 105 pairwise correlations (or 19,900 correlations with 200 variables).

In SPSS, the printout from *[Analyze, Correlate, Bivariate]* is organized such that with fifteen variables it fills three pages and has 225 cells. Since the matrix is symmetric with unities along the main diagonal (a variable correlates 1 with itself), only 105 correlations are unique but each cell by default contains three figures (the Pearson correlation, a two-tailed significance test and the sample size for the comparison).

Unfortunately, the size of the output grows exponentially when increasing number of input variables: the comparable printout when running a problem with 200 variables will be 480 pages.

This is where factor analysis comes in. Indeed, factor analysis was developed for handling situations where the researcher wants to analyze relations and interactions between variables in cases where many – usually interval-scaled – variables are involved. Factor analysis facilitates an understanding of the data analysis problem by reorganizing and reducing the amount of output. Therefore, the method is also known as a **data-reduction technique**. The idea is to structure the explained variance and present it in a table in such a way that there is no redundancy or double-counting of variance. The process of factor analysis aims to discard as much as possible of the *quantitative* amount of the data, as measured by the variables, and at the same time keep as much as possible of the *qualitative* characteristic of the data, as measured by the variance explained and as indicated by the – yet to be introduced – factors.

The idea behind factor analysis is to reorganize the data and to establish a matrix or table where the correlations of the involved variables are to be compared, not with another variable like *X2* above, but with something new, which we could regard as a 'super variable'. This 'super variable' – usually called a factor, a principal component or a dimension – is computed by way of subsequent steps involving mathematical and statistical procedures.

Alas, covering the more technical aspects of factor analysis necessitates some knowledge of matrix algebra, which few students possess. Therefore – in contrast to ANOVA and regression in Chapters 9 and 10 – we will not provide a complete technical introduction to the method by way of a small numerical example. In the next section a numerical example is nevertheless introduced. However, the detailed statistical computations have been placed in Appendix 11-A (see www.pearsoned.co.uk/schmidt). The reader who wants to get a better insight into the technical aspects of the method is encouraged to read this appendix.

Table 11.3 shows excerpts from the output of a factor analysis based on the banking case.

Consider how Table 11.3 differs from Table 11.2:

■ The column heading ("Correlation with X2/friendly") has changed and now has two columns, Factor 1 and Factor 2.

Table 11.3 Factor analysis of the bank data

	Variables	*Factor 1*	*Factor 2*
X1	Modern	0.76	0.16
X2	Friendly	0.82	0.16
X6	Successful	0.77	0.20
X7	Good advice	0.77	0.42
X8	Stagnant	−0.75	−0.17
X9	Kind	0.80	0.21
X12	Good housing advice	0.31	0.77
X13	No good tax advice	−0.12	−0.87
X14	A bank for me	0.76	0.24

- The variable "*X2*/Friendly" that was a column heading in Table 11.2 has now changed its place and appears aligned with the other variables in a row.
- Table 11.3 contains two new variables, *X12* and *X13*.
- Finally, the numbers in the cells differ.

Take a closer look at the numbers appearing in Table 11.3. It turns out that a cell entry, say 0.76, is a simple correlation of *X1* and the newly established but yet-to-be-explained Factor 1.[1] What currently confuses us is that we do not know what *Factor 1* represents. It was no problem for us to understand what a correlation of 0.65 between *X1* (modern) and *X2* (friendly) means.

But how do we explain a correlation between a variable that has a name that we can refer to, and a Factor 1 that has no name referring to its meaning? The trick is that we must ourselves – by way of our own interpretation – give the factor a name. But how do we do that?

In factor analysis, it is usual to name a correlation between a variable and a factor for a **factor loading** or an **indicator loading**. Technically, it is a simple correlation and consequently the loading – like a correlation – has a value between -1 and $+1$.

Since Table 11.3 contains nine variables, an inspection of all possible correlations involves the examination of thirty-six cells. Assume for a moment that we choose to skip the investigation of the thirty-six pair correlations and instead concentrate on making sense of the two factors. This task is made possible by using the information provided by the factor loadings and especially by looking at relations between them.

We note that seven variables in Table 11.3 have high loadings (better than 0.5) on Factor 1. They are: *modern, friendly, successful, good advice, (not) stagnant, kind, a bank for me*. One of these loadings (*stagnant*) has a negative sign indicating a negative correlation between the variable and the factor. We correct for this by letting a negation precede the word.

Despite being involved in the analysis of a statistical problem, it is now time for some creativity. We must try to identify and uncover the "supervariable" or factor that simultaneously correlates highly with the seven variables mentioned above. Suppose we were asked to substitute the terms *modern, friendly, successful, good advice, (not) stagnant, kind, a bank for me* with one single term. How could we "summarize" the seven terms? Well, none of them is very specific. Indeed all of them deal with broad image aspects (and all but one have a positive value orientation). Couldn't we agree upon a summarizing term like *Customer-oriented service* as a description of the seven variables? If we can, then we have a name for Factor 1!

But the interpretation of Table 11.3 is not finished yet, because Factor 2 needs a name. Only two variables – *X12* and *X13* – possess high loadings on Factor 2 (0.77 and -0.87 respectively). Interestingly, the same two variables did not have high loadings on Factor 1 (0.31 and -0.12). This is a general tendency in factor analysis: it is impossible for a single variable to have very high loadings on (correlations with) two or more factors simultaneously. Why? Because factors by definition are uncorrelated. Assume that *X1* in Table 11.3 correlated perfectly (1.0) with Factor 1 and Factor 2 at the same time. Consequently, the correlation between Factor 1 and Factor 2 would also have to be 1.0. But this correlation is *always* 0.0.

Table 11.4 Factor analysis of the bank data

Variables		Factor 1	Factor 2
X1	Modern	0.76	0.16
X2	Friendly	0.82	0.16
X6	Successful	0.77	0.20
X7	Good advice	0.77	0.42
X8	Stagnant	−0.75	−0.17
X9	Kind	0.80	0.21
X12	Good housing advice	0.31	0.77
X13	No good tax advice	−0.12	−0.87
X14	A bank for me	0.76	0.24
Name given to factor:		Customer orientation	Financial advice
Percent of variance explained		56%	11%

It can also be shown that the following holds: concerning each variable (in each row) the sum of all squared loadings is unity. For instance, in the first row of Table 11.3: $(0.76)^2 + (0.16)^2 + ... + = 1.0$. From this it can be deducted that if we, as in Table 11.3, have two factors, both loadings in a given row cannot exceed 0.707 at the same time, since $(0.707)^2 + (0.707)^2 = 1.0$ (comparable upper limits for three and four factors are 0.577 and 0.5). In the majority of cases then, a variable will have or a high loading on one factor only and then have small or insignificant loadings on the remaining factors. A variable, so to speak, spends most of its fixed loading amount on one factor.

Now let us find a name for Factor 2. The variables *X12* and *X13* have high absolute loadings on Factor 2. (Since *X7* has a loading of almost 0.5 it is included here.) What do the variables addressing *good housing advice*, (no) *good tax advice²* and *good advice* have in common? All contain the word advice and two of them refer to a specific type of financial advice. Therefore, we suggest the name *(State of) financial advice*.

To complete the interpretation, all high loadings could be highlighted and the factor name put in the table. It is also usual to provide information concerning the importance in means of variance explained by each factor. This has been done in Table 11.4. Verbally, the interpretation could be presented thus: a factor analysis was carried out based on 114 customers' responses to a set of nine bipolar items such as modern/old-fashioned, friendly/unfriendly, etc.

It appears that the nine items can be properly summarized by two factors, including an image-related factor that deals with customer orientation. This is the most important factor and it accounts for more than half of the variance explained. The second factor addresses the state of financial advice and accounts for little more than 10 percent. When combined, the two factors or dimensions account for two-thirds of the variance.

When interpreting and presenting results of a factor analysis, a graphical interpretation is helpful – provided that enough variance can be summarized in two factors.

In Figure 11.2, the factor loadings of Table 11.4 are displayed or treated as (*x1*, *x2*) coordinates in a two-dimensional factor space. Figure 11.3 proposes a four-stage process:

■ In panel (a) digits and variable references (*X12* etc.) are removed.

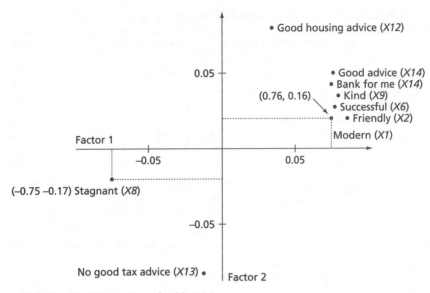

Figure 11.2 Graphical illustration of Table 11.4.

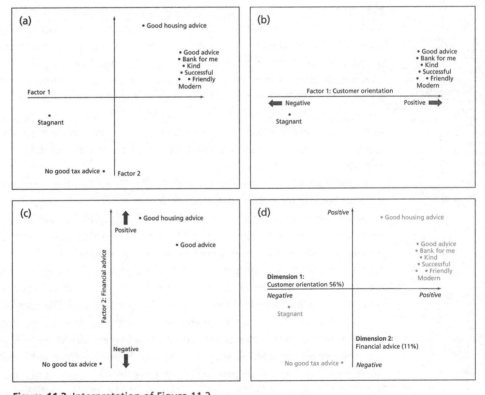

Figure 11.3 Interpretation of Figure 11.2

■ Panel (b) concentrates on variables with high loadings on Factor 1 according to Table 11.4. Moreover, an explanation of the primary axis is offered including a directional orientation.

Table 11.5 Factors and their relative importance

Factor numbering in output		Variance explained	Root (Kaiser criterion)
Factor 1		56%	5.07
Factor 2		11%	1.01
Factor 3		7%	0.64
Factor 4		7%	0.61
Factor 5		6%	0.51
Factor 6	33%	5%	0.40
Factor 7		3%	0.30
Factor 8		3%	0.28
Factor 9		2%	0.18
Factors 1–9 total		100%	9.00

- In panel (c) the process is repeated, this time focusing on variables that have high loadings on Factor 2.
- Finally, panel (d) tries to clarify and summarize the interpretation.

The reader might ask, why the above analysis is based on two factors? Theoretically, it is possible to select ("extract") up to as many factors as there are variables. Therefore, in the example with nine variables (Table 11.4) the interpretation could rely on up to nine factors. However, in real-life, researchers would never be interested in doing this because of two related reasons. First, factors that appear in the far-right columns of the output – like factors three to nine in the bank case (not shown) – explain smaller and smaller amounts of the total variance. It is common to speak about factors that are extracted late in the process. None of the remaining seven factors in the above example explains as much as the 11 percent explained by Factor 2, and most of them explain much less. By definition, factors are ordered or sorted according to decreasing variance explained. On average they explain less than 5 percent (33/7).

In Table 11.5 the factors above the dotted line are called the "extracted" factors while the ones beneath the line are discarded or ignored.

According to many analysts, an extracted factor must be able to explain *at least* as much variance as a variable. Regarded from this perspective, every variable has the same importance and so each variable contributes with a "weight" of 1. As a consequence, each factor extracted as a minimum should pass this threshold value. In factor analysis the importance of a factor is determined by the size of the so-called "Root" or "Kaiser criterion" – a statistical measure that will be discussed below. The root is computable by solving a mathematical system that contains as many equations as there are unknowns. In technical terms, each factor is treated as an unknown. In the early stage of the factor analysis process, there are as many variables as there are factors and therefore the number of unknowns also equals the number of variables. In a way, output of a factor analysis (the so-called column with factor scores) is just a different or more efficient (optimal) way of representing the variance that is embedded in or "nested" in the variables.

While each variable is treated as explaining an "average" amount of variance, factors are extracted such that the first factor explains the biggest amount of variance, the second variable explains the next most variance and so on. Figure 11.4 shows how the variance

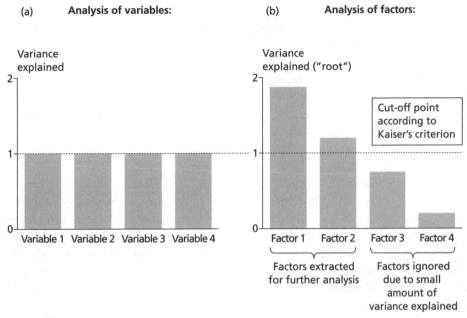

Figure 11.4 Variance explained by variables and by factors

explained is treated in the analysis of variables and how it is restructured in factor analysis. Note that each of the first two factors of panel (b) explains more variance than any of the variables in panel (a). Factor 1 explains almost twice as much as any of the variables.

Below we display the results of two sets of factor analyses based on the image study for the bank and involving all fifteen statements used. The data file is available at www.pearsoned.co.uk/schmidt. It is named Southern_Bank.sav in SPSS format and Southern_Bank.xls in Excel format. Note that the SPSS file has labels that disappear when saving in Excel format. The variable names *X1–X15* are the same as in Table 11.6 below. The variables have been scaled according to a seven-point bipolar semantic differential of which only the left side is shown in Table 11.6. In the original questionnaire it ran (Very) Modern = 1 to (Very) Old-fashioned = 7, (Very) Friendly = 1 to (Very) Unfriendly = 7 and so on. The data file also contains a metric age variable and gender variables where 1 = males and 2 = females.

How do we run an analysis that is not based on all observations but, say, on the subset of males? That is easy to do.

1. Load the file Southern_Bank.sav into SPSS screen editor.
2. Tab *[Data, Select Cases]*.
3. Select "If condition is satisfied" and tab *[If]*. The calculator-like pop-up that appears can be used for selecting subgroups of a data set.
4. Scroll down the variables field on the left and click "Gender" into the empty field on the right.
5. Simply use the buttons of the "calculator" for tabbing "=1" so that the white field reads exactly "gender=1" (without the quotation marks!).

6. Click *[Continue, OK]*. Note that the data screen now entails a new variable called "*filter_$*" as the rightmost column. This variable contains the value 1 if the gender variable has the value 1 and 0 when gender has the value 2. So, the males have been filtered out (the females are ignored). If you run the factor analysis again or any kind of analysis it is solely based on the male subset.

7. Note that if you want to include all responses again, click *[Data, Select Cases]* and select "All cases." And *[OK]*.[3] *Do remember to carry out this last step, since otherwise subsequent analyses are flawed. Only if you exit and restart SPSS will all cases be automatically included again!*

Table 11.6 compares a factor analysis of the male subset with that of the female subset.[4] Table 11.7 comprises a different split of the sample, namely a split into two different age groups (though with age being a metric variable, this selection is artificial).

To aid interpretation, the results presented in Tables 11.6 and 11.7 have been edited. Compared with Table 11.4, all factor loadings have been multiplied by one-hundred and rounded to the nearest integer while loadings lower than 0.5 are not shown. Figure 11.7 (to be discussed below) shows that SPSS has a facility in the options box called "Suppress absolute values less than." This we can flag and then tab in 0.5.[5]

In bigger matrices it may provide further help to flag loadings that are *higher* than a threshold value, say, with an asterisk. SAS Proc Factor offers this option and the default is the root mean square of all values in the data matrix. Applying this technique to Table 11.7 implies that all loadings (18–34 years run, fifteen variables times four factors) are squared and added, including the ones with loadings less than 0.5. Next, this summarized value is divided by the number of cells (60). Finally, one takes the square root of the number.[6]

It should be noted that Tables 11.6 and 11.7 – like most output tables and figures in this book – have *not* been manually produced.

- For instance, with regard to Table 11.6 we can click the so-called Rotated Component Matrix ("Varimax") – to be explained below – that can be requested as part of the output of SPSS's Factor Analysis program.

- Next we copy/paste this table directly into Excel where it appears as a "raw" table to be used for further editing. Assumed that this "raw" table contains the output from the analysis of, say, the male subset, then we can copy/paste the column with the variable explanations, into a new selection area or Excel sheet for further refining (the variable explanations – called labels by SPSS – are included in the file Southern_Bank.sav at www.pearsoned.co.uk/schmidt).

- We can also copy/paste the four loading columns (F1–F4) multiplied by the 15 variable rows to the same selection and place them to the right of the column with the labels/variable explanation.

- Using Excel's formula editor, we can multiply all relevant cells by 100 and set the number of decimal cells to 0. After this the four columns look exactly as in Table 11.6.

- In another part of the SPSS factor output we find a table called "Total Variance Explained." This is copied into Excel, then we select and copy the relevant part of it and use *[Paste Special, Transpose]* for pasting it into the refined table. The latter two steps produces the figures appearing in the bottom three rows of columns F1–F4 in Table 11.6.

To sum up, Tables 11.6 and 11.7 can be almost completely produced solely based on the output of the four factor analyses runs, followed by copying and pasting output tables into Excel and refining the tables. Once the Excel-edited tables appear complete, they can be copied into a word processor or presentation package for final editing.

In Table 11.6, in the analysis of the male run, four factors passed the Kaiser criterion (a root of 1.0) compared with only three factors in the female run. However, from the corresponding variance, the first female factor explains much more variance (56 percent) than the first male factor (35 percent). The first female factor has twice as many high loadings as the first male factor.

All variables that load (beyond fifty) on the first female factor also load on the male factor but, on average, the female loadings are about 10 percent higher than those of males (76.5 to 67.2). Apparently, the first factor in both the female and the male run resembles the first factor in Table 11.4 and covers customer orientation. But it seems that the first factor in the analysis of the female subset is much more important compared with the male run. And while the first three factors in the female run explain 73 percent of variance, they only account for 53 percent in the analysis of the male subset.

The second factor in the male run appears to refer to matters of exclusivity versus nonexclusivity. (Recall that factor analysis is a purely statistical technique and it happens that a variable has a high loading on a factor where the correspondence between the variable and the factor seems odd or unexplainable.) The third male factor resembles the second

Table 11.6 Factor analysis of males' and females' statements about their bank

	Variable explanation	Males (n=69)				Females (n=31)		
		F1	F2	F3	F4	F1	F2	F3
X1	Modern		−54			85		
X2	Friendly	59			59	84		
X3	No family bank		69				−81	
X4	Interesting window displays				89			86
X5	For rich customers		63					
X6	Successful	77				80		
X7	Providing good advice	69				86		
X8	Stagnant	−67				−81		
X9	Kind	64				85		
X10	Good for workers			56			86	
X11	Not interested in customers		67			−56		
X12	Good housing advice			79		63		
X13	No good tax advice			−75		−56		
X14	A bank for me		−56			89		
X15	Good for children			56				65
	Eigen value (Root)	5.3	1.5	1.2	1.1	8.3	1.5	1.0
	Explained variance (%)	35	10	8	7	56	10	7
	Accumulated explained (%)	35	45	53	60	56	66	73

Table 11.7 Factor analysis of two different age groups (bank statements)

	Variable explanation	18–34 years (n=42)				35–54 years (n=45)		
		F1	F2	F3	F4	F1	F2	F3
X1	Modern	62				69		
X2	Friendly	58		66		84		
X3	No family bank	−57						−73
X4	Interesting window displays			81				74
X5	For rich customers	−61				−80		
X6	Successful	75				80		
X7	Providing good advice	78				83		
X8	Stagnant	−79				−75		
X9	Kind	70				79		
X10	Good for workers		73					
X11	Not interested in customers					−64		
X12	Good housing advice		81			69		
X13	No good tax advice				−74		−71	
X14	A bank for me	78				74		
X15	Good for children		67					59
	Eigen value (Root)	6.2	1.4	1.3	1.1	7.1	1.5	1.2
	Explained variance (%)	41	10	9	7	47	10	8
	Accumulated explained (%)	41	51	60	67	47	57	65

factor of Table 11.4. It reflects aspects of financial advice. When inspecting the female run we observe that there are no factors that resemble the male factors two and three.

However, we also note that the two variables loading on the third female factor, *X4* (interesting window displays) and *X15* (good for children) do not load on the same factor in the male run. One might ask if there is any connection or link between these two variables. Maybe there is: none of the variables deals with what one could call the bank's core business. Instead, both issues address secondary product features: how the bank looks and how it handles or takes care of children. When a male faces the issue "good for children" he might think about financial aspects, such as a children's savings account. But when a female (mother) is exposed to "good for children" she might tend to focus on more everyday concerns: does the bank have facilities that are capable of entertaining a child while the mother talks to the bank's personnel?

In Table 11.6, in both runs, the first factor mirrors customer orientation. That is just like in the other runs (the size of the loadings may differ though). But, from the second factor in the 18–34 years age group (Table 11.7), we note that it does not resemble one of the two remaining factors in the analysis of the 35–54 age group. The factor has high loadings on:

■ good for workers (*X10*);
■ good housing advice (*X12*); and
■ good for children (*X15*).

Unlike the male run above, *X13*, "no good tax-advice," does not load on the same factor as does "good housing advice". Instead, it loads on a separate factor where it is the only variable with a high loading.

Is there an explanation for these differences in factor-pattern? Consider the three high variable loadings on Factor 2 in the 18–34 age group. Do they have something in common? What connects "workers," "housing advice," and "children"? Perhaps they all address issues of special interest and importance to the young family:

■ most young couples are in work;
■ they have often just bought a house or are thinking about doing so; and
■ young families tend either to have small children or plan to have some soon.

11.3   Numerical example of factor analysis

This section explains the basics of factor analysis by way of a small numerical example. Unlike analysis of variance and regression, covered in Chapter 9, the mathematical and statistical computations involved in factor analysis are regarded as too complex for even a postgraduate textbook for business students. It is hardly possible to explain the principles of factor analysis without assuming some familiarity with matrix algebra and vector analysis. Normally, therefore readers will be referred to specialized and comprehensive but still not too complicated texts such as Harman (1976) or Rummel (1988). Kim and Mueller (1979) is also dedicated to factor analysis.

Students who do not want to read a whole book dedicated to these topics should consider Green (1978, Chapters 8 and 9), Hair et al. (1998, Chapter 3) or Lattin, Carroll and Green (2003, Chapters 4 and 5). Green (1978) is the classic text and assumes only limited insight into matrix algebra. Hair et al. (1998) is the easiest for someone who does not like formulae. However, it does not have all answers for someone with technical questions. Lattin, Carrol and Green (2003) is up to date but it is also the most difficult of the three texts.

Table 11.8 shows three variables used in the bank image analysis introduced earlier. The filled-in response applies to the first respondent in Table 11.9. See columns II–IV. The example is based on a sample of twenty respondents. The bottom of the respective columns has the average and standard deviation of each variable column. Columns V–VII provides the standardized values of columns II–IV. For instance, the first entry in column V, -0.42, is computed as $(2-2.6)/1.4$. That is the corresponding entry from column II (2) minus the mean or average of the same column (2.6) divided by the column's standard deviation (1.4). By repeating this operation for all twenty values in the first row and then for the remaining two columns (using the respective row's average and standard deviation), results in the entries of columns V–VII. Note that the averages of these columns are zeros while the standard deviations are unities. The reader is encouraged to check that this is correct.

Note that the calculations and formulae shown from now on often only display two decimal places in tables and figures. The computations, however, are based on a much higher level of precision (typically six to eight digits). The operations carried out below involve series of calculations where an output figure from one computation is used as input for a subsequent calculation. Therefore, even small rounding errors "add up", so

Table 11.8 Three variables from the bank research

My bank is (has)...	1	2	3	4	5	6	7	
X1 Modern			X					Old-fashioned bank
X4 Interesting window displays	X							Uninteresting window displays
X8 Stagnant bank						X		Dynamic bank

Table 11.9 Original observations and standardized values

I	II	III	IV	V	VI	VII
Observation	X1	X4	X8	X1_s	X4_s	X8_s
1	2	1	6	−0.42	−1.44	0.63
2	3	2	7	0.28	−0.99	1.23
3	4	3	4	0.98	−0.54	−0.57
4	1	3	7	−1.12	−0.54	1.23
5	3	7	5	0.28	1.26	0.03
6	3	1	6	0.28	−1.44	0.63
7	1	4	4	−1.12	−0.09	−0.57
8	5	2	3	1.68	−0.99	−1.17
9	7	6	1	3.08	0.81	−2.37
10	3	7	3	0.28	1.26	−1.17
11	2	7	2	−0.42	1.26	−1.77
12	2	3	6	−0.42	−0.54	0.63
13	2	6	6	−0.42	0.81	0.63
14	2	7	6	−0.42	1.26	0.63
15	2	7	6	−0.42	1.26	0.63
16	2	2	5	−0.42	−0.99	0.03
17	1	4	6	−1.12	−0.09	0.63
18	2	4	4	−0.42	−0.09	−0.57
19	2	6	6	−0.42	0.81	0.63
20	3	2	6	0.28	−0.99	0.63
Average	**2.6**	**4.2**	**5.0**	**0.00**	**0.00**	**0.00**
Std dev.	**1.4**	**2.2**	**1.7**	**1.00**	**1.00**	**1.00**

Note that observation 1's value on $X1\_s$ is found as $(2-2.6)/1.4 = -0.42$

calculations based on only two decimal places throughout would lead to imprecise results. Also, dividing or multiplying small figures causes accuracy problems: for example, 0.00015/0.00014 yields 1.07 when using five decimal places. The same operation, however, results in 2.00 with only four decimal places (0.0002/0.0001).

Computer programs tend to display only relatively few figures (this may be changed in the software's set-up, though). In SPSS, double clicking a figure, say in the factor output table, triggers several more digits. Note that these digits are kept and reappear when the SPSS output table is copy/pasted into Excel.

In Appendix 11-B on the website (www.pearsoned.co.uk/schmidt), which concentrates on a technical issue in factor analysis (VARIMAX rotation), eight decimal places are used in computations.

Now consider Table 11.10. It has nine columns. Columns I–III are identical to columns V–VII of Table 11.9. The three rows at the bottom constitute a symmetric matrix of correlations among the three data columns. For instance, -0.60 is the correlation of $X1\_s$ and $X8\_s$. Since correlation is unaffected by (insensitive to) standardization of values, the correlation between $X1$ (row II) and $X8$ (row IV) of Table 11.9 is also -0.60. (As always, the reader is encouraged to check this.)

Columns IV to VI of Table 11.10 comprise a three-by-three matrix. How these values were obtained will be addressed later. Consider the systematic procedure governing the computations below:

First row of column I (-0.42) times first row of column IV (0.62) +
first row of column II (-1.44) times second row of column IV (0.33) +
first row of column III (0.63) times third row of column IV (-0.71) = -1.18 etc.

$$Z01.1 = (-0.42) * (0.62) + (-1.44) * (0.33) + (0.63) * (-0.71) = -1.18$$
$$Z02.1 = (0.28) * (0.62) + (-0.99) * (0.33) + (1.23) * (-0.71) = -1.02 \text{ etc.}$$

...

$$Z01.2 = (-0.42) * (-0.47) + (-1.44) * (0.88) + (0.63) * (-0.01) = -1.08$$
$$Z02.2 = (0.28) * (-0.47) + (-0.99) * (0.88) + (1.23) * (-0.01) = -1.01 \text{ etc.}$$

...

$$Z01.3 = (-0.42) * (0.62) + (-1.44) * (0.34) + (0.63) * (0.71) = -0.31$$
$$Z02.3 = (0.28) * (0.62) + (-0.99) * (0.34) + (1.23) * (0.71) = 0.70 \text{ etc.}$$

...

$$Z20.3 = (0.28) * (0.62) + (-0.99) * (0.34) + (0.63) * (0.71) = 0.28$$

Using this computational method produces columns VII–IX.

Next, correlate the columns of VII to IX (from now on, call them $Z1$ to $Z3$) – and observe that, – unlike columns I–III, they are uncorrelated! For instance, the correlation of $Z1$ and $Z2$ is 0.00. The three-by-three matrix at the bottom of columns VII–IX is called an **identity matrix**. It has unities along the main diagonal and zeros in all off-diagonal entries.

Somehow the computation based on the small three-by-three matrix of columns IV–VI has removed the correlation. This matrix is usually called a **U-matrix** or an **eigenvector matrix**.

Finally, at the bottom of columns IV–VI there is another three-by-three matrix. Note that this matrix is non-symmetric. As a matter of fact, this matrix is a matrix of cross-correlations between columns I–III and VII–IX. For instance, the value 0.81 is a correlation between column I ($X1\_s$) and column VII ($Z1$).

This matrix is called the **F-matrix**, or **Factor matrix**. It is reproduced as Table 11.11. Recall that we have been encountering this type of matrix or small table earlier in this chapter. It turns out that Table 11.11 has the same structure as Table 11.4. The main difference between Table 11.11 and Table 11.4 (reproduced again here as Table 11.12) is that in the latter the factors that did not pass the threshold level of 1.0 concerning the root or eigenvalue have been discarded and are not displayed.

Table 11.10 Standardized values and the computation of uncorrelated factor scores

I	II	III	IV	V	VI	VII	VIII	IX
X1_s	X4_s	X8_s	U1	U2	U3	Z1	Z2	Z3
−0.42	−1.44	0.63	0.62	−0.47	0.62	−1.18	−1.08	−0.31
0.28	−0.99	1.23	0.33	0.88	0.34	−1.02	−1.01	0.70
0.98	−0.54	−0.57	−0.71	−0.01	0.71	0.84	−0.94	0.02
−1.12	−0.54	1.23				−1.75	0.05	−0.01
0.28	1.26	0.03				0.57	0.98	0.62
0.28	−1.44	0.63				−0.75	−1.41	0.13
−1.12	−0.09	−0.57				−0.32	0.45	−1.13
1.68	−0.99	−1.17				1.55	−1.66	−0.12
3.08	0.81	−2.37				3.86	−0.73	0.52
0.28	1.26	−1.17				1.42	0.99	−0.22
−0.42	1.26	−1.77				1.41	1.32	−1.08
−0.42	−0.54	0.63				−0.89	−0.28	0.00
−0.42	0.81	0.63				−0.44	0.91	0.46
−0.42	1.26	0.63				−0.29	1.31	0.61
−0.42	1.26	0.63				−0.29	1.31	0.61
−0.42	−0.99	0.03				−0.61	−0.68	−0.58
−1.12	−0.09	0.63				−1.17	0.45	−0.28
−0.42	−0.09	−0.57				0.11	0.12	−0.69
−0.42	0.81	0.63				−0.44	0.91	0.46
0.28	−0.99	0.63				−0.60	−1.01	0.28
1.00	−0.01	−0.60	0.81	−0.47	0.35	1.00	0.00	0.00
−0.01	1.00	−0.32	0.43	0.88	0.19	0.00	1.00	0.00
−0.60	−0.32	1.00	−0.92	−0.01	0.39	0.00	0.00	1.00

Table 11.11 Factor analysis of the numerical example

		Factor 1	Factor 2	Factor 3
X1	Modern	0.81	−0.47	0.35
X4	Interesting window displays	0.43	0.88	0.19
X8	Stagnant bank	−0.92	−0.01	0.39
Percent of variance explained		56%	34%	10%
(Eigenvalue or root)		1.68	1.01	0.31

Table 11.12 Factor analysis of the bank data (from Table 11.4)

Variables		Factor 1	Factor 2	Factors 3–9
X1	Modern	0.76	0.16	
X2	Friendly	0.82	0.16	
X6	Successful	0.77	0.20	
X7	Good advice	0.77	0.42	Discarded
X8	Stagnant	−0.75	−0.17	(not further
X9	Kind	0.80	0.21	discussed)
X12	Good housing advice	0.31	0.77	
X13	No good tax advice	−0.12	−0.87	
X14	A bank for me	0.76	0.24	
Percent of variance explained		56%	11%	33%

Below is the three-by-three matrix, called U, from Table 11.10. It is followed by one more data matrix, called D. This is a so-called diagonal matrix since all entries or cells but the ones that are situated along the main diagonal are zeros.

$$U = \begin{vmatrix} 0.62 & -0.47 & 0.62 \\ 0.33 & 0.88 & 0.34 \\ 0.71 & -0.01 & 0.71 \end{vmatrix}$$

$$D = \begin{vmatrix} 1.68 & 0 & 0 \\ 0 & 1.01 & 0 \\ 0 & 0 & 0.31 \end{vmatrix}$$

The values that appear in the main diagonal are **roots**. They are solutions or 'zero-points' in a mathematical system of equation that can be constructed, based on the matrix of simple correlations (Table 11.10 – bottom of the first three rows). You might remember a time at school when the teacher explained how to solve a system of n equations with n unknowns. It happens that the same technique has been used for computing the matrix D. The example has three variables. The matrix of correlations between $X1$, $X4$ and $X8$ can be treated as three equations with three unknowns. It turns out that the three unknowns to be found are the three factors. The key to computing the factors is to solve the system of equations. Technically, the system of equations can be summarized or rewritten as a polynomial of the same power as the number of unknowns. In the numerical example the polynomial is of third power and the expression that is to be solved is:

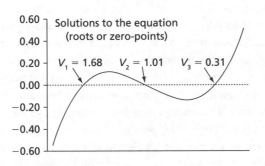

Functional values when
V is between 2 and 0

V	Function
2.0	−0.53182
1.9	−0.30790
1.8	−0.13798
1.7	−0.01606
1.6	0.06386
1.5	0.10778
1.4	0.12170
1.3	0.11162
1.2	0.08354
1.1	0.04346
1.0	−0.00262
0.9	−0.04870
0.8	−0.08878
0.7	−0.11686
0.6	−0.12694
0.5	−0.11302
0.4	−0.06910
0.3	0.01082
0.2	0.13274
0.1	0.30266
0.0	0.52658

Solutions to the equation (roots or zero-points)

$V_1 = 1.68$ $V_2 = 1.01$ $V_3 = 0.31$

Note: 1.68 + 1.01 + 0.31 = 3
1.68 is the eigenvalue of the first factor.
It explains (1.68/3)*100% = 56% of the variance

Figure 11.5 Mathematical expression of variance explained

$$-V^3 + 3V^2 - 2.5292V + 0.52658 = 0$$

This expression usually has three solutions (also called roots or zero-points). In this case the roots are 1.68, 1.01 and 0.31 (see Figure 11.5). Substituting 1.68, 1.01 or 0.31 for V in the above expression makes it a true expression.

Appendix 11-A shows the involved computations using simple matrix algebra. Visit www.pearsoned.co.uk/schmidt.

There is a direct correspondence between the size of the roots, say 1.68, and the amount of variance explained by the appropriate factor as compared to a variable. In the example there are three variables. Then, a factor analysis tells us that the first factor explains 56 percent of the variance. This value, computed as a percentage, gives:

$$\left(\frac{1.68}{3}\right) * 100 = 56\%$$

When running a factor analysis with three variables, a factor should *at least* be able to explain as much variance as a variable (1.00). Otherwise there is no benefit to analyzing a factor rather than analyzing a variable. And there should be some benefit from running a complicated technique like factor analysis. The first factor does quite a good job in explaining 56 percent of the variance, clearly better than 33 percent. The second factor explains 34 percent – just a little better than expected. But with a value of 1.01, it passes the threshold value of 1.0 and therefore one would usually keep this factor for further analysis. However, the last factor only explains 10 percent of the variance, much less than that of a variable.

Note also that – unlike Factor 1 and Factor 2 – no variable has a high loading or correlation (say, better than 0.5) with *Factor 3*. It is not really related to any variable and therefore high loadings between a variable and a factor cannot help interpret the factor. Factor 1 has high loadings on variables *X1* and *X8*, and *factor 2* has at least one high loading on *X4* and therefore these high loadings can be used to help understand the factors. But *Factor 3* has no high loading connected with its column and since the amount of variance explained is small, it is usually discarded. Discarding *Factor 3* makes also good sense from a simple cost-benefit point of view: drop 33 percent of the factors (from three to two) but keep 90 percent of the variance explained (56 percent + 34 percent). Stated differently, drop one-third of the *quantity* of information but keep 90 percent of the *quality* of information. In a small numerical example, the gain in this regard is modest. But in real life, one might have one hundred statements or variables and from a factor analysis we might be able to explain more than half of the variance by using only ten factors. In such a case, one discards 90 percent of the information quantity and keeps 50 percent of the information quality.

One could also argue that a factor yields an even better or more correct picture, say, of consumers' most important perceptual dimensions or of how they weigh primary decisional criteria. While variables emanate from questionnaires, factors uncover the underlying structure of a phenomenon. Some simple computations provide a better understanding of how interrelated the output matrices of factor analysis are. First, multiply matrix U by D. Do this by applying the same computational procedure introduced earlier:

$$UD1.1 = (0.62) * (1.68) + (-0.47) * (0) + (0.62) * (0) = 1.05$$
$$UD2.1 = (0.33) * (1.68) + (0.88) * (0) + (0.34) * (0) = 0.56$$

... .

$$UD3.3 = (0.71) * (0) + (-0.01) * (0) + (0.71) * (0.31) = 0.22$$

$$\begin{matrix} \textbf{U} & * & \textbf{D} & = & \textbf{UD} \end{matrix}$$

$$\begin{vmatrix} 0.62 & -0.47 & 0.62 \\ 0.33 & 0.88 & 0.34 \\ 0.71 & -0.01 & 0.71 \end{vmatrix} * \begin{vmatrix} 1.68 & 0 & 0 \\ 0 & 1.01 & 0 \\ 0 & 0 & 0.31 \end{vmatrix} = \begin{vmatrix} 1.05 & -0.48 & 0.19 \\ 0.56 & 0.89 & 0.11 \\ 1.19 & -0.01 & 0.22 \end{vmatrix}$$

Finally, multiply the product of this computation UD by U', called U transposed. U' deviates from U in that the rows and columns have changed place. But the values appearing in the matrix are the same. They have been laterally reversed along the main diagonal.

$$R1.1 = (1.05) * (0.62) + (-0.48) * (-0.47) + (0.19) * (0.62) = 1.00$$
$$R2.1 = (0.56) * (0.62) + (0.89) * (-0.47) + (0.11) * (0.62) = -0.01$$

... .

$$R3.3 = (1.19) * (0.71) + (-0.01) * (-0.01) + (0.22) * (0.71) = 1.00$$

$$\begin{matrix} \textbf{UD} & * & \textbf{U'} & = & \textbf{R} \end{matrix}$$

$$\begin{vmatrix} 1.05 & -0.48 & 0.19 \\ 0.56 & 0.89 & 0.11 \\ 1.19 & -0.01 & 0.22 \end{vmatrix} * \begin{vmatrix} 0.62 & 0.33 & 0.71 \\ -0.47 & 0.88 & -0.01 \\ 0.62 & 0.34 & 0.71 \end{vmatrix} = \begin{vmatrix} 1.00 & -0.01 & -0.60 \\ -0.01 & 1.00 & -0.32 \\ -0.60 & -0.32 & 1.00 \end{vmatrix}$$

Now it is time to recapitulate. When multiplying the matrix U (called the matrix of eigenvectors) first with the matrix D (the diagonal matrix of eigenvalues or roots) and subsequently with the transposed or laterally reversed matrix U, the product obtained turns out to be the correlation matrix regarding *X1*, *X4* and *X8* (bottom of Table 11.10).

$$\begin{matrix} \textbf{U} & * & \textbf{D} & * & \textbf{U'} & = & \textbf{R} \end{matrix}$$

$$\begin{vmatrix} 0.62 & -0.47 & 0.62 \\ 0.33 & 0.88 & 0.34 \\ -0.71 & -0.01 & 0.71 \end{vmatrix} * \begin{vmatrix} 1.68 & 0 & 0 \\ 0 & 1.01 & 0 \\ 0 & 0 & 0.31 \end{vmatrix} * \begin{vmatrix} 0.62 & 0.33 & 0.71 \\ -0.47 & 0.88 & -0.01 \\ 0.62 & 0.34 & 0.71 \end{vmatrix} = \begin{vmatrix} 1.00 & -0.01 & -0.60 \\ -0.01 & 1.00 & -0.32 \\ -0.60 & -0.32 & 1.00 \end{vmatrix}$$

The above sequence of computations is known as the Eckart-Young **singular value decomposition** technique. By way of a series of appropriate mathematical manipulations the correlation matrix has been split (decomposed) into three matrices that possess certain merits regarded from a statistical perspective. Multiplying the standardized data matrix (X_S) by the matrix (U) produces matrix Z, the matrix of factor scores. As can be checked in Table 11.10, columns VII–IX are uncorrelated. The matrix D is a diagonal matrix of eigenvalues with entries that correspond to the variance explained by the factors. Finally, the U' matrix is a mirror of the U matrix.

Two other computations provide interesting findings:

$$\begin{array}{ccccc} \mathbf{U} & * & \mathbf{U'} & = & \mathbf{I} \end{array}$$

$$\begin{vmatrix} 0.62 & -0.47 & 0.62 \\ 0.33 & 0.88 & 0.34 \\ -0.71 & -0.01 & 0.71 \end{vmatrix} * \begin{vmatrix} 0.62 & 0.33 & 0.71 \\ -0.47 & 0.88 & -0.01 \\ 0.62 & 0.34 & 0.71 \end{vmatrix} = \begin{vmatrix} 1 & 0 & 0 \\ 0 & 1 & 0 \\ 0 & 0 & 1 \end{vmatrix}$$

Post-multiplying U (the matrix of eigenvectors) by its own transposed matrix yields the **identity matrix**.[7] Finally, multiplying U by the square root of D gives the factor matrix (bottom of Table 11.10, columns IV–VI).

$$\begin{array}{ccccc} \mathbf{U} & * & \mathbf{D^{0.5}} & = & \mathbf{F} \end{array}$$

$$\begin{vmatrix} 0.62 & -0.47 & 0.62 \\ 0.33 & 0.88 & 0.34 \\ -0.71 & -0.01 & 0.71 \end{vmatrix} * \begin{vmatrix} \sqrt{1.68} & 0 & 0 \\ 0 & \sqrt{1.01} & 0 \\ 0 & 0 & \sqrt{0.31} \end{vmatrix} = \begin{vmatrix} 0.81 & -0.47 & 0.35 \\ 0.43 & 0.88 & 0.19 \\ -0.92 & -0.01 & 0.39 \end{vmatrix}$$

11.4 Running the example in SPSS

The above example can be run in SPSS. Excel's Analysis Toolpak does not offer factor analysis. However, add-ons such as Winstat (www.winstat.com), statistiXL (www.statistixl.com) and XlStat (www.xlstat.com) provide this option.

Figure 11.6 displays the factor analysis facility within the SPSS *[Analysis]* dropdown menu.

Figure 11.7 shows appropriate settings concerning three of the available five dialogue boxes. Note that in each of the boxes settings have been changed from the default:

- In the *[Descriptives]* box we have flagged "Univariate descriptives," "coefficients" and unflagged "Initial solution" (since we do not need it here).
- In the *[Extraction]* box we have changed the default radio button from "Eigenvalues over" to "Number of factors" and tabbed 3 (during the introductory analysis we want to keep all three factors).
- Finally, in the *[Scores]* box "Save as variables" has been flagged.

Note that none of these changes is strictly necessary. Immediately after we have tabbed the three variables into the *[Variable]* field, the OK button is clicked and the analysis can be

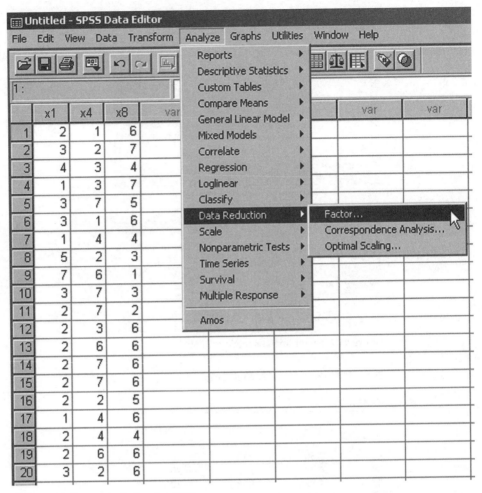

Figure 11.6 Factor analysis using SPSS

run. However, we have changed some settings to alter the output so it fits better with the present discussion.

The resulting output appears in Table 11.13. Compare Table 11.13 with the manual computations of the example introduced in the previous section and note that most of the figures are the same (apart from rounding errors):

- Descriptive statistics appear in Table 11.9 (bottom).
- The correlation matrix is found in Table 11.10 (lower left three-by-three matrix).
- The component or factor matrix also appears in Table 11.10 (lower middle three-by-three matrix).
- Communalities are not of interest here but are discussed below in Section 11.5 on rotation.
- Total variance explained was earlier seen in Table 11.11 and in Figure 11.5.

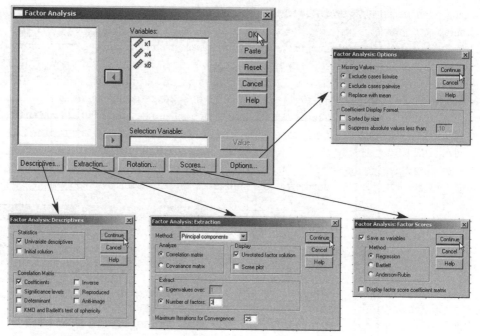

Figure 11.7 Factor analysis settings in SPSS

Table 11.13 SPSS factor analysis output

Descriptive statistics

	Mean	Std dev.	Analysis N
X1	2.60	1.429	20
X4	4.20	2.215	20
X8	4.95	1.669	20

Correlation matrix

		X1	X4	X8
Correlation	X1	1.000	−0.007	−0.605
	X4	−0.007	1.000	−0.325
	X8	−0.605	−0.325	1.000

Component matrix

	Component		
	1	2	3
X1	0.809	−0.474	0.347
X4	0.429	0.883	0.189
X8	−0.919	−5.372E-03	0.394

Extraction method: principal component analysis.
Three components extracted.

Communalities	Extraction
X1	1.000
X4	1.000
X8	1.000

Extraction method: principal component analysis.

Total variance explained

	Extraction sums of squared loadings		
Component	Total	% of variance	Cumulative %
1	1.683	56.112	56.112
2	1.006	33.518	89.630
3	0.311	10.370	100.000

Extraction method: principal component analysis.

Once the output window is closed, we discover that three new variables have appeared next to the variables with the original data. Table 11.14 shows the first five rows of this twenty-by-three matrix.

Table 11.14 First five rows of new matrix

Obs.	Fac1_1	Fac2_1	Fac3_1
1	−0.91324	−1.07478	−0.54959
2	−0.78906	−1.01135	1.26327
3	0.64361	−0.93511	0.0446
4	−1.34668	0.04551	−0.02471
5	0.44014	0.97859	1.11747

It turns out that this matrix is a matrix of factor scores and that its values are closely related to the values appearing in columns VII–IX of Table 11.10. To see how, consider Table 11.15 showing the first five rows of columns VII–IX.

Table 11.15 First five rows of columns VII–IX

	VII	VIII	IX
Obs	Z1	Z2	Z3
1	−1.18488	−1.07776	−0.30653
2	−1.02376	−1.01415	0.70459
3	0.83505	−0.93770	0.02488
4	−1.74725	0.04564	−0.01378
5	0.57106	0.98130	0.62327

Earlier in this chapter (page 290) we presented the expression $U*D^{0.5} = F$. As a matter of fact, the matrix $D^{0.5}$ – a diagonal matrix – constitutes the link between the two columns of data or factor scores.

$$
\begin{vmatrix}
-0.91324 & -1.07478 & -0.54959 \\
-0.78906 & -1.01135 & +1.26327 \\
+0.64361 & -0.93511 & +0.04460 \\
-1.34668 & +0.04551 & -0.02471 \\
+0.44014 & +0.97859 & +1.11747
\end{vmatrix}
*
\begin{vmatrix}
\sqrt{1.683} & 0 & 0 \\
0 & \sqrt{1.006} & 0 \\
0 & 0 & \sqrt{0.311}
\end{vmatrix}
=
\begin{vmatrix}
-1.18488 & -1.07776 & -0.30653 \\
-1.02376 & -1.01415 & +0.70459 \\
+0.83505 & -0.93770 & +0.02488 \\
-1.74725 & +0.04564 & -0.01378 \\
+0.57106 & +0.98130 & +0.62327
\end{vmatrix}
$$

$$
\sqrt{1.683} = 1.2974; \quad \sqrt{1.006} = 1.0028; \quad \sqrt{0.311} = 0.5578
$$

11	−0.91324	*	1.2974	+	(−1.07478)	*	0	+	(−0.54959)	*	0	=	−1.18488
21	−0.78906	*	1.2974	+	(−1.01135)	*	0	+	(+1.26327)	*	0	=	−1.02376
.	.		.		.		.		.		.		.
12	−0.91324	*	0	+	(−1.07478)	*	1.0028	+	(−0.54959)	*	0	=	−1.07776
22	−0.78906	*	0	+	(−1.01135)	*	1.0028	+	(+1.26327)	*	0	=	−1.01415
.	.		.		.		.		.		.		.
13	−0.91324	*	0	+	(−1.07478)	*	0	+	(−0.54959)	*	0.5578	=	−0.30653
23	−0.78906	*	0	+	(−1.01135)	*	0	+	(+1.26327)	*	0.5578	=	+0.70459
.	.		.		.		.		.		.		.

In the present case it is not necessary to provide the computations in matrix mode. It is sufficient to multiply the first column of data in the SPSS screen by 1.2974, the second by 1.0028 and the third by 0.5578. This is easy to do in SPSS and in Excel. However, using matrix terms usually makes it easier to understand how the computer performs the computational steps that lead to the result. The computer is programmed to "think," act and behave in pure matrix language. Note that the correlation between the factor score columns (Fac1_1, Fac2_1 and Fac3_1 of Table 11.14) is 0. That is, the twenty-by-three matrix of factor scores is uncorrelated.

11.5 Rotation of factors

To most students, factor analysis theory is a difficult topic. It can be hard to obtain an appropriate understanding of the method's principles unless one possesses knowledge of matrix algebra. The same holds with regard to a comprehension of factor rotation. Advanced texts such as Harmann (1976, chapter 14) and Lattin, Carroll and Green (2003, chapter 5) provide an in-depth discussion of approaches to the rotation of factors.

Most factor analyses presented in the academic literature and in empirical settings involve rotation. Very often, the interpretation of the results is based on the table or matrix containing the **Varimax-rotated solution**. Therefore, a proper understanding of factor analysis necessitates at least some non-technical introduction to the principles governing rotation. Readers wanting to gain a better understanding of how the technique works, are encouraged to inspect Appendix 11-B.

Appendix 11-B shows how to manually compute the Varimax rotated factor matrix, based on the unrotated matrix. As the reader will see, the calculations are cumbersome, especially for a handheld calculator. Even when using Excel's formula editor, it takes some time before the manually computed results fit with SPSS or SAS. Visit www.pearsoned.co.uk/schmidt.

Example of pure simple structure

Variable	Factor 1	Factor 2	Factor 3
X1	0	1	0
X2	1	0	0
X3	0	0	1
X4	1	0	0

The purpose of factor rotation is to make the interpretation of the output easier. A rotation technique like Varimax aims to improve interpretation using **simple structure**. The computations are complex, but the underlying principles may be explained using a hypothetical example, supplemented by some tables and figures. See the table above (Example of pure simple structure).

The idea behind simple structure is that each variable ought to have a loading of 1.00 on one factor and 0.00 on all the remaining factors. In a perfect world, a factor would be completely explained by (correlate 1.00 with) a certain variable. For instance, in the hypothetical example of Table 11.15, Factor 2 is perfectly explained by *X1*. Since factors themselves by way of definition are uncorrelated, a loading (correlation) of 1.00 by *X2* on, say, Factor 1 and *Factor 3* simultaneously (in the same row) is impossible, because this would imply that the R-square between Factor 2 and *Factor 3* was 1.00, while any set of two factors by way of definition have a bivariate correlation of 0.00. Note also, that *X2* and *X4* both correlate perfectly with Factor 1. This implies that the correlation between *X2* and *X4* is 1.00 also.

While the table above represents an ideal situation, Table 11.16 symbolizes a worst-case scenario from an interpretational perspective (the present example is hypothetical and therefore the correspondence between variable notation – *X1*, *X2*, etc. – and variable text differs from the example on bank image analysis).

Unfortunately, all variables correlate equally well or badly (numerically) with both factors. In other words, all variables contribute with the same amount (weight) to the interpretation of the two factors, and neither of the loadings is of impressive size. So, how can we use *X1* to *X4* to explain the factors? An interpretation based on Table 11.16 does not make any sense. Figure 11.8 (panel (a)) provides a graphical illustration of Table 11.16. Now assume that the two axes were rotated by an angle of $45°$ while keeping a $90°$ perpendicular relationship between the two axes. To prevent confusion, we will call the original axes "old" and the rotated axes "new." This is illustrated in panel (b).

In panel (c) of Figure 11.8 the old axes have been removed. Finally, in panel (d), the rotated space of panel (c) has been reversed or rotated back to an upright or horizontal/vertical perspective. Table 11.17 shows the co-ordinates or rotated loadings of Figure 11.8 (d) (Rotated solution). Note how close the solution comes to the ideal state of simple structure.

Table 11.16 Worst case scenario when interpreting a factor analysis

Variable		Factor 1	Factor 2
X1	(modern)	0.5	0.5
X2	(no good tax advice)	0.5	−0.5
X3	(good housing advice)	−0.5	0.5
X4	(stagnant)	−0.5	−0.5

Table 11.17 Variable loadings after rotation of factors

	Rotated solution		Simple structure	
Variable	Factor 1	Factor 2	Factor 1	Factor 2
X1 (modern)	0.90	0.10	1.00	0.00
X2 (no good tax advice)	0.05	−0.95	0.00	−1.00
X3 (good housing advice)	−0.05	0.95	0.00	1.00
X4 (stagnant)	−0.95	0.05	−1.00	0.00

In Figure 11.9 we provide an interpretation of the rotated two-dimensional space. An interpretation of Figure 11.8 seems easy. It appears that the four (hypothetical) variables constitute "extreme" observations along two (uncorrelated) dimensions:

■ a traditional/progressive dimension; and
■ a technical/financial dimension.

While introducing the concept of factor analysis above, factor rotation was not addressed. However, without being aware of it, we were indeed using output that was based on a Varimax rotation. For instance, the interpretation of the factor analysis concerning the image of banks in Table 11.6 and Table 11.7 was based on three and

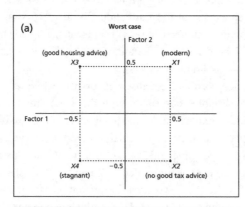
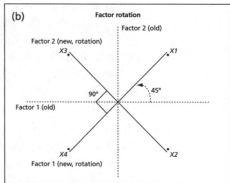
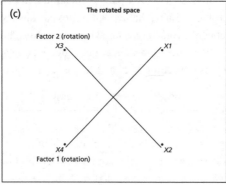
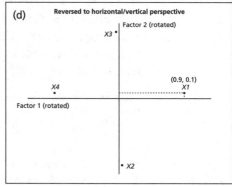

Figure 11.8 The process of factor rotation

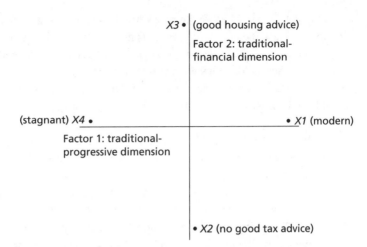

Figure 11.9 Making sense of the space

four-dimensional spaces that were indeed Varimax rotated before analysis. No mention was made of this because it would have complicated the discussion.

Now, reconsider the example with the variables $X1$ (Modern), $X4$ (Interesting window displays) and $X8$ (Stagnant). Figure 11.6 showed where to find factor analysis in the SPSS *[Analyze]* dropdown. Figure 11.7 displayed the dialogue box settings that produced the

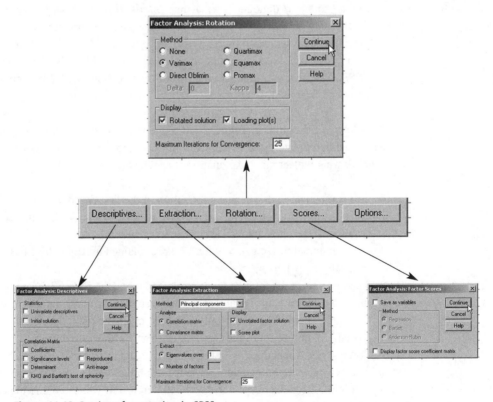

Figure 11.10 Settings for rotation in SPSS

output of Table 11.13. Note that while Figure 11.7 shows four of the five available dialogue boxes, the box *[Rotation...]* is not explained. This will be done now. And since we do not want to obtain the output Table 11.13 again, we will need to change settings in some of the other dialogue boxes. See Figure 11.10.

Before discussing the output of Table 11.18, briefly compare the settings of Figure 11.10. with those of the unrotated solution (Figure 11.7).

- In the *[Descriptives]* box, unflag *[Univariate descriptives]* and *[Coefficients]* because they are not necessary for a discussion of rotation. *[Initial Solution]* should also be unflagged.
- In the *[Extraction]* dialogue box, change *[Extract]* from *[Number of Factors]* = 3 to *[Eigenvalues over]* = 1. When explaining the basics of an unrotated factor output, one usually wants to keep all factors in the solution (this especially applies when dealing with a small numerical example). However, when the topic changes to an explanation of the purpose of rotation, then it is common to have fewer factors than variables in the final solution. Here, use SPSS's default setting, namely to extract factors with eigenvalues of at least 1.00. (Readers who still experience trouble with understanding what an eigenvalue is should once more check Figures 11.4 and 11.5.) In the same box flag *[Display unrotated factor solution]* if it is not flagged.
- *[Scores]* dialogue box: do not save the (rotated) factor scores as variables to the screen editor. They are unnecessary for an understanding of rotation.
- In the *[Rotation]* dialogue box, change *[Method]* from *[None]* to *[Varimax]*.
- Finally, flag *[Loading Plot]*. Note that to compare the unrotated and the rotated loading plots, the analysis has to be run twice, once while *[Method]* is set to *[None]* and once with *[Varimax]*. Note also, that the plots of Figure 11.11 have not been produced by SPSS. Instead, the component matrix was copied from the SPSS output into Excel and produced from there.

Now look at the output in Table 11.18. Some numbers that appear in Table 11.14 are not explained here. (Interested readers can inspect Appendix 11-B at www.pearsoned.co.uk/schmidt where a technical explanation is provided.)

- The component matrix is just a repetition of the first two data columns in the unrotated component matrix of Table 11.13. Since the eigenvalue of the third component is less than the Kaiser criterion of 1.0, it is ignored here.
- The communalities, e.g. 0.879 for *X1*, are explained in Appendix 11-B. The value 0.879 is usually known as hj^2.
- The first part of the total variance explained table, the Extraction sums of squared loadings also appears in Table 11.13 (the reader should not be confused by the word "loadings" here. This table only contains eigenvalues and variance explained). The "Total" column contains the eigenvalues. These values are discussed in connection with Figure 11.5. Appendix 11-A shows how the eigenvalues are calculated.
- The second part of the total variance explained table, the rotation sum of squared loadings, differs from the unrotated extraction sum values. While the cumulative variance explained (89.63 percent) of the first two components remains unchanged, the first

Table 11.18 Varimax rotated factor solution

Component matrix

Component	1	2
X1	0.809	−0.474
X4	0.429	0.883
X8	−0.919	−0.005

Extraction method: principal component analysis. Two components extracted.

Communalities

	Extraction
X1	0.879
X4	0.964
X8	0.845

Extraction method: principal component analysis.

Total variance explained

Component	Extraction sums of squared loadings			Rotation sums of squared loadings		
	Total	% of Variance	Cumulative %	Total	% of Variance	Cumulative %
1	1.683	56.112	56.112	1.584	52.786	52.786
2	1.006	33.518	89.630	1.105	36.844	89.630

Extraction method: principal component analysis.

Rotated component matrix

	Component	
	1	2
X1	0,929	−0,128
X4	0,057	0,980
X8	−0,847	−0,358

Extraction method: principal component analysis. Rotation method: Varimax with Kaiser normalization. Rotation converged in three iterations.

Component transformation matrix

Component	1	2
1	0.923	0.384
2	−0.384	0.923

Extraction method: principal component analysis. Rotation method: Varimax with Kaiser normalization.

factor now explains relatively less and the second one relatively more. The rotation has changed the explanatory power of the factors. In the unrotated case (extraction sum of squares), a factor that is extracted later (say, component 2) will always have a lower eigenvalue and therefore explain less variance than a factor that was extracted earlier (say, component 1). After rotation this need not always be the case. The requirement of monotonically decreasing variance is sacrificed in the interest of obtaining better inter- pretability of the factor loadings and, hence, the re-orientated dimensions themselves (Green, 1978, 379).

- The rotated component matrix has not appeared elsewhere in this chapter. However, Appendix 11-B explains in technical detail how this matrix can be calculated, based on the unrotated matrix.

- The component transformation matrix is necessary for computing the rotated matrix. Appendix 11-B also shows how this matrix is computed. The arccosine of 0.923 and the arcsine of 0.384 are both 22.6° corresponding to the angle of rotation in the present example (ignore the sign of the rotation angle being negative). See Figure 11.11.

Figure 11.11 shows the unrotated and the rotated factor matrix (it is called component

Component matrix

	Component	
	Factor 1	Factor 2
X1	0.809014	−0.474300
X4	0.428724	0.883492
X8	−0.919270	−0.005370

Extraction method: principal component analysis. Two components extracted.

Rotated component matrix

	Component	
	Factor 1	Factor 2
X1	0.929073	−0.127610
X4	0.056951	0.980367
X8	−0.846860	−0.357650

Extraction method: principal component analysis. Rotation method: Varimax with Kaiser normalization. Rotation converged in three iterations.

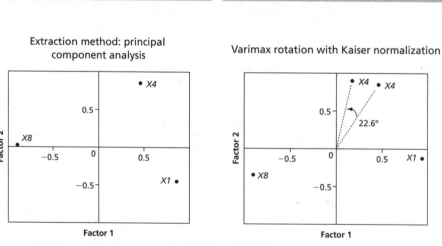

Figure 11.11 Comparing unrotated and rotated solution

matrix in the SPSS output) as well as the corresponding two-dimensional factor spaces. When comparing the rotated with the unrotated plot, note that $X1$ and $X4$ have come nearer to the simple structure criterion (close to 1 on one axis and close to 0 on the other). Unfortunately, $X8$ is worse off after rotation. However, the better fit on $X1$ and $X4$ more than offsets this.

In the present example, rotation does not change the interpretation of the factor analysis results. It only makes the interpretation a little clearer. Before rotation, variables $X1$ and $X4$ have loadings on Factor 2 (-0.4743) and Factor 1 (0.4287) respectively near $+/-0.5$ – loadings that seem too high (see Table 11.16 and panel (a) of Figure 11.8). After rotation they are much less (-0.12761 and 0.05695). Note also that by post-multiplying the unrotated component matrix by the component transformation matrix we obtain the rotated component matrix. The reader should check this by using a handheld computer or via Excel. See Table 11.18 for instance $(0.809*0.923) + (-0.474*-0.384) = 0.929$ and so on.

11.6 Additional issues in factor analysis

Is the input matrix suitable?

The reader may find the current chapter (and the two attached appendices) difficult to understand and wonder whether all the computations are necessary for solving applied and

Table 11.19 Data from the old and the new survey of bank customers

	I	II	III	IV	V	VI
Obs.	X1	X4	X8	X1new	X4new	X8new
1	2	1	6	2	2	3
2	3	2	7	2	2	4
3	4	3	4	4	2	3
4	1	3	7	1	3	3
5	3	7	5	4	4	4
6	3	1	6	2	2	3
7	1	4	4	3	3	2
8	5	2	3	5	1	3
9	7	6	1	7	2	4
10	3	7	3	4	4	3
11	2	7	2	4	4	2
12	2	3	6	2	3	3
13	2	6	6	3	4	3
14	2	7	6	3	4	4
15	2	7	6	3	4	4
16	2	2	5	2	2	2
17	1	4	6	2	3	3
18	2	4	4	3	3	2
19	2	6	6	3	4	3
20	3	2	6	2	2	3
Mean	2.6	4.2	4.95	3.05	2.9	3.05
Std dev.	1.429	2.215	1.669	1.356	0.968	0.686

Table 11.20 Test on the adequacy of factor analysis in SPSS

KMO and Bartlett's test		Columns I–III (original)	Columns IV–VI (new)
Kaiser-Meyer-Olkin measure of Sampling adequacy		0.419	0.476
Bartlett's test of sphericity	Approx. chi-square	11.010	1.066
	df	3	3
	Sig.	0.012	0.785

empirical problems. In fact, only those techniques that are absolutely necessary have been introduced. More technical topics are in appendices that can be skipped by readers who are not interested. However, factor analysis is a complex, yet popular technique. It should be noted that comprehensive and rather non-mathematical textbooks such as Harman (1976) and Rummel (1988) dedicate up to 600 pages to the method.

Before finishing with factor analysis, there are some important issues that have not been addressed yet. In theory, one should not spend much time on a factor analysis *before assessing whether the data are suitable*. Assume that we have collected a new set of twenty responses to the three questions of our numerical example (Table 11.9). Columns I–III of Table 11.19 display the old data, while IV–VI contain the new data.

We now want to assess the *suitability* of running a factor analysis – first based on our original data and then on the new data.

Two appropriate tests are called **KMO (Kaiser–Meyer–Olkin)** and **Bartlett's test of sphericity**. Both are available in SPSS. See Figure 11.7 on the bottom-left of the *[Descriptives]* dialogue box. After loading the data columns of Table 11.19 into the screen editor, flag the checkbox *[KMO and Bartlett's test of sphericity]*. The result of both runs is shown in Table 11.20.

Before trying to interpret Table 11.20, a few words about the two measures. KMO ranges from 0 to 1. If KMO is 1, each variable is perfectly predicted by the other variables. If there is no correlation among variables, that is, if the correlation matrix is an identity matrix, then KMO is 0.5 (*not* 0.0). With very small empirical sample sizes, the measure may be approaching 0. Moreover, KMO increases "automatically" as:

- the sample size increases;
- the average correlation increases;
- the number of variables increases; and
- the number of factors *decreases*.

According to Kaiser, a KMO measure of 0.9–1.0 is marvellous, 0.8–0.9 meritorious, 0.7–0.8 middling, 0.6–0.7 mediocre, 0.5–0.6 miserable and below 0.5 unacceptable. However, these rules of thumb seem to have been developed for analyzing empirical sample sizes with more than one hundred or so cases. The measure cannot be used for very small samples, and therefore the KMO-analysis based on the data of Table 11.19 is not valid. For more on KMO see Kaiser (1970, 1974a, 1974b).

We believe that Bartlett's test of sphericity is preferable to KMO if the sample size is small (less than one hundred), especially when the number of variables is relatively large

Table 11.21 Bartlett's test of significance between R and I

		R: Correlation matrix (from Table 11.13)			I: Identity matrix		
		X1	X4	X8	I1	I2	I3
Correlation	X1	1.000	−0.007	−0.605	1.000	0.000	0.000
	X4	−0.007	1.000	−0.325	0.000	1.000	0.000
	X8	−0.605	−0.325	1.000	0.000	0.000	1.000

(ten to twenty). For bigger sample sizes, Bartlett's chi-square is almost sure to reject the null hypothesis (namely that the data matrix is uncorrelated, more on this below) – even if the average correlation is less than 0.10 or so, that is, if R-square is 0.01! See Cooley and Lohnes (1974).

Table 11.21 displays the correlation matrix of the example (from Table 11.13) and an identity matrix (a case where there is no correlation between the variables).

Bartlett's test of sphericity assesses whether the difference between the R and I matrices is significant. For instance, could the off-diagonal cells (−0.007, −0.605 and −0.325) reasonably be attributed to random chance, given that $n = 20$? Or are these correlations when combined (numerically) higher than can be expected by random chance? Normally we would hypothesize that there is no significant difference between R and I (more formally H–0: R=1). If the correlation matrix cannot be clearly distinguished from an uncorrelated identity matrix, then factor analyzing it is meaningless. If a matrix of uncorrelated component or factor scores is used as input for a factor analysis then Bartlett's chi-square equals 0.000 while the significance value equals 1.000. For more on the test of sphericity, see Bartlett (1950).

While most multivariate textbooks cover Bartlett's test in some detail, not all mention KMO. Sometimes the Kaiser–Meyer–Olkin measure is called **Measure of sampling adequacy (MSA)** without reference to KMO.

Look back at Table 11.20. For both the original and the new study, KMO is disappointingly low (less than 0.5). But the samples only included twenty cases and since the KMO measure is unstable when the number of cases is less than one hundred, there is no need to worry. What is perhaps more interesting is that Bartlett's test shows significance concerning the original study but not with regard to the new study. So, according to Bartlett's test, a factor analysis is justified on the original data but not on the new data. Why does this happen? Consider the correlation matrix of the new data in Table 11.22.

Comparing this correlation matrix with the one based on the original data (Table 11.21), note that the correlation on average is much lower. The average numerical

Table 11.22 Correlation matrix

		R(new) – Correlation matrix		
		X1new	X4new	X8new
Correlation	X1new	1.000	−0.036	0.223
	X4new	−0.036	1.000	0.087
	X8new	0.223	0.087	1.000

(off-diagonal) correlation among the original variable-columns is 0.312 but it is only 0.115 among the variables in the new data. Also, note from Table 11.19 that the difference in means and the absolute size of the standard deviations is smaller in the new study as compared with the original one. If the difference in means is insignificant and both variance and correlation coefficients are of modest size, then a factor analysis is not an option.

But why is the new study so unsuitable for a factor analysis? Well, the authors must admit to "cheating" a little in obtaining the new sample. The first cell entry of column IV in Table 11.19 is 2. This figure has been constructed by taking the first cell value in the matrix that contains the uncorrelated factor scores based on the original example (column VII of Table 11.10). This value is -1.18 or more precisely, -1.184880489. Then we added the number $+3$ to this value and obtain 1.815119511. We then rounded to the nearest integer, which is 2. This then becomes the first cell entry of column IV in Table 11.19. And so on. Thus, the new study is a "concealed" (rounded or rough) version of the uncorrelated factor scores, based on the original study. Knowing this, it can be no surprise that the new data are not suitable for factor analysis. But why then is there any correlation in the new data columns? The value 0.115 on average is not 0.000. That is caused by the rounding process that is involved in constructing the new "observations." But if we had used precise figures, such as 1.815119511 instead of 2, etc., then the outcome of the factor analysis would be as shown in Table 11.23.[8]

While the mean, the correlations matrix, KMO, and Bartlett's test makes sense, why is the standard deviation not 1.000 as is usually the case when figures are standardized (and computing factor scores involves a standardization)? There is a good reason for this: do you recall having seen the values earlier in this chapter (1.29745, 1.00277 and 0.55775)? Squaring the values gives $(1.29745)^2 = 1.6834$, $(1.00277)^2 = 1.0055$ and $(0.55775)^2 = 0.3111$. These values are the eigenvalues that show how much variance a given factor explains. The first time the eigenvalues appeared was in Table 11.11 and in Figure 11.5. The square roots of the eigenvalues also first appeared on page 294.

Figure 11.24 shows the result of three subsequent factor analyses based on random numbers (scaled between one and seven) using the uniform distribution of Excel's random

Table 11.23 New data (Table 11.19) using exact data

	Mean	Std deviation	Analysis N
X1new exact	3.0000	1.29745	20
X4new exact	3.0000	1.00277	20
X8new exact	3.0000	0.55775	20

Correlations	X1new exact	X4new exact	X8new exact
X1new exact	1.000	0.000	0.000
X4new exact	0.000	1.000	0.000
X8new exact	0.000	0.000	1.000

KMO		0.500	
Bartlett's test	Chi-square	0.000	
	Df	3	
	Sig.	1.000	

Table 11.24 Monte Carlo assessment of KMO and Bartlett's test with three variables

N	Run	10	100	1,000	10,000	30,000
Determinant	1	0.481	0.888	0.998	1.000	1.000
	2	0.415	0.993	0.999	0.999	1.000
	3	0.534	0.981	0.997	1.000	1.000
KMO	1	0.283	0.436	0.497	0.502	0.500
	2	0.520	0.504	0.499	0.502	0.500
	3	0.324	0.501	0.495	0.501	0.501
Bartlett chi-square	1	4.519	11.389	1.730	2.458	0.422
	2	4.997	0.656	0.842	7.276	4.419
	3	4.502	1.874	3.366	2.172	4.843
Bartlett's significance	1	0.211	0.010	0.630	0.483	0.936
	2	0.172	0.884	0.839	0.064	0.200
	3	0.212	0.600	0.339	0.537	0.184

number generator that is included in the Analysis Toolpak. Every run involves sample sizes from 10 to 30,000.

Since a correlation matrix based on an infinite amount of random numbers equals an identity matrix, its determinant must be 1.000. Likewise, KMO must approach 0.500. Note that the values of KMO are unstable for ten and even for one hundred observations. From 1,000 and upwards the figure stabilizes at 0.500. Bartlett's chi-square and the corresponding significance value fail to converge to 0.000 and 1.000 respectively. The measure is probably more unstable and it unexpectedly finds one run highly significant and thus suitable for factor analysis (run 1, 100 cases) while another run is found marginally significant (run 2, 10,000 cases). While this is not a flaw in Bartlett's test but a consequence of working with random numbers, it shows the sensitivity of the test especially as the number of cases increases (in the first case the average numeric correlation was 0.17). Obviously, three simulated runs with only five different sample sizes are not enough to make conclusions. To do this, one would have to perform 100 or so runs and then compute the average and standard deviations of the KMO and Bartlett's test. The reader is encouraged to do this.[9]

Finally, we show how to compute Bartlett's test of sphericity and the KMO measure manually.

First, Bartlett's test of sphericity:

$$\chi^2{[0.5(n^2-n)]} = -\left[m - 1 - \frac{1}{6}(2n+5) \times \ln|R|\right]$$

where n = number of variables (3)
  m = sample size (20)
  $\ln|R|$ = determinant of sample correlation matrix R

Appendix 11-A shows how to compute the determinant of a three-by-three matrix. Instead of the matrix $|A|$ and its general notation, substitute the values of the three-by-three correlation matrix from Table 11.13.[10] The result is $|R| = 0.527$. So, we have:

$$\chi^2 \left[_{0.5(3^2-3)}\right] = -\left[20 - 1 - \frac{1}{6}(6+5)\right] \times \ln |0.527| = 11.0 \text{ with 3 degrees of freedom}$$

The appropriate significance value is 0.012 (chi-square distribution).

The KMO (Kaiser–Meyer–Olkin) test of sampling adequacy is the ratio between the sum of squared simple correlations and (the sum of squared simple correlations + [the sum of {sign reversed} squared *partial* correlations]). A partial correlation between two variables is a correlation, which has been corrected for the two variables' correlations with all other variables in the analysis. For instance, the partial correlation of $X1$ and $X4$ is "net of" $X8$'s correlation with $X1$ and $X4$.[11] The key to performing this correction is a regression among residuals of the involved variables. For details on how to compute the partial correlation, see Appendix 9-D on stepwise regression.

In the numerical example KMO is computed so:

$$\left[\frac{(-0.066517)^2 + (-0.604508)^2 + (-0.324559)^2}{(-0.066517)^2 + (-0.604508)^2 + (-0.324559)^2 + (0.269)^2 + (0.641)^2 + (0.412)^2}\right] = 0.419$$

This figure appears in Table 11.20.

Earlier in this chapter an empirical factor analysis concerning customers' perception of their bank's image based on fifteen criteria was used to run two sets of factor analyses, one concerning gender (Table 11.6) and another concerning age (Table 11.7). At that time no check was made as to whether the data were suitable for running a factor analysis.

Now, the results of assessing the suitability of these runs is shown in Table 11.25.

According to both KMO and Bartlett's test, it seems justified to conduct a factor analysis based on the bank image data (note that the sample sizes of Table 11.25 are less than one hundred and strictly the KMO measure does not apply). Bartlett's sphericity test is highly significant and KMO is nearer to 1.0 than 0.5. According to the rules of thumb suggested by Kaiser (see above), all four runs are in the marvellous to meritorious range.

Table 11.25 KMO and Bartlett's test on bank image analysis

	Gender		Age	
	Male	*Female*	*18–34*	*35–54*
n	69	31	42	45
KMO	0.795	0.810	0.824	0.773
Bartlett's chi-square	353.3	360.9	286.9	402.0
Significance	0.000	0.000	0.000	0.000

In all runs the number of degrees of freedom is $0.5(m^2-m) = 0.5(15^2-15) = 105$, where m is the number of variables. The sample size is not needed for calculating degrees of freedom.

Selecting input matrix, extraction method and number of factors to extract

See Figure 11.10. The default input matrix in SPSS is the matrix of correlation among variables. However, one might also use the covariance matrix, or the raw sum of squares and cross products matrix, or the mean corrected sum of squares and cross product matrix (the latter two are presently not available in SPSS). Green (1978, 358–359) shows the effects of using the other input matrices. While the results usually differ, deviations tend to be minor. We recommend using the correlation matrix.

The extraction method is used to find the eigenvalues (roots) and to compute the (unrotated) factor matrix. This can be done in several ways. The default method in SPSS is known as "Principal Component" and this method is used in Appendix 11-A. It is more or less standard in applied marketing research.

However, a lot of other methods have been developed and in SPSS six other approaches are available. They can be selected from the *[Method]* menu in the *[Extraction]* dialogue box. Table 11.26 provides a brief description of the methods. To learn more about other extraction methods, see Harman (1976) or Rummel (1970).

Earlier, the Kaiser criterion (eigenvalues of at least 1.00) was used for selecting factors. While this method is both simple to apply and comprises the default setting in most software, it is in some ways an arbitrary cut-off value. Another popular method is **Cattell's scree plot**. It can be requested in SPSS *[Analyze, Data Reduction, Factor, Extraction, Scree Plot]* (see Figure 11.7). The rationale behind this plot is simple. All eigenvalues are listed in a

Table 11.26 Extraction methods in SPSS

Principal components	Recommended to find a small number of factors that can explain a maximum amount of variance
Maximum likelihood (ML)	Produces parameter estimates that are most likely to have generated the observed correlation matrix. Unlike other extraction techniques the method provides statistical goodness-of-fit tests (based on a chi-square approximation for determining the number of factors to retain). Moreover, factor estimates are independent of the scale of measurement. ML is used in the popular LISREL method
Unweighted and generalized least squares (GLS)	Based on the same algorithm as is ML. They differ with regard to the structure and scaling of the input matrix
Principal axis factoring (common factor analysis)	Recommended to detect the underlying dimensions and when the common variance is of interest. Popular among psychologists
Alpha factoring	Maximizes the reliability (Cronbach's coefficient alpha) of the common factors. Produces a first factor with the highest possible reliability, a second factor with the second highest reliability, and so on
Image factoring	Variables are split into a common and a unique part, called image and anti-image respectively. Computations based on partial correlations

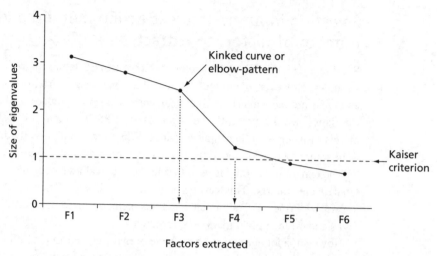

Figure 11.12 Catell's scree plot in SPSS

descending way along the *x*-axis while the size of the eigenvalue is plotted along the *y*-axis. See Figure 11.12.

In this hypothetical case, applying the visual recommendation of Catell implies extracting three factors, up to just before the kink. According to this approach, a kink indicates a "dramatic" or at least a visually observable decline in importance (variance explained) between two factors. In the present case, choosing the number of factors according to the Kaiser criterion would qualify four factors. In fact, the two approaches do not normally recommend extracting the same number of factors. While the scree plot is less arbitrary than the Kaiser criterion, it often suggests extracting too few factors. For instance, applying the scree plot to the factor analysis of bank customers would request only one factor. Regardless of whether one chooses to factor analyze all 102 valid responses or uses the splits shown in Table 11.6 and Table 11.7, the result is the same: one factor (customer-friendly service) dominates, explaining between 56 percent and 35 percent of the variance; the second factor explains 10 percent; and factors three and four account for 9–7 percent. This pattern with a first dominating factor and a number of subsequent factors of almost equal but of much less importance is not untypical. However, in almost all practical cases it is of no interest to extract a single factor or to extract a number of factors that only explain between one-third and one-half of the variance. Needless to say that it is not possible to rotate one factor.

An additional difficulty with applying the scree test concerns the nature of empirical problems. Real-life data often show a smooth curve within no clear kink, especially when a relatively large number of factors is involved.

Another test is known as Horn's test (Horn, 1965; Crawford and Koopman, 1973). While this test is rarely used, it has some algorithmic appeal and is easy to apply:

1. Plot the eigenvalues of the empirical data set as in a scree test (Figure 11.12).
2. Next, draw *k* random samples with the same number of observations (*n*) and variables (*m*) – and variable scaling – as the empirical data set.

3. Run a factor analysis on each of the n random samples and save the vector of eigenvalues (it typically will be part of the output).

4. Compute the average of the k columns of eigenvalues, based on the random samples. Thus a vector of m averaged eigenvectors is established (all factors are extracted in this test).

5. Plot these averaged random eigenvalues in the same plot as the empirical eigenvalues.

6. Note where the two functions intersect. Find the empirical eigenvalue just left of the intersection and stop extraction after this empirical eigenvalue has been extracted.

Assuming that the correlation matrix is an identity matrix (no correlation among variables), the so-called determinant (see Appendix 11-A) is 1.000. Moreover, all eigenvalues will be of size 1.000.

However, variables that do not correlate at all do not exist in the real world. But we could approach such a situation by drawing a randomized sample consisting of m variables and n observations (sometimes this process is called a **Monte Carlo simulation**). While variables with randomized observations will, in principle, be uncorrelated, the corresponding correlation matrix will in practice contain correlation due to sampling error. Not much but some, and the smaller the sample size, the bigger the error-based correlation will be. If one now factor-analyzes this randomized correlation matrix, the vector of eigenvalues will not be m unities. Some will be bigger and some smaller than 1.0 – reflecting the size of the error-based non-zero correlation.

When repeating this process k times we can compute a measure of average randomized eigenvalues. As noted above, these random eigenvalues are plotted in the same plot that has the empirical eigenvalues. As long as the empirical function is above the random function, it does better than randomness and is therefore extracted.

Table 11.27 shows how to perform Horn's test (plus another test to be discussed afterwards). Column III contains the eigenvalues from the factor analysis of the fifteen bank items concerning the male subset. The first four eigenvalues also appear – rounded – in Table 11.6. Column II has been produced so:

1. Start Excel *[Tools, Data Analysis, Random, Number Generator]*.
2. Set the number of random variables to 15 (= number of items in bank case).
3. Set the number of observations to 69 (= valid respondents in male subset).
4. Select *[Uniform]* distribution.
5. Choose a range from 0.5 to 7.5 (!).[12]
6. Copy or put the 69*15 matrix into a separate Excel sheet.
7. Repeat steps 2–6 nine times to produce ten sheets with random numbers.
8. Copy/paste the data in each sheet to the screen editor of SPSS and run a factor analysis based on the 69*15 data matrix with random scores.
9. After each run, save the column "Total" that appears in the "Total variance explained" table. This column contains the eigenvalues of the run. Copy/paste the table back into Excel, select the column with the eigenvalues and save it in a separate sheet (you can then delete the table "Total variance explained").
10. After all runs are completed, the result is a fifteen row (eigenvalues) times ten column

Table 11.27 Procedures for factor extraction

I	II	III	IV	V	VI
EV	Rand	Male	Chi	df	Prob
1	1.83	5.25			
2	1.70	1.49	143.64	104	0.006
3	1.51	1.21	114.37	90	0.042
4	1.37	1.07	94.71	77	0.083
5	1.27	0.98	77.55	65	0.137
6	1.13	0.88	60.96	54	0.240
7	1.04	0.78	45.82	44	0.397
8	0.95	0.66	32.92	35	0.569
9	0.87	0.61	23.28	27	0.670
10	0.77	0.53	13.52	20	0.854
11	0.69	0.40	5.57	14	0.976
12	0.59	0.37	3.15	9	0.958
13	0.52	0.31	0.61	5	0.987
14	0.43	0.26	0.00	2	1.000
15	0.34	0.20			

(runs) matrix. Use Excel's formula editor to compute an average column. This is the way that column II in Table 11.27 was produced.

11. In Figure 11.13 the data of column II have been plotted against the empirical values of column III.

In the present case the two curves intersect at the second eigenvalue. Therefore, according to Horn, one would extract two factors (strictly speaking, we should only extract one factor, because only the first empirical EV exceeds the random EV). Note that, according to the Kaiser criterion, one would extract no less than seven factors concerning the randomized data (or $m/2$ factors since one half of the eigenvalues in a randomized sample is expected to be higher than unity while the other half is expected to be less than unity). Since column II of Table 11.27 is the result of a randomization process, the reader will be unable to obtain precisely the same values.

Finally, one could apply a chi-square test that assesses whether the difference between two or several eigenvalues is significant. A proper test – an extension of a test developed by Bartlett – has been suggested by Lawley and Maxwell (1971). Referring to our small numerical example, we could test whether the difference between the second and the third eigenvalue is significant. The eigenvalues were: $EV1 = 1.683$, $EV2 = 1.006$ and $EV3 = 0.311$. The second eigenvalue is almost exactly 1, and had it been a little bit smaller, it would not have been extracted according to the Kaiser criterion, which only extracts values of at least unity. Since the second factor is "sensitive to the extraction level" consider if it is worth extracting at all. One way of approaching the problem is to assess whether the difference between 1.006 and 0.311 is statistically significant.

The appropriate generalized test is the following measure:

$$n \times \left[-\ln(EVi \times EVj \times ... \times EVm) + (p-k) \times \ln\left\{ \frac{(EVi + EVj + ... + EVm)}{m} \right\} \right]$$

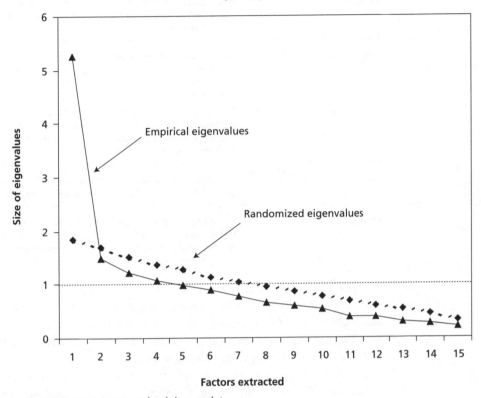

Figure 11.13 Horn's test on bank image data

where n is the sample size, EVi, EVj …EVm, are eigenvalues to be tested for equality, p is the total number of factors (or variables) and k is the number of factors already extracted before the test (so $m = p-k$).

This measure is chi-square distributed with $\frac{1}{2}(p - k + 2) \times (p - k - 1)$ degrees of freedom.

The numerical example gives:

$$20 \times \left[-\ln(1.006 \times 0.311) + (3 - 1) \times \ln\left\{ \frac{1.006 + 0.311}{2} \right\} \right] = 6.528$$

with $\frac{1}{2}(3 - 1 + 2) \times (3 - 1 - 1) = 2$ degrees of freedom. The corresponding probability value is 0.0382. Therefore, on the 0.05 level we reject the hypothesis of equality of the two eigenvalues – the second EV is significantly higher than the third. For specifics, see Lawley and Maxwell (1971, 20–22) and Bartlett (1951).

In columns IV–VI of Table 11.27 the same chi-square test has been applied to the bank image data (male subset). In the second row the chi-square value of 143.64 with 104 degrees of freedom transforms to a probability value of 0.006. It indicates the probability

Table 11.28 Rotation methods in SPSS

Varimax	Rotates factors so that the variation of the squared loadings is made large for a given factor and small for the remaining factors (simple structure)
Direct oblimin (oblique)	A direct procedure for improving orthogonal solutions. Involves a series of complex computations making those of Appendix 11-B appear easy
Quartimax	Rotates in such a way that a given variable has only one major loading on a given factor. It has an undesirable tendency to generate a dominant general factor with most factors having high loadings
Equamax	Attempts to achieve simple structure with respect to both rows and columns of the factor matrix. Also called Equimax
Promax (oblique)	A Varimax rotation is used to identify a preliminary pattern. Subsequently, the assumption of orthogonality is relaxed so that the final solution comes closer to a simple structure

that the eigenvalues of factor two to factor fifteen are all equal. The value 0.042 in the next row denotes that the factors three to fifteen are equal and so on. According to this measure, one ought to extract three factors. Extracting four factors could also be justified since the fourth eigenvalue has a marginal probability of 0.083 – between 0.05 and 0.10 – (four factors is what the Kaiser criterion recommends).

Above, the Varimax method was used to rotate the initial (unrotated) factor or component matrix (Table 11.18). Kaiser's Varimax rotation is probably the most popular technique. However, other methods exist and several of them are available in SPSS (Table 11.28).

Methods such as Oblimax, Quartimin, Biquartimin, Covarimin, and Procrustes (all oblique rotations) are not supported by SPSS. For a detailed and technical explanation of rotation methods, see Harman (1976) or Rummel (1970).

Case study: Dream Holiday (part 1)

Investigating European consumers' perceptions of tourism and reassessing promotional strategy

A big European travel agency, Dream Holiday Inc., asked its market research agency to conduct a large cross-country study dealing with tourists' opinions, attitudes and behaviour concerning travel related issues.[13] The rationale of the study was to improve management's insight into the tourists' attitudes towards topics such as holiday, vacation, tourism, spare time, experiences, culture, attractions, entertainment, sun and bathing. The aim was to gain knowledge about the perceptual–cognitive system and about how tourists made decisions.

According to managers, the findings would constitute a decisive input with regard to the agency's next marketing campaign, aimed at attracting Northern European tourists. Therefore, the agency was asked to conduct interviews with tourists in the Scandinavian and Baltic countries, in Poland, in the British Isles, in the Benelux countries and in Germany. About four hundred interviews were to be collected in each country.

The travel agency's marketing manager met the research agency. The research agency was an international company and had subsidiaries and/or affiliations in all the countries included in the research design.

After an introductory meeting, Dream Holiday's marketing manager and a team of consultants from the research agency – supplemented by a consumer psychologist and a professor of tourism marketing – agreed on a research process. First, a single focus group involving 8–12 tourists was conducted in each country (4–6 people of each sex; 4–6 persons aged 18–44 and 45+. At least half of them should travel abroad almost once a year). Each focus group was transcribed and translated into English.

The agency's consultants – assisted by the psychologist and the professor – used the reports to develop a comprehensive list of statements that could be tested quantitatively by way of a questionnaire. Eight weeks after the research process was initiated, the focus groups had been conducted and the transcript translated. Then, after intense e-mail communication between the consultants and the marketing manager, the final questionnaire was ready for the field phase.

The full questionnaire included questions concerning background characteristics and referred to behaviour and intentions (destination of last vacation, plans for coming vacation, satisfaction with last trip, etc.). The present case study only reports on eighty-eight tourism-related statements (plus some background data). All statements were structured according to a five-point Likert scale implying an interval measure ranging from "agree strongly" to "disagree strongly." The eighty-eight statements were arranged into the following categories:

- General statements about holidays and vacations (*X1–X22*).
- Statements related to taking a vacation within one's native country versus travelling abroad – for instance to Southern Europe (*X23–X35*).
- Statements about taking a vacation to other European countries – for instance travelling to countries in Southern Europe (*X36–X51*).
- Statements on experiencing the local atmosphere in an "exotic" environment – i.e. when travelling to countries outside Europe (*X52–X58*).
- Statements adressing package tourism (charter) versus individual travel (*X59–X68*).
- General statements about one's perception of life, career, family, leisure, politics, etc. (*X69–X88*).

Interviews were carried out as face-to-face interviews. With regard to the eighty-eight statements, the interviewer was instructed to hand over the questionnaire to the respondent and to let her/him fill in the questions. A total of 4,077 usable interviews were received. The interviews were done in four waves of random samples of approximately 1,000 omnibus interviews. Some background variables were included in the study: gender, age, household size, marital status, household income, whether the respondent was part of the

Table 11.29 The eighty-eight statements used in the tourism analysis

X1	I prefer travelling less often and then have a better holiday instead
X2	I primarily want to spend my holiday with my family
X3	It becomes more and more difficult to visit places where nature is unspoiled and the environment is unharmed
X4	It is important for me to have joy and fun during my holiday
X5	I prefer inns and small hotels to big hotels
X6	I feel that it is important to get in contact with other tourists
X7	The quality of a holiday trip is more important to me than the price
X8	I prefer having my holiday organized (charter) by a travel agent instead of doing all the planning myself
X9	When on holiday I want to be at places where there is not much tourism
X10	I really want to relax ("do nothing") when I am on holiday
X11	During my holiday it is important for me to be independent and free
X12	I need my holiday to recover and to gain strength for my work
X13	During my holiday I want as many experiences as possible
X14	When on holiday I look for a life that differs as much as possible from my everyday life
X15	I like entertainment and to have contact with other people during my holiday
X16	I prefer to plan my holiday in detail, so that nothing goes wrong
X17	One of my biggest dreams is to go round the world for a whole year
X18	While on holiday I am ready to accept less comfort than when I am at home
X19	During my holiday I want to live in as close a contact with nature as possible
X20	I am very active during my holiday
X21	To me a real summer holiday implies sun, beach and water
X22	When on holiday I do not want to think about money (how much things cost)
X23	Even when the sun does not shine it is possible to have a good holiday in my native country
X24	One of the reasons for me not to travel abroad is that the distances at home are shorter
X25	There are many sights and attractions in my native country
X26	Nature in my native country is not very interesting
X27	The weather in my native country is too unpredictable
X28	With children, it is best to have a holiday in one's native country
X29	My native country is not so different, and therefore I travel abroad
X30	Referring to the cost of taking a holiday in my native country, I get more "value for money" abroad
X31	One ought to get familiar with one's own country first
X32	I don't like to take a holiday in my native country because I will have to do all the planning myself
X33	One ought to take one's holiday in one's native country because employment and GNP benefit from it
X34	The weather in my native country is not that bad, it is pleasant and varied
X35	It is possible to take a good and cheap holiday in my native country
X36	I prefer to take my holiday abroad because the weather is more stable and it is warmer
X37	It is cheaper to take one's holiday abroad
X38	In a way, only a holiday abroad is a real holiday
X39	I want to see and experience foreign cultures
X40	I take my holiday abroad because I want to experience interesting and different nature
X41	When travelling abroad one is often exposed to crime and confidence tricks
X42	I take my holiday abroad because foreign countries have many more sights and attractions
X43	Travelling abroad often implies difficulties understanding the language, the traffic systems, etc.
X44	I take my holidays abroad because I want to visit museums, exhibitions, concerts, etc.
X45	I take my holiday abroad because I want to have challenging and untraditional experiences
X46	I find it important to socialize with the local people
X47	The weather is often too hot in Southern Europe
X48	I take my holiday abroad because it is so easy to buy a prepackaged tour
X49	Travelling abroad often implies health risks due to spoiled food or water

X50   A real summer holiday with sun, beach and water is practically only possible abroad
X51   I prefer travelling to places that are not for everybody

X52   I prefer staying at a luxury hotel with an international atmosphere and comfort
X53   I prefer to travel with a travel agent and a guide, who have been organizing the trip in advance
X54   I am primarily interested in the country's tourist attractions but not in its political and social conditions
X55   I am interested in getting in contact with the local people, because I want to learn about the country
X56   I prefer staying at a small hotel with the country's typical atmosphere, even if it is less comfortable
X57   I prefer to travel individually and to do much of the planning myself (except for plane and hotel)
X58   Apart from the country's tourist attractions I am also interested in the political and social conditions

X59   A prepackaged holiday (charter) is fairly cheap
X60   On a package tour one is forced to adapt oneself to the other passengers
X61   On a package tour everything is organized according to a schedule
X62   When being on a package tour one does not have to bother about anything. Everything is organized
X63   Package tours are organized such that they match the needs of average tourists
X64   Trips to distant countries are almost impossible to organize by oneself
X65   A charter tour can definitely also be an individual trip
X66   It is cheaper to do the planning by oneself (since travel agents must earn money, too)
X67   On a package tour, only transport, hotel, etc. are organized. Apart from this one can do as one pleases
X68   Charter tourism equals mass tourism

X69   I prefer spending my spare time away from home because I like variety and to get to know new people
X70   I am satisfied with my present job and do not want to get new tasks and responsibilities
X71   I am not very interested in current political issues, as long as they do not affect my family
X72   I find it important to obtain a higher income and better standard of life
X73   I often do things only because I want to convince myself that I can do it
X74   During my spare time I am usually occupied with activities like sports, going to town, visiting exhibitions, etc.
X75   Nowadays, too many people are indulged in pleasure while too few are working hard to make a difference
X76   I am setting myself difficult objectives which I subsequently try to achieve
X77   It is important for me to have at least one and preferably two real holiday trips each year
X78   One should do whatever possible to preserve regional and national differences in language, food, etc.
X79   I like to work hard and make a difference
X80   I prefer spending my spare time at home together with family and close friends
X81   For me, my work counts more than my family
X82   The economic growth must be ensured by industrial expansion, even if it means more pollution
X83   My personal development (self-fulfilment) is more important than my career
X84   I like to take risks and try new things
X85   I believe that my country contributes too much to foreign aid
X86   I think that more leisure is more important than higher income
X87   In my spare time, I am often relaxing at home reading a good book or watching a good film on TV
X88   I agree with the statement "To travel is to live"

Note: All statements scaled 1 = Agree strongly, 2 = Agree somewhat, 3 = Neither agree nor disagree, 4 = Disagree somewhat, 5 = Disagree strongly

Table 11.30 The first 25 eigenvalues

Factor	Eigenvalues		Cumulative
	Random	Empirical	Variance
1	1.30	7.42	8.4
2	1.29	6.61	15.9
3	1.27	5.09	21.7
4	1.26	2.99	25.1
5	1.25	2.61	28.1
6	1.23	2.29	30.7
7	1.22	2.02	33.0
8	1.22	1.92	35.2
9	1.21	1.57	36.9
10	1.20	1.50	38.6
11	1.19	1.46	40.3
12	1.19	1.40	41.9
13	1.18	1.34	43.4
14	1.17	1.27	44.9
15	1.17	1.20	46.2
16	1.16	1.18	47.6
17	1.15	1.13	48.8
18	1.14	1.12	50.1
19	1.14	1.07	51.3
20	1.13	1.05	52.5
21	1.12	1.01	53.7
22	1.11	0.99	54.8
23	1.11	0.97	55.9
24	1.10	0.95	57.0
25	1.10	0.94	58.0

workforce, occupational status, whether there was a video in the household, housing conditions, whether there was a garden in the household, and level of education. The background variables are included in the SPSS data file Dream_Holiday.sav as well as in the Excel files Dream_Holiday.xls and Dream_Holiday_Statements.xls. Both files can be downloaded from www.pearsoned.co.uk/schmidt.

Introductory factor analysis revealed a remarkable similarity or stability concerning the factor pattern when run on each country. Therefore, Dream Holiday's marketing manager decided that further analysis would be based on the pooled cross-country data. Doing so has the obvious advantage that the findings could be used as input and presented to managers in the travel agency's subsidiaries all over Europe.

The wording of the eighty-eight statements is provided in Table 11.29.

Table 11.30 lists the first 25 eigenvalues of the empirical study along with the accumulated variance explained and a column with the average eigenvalues derived from three randomized factor analysis based on a 4,077 cases by 88 variables matrix. Figure 11.14 displays the columns containing the empirical and the randomized eigenvalues.

There appear to be two kinks in the curve, a major one (between factors three and four) and a minor one (between factors eight and nine). Thus, according to the scree test, we should extract either three or eight factors. However, by doing so, either three-fourths respectively more than two thirds of the variance would be unaccounted for. Therefore, the marketing

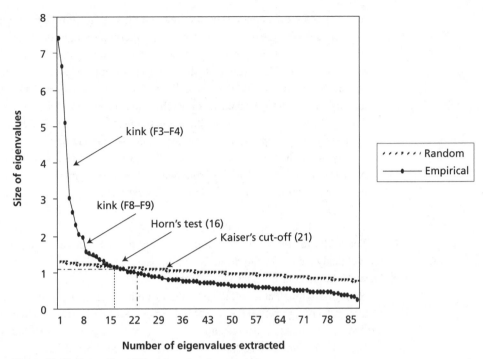

Figure 11.14 Extraction of factors – tourism analysis

manager rejects both scree test recommendations as unacceptable. Horn's test recommends sixteen factors while Kaisers test suggests twenty-one (see Figure 11.14 and Table 11.30).

The research agency's consultants carry out both runs (sixteen and twenty-one factors). After a preliminary analysis based on the Varimax solution they decide to use the twenty-one-factor solution, since several factors of the sixteen-factor solution appear strange. At least some of the factors seem difficult to explain. While several factors of the twenty-one-factor solution still constitute an interpretational challenge, all agree that twenty-one factors provides the best solution. So, the twenty-one-factor solution is chosen for interpretation. Results are Varimax-rotated and SPSS's default method, Principal components, is selected for extraction.

The Varimax-rotated component space is displayed in Table 11.31. Some deviations from the SPSS factor default have been made (defaults can be restored by the Reset button seen in Figure 11.7).

- *[Descriptives]*: KMO and Bartlett's test is *flagged*.
- *[Extraction]*: display "unrotated factor solution" is *deflagged* while "Scree plot" is flagged.
- *[Rotation]*: method is changed from "None" to "Varimax."
- *[Scores]*: default settings left unchanged.
- *[Options]*: since each of the 88 statements had between 20 and 80 missing – of which a portion were multiple missings, a factor analysis of the 4,077*88 matrix would have been based on fewer observations, namely the complete cases ($n = 3,344$). Since the number of missing observations per variable on average is small (60 cases or 1.5

percent) and seems non-systematic, the default setting for missing values was changed to "Replace with mean." Moroever, to aid interpretation, both checkboxes concerning the "Coefficient display format" are activated. The first one, "Sorted by size" has the effect that variables loading on the same factor appear as grouped or ordered in the output (see Figure 11.7). The second one, "Suppress absolute values less than" causes loadings less than the chosen value (between 0 and 1) to be ignored in the output display. In the tourism analysis the value 0.5 was chosen. The latter two output display requests greatly help interpretation, especially when many variables are involved.

■ Finally, to further ease interpretation, all data values of the rotated factor matrix have been multiplied with 100 and rounded to the nearest integer (to do this, the output matrix was exported to Excel where this operation is easy to do with the formula editor).

Table 11.31 shows the rotated matrix.

The KMO measure is 0.879, indicating that the data set according to theory is almost marvellously suited for factor analytic purposes. Bartlett's test value of 0 is of no interest because the number of cases is too large.

Note that while Table 11.29 lists eighty-eight statements, Table 11.31 only contains results concerning sixty-three variables. Since loadings of twenty-five variables did not exceed the 0.5 threshold across any of the twenty-one factors extracted, they are ignored in Table 11.31. Notice also that two factors (numbers 13 and 18) load with just one variable. Moreover, nine factors share loadings with only two variables. According to factor analysis theory, one should be cautious about interpreting a factor that has loadings with less than three variables. In the present analysis the first ten factors pass this criterion, which, however, is at best a rule of thumb.

Questions

The marketing manager of Dream Holiday acknowledges that he is unfamiliar with advanced marketing techniques like factor analysis, so some of the findings appear strange to him. A lack of expertise means he is unable to figure out if there is anything wrong with the results. He cannot rule out that everything has been done appropriately, but he wonders if something has been carried out improperly: maybe the questionnaire (the choice of statements) was not successful. Or something may have gone wrong during the data analysis. Finally, the consultants' interpretation of the output may be erroneous. The marketing manager simply does not know. He calls the professor of tourism who is affiliated to the study. However, it turns out that he is not an expert in quantitative methods – his own doctorate dealt with a Freudian approach to decision-making by tourists.

Fortunately, the marketing manager learns that you have recently been hired by Dream Holiday. Therefore, he asks you to interpret the data. However, since he wants to compare your analysis with the one provided by the research agency's consultants, you are not allowed to see their report before you have delivered your own interpretation. You are requested to address the following questions:

1. You are asked to perform an interpretation of Table 11.31 (using the statements in Table 11.29).

Table 11.31 Varimax-rotated solution of statements used in the tourism analysis (21 factors)

	1	2	3	4	5	6	7	8	9	10	11	12	13	14	15	16	17	18	19	20	21
X29	73																				
X26	66																				
X23	-65																				
X38	62																				
X27	59																				
X25	-59																				
X34	-54																				
X32	52																				
X35	-50																				
X39		73																			
X40		72																			
X45		69																			
X42		53																			
X8			67																		
X16			53																		
X48			50																		
X76				73																	
X73				67																	
X79				66																	
X84				64																	
X61					78																
X62					74																
X63					64																
X60					61																
X68					54																
X49						68															
X41						68															
X43						59															
X47						56															
X6							78														
X15							78														
X4							58														
X58								-75													
X54								68													
X71								54													
X52									82												
X56									-76												
X53									58												
X57									-57												
X80										75											
X87										66											
X2										52											
X74										-52											
X12											63										
X11											54										
X55												60									
X46												58									
X37													74								
X30													72								
X31														50							
X67															76						
X65															71						
X82																63					
X81																53					
X86																	67				
X83																	65				
X20																		72			
X7																			68		
X22																			65		
X1																				67	
X77																				-56	
X66																					71
X59																					-56

2. What do you think about the eighty-eight statements? What about the weighting of statements? Does the selection or sum of statements constitute a fair representation or random sample of the tourism and vacation universe of statements and attitudes?

3. (Optional) Go to the website connected to this book, www.pearsoned.co.uk/schmidt. Download the SPSS file Dream_Holiday.sav. Try to run the analysis using the above settings but with a different number of factors, say, with eight factors. How do you find this solution compared with your interpretation based on Table 11.29?

4. (Optional). Assume that you have downloaded Dream_Holiday.sav: recall that the eighty-eight statements belong to six topics. Would the interpretation be helped if one carried out, say, a factor analysis on each subtopic?

5. What clues or ideas does the output of Table 11.31 give with regard to an advertising strategy? Can you come up with 2–3 themes for: advertisements in printed media (and if so, which type of media); 2–3 themes (overall promotional message) for a TV-advertisement campaign (and if so, which type of TV-channel would you select)?

6. How could one use the results of the study to launch a campaign based on the internet? How could such a campaign be orchestrated?

11.7 Summary

The chapter deals with an important method in modern behavioural research and factor analysis.

In market research one often faces two related problems: summarizing the number of columns (variables); and classifying the number of rows (observations). Factor analysis is appropriate for addressing the former problem while cluster analysis (Chapter 12) is a proper method for dealing with the latter.

Factor analysis is used for "trimming down" the number of variables of a matrix into a smaller subset of **principal components** or factors. Factor analysis intends to keep as much as possible of the qualitative amount of information (explained variance) while discarding as much as possible of the quantitative amount of information (reduce the m variables to k factors were k is several times smaller than m). A factor is a linear composite of variables. The link between a variable and a factor is called a loading. In technical terms, the loading is the simple correlation between a variable and a factor. Whereas a variable possesses a known content (age, gender, agreement on an item, etc.), a factor is a mathematical–statistical construct. A factor (F) is named or identified by way of those out of the m variables that correlate/load highly with the factor.

The input to factor analysis is an observations-by-variables matrix while the output is a variables-by-factors matrix or factor matrix. The importance of a factor is indicated by its eigenvalue. The eigenvalue is a mathematical expression of a factor's ability to explain variance. The factors in the factor matrix are ordered according to descending size of the eigenvalues: the first factor has the highest eigenvalue, the second factor has the second highest and so on. Several methods exist for computing the factor matrix. The present chapter is based on principal components (Eckart–Young's singular value decomposition). The input used is the correlation matrix among variables (several other matrices could have be used instead). Appendix 11-A shows how the principal components technique works.

Theoretically, if a matrix has m variables it can have between one and m factors. Usually, though, the interest will focus upon a certain (low) number of factors. No statistical operator exists for determining the best number of factors to be extracted for final analysis and interpretation. However, several measures can be used for assessing the most appropriate number of factors, given the data set under scrutiny.

The measures discussed are:

- Kaiser criterion, an arbitrary cut-off procedure that exclusively considers factors with an eigenvalue of at least 1.0.
- Catell's scree plot plots the size of the eigenvalues (y-axis) against the number of factors extracted (x-axis). In the functional plot, which goes from upper left to lower right, one looks for a downward kink or an "elbow-structure." The objective is to stop the extracting factors just before the kink. So, if the kink appears between factor 4 and 5, one should stop at four factors.
- Horn's procedure involves computations where the empirical data set is compared with a measure obtained by way of a randomized process. The randomized data matrix has the same size (variables and observations) as the empirical data matrix. According to Horn's procedure, an empirical factor is only extracted if its eigenvalue exceeds the eigenvalues of the corresponding randomized run.

As a rule of thumb, the number of factors used for interpretation in a factor analysis should at least be able to explain half the variance and, preferably three-fourths of it. Moreover it should be able to do this with a k/m ratio of at least 1/3, or less.

Some data are more suited for factor analysis than others. The less the correlation between variables is, the less successful the factor analysis. A statistic like KMO can help the analyst to evaluate how suitable an empirical data set is for conducting factor analysis. A KMO statistic of 0.8 (the maximum is 1.0) indicates that the data are well suited for factor analysis. A statistic of less than 0.6 indicates that the data is not apt for factor analysis.

For matters of interpretation it is preferable that a variable loads highly on one factor only. This is a favourable situation because it implies that the variable can be explained fairly well by one factor. However, when inspecting the raw factor matrix it often happens that a variable's loading does not exceed 0.5 on any of the factors. Sometimes, few factors possess several loadings better than 0.5. In such a case it will help to manipulate the structure of the factor matrix such that an explanation of factors is made easier. It turns out that a rotation of the raw factor matrix in n-dimensional space by way of some statistical criteria (called simple structure) helps provide an interpretation. Several rotation methods exist. Some of them perform an orthogonal rotation while others rotate obliquely. In the present chapter a popular orthogonal method called Varimax is used. Appendix 11-B offers a technical explanation of how this rotation method works.

Questions

1. One of the cases in the book's main appendix is Appendix A-2, the Zaponia customer survey. Before proceeding, read this case carefully – particularly the comments on missing values – and download the appropriate files from www.pearsoned.co.uk/ schmidt. The data files are available in SPSS (.sav) and Excel (.xls) format. This study has a battery of variables that are suitable for conducting factor analysis (c1–c41). You are asked to carry out a factor analysis, name the factors and establish a list of the most important criteria concerning purchase and maintenance of a copier. The list should be usable as input for an advertising agency's consultant (a person without any knowledge of statistics). If you compare the variables list with the (Varimax rotated) output from the factor analysis, is there something that looks rather strange?

2. One of the first marketing applications of factor analysis appeared in the *Journal of Advertising Research* (Stoetzel, 1960). The author had conducted a factor analysis of the liquor preferences of French consumers. Some issues later, another author had a paper published in the same journal, which made critical comments with regard to how Stoetzel commented on and concluded his study (Vincent, 1962). Locate the two original studies.

    ■ Copy or print them.
    ■ Read both papers.
    ■ Provide a few comments that justify Vincent's critique.

3. Another case in Appendix A-3 is the Radio Store survey. Read this carefully and download the appropriate files. This study has a battery of variables that are suitable for conducting factor analysis cluster analysis (*v1–v55*). This file has no missing values and all 216 observations have valid responses. Carry out a factor analysis, name the factors and establish a list of issues that can be used as input for a description of what goes on in the mind of a typical consumer who enters a Radio Store outlet. The list should be usable as input for an advertising agency's consultant who is responsible for Radio Store's advertising. What should the five main themes centre on?

References

Aaker, D. A., Kumar, V. and Day, G. S. (2002) *Marketing Research*. John Wiley, New York.

Bartlett, M. S. (1950) "Test of Significance of Factor Analysis." *British Journal of Psychology* (statistical section). Vol. 3. 77–85.

Bartlett, M. S. (1951) "The effect of standardization on an approximation in factor analysis." *Biometrika*. Vol. 38. 337–344.

Bartlett, M. S. (1954) "A Note on the Multiplying Factors for various Chi-Square Approximations," *Journal of the Statistical Society*. Vol. 16 (Series B). 296–8.

Catell, R. B. (1966) "The Scree Test for Number of Factors," *Multivariate Behavioral Research*. No. 1. 245–76.

Cooley, W. W. and Lohnes, P. R. (1974) *Multivariate Data Analysis*. Wiley, NY.

Crawford, C. B. and Koopman, P. (1973) "A note on Horn's test for the number of factors in factor analysis." *Multivariate Behavioural Research*. Vol. 8. 117–125.

Dillon, R. W. and Goldstein, M. (1984) *Multivariate Analysis: Methods and Applications*, New York: John Wiley.

Green, P. E. (1978) *Analyzing Multivariate Data*, Hinsdale, Ill.: Dryden Press.

Hair, J. F., Anderson, R. E., Tatham, R. L. and Black, W. C. (1998) *Multivariate Data Analysis*. Prentice-Hall, Upper Saddle River, NJ.

Harman, H. H. (1976) *Modern Factor Analysis*. University of Chicago Press.

Horn, J. L. (1965) "A rationale and test for the number of factors in factor analysis." *Psychometrika*. Vol. 30. 179–186.

Kaiser, H. F. (1970) "A second-generation little jiffy." *Psychometrika*. Vol. 35. 401–415.

Kaiser, H. F. (1974a) "An index of factorial simplicity." *Psychometrika*. Vol. 39. 31–6.

Kaiser, H. F. (1974b) "Little jiffy, mark IV." *Educational and Psychology Measurement*. Vol. 34. 111–117.

Kim, J. O. and Mueller, C. W. (1979) *Introduction to Factor Analysis*. Sage.

Kruskal, J. B. and Shepard, R. N. (1974) "A non-metric variety of linear factor analysis." *Psychometrika*. Vol. 38. 123–157.

Lattin, J., Carroll, J. D. and Green, P. E. (2003) *Analyzing Multivariate Data*. Thomson Learning, Pacific Grove, CA.

Lawley, D. N. and Maxwell, A. E. (1971) *Factor Analysis as a Statistical Method*. Butterworth, London.

Lazarsfeld, P. F. and Henry, N.W. (1968) *Latent Structure Analysis*. Houghton Mifflin, Boston, MA.

Lingoes, C. and Guttmann, L. (1967) "Nonmetric Factor Analysis: A Rank Reducing Alternative to Linear Analysis." *Multivariate Behavioural Research*. Vol. 2. 485–505.

Rummel, R. J. (1988) *Applied Factor Analysis*. Northwestern University Press.

SAS/STAT Users Guide (1990) Version 6, Fourth Edition, Vol. 1. SAS Institute: Cary, NC.

Shavelson, R. J. and Webb, N. M. (1991) *Generalization Theory – A Primer*. Sage, Newbury Park, CA.

Stewart, D. W. (1981) "The Application and Misapplication of Factor Analysis in Marketing Research," *Journal of Marketing Research*. Vol. 18 (February). 51–62.

Stoetzel, J. (1960) "A Factor analysis of the liquor preferences of French consumers." *Journal of Advertising Research*. Vol. 1, no. 1. 7–11.

Tabachnick, B. G and Fidell, L. S. (1996) *Using Multivariate Statistics*. HarperCollins, New York.

Vincent, N. L. (1962) "A note on Stoetzel's factor analysis of liquor preferences." *Journal of Advertising Research*. Vol. 2, no. 1. 24–27.

End notes

[1] Or, more correctly, 0.76 is the correlation between *X1* and the column of data containing the so-called *factor scores* on Factor 1 (this column is not shown, but we will have more to say about factor scores later). Factor scores may be regarded as numerical weights that are not confined to values between +/− 1.

[2] The variable's original name is "no good tax advice" but since its loading on Factor 2 has a negative sign it seems justified to disregard the preceding negation.

[3] When using *[Select Cases]* one must be careful. For instance, to select the age group 35–54 based on the age variable, you must either tab in the logical operator "age > 34 and age < 55" or "age >= 35 and age <= 54." In any regard you should check if the selection variable contains the correct data by comparing values of the selection variable with values in the same row of the age variable.

[4] In both the factor analysis of gender and in that of age, fourteen responses were excluded due to missing values (in factor analysis by default, every observation that has a missing values is excluded). Moreover, in the analysis of age, thirteen respondents were older than fifty-four and were therefore also excluded. We could have used *[Analyze, Data Reduction, Factor, Options, Replace missing with mean]*.

[5] We could also have flagged "Sorted by size" in the same box. Doing so causes the rows or variables of various factor matrices to be reordered on the printout. Variables that have highest absolute loading on the first factor are printed first, from largest to smallest loading, followed by variables with their highest absolute loading on the second factor and so on. Factors are not reordered.

[6] In the example below, we have the following matrix:

	Factor 1	Factor 2
X1	0.81	−0.47
X4	0.43	0.88
X8	0.92	0.01

If we apply the rule used by SAS it implies that values of 0.67 and higher be flagged, since

$$\sqrt{\frac{\left[(0.81)^2 + (0.43)^2 + (0.92)^2 + (-0.47)^2 + (0.88)^2 + (0.01)^2\right]}{6}} = 0.67$$

[7] Note that U'*U also generates 1, although the law of multiplication [A=B always equals B=A] does *not* apply to matrix algebra. In our example it only holds because one of U's properties is that it is *orthogonal*.

[8] To check the argument, load the old or original data from Table 11.19 and run a factor analysis in SPSS. In *[Extraction]* set the number of factors to 3, in *[Scores]* choose *[Save as variables]*, *[OK]*. In the data screen, three new variables appear, the factor scores. They are called *fact_1*, *fact_2* and *fact_3*. Now request another factor analysis, deselect the original variables *X1*, *X4* and

X18 and instead select the new score variables. The first one is called "REGR factor score 1 for analysis 1 [FACT1_1]." In the *[Scores]* box *deselect [Save as variables]*. In the *[Extraction]* box keep the number of factors at 3, in the *[Descriptives]* box, request *[KMO and Bartlett...]* and also request *[Univariate Descriptives]* and *[Coefficients]*. Now run the analysis. In the output, KMO will be 0.500, Bartlett's chi-square will be 0.000, the significance value will be 1.000. The correlation matrix will be an identity matrix, with unity diagonal entries and zeros off-diagonal entries. Unlike Table 11.23, the mean is now 0.000 and not 3.000. But that is only because we have not added the value 3 to all scores before running the final analysis. Moreover, the standard deviation is 1.000 for all variables, while in Table 11.20 the standard deviation of a factor is the square root of the factor's eigenvalue. So, the difference is caused by a difference in the way SPSS scales the factor scores and the "more direct" computation in Table 11.10.

[9] Note that the range of the upper and lower parameter in the uniform distribution must be set to 0.5 and 7.5 instead of 1 and 7. Otherwise the sample will contain only half as many numbers that represent the first and the last interval as compared to the other intervals (1–1.5, 1.5–2.5, etc.).

[10] The computations are:

$$
|R| = \underset{\text{1}}{(1*1*1)} + \underset{\text{2}}{(-0.007)*(-0.325)*(-0.605)} + \underset{\text{3}}{(-0.605)*(-0.007)*(-0.325)}
$$

$$
- \underset{\text{4}}{(-0.605)*(-0.605)*(1)} - \underset{\text{5}}{(-0.325)*(-0.325)*(1)} - \underset{\text{6}}{(-0.007)*(-0.007)*(1)} = 0.527
$$

[11] The *partial correlation* of *X4*, say, is computed according to the formula:

$$
R_{X1X4 \bullet X8} = b_{X4} \left[\frac{(SD_{X4})\sqrt{1 - R_{X4X8}^2}}{(SD_{X1})\sqrt{1 - R_{X1X8}^2}} \right]
$$

$R_{X1X2 \cdot X8}$ refers to a correlation of *X1* and *X4* that is adjusted of ("net of") *X8*'s correlation with *X1* and *X4*, respectively. b_{X4} is the unstandardized regression coefficient of *X4* when regressing *X1* on *X4* and *X8*. Necessary requisites for computing the partial correlation coefficient:

$$
X_1 = -0.146X_4 - 0.580X_8 + 6.088
$$

b_{X4}	$= -0.146$
$SDX4$	$= 2.215$ (standard deviation of *X4*)
$SDX1$	$= 1.429$ (standard deviation of *X1*)
$R^2_{X1, X8}$	$= -0.605$ (regressing *X1* on *X8*)
$R^2_{X4, X8}$	$= -0.325$ (regressing *X4* on *X8*)

Inserting the appropriate values into the formula yields:

$$
R_{X1X4 \bullet X8} = -0.146 \left[\frac{(2.215)\sqrt{1 - 0.1056}}{(1.429)\sqrt{1 - 0.366}} \right] = -0.269
$$

Since the KMO formula uses the negative signed partial correlation (also called the **anti-image correlation**), the appropriate value on *X4* for the formula becomes 0.269.

[12] The semantic differential applied in the bank questionnaire used a 1–7 scale. However, since we want the two extremes of the interval scale (1 and 7) to appear in the random selection with a probability corresponding to the other interval-points (2–6), we need to expand the range beyond 1 and 7. Otherwise only values from 1 to 1.49999 will represent 1 and only values from 6.5 to 7 will represent 7, while all the remaining values in the interval will be represented by one full score point and not only by a half score point. For instance, 2 will be represented from 1.5 to 2.4999. Therefore, if one selects 1,000 values and they are to be rounded to integers, 1 and 7 appear only

about 83 times while 2–6 appear approximately 166 times. But if the width of the range goes from 0.5 to 7.5 then all 7 intervals will be represented about 143 times each.

[13] While the name is fictitious, the underlying data set is based on a large empirical project carried out some years ago.

12 Cluster analysis and segmentation of customers

Learning objectives

After studying this chapter you should be able to:

- Explain the purpose of cluster analysis.
- Explain the difference between hierarchical and non-hierarchical methods.
- Give an overview of tools for selecting the best number of clusters.
- Outline how cluster analysis can be used in marketing.
- Show how to run cluster analysis in SPSS.
- Discuss generalizability in relation to factor analysis and cluster analysis.

12.1 Using factor analysis for clustering observations

Chapter 11 addressed the similarities of factor and cluster analysis from a methodological perspective. Having covered factor analysis it is now time to deal with its "transposed cousin," cluster analysis. This chapter uses the terms segment/segmenting and cluster/clustering interchangeably. When discussing fragments of a market the term "segment," is preferred while "cluster" is used when categorizing a sample by statistical techniques.

Cluster and factor analysis may be perceived as opposing sides of the same coin (look back to Figure 11.1). Indeed, data from the bank of Chapter 11 (Table 11.9) could be used to cluster our respondents by way of a factor analysis. This is known as a **Q-type** factor analysis (to denote the contrast to the usual type of factor analysis, the R-type). To illustrate this, panels (c) and (d) of Figure 11.1 display the underlying principles of performing an R-type factor analysis. In panel (c) the raw data matrix is structured so that the variables appear along the columns (horizontal) while the observations are placed in the rows (vertical). This type of matrix is used as input for a factor analysis that results in an output format corresponding to panel (d) where the variables are now placed in the rows while the factors appear in the column (the observations as such are of no interest in the factor analysis output, since we factor analyze across subjects or respondents). The cells in panel (d) contain the correlation (loadings) between the specific variable and a factor.

Table 12.1 Input matrix for factor analysis

									Observations											
	1	2	3	4	5	6	7	8	9	10	11	12	13	14	15	16	17	18	19	20
X1	2	3	4	1	3	3	1	5	7	3	2	2	2	2	2	2	1	2	2	3
X4	1	2	3	3	7	1	4	2	6	7	7	3	6	7	7	2	4	4	6	2
X8	6	7	4	7	5	6	4	3	1	3	2	6	6	6	6	5	6	4	6	6

Now assume for a moment that the rows and the columns of panel (c) and (d) are reversed. In panel (c) the observations appear in the columns while the rows become the variables. In panel (d) the observations appear in the rows instead of the variables (the variables are of no specific interest here since we now want to factor analyze across variables). The columns in panel (d) would still contain the factors. However, a factor loading would no longer indicate a correlation between a variable and a factor but would refer to a correlation between the observation (respondent) and the factor. If, say, three factors were extracted some observations would load highly on Factor 1, some on Factor 2 and so on. From an interpretational viewpoint all observations with high loadings on Factor 1 would be regarded as a "member of cluster 1" and so on.

Again from Chapter 11, the input matrix of Table 11.6 for factor analysis would look like Table 12.1.

A factor analysis of this matrix produces the output shown in columns II–III of Table 12.2 (the reader is encouraged to check this).

Table 12.2 Q-type factor analysis of numerical example

I	II	III	IV	V	VI	VII
	Varimax rotation					
	F1	F2				"CLUSTER"
Observation 1		1.00	2	1	6	2
Observation 2		1.00	3	2	7	2
Observation 3	−0.73	0.69	4	3	4	−1/2
Observation 4	0.54	0.84	1	3	7	1/2
Observation 5	0.97		3	7	5	1
Observation 6		0.98	3	1	6	2
Observation 7	0.96		1	4	4	1
Observation 8	−1.00		5	2	3	−1
Observation 9		−0.92	7	6	1	−2
Observation 10	0.73	−0.69	3	7	3	1/−2
Observation 11	0.73	−0.69	2	7	2	1/−2
Observation 12		0.89	2	3	6	2
Observation 13	0.96		2	6	6	1
Observation 14	1.00		2	7	6	1
Observation 15	1.00		2	7	6	1
Observation 16		0.97	2	2	5	2
Observation 17	0.77	0.64	1	4	6	1/2
Observation 18	0.96		2	4	4	1
Observation 19	0.96		2	6	6	1
Observation 20		1.00	3	2	6	2
EV	11.5	8.5	(all other eigenvalues approach 0)			

From a methodological perspective this way of conducting a factor analysis causes problems. Most multivariate procedures, including factor and cluster analysis, assume that the number of rows or observations exceeds the number of columns or variables by a factor of at least five. This rule of thumb holds for a normal factor analysis with three variables and twenty observations. However, the factor analysis above is technically based on only three rows and twenty columns implying that the number of "variables" (twenty) by far exceeds the number of "observations" (three).

While software usually accepts a factor analysis based on the above "flat" matrix, they tend to flag an alert to the potential problem. In SAS, the log file provides the following message: "Warning: The number of observations is not greater than the number of variables." When running the problem in SPSS, the output may begin with the message: "Correlation matrix: This matrix is not a positive definite." According to statistical theory, a matrix that possesses the merits of being a positive definite must not contain columns or variables that are linearly dependent (i.e. identical).

This assumption does not hold in the present case. The two pairs of observations, 13 and 19, and 14 and 15, are identical, so their correlations are 1.00. Columns IV–VI of Figure 12.2 display the raw data of the numerical example. Finally, column VII suggests a cluster membership of the twenty respondents, based on their two factor loadings. As before, loadings of less than 0.5 (numerically) have been ignored. In some cases both loadings pass the 0.5 threshold and in such situations the respondent is affiliated with both clusters by means of a weight corresponding to the loading. Contrary to the clustering methods to be discussed below, the Q-type factor analysis does not assume exclusivity concerning cluster membership (therefore it is usually regarded as belonging to the class of **overlapping cluster analyses**). For instance, Observation 4 possesses loadings or weights better than 0.5 on both factors. However, association with Factor 2 (0.84) is higher than with Factor 1 (0.54). Note that this way of perceiving categories fits much better with intuitive reasoning than does traditional cluster analysis, discussed below. According to Q-type factor analysis a respondent can be a member of several clusters simultaneously and the loading indicates the weight or affiliation with the specific cluster. In traditional cluster analysis a respondent is either a member of one cluster or another.

Column VII of Figure 12.2 is an attempt to translate the loadings pattern of columns II and III to cluster membership. Unfortunately, two problems cause interpretational problems. First, if a respondent loads highly on two factors, which one is that person to be regarded a member of?[1] The only way is to regard them as a member of the cluster with the highest loading. For instance, Observation 4 would be regarded as a member of cluster two rather than cluster one. Note also that in several cases the sign of a respondent's loading is negative, implying that the person's response is a "negation" of the respondents with positive signs on the same factor. From an interpretational viewpoint this is difficult to handle. A value of -1.00 on Factor 1 does not imply that the respondent belongs to cluster two. For instance, Observation 8's value on Factor 1 is -1.00 while his/her response profile (columns IV–VI) does not at all resemble that of Observations 1, 2 and 20, all of which load $+1.00$ on Factor 2. (Nor does it fit observations 14 or 15 of Factor 1). Another example: while Observation 9's negative sign on Factor/Cluster 2 apparently does not transform to or fit with Factor/Cluster 1, its value actually constitutes a negation of the variables having a positive sign on Factor 2.

Roughly speaking one could say that Factor/Cluster 1 implies a low value on variable one and a high value on variables two and three; whereas Factor/Cluster 2 implies a low value on the first two variables and a high value on the third (note that observation 9 fits "inversly" with this pattern). A loading plot of the Varimax rotated solution shows a curious pattern: the observations form a circular structure along the borders of the rectangular solution space.

To sum up, the advantage of a cluster analysis based on a Q-type factor analysis is that it allows for a simultaneous membership of several clusters. The disadvantage concerns interpretation. In the above numerical example only about half of the respondents could be clearly identified as belonging to a certain cluster, while the rest either seemed to be split between two clusters or possessed a loading that appeared difficult to make sense of when compared with the response profile.

According to some researchers (Green, 1978) using the Q-type factor analysis for clustering of respondents causes additional problems. First, each individual must be measured across a large number of variables to obtain stability between person correlations. The more limited the sample of variables, the less useful is the classification of individuals into "types" by their factor loadings. Second, it is not infrequently the case (not here though) that real individuals do not load highly on any factor/cluster.

The big problem with Q-type factor analysis is that, due to the extraction process, it produces factors/clusters of decreasing size. The bank image analysis above is based on fifteen variables and one-hundred-and-fourteen observations. A Q-type analysis on this matrix would give fourteen ($m-1$, or $15-1$) non-zero eigenvalues that explain all of the variance. The first factor explains more than half (56 percent) of the total variance, while the next thirteen factors explain between 12 percent and 1 percent. The remaining 100 factors explain nothing at all. Note, that if you want to run this example in SPSS you must use two options, namely *[Factor, Options, Missing values: Replace with mean]* and then in the *[Rotation]* box set the *[Maximum iterations for convergence]* to, say, 500. Otherwise SPSS will not produce an output. And, of course, you must transpose the data matrix first. This is easy to do in SPSS *[Data, Transpose]*.

12.2 Traditional clustering of subjects or cases (respondents)

As seen in the previous section, the applicability of factor analysis for clustering people is limited. Fortunately, other clustering methods are available. The remainder of this chapter will be dedicated to these.

Stated briefly, the purpose of all clustering methods is to maximize the homogeneity or similarity of observations *within* a cluster and simultaneously maximize the heterogeneity or dissimilarity *between* clusters. Cluster analysis is a statistical tool that an analyst can use to test empirically whether there are patterns in the data. Examples might include:

- A producer of soft drinks might want to assess if the market or the product category can be segmented with regard to lifestyle.

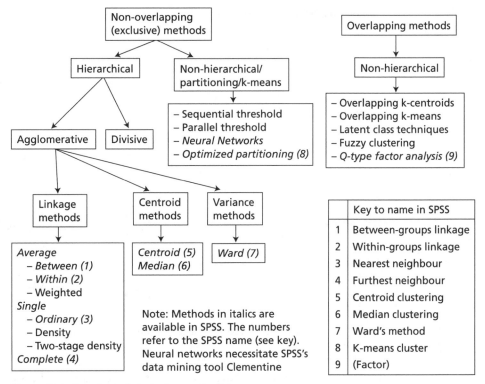

Figure 12.1 Overview of clustering methods

- An insurance company could be interested to know if its own customers could be categorized into sub-segments according to specific characteristics.
- A charity might want to segment its members or its target market into categories that need different communication channels (personal selling or online promotion).
- A producer of business software could be interested in categorizing customers into two or three categories with regard to their need for online maintenance.
- Sometimes an international marketer would like to know if primary customer segments in foreign markets are similar to the marketer's home market or if foreign markets differ in ways justifying a different approach to advertising and sales promotion.

Today, all statistical software can categorize objects (respondents, companies, occasions, census statistics, etc.). Most programs intend to cluster observations or cases but usually they can also be used for clustering of variables. When working with SAS/STAT one can choose between fifteen to twenty methods, distributed across several general procedures, while SPSS has 8–9 methods depending on how one defines a cluster analysis.

Data-mining software (SAS and SPSS supply special modules) contains k-means clustering, fuzzy clustering and neural networks. Furthermore, stand-alone programs, special purpose software and Excel add-ins can do cluster analysis. Therefore, before beginning a detailed coverage of selected methods, a systematic overview of approaches may facilitate the understanding of the problem. See Figure 12.1. Figure 12.2 displays the basic characteristics of the clustering methods shown in Figure 12.1.

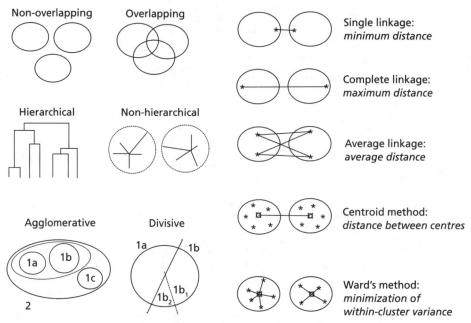

Figure 12.2 Illustration of important clustering issues in Figure 12.1

Overlapping versus non-overlapping methods

The first question that faces the analyst concerns the exclusivity of cluster membership. Is it possible for a case, say a respondent, to be a member of several clusters at the same time? From an intuitive point of view an overlapping algorithm appears to constitute a superior description of the real world compared with a non-overlapping approach. Just as few phenomena in the real world are either black or white, hardly any customer belongs 100 percent to a price-conscious segment and 0 percent to a luxury segment. It depends on situational factors (time, occasion, etc.). Ideally, a consumer's membership of a specific cluster changes in accordance with her/his financial resources, with the stage in their life, mood and so on. An example: at the end of the month before the person gets paid, she/he may be a very price conscious customer. The day after the pay cheque arrives, the person suddenly turns into a luxury customer. Consequently, she/he buys something for immediate pleasure, say an expensive wine or a computer.

According to overlapping methods, a weight indicates the respondent's association with a specific cluster. The issue was mentioned above in the section dealing with Q-type factor analysis. Due to interpretational problems, overlapping methods are rarely used in applied settings – in spite of the theoretical merits of the overlapping approach (imagine the difficulty of making sense of five clusters where a respondent's weight concerning each one is 0.2). Therefore overlapping methods will not be covered here. However, the techniques are reviewed in Shepard and Arabie (1979), Arabie, DeSarbo and Wind (1981) and Chaturvedi et al. (1997). The last two papers discuss overlapping methods and their applicability in relation to market segmentation.

Hierarchical versus non-hierarchical methods

Due to their structure, hierarchical methods are sometimes called "vertical" methods to differentiate them from non-hierarchical "horizontal" methods. In a hierarchical system, the trait can be followed all through the branches and at any time it is possible to trace the history of every case. From an analytical viewpoint this is a definitive advantage. However, a drawback of this "over-reliance" on the individual case is that it becomes difficult to handle as the number of cases becomes too big to view or grasp at a glance. One runs the risk of getting lost in the details.

The smaller the sample the more sense it makes to use hierarchical methods. If the sample size is less than one hundred, non-hierarchical techniques may cause difficulties because the result may be highly sensitive to the order of the observations in the data set (SAS/STAT, 1990). If, on the other side, the sample size exceeds two hundred, interpretation of the hierarchical method becomes difficult, especially when using some of the output options. Therefore, when the sample size exceeds two hundred (or even one hundred), as often is the case in applied settings, a non-hierarchical method may be a better choice.

Agglomerative versus divisive approaches

Hierarchical methods represent a hierarchical way of categorizing cases. Usually the algorithm works from bottom to top. First, each case is treated as a cluster. In the next step, the two closest cases are clustered, etc. The procedure stops when all cases or observations appear as part of a supercluster. This approach, proceeding from many clusters to one, is called **agglomerative clustering**. It is possible to reverse the clustering process, by starting with a supercluster and splitting it into two subclusters. Next, one of the subclusters is split into a sub-subcluster. In successive steps cases that are most dissimilar are split off and put into smaller clusters. This process continues until every cluster consists of a single case. In any case, divisive (hierarchical) methods work almost as agglomerative (hierarchical) methods in reverse. Note also that it is always possible to split a subcluster by way of a non-hierarchical method. One just needs to pre-define the number of clusters that the subcluster is to be split into.

Linkage, centroid and variance methods

Linkage methods focus on linking cases to other cases or to existing clusters or merging clusters with other clusters. They concentrate on the measurement of interpoint/intercluster distance and how this is done in the most efficient way when considering specific presumptions. In linkage methods the measurement of interpoint distances plays a crucial role, whereas in centroid methods they are ignored in favour of average distances. As follows from the name, variance methods centre on (intra-cluster) variance while the distance between clusters plays no role at all. Since linkage, centroid and variance methods are available in most statistical computer packages they will be discussed in some detail below.

There are other clustering techniques that are not covered here. These include maximum-likelihood hierarchical clustering, Lance-Williams flexible-beta, McQuitty's similarity analysis, Howard-Harris's method and S. C. Johnson's hierarchical clustering (Gower's median). The interested reader should inspect specialized texts such as Everitt (2001), Romesburg (1990), Lorr (1983), Aldenderfer and Blasfield (1985), Jajuga, Solokowski and Bock (eds, 2002), Anderberg (1973), Späth (1980) or Jamby and Lebeaux (1983). Most of these books also cover non-hierarchical methods. The first three books are

Table 12.3 Pilot study of managers risk aversion and propensity to internationalize

Manager	Risk aversion (X1)	Propensity to internationalize (X2)
A	2	6
B	3	9
C	7	1
D	8	3
E	2	2

recommended for the reader who is not a statistical expert and who is not very familiar with matrix algebra. Everitt is the classic treatise on the subject. Späth is "The Harman of Cluster Analysis," but difficult to read. Much insight into clustering techniques can be obtained by studying the *Journal of Classification*, published by Springer Verlag, New York.

12.3 Hierarchical cluster analysis: an example

Assume a pilot study among five knowledgeable export managers has been done. The purpose of the study is to obtain input for a large-scale study. Each manager is asked to provide answers to two statements: management's risk-aversion in general, *X1* and management's propensity to launch products on the international market, *X2*. So far, none of the involved companies has engaged in international sales. The statements are marked on a ten-point scale: 1 = Very high risk-aversion to 10 = No risk-aversion at all for *X1*; and 1 = No propensity at all to internationalize to 10 = very high propensity to internationalize for *X2*. The result of the pilot study is shown in Table 12.3.

Soon, a large-scale survey is to be conducted, based on the results of the pilot study. The purpose of the large-scale study is to categorize or cluster managers according to their attitude towards an array of issues dealing with economic and international behaviour. Before carrying out the large-scale study, however, the responses of the pilot study will assess the usefulness of (hierarchical) cluster analysis.

For illustrational purposes the way to measure the distance between the two points A and B is shown in panel (a) of Figure 12.3. Usually (but not always) one would employ the measure known as Euclidian distance. Generally, the formula is defined thus:

$$d_{ij} = \sqrt{\sum_{k=1}^{r} (x_{ik} - x_{jk})^2}$$

Where *k* refers to the number of dimensions. However, readers may be more familiar with the two-dimensional version of the formula:

$$d_{AB} = \sqrt{(x_1 - x_2)^2 + (y_1 - y_2)^2}$$

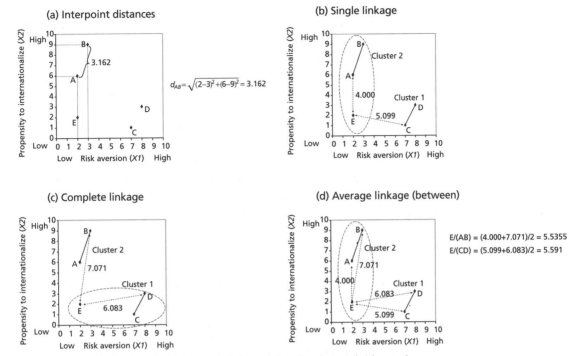

Figure 12.3 Five managers' attitudes towards internationalization and risk aversion

The plot of Figure 12.3 has two dimensions, X1 and X2. Consequently, the distance A to B is measured as:

$$d_{AB} = \sqrt{(2-3)^2 + (6-9)^2} = 3.162$$

Table 12.4 shows all ten possible interpoint distances of Figure 12.3.

Generally, with n points, there will be $[n*(n-1)]/2$ distances. In this example there are only two variables, implying that distances are measured in a two-dimensional space. While this is quite easy, imagine the empirical sample of the Dream Holiday case study in Chapter 11. That sample has 4,077 observations, so (ignoring missing observations), it would need to perform $(4,077*4,076)/2 = 8,308,926$ measurements. Usually one would

Table 12.4 Interpoint distances of Figure 12.3

AB	3.162
AC	7.071
AD	6.708
AE	4.000
BC	8.944
BD	7.810
BE	7.071
CD	2.236
CE	5.099
DE	6.083

base a cluster analysis on lifestyle items or statements. The Dream Holiday study has eighty-eight such variables. So each interpoint distance is a compound measure consisting of 87 ($n - 1$) variable-to-variable measures on a subject or case level. In summary that becomes 722,876,562 "submeasures." Fortunately, this can be done in seconds on a computer.

To cluster the five points in Figure 12.3(a), it is not even necessary to inspect the ten measurements of Table 12.4 to see that C and D ($d_{CD} = 2.236$) are clustered first, followed by A and B (($d_{AB} = 3.162$). However, having formed clusters D/C (cluster 1) and A/B (cluster 2), which of the two clusters is E going to be put into? This question immediately brings up a subsequent issue: which place or co-ordinate in the new clusters represents the point of reference? As long as a cluster only consists of a single point, a reference problem does not arise. The measurement is from point to point. But how can the distance, say, from point E to cluster 1, be measured? Several possibilities exist:

1. Measure from E to C. With other words from E to the *closest* point in Cluster 1. This would be the distance E/C (5.099) because the distance from E to the other point, D, in cluster 1 is longer (6.083). This approach is called **single linkage** or **nearest neighbour** [SPSS-name: nearest neighbour]. See Figure 12.3(b). In the present case, E would be merged with the cluster 2 because the distance AE is smaller than EC.

2. Measure from E to D. That is, from E to *the most distant* or furthest away point in cluster 1. While it appears odd to use the farthest away point in a cluster as the point of reference, the approach ensures that a new case that is added to the cluster is relatively close to all cases in the cluster and not only close to one. If E consists of several points, the appropriate distance is from furthest point in E to furthest point in cluster 1. The maximum distance between points in each cluster represents the smallest distance (minimum diameter) that can enclose all cases of both clusters. This technique is named **complete linkage**, **farthest** or **furthest neighbour** or **diameter method** [SPSS name: furthest neighbour]. See Figure 12.3(c).

3. Another way would be to measure every existing distance between E and points in cluster 1 and then use the average distance between E and the points in the clusters as a reference. This is the **average linkage between groups** method [SPSS name: between-groups linkage]. See Figure 12.3(d).

4. When measuring all distances between clusters one might ask if this is the best way. A different approach is to assume E to be part of the new cluster and subsequently compute the average intra-cluster distance of clusters ECD and EAB, respectively. This method is called **average linkage within groups** [SPSS name: within-groups linkage]. See Figure 12.4(a).

5. Instead of measuring distances between E and individual points in a cluster one could use the midpoint or centroid of a cluster as a reference for measuring the distance between E and the cluster. This is the **Centroid** method [SPSS name: centroid clustering]. See Figure 12.4(b).

6. Another school of methods ignores the distance between clusters. Instead, it aims at minimizing intercluster variance. One such method is known as **Ward's** [SPSS name: Ward's method]. See Figure 12.4(c) and (d).

7. **Median clustering** resembles the centroid method with the exception that the centroid

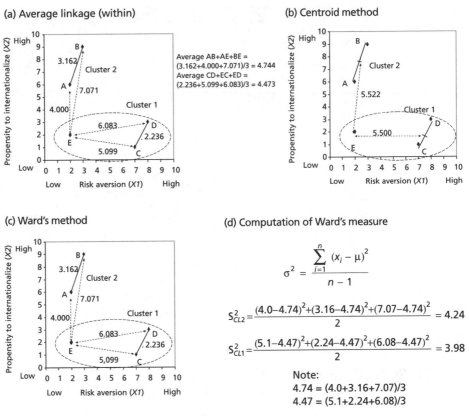

Figure 12.4 Additional clustering methods

or weighted average is replaced by the median. According to this approach, equal weighting is used to construct the joined cluster (as if the two clusters had equal size). The median method is the appropriate technique for handling nominal and ordinal variables [SPSS name: median clustering].

Hierarchical cluster analysis in SPSS

This section shows how to run hierarchical methods using SPSS. Figure 12.5 shows the data of Table 12.3 in the screen editor of SPSS. Clustering methods are found in the *[Analyze]* menu. (K-means cluster will be covered in the next section.) Discriminant is not a clustering method but is listed because, like cluster methods, it can be used for categorizing. Discriminant analysis was discussed in Chapter 10. If your version of SPSS possesses the necessary licence, the *[Classify]* list in the *[Analysis]* dropdown will also include a program called *[Tree]*. This is a systematic procedure for splitting big data sets. It will be covered in Chapter 15, Section 1.

Figure 12.6 displays the dialogue boxes for running hierarchical cluster analysis.

■ In the main box, click *X*1 and *X*2 into the *[Variables]* field. Sometimes, it is a good idea

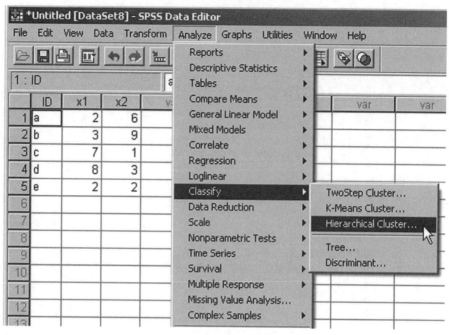

Figure 12.5 Running hierarchical cluster analysis in SPSS.

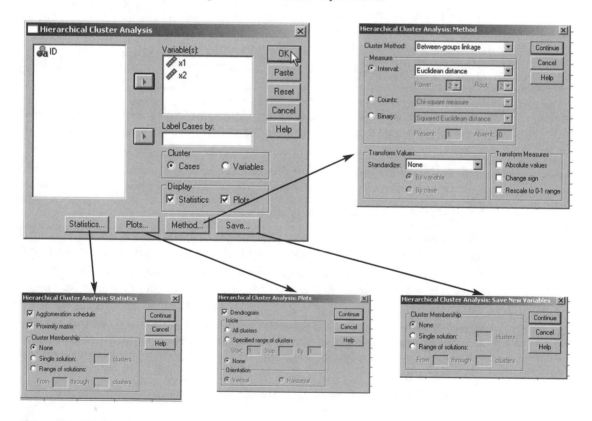

Figure 12.6 SPSS hierarchical cluster analysis dialogue boxes

Table 12.5 Distance measures for interval-scaled data

Euclidean distance	See panel (a) of Figure 12.3
Squared Euclidean	Square of the Euclidean distance
Cosine	According to the cosine similarity measure a small angle between two sets of points implies that the points are close and vice versa. This similarity measure is a semi-metric that obeys some of the rules of non-Euclidean metrics
Pearson correlation	Two sets of points can be compared by their components with the Pearson correlation coefficient. The measure is confined to the interval -1 to $+1$. The metric is independent of the set of points' relation to the origin, and thus it is invariant under linear transformation of the data
Chebychev	The Chebychev distance between two objects is the maximum absolute difference in values for each variable in any single dimension
Landahl's city block (Manhattan)	The city block distance between two objects is the sum of absolute differences in values for each variable
Minkowski	The distance between two objects is the pth root of the sum of the absolute differences to the pth power between the values for the objects. When $p=1$ the Minkowski distance equals city block distance. When $p=2$, Minkowski equals Euclidean distance and when $p=\infty$, Minkowski equals Chebychev distance
Customized	In the case of the Euclidean distance, differences between points are first squared and then added. Finally, one takes the square root of the result. When selecting customized, one can vary both the power and the root from 1 to 4. Only recommended for experienced users. In Minkowski, one can change the power only. In all cases, the default setting is 2

to use a label that helps interpret the output. Therefore, add a label called "id," referring to the five data points of Table 12.3. Next, click the "id" variables into the *[Label Cases by]* field. Leave the default settings in this box unchanged.

- In the statistics box, flag the *[Proximity matrix]*. It gives the Euclidean distances between points.
- In the Plots box, flag *[Dendrogram]* and change *[Icicle]* to "None" to target and reduce the output.
- In the *[Save New Variables]* box, leave default settings untouched.
- The Method box is the most important. One can choose between seven methods. The default method is "Between-groups linkage" (SPSS notation for average linkage). All the available methods have been explained above. For the present run, keep the default settings.
- Another rather important setting concerns the *[Measure]*. Default setting is "Squared Euclidean distance." Available choices are shown in Table 12.5.

The Euclidean distance – squared or not – is the most popular measure. However, one should note that the Euclidean distance takes no account of any pattern of covariance that exists in the data. Moreover, it is not scale-invariant.[4] Therefore, other distance measures may be more appropriate in some cases. For illustrative purposes, change the default setting from "Squared Euclidean distance" to "Euclidean distance."

It is worth discussing the Method options in more detail; first, the *[Measure]* choices. Usually the distances to measure are interval-scaled. But sometimes they may be non-metric, e.g. frequencies ("counts" in SPSS terminology) such as purchase of different brands or marital status. In this case we would have to employ other, less ambitious distance measures. Assume that in Figure 12.3(a) the variables had been purchases of Coke (*X1*) and Pepsi (*X2*) within the last month. Here the exact difference of 3.162 between points A (2 Cokes and 6 Pepsi) and B (3 Cokes and 9 Pepsi) simply makes no sense. SPSS provides two measures for assessing the difference between objects that are nominal scaled:

- Chi-square measure of equality for two sets of frequencies.
- Phi-square measure. This is the chi-square measure normalized by the square root of the combined frequency.

If data are confined to 0 and 1 (e.g. gender, where 0 = female and 1 = male) distance measures must be used for calculating distances between binary data ("binary" in SPSS terminology). There are many (dissimilarity) measures available for binary data. SPSS lists no less than twenty-seven measures. All of these binary-based measures use two or more of the values obtained from a simple 2*2 matrix of agreement, where four outcomes are possible (0,0), (1,0), (0,1) and (1,1). Many of these measures differ with regard to how to handle negative values. Since binary data are rarely used for distance measurement in marketing research, they will not be covered here.

The *[Transform Values/Measures]* options. All cluster measurements can be transformed, for example, to factor scores; they can be rescaled to values between −1 and 1 or to values between 0 and 1; signs may be changed; and so on. We doubt that the reader will need to use these features and therefore they are ignored here.

Now tab the *[Continue]* button of the Methods box and the *[OK]* button of the main box. The output is presented in Table 12.6 and Figure 12.7.

Table 12.6 and Figure 12.7 are to be compared with Figure 12.3(d). Based on the manual computations in (d), the average linkage (between groups) method implies putting point E (the manager from company E) into cluster 2.

Table 12.6 also shows the proximity matrix requested in Figure 12.6 (statistics box). It is symmetric and provides all pairwise measurements between points, including distances, say between A and D (not shown in Figure 12.3(d)). The agglomeration schedule is to be used with Figure 12.7, which shows a so-called dendrogram. A dendrogram shows at which distance an observation joins another observation or a cluster or at which distance clusters join other clusters. Since SPSS applies some rescaling, the values in the agglomeration schedule of Table 12.6 do not fit with the distances that can be manually read in Figure 12.7. For instance, in the proximity matrix of Table 12.6, the difference between A and B is 3.162. However, in Figure 12.7 they appear to join at a numerical distance of approximately 5. To make matters worse, SPSS appoints numbers to observations beginning with the first case in the file (so A becomes 1), which may be confusing.

Table 12.6 SPSS output tables from hierarchical cluster analysis

Method: Between-groups linkage (average linkage)

Case processing summary

Cases

Valid		Missing		Total	
N	*Percent*	*N*	*Percent*	*N*	*Percent*
5	100	0	0	5	100

Average linkage (between groups)

Proximity matrix

Euclidean distance

Case	1	2	3	4	5
1	0.000	3.162	7.071	6.708	4.000
2	3.162	0.000	8.944	7.810	7.071
3	7.071	8.944	0.000	2.236	5.099
4	6.708	7.810	2.236	0.000	6.083
5	4.000	7.071	5.099	6.083	0.000

This is a dissimilarity matrix

Agglomeration schedule

	Cluster combined		Coefficients	Stage cluster first appears		Next stage
Stage	*Cluster 1*	*Cluster 2*		*Cluster 1*	*Cluster 2*	
1	3	4	2.236	0	0	4
2	1	2	3.162	0	0	3
3	1	5	5.536	2	0	4
4	1	3	6.953	3	1	0

The agglomeration schedule of Table 12.6 tells us that auto-number 3 (C) and 4 (D) are the first two 'clusters' to join at a distance of 2.236 – their Euclidean distance. Second, points 1 (A) and 2 (B) are to join – at a distance of 3.162. Third, point 5 (E) is to join the cluster consisting of A and B. This happens at 5.536 (this value first appeared in Figure 12.3 (d)). Finally, the two clusters A/B/E and C/D join at the distance of 6.953. This number can be computed based on the values in the proximity schedule of Table 12.6 as (7.071 + 6.708 + 8.944 + 7.810 + 5.099 + 6.083)/6. The proximity matrix has ten pairwise distances. When computing the distance between two clusters A/B/E and CD the four intra-cluster distances A/B, AE, BE and CD are ignored.

The reader is encouraged to check if the manual computations concerning the remaining six linkage methods of Figure 12.3 and Figure 12.4 are correct. Note that before applying the centroid method and Ward's method, one should first change *[Measure/Interval]* in the Methods dialogue box from "Euclidean distance" to "Squared Euclidean distance."

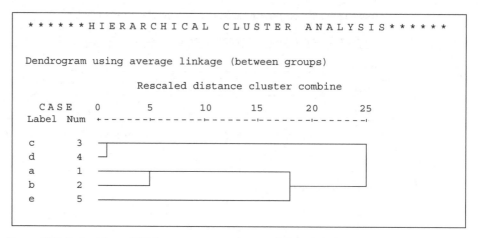

Figure 12.7 Output from SPSS between-groups (average) linkage

Clustering methods rarely yield the same or even similar results when applied to empirical data. Depending on the nature of the data, each method has its advantages and disadvantages. Table 12.7 provides some clues. Note though that they are rough rules of thumb at best. As a matter of fact what appears to be a disadvantage in some situations may be advantageous in others. For example, single linkage's tendency to produce snake-like clusters is usually regarded as a disadvantage of the method. However, it need not necessarily be so, provided that the snake-like pattern reflects a characteristic in the data set.

Returning to the bank image data of Chapter 11, this time by applying cluster analysis on the data, the data are reproduced in Table 12.8 (recall that lower values indicate higher agreement with regard to the left side of the semantic differential). Above, it was con-

Table 12.7 Some properties of hierarchical cluster analyses

Average linkage	Tends to combine clusters with small within-cluster variance. Tends to be biased towards establishing clusters with about the same variance
Single linkage	While possessing intuitive appeal, it is known to produce big clusters that resemble a banana or snake, and where observations at opposite ends of the cluster may be much closer to observations that are not part of the cluster. The phenomenon is sometimes called chaining. The method does not require metric data; for instance, ordinal data (preferences or similarities) can be used
Complete linkage	Highly sensitive to outliers in the data. Like single linkage, it does not require metric data
Centroid	The method sometimes produces muddled results. However, it seems less affected by outliers than other hierarchical techniques
Median	Appropriate for non-metric data
Ward	Tends to combine clusters with a small number of observations. It also tends to produce clusters with about the same number of observations

Table 12.8 Bank image analysis

	Modern	Interesting displays	Stagnant	Cluster number
	X1	X4	X8	CL = 3
obs1	2	1	6	1
obs2	3	2	7	1
obs3	4	3	4	1
obs4	1	3	7	1
obs5	3	7	5	2
obs6	3	1	6	1
obs7	1	4	4	1
obs8	5	2	3	1
obs9	7	6	1	3
obs10	3	7	3	2
obs11	2	7	2	2
obs12	2	3	6	1
obs13	2	6	6	2
obs14	2	7	6	2
obs15	2	7	6	2
obs16	2	2	5	1
obs17	1	4	6	1
obs18	2	4	4	1
obs19	2	6	6	2
obs20	3	2	6	1

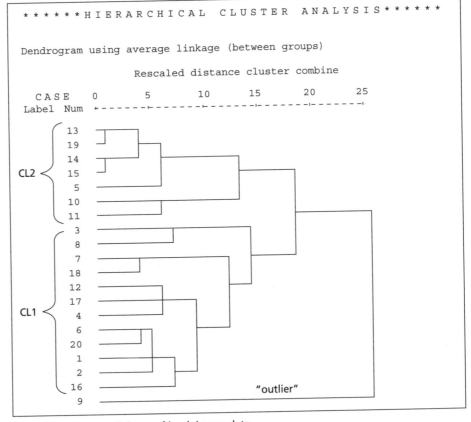

Figure 12.8 Average linkage of bank image data

Table 12.9 Bank image analysis categorized by cluster membership

		Case	X1	X4	X8
Outlier		obs 9	7	6	1
CL2 n = 7		obs13	2	6	6
		obs19	2	6	6
		obs14	2	7	6
		obs15	2	7	6
		obs5	3	7	5
		obs10	3	7	3
		obs11	2	7	2
		mean	2.29	6.71	4.86
		SD	0.49	0.49	1.68
CL1 n = 12		obs3	4	3	4
		obs8	5	2	3
		obs7	1	4	4
		obs18	2	4	4
		obs12	2	3	6
		obs17	1	4	6
		obs4	1	3	7
		obs6	3	1	6
		obs20	3	2	6
		obs1	2	1	6
		obs2	3	2	7
		obs16	2	2	5
		mean	2.41	2.58	5.33
		SD	1.24	1.08	1.30
Z-test for differences		z-value	−0.33	11.37	−0.64
		p-value (two tails)	0.74	0.00	0.52

cluded that a Q-type or reversed factor analysis yielded "clustering" results that were difficult to understand. But what about a hierarchical cluster analysis, say a between-groups average linkage with Euclidean distance?

Figure 12.8 shows the dendrogram from running average linkage cluster analysis. (*[SPSS: Analyze, Classify, Hierarchical Cluster]*, Method: Between Group Linkage: Measure: Squared Euclidean Distance). There appear to be two clusters in the data, plus one outlier (observation 9). The far right column of Table 12.8 displays the cluster number of each observation provided that three clusters are selected.[5] In Table 12.9 we have rearranged the observations in accordance with cluster membership.

Note from Table 12.6 that the cluster analysis has correctly identified both extreme and systematic patterns in the data. Respondents 13 and 19 plus respondents 14 and 15 are clustered first. This is because their responses are identical – and the four observations only differ by one scale point across the three variables. In general, members of cluster 2 have a quite similar response profile – apart from respondents 10 and 11, which differ on *X8*. Note that the standard deviation is much less on *X1* and *X4* in cluster 2 than in cluster

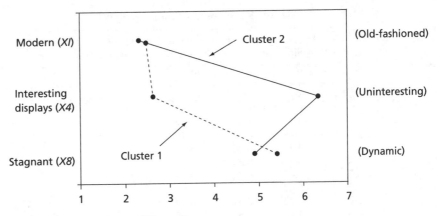

Figure 12.9 Visualizing cluster differences

1. The sample is small and therefore mean differences across clusters on *X1* and *X8* are not significant. Note though, that there is a significant difference (with a z-test) concerning how the respondents of the two clusters perceive the window displays of their bank (*X4*). See Figure 12.9.

While cluster 2 is very critical, cluster 1 is positive. If the sample had been bigger it might have been worthwhile to analyze further why members of cluster 2 are more critical. Is it because all or most of them have a bank that is known for being conservative (boring) with regard to window displays? Or does cluster 2 primarily consist of young females who pay much more attention to window displays? If the former holds, and they happened to be customers at the bank, it might be worth doing something about it (say, exhibit modern art in the windows). Remember though, that *X4* is a semantic differential that says nothing about whether respondents of cluster 1 regard window displays as something that might make them consider changing to another bank (probably it is not).

12.4 Non-hierarchical cluster analysis: an example

Many researchers prefer to apply hierarchical methods as long as the number of cases is less than one hundred. By way of the dendrogram it is possible to get a kind of bird's-eye view of the clustering process from beginning to end. However, imagine clustering the 4,077 respondents of the Dream Holiday study in Chapter 11. The dendrogram alone would fill almost one hundred pages. To obtain a bird's-eye view of the printout, for instance by placing the pages in a line, then the length of the dendrogram would be about thirty metres. Such a dendrogram is un-interpretable.

If the number of cases exceeds two hundred, hierarchical methods become too difficult to use for the applied researcher. Instead, she or he would have to employ **non-hierarchical methods**. Synonyms for these methods are k-means, partitioning and nearest centroid sorting. Like hierarchical methods they are non-overlapping.

To illustrate how a non-hierarchical method works, assume a study has been made

Table 12.10 Managers' responses to two statements

X1: Expected market development (0 = very negative, 6 = very positive)
X2: Willingness to export (0 = none, 6 = very high)

I	II	III	IV	V	VI
Industry	X1	X2	Seed (X1 + X2)	Cluster (iteration 1)	Cluster (iteration 2)
1	1.19	2.33	3.52	1	1
2	1.25	4.50	5.75	1	1
3	1.17	5.06	6.23	1	1
4	4.72	5.35	10.07	2	2
5	1.47	0.95	**2.42**	1	1
6	0.82	3.24	4.06	1	1
7	1.50	2.64	4.14	1	1
8	1.60	4.86	6.46	1	1
9	0.51	2.20	2.71	1	1
10	3.89	2.89	6.78	2	2
11	2.07	4.53	6.60	**2**	**1**
12	3.06	5.30	8.36	2	2
13	5.07	4.67	9.74	2	2
14	1.54	4.35	5.89	1	1
15	1.71	1.56	3.27	1	1
16	0.83	5.12	5.95	1	1
17	2.78	5.27	8.05	2	2
18	2.73	4.03	6.76	2	2
19	1.04	4.02	5.06	1	1
20	5.45	5.40	**10.85**	2	2

Note that observations on X1 and X2 are averages on an industrial level.

among export managers within twenty industries (pharmaceuticals, industrial machinery, banking, etc.). Within each industry, interviews were carried out with ten to twenty managers. Each manager was asked to comment on two statements. The two statements are shown in the first two rows of Table 12.10, while columns II–III shows the average response within each industry (columns IV–VI will be explained later).

Figure 12.10(a) displays the average responses of Table 12.10.

Now assume we would like to classify the twenty responses into two clusters. However, this time k-means clustering is used instead of a hierarchical method. A non-hierarchical method must be told how many clusters or categories the analyst wants to establish before each run (between two and nineteen clusters could be chosen). Once the number of clusters is decided on – in this case, two – the k-means method typically selects two extreme observations and uses ("appoints") them as temporary centres of the new clusters. Usually, these cluster centres are called **cluster seeds**. The technical aspects of the procedure are demonstrated in column IV of Table 12.10. For each observation, the X1 and X2 values are added. The *smallest* value (2.42 – industry 5) becomes the first seed while the *biggest* value is made the second seed (10.85 – industry 20). The process is shown graphically in Figure 12.10(b). Note that if three clusters are selected, the third seed will be observation 16, because, of the remaining 18 observations, it has the farthest combined distance to 5 and 20. (The fourth seed is 10 since that point is farthest apart from 5, 20 and 16 in combination, and so on.) The (X1, X2) co-ordinates of observations 5 and 20 are called **initial cluster centres** or **seeds of iteration 1** (sometimes called iteration 0).

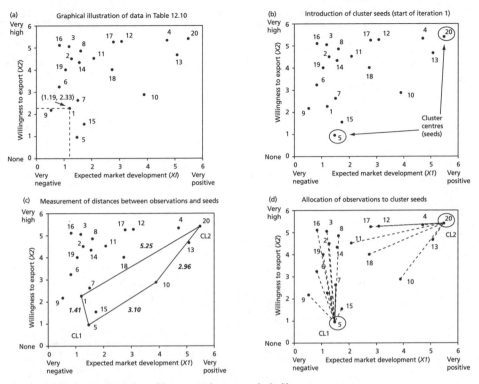

Figure 12.10 Basic principles of k-means cluster analysis (I)

Having found the cluster centres, the next task is to measure the distance from each of the eighteen points to cluster 1/observation 5 and cluster 2/observation 20, respectively. This implies 36 – or generally $(n-k)*k$ measurements – far fewer than 190 measurements – or generally $[n*(n-1)]/2$ – that are necessary when employing a hierarchical method. In (c) two measurements are illustrated, from observation 1 and 10 to the two clusters. While observation 1 is close to cluster 1 (observation 5), observation 10 is closer to cluster 2 (observation 20). Consequently, observation 1 is put into cluster 1 and observation 10 into cluster 2. In (d) each observation has been assigned to the nearest cluster seed. But the process is not yet finished or stable. After all observations have been assigned to the two clusters, a new cluster centre or centroid of each of the two clusters is calculated. See Figure 12.11(a).

The table below panel (a) of Figure 12.11 shows how the centroid of cluster 2 is calculated. Note that observations 5 and 20 have been downgraded to manual observations. The $(X1, X2)$ co-ordinates of the centroids are called **final** cluster centres or seeds of iteration 1 (the *final* cluster centres of *iteration 1* = the *initial* cluster centres of *iteration 2*).

During iteration 2 the new centroids serve the same purpose as did the original seeds during iteration 1 (panels (b) to (d) in Figure 12.10). This time the distance is measured from each observation to both of the new centroids. Let us focus on a specific case, observation 11, that has an interesting characteristic. See panel (b) in Figure 12.11. During iteration 1 (panel (d) of Figure 12.10) observation 11 was assigned to cluster 2. But the initial cluster centres of iteration 2 differ from those of iteration 1, and this change implies that observation 11 now is closer to the centre of cluster 1 (Euclidean distance = 1.41) than it is to cluster 2

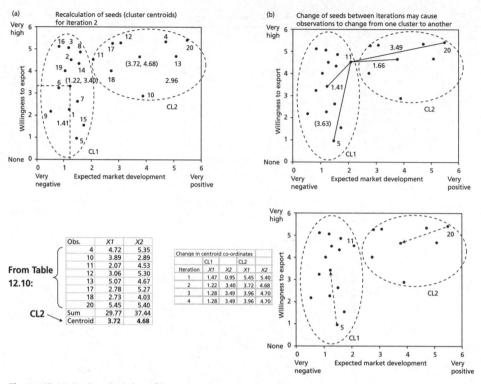

Figure 12.11 Basic principles of k-means cluster analysis (II)

(Euclidean distance = 1.66). Therefore, observation 11 is reassigned to cluster 1. Panel (b) of Figure 12.11 shows the distances from observation 11 to the seeds during iteration 1.

In Figure 12.11, the diagram below panel (b) illustrates how the cluster centres move between iterations 1 and 2: cluster 1's centre moves north and slightly west, while cluster 2's centre moves west and slightly south. The small table to the left of the diagram shows the change in centroid co-ordinates from iterations 1 to 4. From iteration 1 to 2, the change is substantial, from 2 to 3 there is still a minor change, caused by the change in cluster affiliation of observation 11. From iteration 3 to 4 no observation changes cluster affiliation, implying that the centroid co-ordinates of iteration 3 and 4 are the same since all distances from observations to clusters are unchanged. Consequently, convergence has appeared. Cluster membership of each case in iteration 1 and iteration 2 is shown in columns V and VI of Table 12.10.

Intuitively, the use of extreme observations as cluster seeds (panel (b)) seems problematic. What if observation 20's co-ordinates had been a real outlier or influential observation with co-ordinates, say, (50.00, 50.00) – ignoring that this observation falls far beyond the allowable range concerning our numerical example? Like hierarchical methods, k-means cluster immediately detects such an outlier. Had a two-cluster solution been chosen, eighteen observations would be assigned to observation 5 (seed 1) while seed 2 would only contain observation 20. One would then have to select three clusters and rerun the analysis. One of the clusters would still consist of one case, observation 20.

Another possibility would be to remove the outlier and rerun the analysis, again selecting two clusters. Indeed, some computer manuals advise the analyst to use a clustering method like k-means for removing up to 10 percent of observations. This is done by way of a preliminary k-means cluster analysis, where the number of clusters is set to 10 percent of the number of observations (for instance thirty clusters when there are three hundred observations). Often, a lot of these clusters consist of only a single or of a few cases. Such cases are then treated as outliers and are deleted before running the final cluster analysis.[7]

It seems that k-means clustering is able to detect outliers in most cases. The bank image data analysis contained an outlier (Figure 12.8). Note that this outlier is detected when choosing three clusters (see far right column of Table 12.8). However, note that the outlier is *not* detected when only inspecting a two-cluster solution. But from 3–5 clusters it appears as the only cluster consisting of a single observation. This latter finding underscores the importance of scrutinizing all possible cluster solutions from two to at least five clusters (ten if the sample size exceeds five hundred).

Running the k-means cluster in SPSS

Figure 12.12 shows where to find the k-means cluster analysis in the *[Analyze]* dropdown of SPSS.

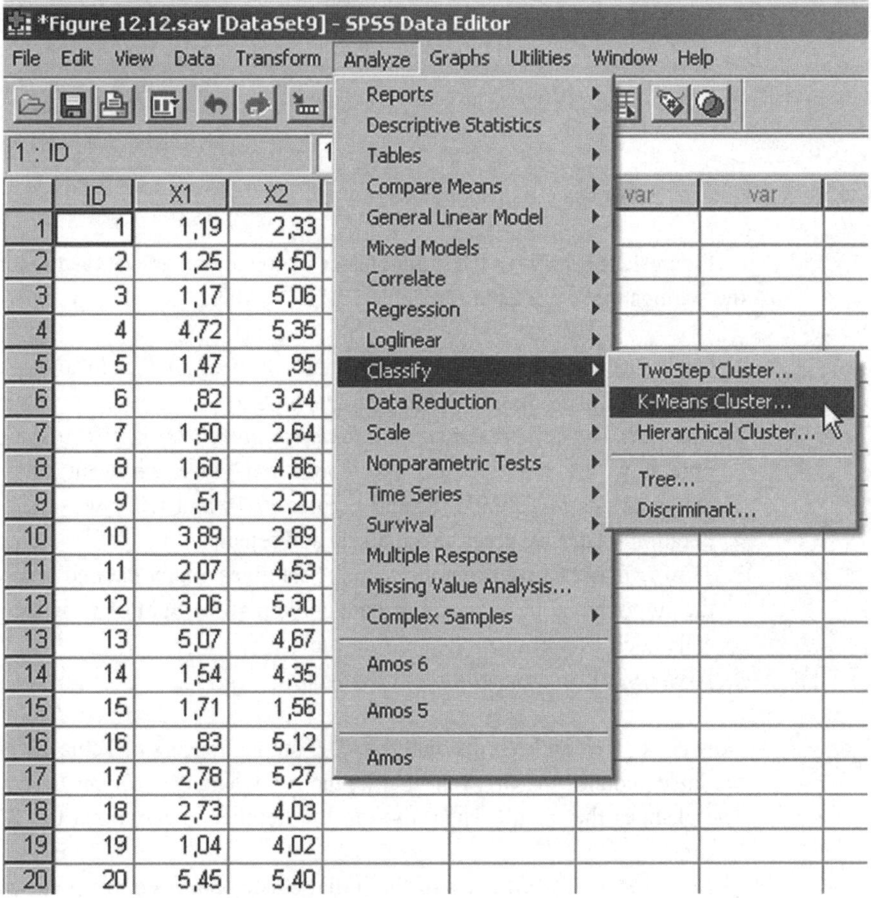

Figure 12.12 Running k-means cluster analysis in SPSS

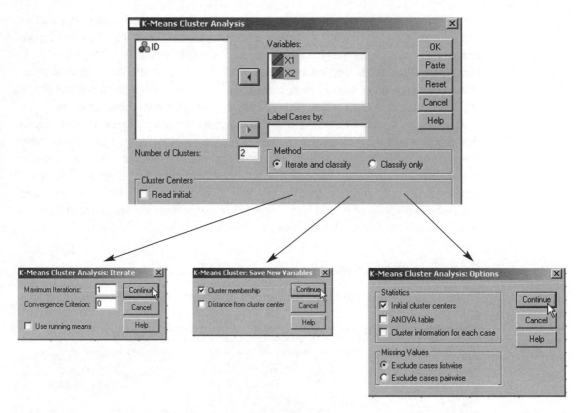

Figure 12.13 SPSS k-means cluster analysis dialogue boxes

Figure 12.13 displays the main cluster dialogue box as well as the three sub-boxes and the settings that were used for Table 12.11.

1. Click the two variables $x1$ and $x2$ into the variables field and leave other settings unchanged, including the *[Number of Clusters]*.
2. *[Iterate]:* The default setting of *[Maximum Iterations]* is "10." (Since we want to illustrate how the iterative process works and since we want to check our manual computations of Table 12.10 and Figures 12.10 and 12.11 we change the value to "1" iteration – later we rerun the analysis and select "2".)
3. *[Save]:* Flag "Cluster membership." This gives a new data column that is not part of the output but appears as a new data column at the right of $x2$ in the screen editor. It is called qcl_1 (for quick cluster, first run).
4. *[Options]:* Leave everything unchanged.

Now click *[OK]* and run the analysis. The output appears in Table 12.11. The first part of the table contains the first run, that is, the run where *[Maximum Iterations]* is set to "1." The changes that result when altering the number of iterations to "2" are given at the bottom.

Note that the co-ordinates of the initial cluster centres correspond with observations 5 and 20 and that the final cluster centres of iteration 1 fit with the co-ordinates of panel (a)

Table 12.11 Output from k-means cluster (SPSS quick cluster)

Initial cluster centres

	Cluster	
	1	*2*
X1	1.47	5.45
X2	0.95	5.40

Iteration history[a]

	Change in cluster centres	
Iteration	1	2
1	2.34	2.09

[a] Iterations stopped because the maximum number of iterations was performed. Iterations failed to converge. Maximum distance by which any centre has changed is 2.320. The current iteration is 1. The minimum distance between initial centres is 5.970.

Final cluster centres

	Cluster	
	1	2
X1	1.22	3.72
X2	3.40	4.68

Number of cases in each cluster

Cluster	1	12
	2	8
Valid		20
Missing		0

Below: new run with two iterations

Final cluster centres

	Cluster	
	1	*2*
X1	1.28	3.96
X2	3.49	4.70

Number of cases in each cluster

Cluster	1	13
	2	7
Valid		20
Missing		0

in Figure 12.11. The final cluster centres in the run with two iterations at the bottom of Table 12.11 appear as (initial cluster centres for) iteration 3 in the small table below panel (b) in Figure 12.11. Comparing the small table "Number of Cases in each cluster" of the 1-iteration run with the 2-iteration run, note that one case has changed from cluster 2 to cluster 1. Inspecting the qcl_1 and qcl_2 columns of the data screen shows that it is indeed observation 11 that has changed from cluster 2 to cluster 1 – as demonstrated in panels (a) and (b) of Figure 12.11.

Compared with factor analysis, cluster analysis in general and k-means cluster analysis in particular is characterized by ease of use. It should be noted that when loading the present numerical example into SAS and running Proc Fastclus, one yields the same results concerning co-ordinates of seeds, cluster membership of individual cases with regard to iteration 1, 2 and so on. This need not be the case due to the existence of different k-means algorithms. Basically, three different approaches exist:

■ **Sequential threshold:** this method begins with selecting one cluster seed. Then all cases within a previously specified distance are assigned to the cluster. Next, a second cluster is established and again, cases within a specified distance are assigned to the new seed, and so on. Usually, the process ends before all cases are clustered. Once a case is assigned to a seed it is no longer considered for clustering.
■ **Parallel threshold:** several introductory seeds are established instead of just one. Pre-specified distances may be changed so that more or fewer cases are included in a specific cluster. Again, some cases may never enter a cluster and be regarded as outliers.
■ **Optimizing partitioning:** this method differs from the two others in that it allows for reassignment of cases. This may happen if a case during the iterative clustering process comes closer to another seed. It then switches to another cluster. This method has received most coverage.[8]

Assessing the success of the clustering

How successful is our k-means clustering based on the small sample? A straightforward way of assessing the strength of the model is to test whether the difference in means between the two clusters is statistically significant. This can be done in several ways.

One method is to employ a Z-test: this tests whether the differences between the mean of cluster 1 and 2 are significant concerning each of the two variables $x1$ and $x2$.

The Z-test is explained in Session 2 of Appendix D (see www.pearsoned.co.uk/schmidt). Using the final clustering (column VI of Table 12.10) for the analysis we can conduct two Z-tests, one on each of the two variables, and then we hypothesize that

Table 12.12 Results of Z-test on means

	CL1		CL2		
		Mean		Z-value	Probability
X1	1.28		3.96	−6.01	0.000
X2	3.49		4.70	−2.29	0.01
n	13		7		

Table 12.13 Result of F-test discriminant analysis

	F-test	df1	df2	Probability
X1	59.1	1	18	0.000
X2	4.1	1	18	0.058

the group means are equal. The test can be conducted using the Excel Analysis ToolPak. As shown in Table 12.12, the differences in mean are statistically sigificant with regard to both variables, so the clustering has been successful.

Another test is to run a discriminant analysis. Here, the cluster variable (column VI in Table 12.10) is treated as a grouping or dependent measure. The model then uses $X1$ and $X2$ as predictors. Once more the analysis is successful, as seen in Table 12.13. In discriminant analysis an F-test is the appropriate measure, so while the two tests cannot be compared directly, they lead to the same conclusion. The difference in cluster means is highly significant on $X1$ and significant at about the 0.05 level on $X2$. The findings are further confirmed when inspecting the classification table that can be requested in discriminant analysis. The grouping results in only one misclassification of the twenty cases. In other words, 95 percent of cases are correctly classified (the reader may check the above results).

To sum up: the clustering has been successful. There is a problem, though: the numerical example used was generated by way of Excel's random number generator! The data of columns $X1$ and $X2$ of Table 12.10 were obtained by: requesting two variables and twenty random numbers; selecting a uniform distribution; and choosing a data range from 0.5 to 5.5 (to fake a 1–5 Likert scale). It may appear that the data structure of Figure 12.11 provides some kind of pattern. And indeed, the Pearson correlation between $X1$ and $X2$ is 0.41 with an associated marginal probability of 0.07. However, such a pattern is not at all exceptional when analyzing small samples based on random numbers.

What is the lesson of this validation of the cluster analysis? Unlike in analysis of variance, regression, discriminant analysis, etc., usual model fit statistics are invalid or opportunistic in cluster analysis. For instance, the F-test is upwards inflated and cannot be used as a test for differences in cluster means. As mentioned at the beginning of the chapter, this is because cluster analysis is an *independence* method and not a *dependence* method (like analysis of variance and regression). In independence methods the "data speak for themselves." Cluster analysis methods are optimized at separating or categorizing cases, *solely based on patterns prevailing in the actual data set*. It is not a valid research strategy to first use a method (cluster) for maximizing differences in the specific data set under scrutiny and then subsequently use a different method (z-test, discriminant analysis) to prove that the differences just detected exist and are significant. This research strategy possesses no generalizability whatsoever.

Note that in the SPSS k-means cluster an ANOVA table could have been requested (the results are identical with the F-test conducted above). One just needs to flag "ANOVA-table" in the Options dialogue box in the k-means set-up (see Figure 12.13).

12.5 How many clusters should be used?

One of the most important questions in cluster analysis concerns the number of clusters. In a way, the question resembles the extraction or number of factors problem in factor analysis. Recall, that in factor analysis the analyst can choose between several measures: Kaiser's criterion, Bartlett's scree-test and Horn's test. None of them seems to possess distinguished characteristics compared with the others, though.

A related problem exists with regard to cluster analysis. While several statistical approaches have been developed, none of them appears to have outstanding qualities. The following section briefly covers three well-known cluster measures. Since the number of clusters problem is related to the validity of the cluster solution, the two problems will be addressed in unison.

Error sum of square (ESS) is an obvious, easy way of evaluating the performance of a cluster solution. The underlying philosophy of this measure is to estimate the average Euclidean distance from observations to their respective cluster centre. Each deviation from the centre represents an error – compared with the "perfect cluster," where all observations of a cluster have exactly the same co-ordinates, for instance the same response profile if respondents are involved. This procedure is repeated for all clusters and finally the distances are added. The practice needs to be replicated for as many cluster solutions as the analyst deems relevant. We will now explain how the procedure works by way of columns II and III in Table 12.10. Strictly speaking, the square root of ESS is calculated (the outcome is the same, though).

In the SPSS *[Classify, K-Means Cluster]* setup (Figure 12.13) flag the "Distance from cluster center" in the *[Save]* dialogue box together with "Cluster membership." *[Iterate]:* for simplicity set the "Maximum iterations" to two. Moreover, start by selecting two clusters. Click *[OK]*. Now the screen editor – not the output – contains two new columns, "qcl_1" (cluster membership) and "qcl_2" (distance from cluster centre). The values in qcl_1 should look like the first twenty data cells in column IV of Table 12.14. This column lists the cluster assignment of each observation, assuming two iterations. It is just a repetition of column VI of Table 12.10. The column in the SPSS screen editor called qcl_2 should – apart from the number of decimals – look like the first twenty data cells of column V in Table 12.14. Each cell of column V has the Euclidean distance from the observation to the respective cluster centre. For instance, the first cell value of 1.07 is calculated accordingly:

$$d_{AB} = \sqrt{(x_1 - x_2)^2 + (y_1 - y_2)^2}$$

$$d_{AB} = \sqrt{(1.19 - 1.22)^2 + (2.33 - 3.40)^2} = 1.07$$

Where (1.22, 3.40) is the centre of cluster 1 at the end of iteration 1 – the values appeared in the SPSS output of Table 12.11 and in panel (a) of Figure 12.11. The value 1.07 is the Euclidean distance from observation 1 to the centre of cluster 1. Note that for all observations belonging to cluster 2, the appropriate centre is (3.72, 4.68). The final cell of column V in Table 12.14 – 26.59 – contains the sum of the twenty data values.

Table 12.14 Computing ESS-measure for assessing best clustering

I	II	III	IV	V	VI	VII	VIII	IX	X	XI
	X1	X2	CL2	e_2	CL3	e_3	CL4	e_4	CL5	e_5
1	1.19	2.33	1	1.07	1	0.18	2	0.18	5	0.40
2	1.25	4.50	1	1.10	2	0.59	3	0.53	3	0.06
3	1.17	5.06	1	1.66	2	0.73	3	0.60	3	0.61
4	4.72	5.35	2	1.20	3	0.78	4	0.42	4	0.42
5	1.47	0.95	1	2.47	1	1.23	2	1.23	5	1.00
6	0.82	3.24	1	0.43	1	1.15	2	1.15	3	1.31
7	1.50	2.64	1	0.81	1	0.57	2	0.57	5	0.74
8	1.60	4.86	1	1.51	2	0.26	3	0.13	3	0.51
9	0.51	2.20	1	1.40	1	0.69	2	0.69	5	0.81
10	3.89	2.89	2	1.80	3	1.91	1	0.81	2	0.00
11	2.07	4.53	1	1.41	2	0.32	3	0.44	3	0.78
12	3.06	5.30	2	0.91	2	1.39	3	1.45	1	0.48
13	5.07	4.67	2	1.35	3	0.30	4	0.47	4	0.47
14	1.54	4.35	1	1.00	2	0.44	3	0.46	3	0.27
15	1.71	1.56	1	1.91	1	0.78	2	0.78	5	0.57
16	0.83	5.12	1	1.76	2	1.06	3	0.94	3	0.80
17	2.78	5.27	2	1.11	2	1.13	3	1.18	1	0.41
18	2.73	4.03	2	1.19	2	1.14	1	0.81	1	0.85
19	1.04	4.02	1	0.64	2	1.03	3	1.01	3	0.51
20	5.45	5.40	2	1.87	3	1.06	4	0.45	4	0.45
ESS measure				26.59		16.74		14.33		11.45

Columns VI–VII, VIII–IX and X–XI are repetitions of the procedure just described but with three, four, and five clusters, instead of two (however, still with two iterations).

ESS equals 0 (the actual value is 26.59), provided that the homogeneity within clusters is perfect, that is, if all observations have precisely the same co-ordinates as has the cluster centre (perfect homogeneity). There is no upper limit with regard to ESS. ESS is a relative measure. Therefore, the numeric size of it will depend on sample size, number of clusters, scaling, etc.

Figure 12.14(a) shows the ESS measure against the corresponding number of clusters selected. Panels (b), (c) and (d) visualize the solutions with two, three and four clusters, respectively. According to theory, we should look for a kink or drop in the function of (a) and then choose the number of clusters immediately after the kink, which here obviously is at three clusters. When inspecting panels (b), (c) and (d), it indeed appears that the three-cluster solution looks "better" than both the two- and the four-cluster solutions. The two-cluster solution "forces" disparate cases like observations 16 and 5 (CL1), and 11 and 20 (CL2) to be part of the same cluster. The four-cluster solution on the other hand has clusters consisting of only two and three cases. So, given the numerical example, three clusters appear to represent the best clustering.

Cubic clustering criterion (CCC) and **pseudo F-statistic** in the SAS/STAT procedures Proc Cluster and Proc Fastclus provide a measure that helps the analyst to decide upon the best number of clusters. The CCC statistic assumes that the empirical data set has been sampled from a uniform distribution.

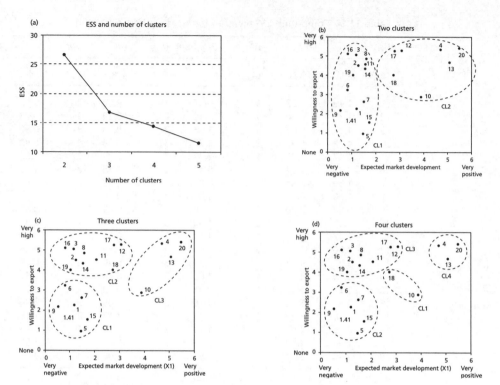

Figure 12.14 Assessing the best clustering

A uniform distribution deviates from a normal distribution in that it is possible to define allowable ranges for observations. So, if one wants observations to fall with a range of, say, 1 and 10, the uniform distribution assumes a sample to consist of random values between 1 and 10 (e.g., 1.345, 9.684, 4.527). In some cases, the uniform distribution is preferred to the normal distribution because the latter may obtain observations that are beyond the allowable range. For instance, assume that a researcher wants to draw a random sample of 1,000 cases concerning the variable age and a mean of 40 years is selected. In such a case the normal distribution usually will come up with some negative values, for instance -11.719, which does not make any sense. On the other hand, when using the uniform distribution one can specify a lower limit of, say, 16 (years).

A problem with the ESS measure is that by definition it *decreases* as the number of clusters *increases*: the more clusters the lower the within-cluster heterogeneity (Lattin, Carroll and Green, 2003). The CCC measure and the related pseudo F-statistic may increase and decrease as the number of clusters increase.

The CCC measure and the pseudo F-statistic are not quite as straightforward to use as ESS. The former two statistics assume that the involved variables are uncorrelated (recall that the Pearson correlation between $X1$ and $X2$ in our numerical example is 0.41.) Therefore, if a numerical example is to be analyzed by means of the CCC measure, it cannot be based on the correlated $X1$ and $X2$ variable columns. Instead, it ought to be founded on the corresponding columns that contain the uncorrelated principal component scores or factor scores – Prin1 and Prin2 in SAS terminology.

Table 12.15 Results of running CCC measure and pseudo F-statistic

Number of clusters	CCC measure	Pseudo F-statistic
2	1.80	14.4
3	5.83	27.8
4	6.12	25.5

Table 12.15 results from the following:

1. Run SAS/STAT Princomp based on *X1/X2* and request the uncorrelated component scores matrix as output.
2. Run SAS/STAT Fastclus based on these uncorrelated component score columns (input) instead of variables.
3. Run Fastclus based on two iterations with two-, three-, and four-cluster solutions (SAS notation: maxiter = 2 and maxc = 2, etc.).

In the present case it turns out that this formally correct procedure fits with the simpler ESS measure. The pseudo-F statistics peaks at three clusters (in the range between two and four clusters). The CCC does not peak at three clusters, but the *relative* increase from two to three clusters (4.03) is much bigger than from three to four clusters (0.29). According to theory on the CCC-criterion, one should look for a considerable functional increase, followed by a decline or decreasing steepness in the function. The best number of cluster then is the number immediately after the marked increase (see SAS/STAT, 1983). In the present case a kink or elbow appears at three clusters. Therefore, three clusters seems to be the superior choice, given the data.

When requesting a case-by-case list of the above SAS k-means cluster solutions, the assignment of cases to clusters almost matches that of Table 12.14 (columns IV, VI and VIII).[9] Readers with access to both SPSS and SAS should check this.

Replicated or consensus clustering, **Rand index** and **adjusted Rand index** are three related approaches that can also be explained by example. To simplify things, computations will be based on only one iteration. However, additional iterations do not complicate matters, they just result in a tremendous increase in the number of manual computations.

First, look at Figure 12.15. Panel (a) is the same as (d) in Figure 12.10. Panel (b) shows the result of a new k-means cluster analysis. But this time the default seeds suggested by SPSS are not used. Instead, there is a new set of arbitrary seeds. To be specific, observations 10 and 16 are the initial cluster seeds and subsequently all remaining eighteen observations have been assigned to the nearest seed.

Panel (c) displays the corresponding cluster assignment of observations according to *Rep_1* and *Rep_2*. The first table of panel (d) is a crosstab between the two clusterings. Note that eight observations (2, 3, 6, 8, 9, 14, 16 and 19) are grouped into cluster 1 in *Rep_1* and into cluster 1 in *Rep_2*. However, four observations (1, 5, 7, 15) appear in cluster 1 in *Rep_1* but in cluster 2 in *Rep_2*. Somehow the congruence of the two clusterings does not appear to be too good. Observations that are assigned to cluster 1 in one clustering need not be assigned to cluster 1 in the other clustering since cluster names are

(a) Clustering of numerical example using SPSS default seed and one iteration

(b) New Clustering of data this time using observations 10 and 16 as initial seeds (one iteration)

(c) Listing of cluster assignment of observations in both cluster runs

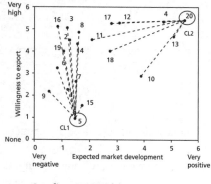

See figure 12.11(a)

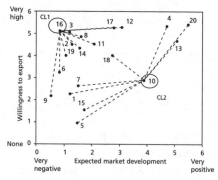

Obs.	Rep_1	Rep_2	Rep_3
1	1	2	2
2	1	1	2
3	1	1	2
4	2	2	1
5	1	2	2
6	1	1	2
7	1	2	2
8	1	1	2
9	1	1	2
10	2	2	1
11	2	1	1
12	2	1	1
13	2	2	1
14	1	1	2
15	1	2	2
16	1	1	2
17	2	1	1
18	2	2	1
19	1	1	2
20	2	2	1

See Table 12.10, column V

	Cluster 1 seed	Obs. 16	Obs. 4
	Cluster 2 seed	Obs. 10	Obs. 9

(d) Crosstab of clusterings

Replication 1 versus 2

		REP_2		Total
		CL1	Cl2	
REP_1	CL1	8	4	12
	CL2	3	5	8
Total		11	9	20

Replication 1 versus 3

		REP_3		Total
		CL1	Cl2	
REP_1	CL1	0	12	12
	CL2	8	0	8
Total		8	12	20

Figure 12.15 The principle of replicated clustering

arbitrary. But all observations that are assigned to cluster 1 in one clustering ideally ought to appear in the same cluster (i.e. cluster 2) in another clustering. What is important here is cluster consistency.

Now assume a third cluster analysis, this time with observation 4 as cluster seed 1 and observation 9 as cluster seed 2. While this clustering is not shown in Figure 12.15, the far right column of panel (c), *Rep_3* lists the corresponding cluster assignment (as always, the reader is encouraged to check this).

The second table of panel (d) shows the cross-tab of *Rep_1* and *Rep_3*. This time there is a systematic pattern: all observations that were assigned to cluster 1 in *Rep_1* are assigned to cluster 2 in *Rep_2* and vice versa. It looks as if *Rep_3* corresponds better with *Rep_1* than does *Rep_2*. However, proof is needed to substantiate the proposition. Generally speaking, a proper measure is needed for assessing the quality or stability of two or more clusterings. Otherwise, one empirical clustering cannot be compared with another.

The Rand index (Rand, 1971) is the appropriate tool for testing the convergent validity of several clusterings.[10] Sometimes the measure is called an *unadjusted* Rand index. It runs:

$$A = \frac{n(n-1)}{2} + \sum_{i=1}^{R}\sum_{j=1}^{C} n_{ij}^2 - \frac{1}{2}\left(\sum_{i=1}^{R} n_{i.}^2 + \sum_{j=1}^{C} n_{.j}^2\right)$$

where n is the number of observations, R and C refers to row and columns of the crosstab, n_{ij} refers to a cell entry, $n_{i.}$ and $n_{.j}$ relate to row and column marginal frequencies.

This measure can evaluate the validity of *Rep_1* and *Rep_2*. All input figures appear in the first table of panel (d) in Figure 12.15. For matters of comparison we could call *Rep_1* the "true structure" and *Rep_2* the sample or "test structure."

$$A_{R1/R2} = \frac{20(19)}{2} + 8^2 + 4^2 + 3^2 + 5^2 - \frac{1}{2}\left(11^2 + 9^2 + 12^2 + 8^2\right) = 99$$

It can be shown that 99 is the number of consistent pairs, that is, pairs of observations appearing in the same cluster across both groupings (*Rep_1* and *Rep_2*). This figure must then be divided by the total number of pairwise groupings. With twenty observations the total number or pairs is $(20*19)/2 = 190$.

Consequently, the Rand index in this case is $99/190 = 0.52$. This figure is not impressive, since with two clusters the minimum value is 0.47 (recall that the data consist of random numbers).[11]

Finally, to compute the validity of *Rep_1* and *Rep_3*.

$$A_{R1/R2} = \frac{20(19)}{2} + 0 + 144 + 64 + 0 - \frac{1}{2}(64 + 144 + 144 + 64) = 190$$

This time 190 out of 190 possible pairs of groupings are consistent. In other words, the groupings are identical, implying a Rand index of 1.0. This is the upper range of the index.

Returning to the numerical example, the validity of *R_1* and *R_3* is perfect while the validity of *R_1* and *R_2* is not good and not much better than chance. Unfortunately, the above validity test is far from universal. It is confined to:

■ Three sets of two initial seeds (each consisting of two, two-dimensional co-ordinates) used for *R_1*, *R_2* and *R_3* respectively. However, with twenty observations it is possible to establish one hundred and ninety such seeds. For the test to be exhaustive, all 190 runs are needed with computations of an average Rand index (with 4,000 observations and three clusters, there are more than ten billion possible ways of establishing initial seeds). In a practical setting, one draws a random sample of, say, one hundred or so seeds and then computes an average Rand index.
■ One iteration. Typically one would use several iterations. Recall, that *Rep_1*, which was first introduced in column V of Table 12.10, represents a clustering where convergence was not obtained. Convergence was first achieved when an additional iteration was carried out. In SPSS k-means, the default is ten iterations.
■ In the export manager example there were only twenty observations and two variables, whereas in the Dream Holiday case study of Chapter 11 there were more than 4,000 observations and almost one hundred variables.
■ Only a two-cluster solution has been considered. Normally one would assess clusterings between two and ten or at least between two and five.

Hubert and Arabie (1985) have suggested a modification of the Rand index, known as the **modified Rand index**. This is a more complex measure and is not be discussed here, but is covered in Helsen and Green (1991).

As follows from this section, deciding upon the best number of clusters is a difficult question and sometimes, different measures or rules of thumb lead to contradictory conclusions. The reader should keep in mind, that ESS, CCC and the Rand index are based on a *statistical interpretation* of the data. But once it comes to interpretation of the results, namely once the clusters are to be profiled across socio-economic background characteristics, and batteries of statements used as input for clustering and so on – then one needs to focus on sense making, that is, on an *operational interpretation*.

Fortunately, a cluster solution that has statistical merits often makes good sense from an interpretational perspective as well. Assume that the five-cluster solution from a statistical perspective looks better than the four-cluster solution. Should the analyst automatically prefer the five-cluster solution? Not necessarily. First, the five-cluster solution should not only be marginally better. Statistically, the difference should be "distinctive" (statistical significance does not make sense here). Second, after the analyst has tried to profile both cluster solutions, the one with five clusters should make more sense than that with four. At this phase it might be a good idea to let three or four people try to do the profiling – and preferably, they should arrive at the same conclusions, be it four or five clusters/segments. Third, if two cluster solutions seem to be equally qualified, managers should ask themselves how they would like to use the results (ideally this consideration should have been done before the study was initiated). Is it realistic or even preferable to consider the market as consisting of five segments instead of four?

Maybe it is, and perhaps a manager is only interested in two or three of these segments. In the real life study that Chapter 11's Dream Holiday is based on, managers chose an eight-cluster solution initially. They then decided to ignore three segments with regard to target marketing and to regard only three segments as the core market. The managers felt it was not realistic for the tour operator to attract segments that appeared to be very prone towards charter tourism in Southern Europe. Instead, they decided to concentrate on segments that seemed to be favourable to promotional messages concerning short weekend trips, bus tours for retired people, families with children and people who preferred travelling to neighbouring countries, and to capital cities.

If the five-cluster solution is only slightly better than the four-cluster solution, then *Occam's razor*, also called the **principle of parsimony** recommends four clusters rather than five.

The next section reports on a real study where cluster analysis was used for segmenting customers.

12.6 An empirical example of k-means cluster: segmenting readers of sales flyers

Table 12.16 shows the result of a k-means cluster analysis of recipients of sales flyers. The study was based on 1,089 responses from members of a representative household panel (Schmidt and Bjerre, 2003). A section of the questionnaire contained ten items addressing consumers' usage of and attitudes towards flyers (on a four-point Likert scale).

First, data were factor analyzed and a 1,089 * 10 matrix of non-correlated principle component scores was generated. Components or factor scores were used instead of ordinary variables since scores are uncorrelated and because central k-means statistics (i.e. the pseudo F-statistic) are invalid for correlated variables. A few missing observations per item were substituted by the mean.

Next, this matrix was clustered using the k-means algorithm. Before the final clustering, outliers were removed in accordance with recommendations typically provided in software manuals.[12] In a preliminary k-means cluster analysis, the number of clusters was set to about 10 percent of observations – 100 clusters. This run revealed a lot of outliers in the form of clusters that only consisted of one, two or three observations.

This outlier detection procedure indicated 84 outliers, which were removed before final analysis. An inspection of cluster solutions between two and ten clusters indicated a global peak at three clusters.[13]

Note from Table 12.16 that members of cluster 2 possess quite critical attitudes toward flyers: they think that consumers today receive too many flyers. They regard them as a waste of money and as harmful to the environment. Flyers should either be forbidden or be taxed. Cluster 1 on the other hand is more flyer-prone: flyers help them get ideas, help saving money, constitute good consumer advice. Cluster 3's views come closer to those of cluster 1 than to those of cluster 2. But cluster 3 is more difficult to profile.

The far right columns of Table 12.16 display the results from a stepwise multiple discriminant analysis treating the cluster-membership as the classification or grouping variable. While some differences between group-averages are small (statements 2, 6, 8 and 10), all predictors contribute significantly to the model.[14] The reader should keep in mind that the nice significance statistics are caused primarily by the relatively big sample size

Table 12.16 K-means cluster analysis of recipients of sales flyers

Statements involved in the study	CL1	CL2	CL3	Partial R^2	Sign. Level
1. Today, we receive too many flyers	1.7	_1.3_	2.0	0.03	0.01
2. I prefer reading flyers to newspaper supplements	_2.0_	2.3	2.3	0.01	0.01
3. The government ought to put an environmental tax on flyers	2.1	_1.7_	2.4	0.01	0.02
4. Flyers help me get ideas on what I shall buy	_2.1_	3.0	2.0	0.06	0.01
5. Flyers are a waste of consumers' money	2.6	_1.9_	2.7	0.01	0.01
6. Flyers make it possible to save money and buy cheaper	_1.8_	2.0	2.0	0.17	0.01
7. Flyers ought to be forbidden	3.5	_2.6_	3.6	0.24	0.01
8. Flyers constitute good consumer advice	2.4	2.5	2.4	0.08	0.01
9. The growing number of flyers is harming the environment	2.1	_1.6_	1.9	0.04	0.01
10. I often read the flyer in the store, prior to shopping	_3.2_	3.4	3.5	0.02	0.01

A four-point item was used: 1. Strongly agree, 2. Agree somewhat, 3. Disagree somewhat, 4. Strongly disagree.

Table 12.17 A few socio-demographic differences between clusters

(All differences shown are significant on the 0.01 level)	CL1	CL2	CL3
Education:			
Elementary school/college	56%	64%	55%
Higher education	44%	36%	45%
Employment:			
White-collar workers	38%	33%	43%
Pensioners	22%	32%	18%
Other	40%	35%	39%
Read almost all flyers that I receive	53%	40%	54%
Read flyers rarely or never	47%	60%	46%
Average household size	2.5	2.2	2.3
Age	47 years	54 years	47 years
Relative size of cluster	26%	25%	49%

($n=1,089$). Note also that one important statement (10 – readership of flyers before shopping) indicates minor or little stated behaviour from *all* clusters.

It may appear strange that small differences between clusters (item 6) transform to "big" partial R-squares while bigger differences (item 5) produces much smaller R-squares. This is caused by the inter-correlation of items. One should also remember that forward stepwise procedures are sensitive to the order in which the variables enter the model.

The findings of Table 12.17 correspond to those of Table 12.16: clusters 1 and 3 resemble each other while cluster 2 differs. Compared with the flyer-prone cluster 1 and the moderately flyer-prone cluster 3, customers of cluster 2 are on average older and less educated. Moreover cluster 2 is over-represented with regard to pensioners and non-readers of flyers.

Case study: Dream Holiday (part 2)

Using cluster analysis for segmenting European consumers

The management of Dream Holiday wants to segment the European tourist market. So it has asked you to carry out a cluster analysis, based on a completed study (see Chapter 11). The eighty-eight statements involved are displayed in Table 11.29. The purpose of the new cluster analysis is to identify a few segments that can be found across European markets. At this stage, the management is not interested in knowing whether a specific segment is relatively bigger in one country than another.

Once again recall that the SPSS file, Dream_Holiday.sav is available at www. pearsoned.co.uk/schmidt. The file has 4,077 responses, but only 3,344 are used with regard to clustering, since in SPSS *[K-means cluster]* – unlike in *[Regression]*, *[Discriminant]* and *[Factor]* – there is no automatic feature to substitute missing observations with the mean of valid observations. However, SPSS Base provides a general and very user-friendly procedure for substituting missing values with the mean (or with several other related measures). The procedure is shown in the case, Zaponia. See Appendix-A on the website. This procedure is not used here, however.

Dream Holiday's market research agency has conducted some preliminary cluster analyses, based on the data. One of the issues that the management has asked the agency to consider concerns the number of clusters. Managers have told the agency that all solutions between two and five are acceptable, but they are interested in obtaining the best clustering.

The agency decides to commit the appropriate resources for identifying the best clustering. First, the agency loads the 4,077 (observations) * 88 (statements/variables) file into SAS/STAT. The (original) file that is *used* for clustering procedure is of size 3,344*88 (observations with missing cells are excluded). Next, a principal component analysis (Proc Princomp) is run based on this 3,344*88 matrix. The output contains a matrix of principal component (factor) scores, which is saved to a file. The new file is still of size 3,344*88. But unlike the original observations*variables matrix – containing *correlated* variables – the columns of the new matrix consist of uncorrelated "equally weighted" principal component scores (rescaled such that the mean of each column is 0 and the variance is 1). The original and the new matrix are based on the same input, the matrix of correlations among variables, and they both contain the same information. But in the latter matrix, the data are structured so that certain statistical assumptions are met.

The new matrix is then used as the input matrix for Proc Fastclus, the SAS k-means method. Here, the CCC-measure and pseudo-F are requested as part of the output. Recall that these measures are invalid for correlated variables. But they are valid for uncorrelated variables – and this is exactly what the principal component scores of the new matrix are.

No outlier detection procedure is carried out, so all 3,344 valid observations are included in the cluster analysis. The number of clusters are set to 2, 3, 4 and 5.[15] Table 12.18 shows the result.

As can be seen, the pseudo F-statistic peaks at three clusters while the CCC-measure improves markedly from two to three clusters and thereafter it decreases a little from three to four clusters. Both figures favour three clusters. Note that the two-cluster solution basically consists of one supercluster plus a few outliers in a separate cluster. This solution is definitely inappropriate. The negative signs of the CCC-measure is a technical consequence of using scores instead of variables.

Table 12.18 Dream Holiday analysis from Proc Fastclus

No. of clusters	Pseudo-F	CCC	Size of clusters (n)
2	3.53	−82.1	5 – 3339
3	21.64	−26.5	1107 – 1473 – 764
4	20.05	−27.2	516 – 758 – 1047 – 1023
5	19.75	−25.3	884 – 421 – 481 – 687 – 871

The three-cluster solution is selected and imported into SPSS. It is present in the file Dream_ Holiday.sav and is contained in the column called *sas_cl3* (far right).

The clustering of the eighty-eight tourism statements can also be carried out using SPSS k-means (Figure 12.13). The default number of iterations (10) was used.[16] The three-cluster solution was chosen. "Cluster membership" was flagged. The result of the SPSS run is displayed in the column called *spss_cl3* (placed next to the SAS run). Unlike the SAS run, the SPSS run was based on the raw (correlated) variables.

In the next column of the file, outliers, the following has been done. First, a preliminary cluster analysis is run using SPSS k-means and by selecting the default number of iterations (10). This time the number of clusters is set to one hundred (!). Cluster membership is saved (SPSS calls the variable *qcl_1*). Then *[Descriptive Statistics, Frequencies]* is selected and *qcl_1* is selected as variable. The output of this run shows the frequency of each cluster. It turns out that twenty-four clusters have fewer than ten observations (out of these, ten clusters contain only one observation). The twenty-four clusters contain a total of seventy-five observations. They are regarded as outliers and must be identified using a separate variable.

Therefore, a new variable called *outliers* is established. This variable will contain one value, 1, as the standard value, and another value, 9, every time an outlier observation appears. For instance, the output from *[Descriptive Statistics, Frequencies]* of *qcl_1* with one hundred clusters shows that cluster 3 has only one observation. If one selects the

Table 12.19 Cluster mean on fifty-four significant statements

Variable	CL1	CL2	CL3	Variable	CL1	CL2	CL3
X2	1.8	2.2	2.5	X48	4.0	2.8	4.1
X5	2.0	2.1	2.0	X49	2.8	2.6	3.5
X6	3.1	2.2	2.6	X50	3.9	2.5	2.9
X7	2.5	1.9	2.3	X52	3.1	2.3	3.5
X8	3.5	2.1	3.7	X53	2.4	1.6	3.5
X10	2.7	2.2	3.2	X54	2.3	1.8	3.2
X13	2.2	1.6	1.7	X56	2.6	2.8	2.0
X15	3.2	2.2	2.5	X57	3.4	3.8	2.2
X16	3.3	2.4	3.6	X58	3.6	3.9	2.6
X17	4.1	3.5	2.4	X59	2.5	2.0	2.4
X18	2.2	2.4	1.9	X60	1.8	1.6	2.4
X20	3.0	2.8	2.4	X62	2.4	1.9	2.8
X21	3.0	1.9	2.6	X64	2.7	2.2	4.0
X22	3.1	2.2	2.7	X68	1.8	1.6	1.9
X24	2.3	2.1	3.0	X69	3.7	2.6	2.4
X25	1.3	1.4	1.7	X70	2.2	2.1	3.1
X27	4.0	2.6	3.1	X71	2.9	2.4	3.8
X28	2.5	2.6	3.3	X73	3.0	2.1	2.5
X30	3.4	2.3	2.8	X74	3.7	2.9	2.5
X32	4.6	3.8	4.3	X77	3.9	2.8	2.8
X33	2.5	2.4	3.1	X80	1.6	1.9	2.7
X34	1.9	2.3	2.7	X82	3.9	3.5	4.1
X36	3.7	1.9	2.3	X83	2.2	1.9	2.1
X37	3.5	2.3	2.8	X84	2.9	2.2	1.9
X39	2.7	1.8	1.7	X85	2.9	2.5	3.4
X40	2.8	1.8	1.9	X87	1.6	1.6	2.3
X45	3.0	2.1	1.9	X88	2.9	1.9	1.9

column *qcl_1* and searches for (cluster) "3," it turns that the outlier observation is 2382 (first column of the file).

The outlier variable consists mostly of ones, and seventy-five cases of nine. The variable has a third level or value, "five." This value indicates that the observation was not included – that is, treated as missing – in the cluster analysis (due to missing values on *X1–X88*). Level 5 has 716 cases. To sum up, 3,286 cases are regarded as "valid non outliers," seventy-five are treated as "valid outliers" and 716 cases are coded as missing (3,286+75+716=4,077).

The variable *outliers* can be used to assess the influence of outliers and missing observations on the analysis. Note that the definition of outliers is *only* based on the eighty-eight statements. Likewise, a missing observation *only* indicates that the observation has at least one missing response concerning *X1–X88*.

Finally, a Ward hierarchical cluster analysis has been run using three clusters. Figure 12.6 displays the available settings for the hierarchical cluster method. In the *[Methods]* dialogue box cluster method is changed from "Between-groups linkage" to "Ward's method." Concerning *[Save new variables]* the "Single solution" is selected and set to 3. In the main dialogue box, "Statistics" and "Plots" are unflagged.

After the run is completed, the screen editor contains a new column called clu3_1. The result of this run is also contained in the file Dream_Holiday.sav as column ward_cl3.

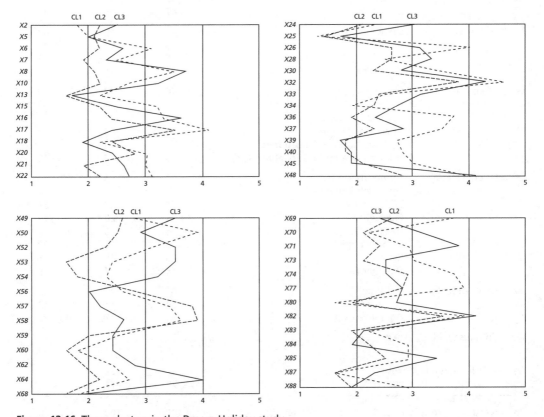

Figure 12.16 Three clusters in the Dream Holiday study

The cluster solution spss_cl3 was selected as the definitive run, not because it is the best solution, but because differences in performance were found to be rather marginal and because the present text encourages using Excel and SPSS Base for checking results involving numerical examples as well as empirical data files.

In a following step a discriminant analysis *[SPSS: Classify, Discriminant]* is run using the variable spss_cl3 as the "grouping variable" and treating *X1–X88* as "independents." Figure 10.6 of Chapter 10 shows the dialogue boxes of the discriminant method. Concerning the grouping variable the *[Define Range]* is set to 1 for "Minimum" and 3 for "Maximum." In the *[Statistics]* box, "Means" is flagged. In the *[Classify]* box "Prior Probabilities" is changed from the default to "Compute from group sizes" and the "Summary table" is flagged. "Replace missing values with mean" is *not* flagged this time. In the main box the method is changed to "Use stepwise method."

The output contains a table called "Group statistics." This table can be pasted directly

Table 12.20 Background information on the three clusters

		CL1	CL2	CL3	Total
Age	(Years)	48	49	33	43
Household size	(Number of persons)	2.7	2.4	2.5	2.5
Household income (€)	(Annual average)	61,591	55,828	65,196	60,417
Gender	Female	53	55	51	53
	Male	47	45	49	47
Marital status	Single	12	18	42	25
	Married	73	62	48	60
	Divorced	5	6	7	6
	Widow(er)	10	14	3	9
Level of education	Elementary school	40	47	10	32
	College	44	41	50	45
	Bachelor of science	9	5	15	10
	University degree	4	3	7	5
	Under education (i.e. students studying at an educational institution)	3	4	18	8
Occupational status	Farmer/fisherman	3	1	1	2
	Other self-employed	3	3	4	4
	White collar	34	27	39	34
	Blue collar	21	20	19	20
	Housewife	5	6	2	4
	Student/pupil	3	6	22	11
	Retired	26	30	5	20
	Unemployed	5	7	8	7
Part of workforce	Full-time	47	42	55	48
	Part-time	14	11	13	13
	Do not work	39	47	32	39
Video in household	Yes	75	69	71	72
	No	25	31	29	28
Garden in household	Yes	22	29	33	28
	No	78	71	67	72
Total (vertical percent sums to 100 within each variable)		100	100	100	100

into an Excel editor. It is – edited – shown as Table 12.19. Figure 12.16 displays the same data by way of a graphical representation. Due to the chosen method, variables that do not significantly contribute to the discriminant model are ignored. Recall, that the eighty-eight statements are shown in Table 11.29.

Table 12.20 provides some background characteristics on the three clusters. Except gender, the differences between clusters are significant on the 0.001 level.

As always, the reader is encouraged to check all the results by downloading the file Dream_Holiday.sav from the website.[17]

Questions

1. Table 12.21 below is a cross-tab of the two-cluster analysis discussed above, the one by SPSS and the other one by SAS. The Pearson chi-square of the table is 14.5 implying significance on the 0.6 percent level. What does this figure tell us?

Table 12.21 Crosstab of two-cluster analysis

		SPSS_CL3			Total
		1	2	3	
SAS_CL3	1	371	331	405	1,107
	2	482	472	519	1,473
	3	300	194	270	764
Total		1,153	997	1,194	3,344

2. Compute the Rand index of the two clusterings. How valid or stable is the three-cluster solution? Note that cluster numbers are arbitrary. For instance, a respondent that is put into cluster 1 by SAS may most appropriately appear in cluster 2 by SPSS and so on. So, unlike in discriminant analysis it is not sufficient to only inspect the main diagonal. The best correspondence between validating (SAS) and calibrating (SPSS) clustering may be off-diagonal.

3. The crosstab of Table 12.22 compares the SPSS k-means clustering using three clusters ("spss_cl3") – see Table 12.21 – with a three-cluster solution generated by SPSS using Ward's hierarchical method ("ward_cl3") – also based on three clusters. The Pearson chi-square of this table is 2,184.7. Compute the Rand index of the clusterings. Which of the two is most successful (sas_cl3/spss_cl3 or spss_cl3/ward_cl3)? Assume that the above variables "spss_cl3" and "ward_cl3" were not output from a

Table 12.22

		SPSS_CL3			Total
		1	2	3	
WARD_CL3	1	930	150	215	1295
	2	148	833	421	1402
	3	75	14	558	647
Total		1153	997	1194	3344

cluster analysis. Instead, assume that both variables were scaled 1–3 but that the observations were actually random numbers generated from a uniform distribution. What would the size of the Rand index be? (You need not run the example in Excel. Theoretical reasoning should suffice.)

4. You are asked to profile the three-cluster solution, based on SPSS k-means. It is recommended that you do the following: either photocopy the statement list of Table 11.29 or download it in Excel format from www.pearsoned.co.uk/schmidt. Place this statement list in front of you and next to Table 12.19 (mean across clusters on all eighty-eight statements), Figure 12.16 (corresponding graphical display) and Table 12.20 (background). Simultaneously, use a spreadsheet or wordprocessor to plug in keywords where each of the segments has extreme values – when compared with one or both of the other clusters and/or where the differences between two (or three if you can handle that) is big. Finally, come up with a cluster profiling of all three clusters. The description need not to be exhaustive but should address key differences concerning both the statement list and the background data.

5. Provide a list containing five or six recommendations so that Dream Holiday's marketing strategy can be optimally targeted towards each of the three segments individually. The list should include suggestions with regard to advertising and promotional strategy.

6. Use the variable *outliers* (included in the file Dream_Holiday.sav) to profile the 716 missing observations and the 75 outliers. Compare them with the 3,286 valid observations. Can you reveal any interesting differences?

12.7 Summary

Often, managers would like to split a market or its customers into a small subset of segments with different preferences and behaviour. If this can be done, and provided that the segments can be identified and targeted, then the company might improve revenues by developing and marketing different products and services for specific segments.

Segmentation can be done *a priori*, implying that one pre-specifies how the customers or the market are to be segmented. In such a situation a discriminant analysis is an option. One specifies in advance, say, that loyal customers are to be compared with non-customers and/or former customers. The customer–type (loyal/non-/former) is treated as the classification or dependent variable and then one selects the list of predictor variables (age, income, statement A, etc.).

Another way of segmenting a market is *a posteriori*. That is, we do not have any clues or pre-specified prejudices with regard to how the segmentation is done. In other words, we let the data speak for itself: we use an algorithm that looks for patterns in the data and then we let the method suggest a few numbers of appropriate clusters.

An empirical approach involves the construction of a questionnaire consisting of a battery of items (for instance scaled from "totally agree" to "totally disagree"). The items should address the problem under scrutiny. If the company is involved in the automotive insurance business, then items should deal with price and coverage of a policy, with people's risk aversion, what might make people change to another insurance company, with attitudes towards driving and traffic, and so on. The questionnaire could then be sent to a sample of respondents and the responses could be used as input for a cluster analysis.

A cluster analysis can be either **non-overlapping** or **overlapping**. In a non-overlapping analysis a respondent can only be part of one cluster at the same time. While overlapping cluster methods possess intuitive merits, they are difficult to use and are rarely applied. This text recommends using non-overlapping methods.

Non-overlapping methods can be categorized into two types, **hierarchical** methods and **non-hierarchical** methods. Hierarchical methods start with assuming that each observation is a cluster. Then close observations are clustered. Next clusters are joined with observations or with other clusters and so on. In the end, all observations are part of one supercluster. As follows from the name, hierarchical methods proceed hierarchically subject to a distance measurement criterion. Some popular hierarchical methods are **single linkage**, **average linkage**, **complete linkage**, and **Ward's** method.

The second type of cluster analyses concerns the non-hierarchical methods. They are also called **k-means** techniques or **partitioning** methods. These methods are faster to carry out and involve considerably fewer calculations compared with hierarchical methods. Since a k-means method does not carry out all possible distances between pairs of observations but rather a small fraction (it is an iterative procedure) it may happen that the outcome of the analysis is a local optimum. In most cases, though, the outcome will approach optimum.

Figure 12.1 and Figure 12.2 display important aspects of cluster analysis.

An important question in cluster analysis concerns how many clusters should be used. The question resembles the number-of-factors problem in factor analysis. Like in factor analysis, no undisputed approach exists. The present text discusses three measures:

- the error sum of squares (ESS);
- the cubic clustering criterion and the pseudo F-statistics; and
- the Rand index.

The first two measures involve looking for a kink or a peak – and then one should select the number of clusters right after (not before) the kink. The latter measure tests the stability of a clustering by comparing different cluster methods or settings based on the same data and number of clusters.

Questions

1. Figure 12.8 shows the result of running an average linkage cluster analysis based on the bank image data of Table 12.8. The far right column of Table 12.8 shows the cluster membership of each observation when selecting three clusters. Compare this

three-cluster solution to comparable solutions based on: single linkage; complete linkage; and Ward's method. Choose the default distance measure (squared Euclidean distance). Finally, use the same data as input for a k-means cluster analysis. Select three clusters and keep the number of iterations at ten (default). Remember to flag "Cluster membership" in the *[Save New Variables]* box each time. Hint: with regard to hierarchical methods, in the *[Save New Variables]* box of Figure 12.6, select "Single solution" and choose 3. It is recommended that you rename the cluster variable as soon as it appears in the screen editor. For instance you should rename "clu3_1" – the SPSS system name for the variable that contains the cluster membership name – to, say, "average3." However, when shifting from *[Data View]* to *[Variable View]* in the screen editor, the cluster method that generated the column appears as a label. Which of the four cluster runs comes closest to that of Table 12.8?

2. Table 12.23 shows the result of asking a small sample of managers two questions, on a nine-point scale. *X1*: export market development (from very negative to very positive); and *X2*: willingness to export (from very low to very high). First, run a single linkage cluster analysis (nearest neighbour), and then an average linkage analysis (between Groups Linkage) (select squared Euclidean distance). Compare the results. Provide a scatter plot of the raw data. Discuss the appropriateness of the two clusterings. Which one would you choose?

Table 12.23

	X1	X2
a	1	5
b	2	6
c	3	7
d	4	8
e	5	9
f	6	8
g	7	7
h	8	6
i	9	5
j	8	4
k	7	3
l	6	2
m	5	1
n	4	2
o	3	3
p	2	4
q	6	5

3. As a marketing manager you are responsible for advertising the country's biggest retail chain. The chain distributes a weekly flyer to most households. So far the company has used the shotgun approach to marketing. Basically, it has regarded all consumers as one big market. Based on the cluster analysis presented in Table 12.16 and Table 12.17 you are asked to discuss whether this approach should be upheld or not. Can you recommend alternatives to the shotgun approach? And if so, which? Specify. Briefly discuss appropriate advertising themes and overall message content of a promotional campaign based on your suggestions.

4. Recently, a new and comprehensive segmentation study was published by a leading international research agency, Constellation. According to the study, twenty-first century consumers can be "universally" segmented into no less than thirteen groups – in Constellation's promotional material they are called "micro segments." Earlier in this chapter, use of a number of clusters between two and five was recommended. While a small number of clusters is preferable in most situations, especially if the analyst is not an expert in advanced clustering methods, situations may appear where using a bigger number of segments seems advantageous. Usually, only some of the thirteen segments make sense on a specific market. The advantage of the micro segments system is that it roughly applies across most markets for products and services. The development of the system involved intense and repetitive interviews with a representative sample of 1,200 respondents (for details, see *Quarterly Journal of Market Research*, vol. 27 no. 3, 2003). Tables 12.24 and 12.25 display a small selection of findings based on the study. Table 12.24 covers selected behaviour and opinions while Table 12.25 provides some socio-demographic information on the thirteen segments. Note that in empirical studies, cell differences across segments are often rather marginal in size. But since the present sample is relatively big ($n = 1,200$), differences in cell percentages exceeding 3–4 percent in most cases will be statistically significant on an alpha level of 0.05. You are asked to perform a brief profile of the thirteen clusters, based on Table 12.24 and Table 12.25. Hint: use the bold column of Table 12.24 and the bold row of Table 12.25 as a baseline for identifying differences. Suggest three target segments concerning:

- a new brand of decaffeinated coffee;
- a DVD of fitness programmes;
- a liberal politician's election campaign.

Table 12.24 The thirteen clusters broken down on selected behaviour and attitudes

	Total	C1	C2	C3	C4	C5	C6	C7	C8	C9	C10	C11	C12	C13
Daily behaviour:	Positive response (%) (multiple responses)													
Taking shower	58	63	65	53	58	57	57	53	55	57	64	64	51	60
Drink coffee	58	64	59	57	53	58	66	51	59	60	57	61	57	49
Drink tea	20	15	20	19	20	16	20	21	24	19	18	17	25	28
Eating rolls	11	9	16	7	10	9	15	9	12	10	8	14	13	23
Eating egg	4	4	5	7	4	4	5	2	4	3	2	2	2	2
Drinking juice	10	9	9	12	10	12	6	10	11	9	14	10	8	4
Eating yogurt	18	21	10	12	21	25	17	21	22	17	15	23	17	9
Reading newspaper	25	24	29	25	19	25	25	23	22	23	25	32	31	26
Listening to radio	72	76	76	71	64	66	72	69	82	73	65	66	76	62
In favour of casinos	52	51	59	53	56	38	56	47	56	56	54	44	51	60
Alcohol prohibition at work OK	33	33	32	37	40	27	31	34	37	24	28	38	37	34
Feels stressed (too busy)	30	26	27	31	36	22	39	24	31	34	22	41	32	19
Wear gloves regularly	21	25	21	15	24	23	15	24	21	15	24	23	14	23
We sometimes bake cakes	59	61	61	61	61	47	62	52	54	63	65	54	65	66
Car ownership	59	64	52	65	63	65	57	52	58	61	59	59	52	64

Table 12.25 The thirteen clusters broken down on selected background characteristics

Cluster number	C1	C2	C3	C4	C5	C6	C7	C8	C9	C10	C11	C12	C13	Total
Horizontal percent	8	9	6	8	9	6	9	8	7	9	8	8	4	100
18–24 years	9	8	11	10	6	6	8	10	3	15	6	8	0	100
25–29	7	8	8	6	9	10	8	7	13	7	7	10	0	100
30–39	10	6	5	11	11	4	11	10	8	7	11	6	1	100
40–49	9	10	6	7	8	5	12	7	5	12	7	9	2	100
50–59	7	16	7	9	10	7	6	5	8	8	7	7	3	100
60–69	8	6	2	9	8	7	8	6	11	8	9	11	7	100
70 +	5	9	7	4	9	5	7	9	5	9	10	9	13	100
Male	7	10	5	10	8	7	8	8	7	11	7	7	5	100
Female	9	8	8	6	9	5	10	8	8	8	9	10	2	100
Resident of capital	7	9	6	7	9	8	7	9	9	10	9	9	2	100
Resident of city	8	11	3	10	3	6	17	5	5	8	8	7	4	100
Resident of village	10	7	5	9	10	7	8	8	8	14	8	8	3	100
Farmer	11	9	10	7	9	4	9	7	7	6	8	8	6	100
Entrepreneur	12	7	4	7	9	4	8	6	3	5	5	14	15	100
White-collar	11	8	4	6	12	7	8	11	2	14	9	7	1	100
Blue-collar	8	11	8	14	8	6	9	10	7	7	6	7	2	100
Housewife	10	5	4	8	7	5	14	9	4	12	4	15	2	100
Retired	5	11	4	9	8	4	9	9	10	8	11	6	11	100
Student	7	9	14	6	6	6	10	9	2	12	9	7	0	100

For each chosen segment, outline a media strategy in five key words.

5. One of the case studies in the online appendix is Appendix A, the Zaponia customer survey (www.pearsoned.co.uk/schmidt). Before proceeding, read this carefully – particularly the comments on missing values – and download the appropriate files. This study has a battery of variables that are suitable for conducting factor analysis and cluster analysis ($c1$–$c41$). First, carry out a factor analysis, name the factors and establish a list of the most important criteria concerning purchase and maintenance of a copier. The list should be usable as input for an advertising agency's consultant (a person without any knowledge about statistics). Second, if you compare the variables list with the (Varimax-rotated) output from the factor analysis, is there something that looks strange? Third, conduct a cluster analysis and profile the clusters (note that a few background criteria are available in the file). Your solution should be the best possible considering the data. Zaponia wants to improve targeting of its promotional messages and its service strategy. Do you think that segmenting its customers (and current non-customers) – based on your suggestions – could facilitate this strategy? Say why.

6. Read Appendix A, the Radio Store survey, carefully and download the appropriate files (from www.pearsoned.co.uk/schmidt). This study has a battery of variables that are suitable for conducting factor analysis and cluster analysis ($v1$–$v55$). This file has no missing values so all 216 observations have valid responses. First, carry out a factor analysis, name the factors and establish a list of the issues that can be used as input for a description of what goes on in the mind of a typical or 'average' consumer who enters

a Radio Store shop. The list should be usable as input for an advertising agency's consultant who is responsible for Radio Store's next advertising campaign. For instance, what should the five main themes be? Next, conduct a cluster analysis and profile the clusters (note that no background criteria are available). Is there any way to profile the clusters solely based on the fifty-five items? Which differences between clusters based on the statements used do you find important? Why? If the identified differences between clusters are "impressing" how could they be used for targeting an immediate multimedia advertising campaign, as input for a brainstorming session by management that aims at suggesting new follow-up studies, based on the first survey.

7. One of the early applied clustering studies was presented at a marketing conference by Neidell (1970). His subjects–times–objects matrix was small and unusual. The twelve subjects were the Playmates of the Month appearing in *Playboy* magazine during 1969. The variables of the study were the prospect's age, as well as several body characteristics: weight, height, bosom, hips and waist. Note: weight is measured in pounds, whereas the other variables are measured in inches. The data matrix is shown in Table 12.26. The measurement unit in columns IV to VII is inches and column VIII is in pounds, whereas the measurement unit in columns IX–XII is centimetres while column XIII is kilograms. The data are the same but they have been converted (1 inch = 2.5 centimetres; 1 pound = 0.454 kilograms). Now, first do a hierarchical cluster analysis (choose SPSS default settings, request a dendrogram as part of the output). Use the following variables: columns III to VIII. Inspect the results and discuss the output. Next, conduct a cluster analysis based on columns III and IX to XIII. Do not change any settings. Compare the results of the two analyses. Discuss your findings. (Hint: the scale of measurement plays an important role for answering the question.) The datafile is on the book's website (www.pearsoned.co.uk/schmidt) as Table 12.26.sav (and .xls).

Table 12.26 Female body proportions/characteristics

Playmate	ID	Age	Bosom	Waist	Hips	Height	Weight	Bosom	Waist	Hips	Height	Weight
I	*II*	*III*	*IV*	*V*	*VI*	*VII*	*VIII*	*IX*	*X*	*XI*	*XII*	*XIII*
January	1	22	36	24	37	67	130	91.4	61.0	94.0	170.2	59.0
February	2	21	36	21	36	66	118	91.4	53.3	91.4	167.6	53.6
March	3	22	36	24	34	64	120	91.4	61.0	86.4	162.6	54.5
April	4	19	35	23	34	64	105	88.9	58.4	86.4	162.6	47.7
May	5	22	36	24	35	64	110	91.4	61.0	88.9	162.6	49.9
June	6	20	35	24	34	63	110	88.9	61.0	86.4	160.0	49.9
July	7	22	36	24	34	62	105	91.4	61.0	86.4	157.5	47.7
August	8	21	36	24	36	63	112	91.4	61.0	91.4	160.0	50.8
September	9	22	36	23	34	63	110	91.4	58.4	86.4	160.0	49.9
October	10	22	34	23	36	64	117	86.4	58.4	91.4	162.6	53.1
November	11	21	35	23	36	66	115	88.9	58.4	91.4	167.6	52.2
December	12	21	34	23	34	62	105	86.4	58.4	86.4	157.5	47.7
Mean		21.25	35.42	23.33	35.00	64.00	113.08	90.00	59.30	88.90	162.60	51.30
Standard dev.		0.97	0.79	0.89	1.13	1.60	7.40	2.01	2.25	2.87	4.05	3.36

References

Aldenderfer, M. S. and Blasfield, R. K. (1985) *Cluster Analysis*. Sage, Beverly Hills, Ca.

Anderberg, M. (1973) *Cluster Analysis for Applications*. Academic Press, New York.

Arabie, P., DeSarbo W. and Wind, J. (1981) "Overlapping clustering: A new method for product positioning." *Journal of Marketing Research*. Vol. 18 (August). 310–17.

Chaturvedi, A., Carroll, J. D., Green, P. E. and Rotondo, J. A. (1997) "A feature-based approach to market segmentation via overlapping k-centroids clustering." *Journal of Marketing Research*. Vol. 34 (August). 370–7.

Dillon, R. W. and Goldstein, M. (1984) *Multivariate Analysis: Methods and applications*. John Wiley, New York.

Everitt, B. S. (1979) "Unresolved Problems in Cluster Analysis." *Biometrics*. Vol. 35, 169–81.

Everitt, B. S. (2001) *Cluster Analysis*. Edward Arnold, London.

Green, P. E. (1978) *Analyzing Multivariate Data*. Dryden Press, Hinsdale, Ill. 405.

Green, P. E. and Krieger, A. M. (1999) "A cautionary note on using internal cross validation to select the number of clusters." *Psychometrika*. Vol. 64, no. 3. 53.

Hair, J. F., Anderson, R. E., Tatham, R. L. and Black, W. C. (1998) *Multivariate Data Analysis*. Prentice-Hall, Upper Saddle River, NJ. 497.

Helsen, K. and Green, P. E. (1991) "A computational study of replicated clustering with an application to market segmentation". *Decision Sciences*. Vol. 22. (November). 1124–41.

Hubert, L. and Arabie, P. (1985) "Comparing Partitions." *Journal of Classification*. Vol. 2. 193–218.

Jajuga, K., Solokowski, A. and Bock, H. (eds) (2002) *Classification, Clustering and Data Analysis*. Springer, New York.

Jamby, M. and Lebeaux, M. O. (1983) *Cluster and Data Analysis*. Elsevier, Oxford.

Lattin, J., Carroll, J. D. and Green, P. E. (2003) *Analyzing Multivariate Data*. Thomson Learning, Pacific Grove, CA. 291.

Lorr, M. (1983) *Cluster Analysis for Social Scientists*. Jossey-Bass, San Francisco, CA.

Neidell, L. A. (1970). "Procedures and pitfalls in cluster analysis." *AMA Summer Educator's Conference*. AMA, Chicago.

Punj, G. and Stewart, D. W. (1983) "Cluster analysis in marketing research: review and suggestions for application." *Journal of Marketing Research*. Vol. 20 (May). 134–48.

Rand, W. M. (1971) "Objective criteria for the evaluation of clustering methods." *Journal of the American Statistical Association*. Vol. 66. 846–850.

Romesburg, H. C. (1990) *Cluster Analysis for Researchers*. Krieger, Melbourne, Fl.

SAS/STAT *User's Guide* (1990) version 6, 4th edn. Vol. 1. SAS Institute, Cary, NC. 824.

SAS/STAT Technical Report (1983) *A 108: Cubic clustering criterion*. SAS Institute, Cary, NC.

Schmidt, M. and Bjerre, M. (2003) "Can recipients of sales flyers be segmented?" *International Journal of Advertising*. Vol. 22. 375–391.

Shepard, R. N. and Arabie, P. (1979) "Additive clustering representation of similarities as combinations of discrete overlapping properties". *Psychological Review*. Vol. 86. 87–123.

Späth, H. (1980) *Cluster Analysis Algorithms*. Halsted Press, New York.

End notes

[1] Two loadings cannot simultaneously exceed 0.707 because $(0.707)^2 + (0.707)^2 = 1$ which is the upper limit (communality) concerning accumulated loadings of a variable.

[2] It resembles a horseshoe that is known from multidimensional scaling and is an indicator of an inappropriate choice of dimensionality.

[3] Factor analysis can be used for clustering observations across variables. Correspondingly, cluster analysis can be used for clustering variables across observations. SAS/STAT has a procedure called Varclus and in SPSS's *[Hierarchical Cluster]* one can change the default "cluster cases" to "cluster variables."

[4] Consider three people each with the following weights in pounds and height in feet: A (160; 5.5), B (163; 6.2) and C (165; 6.0). Employing the Euclidean yields: $d_{AB} = 3.08$; $d_{AC} = 5.02$ and $d_{BC} = 2.01$. Expressing these weights in kilo and heights in centimetres gives: A (72.64; 167.64), B (74; 188.98) and C (74.91; 182.88). Now, the Euclidean distance becomes $d_{AB} = 21.38$, $d_{AC} = 15.41$ and $d_{BC} = 6.17$. When the distance is measured according to the Imperial units, the order of the distances is BC < AB < AC while it is BC < AC < AB when expressed in kilos and centimetres. The example is adapted from Dillon and Goldstein (1984, 162ff).

[5] One can select any number of clusters between 2 and $n - 1$ by selecting "Single solution" in the *[Save New Variables]* box of Figure 12.6. Here, choose three clusters.

[6] Remember that hierarchical methods are exact approaches, while non-hierarchical methods are iterative. In the present case the first iteration does not yield convergence when run in SPSS. Indeed 4 iterations or 156 (36 +40+40+40) measurements are necessary. This is not much less than 190 – the total number of measurements in hierarchical cluster analysis. But assume we had to cluster the 4,077 observations of Dream Holiday in Chapter 11. Here the hierarchical method would need 8,308,926 measurements compared with 32,612 assuming two clusters and four iterations – when employing the non-hierarchical method – corresponding to 255 times fewer measurements. However, using today's software the time taken is hardly noticeable.

[7] "It often helps to remove all clusters with small frequencies even though the clusters may not be remote enough to be considered outliers. Removing points in low-density regions improves cluster separation and provides visually sharper cluster outlines in scatter plots" (SAS/STAT, version 6, volume 1, 833). "As a clustering algorithm includes more and more observations, its performance tends to deteriorate, particularly at high levels of coverage, 90 percent or above. This effect is probably the effect of outliers beginning to come into the solution. Clustering all observations may not be a good practice. Rather, the identification and elimination of outliers or the use of a decision rule to stop clustering short of the inclusion of all observations is probably advantageous." (Punj and Stewart, 1983).

[8] According to Hair et al. (1998) the k-means method in SPSS, also called quick cluster, is a parallel threshold method, while Fastclus in SAS is a sequential threshold procedure. We think both methods are optimizing partitioning methods in newer versions.

[9] When using two iterations, the three- and four-cluster assignments are the same. With two clusters, there is one disagreement, observation 11. With three or more iterations in SAS Fastclus, the two-cluster assignment of SAS fits perfectly with the SPSS-based ESS measure shown in Table 12.14.

[10] Some researchers stress that the measure is designed for validity purposes and *not* for validating the number of clusters. See Lattin, Carroll and Green (2003, 302), Green and Krieger (1999).

[11] Had the data set been "perfectly" randomized there would have been five observations in each of the four cells in the small 2*2 crosstab of Figure 12.15, panel (d). In that case the number of consistent pairs would have been:

$$A_{R1/R2} = \frac{20(19)}{2} + 5^2 + 5^2 + 5^2 + 5^2 - \frac{1}{2}\left(10^2 + 10^2 + 10^2 + 10^2\right) = 90$$

Now, 90/190 = 0.47.

[12] See for instance SAS/STAT User's Guide (1990) 832–34.

[13] The statistical program used, Fastclus (SAS/STAT) provides a measure (cubic clustering criterion) that helps to identify the most appropriate number of clusters.

[14] It is important to recall, though, that assessing the success of the clustering by running a discriminant analysis, although often used, violates "statistical correctness."

[15] The SAS code used for analysis is:

data sasspss; input $X1 - X88$; cards;

2 1 2... (start of observation 1)

...3 3 3 (end of observation 4077) ; run;

PROC PRINCOMP std out = pscore; var $X1–X88$;

PROC FASTCLUS data = pscore maxc = 2 out = cluster conv = .01 maxiter = 25 short summary;

var prin1-prin88; run;

[16] Note that using ten iterations does not imply convergence here. Indeed, twenty-eight iterations must be conducted before convergence is obtained. However, the default setting is used for simplicity, even though several hundred observations change cluster between the tenth and the twenty-eighth iterations.

[17] For the nominal variables a Pearson chi-square test was used *[Descriptives, Crosstabs, Statistics]* – "Chisquare" should be flagged. For the metric variables (age, household size and income) an ordinary ANOVA is an appropriate test *[Compare Means, One-Way ANOVA]*. "spss_cl3" must be put into the factors field while age, households size and income must appear on the "Dependent List." Within *[Options]*, "Descriptives" needs to be flagged. Alternatively, *[General Linear Model, Univariate]* may be used.

13 Positioning the product: MDS

Learning objectives

After studying this chapter you should be able to:

- Explain why product positioning is a significant competitive tool.
- Explain the basics of multidimensional scaling (MDS).
- Clarify how a product space is to be interpreted.
- Describe how properties and preferences fit into the product space.
- Explain the underlying principle of correspondence analysis.

13.1 The importance of product positioning

As the competition increases, the positioning of a company's brands becomes an even more important issue for managers. A company that is unable to continuously launch new brands or services or reposition and adjust its existing product line is heading for trouble.

Positioning of a product is a necessity because:

- Consumers' preferences (taste) change over time.
- Consumers' expectations and demands become more sophisticated.
- The company's brands need to be revitalized.
- Competitors are aggressively launching new products.

No company can ignore rivals and their products, and therefore competitiveness becomes a necessity for survival.

For more than thirty years it has been common within marketing to use terms such as perceptual space, cognitive map, and multidimensional scaling (MDS) in connection with the analysis of products, services, markets and brands.

Before examining the technical issues involved in product positioning, read the following Marketing research in action box.

Marketing research in action

Product positioning at Dream Holiday

Historically, the management of Dream Holiday (see Chapter 11 and Chapter 12) has classified its customers into seven business segments with regard to tourists' and travellers' preferred destinations:

1. Scandinavia: Norway, Sweden, Finland, Iceland.
2. Western European islands and coasts: England, Ireland, Scotland, Normandy.
3. Central Western Europe: Alsace, the Harz, the Rhine, Lake Garda, the Alps.
4. Western part of Southern Europe: Spain, Portugal, French Riviera, Italy.
5. Eastern part of Southern Europe: Croatia, Greece, Aegean Islands (Turkey).
6. Eastern Europe (other): Poland, Czech Republic, Russia.
7. Rest of the world: North America, South America, Asia and Africa.

Up to now, Dream Holiday's marketing strategy has been organized in accordance with the seven segments. Sales catalogues, brochures, websites and other promotional material focuses on the above segments. For instance, there is a specialized brochure in several languages that promotes each segment: one covers Scandinavia, another focuses on Normandy and the British Isles, and so on.

However, Dream Holiday's directors were recently forced to resign due to declining sales and accelerating losses in day-to-day operations. During recent years Dream Holiday has lost market share to its big European competitors: TUI/Thomson, Thomas Cook/Neckermann, MyTravel/Airtours, First Choice and Kuoni. (Strictly speaking, these companies are not "travel agencies" but rather pan European travel companies. For instance, with regard to TUI, Thomson and TUI Nordic are main operators, Lunn Poly and Nouvelles are travel agencies while Hapag Lloyd and Britannia AB are in-house carriers.)

The new leadership wonders if the former management's perception of the market and the segmentation is still appropriate (or if it ever was). So far Dream Holiday has been targeting all markets, or more correctly, no segment has been ignored. For instance there is a brochure for each of the seven segments distributed to all European sales offices and agents. However, some questions arise. If the seven segments represent a good market categorization, should Dream Holiday target all of them? If the seven segments do not appear valid or reasonable from a marketing or consumer behaviour perspective, what are the alternatives?

Based on the answers to these questions, should Dream Holiday redefine its perception of market segments? And if so, should it reposition its offer platform?

To answer the above questions, the new management asked its research agency to carry out a product positioning analysis in accordance with the market research technique called multidimensional scaling (perceptual mapping). Ten interviews were carried out in each of the five countries England, Germany, France, the Netherlands and Norway. Each of these was carried out as a "self explicated interview" – a questionnaire handed out to respondents at the end of a focus group dealing with a family's holiday choice. All respondents had been recruited for the focus groups on the basis that they had been on holiday abroad at least once a year for the past three years.

So, a total of fifty interviews were conducted. While fifty interviews seems to be a small sample, MDS is known to be rather robust with regard to placing objects in two or three dimensional space. Whether the analysis is based on ten or 100 interviews does not matter that much (Büyükkurt and Büyükkurt, 1990). MDS is also known to be rather insensitive to outliers (Spence and Lewandowsky, 1989). See also Green (1975), Malhotra (1987) and Malhotra, Jain and Pinson (1988). Obviously the methodological robustness of MDS is caused by technical reasons. In an MDS-based questionnaire one asks respondents to compare products/services with regard *not* to preferences, but with regard to closeness/similarity/proximity (say, whether two products/services taste/look alike). It is well known within psychology that it is much easier for people to agree upon perceived proximity than on preferences.

The managers meet with the research agency's consultants and after a few day of e-mail correspondence, the questionnaire is approved. For matters of convenience, twelve well-known tourist destinations were selected for the analysis. During the interview, respondents were asked to rate the destinations in pairs with regard to perceived similarity. With twelve items, a total of sixty-six comparisons were needed – $[n*(n-1)]/2 = (12*11)/2$.

A one to ten rating scale was used, where a small number implies great similarity and vice versa.

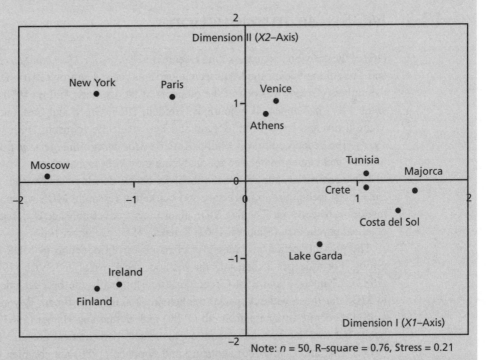

Note: $n = 50$, R-square = 0.76, Stress = 0.21

Figure 13.1 Perceptual space of selected holiday destinations

Figure 13.1 displays the (two-dimensional) perceptual space based on the MDS analysis. (The technique is explained in detail later in this chapter.)

Questions
1. Provide an interpretation of Figure 13.1. Note that the axes are arbitrary. The origin only serves as the centre of the structure. Also, left/right and up/down are arbitrary. What counts is the positioning of products (here: destinations) in relation to other products. Closeness indicates similarity and vice versa. One should keep in mind that the placement of destinations in Figure 13.1 is *not* based on, say, a cluster analysis of respondents' preferences. So, strictly speaking, the positioning of destinations does not correspond to segments. Input for the analysis was fifty respondents' similarity/dissimilarity rating of all twelve destinations in pairs.
2. Based on your interpretation, does Figure 13.1 support the old management's segmentation (the seven segments). Or do you think that the new management should change the company's segmentation strategy? And if so, how could this be done?
3. Based on your interpretation of Figure 13.1 you are asked to provide input for a new multimedia advertising campaign. Which overall themes should be targeted at which segments?

13.2 MDS – an introduction

One of the early books in marketing research, *Research for Marketing Decisions* by Green and Tull, did not cover the MDS technique in its second edition (1970). However, one of the authors (Green) was one of the pioneers of the method. And by 1970 the first papers about MDS had appeared in journals (Neidell, 1969; Green and Carmone, 1969; Green, Maheshwari and Rao, 1969; Morgan and Purnell, 1969; Johnson, 1971; Green and Rao, 1972). The second edition of Philip Kotler's *Marketing Management* from 1972 shows how the technique can be used for analyzing the US beer market.

Early marketing publications were inspired by developments within psychometrics. Like many techniques in marketing and marketing research, MDS was not developed by marketing researchers. The first MDS algorithms were established by researchers in mathematical psychology (Shepard, 1962; Kruskal, 1964; Coombs, 1964).

The present section provides a brief hands-on introduction to MDS in a marketing setting. For a deeper insight into the method, see Kruskal and Wish (1978) and Coxon (1982). Chapters 2 and 3 of Coxon constitute probably the best technical introduction to MDS for those without special mathematical skills. Schiffman, Reynolds and Young (1981), Green, Carmone and Smith (1989) and Young and Hamer (1987), are advanced books but can also be read without sophisticated mathematical presumptions. Davidson (1992), Cox and Cox (2000) and Borg and Groenen (1989) are complex treatises on the topic.

Basic theory of multidimensional scaling

This discussion of MDS begins with a type of example used a decade or two ago (see Green and Tull, 1978; Coxon, 1982). Table 13.1 shows the approximate distances in kilometres between fifteen European capitals.

According to the table, the distance between Stockholm and Vienna is 1,165km, between Rome and Vienna it is 582km and so on. Since Table 13.1 contains all possible pairs of distances, it has $[n*(n-1)]/2$, here $(15*14)/2 = 105$ cells. The shortest distance, 146km, is between Brussels and Luxembourg de Ville, while the longest distance is between Helsinki and Lisbon (2,912km). The information has come from a map that displays the correct linear geographical distances between the European capitals. The matrix of Table 13.1 contains the same information about distances between the fifteen cities but in tabular form.

Now, assume for a moment that a despotic regime took over power in a United States of Europe. The iconoclastic leaders deem all maps to be the work of aliens and order them destroyed. The new regime also decides that mouth-to-mouth interaction is the only legal way of communication, implying that all other means of obtaining information, such as TV, radio, newspapers and satellites are forbidden. If a person is caught sending an e-mail he is immediately shot. A hundred years pass under the regime. New generations grow up. Any teaching of geography is forbidden. Moreover, all teachers and scholars of geography have died. So, knowledge of Europe's topography has disappeared. Inhabitants of Brussels may know from tradesmen that Luxembourg is rather close, but they will probably not know where Helsinki is let alone if, say, Rome is closer to Vienna than it is to Madrid. Neither will they know if Lisbon – when regarded from Brussels – is in the opposite direction to Helsinki.

Eventually, the European citizens succeed in revolting against the oppressive regime and the despots are overthrown.

One of the most important issues is to regain knowledge of European topography. Unfortunately, the last person with knowledge of geography died in a prison cell many years ago.

Table 13.1 Linear or "airline" distances between fifteen European capitals (km)

	Vie	Sto	Rom	Par	Mad	Lux	Lon	Lis	Hel	Dub	Cop	Bru	Ber	Ath	Ams
Vienna	0	–	–	–	–	–	–	–	–	–	–	–	–	–	–
Stockholm	1165	0	–	–	–	–	–	–	–	–	–	–	–	–	
Rome	582	1731	0	–	–	–	–	–	–	–	–	–	–	–	
Paris	857	1456	857	0	–	–	–	–	–	–	–	–	–	–	
Madrid	1391	2248	987	809	0	–	–	–	–	–	–	–	–	–	
Luxembourg	663	1262	793	226	987	0	–	–	–	–	–	–	–	–	
London	1051	1391	1148	291	1003	404	0	–	–	–	–	–	–	–	
Lisbon	1747	2556	1359	1100	372	1310	1229	0	–	–	–	–	–	–	
Helsinki	1375	421	1957	1812	2588	1601	1779	**2912**	0	–	–	–	–	–	
Dublin	1472	1634	1553	696	1165	841	437	1294	2038	0	–	–	–	–	
Copenhagen	793	534	1278	922	1698	712	873	2022	922	1181	0	–	–	–	
Brussels	776	1245	938	194	1019	**146**	275	1310	1618	696	712	0	–	–	
Berlin	453	809	954	760	1488	534	825	1828	1100	1213	340	582	0	–	–
Athens	971	2054	744	1585	1666	1472	1876	2006	2135	2281	1747	1618	1423	0	–
Amsterdam	809	1116	1035	356	1165	259	307	1456	1504	696	582	162	518	1698	0

Then something unexpected happens. On an old fragment someone finds a table that is an exact copy of Table 13.1. The question now arises: can this tabular information be used to regenerate a map of Europe?

Well maybe, but how? Fortunately another thing happens that may help: an intact PC is found. It is turned on and – hardly believable – it still works. Moreover, it turns out that it has SPSS 14 installed. Someone remembers being told by her grandfather that SPSS contained a program that could transform tabular information into geographic information. So in a state of expectancy, SPSS is loaded and the figures of Table 13.1 typed into the SPSS data editor. The file is available at www.pearsoned.co.uk/schmidt and is called Figure 13.1.sav.

1. Begin by tabbing *[Analyze]* on the main menu bar and select *[Scale]* and *[Multidimensional Scaling (ALSCAL)]*.[1] See Figure 13.2. Note that the data must appear as a lower triangular matrix, exactly as shown in the screen editor. Zeros must appear along the main diagonal. Dots for missing values in the upper triangular matrix are automatically generated by SPSS. For matters of convenience all cities have been abbreviated in the variable list to the first three letters of the name.

2. Selecting *[Multidimensional Scaling]* triggers the method's main dialogue box. See the upper box of Figure 13.3. Now highlight all cities in the list box at the left and click them into the variables list. Before running the analysis two settings are changed. First, click the *[Model]* box and flag "Untie tied observations." This needs to be done because there are several ties in Table 13.1. For instance, the distance between Vienna and Stockholm is 1,165 km – the same as the distance between Amsterdam and Madrid as well as between Dublin and Madrid. SPSS must be told how to handle ties.[2] From a

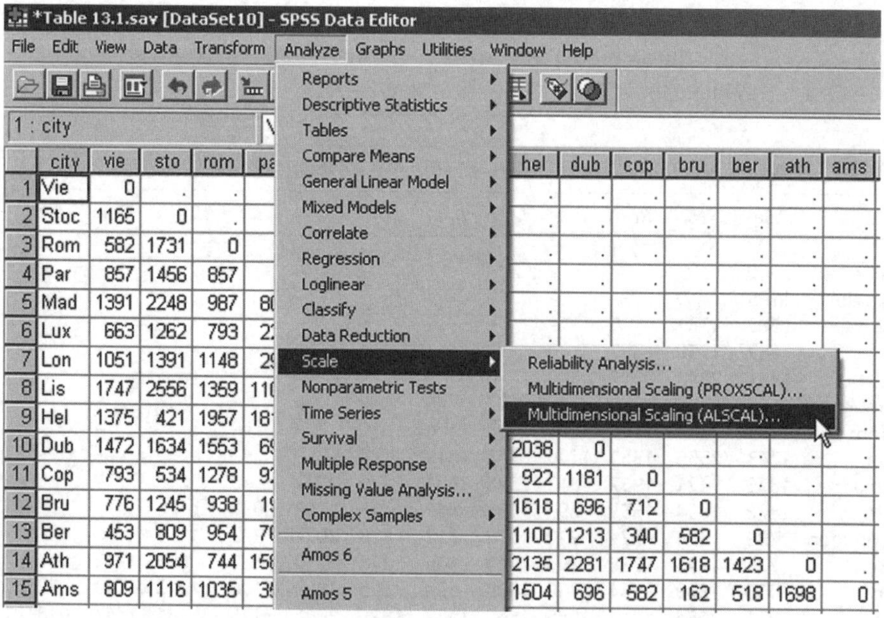

Figure 13.2 Running MDS in SPSS

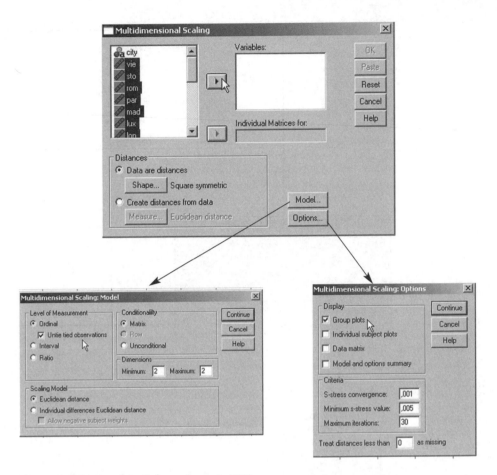

Figure 13.3 Appropriate dialogue boxes in SPSS

    modelling perspective the "Level of Measurement" ought to be changed from "Ordinal" to "Ratio" – kilometre is ratio-scaled – but that can be left unchanged. Click *[Continue]*.
3. Next, tick the *[Options]* button and flag "Group plots" – the result is that a two-dimensional plot appears in the output.
4. Click *[Continue, OK]*.

Figure 13.4 shows the result.[3] The output has been abbreviated and edited.[4] Indeed, it appears that important aspects of the European topography can be re-established solely based on the plot. The statistics in Figure 13.4 show the recovery is perfect. Basically, the accuracy of the recovery is measured as the correspondence between Table 13.1 and a reconstruction of Table 13.1 that is based on the co-ordinates of Figure 13.4. Figure 13.5 illustrates the computational procedures.

    The x/y co-ordinates of the cities according to the reconstructed map of Figure 13.4 are used for measuring inter-city distances. By multiplying the Euclidean distance with a rescaling factor (620), the recovered distances can be computed (reconstructed Table 13.1 in Figure 13.5). In the present case the fit of original values and reconstructed values is almost perfect.

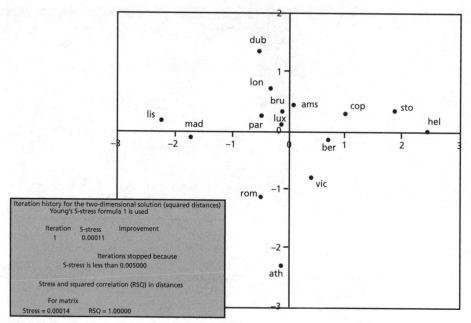

Figure 13.4 Output from SPSS multidimensional scaling

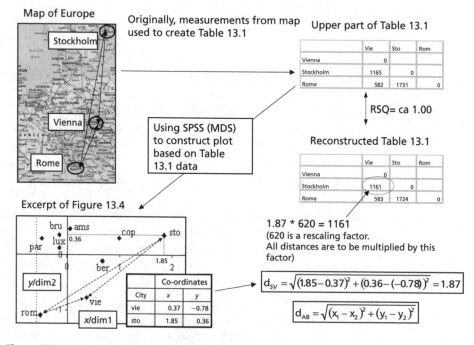

Figure 13.5 From original to reconstructed distances

The RSQ (R-square) is 1.00000 and the stress (a badness of fit measure) is 0.00014, approaching the lower limit of 0. In other words, the geographical plot of Figure 13.4 corresponds perfectly to the information in Table 13.1. However, no information is known about relative directions, so the plot of Figure 13.4 is arbitrary. In fact, rotating Figure 13.4 by about 45 degrees counterclockwise shows that the placement of the fifteen cities fits a corresponding map.

Now, assume for a moment that the actual distances of Table 13.1 are not known. Instead, there is only non-metric or rank-ordered information of the city-distances. So, the shortest distance (Brussels–Luxembourg, 146km) appears as "1"; the second shortest distance (Amsterdam–Brussels, 162km) is a "2"; etc., and the longest distance (Helsinki–Lisbon, 2,912km) is represented by the number "105". Table 13.2(a) displays all distances of Table 13.1 as ranks.

In Table 13.2(b) the distances of Table 13.1 have been transformed to a one to nine interval scale according to the following principle: the longest distance in Table 13.1 is 2,912km (Helsinki–Lisbon) and the shortest is 146km (Brussels–Luxembourg). We now treat 146 as the lower end and 2,912 as the upper end of an interval scale, consisting of nine equally sized intervals, implying that each interval has the length of $(2,912 - 146)/9 = 307$km. So all distances in Table 13.1 between 146 and 453 ($146 + 307$) appear as "1" in Table 13.2(b), all distances between 454 and 760 ($146 + 2*307$) appear as "2" and so on. Note how imprecise or even misleading Table 13.2(b) is at representing the distances of Table 13.1. An example: according to Table 13.1, the distance between Berlin and Vienna is 453km. This distance is more than three times that of Brussels and Luxembourg (146km). Yet according to Table 13.2b the two distances are the same ("1" interval distance unit)! Note that the data of Table 13.2(a) and 13.2(b) are available for download on the book's website.

Figure 13.6 shows the result of running MDS based on both the ranked data (Table 13.2(a)) and the interval-scaled data (Table 13.2(b)). Despite a less precise input data structure, it is impressive how successful the fits are. The plot based on the ranked data

Table 13.2(a) Non-metric (rank ordered) distances between the fifteen capitals

	Vie	Sto	Rom	Par	Mad	Lux	Lon	Lis	Hel	Dub	Cop	Bru	Ber	Ath	Ams
Vienna	0	–	–	–	–	–	–	–	–	–	–	–	–	–	–
Stockholm	56	0	–	–	–	–	–	–	–	–	–	–	–	–	–
Rome	19	88	0	–	–	–	–	–	–	–	–	–	–	–	–
Paris	38	73	39	0	–	–	–	–	–	–	–	–	–	–	–
Madrid	70	101	46	35	0	–	–	–	–	–	–	–	–	–	–
Luxembourg	22	63	32	4	47	0	–	–	–	–	–	–	–	–	–
London	51	71	55	7	48	12	0	–	–	–	–	–	–	–	–
Lisbon	89	103	68	52	11	66	61	0	–	–	–	–	–	–	–
Helsinki	69	13	95	92	104	81	91	105	0	–	–	–	–	–	–
Dublin	75	84	79	23	57	37	14	65	98	0	–	–	–	–	–
Copenhagen	31	17	64	41	86	26	40	97	42	59	0	–	–	–	–
Brussels	30	62	43	3	49	1	6	67	82	24	27	0	–	–	–
Berlin	15	34	44	29	77	18	36	93	53	60	9	21	0	–	–
Athens	45	99	28	80	85	76	94	96	100	102	90	83	72	0	–
Amsterdam	33	54	50	10	58	5	8	74	78	25	20	2	16	87	0

Table 13.2(b) Interval distances (scaled 1–9) between the fifteen capitals

	Vie	Sto	Rom	Par	Mad	Lux	Lon	Lis	Hel	Dub	Cop	Bru	Ber	Ath	Ams
Vienna	0	–	–	–	–	–	–	–	–	–	–	–	–	–	–
Stockholm	4	0	–	–	–	–	–	–	–	–	–	–	–	–	–
Rome	2	6	0	–	–	–	–	–	–	–	–	–	–	–	–
Paris	3	5	3	0	–	–	–	–	–	–	–	–	–	–	–
Madrid	5	7	3	3	0	–	–	–	–	–	–	–	–	–	–
Luxembourg	2	4	3	1	3	0	–	–	–	–	–	–	–	–	–
London	3	5	4	1	3	1	0	–	–	–	–	–	–	–	–
Lisbon	6	8	4	4	1	4	4	0	–	–	–	–	–	–	–
Helsinki	5	1	6	6	8	5	6	9	0	–	–	–	–	–	–
Dublin	5	5	5	2	4	3	1	4	7	0	–	–	–	–	–
Copenhagen	3	2	4	3	6	2	3	7	3	4	0	–	–	–	–
Brussels	3	4	3	1	3	1	1	4	5	2	2	0	–	–	–
Berlin	1	3	3	2	5	2	3	6	4	4	1	2	0	–	–
Athens	3	7	2	5	5	5	6	7	7	7	6	5	5	0	–
Amsterdam	3	4	3	1	4	1	1	5	5	2	2	1	2	6	0

needs to be rotated about 135 degrees clockwise and the interval scaled plot must be rotated about 45 degrees counterclockwise. Then both plots correspond with the hemisphere. Note how close the plot with the interval data fits the metric based plot of Figure 13.4. The principle of recovering a geographical space is based on numeric distances by way of a geometric technique called naval triangulation. This is a technique for distance measurement that has been known at least since the seventeenth century, but whose origins can be tracked back to the ancient Greek mathematicians. Since the middle of the last century the method has been replaced by more modern methods, most recently by GPS.

How does this work? Figure 13.7(a) shows a fraction of Table 13.2b, the table with the interval scaled distances between the European capitals. We know that there are four – linear – distance units between Vienna and Stockholm and therefore we begin with drawing this distance (say, by using centimetres) on a piece of paper. Next, we wish to determine where Rome is going to be placed. Since we know that there simultaneously are

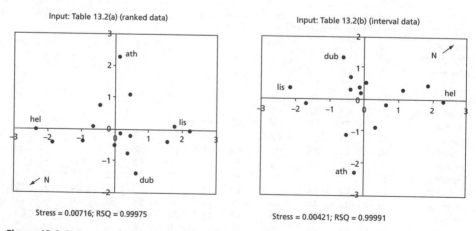

Input: Table 13.2(a) (ranked data)   Input: Table 13.2(b) (interval data)

Stress = 0.00716; RSQ = 0.99975   Stress = 0.00421; RSQ = 0.99991

Figure 13.6 Recovery of ranked and interval distances

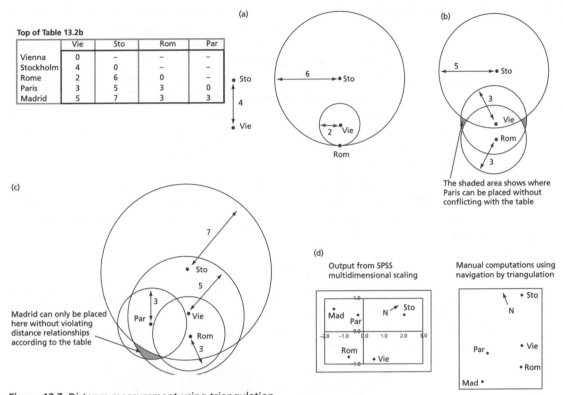

Figure 13.7 Distance measurement using triangulation

two units from Vienna to Rome and six units from Stockholm to Rome, we can use a caliper to draw circles with radii of two and six units around Vienna and Stockholm, respectively. We then place Rome at the intersection of the two circles.

In Figure 13.7 (b) the relative positioning of Vienna, Stockholm and Rome is assumed to be known. Table 13.2b also contains the distances from Paris to Vienna (3), Stockholm (5) and Rome (3). Once more we draw circles. However, this time we are unable to identify a single point with regard to placing Paris. This is because the three circles do not intersect at the same point. In the present situations, Paris can be placed anywhere within the two grey zones. We choose the centre of one of them and assume Paris to be located there. In (c) the procedure is once more repeated, this time with the purpose of placing Madrid.

This time the measurement results in a single but bigger zone. The zones of indetermination are caused by measurement error. They appear partially because we use imprecise information. Moreover, in Figure 13.7 we only use five points. If there are ten points or more, areas of indetermination rarely constitute a methodological problem. Finally, in (d) we compare our manual positioning of the cities with a run by SPSS Multidimensional Scaling. Apart from the usual unpreventable differences in hemispheric direction and apart from divergences in scale-length (caused by SPSS), the two plots match nicely.

The underlying algorithm of multidimensional scaling is an individual model and therefore – unlike regression or ANOVA – it makes sense to run the analysis on the subject level. The MDS method belongs to the class of iterative or optimizing procedures, so it aims to produce the best fit between tabular and figurative representation of numerical information. With regard to approaching the optimum – and being sensitive to local optima – MDS resembles the simplex linear programming technique that is often used in economics. In *[SPSS, Scale, Multidimensional Scaling (PROXSCAL), Define, Options]* the default initial configuration is indeed "Simplex" – a linear programming algorithm. A fine technical introduction to MDS for non-mathematicians is given by Coxon (1982, 10–92).

The city geography example has introduced the theory in a non-technical way. Now, the same method will be used to construct a "psychographic" map of a market. The only difference is that perceived distances between brands, products or services are used instead of metric distances between cities.

It is quite easy to construct a questionnaire where a respondent is asked to rate the perceived degree of (dis)similarity between a set of brands. These similarities are then treated as perceived tabular distances and used as input for establishing a cognitive map of the product market.

The product space for alcoholic bitters

Below an empirical study is introduced. The involved data on proximities and preferences are available at www.pearsoned.co.uk/schmidt as nautic.xls. The Excel file has several worksheets with raw data, a format that is ready for loading into SPSS, etc. The necessary instructions appear in the file.

Figure 13.8 A selection of alcoholic bitters

Some years ago, the leading marketer of drinks on the Danish market, Danisco wanted to launch an alcoholic bitter. An alcoholic bitter differs from schnapps, vodka, whisky and gin in that it has a brown/dark colour. Moreover, bitters are characterized by having a bitter flavour and a spicy taste.

The producer's leading brand within alcoholic bitters is Gammel Dansk. While Gammel Dansk is almost unknown outside Scandinavia and Northern Germany it is very popular on the Danish market. Since it was introduced in 1964 it has gained a dominant market share, at some times approaching 80 percent. During the late 1980s, its market share began to decline slowly while a small competitor, Vinhuset Norden, succeeded in gaining share with its Nordsøolie brand, a drink that is known to be especially popular in bars and cafés. When Danisco decided to counterattack, its market share was down to 65 percent while Nordsøolie had a share of about 15 percent. While a 15 percent share seems modest, no other bitter brand on the Danish market has more than 1–2 percent share. After a long period of development, the new brand, Nautic, was ready to be launched. Before the final launch, managers decided to conduct a product positioning analysis. Figure 13.8 shows a selection of alcoholic bitters available in Denmark at the time of the study (seven of them were included in the study). The leading brand, Gammel Dansk, is in the middle of the first row. The new brand, Nautic, is just behind it.

First, a list of brands to be included in the study was agreed upon. Next, a questionnaire was mailed to about one hundred respondents. (All respondents were members of a panel of tasters that occasionally received a small package containing two to three alcoholic bitters in 10cl bottles. The respondents were asked to taste the bitters and then to fill in a questionnaire. Respondents did not know the contents of the specific bottles. So it was a blind test.) The members of the panel were recruited on the basis that they were knowledgeable about alcoholic bitters. So, while the respondents did not constitute a random sample of the population, Danisco ensured that basic background characteristics, such as age, gender, marital status, were met.

As part of the questionnaire, the respondent was asked to compare the ten selected brands in pairs. For each of the 45 comparisons a one-to-nine interval scale was used, where 1 indicated that two brands were "very similar" and 9 stood for "very dissimilar." Table 13.3 shows how the comparisons were structured.

According to the philosophy of MDS, the respondent is given no advice with regard to which criteria or what specific characteristics to use as a baseline for comparison (price, quality, etc.). An MDS analysis is carried out as we wish to determine the most important aspects or dimensions of the respondent's perceptional space. Therefore, we should not

Table 13.3 Bitters taste comparison

Comparison	1	2	3	4	5	6	7	8	9
	Very similar			Neither/nor			Very dissimilar		
1. Underberg/Jaegermeister 2. Underberg/Gammel Dansk (3–44 are not shown) 45. "Dummy"/Nautic					X			X	X

	U	J	G	K	L	V	F	N	D	NB
Underberg	0									
Jaegermeister	8	0								
Gammel Dansk	5	6	0							
Krabask	6	6	6	0						
Landsoldat	9	3	8	7	0					
Von Oosten	5	5	5	3	8	0				
Fernet Branca	4	7	4	3	8	3	0			
Nordsøolie	9	5	9	5	3	9	9	0		
Dummy (G .Dansk)	5	5	2	6	8	6	6	7	0	
Nautic (new brand)	6	4	8	3	4	5	4	3	7	0

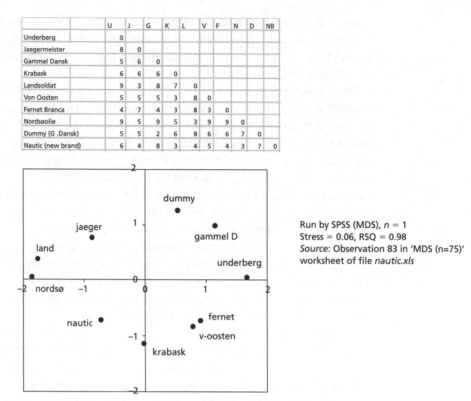

Run by SPSS (MDS), $n = 1$
Stress = 0.06, RSQ = 0.98
Source: Observation 83 in 'MDS (n=75)'
worksheet of file *nautic.xls*

Figure 13.9 An individual's product space of alcoholic bitters

give the respondent any clues or premises concerning the comparison of brands. The respondent should rate the brands in pairs and then the analyst should carry out the MDS analysis. Thereafter it is up to the analyst to make sense of the most important two or three dimensions. Due to practical reasons one usually chooses to look at a space that comprises the first two dimensions. Sometimes, a third dimension may aid interpretations.[5]

Figure 13.9 displays the two-dimensional product positioning map, based on one respondent's responses. The input matrix is shown above the positioning map.

The package that contained the questions for the positioning analysis usually included two small sample bottles with bitters. One of them was the new brand, Nautic, while the other one contained Gammel Dansk (recall that it was a blind test). So, when respondents were asked to compare one of the two samples with the other eight brands in the question-naire, they were unknowingly comparing the well-known brand Gammel Dansk with itself. This was done in order to evaluate the validity of the positioning analysis. If respon-dents were unable to detect the similarity of Gammel Dansk and the dummy sample that contained Gammel Dansk, then one might question the validity of using the MDS method in the present case. (Fortunately, most respondents regarded the two identical brands as being similar.)

According to the respondent in Figure 13.9, Underberg and Jaegermeister seem to be dissimilar (as indicated by the "8" on the interval scale). Also, she/he has detected that Gammel Dansk and the dummy brand are similar ("2") – as should be the case. With some exceptions, brands that appear to be dissimilar according to the table (indicated by big

	under	jaeger	gammel_d	krabask	land	van_oost	femet	nordsoe	dummy	nautic
1	0	.	.	.	.	.	.	.	.	.
2	9	0	.	.	.	.	.	.	.	.
3	4	9	0	.	.	.	.	.	.	.
4	5	7	4	0	.	.	.	.	.	.
5	9	1	9	9	0	.	.	.	.	.
6	3	8	4	7	9	0	.	.	.	.
7	3	9	8	8	8	3	0	.	.	.
8	9	9	9	8	7	7	9	0	.	.
9	7	9	6	5	9	9	9	9	0	.
10	9	7	9	9	4	9	1	4	9	0
11	0	.	.	.	.	.	.	.	.	.
12	9	0	.	.	.	.	.	.	.	.
13	6	9	0	.	.	.	.	.	.	.
14	4	9	4	0	.	.	.	.	.	.
15	8	2	8	9	0	.	.	.	.	.
16	9	9	8	9	9	0	.	.	.	.
17	9	8	9	9	9	9	0	.	.	.
18	8	3	7	9	3	9	9	0	.	.
19	4	5	3	7	5	9	9	5	0	.
20	8	8	8	9	8	9	2	8	9	0
740	.	.	.	.	.	.	.	.	.	.
741	0	.	.	.	.	.	.	.	.	.
742	8	0	.	.	.	.	.	.	.	.
743	6	9	0	.	.	.	.	.	.	.
744	8	8	7	0	.	.	.	.	.	.
745	9	5	8	5	0	.	.	.	.	.
746	7	9	6	9	8	0	.	.	.	.
747	5	9	7	8	8	7	0	.	.	.
748	9	5	9	9	6	9	9	0	.	.
749	6	9	1	8	9	7	5	9	0	.
750	6	9	2	8	9	7	5	9	2	0

Figure 13.10 Loading multiple observations into SPSS/MDS

values) are placed far from each other in the positioning plot and vice versa. The respondent obviously is better at determining what is dissimilar than what is similar: the rating contains five cases of 9 and six of 8 but no "1" and only a single case of "2." However, this is a pattern often observed when rating by pairs.

In Figure 13.9 the fit between the distances in the table and the co-ordinate-based distances of the figure is very high: the R-square is approaching unity and the stress is close to 0. The reader should try to run the sample problem using *[SPSS Scale, Multidimensional Scaling (ALSCAL)]* by proceeding exactly as shown in Figure 13.2 and Figure 13.3. Note that although the data of Figure 13.9 are interval-scaled, ties are involved and therefore we use the default, *[Ordinal data]*, and flag "Untie tied observations" in the *[Model]* box. Remember to request a plot in the *[Options]* box.

Figure 13.10 shows how the input data file for MDS must be structured to base the analysis on several observations at a time. Note that the lower triangle matrices are simply stacked. At www.pearsoned.co.uk/schmidt the file with all seventy-five usable responses is available (the file also includes the data from the respondent of Figure 13.9, lines 571–80).

Figure 13.11 displays the output based on all seventy-five observations.

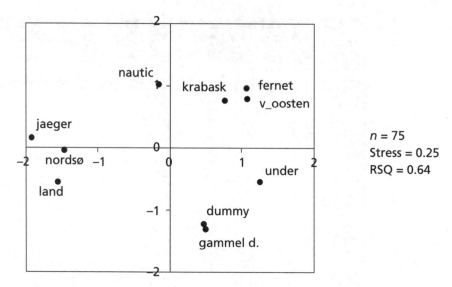

Figure 13.11 The product space based on 75 observations

The plot in Figure 13.9 had an excellent fit. But this is not surprising for fitting an individual's similarity rating to an individual subject space. On the other hand, a product space that has been accumulated across many respondents will always provide higher stress and a lower R-square. In the present case, the stress (0.25) and the R-square (0.64) seem acceptable.[6]

When comparing Figure 13.11 with Figure 13.9, note a similar pattern. In both plots the same products are placed relatively close to each other and vice versa. (We did select an individual plot that resembled the aggregated plot.)

But let us concentrate on Figure 13.11.

What do the brands "jaeger," "land" and "nordsø" have in common? Well, all have a relatively sweet flavour. Sometimes such brands are categorized as "half-bitters." "Land" was originally designed as a "me-too" product by Danisco, which felt threatened by the increasing Danish sales of "jaeger." At the opposite side of the first axis we find brands like "fernet," "v_oosten" and "underberg." These bitters are more spicy and are sometimes called "morning bitters" – for when you need something to really make you feel better, especially when you have a hangover.

The second axis appears to be more complex to interpret. But we note that on average the respondents have identified the similarity of "gammel_d" and "dummy." It appears that "gammel_d" is perceived as being different from the two other main clusters of brands on the market (jaeger, nordsø, land) and (krabask, fernet, v_oosten). The positioning of "under" relatively far from the group "krabask, fernet, v_oosten) seems a bit surprising. Maybe it is because "under" is sold exclusively in a 2cl bottle.

Is the perceived positioning of nautic as expected? At least it seems not to be positioned too closely to fernet and v_oosten. However, the relative closeness to krabask (also sold by Danisco) may worry management with regard to the danger of cannibalization of an existing product. It might be recommended to modify the flavour of nautic a little with the purpose of moving it in the direction of Danisco's main competitor nordsø.

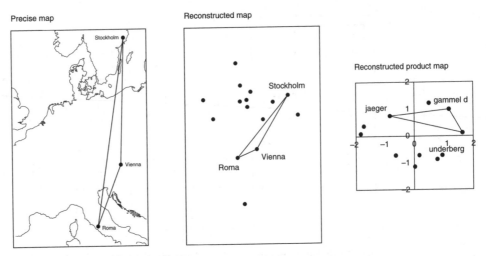

Figure 13.12 From cities to products

By moving nautic in the direction of nordsø and jaeger, Danisco could pursue a strangulation strategy. But then again there is the danger of cannibalizing another of its own brands, land.

What actually happened? The empirical study on which the bitter case is based was carried out during the spring of 1988. The product that was the focus of the managerial problem, nautic, was launched in late 1988. During the same months, coincidentally, the company was bought by another and both the product manager and the marketing manager in charge of alcoholic bitters, left. As a result, the launch of nautic did not get the marketing support that two years of intensive product development seemed to justify. Eventually, nautic was withdrawn in the mid-1990s. Some years later, the main competitor to gammel dansk, nordsø, was bought by Danisco.

Figure 13.12 summarizes the link between the city example and the example with alcoholic bitters.

Unlike the geographical model, the psychographical model does not have a "precise" product map. It does not make sense to talk about an exact perceptional map or, say, of a metric distance between products. Consequently, it is not possible to produce a metric table of distances in the psychographical model. What we can do, however, is to obtain interval measurements of the type used in Table 13.2(b). Based on this table, we can use SPSS for obtaining Figure 13.9 with perceived distances between products. Finally, we make the crucial assumption: since the reconstructed European map is an accurate description of the known map, the reconstructed product map is an acceptable proxy of the unobtainable product map. Provided we can accept this final assumption, the concept of product positioning makes good sense from a methodological perspective.

Preferences (ideal vectors)

Multidimensional scaling can help determine how a product space looks. If properly applied it helps us to identify which are the closest competitor(s) to a brand(s) – as perceived by a sample of knowledgeable customers. However, being a proximity method that

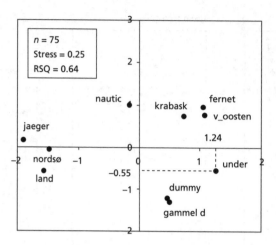

	Co-ordinates		Rankings	
	X1	X2	Y40	Y84
under	1.24	−0.55	6	2
jaeger	−1.91	0.16	1	8
gammel d.	0.51	−1.29	9	4
krabask	0.76	0.74	3	7
land	−1.56	−0.54	4	5
v_oosten	1.07	0.79	8	6
fernet	1.05	0.94	7	9
nordsø	−1.48	−0.04	2	1
dummy	0.47	−1.21	10	3
nautic	−0.14	1.01	5	10

Figure 13.13 Fitting preferences into the product space (1)

focuses on similarities/dissimilarities, it does not say anything about preferences in the marketplace. For instance, while most customers agree that underberg clearly differs from jaegermeister (probably due to differences in taste), this information does not say which of the two brands they would prefer if they had to choose between them.

To get an idea about preferences, the product space has to be combined with preference data. Assume preference data has been collected on the ten alcoholic bitters. The data has come from 161 respondents who were members of the bitters' tasting panel mentioned earlier.

All respondents were asked to rank the ten brands from 10 = best to 1 = worst. Figure 13.13 repeats the product space of Figure 13.11 with a table showing the co-ordinate vectors of the two-dimensional space. For instance, (1.24; −0.55) indicates the positioning of 'under' in the X1/X2 space. The table also contains the preferences of two respondents (Y40 and Y84).

The data in the table is used to establish preference vectors ("idle points") for the two respondents. This is done by way of a multiple regression on the individual level. Technically, one respondent's preference ranking, say Y40, is treated as the dependent measure and the (X1, X2) co-ordinates of the group plot as the predictor variables. The ten brands' co-ordinates in the product space then explain Y40's preference ranking. It is an easy task to regress Y40 on X1 and X2. Figure 13.14 shows the regression model, the estimated parameters and the fit for Y40 and Y83. The model fit is quite good, implying that the ranking corresponds with the positioning of the products. Now, treat the parameter estimates of X1 and X2, namely b1 and b2 as co-ordinates in the product space and then draw a straight line from the origin to the b1, b2 co-ordinates (here: 1.87, −1.57), with the line ending at an arrow pointing towards the co-ordinate. This is respondent Y40's preference vector. Because he prefers the dummy brand and gammel dansk, the vector is drawn pointing south. A relative liking of von oosten, fernet branca and underberg draws the arrow towards the east. Y40's least-liked brands are jaegermeister and nordsø – brands that are placed almost in the opposite direction to Y40's preference vector.[7]

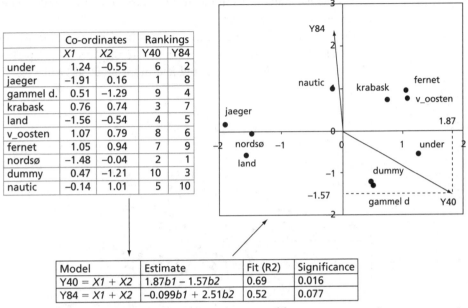

	Co-ordinates		Rankings	
	X1	*X2*	Y40	Y84
under	1.24	–0.55	6	2
jaeger	–1.91	0.16	1	8
gammel d.	0.51	–1.29	9	4
krabask	0.76	0.74	3	7
land	–1.56	–0.54	4	5
v_oosten	1.07	0.79	8	6
fernet	1.05	0.94	7	9
nordsø	–1.48	–0.04	2	1
dummy	0.47	–1.21	10	3
nautic	–0.14	1.01	5	10

Model	Estimate	Fit (R2)	Significance
Y40 = X1 + X2	1.87b1 – 1.57b2	0.69	0.016
Y84 = X1 + X2	–0.099b1 + 2.51b2	0.52	0.077

Figure 13.14 Fitting preferences into the product space (2)

Strictly speaking, the regression analysis of Figure 13.14 has several methodological problems. First, the sample is small so that in most cases the regression model does not yield significance. Second, the dependent variable is non-metric scaled. Therefore we ought to use a regression algorithm that properly appreciates the scaling of dependent measure, such as SAS/STAT's Proc Transreg. Third, the "idle point" (and the MDS analysis as such) assumes that all relevant products are included in the analysis. This rarely is the case. For instance, the empirical study did not include the brands boonekamp, branca

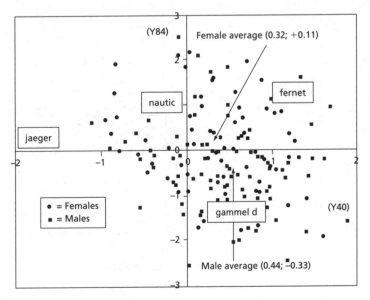

Figure 13.15 Preferences across gender

menta, and halvbitter (seen in Figure 13.8) nor did it incorporate arnbitter, ratzeputz and st margarethener wurzelbitter.

The study is based on preference rankings from 161 respondents, of whom ninety-five were males and sixty-six females. Figure 13.15 displays all 161 preference points along with the gender-specific averages and four of the products. While the overall plot appears

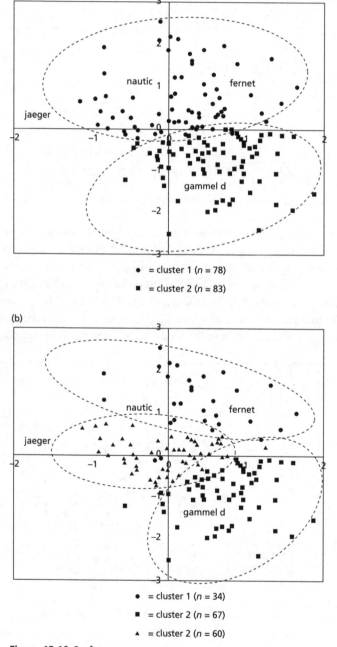

Figure 13.16 Preference segments

to be "blurred", there is a two-to-one over-representation of male points in the bottom-right quadrant. The two left-hand quadrants each contain one eighth of the points; the top-right quadrant has about a quarter and the bottom-right almost half of the points. This distribution appears roughly to fit with the market share at the time of the study where gammel dansk had a market share of 60–70 percent.

The idle-point analysis should make the marketers of the nautic worry, because the area surrounding the new brand appears to be thinly populated with ideal points – unlike the area of Danisco's flagship, gammel dansk.

Figure 13.16 attempts to classify the 161 ideal points into two and three clusters, respectively. While nautic appears to be somewhat better positioned than jaegermeister and fernet – both brands have shares of 1 percent or so – it is not nearly as favourable as the positioning of gammel dansk. The two-cluster solution seems to categorize the ideal points into two segments, "gammel dansk" and "non-gammel dansk." This is not surprising but it shows that the "non-gammel dansk" segment consists of 48 percent of the respondents. So, if the sample is representative, there is potential for this heterogeneous preference segment, since the combined market share of the 'non-gammel dansk' brands is only 20–30 percent. All managerial deductions based on *ideal points* should be treated with care. It is more realistic to regard the points as "tendencies" or "indications" since the majority of ideal points, especially those at the centre, are grounded on regression analyses that are not, and in many cases not even nearly, significant. Indeed, the preference rankings of Y40 and Y84 were exceptions: of the 161 regressions only thirty-three had an R-square better than 0.3 and only in ten cases was the model's significance lower than 0.10. This is caused by the small sample size ($n = 10$) of the individual regressions.

Another way of establishing a product space is to base the analysis on the file that contains the 161 respondents' preference ranking of the ten brands. This 10 variables * 161 observations matrix is then loaded directly into the SPSS. The appropriate data file is available at www.pearsoned.co.uk/schmidt as a separate sheet "Preferences(raw)" in nautic.xls. When these data appear in the SPSS screen editor, tab *[Analyze, Scale, Multidimensional Scaling]*, in the main dialogue box, and change *[Distances]* to "Create distances from data." Do not change *[Measure]*. As usual, select "Untie tied observations" in the *[Model]* box and request a "Group plot" in the *[Options]* box. Clicking *[OK]* gives a product space *based not on proximities but on preferences alone*. The methodology that uses preferences for establishing a product space is known as MDPref. While the model fit is fine (RSQ=0.94 and Stress = 0.11) it is very problematic to provide a useful interpretation to such output.

The above approach to fitting of ideal vectors based on respondents' rankings and running individual regressions is documented in separate sheets of nautic.xls. "MDS(n = 75)" has the raw data (Figure 13.10) used as input for producing Figure 13.11. The sheet "Preferences(raw)" contains the raw preference data as well as some information on how to handle them. Finally, the sheet "Preferences(OLS)" contains the data used in Figures 13.13–13.16. The sheet contains co-ordinates – the ideal vector – of all 161 respondents, based on an OLS regression of each of the 161 individuals. The file also includes the respondents' gender (Figure 13.15) plus a cluster variable for a two- and a three-cluster solution (Figure 13.16).

Property fitting

A "complete" product positioning analysis can be seen as having three parts:

- A section consisting of the ordinary perceptual mapping of distances (peceived similarities) where pairs of brands are rated using an interval scale.
- A section where respondents have been asked to rank or rate the brands according to preferences.
- A section where respondents rate the brands on a selection of appropriate properties that characterize the brand or the product environment.

The first two parts have been discussed above. The task now is to show how respondents' responses to a selection of statements or properties can be merged with the product space. The technique used is the same (regression) as was used for estimating ideal points and fitting them into the product space. First, recall the product space concerning holiday destinations that was introduced at the beginning of the chapter (Figure 13.1).

Assume that the management of Dream Holiday would like to obtain a better interpretation of the product space. The placement of the two principal axes is arbitrary and their intersection just indicates a centre of gravity. Therefore, it is decided to carry out an analysis to supplement the first MDS analysis (Figure 13.1). Fortunately, the research agency's consultant, having a certain experience with MDS analysis, foresaw that Dream Holiday might want to dig deeper into the MDS analysis and therefore decided to place ten statements and a preference ranking of the twelve destinations in the original questionnaire. So, the data is already available and needs only to be analyzed.

Table 13.4 displays the ten statements. There are eleven other destinations, so consequently a complete questionnaire implies one-hundred-and-twenty ratings. While this might appear to be a burden for a respondent, the rating section can be split into several parts and filled in by two or more different respondents. For illustrative purposes, Table 13.4 shows the response pattern of one respondent.

Table 13.5 shows the average ratings across destinations. The far-right columns of Table 13.5 display the ($X1$, $X2$) co-ordinates of the twelve destinations in the perceptual

Table 13.4 Statements about destinations by one respondent

	Totally disagree				Totally agree
I think that ... Majorca ... is/has ...	1	2	3	4	5
S1 A good place to relax			X		
S2 Has low prices	X				
S3 For people who love culture and art			X		
S4 Good for shopping			X		
S5 Risk of stomach trouble			X		
S6 Has beautiful nature					X
S7 Exciting night life					X
S8 Good for a walk				X	
S9 Good to visit without (girl-) friend					X
S10 Here you can meet interesting people				X	

Table 13.5 Cross-tab of holiday destinations and averaged statements

	Responses averaged across subjects (n=52)										Co-ordinates of places	
	S1	S2	S3	S4	S5	S6	S7	S8	S9	S10	X1	X2
Majorca	4.40	3.67	1.62	2.25	3.46	3.10	4.25	2.92	4.19	3.21	1.5239	−0.1517
Venice	3.27	2.56	4.38	3.73	3.13	2.98	3.21	2.94	2.42	3.52	0.2662	1.0123
Costa d. S.	4.54	3.58	1.60	2.35	3.62	3.04	4.04	2.98	4.02	3.27	1.373	−0.3975
Paris	2.77	2.15	4.63	4.33	2.10	2.02	4.46	3.63	3.19	4.25	−0.6585	1.0752
Lake Garda	4.46	3.10	2.23	2.52	2.83	4.27	2.96	4.25	3.04	2.96	0.6621	−0.8472
Moscow	2.04	3.67	4.13	2.56	2.48	2.44	1.96	2.98	1.77	2.77	−1.7625	0.0423
New York	2.15	1.98	3.94	4.04	2.29	2.04	4.50	3.13	3.04	4.25	−1.3085	1.1344
Crete	4.56	3.73	3.38	3.38	3.48	4.27	3.69	4.06	3.31	3.48	1.0693	−0.1039
Finland	3.15	2.65	2.94	2.98	1.94	4.56	2.37	4.56	2.33	2.96	−1.3101	−1.3738
Athens	3.12	3.58	4.65	4.06	3.54	3.38	3.63	3.40	2.62	3.62	0.1793	0.8577
Tunisia	4.17	4.06	2.69	3.27	4.29	3.44	2.71	3.21	2.60	3.06	1.0788	0.0717
Ireland	3.10	2.96	2.71	2.83	2.02	4.63	2.67	4.50	2.38	3.37	−1.109	−1.3193
R-square	0.97	0.40	0.77	0.63	0.75	0.69	0.44	0.51	0.50	0.51		
Significance	0.00	0.10	0.00	0.01	0.00	0.01	0.08	0.04	0.04	0.04		

space. While they were not shown explicitly in Figure 13.1 they are part of the MDS default output in SPSS. The reader can check this because the fifty observations used as input for Figure 13.1 can be downloaded from www.pearsoned.co.uk/schmidt. The Excel file Dream_Holiday_MDS.xls has several worksheets. The first is called MDS.[8]

Table 13.5: note that while Majorca scores highly on "A good place to relax"/*S1* (4.40) – the maximum is 5.00 – it is not regarded as "A place for people who love art"/*S3* (1.62).

Note: *n* = 50, R–square = 0.76, stress = 0.21

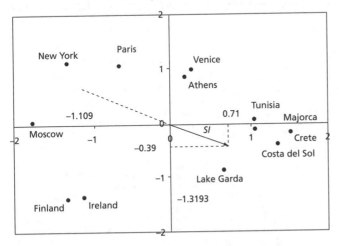

	Co-ordinates of places		
	X1	X2	S1
Majorca	1.5236	−0.1517	4.40
Venice	0.2662	1.0123	3.27
Costa d. S.	1.373	−0.3975	4.54
Paris	−0.6585	1.0752	2.77
Lake Garda	0.6621	−0.8472	4.46
Moscow	−1.7625	0.0423	2.04
New York	−1.3085	1.1344	2.15
Crete	1.0693	−0.1039	4.56
Finland	−1.3101	−1.3738	3.15
Athens	0.1793	0.8577	3.12
Tunisia	1.0788	0.0717	4.17
Ireland	−1.109	−1.3193	3.10

Property S1: This is a good place to relax

Model	Estimate	Fit (R²)	Significance
$S1 = X1 + X2$	$0.71b1 - 0.39b2$	0.97	0.000

Figure 13.17 Fitting a property into product space

Many of the differences in mean will be statistically significant, which the reader can verify by way of a t-test.[9] The reader can verify this by using Excel *[Tools, Data Analysis, t-test: Paired Two Sample for Means]*.

However, little time need be spent on Table 13.5. Instead, look at Figure 13.17. The perceptual plot is similar to Figure 13.1. The table to the right of the plot repeats the (X1/X2) co-ordinates of Table 13.5 together with the first column (S1). This column or data vector contains the averages across respondents with regard to "A good place to relax" for the twelve destinations. Note that Crete (4.56), Costa del Sol (4.54) and Lake Garda (4.46) have the highest ratings while Moscow (2.04), New York (2.15) and Paris (2.77) have the lowest ratings.

The table at the bottom of Figure 13.17 shows the result of regressing column S1 on X1 and X2. It is a simple multiple regression with two predictors (X1 and X2) and one dependent variable (S1) comprising twelve observations.

Next, use the same procedure as was used for fitting ideal points into the product space (Figure 13.14). The only difference is that a vector or property instead of an ideal point vector is fitted into the group or product plot. As before, use the estimated parameters – the regression coefficients – to draw a line that starts at the origin and ends with an arrow pointing at the co-ordinate of S1 (0.71, −0.39). For the present vector the fit is excellent, with R-square almost 1.0 and the significance approaching 0. This corresponds nicely with the way the destinations are positioned in the plot: the vector points towards the destinations that have the highest rating on vector S1 and points away from the destinations that have the lowest ratings on S1. To sum up: Crete, Costa del Sol and Lake Garda are places that the respondents associate with relaxing. New York on the other hand is not for relaxing.

Figure 13.18 shows the result of regressing all ten vectors of Table 13.5 individually on the (X1, X2) co-ordinates and fitting them into the product space. For clarity, axes have

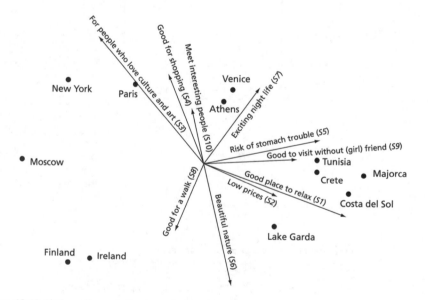

Figure 13.18 Fitting all properties into the product space

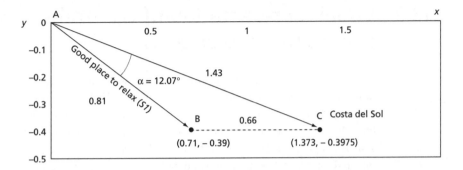

A distance say, AB is computed thus: $d_{AB} = \sqrt{(0-0.71)^2 + (0-[-0.39])^2} = 0.81$

The angle α is computed as:

$$\cos\theta_{AB:AC} = \frac{|AB|^2 + |AC|^2 - (|BC|)^2}{2 \times |AB| \times |AC|} = \frac{(0.81)^2 + (1.43)^2 - (0.66)^2}{2 \times (0.81) \times (1.43)} = 0.9779$$

0.9779 is the correlation of the vectors representing the item Costa del Sol and the vector representing the property "A good place to relax" (*S1*).
The arccosine of 0.9779 is 12.07°. This is the angle between the vectors.

Figure 13.19 Geometric relationships between properties and objects

been left off and the length of the arrows doubled. Note that the length of a vector corresponds with the size of R-square (the higher the R-square, the longer the vector).[10] Note also that the angle of a property vector and of a destination corresponds with the correlation between the two. For instance, if in Figure 13.17 a straight line is drawn between (0.0) and the co-ordinate of Costa del Sol (1.373–0.3975), the angle between this line and vector *S1* turns out to be 12.07 degrees. The directional cosine of 12.07° is 0.9779. This is the correlation between the destination vector Costa del Sol and the property vector *S1* ("A good place to relax"). Figure 13.19 has the geometric and computational details.[11] For details on geometric aspects of vectors see Carroll, Green and Chaturvedi (1997).

Curiously, the vector "For people who love culture and art" points away from Crete and Majorca, both destinations renowned for their history. Nevertheless, assuming that our sample of respondents is representative it will probably not be wise to persuade a mass audience to choose, say, Majorca because of its many old churches.

Once more it should be noted that all output discussed here on MDS and property fitting concerning the tourism data can be checked since all raw or input data appear in the file Dream_Holiday_MDS.xls.

13.3 Visual representation of cross-tabs: correspondence analysis

If handled carefully, MDS is a powerful and flexible tool for assessing how a brand is positioned against its competitors. The disadvantage of MDS is that it necessitates a detailed questionnaire that most respondents find rather strange, time-consuming and boring. When the number of brands to be analyzed is, say, twenty, then the number of pairwise comparisons is one hundred and ninety. If a property analysis with twenty items is involved, four hundred questions (twenty brands times twenty items) must be filled in. Finally, the preference ranking or rating of the brands necessitates twenty more responses. To sum up, a comprehensive MDS analysis that includes property fitting and an idle product analysis necessitates that the respondent provides answers to 610 questions. Consequently, one must read a monotonous text of 20–30 pages.

Because of the complexity of the questionnaire, MDS is often ruled out as an option during the idea-screening phase of the research process. Another methodological drawback is that MDS usually cannot be used for analyzing data from questionnaires that have not been specifically designed for the purpose. Note how odd the data structure of Figure 13.10 is. Limited raw data originate or exist as lower-triangular matrices or can easily be transformed or rescaled in such a way.

This implies that the MDS method can rarely be used for the analysis of secondary data or for renewed scrutiny of existing primary data (this at least holds in a marketing context). So, if a company wants to analyze data gathered some time ago for a different purpose, or if it wants to produce a perceptional map from data found on a website, or it wishes to analyze data obtained, say, from Eurostat, MDS is not suitable.[12] Fortunately, other methods can provide a graphical impression of such data.

As long as the data are metric or interval-scaled, it is almost always possible to establish a geographical space to help understand the relationship between objects or/and subjects – even if MDS is not applicable. Factor analysis, presented in Chapter 11, could be an option.

However, when working with qualitative data, a graphical representation of associations is not quite as straightforward.[13]

Sometimes an analyst is interested in untangling relationships that appear to be "embedded" in relations between nominal data. While associations between variables in a small and simple cross-tab usually can be handled without sticking to complex analytical methods, problems arise as soon as the number of levels exceeds five and whenever the cross-tab involves more than two variables. Since a person's perceptual system is better at processing geographical rather than tabular information, it seems natural to look for a method that can display any kind of cross-tables. Correspondence analysis fulfils this need.

Several books are available on correspondence analysis. The best known texts include Greenacre (1984, 1993) and Lebart, Morineau and Warwick (1984, translated from French). Greenacre (1993) is an excellent non-technical introduction.

First, consider an example. At the end of two focus groups, respondents are asked to fill in a sheet of paper containing three simple dichotomous questions on gender, smoking and preferred beverage. Table 13.6 shows the result.

Table 13.6 Gender, smoking and beverage preference of a small sample

Respondent	Gender 1=male 2=female	Smoking 1= smoker 2=non-smoker	Beverage 1=beer 2=wine
1	2	1	2
2	1	2	2
3	1	1	1
4	1	2	1
5	2	2	2
6	1	2	1
7	2	1	2
8	2	2	2
9	1	2	2
10	1	2	1
11	2	2	1
12	2	1	2
13	1	2	1
14	2	2	2
15	1	2	2
16	2	1	2
17	1	2	1
18	1	1	1
19	2	2	2
20	2	1	1

At a first glance, it is almost impossible to detect a pattern in the three-by-twenty matrix. According to cross-tabs (see Table 13.7), it appears that the male subset contains fewer smokers and more beer drinkers (ignore the fact that the number of observations is very small). Conversely, half the females smoke and 80 per cent prefer wine to beer. With regard to the cross-tab of beverage and smoking a pattern seems to be lacking.

To find patterns and to obtain a better interpretation, we carry out a correspondence analysis in SPSS.

- Start SPSS and tab in the data of Table 13.6. (Below we use SPSS version 14. In earlier versions the dialogue boxes of this method look rather different.)
- Select *[Analyze, Data Reduction, Optimal Scaling]*. See Figure 13.20.
- In the *[Optimal Scaling]* dialogue box tab *[Define]*. See Figure 13.21.
- In the *[Multiple Correspondence Analysis]* box highlight "gender", "smoking" and "beverage" and tab them into the "Analysis Variables" field.
- Tab the *[Plots: Variable]* tag.
- In the *[MCA: Variable Plots]* box highlight the three variables and tab them into the *[Joint Category Plots]* field.
- Tab *[Plots, Object]* and in the *[MCA: Objects Plots]* change *[Label Objects]* from "Case Number" to "Variable". *[Continue]*.
- Tab the *[Output]* tag and in the *[MCA: Output]* dialogue box tab the three variables into the *[Category, Quantifications and Contributions]*.
- Tab *[Continue]* and *[Ok]*.

Table 13.7 Cross-tabs of responses

		Smoking		
		Smoker	Non-smoker	Total
Gender	Male	2	8	10
	Female	5	5	10
	Total	7	13	20

		Preferred beverage		
		Beer	Wine	Total
Gender	Male	7	3	10
	Female	2	8	10
	Total	9	11	20

		Preferred beverage		
		Beer	Wine	Total
Smoking	Smoker	3	4	7
	Non-smoker	6	7	13
	Total	9	11	20

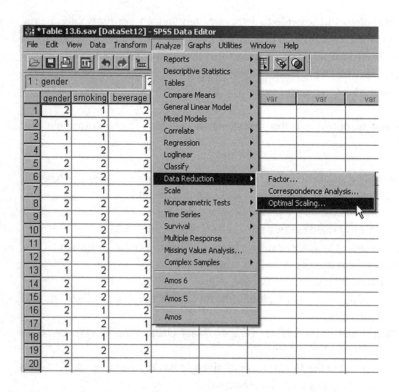

Note: SPSS has two programs for correspondence analysis: correspondence analysis has two-group correspondence analysis (for simple cross-tabs). Optimal scaling can be used for carrying out a multiple correspondence analysis (MCA).

Figure 13.20 Running multiple correspondence analysis (MCA) in SPSS

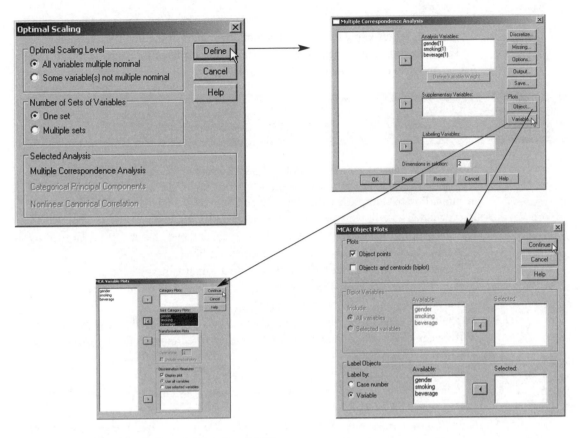

Figure 13.21 Dialogue boxes in optimal scaling (MCA)

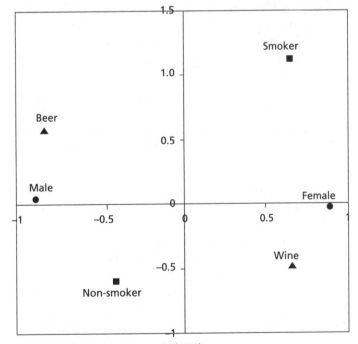

Figure 13.22 MCA plot of numerical example (SPSS)

Figure 13.22 displays an abridged and refined output. The output contains the co-ordinates of the points representing the row and column marginals of the involved variables.

The following Marketing research in action box explains the steps involved in producing an Excel chart based on SPSS output tables.

Marketing research in action

Producing an Excel chart based on SPSS output tables

SPSS output may be edited in SPSS. SPSS also has a *[Graphs]* button in the main toolbar. However, if one wants to integrate output graphs into a report created in Word or into a PowerPoint presentation, it may be better to change the SPSS graph into an Excel chart. The following description is based on Excel 2000.

1. The output from running MCA in SPSS contains tables that are rarely needed by market researchers, so they will not be discussed here.
2. The section "Quantifications" consists of three small tables: "Gender", "Smoking" and "Beverage" . The tables contain the two-dimensional co-ordinates of the row and column points. They can be copied into Excel.
3. The tables need to be joined into one table. This is done by deleting unnecessary rows/columns. A little editing (variable heading, rearrangement of columns) also helps.
4. Now select the cells containing all co-ordinates, (i.e. C2–D7).
5. Select Excel's Chart Wizard. Choose XY (Scatter) as chart type *[Chart Wizard – Step 1 of 4 Chart Type]*, Tab *[Next]*.
6. In *[Chart Wizard Step 2 of 4 Chart Source Data]* the Data Range field should contain the range C2–D7 (Series in Columns). *[Next]*.
7. In *[Chart Wizard – Step 3 of 4 – Chart Options]* the chart can be refined if, for example, we want to move the legend or if we do not want gridlines.
8. If we tab *[Next]*, *[Chart Wizard Step 4 out of 4]* appears. Here we can choose where to place the chart. Default is the active sheet. Press *[Finish]* and the chart appears.
9. The chart can now be edited by double clicking/right clicking on The Chart Area, The Plot Area, Value (X) axis, Value (Y) axis. When double clicking the axes and next clicking *[Scale]* one can alter the scaling of the axes. Inexperienced Excel users should spend time getting used to the Chart Wizard.

Correspondence analysis aims at establishing a match between tabular and geographical information. The method transforms frequencies in a table to distances in a perceptual space such that big cell frequencies (close association) imply small distances between row and column points of the cell and vice versa.

When looking at Figure 13.22 note the correspondence between the gender points and the smoking points: half of the females smoke and most males are non-smokers. Consequently, it is approximately the same distance from the female point to the smoker point than it is from the female point to the non-smoker point (note that the dimensions are scaled differently). The male point however, is placed closer to the non-smoker point. The beverage points are also positioned in accordance with the respective cell frequencies: most females prefer wine and most males prefer beer. One should bear in mind that the within-variable distance has no meaning. Obviously, it does not make sense to look at distances between the female and the male point, between smokers and non-smokers or between wine and beer. It only makes sense to compare a level of one variable with another, for example males (or females) in relation to beer and wine, respectively.[14] To sum up, males are associated with beer and nonsmoking, whilst females are associated with wine.

The present example is small and fictitious. In a real life study, there would be several hundred observations and a lot of categorical variables. Moreover, many variables will have more than two levels. If the analysis has thirty variables, an analysis of all cross-tabs would require no less than 435 tables. Moreover, since some tables – occupation, education, available brands, etc. – may have ten or more levels, SPSS will generate more than one hundred pages of printout. In such cases correspondence analysis becomes a powerful analytical tool.

The reader may recall that correspondence analysis was introduced in Chapter 1 (Exhibit 1.2, Figure 1.1a and Figure 1.1b). A simple correspondence analysis *[Analyze, Data reduction, Correspondence Analysis]* was used that only investigated two variables at a time. However, multiple correspondence analysis *[Optimal Scaling]* could have been used.[15] Figure 13.23 shows the outcome.

For a better understanding the reader might need to re-read Exhibit 1.2.

Certain important aspects of the simple correspondence analyses of Figure 1.1(a) and 1.1(b) also appear in the MCA-plot of Figure 13.23: a correspondence between public ownership and polycentric marketing strategy; and an association between national ownership and a regiocentric strategy. However, according to Figure 1.1(b), the ethnocentric

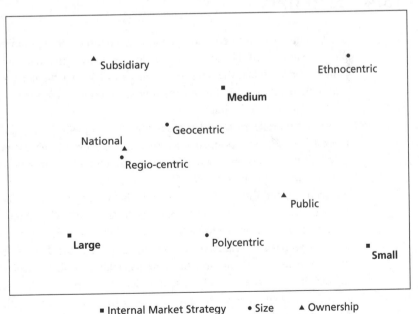

Figure 13.23 MCA plot of numerical examples (SPSS)

point is also close to public ownership. This is not the case in the MCA plot of Figure 13.23. From the cross-tabs (not shown), note that the public/polycentric cell ($n = 101$) has more than twice as many observations as has the public/ethnocentric cell ($n = 46$). So the ethnocentric point should be further away from the public point than the polycentric point.

As long as the number of variables involved in the analysis is manageable, it is recommended that the analyst carries out both the MCA and the simple correspondence analyses and compares the results. If the number of variables exceeds five or so, the analyst should select a sample of cross-tabs for cross-checking results by comparing the MCA plot with the cross-tabs and with simple correspondence analysis plots.

The analyst should abstain from any uncritical deduction based on an MCA plot. One should also keep in mind that the plot of Figure 13.23 has two limitations. First, responses to the involved question are based on self-reported behaviour (did all interviewed managers understand concepts such as regiocentric and geocentric?). Second, Figure 13.23 shows a two-dimensional solution. This choice of dimensionality is convenient, but it is arbitrary and may be inappropriate. Thirdly, the employment/firm size variable has been discretized (transformed to nominal scale).

In some cases a conventional analysis of an ordinary two-dimensional MCA space does make sense from an interpretational viewpoint. In other situations an extension of the solution space to three dimensions may facilitate interpretation, usually at the cost of simplicity, though.

Appendix 13-A (on the book's website www.pearsoned.co.uk/schmidt) provides a commercial case study involving the interpretation of a three-dimensional MCA space.

13.4 Summary

Most companies face fierce competition on a national or on a global scale. Obviously, the phrase "survival of the fittest" applies to competitive markets. Whenever there are competitors for a market, the question arises as to whether the company's current product is optimally positioned or if its competitive positioning, in terms of consumer perception or market share, could be improved.

An appropriate method for assessing the competitive positioning of products on a market is MDS – multidimensional scaling. This usually necessitates a special questionnaire where brands are compared via rating or ranking in pairs with regard to overall product similarity/dissimilarity. The number of brands in an MDS analysis usually varies between five and fifteen. One should note that the MDS analysis focuses on perceived differences between brands. MDS belongs to the class of proximity analyses; it tells us nothing about consumer preferences or about the size of market segments.

After all pairs of brands have been given a score, the data can be analyzed. The MDS program reads the file or table (a triangular matrix) with the scores and establishes a low dimensional surface (usually a two-dimensional space). The program aims to fit the Euclidean distances between products in the triangular matrix with the distances between brands in the two-dimensional space or map. The two-dimensional space is known as cognitive map or product space. Theoretically, product maps may have more than two dimensions and sometimes three-dimensional solutions need to be inspected because two dimensions do not reveal a pattern. However, two dimensions are standard.

Brands that respondents regard as being similar would be placed close to each other in the map, implying that they address the same product attributes. A close scrutiny of the product space can help a company optimize its product positioning strategy. It may both help the company to prevent cannibalizing its existing brands and help strangle the competitor's brands. In an MDS analysis it is critical to select the relevant brands. If an important brand has been ignored the analysis may be flawed.

While a product space helps a company's comprehension of the competitive environment of its brand, the MDS analysis neither says anything specific about why products are placed where they are, nor does it address preferences and segments. The former issue can be assessed by way of property fitting while the latter is approached via a preference mapping.

In property fitting, subjects are asked to indicate whether a selection of properties or statements are suitable at characterizing an individual brand. After the responses have been collected, a computer program via regression fits the estimated parameters – also called property vectors – into the MDS product space. A property vector is visualized as a straight line starting at the centre of the Cartesian system and ending with an arrow pointing into the MDS space. If a property vector points in the direction of, or comes close to a brand, then there is an association between the property (statement) and the brand. If this is the case, the property is suitable for characterizing the brand. If the property is somehow regarded as favourable (good place to relax – Costa del Sol), then the company can use the property for targeting its promotional messages. Conversely, if the property is regarded as unfavourable (risk of stomach trouble – Tunisia), the company can use this insight for either repositioning the product, of if that is not an option, for adjusting consumers' perception of the product.

Preference mapping – sometimes called ideal point analysis – necessitates that the respondent ranks or rates the analyzed brands according to preference. Next, the respondent's preference scores are fitted into the MDS product space via regression. The regression parameters are treated as co-ordinates depicting the respondent's preference vector in the MDS space. When a sample of respondents is involved it may make sense to cluster their preference co-ordinates to end up with, say, two or three cluster-based preference vectors. Each of the segments can then be targeted by tailored promotional strategies. It is also possible that clustering of preferences reveals a "hole" in the market referring to a concentration of ideal points without a corresponding concentration of actual brands.

The combined use of MDS, property fitting and preference mapping may be of great help in formulating or reconsidering the company product positioning and marketing strategy. However, results should be interpreted with caution. One of the first large scale MDS-studies ($n = 1000$), conducted before the 1968 US presidential elections, indicated that Senator McCarthy's "brand" positioning was close to favourable properties compared with other candidates. Moreover, several candidates, including Reagan and Wallace, were placed inside or close to big clusters or segments of ideal points (voter preferences). Nevertheless, they ended up getting only 10–20 percent of the votes of these clusters (which could be checked because respondents were from a panel). Nixon, who won, did not appear to be well positioned with regard to properties and ideal points. Was it because the analysis did not catch elements such as personality, style, charisma or statesmanship? No one knows. See Johnson, (1971).[16]

MDS necessitates a specific input structure (paired comparison of brands) whereas correspondence analysis – a related method – has almost no restrictions with regard to input data. Correspondence analysis aims at transforming cell frequencies in a cross-tab to visual distances in a two- (or three-) dimensional space. If, levels of two categorical variables appear frequently together in a cross-tab as indicated by a big cell value, then the levels should be placed close to each other in a correspondence analysis plot and vice versa. This is because categorically scaled data can be used as input in correspondence analysis. The method is ideal for all kinds of existing data. Even metric data can be used after having been recoded to a small number of levels.

Questions

1. A publisher of comics is considering launching a magazine with a hero called Moon Night. The comic-strip hero has been known in the US for many years but – unlike the other ones in the test – this hero has never had its own comic magazine in the present country. The character resembles a black ghost riding on a white horse. Like other heroes, he fights against evil and crime. The company has a study carried out among 120 boys, aged eight to sixteen years. The averaged and rounded ranking of all responses is shown in Table 13.8 (the file is available at www.pearsoned.co.uk/schmidt).

   Run an MDS analysis in SPSS, either *[Scale, Multidimensional Scaling, ASCAL]* or *[Multidimensional Scaling PROXSCAL]*. When running the former use the same setting as in Section 13.2 (Figures 13.2 and 13.3).

Table 13.8 Results from study of comics

	Tarzan	Batman	Dare Devil	Hulk	Spider	Black Panther	Superman	Phantom	The Judge	Conan
Tarzan	0									
Batman	21	0								
Dare Devil	18	9	0							
Hulk	32	36	38	0						
Spiderman	28	4	8	42	0					
Black Panther	27	2	6	40	3	0				
Superman	30	22	25	17	23	26	0			
Phantom	12	14	19	33	13	20	29	0		
The Judge	16	10	1	37	11	7	24	15	0	
Conan	31	41	44	5	43	35	45	34	39	0

(a) Based on the outcome, would you recommend the publisher to launch the comic *Moon Knight*? Specify your reasons.

(b) Which kind of other analyses would you like to have carried out before the comic is launched?

2. Download the file Dream_ Holiday_MDS.xls from www.pearsoned.co.uk/schmidt. This file contains the data discussed in Figure 13.1 and Figures 13.17–13.18. The worksheet Preferences(raw) contains forty-nine individuals' preference ranking of twelve holiday destinations. In the related sheet Preferences(OLS) forty-nine individual regression analyses have been carried out. In each regression the *X1*, *X2* co-ordinates (Figure 13.17) were treated as independent/predictor variables and *Y* (the individual's preference rating) as the dependent variable. The procedure is as in Figures 13.13 and 13.14 (the alcoholic bitter example), combined with the sheets Preferences(raw) and Preferences(OLS) of the file Nautic.xls. Now, go to the worksheet Preferences(OLS) of Dream_ Holiday_MDS.xls. For now, ignore the column R-square. Columns U1 and U2 have the forty-nine respondents' ideal destinations with regard to the twelve holiday places. First, produce an Excel scatter plot that shows how the forty-nine ideal destinations are distributed in the two-dimensional space [hint: the Marketing research in action box on page 406 shows how to produce a plot in Excel based on two x, y co-ordinates series]. Make a printout of the Excel scatter plot with the respondents' ideal destinations. Next, compare the distribution of ideal destinations with Figure 13.1. Also, merge the ideal destinations scatter plot with the MDS-based co-ordinates of the twelve destinations that is also provided in the worksheet Preferences(OLS). This is a bit more tricky, though.

   (a) What do your think about the positioning of the respondents' ideal destinations/ points compared with the actual destinations? Forty-nine points is too few to cluster, but assume that the forty-nine respondents were truly representative for forty-nine million European heavy users of "the foreign tourism product."

   (b) If you were the responsible manager at Dream Holiday Travel, would the analysis of the respondents' ideal destinations cause you to redefine the marketing strategy of the company, as outlined: (i) in the Marketing research in action box on page 378; (ii) your response to the three questions in this box; (iii) Figures 13.1 and 13.18? Would you consider taking any destination out of the program based on the new preference data? Maybe you would consider increasing the promotional efforts regarding certain destinations; if so, which ones?

   (c) It turns out that the respondents were business students. Do you think that the distribution of ideal points would have looked different if the respondents had constituted a random sample of the population? And if so, how? Please specify.

3. A car producer thinks that there is a correspondence between a consumer's car and his/her housing. He supposes that the house owners generally own cars that are more expensive, than consumers who live in rented flats. So, he asks a research agency to phone a sample of consumers. Furthermore, he is only interested in consumers who own a BMW, Honda or a Skoda. Provided that his supposition is correct, he will use the information for direct marketing purposes. The file house_car.sav at www. pearsoned.co.uk/schmidt – has two variables, housing and car ownership. The total number of observations is 784. The two variables are qualitative measures. The response categories are shown in Table 13.9.

Table 13.9 Response categories

Housing	1 = Rented flat
	2 = Multi-ownership flat
	3 = Houseowner/owner occupied flat
Car	1 = BMW
	2 = Honda
	3 = Skoda

You may use SPSS *[Analyze]*, *[Data Reduction]*, *[Optimal Scaling]* for establishing a biplot or visual cross-tab of housing and car ownership. Employ the default settings suggested in Figures 13.20 and 13.21. Alternatively, use *[Data Reduction]*, *[Correspondence Analysis]*. This procedure is limited to analyzing the two variables of a simple cross-tab, so tab one variable into the row field and the other into the column field. The range needs to be defined. In this case, the authors prefer the printout from *[Correspondence Analysis]*. Note that when running SPSS *[Correspondence Analysis]* you are requested to define the range of the two variables. Here you should use 1 for "Minimum value" and 3 for "Maximum value" for both variables. Remember to tab *[Update]*.

(a) Based on the results, how would you recommend using advertising money? Would you place advertisements in the same media, regardless of which car you had to sell? If not, then why not? Please specify. Suggest two types of magazine that are suitable for advertisements with regard to each of the cars.

References

Borg, I. and Groenen, P. (1997) *Modern Multidimensional Scaling: Theory and Applications*. Springer, NY.

Büyükkurt, K. B. and Büyükkurt, M. D. (1990) "Robustness and small-sample properties of the estimators of probabilistic multidimensional scaling (PROSCAL)." *Journal of Marketing Research*. Vol. 27 (May). 139–149.

Carroll, J. D., Green, P. E. and Chaturvedi, A. (1997) *Mathematical Tools for Applied Multivariate Analysis*. Academic Press, New York. 77–124.

Carroll, J. D., Green, P. E. and Schaffer, C. M. (1986) "Interpoint Distance Comparisons in Correspondence Analysis." *Journal of Marketing Research*. Vol. 23 (August). 271–80.

Carroll, J. D., Green, P. E. and Schaffer, C. M. (1987) "Comparing Interpoint Distances in Correspondence Analysis: A Clarification." *Journal of Marketing Research*. Vol. 24. 445–50.

Carroll, J. D., Green, P. E. and Schaffer, C. M. (1989) "Reply to Greenacre's Commentary on the Carroll–Green–Schaffer Scaling of Two-Way Correspondence Analysis Solutions." *Journal of Marketing Research*. Vol. 26 (August). 366–8.

Coombs, C. H. (1964) *A Theory of Data*. John Wiley, NY.

Cox, T. F. and Cox, M. A. A. (2000) *Multidimensional Scaling*. Chapman and Hall/CRC, Boca Raton, Florida.

Coxon, A. P. M. (1982) *The User's Guide to Multidimensional Scaling*. Heinemann Educational, London.

Davidson, M. L. (1992). *Multidimensional Scaling*. Krieger, Malabar, Florida.

Elrod, T. (1988) "Choice map: inferring a product-market map from panel data." *Marketing Science*. Vol. 7, no. 1 (Winter). 21–40.

Green, P. E. (1975) "On the robustness of multidimensional scaling techniques." *Journal of Marketing Research*. Vol. 12 (February). 73–81.

Green, P. E. and Carmone, F. (1969) "Multidimensional scaling: an introduction and comparison of nonmetric unfolding techniques." *Journal of Marketing Research*. Vol. 6 (August). 330–341.

Green, P. E., Carmone, F. and Smith, S. M. (1989). *Multidimensional Scaling*. Allyn and Bacon, Boston.

Green, P. E., Maheshwari, A. and Rao, V. R. (1969) "Self-concept and brand preference: an empirical application of multidimensional scaling." *Journal of the Market Research Society*. Vol. 11. 343–360.

Green, P. E. and Rao, V. R. (1972) "Configuration synthesis in multidimensional scaling." *Journal of Marketing Research*. Vol. 9 (February). 65–68.

Green, P. E. and Tull, D. S. (1978) *Research for Marketing Decisions*. Prentice-Hall, Englewood Cliffs, NJ. 461.

Greenacre, M. J. (1984) *Theory and Applications of Correspondence Analysis*. Academic Press, London.

Greenacre, M. J. (1989) "The Carroll–Green–Schaffer Scaling in Correspondence Analysis: A Theoretical and Empirical Appraisal." *Journal of Marketing Research*. Vol. 26 (August). 358–65.

Greenacre, M. J. (1993) *Correspondence Analysis in Practice*. Academic Press, London.

Greenacre, M. J. and Blasius, J. (eds) (1994) *Correspondence Analysis in the Social Sciences*. Academic Press, London.

Hair, J. F., Anderson, R. E., Tatham, R. L. and Black, W. C. (1998) *Multivariate Data Analysis*. Prentice-Hall, Upper Saddle River, NJ.

Hoffman, D. L. and Franke, G. R. (1986) "Correspondence Analysis: Graphical Representation of Categorical Data in Marketing Research," *Journal of Marketing Research*. Vol. 23 (August). 213–27.

Johnson, R. M. (1971) "Market segmentation: a strategic management tool." *Journal of Marketing Research*. 9 (February). 13–18.

Kaciak, E. and Louviere, J. (1990) "Multiple Correspondence Analysis of Multiple Choice Experimental Data." *Journal of Marketing Research*. Vol. 27 (November). 455–65.

Kotler, P. (1972) *Marketing Management – Analysis, planning, control*. Prentice-Hall, Englewood Cliffs, NJ.

Kruskal, J. B. (1964) "Nonmetric multidimensional scaling: a numerical method." *Psychometrika*. Vol. 29. 28–42.

Kruskal, J. B. and Wish, M. (1978), *Multidimensional Scaling*. Sage. Beverly Hills.

Levy, M. J., Webster, J. and Kerin, R. A. (1983) "Formulating Push Marketing Strategies: A Method and Application." *Journal of Marketing*. Vol. 47 (Fall). 25–34.

Lebart, L., Morineau, A. and Warwick, K. M. (1984) *Multivariate Descriptive Statistical Analysis: Correspondence Analysis and Related Techniques for Large Matrices*. Wiley, NY.

Malhotra, N. (1987) "Validity and structural reliability of multidimensional scaling." *Journal of Marketing Research*. Vol. 24 (May). 164–173.

Malhotra, N. K., Jain, A. K. and Pinson, C. (1988) "The robustness of MDS configurations in the case of incomplete data." *Journal of Marketing Research*. Vol. 25 (February). 95–102.

Moore, W. L. and Winer, R. S. (1987) "A panel-data based method for merging joint space and market response function estimation." *Marketing Science*. Vol. 6, no. 1 (Winter). 25–47.

Morgan, N. and Purnell, J. (1969) "Isolating openings for new products in a multidimensional space." *Journal of the Market Research Society*. 11 (July). 245–266.

Neidell, L. A. (1969) "The use of nonmetric multidimensional scaling in marketing analysis." *Journal of Marketing*. Vol. 33. 37–43.

Schiffman, S., Reynolds, M. and Young, F. W. (1981) *Introduction to Multidimensional Scaling: Theory, methods and applications*. New York: Academic Press.

Shepard, R. N. (1962) "The analysis of proximities: multidimensional scaling with an unknown distance function I." *Psychometrika*. Vol. 27. 125–140.

Shugan, S. M. (1987) "Estimating brand positioning maps using supermarket scanning data." *Journal of Marketing Research*. Vol. 24 (February). 1–18.

Spence, I. and Lewandowsky, S. (1989) "Robust Multidimensional Scaling." *Psychometrika*. Vol. 54, No. 3. 501–13.

Young, F. W. and Hamer, R. M. (eds) (1987) *Multidimensional Scaling, History, Theory and Applications*. Lawrence Erlbaum.

End notes

[1] SPSS provides two procedures for MDS: Alscal and Proxscal. Both yield similar results, but Proxscal offers more options. In SPSS the former method is called *[Multidimensional Scaling]*. In SPSS 14 the order of the two procedures in the list has changed and the Alscal is now named *[Multidimensional Scaling)ALSCAL)...]*

[2] Table 13.1 has 105 cells. Fifteen cells have replications and three values appear three times. So, the table only contains eighty-four dissimilar figures. The great number of ties is caused by the crude measurements that the authors took from a 1:30,000,000-scale map to create Table 13.1.

[3] To check for ties: copy/paste Table 13.1 into Excel, then copy all 14 columns into one variable column that contains all 105 values. Name the column "kilometre." Next, create three more columns. One column must contain an ascending number referring to the appropriate cell. The second column is named "city in row" while the third column is called "city in column." The first line should read: "1, Stockholm, Vienna, 1165"; the second, "2, Rome, Vienna, 582"; the third "3, Paris, Vienna 857"; and the last one "105, Amsterdam, Athens, 1698." Finally, select the four columns and sort them with respect to ascending km. Replicas appear next to each other.

[4] The original SPSS output looks a little different. Figure 13.4 was produced in Excel, based on the co-ordinates from the SPSS's output. The plot has been resized so that a unit has the same absolute length on both axes. If ties appear, the first cell value (column-wise, top down and from left to right) obtains the lowest rank.

[5] SAS Insight includes a fourth dimension by using colours.

[6] The full (original) study contained 105 observations (also on the website). When running this file using *[Ordinal, Untie tied observations]*, the number of ties exceeds the default storage capacity (1,000) and the analysis is not carried out. Note that the individual's response in Figure 13.9 has seven blocks of ties (3–9) on a within respondent basis (then there will ties when measuring distances between respondents). If the range of values is small and the number observations is large, a great number of ties will be involved. An easy way of circumventing the problem is to change the *[Level of Measurement]* to "Interval" or "Ratio." The fit will be lower but the map typically resembles the one obtained using the option "Ordinal – Untie tied observations." Alternatively, one can use SPSS syntax. When the analysis – with the setting "Ordinal – Untie tied observations" is ready for running (but it will not run), type the *[Paste]* button instead of *[OK]*. Then the SPSS Syntax editor appears. Here the criteria line must read exactly: /CRITERIA=CONVERGE(.001) STRESSMIN(.005) ITER(30) CUTOFF(0) DIMENS(2,2) TIESTORE(4000). Compared with the default settings, an option *TIESTORE(2000)* has been added. Click *[Run Current]* and the analysis will run.

[7] It is possible to compute the angle between two vectors. For instance, the angle of the two vectors Y40 and Y84 is computed thus: [Squared distance from (0.0) to $(-0.099, 2.51)$ plus squared distance from origin to $(1.87, -1.57)$ minus squared distance from $(-0.099, 2.51)$ to $(1.87, -1.57)$]/[2 × distance{(0.0) to $(-0.099, 2.51)$} × {(0.0) to $(1.87, -1.57)$}] = -0.6727; arccosine $-0.6727 = 132.28°$. Also, -0.6727 is the correlation between the vectors Y84 and Y40 in the plot (not to be confused with the correlation of ranking Y40 and Y84 in Figure 13.14. That correlation is -0.15). The distance between two points or co-ordinates is computed using the Euclidean distance formula from Chapter 12. Note that the perspective of Figure 13.13 is misleading since the x and y axes are not equally scaled. The rank correlation (Pearson's Rho) between data rows of Y40 and Y84 is -0.152. This figure can be computed in SPSS using *[Analyze, Correlate, Bivariate]*; in the dialogue box, "Spearman" should be flagged. Note that in the present case the Spearman correlation and the Pearson correlation are identical.

[8] The file is in SPSS format so one only needs to copy/paste the cells containing data into the SPSS screen editor. Note that one will have to either rewrite the variable names – the destinations – or save the file several times under different names in Excel format. Next one must delete the other worksheet because SPSS only allows one sheet to be open. When reloading the Excel file format into SPSS one should accept/flag "Read variable names from the first row of data."

[9] The test is in Excel's Analysis ToolPak. The t-test necessitates the variance (standard deviation) of the variable, which is not shown in Table 13.5, but the file Dream_Holiday_MDS includes a worksheet "Properties(raw)" that contains the raw properties data (a 120 variables by 52 respondents file).

[10] The correspondence is not perfect, though. Here, the average correlation between the length of the ten property vectors – as measured by the Euclidean distance from a vector co-ordinate to the origin – and the properties' respective R-square (according to Table 13.5) is 0.75 (not shown).

[11] Note that in Figure 13.19 the scaling of the axes differs, implying that the angle alpha is biased (optically incorrect).

[12] Some publications have appeared, though which report on using MDS algorithms for analyzing scanner and panel data. See Shugan (1987), Moore and Winer (1987) and Elrod (1988).

[13] Chapter 11 mentioned the use of factor analysis for studying qualitative data. See Lingoes and Guttmann (1967) and Kruskal and Shephard (1974) in references to Chapter 11.

[14] There has been some discussion about whether it is possible to compare both within set distances and between set distances, provided that a rescaling technique is employed on the data. See Carroll, Green and Schaffer (1986, 1987), Greenacre (1989) and Carroll, Green and Schaffer (1989). The papers should be read in the listed order.

[15] The raw data file is Export_manager_survey.sav and the variables involved are "owner," "employed" and "eprg." The "employed" variable has been recoded and is included in the datafile as employx.

[16] The method was, strictly speaking, not MDS but rather multiple discriminant mapping.

14 Systematic product development: conjoint analysis

Learning objectives

After studying this chapter you should be able to:

- Discuss how conjoint analysis works.
- Define an experimental design and how it is used in conjoint analysis.
- Show how conjoint concepts are coded so that they can be analyzed via multiple regression.
- Illustrate what a utility value is and how it can be used.
- Explain how findings from a conjoint analysis can be improved by using a cluster analysis.
- Describe how a marketing simulator works.

14.1 Introduction

Conjoint analysis is perhaps the advanced market research technique that has been used most frequently in industry since it was introduced to marketing during the early 1970s. Like most other marketing research methods, conjoint analysis was not developed by marketing scientists but by scholars engaged in other fields of research. The conjoint technique was suggested by J. B. Kruskal in the mid-1960s (he was also one of the founders of multidimensional scaling).

During the method's growth and maturity period, 1975–1995, there were thousands of commercial studies and publications about conjoint analysis or conjoint measurement/trade-off analysis, as it was also called. One of the producers of conjoint programs, Sawtooth Software arranged its own biannual conferences.

Conjoint analysis can be applied to an array of problems. The preconditions are:

1. The problem under scrutiny entails several dimensions or variables. In conjoint terminology they tend to be called *attributes*, or features. Price, volume and delivery time are examples of such attributes.

'hat each attribute can be specified in quantitative terms (this requirement can be inter-
eted in a liberal way) into a small number of discrete *levels*. Two euros, 0.7 litres and
urteen days are levels of price, volume, and delivery time respectively.
e decision-maker must be free to choose which level of the attribute to use when
rketing the product.

The list below illustrates market and company problems where the conjoint technique
either has been applied or where an application appears to be possible.

- A marketer of food products wants to launch a range of sauces for the home
  market.
- A financial company is considering whether one of its accounts can be improved.
- A manufacturer, inexperienced in the toy market, wants to use spare production
  capacity for marketing toys to nurseries.
- An insurance company is losing money and is considering either reducing cover levels
  or raising premiums.
- A sub-contractor wishes to improve the perceived customer satisfaction among its
  industrial buyers.
- A businessman is planning to establish a chain of night clubs in rural districts.
- A board of directors wants to improve employees' job satisfaction.
- A charity is facing declining membership figures and wants to reverse the trend.
- A politician would like to get more votes at the next election.
- The manager of a soccer team is committed to determining which qualities experts and
  audience regard as crucial concerning a new star player.
- A dating agency wants to increase the number of marriages resulting from dates.

Conjoint analysis: finding a new fiancé(e)

To aid understanding of the conjoint method, assume that a woman wants to find a
boyfriend. Such a problem has many attributes and levels, so it forms a good introduction
to conjoint studies.

There are several ways for a woman to meet a prospective partner, including online
dating services.

So she visits a dating website and completes a questionnaire. This helps the site's supplier to narrow the search among 100,000 male profiles stored in its archives. From the
questionnaire, the site's software identifies a shortlist of male profiles, from which the
female can choose a potential date.

Filling in the questionnaire turns out to be a comprehensive process. First, the woman
has to select five preferred "countries of origin" for her latent boyfriend. She chooses
Portugal, Italy, France, Spain and Greece in order of preference.

Next, she is asked to rank preferred heights of the imaginable boyfriend. She chooses:
1.80m, 1.90m, 1.65m, and 2.00m.

The ranking continues with weight of the male, then age and so on. After completing
the ranking part of the questionnaire, the woman has provided rankings for thirty-one attributes. See Table 14.1.

Table 14.1 Attributes and levels characterizing a male

1. Country of origin	8. Hair length	16. Pet	24. 2nd Language
France	Long	Dog	English
Italy	Typical	Cat	German
Greece	Curly	Bird	French
Spain	Short	Aquarium fish	Spanish
Portugal	Bald-headed	No pet	Italian
2. Height	**9. Hair colour**	**17. Music preferences**	**25. Occupation**
2.00m	Blond	Pop	Manager
1.90m	Black	Classical/Jazz	White collar
1.80m	Red	MTV-type	Blue collar
1.65m	Grey	Miscellaneous	Independent
3. Weight	**10. Eye colour**	**18. Beverage**	**26. Sporty**
120kg	Blue	Prefer wine	Very
95kg	Brown	Prefer beer	Moderate
80kg	Grey	Abstainer	Not sporty-
65kg	Green		
4. Age	**11. Face**	**19. Political views**	**27. Occasional sense**
21	Very good looking	Conservative	Good sense
29	Good looking	Liberal	No sense
36	Normal look	Social democrat	
44	Not so good looking	Socialist	
52			
5. Belly	**12. Tattooing**	**20. Wealth**	**28. Mood_1**
Big one	Several big tattoos	Millionnaire	Extrovert
Small	Some small tattoos	Middle class	Introvert
No	No tattoos	Poor	
6. Beard	**13. Children**	**21. Education**	**29. Mood_2**
Full beard	None	Graduate	Humorous
Mustache	One in household	Doctor	Serious
No	Two, with mother	No	
7. Glasses	**14. Smoking**	**22. Urbanization**	**30. Mood_3**
Glasses	Smoker	Urban	Impulsive
No	Non-smoker	Rural	Calm
	15. Status	**23. Intelligence**	**31. Mood_4**
	Never married	High IQ	Altruistic
	Divorced	Normal IQ	Egoistic
	Married	Low IQ	

While thirty-one attributes seems to be a lot, many have not been included at all. The shape of the nose, the hands, the back, the legs, and the style of dress are just some characteristics that have been ignored. Likewise, many psychological dimensions are not included such as interests and hobbies.

Moreover, does it matter whether he once had a drinking disorder? Or that he has once been to prison for some minor offence? Or that he has been involved in adultery? Most women would prefer a male without a shady past. But – and this is where conjoint analysis comes in – can such negative attributes be compensated for by other attractions? Does it matter if the male is a well known actor? Whether he believes in horoscopes? What about his belief in religion and faith?

So much for the *number* of attributes. Now, the question arises *how many levels* should each attribute have, and how should one define and specify a level?

■ Height, weight, and age are on a continuous scale. Indeed, the age attribute might have consisted of one-year levels, or intervals ranging from eighteen to one hundred years. This example only uses five arbitrary, discrete levels. A conjoint research design normally assumes that the different attributes in a design are independent of each other. For instance, that there is no connection – whether perceived or real – between having a beard and wearing glasses, which appears reasonable. Yet there is reason to assume a positive correlation between, say, height and weight.

■ Some of the above attribute levels are mutually exclusive while others are not. It is normally not possible for a person to be both French and Greek. One cannot wear "glasses" and "no glasses" simultaneously. But it is possible to be equally fluent in two languages and a person may like both pop and classical music (from a methodological viewpoint levels ought to be mutually exclusive).

■ A level of one attribute may rule out one or several levels of another attribute, either by definition or because it is improbable. For instance, a bald-headed man cannot have blond hair. While not impossible, it is difficult to imagine that, say, a blue-collar worker who lacks any education and has a low IQ is nevertheless a millionaire. However, he could have inherited a fortune.

■ Some attributes – like height and beard – are visible and indisputable, while others may be subjective, such as the face. Certain attributes are not visible: children, status, music, beverage, etc. However, they will soon be apparent. Other attributes are psychological and may or may not be easily detected, such as sense and mood. There is good reason to believe that such "invisible" attributes are the primary cause of the break-up of many relationships. In a way they compare with a product that becomes defective within the warranty period or to a business contract based on poor descriptions.

■ Several attributes are ratio-scaled (age), some are interval-scaled (face), some nominal-scaled (country of origin) and some are categorical/dichotomous (glasses). A ratio- or interval-scaled attribute need not have a clear direction. Many females prefer a male of average or a little above average height to a very tall or very short person.

■ The number of levels is limited here and may not reflect reality. One can wear contact lenses; some people have white or brown hair; smokers may be divided into heavy and light smokers; a person may be a widower, and so on.

Note that some of the attributes in the design are determined by fate, while others can be changed. A 36-year-old, 1.65m tall, brown-eyed, divorced Italian can do little to change his profile along these dimensions. However, if someone has a big belly, weighs 120kg and smokes, then he – theoretically at least – can alter these "unfavourable" level settings. Finally, some attribute levels can be artificially manipulated: a bald man may buy a wig, the hair may be coloured and the face may be altered, say, the nose straightened, and the belly removed by way of surgery.

Again, this is not unlike the situation of a product: the core product or service and the brand name are difficult, if not impossible, to change. Some parameters, say, protein content, package design, or the guaranteed delivery time can be changed, but only at some cost. Finally, parameters such as price and advertising can be changed almost instantly.

Assume that the dating service possessed at least one person with each possible attribute and across all levels listed in Table 14.1. The first combination of attributes would be:

1. Country of origin: France, 2. Height: 2.00m, 3. Weight: 120kg, ... 31. Mood_4: Altruistic

While the very last concept would be:

2. Country of origin: Portugal, 2. Height: 1.65m, 3. Weight: 65kg, ... 31. Mood_4: Egoistic

If the concepts are numbered consecutively from "1", the very last concept would be numbered 3,095,868,000,000,000. This number of combinations comes from the design having 31 attributes, of which *five* have five levels; *eight* have four levels; *ten* have three levels; and *eight* have two levels. This multiplies out as:

$$5^5 \times 4^8 \times 3^{10} \times 2^8 = 3,095,868,000,000,000$$

That is, 3,095 trillion or a little more than three quadrillion. The number of possible concepts exceeds the number of males in the world, about three billion, by a factor of about a million! Because the dating service has only about 100,000 males registered, the probability that it includes someone who matches the female's preferred level along all the 31 attributes is 1:31 billion.

The experimental design transforms the female's ratings to three quadrillion male concepts, each having an overall utility score. The advantage of the conjoint model is that it can figure out which of the trillions of concepts comes closest to the 100,000 males stored in the dating service's files. For instance, it may turn out that the concept ranked 7,293,534 with regard to the female's preferences matches many of the thirty-one favoured attribute levels of one of the 100,000 males in the dating service's archives. So, if her ultimate preference (out of the three quadrillion) is a young Robert Redford, the best choice among the 100,000 males may turn out to be an anonymous, middle-aged millionaire who supposedly matches her preference along many of the thirty-one attributes.

Such statistics should suffice to demonstrate that the problem is comprehensive. Not only is the number of possible concepts enormous, every concept consists of thirty-one different attributes.

According to psychologists, a person cannot even handle a card that contains ten attribute levels at a time, or at best five per card provided that two cards are to be compared. Basically, most applied conjoint settings and software are differentiated by the technique they employ for reducing the number of attribute levels and concepts that a respondent is exposed to during the interview.

Table 14.2 Removing unacceptable levels

	Number of levels in Table 14.1	After removing unacceptable levels
Belly (5)	3	2
Beard (6)	3	2
Children (13)	3	2
Status (15)	3	2
Political views (19)	4	2
Smoking (14)	2	(removed)
Number of concepts	648	32

Note: The size of the design is reduced by a factor of 20 (648/32)

Procedures for reducing the number of concepts

There are several techniques for reducing the number of levels, attributes and concepts in the design of Table 14.1.

Eliminating unacceptable levels. For some attributes, there may be specific levels that are out of question: perhaps the woman would never consider dating a man with a big belly or a moustache. Likewise, assume the woman is not interested in dating a married man. Nor is she interested in dating a man who has a child from an earlier marriage that is living with him. Moreover, she may abhor people with social democratic or socialist views. Finally she may rule out smokers. By accounting for these unacceptable levels at an early phase in the interview, how is the full design affected? Table 14.2 summarizes the situation.

Discarding irrelevant combinations. Levels of one attribute may rule out one or more levels of another attribute. For example, if the woman prefers an Italian man, the attribute level for second language as Italian does not make much sense. So, it can be excluded, thereby reducing the overall design, but only a little (the number of levels of one attribute changes from five to four).

Removing improbable combinations. Some combination of attribute levels may be theoretically possible but improbable. Consider two attributes, height and weight. In total, the two attributes can be combined in sixteen ways. However, one could argue that the shaded areas of Table 14.3 constitute improbable combinations. The design could specify that only "reasonable" combinations appear. This reduces the design from 16 to 10 cells, and in commercial conjoint studies where different package sizes and prices are included in the design, this way of reducing the design may be important. However, many conjoint researchers warn against excluding combinations of improbable levels, because the levels

Table 14.3 "Reasonable" combinations of height and weight

		Height			
		2.00 m	1.90 m	1.80 m	1.65 m
Weight	120 kg	✓	✓		
	95 kg	✓	✓	✓	
	80 kg		✓	✓	✓
	65 kg			✓	✓

are still of value to the estimation procedure. Excluding certain combinations from the study design corresponds to removing outliers from a regression analysis before estimating the model – the model fit improves but only at the cost of generalizability.

Discarding of unimportant attributes. Another way to reduce the number of concepts in a design involves looking at the relative importance of individual attributes. A woman who is only 1.60m tall may find it important that her boyfriend is not so much bigger than herself. Also, she may consider it quite important that he is not egoistic. Therefore, if she is asked to rate all concepts individually on an importance scale of 4 = very important to 1 = not at all important, she might rate both height and mood_4 at "4". Or she may find that it does not really matter whether the man is French or Italian, as long as he is cute. Likewise she does not care at all whether he wears glasses. This being the case, she would rate those attributes as "1". And so on. Consequently, once the woman has rated all the attributes, the unimportant ones can be eliminated. Further, attributes rated "2" could be downgraded by being given a lower weighting. Ratings of "3" would be left unchanged while ratings of "4" would be upgraded so the attribute would appear more often than others across the number of concepts in the study.

Assume the woman has rated face (11) at "4", hair length (8) at "3", beard (6) at "2" and glasses (7) at "1". Table 14.4 shows a design consisting of twelve concepts (the dashes refer to other attributes appearing on the concepts). If the three concepts face, hair length, and beard had been weighted equally, say, by giving them a score of "3", they would each appear on four of the twelve concepts. But since the respondent regards face as much more important than beard, the design appreciates this difference in importance such that the attribute face appears on three times as many concepts as beard. Note also that hair length appears on a third of the twelve concepts. So it is neither weighted up nor down. Recall also that glasses was rated "1". Therefore it is ignored as long as the current person is interviewed. The weighing procedure of Table 14.4 does not affect the number of concepts but it helps in focusing on the attributes that the respondent regards as being crucial.

Powerful experimental designs. After the respondent has finished the importance rating of the thirty-one attributes, one could finish the interview and compute a score or value concerning each of the 103 attribute levels (according to Table 14.1 there are 103 levels across the 31 attributes). Conjoint analysts call such values *part-worth utilities*. Ranking of levels within attributes combined with importance rating across attributes is called the *self-explicating part* of a conjoint study. However, so far the female has been ranking and rating without being forced to make real choices. For instance, she could give top-ratings to a 29-year-old, very good-looking, altruistic, millionaire with a high IQ. The problem is this: does he exist? And if he does, there is a pretty good chance that he is actually being courted by many other women.

Usually, the results from a conjoint analysis can be improved, provided that the respondent is forced to make choices. For a moment, assume that the woman is only interested in the four attributes that appear in the upper part of Table 14.1: country of origin (1), hair-

Table 14.4 Using a weighting system

– – – 11	– – – 8	– – – 11	– – – 8
– – – 11	– – – 6	– – – 8	– – – 11
– – – 8	– – – 11	– – – 6	– – – 11

Table 14.5 A Graeco-Latin square with five levels and four attributes

			1. Country of origin								
			France		*Italy*		*Greece*		*Spain*		*Portugal*
	Long	1	*1*	2	*4*	3	*2*	4	*5*	5	*3*
	Typical	2	*2*	3	*5*	4	*3*	5	*1*	1	*4*
8. Hair	Curly	3	*3*	4	*1*	5	*4*	1	*2*	2	*5*
length	Short	4	*4*	5	*2*	1	*5*	2	*3*	3	*1*
	Bald	5	*5*	1	*3*	2	*1*	3	*4*	4	*2*
		c	*d*	*c*	*d*	*c*	*d*	*c*	*d*	*c*	*d*

Note: c refers to pets (attribute 16) where 1 = Dog, 2 = Cat etc.
while d refers to levels of second language (24) where 1 = English, 2 = German, etc.
The levels concerning pets and second language appear in the same order as in Table 14.1.

length (8), pets (16) and second language (24). Note that all four attributes have five levels. Therefore, the total number of possible concepts is $5^4 = 625$. This is called the full or complete design. The question now arises whether this design can be reduced and still maintain important statistical properties.

Maybe Table 14.5 can be of some help. It represents an experimental design called a *Greaco-Latin square*. It is one of many useful experimental designs that have been developed (Cochran and Cox, 1957).

This design was created using a program called *Conjoint Designer* (Bretton-Clark). It is not required that there is an equal number of levels (which is the case here). However, if the level numbers are equal, it is possible to obtain a greater reduction in the number of concepts. Table 14.5 is symmetric. Had it not been of type $5 \times 5 \times 5 \times 5$ but, say, of type $5 \times 3 \times 2 \times 2$ it would be asymmetric. An asymmetric design appears if we select attributes country of origin (1), beard (6), glasses (7) and smoking (14). In both cases, the Graeco-Latin square requires 25 cells/concepts but whereas the full design in the first case consists of 625 concepts, the latter only consists of sixty. Consequently, the symmetric design is more than ten times more powerful or more reduced (625/60).

Table 14.5 fulfils certain statistical conditions. Every level of every attribute appears once across the design with every level of every other attribute level. What does that mean? In the table, all cases where attribute c/16/pets has level 1 are shown in bold type and all cases where attribute d/24/second language has level 1 are italicized. Notice that level 1 of attributes (c) and (d) appear *once in every row and once in every column*. The same condition holds with regard to the remaining four levels of attribute (c) as well as with all five levels of attribute (d). Therefore, the design fulfils the necessary and sufficient conditions of being a Graeco-Latin square. The reader should check that this is indeed the case.

It is possible to add two more attributes, each having five levels, into the present design. For instance, age (4) and hair colour (9) could be added – where there could be a fifth level, brown hair. In this case, the full design expands to $5^6 = 15,625$ cells. However, the reduced design still has only 25 cells.

Graeco-Latin squares with four attributes like the one shown in Table 14.5 normally require a number of cells/concepts that is a square of the number of levels. With three

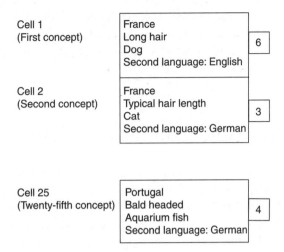

Cell 1 (First concept)	France Long hair Dog Second language: English	6
Cell 2 (Second concept)	France Typical hair length Cat Second language: German	3
Cell 25 (Twenty-fifth concept)	Portugal Bald headed Aquarium fish Second language: German	4

Figure 14.1 How a questionnaire would look

levels it is nine concepts, with four levels it is sixteen concepts and so on. Designs have been developed with up to twelve levels. Curiously, they do not exist (or have so far not been developed) for 6 and 10 levels.

Figure 14.1 shows how a questionnaire containing the concepts could look. Only three of the twenty-five concepts are shown. In the example, assume that all concepts are rated according to a scale ranging from one to ten, where *1 = would I never consider as boyfriend* to *10 = Could very well become my boyfriend*. For illustrative purposes ratings have been filled in.

Later in this chapter we show that the rating score is the key to estimating the parameters or importance of the individual concept levels.

Despite the use of powerful designs, the reader should keep in mind that the full design of Table 14.1 does not consist of a small number of symmetric attributes but of thirty-one attributes (with differing numbers of levels).

Since no one can manage to grasp that number of concepts, the task must be made manageable for the respondent. For instance, the respondent may be able to handle no more than five attributes per concept. So, if a study involves ten different attributes the design must include all ten attributes but the respondent must not be exposed to a sample of concepts that exceeds five attributes per concept. Since the attributes on a specific concept can be treated as part of a "super-design" it is still possible to estimate preference or utility values from the respondent concerning all ten concepts. That is because the five attributes appearing on a concept are systematically varied among the ten concepts.

Later in the chapter we will see an effective way of applying this technique. The drawback of the method, called a ***randomized block design***, is that the total number of concepts, which the respondent needs to rate, is increased. So, while the task becomes more manageable concerning the individual concept, it becomes more time-consuming with regard to the number of concepts that must be rated.

So far, the validity of information that men have provided to the dating service has not been questioned. Assume that the woman's responses are matched with individual profiles that are stored in the dating service's database. Can she trust that a potential boyfriend in fact possesses the profile that the dating service claims? How can she check that he is the good looking person he claims to be? As a matter of fact, she cannot. However, she will find out ...

14.2 Example: conjoint analysis for a red wine

Klaus Bacchus is manager of a family-owned company that produces soft drinks and beers. He has invested in high-tech production machinery, but due to a slump in the market he now has excess capacity. One day, a friend tells him there is a rising demand for wine bottled in smaller sizes than the usual 75cl. Bacchus decides he could use his equipment for bottling wine.

However, he does not know much about the wine market. He has neither the ambition nor financial resources to begin to produce wine on a large scale. His aim is to bottle wine from supplier vineyards. In spite of the cumbersome production process, it appears to be a profitable business. Especially, if he can concentrate on the small niche market for 33cl bottles.

According to his friend, the demand for 33cl bottles is caused by two developments. First, there is a trend all over Europe towards drinking wine on weekdays and during the daytime. However, a 75cl bottle is excessive for lunchtime drinking. Second, there is a growing tendency for young people to hold parties, again creating demand for smaller bottles. Younger women in particular choose mixed drinks or wine instead of beer or spirits.

Bacchus asks a marketing research agency to conduct two focus groups, one with twelve young females aged eighteen to thirty and another with six males and six females between thirty and fifty years of age. Apart from providing input to a market launch, he wants an answer to two questions:

- Should he launch a red wine or a white wine? In view of his resources he wants to concentrate on one or the other.
- What brand name should he choose? His advertising agency has come up with ten names including suggestions for advertising copy.

The outcome of the two focus groups turns out to be confusing. As he had feared, the participants of the two groups seem to reflect two different segments. Despite the bewildering findings, the responses have given him ideas for the marketing campaign. The good thing is that red wine is preferred.

The focus groups also agree on the best brand names and advertising outlines. Participants in both focus groups were asked to rate the ten brand names plus accompanying adverting outline on a preference scale. When responses from the focus groups are averaged it shows that both groups suggest the same three themes.

Bacchus still has some doubts concerning the launch. So, he decides to follow the advice of his marketing research agency to carry out a conjoint analysis before he launches the wine. He has three research questions that he wants to be the focus of the conjoint study:

- His machinery can handle bottles as well as cans and cartons in 33cl size. But which package format will do best in the market?
- He has contacted wine producers in Germany, Italy and France. But what does the market prefer? For instance, a German red wine may appear odd. But the German producer has a reputation outside Germany.
- How price-sensitive is the market? Since the wine is to be sold at supermarkets and petrol stations – the company's current distributional system – it is not relevant to launch the product at a premium price. Presently the price span or price range is significant: while the average market price currently is 1.95 euro, the competitors' prices vary between 1.65 and 2.35 euros.

He decides to include all three brand names in the study.

While a lot of other topics seem relevant Bacchus decides to concentrate on the attributes and levels shown in Table 14.6.

The full design necessitates eighty-one concepts ($3 \times 3 \times 3 \times 3$), which the market research consultant says is too great a number for a respondent to rate or rank. Fortunately, the design is symmetric. Therefore, the consultant selects the Graeco-Latin square shown in Table 14.7. It involves nine cells.

Next, this small design is used for constructing concepts based on Table 14.6. For instance, A1B1C1D1 becomes: "Bottle – Germany – €1.65 – Wine Prince" and so on. Figure 14.2 displays the page of the questionnaire that contains the conjoint design.

Note that concept A1B1C1D1 appears in the second row of the first column – the fourth concept.

Table 14.6 Conjoint design involving a 33cl white wine

Attribute	Level
A. Package	1. Bottle
	2. Can
	3. Carton
B. Country of origin	1. Germany
	2. Italy
	3. France
C. Price	1. EUR 1.65
	2. EUR 1.95
	3. EUR 2.35
D. Brand name	1. Wine Prince
	2. Socrates
	3. White Glory

Table 14.7 Graeco-Latin square design

	B1	B2	B3
A1	C1D1	C2D3	C3D2
A2	C2D2	C3D1	C1D3
A3	C3D3	C1D2	C2D1

Notice that the conjoint questionnaire has been filled in by a respondent, who has ranked the concepts from 1 to 9, where a lower rank indicates higher preference, in circles. The individual likes concept A1B1C1D1 most among the nine concepts. For simplicity, assume that this response is representative of the market.

The analysis will be done by regression analysis, so it is more practical to reverse the ranks and call them scores. This is done by subtracting the rank from the number of concepts plus 1. So the rank 1 for A1B1C1D1 is transformed to a score of $10 - 1 = 9$ and so on.

Before running the analysis, the nine concepts must be coded. Until now, the independent variables of a regression model have been ratio- or interval-scaled. The problem

Figure 14.2 Product concepts used in conjoint wine study

Table 14.8 Dummy coding (effects-type) of wine concepts

	A1	A2	B1	B2	C1	C2	D1	D2	Y
Concept	Bottle	Can	Germany	Italy	1.65	1.95	Wine Prince	Socrates	Score
1	−1	−1	1	0	−1	−1	−1	−1	1
2	1	0	−1	−1	−1	−1	0	1	8
3	0	1	1	0	0	1	0	1	4
4	1	0	1	0	1	0	1	0	9
5	0	1	−1	−1	1	0	−1	−1	7
6	−1	−1	0	1	1	0	0	1	3
7	0	1	0	1	−1	−1	1	0	2
8	1	0	0	1	0	1	−1	−1	5
9	−1	−1	−1	−1	0	1	1	0	6

here is that the attribute levels of the concepts must be treated as independent variables. Unfortunately, the concept levels are not interval-scaled.[1] If the independent variables are nominal or categorical-scaled, we could use logistic regression instead. This would indeed be an option here. However, from Chapter 10, the interpretation of parameters in logistic regression is not as straightforward as it is in normal linear regression.

Interpretation would be easier if the concepts could be coded in such a way that they could be treated as independent variables in a normal linear regression. Luckily, procedures exist for coding levels of a nominal-scaled variable so that they can be used as an independent measure in regression (which is then called *dummy variable regression*). An appropriate procedure for coding the concepts of Figure 14.2 is shown in Table 14.8. It is known as **effects-type dummy coding** (Kerlinger and Lee, 2000; or Kleinbaum, Kupper and Muller, 1988). In this case, the coding technique implies treating each attribute level as a separate variable. Then again, this is strictly not correct since for each attribute, consisting of k levels, only $k − 1$ independent variables are used. Subsequently, the final level is "deduced" based on the parameter estimates connected to the other attribute levels.

This is how it works: in Table 14.8, effects-type dummy coding is used for recoding the attribute levels of the nine concepts in Figure 14.2.

Look at the first concept of Figure 14.2. The wine is German, delivered in a carton, with a price of €2.35 and the brand name White Glory. The design notation of this concept is A3B1C3D3. According to effects-type dummy coding, the three levels of an attribute can be coded by two variables. The levels of the first attribute are coded using the rule in Table 14.9.

Simply define two variables and call them "Bottle" and "Carton" respectively. If the first level of the attribute (Bottle) appears on a concept, code this as (1,0) implying that

Table 14.9 Coding rules

	Bottle	Carton	
A1	1	0	
A2	0	1	
A3	−1	−1	= Can

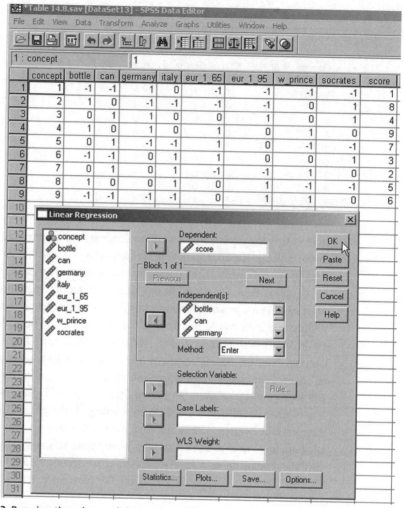

Figure 14.3 Running the wine conjoint study in SPSS

Bottle is present while Can is absent (and so is Carton).[2] Alternatively, if the second level (Can) appears on the concept this is coded as (0,1). Finally, if the third and last level (Carton) is present on a concept, it follows that the first and second levels are missing. This is indicated by -1 in both variable columns. This coding produces eight (effects-type dummy coded) predictor variables. Table 14.6 has twelve attribute levels. When running a regression model based on the eight predictor variables:

$$Y = A1 + A2 + B1 + B2 + C1 + C2 + D1 + D2$$

eight parameter estimates are produced, one for each variable. So how are parameters on A3, B3, C3, and D3 obtained? Thanks to effects-type dummy coding, it holds that A1 + A2 + A3 = 0. So having obtained estimates on A1 and A2, A3 = $-$(A1 + A2).

Table 14.8 used this dummy effects-type technique for coding of all nine concept-levels. Figure 14.3 shows how the problem should look when running *[SPSS, Analyze,*

Regression, Linear]. The variable "score" is to be tabbed into the Dependent field and the eight dummy coded variables are to be put into the Independent(s) field. No settings need to be changed, so tab *[OK]*.

The regression output differs in several ways from the regression example in Chapter 9:

- the R-square is 1.00 (not shown);
- the F-value and significance level for the overall model (ANOVA) are lacking;
- the standard error of the coefficients all equal 0.000; and
- t-values and significance levels of the individual parameters are missing.

These abnormalities are caused by the dummy coding. Basically, a linear regression model is not designed for regressing dummy-coded data on a dependent variable that is metric or non-metric scaled. For instance, an OLS model does not like independent variables that can only assume a limited number of states, such as 1, 0 and -1. Independent variables are intended to be continuous, that is, they may take on an infinite number of states.[3]

Here, these modelling oddities will be ignored. Instead, concentrate on the "coefficients" table in SPSS and specifically the column "standardized coefficients/beta." Observe that the parameter estimates (beta) for the predictors Bottle and Can are 0.738 and -0.211 respectively. Because all three levels within an attribute must sum to 0.00, the missing estimate of Carton must be $-0.527 = -[0.738 + (-0.211)]$. And, of course, $0.738 + (-0.211) + (-0.527) = 0.00$. Now all three levels of the first attribute are known. Next, repeat this process to obtain the third level value of the remaining three attributes. Column III of Table 14.10 displays all resulting values.

Table 14.10 Estimated utilities based on Table 14.8

I	*II*	*III*	*IV=(III/105)*	*V*	*VI (V in pct.)*
Attribute	Level	Standardized coefficients	Utility (rescaled estimate)	Numeric range	Relative importance
A. Package	1. Bottle	0.738	+7		
	2. Can	−0.211	−2	12	34%
	3. Carton	−0.527	−5		
B. Country of origin	1. Germany	−0.105	−1		
	2. Italy	−0.527	−5	11	31%
	3. France	0.632	+6		
C. Price	1. EUR 1.65	0.422	4		
	2. EUR 1.95	0.000	0	8	23%
	3. EUR 2.35	−0.422	−4		
D. Brand name	1. Wine Prince	0.211	+2		
	2. Socrates	0.000	0	4	12%
	3. White Glory	−0.211	−2		
	Sum	0.000	0	35	100%

From column III, the twelve estimates – apart from sign – involve only six different non-zero values: 0.105; 0.211; 0.422; 0.527; 0.632 and 0.738. Moreover, dividing them by the smallest coefficient yields a series of integers: 0.211/0.105 = 2; 0.422/0.105 = 4, etc. Thus, dividing coefficients by the smallest one while leaving any signs unchanged simplifies working with them. See column IV. These values are called *utility values*. Some conjoint analysts call them *part-worths*. Note that the values in column IV still sum to zero. Conjoint programs often differ with regard to how the utility value is scaled.

The interpretation of a utility value is straightforward: the higher the value, the more preferred the attribute level is and vice versa. Since the conjoint model is additive, utilities can be compared across attributes and levels. So, in a way, the model allows pies to be compared with apples. Stated differently, a compound preference score has been collected from the respondent. The dependent score variable is a function of nine observations of a number of independent variables (the concepts). Since the attribute levels have been organized as an experimental design – implying that they vary in a systematic way across the concepts – it is possible to *decompose* the score. The conjoint model splits the overall preference score in such a way that each attribute level is assigned a fraction of the overall score. This is done in accordance with the relative influence that the specific attribute level has on the compound score. The relative effect of an individual attribute level is estimated by the regression analysis. And the effect equals the regression weight or parameter (**utility value** in conjoint terminology).

The conjoint model provides a kind of common denominator that makes it possible to compare the relative importance of the individual product attributes, and to compare levels both within and across attributes. According to the conjoint model, an attribute is scaled from very important to unimportant. There is no preference dimension linked to the attribute as such. The preference appears 'within' an attribute, that is, on the level-stage. The higher the perceived value of a specific level, the better and vice versa. Only for attributes that are regarded as important can there be big differences in the preference for the specific levels. The preference assigned to a specific level indicates the level's utility value. The utility value makes it possible to perform detailed assessments of the elements of the compound product and to estimate how individual product features and settings affect the overall preference for the product.

The relative importance of an attribute across its levels is computed by adding the highest and the lowest value within an attribute while ignoring signs. Concerning the package attribute, the highest utility value is 7 and the lowest is $|-5|$. So the range is 12, and so on. Adding the four ranges yields 35. See column V of Table 14.10. The value 35 may be regarded as an indicator of the combined or overall importance of the four attributes. Notice that the importance varies, that is, some attributes are more important than others. The relative importance of, say, package, is found by dividing this attribute's range by the total range. Here 12/35 = 0.3429 or 34%. See column VI.

Note that the attribute package has the highest importance, followed by country of origin. Both account for about a third of the total importance range. Price explains about a quarter, while brand name accounts for little more than a tenth.

Assuming that the values of Table 14.10 are based on a representative conjoint study, one could argue that Bacchus' best marketing strategy would be to distribute the product development budget in accordance with the importance figures of the individual attributes.

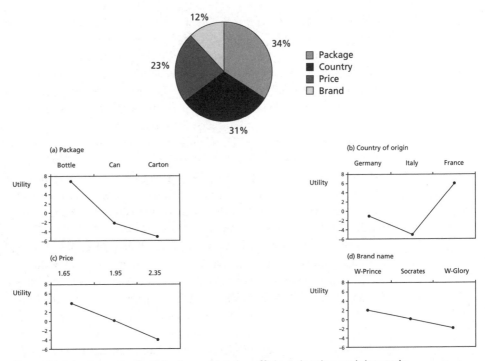

Figure 14.4 Importance of attributes and level coefficients in wine conjoint study

If Bacchus has, €10,000 available for product development, €3,400 should be attributed to package research, €3,100 to investigations related to country of origin, €2,300 to price studies and €1,200 to advertising research. Price and country of origin are important attributes, while brand name is of minor importance. Maybe it would be best to concentrate the limited marketing budget on the most important attributes, implying that no further money is spent on the brand name.

Figure 14.4 provides a graphic illustration of the utilities and importance figures just discussed.

Now let us return to the interpretation of the attribute levels.

In regression analysis, the term regression- or parameter estimate denotes the value that is connected to a predictor variable. Also, recall from Chapter 9 how a regression estimate is to be understood: a one-unit change on the predictor transforms to a change on the dependent, corresponding to the size of the estimate. For instance, if $Y = 0.36X$, then a one unit change on X implies a 0.36 unit change in the scale of Y. This principle, with some modification, applies when interpreting attribute levels, based on the utility value. Consider Table 14.10 (column IV).

Package has three levels of which bottle is preferred whereas can is less preferred and carton the least. The preference for bottle (+7) 'outweighs' the negative utilities of can and carton $(-2) + (-5) = -7$.

Assume that Bacchus originally considered launching the product with the concept settings A2B2C2D2. This concept has a total utility of -7 (= $-2 + [-5] + 0 + 0$). When he obtains the result from the conjoint analysis, he considers changing the product setting to A1B2C3D2. The package is changed from can to bottle improving the overall concept by nine units (from −2 to +7). However, Bacchus knows that this change in package would yield to the product's cost, because glass is more expensive than the thin layer of aluminium board and must be recycled. Moreover, bottles are more difficult to store than cans implying that he will have to give higher discounts to petrol stations and supermarkets. Therefore, if he chooses glass he will need to select a higher price than 1.95 because otherwise he will most probably lose money. However, if he charges 2.35 the product will make a profit. Since the product has a negative price elasticity, Bacchus can only raise the price by sacrificing some of the utility value connected to the price. In the present case he will lose 4 units (from 0 to −4). Nevertheless, according to utility pattern it is recommended to carry out the suggested concept change *because the gain in utility caused by the package change overcompensates the loss in utility emanated by raising the price.* When Bacchus changes the concept as suggested, he gains 9 utility units while he only loses 4. The net change is +5.

Assumed instead that the planned country of origin had been France, but that Bacchus considers compensating changing from can to bottle not with a different price, but, say, with a cheaper wine of lower quality. So he would substitute a French wine with a cheaper Italian wine. Table 14.9 shows that this change cannot be justified since doing so would cost 11 utility points (from +6 to −5), which is more than is to be gained from changing package (+9). Then again, had the planned package been carton, the shift from French to Italian wine would just have been OK, since this shift yields +12 – just one unit more than the loss emanating from country of origin.

Once more, assume that Bacchus wants to change the concept from A2B2C2D2 to A1B2C3D2 but that even a price of 2.35 does not make the shift profitable. Could he raise the price above 2.35 and if so what is the price-threshold where the net utility (+5) is 'used up' or consumed by the higher price? Assuming that the functional relationship of the price attribute is linear (which strictly speaking only applies to prices close to the esti-mated end points) the threshold price can be computed. It is €2.79. How is this figure computed? First, use price and utility of the two extreme levels as (x, y) co-ordinates. So co-ordinate 1 = (1.65, 4) and co-ordinate 2 = (2.35, −4). From basic geometry, the slope of a line is defined as:

$$\alpha = \frac{y1 - y2}{x1 - x2} = \frac{(4 - [-4])}{(1.65 - 2.35)} = \frac{8}{-0.7} = -11.4286$$

Having computed the slope, only one point is needed to determine the line:

$$(y - y1) = a(x - x1) \Rightarrow (y - 4) = -11.4286(x - 1.65) \Rightarrow y = -11.4286x + 22.8752$$

For instance, inserting 2.35 for x gives −3.982 or approximately −4.

Recall that raising the price to 2.35 still leaves +5 utility units that can be used to 'worsen' the overall concept. So, theoretically the lower bound concerning utility loss is −4−(+5) = −9. In other words, y could be as low as −9. Inserting this value into the function:

$$y = -11.4286x + 22.8752 \Rightarrow -9 = -11.4286x + 22.8752 \Rightarrow x = 2.7892$$

File Edit View Insert Format Tools Data Window Help

Statistics ▾ Graphics ▾ Data ▾ Help ▾ » 💾 📊 100% ▾ » Arial   ▾ 10 ▾

| L1 | ▾ | = | =G1+H1+I1+J1 |

	A	B	C	D	E	F	G	H	I	J	K	L	M	N	O	P	Q	R	S
1	A1	B1	C1	D1	*1*		7	-1	4	2		12		A1	B3	C1	D1	19	
2	A1	B1	C1	D2			7	-1	4	0		10		A1	B3	C1	D2	17	
3	A1	B1	C1	D3			7	-1	4	-2		8		A1	B3	C1	D3	15	
4	A1	B1	C2	D1			7	-1	0	2		8		A1	B3	C2	D1	15	
5	A1	B1	C2	D2			7	-1	0	0		6		A1	B3	C2	D2	13	
6	A1	B1	C2	D3			7	-1	0	-2		4		A1	B1	C1	D1	12	*1*
7	A1	B1	C3	D1			7	-1	-4	2		4		A1	B3	C2	D3	11	
8	A1	B1	C3	D2			7	-1	-4	0		2		A1	B3	C3	D1	11	
9	A1	B1	C3	D3			7	-1	-4	-2		0		A1	B1	C1	D2	10	
10	A1	B2	C1	D1			7	-5	4	2		8		A2	B3	C1	D1	10	
11	A1	B2	C1	D2			7	-5	4	0		6		A1	B3	C3	D2	9	*2*
12	A1	B2	C1	D3			7	-5	4	-2		4		A1	B1	C1	D3	8	
13	A1	B2	C2	D1			7	-5	0	2		4		A1	B1	C2	D1	8	
14	A1	B2	C2	D2			7	-5	0	0		2		A1	B2	C1	D1	8	
15	A1	B2	C2	D3	*5*		7	-5	0	-2		0		A2	B3	C1	D2	8	
16	A1	B2	C3	D1			7	-5	-4	2		0		A1	B3	C3	D3	7	
17	A1	B2	C3	D2			7	-5	-4	0		-2		A3	B3	C1	D1	7	
18	A1	B2	C3	D3			7	-5	-4	-2		-4		A1	B1	C2	D2	6	
19	A1	B3	C1	D1			7	6	4	2		19		A1	B2	C1	D2	6	
20	A1	B3	C1	D2			7	6	4	0		17		A2	B3	C1	D3	6	*3*
21	A1	B3	C1	D3			7	6	4	-2		15		A2	B3	C2	D1	6	
22	A1	B3	C2	D1			7	6	0	2		15		A3	B3	C1	D2	5	
23	A1	B3	C2	D2			7	6	0	0		13		A1	B1	C2	D3	4	
24	A1	B3	C2	D3			7	6	0	-2		11		A1	B1	C3	D1	4	
25	A1	B3	C3	D1			7	6	-4	2		11		A1	B2	C1	D3	4	
26	A1	B3	C3	D2	*2*		7	6	-4	0		9		A1	B2	C2	D1	4	
27	A1	B3	C3	D3			7	6	-4	-2		7		A2	B3	C2	D2	4	
28	A2	B1	C1	D1			-2	-1	4	2		3		A2	B1	C1	D1	3	
80	A3	B3	C3	D2			-5	6	-4	0		-3		A3	B2	C3	D2	-14	
81	A3	B3	C3	D3			-5	6	-4	-2		-5		A3	B2	C3	D3	-16	
82																			

Figure 14.5 Sorting concepts according to descending overall utility

Thus, if Bacchus wants to raise the price above €2.79, the gain in preference caused by the change from Can to Bottle is more than offset by the loss in preference due to the price increase.

From Table 14.10 or Figure 14.4, the concept that has the highest combined utility is A1B3C1D1. It has a total utility score of nineteen. The least-liked concept is A3B2C3D3 (score: −16). In Figure 14.2, neither of these concepts was among the nine concepts included in the questionnaire. Nevertheless, estimates have been made of this preference. A great advantage of using experimental designs and the conjoint model is that it allows many concepts to be assessed compared with the number of concepts that are actually included in the questionnaire. A test of nine concepts allows computations for all eighty-one concepts.

Usually, the conjoint analyst wants to obtain a list of all involved concepts (here eighty-one), not only the ones tested (nine). This can be done using Excel.

First, let us look at Figure 14.5.

In columns A–D, all eighty-one concepts are listed.

For illustrative purposes, concepts that appeared in the questionnaire design of Figure 14.2 are highlighted. Column E shows the preference rank of the respective concepts (not the transformed score). The rank also appears in Figure 14.2.

1. Begin by copying cells A1–D81 to G1–J81. Place the pointer at the top of column G and select it (we could highlight columns G–J simultaneously).
2. Next tab *[Edit]* on Excel's menu bar and select *[Replace]* on the scroll-down. In the Replace dialogue box, tab in *A1* for 'Find what' and thereafter tab *7* for 'Replace with'. Tab *[Replace all]*. Consequently all cases of A1 in column G are replaced with 7 – the utility value of attribute level A1. Repeat this procedure with regard to A2 and A3 by exchanging the two levels with –2 and –5 respectively. Next repeat the procedure for the levels of attributes B through D. After this columns G through J should look as they do in Figure 14.5.
3. Move the pointer to cell L1. Tab in '=G1+H1+I1+J1' and *[Return]*. The effect is that Excel adds the content of columns G1 through J1 (= 7 + [−1] + 4 + 2) = 12.
4. Copy cell L1. Next select cells L2 to L81 and *[Return]*. Thereafter column L should look like it does in Figure 14.5.
5. Column L contains the overall utilities of all eighty-one concepts. To sort them with respect to decreasing overall utility, copy/paste cells A1–D81 to, say, N1–Q81. Next copy column L and point at column R.
6. Now tab *[Edit, Past Special]*. In the pop-up, change 'Paste all' to 'Paste values' and *[OK]*.
7. Finally, select columns N through R and tab *[Data]* from the menu bar and *[Sort]* from the scroll down. In the pop-up, click the 'Sort by' field, select Column R and 'Descending' as sorting method. Click OK. Note that column R is the only one that is used for the sorting while columns N through R constitute the selection for the sorting. This ensures that the concept notation in columns N to Q is treated as a slave during the sort.

After the sort, columns N through R should look like they do in Figure 14.5. Values of column R are called an ***overall concept utility***.

Once more, concepts that appeared in the study as well as the original ranking are highlighted. Note that the descended listing of overall concept utilities corresponds with the rankings (overall concept utilities are listed descending while the concept rankings of column S are ascending ranks).

As noted, the concept that has the highest combined utility, A1B3C1D1 is not among the nine concepts that appear in the questionnaire of Figure 14.2. In fact, the top ranking concept according to the questionnaire only obtains sixth place in the descended list of all eighty-one concepts in column R of Figure 14.5.

All top five concepts include the attribute levels "bottle" and "France". Note from comparing A1B3C2D1 with A1B1C1D1 that the difference between the two concepts is that the former is a French wine priced at €1.95 while the latter is a German wine priced at €1.65. Since the former concept obtains a higher overall concept utility (15) than the latter (12), the concept improvement from German to French wine more than compensates for

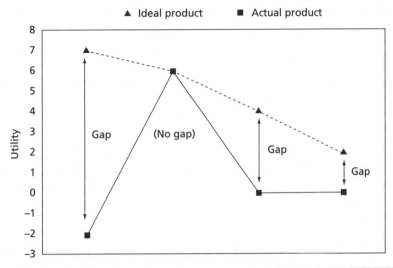

Figure 14.6 Potential for product development

the price increase. The net difference is +3 units. Alternatively, the difference can be found by undertaking the two concept changes based on column IV in Table 14.10. Shifting from Germany (−1) to France (+6) implies a utility gain of 7 while a shift from 1.65 (+4) to 1.95 (+/−0) yields a utility drop of −4. Now 7−4 = 3 = 15 − 12.

Figure 14.6 represents a simple way of illustrating the difference between the product that is being marketed (or about to be launched without the conjoint analysis) and the ideal product (after learning about the conjoint utility values).

According to Figure 14.6 the product that is currently on the market is: A2B3C2D2 or Can/France/1.95/Socrates. From the conjoint analysis, the product can gain significantly in popularity when the package is changed from can to bottle. With regard to the country of origin, the wine cannot be improved because it is a French wine – exactly as the consumers prefer it.

The gap concerning the price attribute is no surprise: a lower price is preferred to a higher one. What is more interesting is that the gaps concerning the price and the brand name are much smaller than the gap regarding the package.

This wine conjoint example has introduced the basic aspects of the method. In several ways the example is oversimplified. It is symmetric in that each attribute has three levels. In a real-life conjoint analysis, the number of levels usually varies: some attributes will be dichotomous (for instance, if a money back guarantee is present or not) while other attributes will consist of 6–8 attributes (for example, brands on a market). However, the conjoint wine design could be expanded with more wines, bottle sizes and so on.

So far, coverage of conjoint analysis has dealt with a simple example based on one person's ranking. This is possible because the conjoint model, like MDS, is an individual model, implying that it makes sense to compute a set or vector of parameters that differentiate an individual from other subjects.

Referring to the wine conjoint example, it is probable that the market for a small white wine ought to be segmented. There may be a price-insensitive segment preferring a Sauvignon in a bottle, a cost-oriented segment that is willing to accept a vin de table in pack, and so on.

Therefore, if a conjoint analysis is based on a sample and the preferences and the market is heterogeneous, then the utilities-times-respondents matrix will need to be clustered. Usually, the researcher wishes to find a small number of clusters containing respondents with similar utility patterns. If such clusters exist then it might make sense to target a market or adopt a product strategy based on individual utility segments.

14.3 Conjoint analysis for a bank account

Northern Bank is a fictional regional bank with a deposit balance of approximately €6 billion. The managers want to evaluate customers' preference for various options for a specific kind of account, a so-called "private cash credit account." The bank operates in a region with fierce competition for this sub-market. The target market being considered is mostly of young and middle-aged blue- and white-collar workers with a two to one majority of males.

According to management, four attributes are of critical importance to the competitiveness of the account:

- *The size of the cash credit.* People lend money on a cash credit account because they need money instantly and temporarily. A crash credit is not intended for financing, say,

Table 14.11 Attributes and levels used in conjoint analysis for bank account

	Attribute		Level
A	Cash credit maximum	1	€16,000
		2	€10,000
		3	€6,000
B	Rate of interest	1	4% of drawing + 2.5% of max
		2	5.5% of drawing and 1.5% of max
		3	8% of drawing
C	Interest on deposits	1	3%
		2	2%
		3	1%
D	Opening fees	1	Free
		2	€100
		3	€200

a car. For such cases a bank offers cheaper loans with pay-back periods ranging from five to thirty years. But assume that a person suddenly needs to have a car repaired. In such a case a person is in urgent need of instant cash. Northern Bank wants to assess consumer preference with regard to the amount of money required. Therefore, it defines three levels for the maximum amount of cash credit. See attribute A in Table 14.11.

- *Rate of interest.* The underlying philosophy of the cash credit account is that sometimes the balance is positive and sometimes it is negative. Depending on whether a person expects the account to be negative or positive, most of the time, the preferred rate of interest may vary. To get a better understanding, look at Table 14.12. Assume that a consumer would like to spend the money on an urgent repair. The cost of the repair is €11,000 so he expects to spend all of the available cash credit (and borrow the rest from a friend), provided that €10,000 is the limit (level A2). In such a case it would be best for the consumer if they could obtain the rate of interest level of B1: the consumer would have to pay 4 percent of the drawing (here €10,000), which is €400. In addition, he would need to come up with 2.5 percent of the maximum (€10,000), which is €250. So, in total, he would have to pay €650. If he obtained condition B2 instead, he would have had to pay an additional €50. It follows that B3 constitutes the most costly option. Next, assume that the consumer does not want to use all of the cash credit maximum, but needs €6,250 for a car. In this case, the consumer will be almost indifferent with regard to which of the three levels of B is offered (though B2 is a bit cheaper than B1 and B3). Finally, assume that the consumer is averse to risk and tends to always keep money in the account. This being the usual situation, the consumer would be recommended to choose B3, because according to this level, he would not have to pay anything, while levels B1 and B2 still require that a specified amount is paid, simply for the "right" to use the credit maximum – whether used or not.
- *Interest on deposits.* The bank pays some interest. The question is, how much is the consumer being offered? In the present case, the management considers an interest of 1, 2 or 3 percent. While a customer will prefer a higher interest rate, one cannot know how important the attribute is.
- *Opening fees.* Like interest on deposits, this attribute has a natural direction. Every consumer prefers something that is free to something that one must pay for. But how

Table 14.12 Differences in payment based on use of the account (cash credit maximum = €10.000)

Level			100%	62.5%	0
			Degree of utilization		
	Drawing	4%	400	250	0
	Maximum	2.5%	250	250	250
B1		Payment	650	500	250
	Drawing	5.5%	550	343.75	0
	Maximum	1.5%	150	150	150
B2		Payment	700	493.75	150
	Drawing	8%	800	500	0
B3		Payment	800	500	0

Table 14.13 Concepts used in the bank account conjoint analysis

Profile and cell:	1. A3B1C3D3	2. A1B3C3D2	3. A2B1C2D2
Cash credit max.:	6,000	16,000	10,000
Rate of interest:	4%+2.5%	8%	4%+2.5%
Interest on deposits:	1%	1%	2%
Opening fee:	200	100	100

Profile and cell:	4. A1B1C1D1	5. A2B3C1D3	6. A3B2C1D2
Cash credit max.:	16,000	10,000	6,000
Rate of interest:	4%+2.5%	8%	5.5%+1.5%
Interest on deposits:	3%	3%	3%
Opening fee:	0	200	100

Profile and cell:	7. A2B2C3D1	8. A1B2C2D3	9. A3B3C2D1
Cash credit max.:	10,000	16,000	6,000
Rate of interest:	5.5%+1.5%	5.5%+1.5%	8%
Interest on deposits:	1%	2%	2%
Opening fee:	0	200	0

important is it that it does not cost anything to open an account? If one needs €10,000 one might not be in a position to decline the offer of a loan, even if there were a charge of €100 or €200 for the service.

Table 14.11 displays the attributes and levels involved in the research design.

The research design of Table 14.11 resembles the design of the conjoint wine study. Like the wine study, it consists of four attributes, each having three levels. Thus a Graeco-Latin square can be used for reducing the design. See Table 14.13.

Note that even the placement of the nine concepts fits the wine study. Compare Table 14.13 with Figure 14.2.

The management did not formulate any hypotheses but it can be noted that the combination A2B2C2D2 was being offered by Northern Bank when the research was carried out.

Personal interviews were conducted with a random sample of customers. A customer was defined as a person who: possessed an account in the bank; and produced at least twenty transactions a year of more than €500.

First, the interviewer explained the purpose of the study. Next, a card containing the attributes and levels of the study (Table 14.11) was handed over to the respondent. Then, the respondent was shown a sheet with the information of Table 14.12, explaining the differences in cost caused by differing degrees of use of the account. Once the respondent understood that, the interviewer handed over a page containing the concepts shown in Table 14.13.

Respondents were then asked to rank the nine credit cash account settings (1 = best to 9 = worst). The analysis resulted in 109 completed interviews. The data presented in this section is available in the file *Northern_Bank.xls* which can be found at www.pearsoned.co.uk/schmidt. The Excel file has several sheets. The worksheet "Design" holds Tables 14.11 and 14.13. The sheet "Rankings" contain the ranks. It is a matrix with nine concept cards times 109 responses.

After the data-gathering was completed, the attribute levels and rankings of the concepts were dummy-coded using the same way of coding as shown in Table 14.8. Again,

Table 14.14 Part of worksheet

			"OLS_dummy_all" (Northern_Bank.xls).							
Row	a1	a2	b1	b2	c1	c2	d1	d1	y	Obs.
1	−1	−1	1	0	−1	−1	−1	−1	3	1
2	1	0	−1	−1	−1	−1	0	1	4	
3	0	1	1	0	0	1	0	1	8	
4	1	0	1	0	1	0	1	0	6	
5	0	1	−1	−1	1	0	−1	−1	7	
6	−1	−1	0	1	1	0	0	1	2	
7	0	1	0	1	−1	−1	1	0	9	
8	1	0	0	1	0	1	−1	−1	5	
9	−1	−1	−1	−1	0	1	1	0	1	
10	−1	−1	1	0	−1	−1	−1	−1	2	2
11	1	0	−1	−1	−1	−1	0	1	8	
12	0	1	1	0	0	1	0	1	7	
13	1	0	1	0	1	0	1	0	6	
14	0	1	−1	−1	1	0	−1	−1	3	
15	−1	−1	0	1	1	0	0	1	5	
16	0	1	0	1	−1	−1	1	0	4	
17	1	0	0	1	0	1	−1	−1	1	
18	−1	−1	−1	−1	0	1	1	0	9	
973	−1	−1	1	0	−1	−1	−1	−1	1	109
974	1	0	−1	−1	−1	−1	0	1	9	
975	0	1	1	0	0	1	0	1	2	
976	1	0	1	0	1	0	1	0	3	
977	0	1	−1	−1	1	0	−1	−1	8	
978	−1	−1	0	1	1	0	0	1	4	
979	0	1	0	1	−1	−1	1	0	5	
980	1	0	0	1	0	1	−1	−1	6	
981	−1	−1	−1	−1	0	1	1	0	7	

the ranking variable was reversed in the coding so that the higher the preference rank the bigger the score (9 = highest preference score to 1 = lowest preference score).

First, an aggregate OLS regression was run on the 981 "respondents rows" of data (9 rows per respondent * 109 respondents) times the 9 columns (8 dummy predictor columns plus the dependent ranking score variable). In the worksheet "OLS_dummy_all" of *Nortern_Bank.xls* ranking-scores of all 109 respondents have been organized so that an OLS regression can be run directly on the data. Table 14.14 shows the top and bottom of the file.

The utilities were computed by employing the same method as in the wine conjoint example: the parameter estimates of the first two levels of an attribute were used for computing the third level (recall that all three levels must sum to zero). Next, all estimates were treated as utilities. The coding of the conjoint wine study was shown in Table 14.8 and Figure 14.3.

Figure 14.7 displays the results of averaging the twelve utilities of the empirical study across all 109 subjects in the bank conjoint.

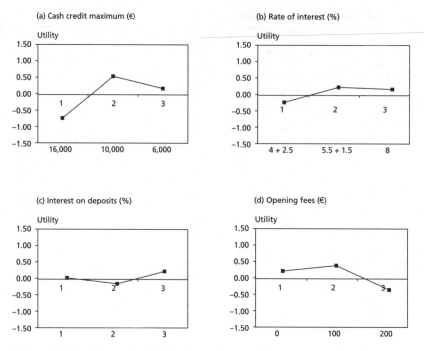

Figure 14.7 Conjoint analysis of bank account

It turns out that the second level produces the highest average utility level for all attributes except C. Unfortunately, differences between levels tend to be small, that is, utility curves appear to be relatively flat – this especially holds for attributes B and C. In other words, there are no striking differences between levels within a concept.

To sum up: in the present case, the aggregate analysis seems to lack a clear pattern. Note also that the utility functions of attributes C and D conflict with rational economic behaviour: while curves are flat, indicating little difference in utility, respondents seemingly prefer an interest on deposits of 1 percent to one of 2 percent! Also, they prefer paying an opening fee of €100 to nothing.[4]

The aggregate model's R-square is disappointingly low: 0.07. The low R-square is a strong indication of heterogeneity of preference among respondents. Since a conjoint model that leaves 93 percent of the variance unaccounted is flawed, it was decided to ignore the aggregate run across all respondents. The authors know of empirical conjoint studies where an OLS on the aggregate data yielded an R-square of more than 0.7. This being the case, it is probably not worth the effort of manipulating the data any further.

Clustering utilities

In the case of the bank account data, is seems obvious to run a cluster analysis based on the matrix containing the 9 concept/card ranks times 109 respondents (the sheet "Rankings" in *Northern_Bank.xls*).[5] So, a cluster analysis was run using SPSS *[Analyze, Classify, K-means cluster]*. The ranks were used as variables. There was only one deviation from the default setting: in the method's *[Save]* dialogue box, "Cluster membership"

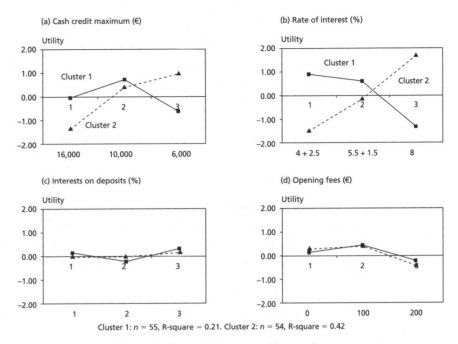

Cluster 1: $n = 55$, R-square = 0.21. Cluster 2: $n = 54$, R-square = 0.42

Figure 14.8 Conjoint analysis of new bank account (clustered)

was flagged and thus saved as a new variable into the screen editor (together with the nine ranking variables). The new system variable is called "qcl_1". The worksheet "Rankings" contains a two- and a three-cluster solution. Only the two-cluster solution is discussed here.

The two-cluster solution yielded two equal sized clusters of fifty-five and fifty-four cases. The sheets called "OLS_dummy_CL1" and "OLS_dummy_CL2" contain the observations from "OLS_dummy_all" that belong to the respective clusters. Running separate OLS regressions on the two clusters yields two new sets of eight regression parameters and deducted from these estimates, two new sets of twelve utilities, one set belonging to each cluster. Figure 14.8 displays the results.

Figure 14.8 shows the mean utilities across the two clusters. The corresponding dummy coded OLS run based on the fifty-five and fifty-four responses yields R-squares of 0.21 and 0.42 respectively – not perfect but much better than the run based on all responses (0.07). It follows that, when separating the data into two clusters, between one and two-fifths of the variance can be accounted for.

Now compare the aggregated analysis of Figure 14.7 with the clustered analysis of Figure 14.8. The obvious differences involve attributes A and B. Note that if an average is

Table 14.15 Aggregated analyses compared

	Level		Utility	
Figure 14.8	A1	Cluster 1	−0.07	[(−0.07)+(−1.36)]/2 = −0.71
	A1	Cluster 2	−1.36	
Figure 14.7	A1	Aggregate	−0.71	

Table 14.16

	(a) Cash credit maximum	(b) Rate of interest
Cluster 1	€10,000 is preferred: second choice is €16,000. Note that in the aggregate analysis €6,000 is second choice	The 4+2.5% level is weakly preferred to the 5.5%+1.5% level. Both are clearly preferred to the 8% level
Cluster 2	An almost inverse linear relationship between utility and level of credit	The 8% level is clearly preferred to 5.5%+1.5% which is clearly preferred to the 4%+2.5% level

taken of the added utility estimates concerning cluster 1 and cluster 2, we obtain the corresponding value in Figure 14.7 results. Table 14.15 shows an example.

The aggregate data of Figure 14.7 blur the existence of two (or more) clusters of respondents with different utility patterns with regard to the new bank account, as shown in Table 14.16.

When exposed to the conditions of the account (Tables 14.11 to 14.12), most respondents obviously begin to think about if and for what purpose they would use the account. Either they would consider using the cash credit or they would not. Depending on which of the two clusters a respondent belongs to, the preferred conditions concerning the rate of interest differs. Since people in cluster 1 prefer the higher levels of the cash credits to the lowest, their preferred rate of interest level behaves accordingly. Cluster 2 on the other hand is made up of consumers who do not need or appreciate being offered a high cash credit. Consequently, they prefer the rate of interest level which guarantees them that they must pay nothing if they do not all use the cash credit option (8 percent). They do not want to pay for a service they do not intend to use.

Besides misrepresenting the utility functions of attribute levels, the aggregate analysis

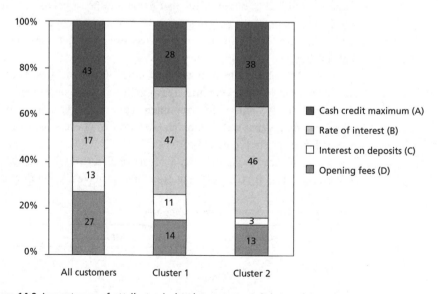

Figure 14.9 Importance of attributes in bank account conjoint

also provides a biased impression of attribute importance. Figure 14.9 presents the same kind of information as the pie chart in Figure 14.4. However, here it is more appropriate shown as a stacked column.

Figure 14.9 clearly shows that the aggregate analysis:

- overestimates the importance of attribute levels A, cash credit maximum, and D, opening fees, compared with the two clusters; and
- underestimates the importance of B, rate of interest.

There can be little doubt that in this case an aggregate conjoint analysis, if used as input for a marketing strategy, would lead to inappropriate decisions.

How then could management use the results from the two clusters? Well, maybe it makes sense to develop two versions of the account, one for "the probable spender" or "loan prone" (cluster 1) and another one for the "save prone" (cluster 2). Provided this makes commercial sense, how should the two segments be reached? In the present case this does not constitute a big problem, since the study can be linked to background characteristics of the respondents (age, gender, etc.). By matching these characteristics with a database of customers (or, if possible, a databases of non-customers), it is possible to establish a profile of customers (and non-customers) that resembles clusters 1 and 2. If all customers have been categorized according to one of the two clusters, the bank can print labels with the names and addresses of the individuals. Each letter would contain the version of the account that, based on the conjoint study and the background profiling, most properly fits the recipient. Those customers who do not seem to be associated with either cluster could just be ignored.

Theoretically, the bank could even target an individual customer. Instead of carrying out the OLS regression on the aggregated data or on cluster level, it could also carry out the conjoint analysis *on the individual level*, that is, estimate a set of utility values on each respondent. Table 14.17 shows individual utilities for the three respondents of Table 14.14.

The worksheet OLS_ind_util of the file *Northern.Bank.xls* contains the file for the 109 respondents. If an SPSS k-means cluster based on this file with a two-cluster solution is done, the result is the same clustering as in the case above (where the clustering was based on the ranks). Moreover, averaging the utilities across each of the two clusters yields the same utilities as in Figure 14.7. In the worksheet OLS_ind_util_CL, the 109 respondents have been separated into the two clusters.

Possessing a utility profile on all 109 respondents constitutes a great opportunity for the bank. However, the 109 respondents will represent only a fraction of the bank's customers. So, the bank could try to establish a fit between the 109 individual utility profiles and the

Table 14.17 Utilities of individual respondents

obs	a1	a2	a3	b1	b2	b3	c1	c2	c3	d1	d2	d3
1	0.00	3.00	−3.00	0.67	0.33	−1.00	0.00	−0.33	0.33	0.33	−0.33	0.00
2	0.00	−0.33	0.33	0.00	−1.67	1.67	−0.33	0.67	−0.33	1.33	1.67	−3.00
109	1.00	0.00	−1.00	−3.00	0.00	3.00	0.00	0.00	0.00	0.00	0.00	0.00

bank's, say, core of 50,000 customers by matching the background characteristics of the 50,000 with the corresponding data of the 109 respondents. Alternatively, the bank could mail the questionnaire containing the nine concepts of Table 14.13 to all 50,000 and use incentives to persuade them to fill in the nine rankings.

When "each" (or a great number of) customers have filled in the questionnaire of Table 14.13, the bank could employ a call-centre to phone all customers and then, based on each customer's utility profile, offer the account settings that matches her/his preferences.

This example has assumed that the 109 respondents are representative of all of Northern Bank's customers. Also, there has been no differentiation between the respondents and the entire universe of banking customers across banks, countries, etc. The reader should bear in mind that the respondents of a study should fairly represent the universe to which results are being deducted.

The marketing simulator

One of management's most important measures of performance concerns changes in the market share of a product.

■ Sometimes, the marketer will be interested in assessing how changes in the setting of concept parameters for products is supposed to change market share. For instance, she/he might want to know how a product launch would alter the market shares of existing products.

■ In other situations, no product launch is involved. Instead, the interest is on how a company's market share is supposed to be affected, by, say, changing the attribute settings of an existing product or service.

Such questions can be assessed (if not answered) by way of a so-called marketing simulator. This is a piece of software that transforms changes in utilities and in preference-based data into changes in market share for specified brands. *Adaptive Conjoint*

Table 14.18 ACA simulator input format (file: util_I.dat)

001	999	0	12
0.000	3.000	−3.000	
0.667	0.333	−1.000	
0.000	−0.333	0.333	
0.333	−0.333	0.000	
003	999	0	12
0.333	−0.333	0.000	
1.667	−1.000	−0.667	
−0.333	−1,667	2.000	
2.333	−0.667	−1.667	.
.	.	.	
107	999	0	12
0.000	0.333	−0.333	
3.000	0.000	−3.000	
−0.667	0.667	0.000	
0.667	0.000	−0.667	

Analysis (ACA) from Sawtooth Software and Bretton-Clark's *Conjoint Analyzer* may be regarded as the pioneers in commercial simulators. In recent years there has been a trend in the direction of what is called "choice-based conjoint" (CBC). CBC differs from the conjoint approach presented here in that the dependent variable is dichotomous scaled (Purchase/Non-purchase).

The utility data from the bank conjoint can be analyzed by a marketing simulator. First, data has to be reorganized so it can be read by the marketing simulator of, say, ACA. An appropriate format is shown in Table 14.18.

In Table 14.18, the data is organized with one response on five rows. The utilities of the first respondent appear in rows two through five – one row for each attribute (the utilities of the first respondent, 001, can also be found in Table 14.17). The first line contains the respondent number (this starts with cluster 1, so respondent 2 is not present in this file because she/he is a member of cluster 2). The next number, 999 (or rather 0.999, but ACA uses the value 999), is an indicator of the individual model fit. Due to the limited size of the bank account conjoint design, the individual model fit concerning each of the 109 respondents is 1.000 (the reader can check this by carrying out the 109 individual regressions based on the worksheet OLS_dummy_all).

Due to technical considerations the model fit is set to a number close to 1,000. When using more complex designs, the model fit estimated from some individuals will be imperfect (i.e., 567 or 0.567). In such situations one can let the program ignore values that do not pass a pre-specified threshold value (i.e., 700 or 0.700). A "0" tells the program that the data are not to be merged with other variables. Since this is not relevant here, it is set to "0". Finally, "12" refers to the fact that there are twelve utilities per respondent.

Having transformed the file to a format like Table 14.18 so it can be recognized by ACA's marking simulator, it is renamed to ACA's system name *util.dat* and placed with

Table 14.19 Simulation set-up menu

1 Enter simulation parameters
2 Enter attribute names and values
3 Enter product specifications
4 Review product specifications
5 Go to simulations menu

Table 14.20 Entering simulation parameter values

Choice model type	1–4	3
Cutoff value	000–999	–
External effects	1 = yes, 2 = no	1

Note: Several facilities on the menu have been omitted

Table 14.21 Simulation choice model type

1 First choice model ("the winner takes it all")
2 Share of preference (no correction for product similarity)
3 Share of preference (with correction for product similarity)
4 Purchase likelihood model

the ACA system files. Also, ACA needs to know how our design looks (Table 14.11). This is done by selecting "Set up interview" from the program's main menu and then selecting "Edit attributes" (not shown). Then the text of the three levels for each of the four attributes is keyed in. Next, from the main menu, "Set up simulation" is selected. This triggers the menu for setting up simulations. It looks similar to Table 14.19.[6]

In the simulation set up menu, select "1. Entering simulation parameters"; a sub-menu like Table 14.20 appears that offers a choice of four simulation models. These choices are (see Table 14.21):

- *First choice model.* In a marketing simulation each product or brand is assigned a specified concept setting, say, brand x: A2B2C2D2, brand y: A1B1C3D1, etc. The simulator then computes a total utility value for each respondent concerning each brand. For instance, using the estimates of the first respondent in Table 14.18, the two concepts just mentioned yield the corresponding overall utility pattern shown in Table 14.22. According to the first choice model, Respondent 1 will buy product x, since its overall utility value is higher than that of product y. The model treats purchases in a way that resembles how votes are treated in the British "first past the post" parliamentary system. The front-runner wins the seat while all other votes are ignored. The first-choice model computes the choices for all respondents in the same way and then computes the market share based on how many first choices a brand has obtained across respondents. While the model appears to possess intuitive merits, it is very sensitive to even minor changes in the product concept.
- *Preference share model (no correction for product similarity).* An individual's overall preference is distributed across the available products. In referring to the above example, the model assumes that products x and y have "market shares" on "the Respondent 001 market" of 0.667 and 0.333 respectively. Put simply, if the product had been a diary it would imply that the person would buy products x and y in a ratio of 2 to 1, that is, out of three purchases she/he would buy x twice and y once. ACA's preference share model uses a logit regression model (Chapter 10).
- *Preference share model (with correction for product similarity).* When two products are regarded as almost identical, a purchase model should be able to adjust for this. Otherwise, the analyst runs the risk of "double counting" a product's share. For instance, a brand may be launched with the aim of strangling a competitor's brands. Or the brand may turn out, unintentionally, to cannibalize one of the company's existing brands. Based on differences (distances) in the utilities matrix, it is possible to correct for similarities between brands. The more the (new) brand, say x, resembles an existing brand, say y, with regard to consumer utilities – and the less the two brands resemble other brands, say z, the more x and y will cannibalize each other and the less will they

Table 14.22 Utility pattern

Respondent 001	Concept	Utilities		Sum	1. Choice	Pref. Share
Product *X*	A2B2C2D2	3.000 + 0.333 −0.333 − 0.333 =		2.667	1	0.667
Product *Y*	A1B1C3D1	0.000 + 0.667 + 0.333 + 0.333 =		1.333	0	0.333
Total				4.000		1.000

affect the share of z. Assume a new brand is introduced that is regarded as identical to an existing brand regarding utility and totally unlike other brands. If the existing brand has a market share of 15 percent, then the combined share of both brands, once the new brand is introduced, will also equal 15 percent. Computational details are to be found in a technical series paper that can be downloaded from Sawtooth's website (www.sawtoothsoftware.com). This model is used in the simulations below.

- *Purchase likelihood model.* This is suitable for situations where no market shares are available, where the term does not make sense and/or when only one product is to be assessed. The model computes a buying probability ranging between 0 and 1.00. The purchase likelihood model, sometimes called a "barometer" of purchase intent, has been used for estimating the popularity of services offered by a hotel chain. For instance, one can estimate an optimal "share of nights" for a specific hotel concept.

Now return to Table 14.20. As noted above, a cut-off value is useful provided that the design is big and when the model fit (R-square) concerning certain responses is deemed to be too low. In such cases, set the cut-off value to, say, 600 (R = 0.6) and the program will only analyze responses with fit above this threshold.

The purpose of the *external effects* parameter is to help the analyst include the effect of marketing and market parameters not incorporated elsewhere in the model. The market share simulator estimates shares that new brands or modified brands are expected to achieve once they have fully penetrated the market. The external factor can be used to estimate shares before full penetration is achieved.

What is the rationale of the external effect? When modelling how concept changes transform to changes in market share, a parameter is needed that adjusts for differences in a company's "seriousness" or power to implement the change. When Procter and Gamble launches its so-called Euro roll-out for a new brand, the effect on the market will be much more significant than when a corresponding launch is performed by a small company. When P&G introduced the Ariel liquid detergent to several European markets, which had been dominated by products based on powder, it was able to "turn the market upside down" and obtain a market share of about 40 percent within months. No other company (maybe apart from Unilever or Colgate) could have done this. Assume that a marketing simulation is being run on the detergent market but without using external effects. Consequently, a market launch or concept change by a small local producer will have the same effect on market share as a corresponding act undertaken by P&G. However, in such a case a launch or concept change by P&G should transform to a bigger change in market share.

At first glance it seems odd that equivalent concept settings (= identical products) yield different market shares. But brands and services on a market often have totally different market shares despite being almost identical. This being the case one can use the external effect as a weight that models the importance of the company or brand. So, by selecting different sizes of the external effect for the different brands it should be possible to arrive at a starting configuration for the simulation where the concept settings of all brands transforms to market shares that are actually relevant (just before the introduction of concept changes or to a product launch). Setting the external effect is based on subjective judgment and should be used with care.

Table 14.23 Entering attribute names and values

	Level	Value	
A. Cash credit maximum	1	1.000	16,000
	2	2.000	10,000
	3	3.000	6,000
B. Rate of interest	1	1.000	4% of drawing + 2.5% of max
	2	2.000	5.5% of drawing and 1.5% of max
	3	3.000	8% of drawing
C. Interest on deposits	1	1.000	3%
	2	2.000	2%
	3	3.000	1%
D. Opening fees	1	1.000	Free
	2	2.000	100
	3	3.000	200

Table 14.24 Entering product specifications (starting configuration)

	A. Creditmax	B. Interest (%)	C. Interest on deposit	D. Opening fee	Market share	External effect
Diamond Bank	2,000	2.0	2.000	2.000	33.3%	100
Northern Bank	2,000	2.0	2.000	2.000	33.3%	100
Labour Bank	2,000	2.0	2.000	2.000	33.3%	100

Table 14.25 Changing product specifications (toward loaner segment – cluster 1)

	A. Creditmax	B. Interest (%)	C. Interest on deposit	D. Opening fee	Market share	External effect
Diamond Bank	2,000	2.0	2.0	2.000	32.5%	100
Northern Bank	1,000	2.0	2.0	2.000	35.1%	100
Labour Bank	2,000	2.0	2.0	2.000	32.5%	100

Now return to Table 14.19. The second action is to "Enter attribute names and values". This is done by putting in the appropriate text. See Table 14.23.

Thereafter, go to "Enter product specifications". See Table 14.24. In this example, three "products" or banks are defined along the four attributes. In the baseline situation, it is assumed that three banks supply accounts that are identical along all four attributes. While this is an oversimplification, it clarifies the following discussion. Usually, however, neither concept settings nor market shares of the company and its competitors will be the same. One company may have a share of 5 percent while another one will have a share of 30 percent. Likewise, the products or services offered will differ along the attribute levels. Nevertheless we will use Table 14.22 as a baseline case since using different settings and shares in the baseline situation complicates the discussion of the strengths and weaknesses of a marketing simulator. So, all banks in the baseline case offer an account consisting of a credit maximum of €10,000, 5.5 percent +1.5 percent rate of interest, 2 percent interest on deposits and charge €100 in opening fees.

The reader should recall that the bank customers fall into two clusters or segments (Figure 14.8). Cluster 1 is a "loan-prone" segment while cluster 2 is a "saver-prone" segment. All marketing simulations will be performed using either one or the other utility file. The worksheet "OLS_ind_util_CL" in the file *Northern_Bank.xls* contains both utility matrices. They can be copied to a different Excel workbook or to the Notepad and then saved in the appropriate file format that fits the format requested by the marketing simulator. The files are available as *util_l.dat* (cluster 1) and *util_s.dat* (cluster 2) in an ASCII format (text delimited) at www.pearsoned.co.uk/schmidt. Both files have a format like the one shown in Table 14.18.

All is now ready to start doing simulations.

Table 14.25: compared with Table 14.24, Northern Bank increases the credit maximum from €10,000 to €16,000. The competitors leave their products unchanged. The outcome of the simulation is a modest increase in market share of Northern Bank (from 33.3 percent to 35.1 percent).

The market shares of Table 14.25 reappear in the top-left cell of Table 14.26. Table 14.26 shows the effect of altering the baseline concept of Northern Bank, each time by one attribute level, while leaving everything else equal. Since the functional relationship of the attribute C, interest on deposits is nearly horizontal (Figure 14.8) this attribute is left unchanged across all runs at 2 percent.

The upper part of Table 14.26 indicates the effect on market share from changing the setting of one attribute level of cluster 1, the loan-prone segment. Increasing the credit limit from €10,000 to €16,000 increases market share by 1.8 percent (35.1 − 33.3), while decreasing it to €6,000 reduces share from the baseline to 27.0 percent, about 6 percentage points. Changing the rate of interest conditions has a bigger effect on share than altering the credit limit. The size of the opening fee has some effect, but not nearly as much as has the rate of interest.

The lower part of Table 14.26 corresponds to the upper part with the difference being the segment that has been loaded by the marketing simulator. The lower part is based on

Table 14.26 The effect of changes in product strategy on market share

	Cash credit max	Share	Rate of interest	Share	Opening fees	Share
LOANER (CL 1)						
Diamond Bank		32.5%		25.1%		30.9%
Northern Bank	A1: €16,000	**35.1%**	B1: 4%+2.5%	**49.9%**	D1: FREE	**38.2%**
Labour Bank		32.5%		25.1%		30.9%
Diamond Bank		36.5%		39.0%		34.5%
Northern Bank	A3: €6,000	**27.0%**	B3: 8%	**22.1%**	D3: €200	**31.1%**
Labour Bank		36.5%		39.0%		34.5%
SAVER (CL 2)						
Diamond Bank		40.1%		38.5%		30.2%
Northern Bank	A1: €16,000	**19.7%**	B1: 4%+2.5%	**22.9%**	D1: FREE	**39.7%**
Labour Bank		40.1%		38.5%		30.1%
Diamond Bank		23.8%		14.8%		34.3%
Northern Bank	A3: €6,000	**52.4%**	B3: 8%	**70.4%**	D3: €200	**31.4%**
Labour Bank		23.8%		14.8%		34.3%

Table 14.27 Simulation of selected strategic scenarios and their effect on market shares (loaner segment)

Scenario		Concept	Strategic activity	Share
1	Diamond Bank	A2**B1**C2D2	Northern raises credit limit to €16.000.	45.6%
	Northern Bank	**A1**B2C2D2	Diamond reacts by changing rate of interest conditions	**26.6%**
	Labour Bank	A2B2C2D2	from 5.5%+1.5% to 4%+2.5%	27.8%
2	Diamond Bank	A2B2C2D2	Northern raises credit limit to €16,000 and simultaneously	35.3%
	Northern Bank	**A1**B2C2**D3**	raises opening fees from €100 to €200. Competitors do not	**29.3%**
	Labour Bank	A2B2C2D2	retaliate	35.3%
3	Diamond Bank	A2B2C2D2	Northern changes rate of interest conditions from 5.5% +	27.4%
	Northern Bank	**A1B1**C2**D3**	1.5% to 4% + 2.5%. Simultaneously it doubles opening	**45.2%**
	Labour Bank	A2B2C2D2	fees from €100 to €200	27.4%
4	Diamond Bank	A2B2C2**D1**	Northern raises credit limit to €16,000. Diamond reacts by	35.3%
	Northern Bank	**A1**B2C2D2	removing opening fees on its account.	**31.0%**
	Labour Bank	A2B2C2D2		33.8%

cluster 2, the savings-prone segment (*util_s.dat*). When comparing the upper and the lower part, note that cluster 2 is much more sensitive to changes. If Northern Bank increases the credit limit from €10,000 to €16,000, its share will decrease dramatically from 33.3 percent to less than 20 percent. Likewise, changing the rate of interest conditions from 5.5 percent + 1.5 percent to 4 percent + 2.5 percent implies that Northern Bank's share will fall to 22.9 percent. Obviously, Northern Bank should abstain from changing the concept in the direction of A1 or B1 when marketing to the savings-prone segment. If the bank offered cluster 2 the concept as A1B1C2D2, its share would plummet to just 14.2 percent (not shown).

Table 14.27 shows four competitive scenarios that represent deviations form the baseline scenario (loaner segment/cluster 1). Scenarios 2 and 3 involve simultaneous concept changes along two attribute levels of the same product. It shows that a change from B2 to B1 (scenario 3) can easily compensate for doubling the opening fees (changing from D2 to D3).

Scenarios 1 and 4 involve competitive reaction from one of the banks. In both cases Northern Bank's competitor is able to neutralize the strategic concept changes by retaliating. Note also that in scenarios 1 and 4 all three banks have different market shares. Also, in both scenarios, Labour Bank performs better than Northern Bank simply by not reacting.

According to scenario 4 the competitor, Diamond, retaliates to Northern's concept change from A2 to A1 by abolishing its opening fees. But *maybe* Diamond only wants to lower the fees to €50. Although €50 does not appear in the experimental design of the bank conjoint analysis (Table 14.23), the marketing simulator can perform linear interpolations between €100 and €0. To include €50 opening fees, just tab in the value "1.5" in Table 14.24, since D1 = 1.000 (= €0/Free) and D2 = 2.000 (= €100). A re-run of the simulation with this setting gives the following shares: Diamond, 32.9 percent; Northern, 33.3 percent; and Labour, 33.7 percent. When comparing these shares with scenario 4 of Table 14.27, we note that lowering the opening fees from €100 to €50 is not a sufficient

Table 14.28 "Primitive" simulation scenarios using Excel (cluster 1, loan segment)

A	B	C	D	E	F	G	H	I	J	K	L	M	N	O	P	Q
													Diamond	Northern_1	Labour	Northern_2
2 obs	a1	a2	a3	b1	b2	b3	c1	c2	c3	d1	d2	d3	A2B2C2D2	A2B1C2D2	A2B2C2D2	A2B1C2D3
3 1	0.00	3.00	−3.00	0.67	0.33	−1.00	0.00	−0.33	0.33	0.33	−0.33	0.00	2.67	3.00	2.67	3.33
4 3	0.33	−0.33	0.00	1.67	−1.00	−0.67	−0.33	−1.67	2.00	2.33	−0.67	−1.67	−3.67	−1.00	−3.67	−2.00
5 5	−0.67	3.00	−2.33	1.00	−1.00	0.00	−0.33	−0.67	1.00	1.00	−0.33	−0.67	1.00	3.00	1.00	2.67
6 6	−0.67	3.00	−2.33	1.00	−1.00	0.00	−0.33	−0.67	1.00	1.00	−0.33	−0.67	1.00	3.00	1.00	2.67
.																
57 106	−2.33	2.67	−0.33	0.67	0.67	−1.33	0.67	−1.33	0.67	0.00	1.00	−1.00	3.00	3.00	3.00	1.00
58 107	0.00	0.33	−0.33	3.00	0.00	−3.00	−0.67	0.67	0.00	0.67	0.00	−0.67	1.00	4.00	1.00	3.33
							Concept utility score across respondents						71.00	89.00	71.00	49.67

retaliatory remedy with respect to compensating for Northern raising the credit limit from €10,000 to €16.000. Diamond will need to remove the opening fee.

The complexity of marketing simulation increases as the number of concepts and products grow. The present example has just eighty-one possible bank account settings (3 × 3 × 3 × 3) and three products. Consequently, a total of 243 brand specific concepts need to be assessed. The reader may imagine the complexity of the marketing simulation problem when thousands of concepts and multiple brands are involved.

A full marketing simulation requires commercial software. However, less sophisticated modelling is possible with Excel's formula editor.

The first twelve data columns of Table 14.28 (B–M) show how the utility file of cluster 1 respondents looks. See also Table 14.18 (the complete data for clusters 1 and 2 appear in the sheet OLS_ind_util_CL of the file *Northern_Bank.xls*). Columns N–Q of Table 14.28 use Excel's formula editor to compute overall concept utilities. For instance, the value 3.00 in the first row of column A2*B1*C2D2 concerning Northern Bank_1 is computed as = C3 + E3 + I3 + L3 = 3.00 + 0.67 + (−0.33) + (−0.33) = 3.00. Summing all values in the column of Northern Bank _1 yields 89.00 utility units. Doing the same in the columns referring to Diamond and Labour yields 71.00 utilities, respectively. Thus, we can infer that the market share of Northern Bank after the rate of interest conditions have been changed from B2 to B1 is 89/(71 + 89 + 71) = 39 percent compared with 31 percent of its competitors. So, under this primitive scenario, the concept change is recommended, provided competitors do not react and that the change is profitable. However, assume that Northern figures out that changing the rate of interest conditions is only profitable if the opening fees are doubled from €100 to €200. The final column of Table 14.28 shows the consequences of this combined concept change: Northern's share after the change is 49.67/(49.67 + 71 + 71) = 26% (compared with 37 percent for its competitors). The combined concept change cannot be recommended because the gain in market share caused by changing the rate of interest cannot compensate for the market share loss caused by doubling the opening fees.

Marketing research in action

Real life conjoint analysis for production of ecological pork

Some years ago the Bacon and Meat Council defined two research topics:

1. Obtain better knowledge about the demand for ecologically produced pork.
2. Acquire a detailed knowledge about the opinions and preferences of consumers with regard to buying ecological pork.

The council is sponsored by the association of pork producers and farmers. One of its responsibilities is to advise pork producers and slaughterhouses about appropriate product adjustments. According to the council, meeting current and emerging market demands is of utmost importance to producers.

The council seriously wants to address the above research questions. Therefore it decides to carry out an analysis to address the need for ecological pork and provide knowledge about factors that are critical for confidence in ecological products. The study should unravel consumer preferences and help to regain faith in products, especially in the intangible quality dimensions.

Survey design

What follows is an outline of the total research design that was employed. The interviewing and data analysis was handled by the multinational market research agency GfK.

1. Pilot phase. Cluster analyses of secondary consumer panel data to select relevant target groups for the explorative phase.
2. Explorative phase. Seven extended focus groups with heavy, medium and light consumers of pork. The focus groups were carried out in accordance with the brainstorming technique, implying that participants ended up with constructing concepts for "ideal pork."
3. Consolidation phase. Internal brainstorming among pork experts to help understand the consumers' values, beliefs, preferences, and buying behaviour.
4. Conjoint phase. Full-profile conjoint analysis of a national representative sample of 1,000 housewives aged 18–74 years.
5. Data analysis. Calculation of utility values by use of SAS/STAT procedure Transreg. Based on the constructed utilities, cluster analyses were applied to find relevant segments for planning future pork demands.
6. Result evaluations. Recommendations and implications for the client.

Statistical design

The conjoint design included ten attributes with number of levels varying from two to five. See Table 14.29. The attribute levels dealt with specific aspects relevant to buying pork. Levels for three attributes are shown in Table 14.30.

Table 14.29 Attributes and number of levels in pork conjoint

	Attribute	Levels					Sum
1	Meat quality	a	b	c	–	–	3
2	Fat content	a	b	c	d	–	4
3	Declarations	a	b	c	d	e	5
4	Environmentally friendly production	a	b	c	–	–	3
5	Medical residuals	a	b	c	–	–	3
6	Pig welfare	a	b	c	–	–	3
7	Feeding	a	b	c	–	–	3
8	Transport to slaughterhouse	a	b	c	–	–	3
9	Prices	a	b	c	d	e	5
10	Salmonella	a	b	–	–	–	2
	Number of levels across attributes						34

Table 14.30 Attributes of pork and levels

	Attributes	Levels
1	Meat quality	a. Everyday meat b. Weekend meat c. Meat to be served for guests
5	Medical residuals	a. Guaranteed never had medicine b. Free from medicine residuals c. Complies with law
10	Salmonella	a. Actual standard b. Guaranteed salmonella-free

The complete design in the present case is of format $5^2 \times 4 \times 3^6 \times 2$, necessitating 145,800 profiles. Clearly, this number cannot be included in a questionnaire. Therefore, it was decided to use an experimental design. However, since the complete design is not symmetric, a simple Graeco-Latin square was not feasible (in sub-designs, a Graeco-Latin square could be used, though).

It turns out, though, that the above design can be reduced to 50 profiles(!) by using the program *Conjoint Designer* from Bretton Clark. Unfortunately, such a design – despite certain statistical merits – cannot be employed in the present situation. Using fifty profile cards each having ten attribute levels is, by far, too much for respondents. The basic problem is not the fifty cards but the number of profiles per card. Conjoint studies rarely use more than five attribute levels per card. Attribute levels sometimes necessitate a whole sentence of explanation. For instance, one declaration ran: "Information on land of origin: Farmer's and farm's name, type of meat, date of slaughtering + maturing".

In the present study, the analysts found that the number of different attributes appearing on an individual profile should not exceed four. So it was necessary to use an appropriate **block design**. A block design can be employed when the number of attributes in the study exceeds the number that can be shown on a profile card. ➤

The experimental design used was a randomized incomplete block design with fifteen blocks and four attributes within every block, each attribute appearing six times across all blocks. Two attributes appear together twice within the same block (Cochran and Cox, 1957, 475), see Table 14.31. These assumptions imply:

- Attribute 1 appears six times (blocks I through VI) in the column below "1" (the first attribute of four to appear on a card). Attribute 1 does not appear anywhere else across the XV blocks. The first attribute has three levels (number in brackets).
- Attribute 1 appears twice together with attribute 2 in the same block (blocks I and II).
- Conditions 1 and 2 hold for all other attributes and combinations of attributes.
  The design of Table 14.31 needs to fulfil the following two conditions:

(1): $v\,r = bk$
(2): $\lambda\,(v - 1) = r(k - 1)$

where:
v is the number of attributes (here: 10);
r is the number of times an attribute appears across blocks (6);
b is the number of blocks (15);
k is the number of attributes within a block (4);
λ is the number of times that two attributes appear within the same block (2).

In the present design this implies:
(1) $10 \times 6 = 15 \times 4$ and
(2) $2 \times (10 - 1) = 6\,(4 - 1)$

Since both equations constitute true statements, the design obeys the statistical conditions that must be fulfilled for using the design.

Because the number of levels varied from two to five and only four attributes were allowed to appear within a block (on a card), the total number of profiles (cards) within a block varied between fifty-four ($3 \times 3 \times 3 \times 2$) in block VI and three hundred ($4 \times 5 \times 3 \times 5$) in block VII. The complete design consisted of 1,917 profiles across the fifteen blocks. This is still too many to handle in an empirical study. Fortunately, one can use statistical designs *within each block* simultaneously, thus reducing the necessary number of profiles across blocks to 316 (Table 14.31).

From the wine conjoint and the bank conjoint, recall that the full design of eighty-one concepts was reduced to nine cells using a $3 \times 3 \times 3 \times 3 = 3^4$ Graeco-Latin square. Note that this is precisely what we do in block XIV. The block consists of attributes 4, 5, 6 and 7 (see Table 14.29). Each of these attributes has three levels. All other blocks have been reduced using the same technique. The only difference is that within each block the attribute with the highest number of levels determines the size of the Graeco-Latin square. Since blocks II, VIII and IX each contain one attribute with four levels, the rule for reducing a full design of size $4 \times 4 \times 4 \times 4 = 4^4 = 256$ cells is to be used. This design can be reduced to sixteen cells by way of a Graeco-Latin square. No less than ten blocks include an attribute with five levels. Consequently, the full

Table 14.31 Incomplete block design (Cochran and Cox plan 11.16)

	Attribute number (number of levels in brackets)				Number of profiles		Pearson's	Kendal's
Block	1	2	3	4	Complete (a)	Reduced (b)	Corr. (c)	Tau b (d)
I	1(3)	2(4)	3(5)	4(3)	180	25	0.74	0.51
II	1(3)	2(4)	5(3)	6(3)	108	16	0.73	0.48
III	1(3)	3(5)	7(3)	8(3)	135	25	0.78	0.62
IV	1(3)	4(3)	9(5)	10(2)	90	25	0.87	0.66
V	1(3)	5(3)	7(3)	9(5)	135	25	0.62	0.44
VI	1(3)	6(3)	8(3)	10(2)	54	9	0.72	0.44
VII	2(4)	3(5)	6(3)	9(5)	300	25	0.49	0.45
VIII	2(4)	4(3)	7(3)	10(2)	72	16	0.84	0.65
IX	2(4)	5(3)	8(3)	10(2)	72	16	0.81	0.69
X	2(4)	7(3)	8(3)	9(5)	180	25	0.71	0.55
XI	3(5)	5(3)	9(5)	10(2)	150	25	0.76	0.58
XII	3(5)	6(3)	7(3)	10(2)	90	25	0.87	0.70
XIII	3(5)	4(3)	5(3)	8(3)	135	25	0.79	0.68
XIV	4(3)	5(3)	6(3)	7(3)	81	9	0.70	0.55
XV	4(3)	6(3)	8(3)	9(5)	135	25	0.75	0.61
Cols a+b = sum; cols. c+d = average:					1,917	316	0.75	0.57

design within block that is that basis for reduction is a 5^4 design with 625 cells. It can be reduced to twenty-five cells. How does one handle a design where the attribute levels vary? Recall that the wine and bank conjoint designs were symmetric. But what, if, say, the wine conjoint only had two packages, bottle and can (but no carton)? It is quite simple. When using Greaco-Latin squares, symmetry is not required. Proportionality suffices. Thus in the wine conjoint of Figure 14.2 simply substitute "carton" in the appropriate three profiles with "bottle" (or can).

Using Graeco-Latin squares within blocks enabled the analysts to reduce the 1,917 concepts to 316. The concepts or profiles were distributed across the fifteen blocks, each containing between nine and twenty-five cards. It was felt that the task of rating (not ranking!) a maximum of twenty-five concepts was something that respondents could handle.

A so-called hold-out card was included within each block (for validating purposes). A hold-out card is a profile or concept card that is ignored when the conjoint program reads the input data. A good conjoint model should be able to correctly predict the utility values of a holdout concept. A holdout concept is independent of the conjoint model (based on the input data).[7] The approximately 1,000 field interviews (by phone) were carried out so that a respondent would be exposed to profiles within one block only (the respondents had received a letter with the concepts a few days earlier). Therefore, respondents were exposed to nine, sixteen or twenty-five profiles/cards depending on the block in which he or she happened to appear. The field interviews were split equally across the fifteen blocks, each block containing sixty-five to sixty- ➤

seven interviews. The respondents were asked to rate the concepts by way of a scale ranging from 1 (no purchase interest), to 9 (great purchase interest).

Cross-validity

Conjoint analysis is a model for predicting choice behaviour. Its empirical validity is based on its cumulative record of providing useful forecasts. Normally, a conjoint study involves a test of cross-validity – i.e. the ability of the model to predict the rating or ranking of first choice of hold out profiles (Green and Srinivasan, 1990).

As mentioned, each block contained a hold-out profile. Table 14.31 (last two columns) displays Pearson's and Kendal's correlations concerning the hold-out cards. As can be seen both the statistics seem quite consistent. Not surprisingly, correlations vary inversely with the volume of the design: the more profiles that are needed in the full design the lower the correlation. The correlation between columns a (complete number of profiles) and c (Pearson) is −0.72. The lowest correlation, 0.49, was found in block VII – a block involving three hundred profile cards. Likewise, blocks with a small number of profiles in the full design (block IV, VIII, IX, and XII) tend to have high correlations. While there is a significant correlation between columns (a) and (c), there is almost no correlation (−0.02) between (b) and (c).

Data collection and findings

Field interviews were conducted according to the telephone-mail-telephone procedure suggested by Levy, Webster and Kerin (1983). The random sample consisted of 1,000 people aged 18–74 years who reported being responsible for the household's purchase of convenience goods. To facilitate respondents' comprehension of the attribute levels, visual clues were included. See Figure 14.10.

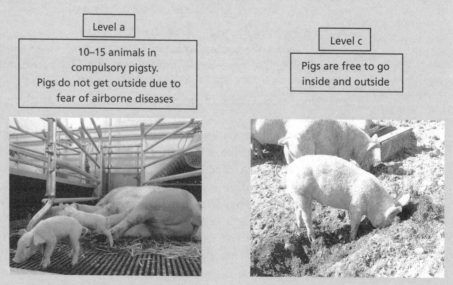

Figure 14.10 Visual clues used in conjoint study on ecological pork (*Source:* GfK, Denmark)

The findings of the present conjoint study are of less importance here. The purpose was to show how powerful statistical designs can be employed in commercial studies where many attributes are involved and where the attributes vary according to the number of levels. The ecological pork conjoint was a so-called "full profile" study (which sounds odd since only four of ten profiles were used on a card).

An alternative to the chosen design would be to base the conjoint interviews on the ACA software from Sawtooth. According to this application, all respondents first are asked to rank levels within an attribute, next they must rate attribute importance. Thereafter they are exposed to a sample of reduced concepts (just like the pork conjoint analysis). In ACA, the concepts appear as pairs where the respondent must indicate which of the two is preferred (and provide a score on how intense the difference in preference is).

The strength of the ACA approach is that it progresses by way of successive steps and thus is able to "learn" about the respondents' preferences and dislikes. ACA's computer interviewing module targets or narrows the design, based on a person's responses. For instance, ACA discards attributes and levels at an early phase, provided that the respondent assigns low scores to the attributes/levels in the introductory section when asked to first rate the importance of attributes and then rank the levels within each attribute.

In the pork conjoint study it was regarded as impractical to apply ACA. It should be noted that both the involved agency (GfK) and one of the authors were familiar with ACA and its electronic interviewing interface. The main obstacle to using ACA was that the client wanted a nationwide random sample of 1,000 interviews. The study was carried out almost a decade before online data collection became an option. However, even if the study had been carried out today, using ACA online would probably still not have been an option, due to the difficulty of obtaining a sample of responses that is nationally representative.

A cluster analysis was carried out based on a utility by respondent matrix (emanating from a so-called self-explicated part not reported here). A five-cluster solution was selected for segmentation purposes. See Table 14.32. The large number of clusters was made possible by the large sample size.

The interview included background characteristics and therefore the segments could be profiled along age, gender, urbanization, etc. Moreover, the agency possessed addresses and phone numbers of the respondents, enabling it to call respondents back and, say, obtain specified data on the respondents' media behaviour. These data could then be merged with the cluster analysis. Doing this would make it possible for the client to target promotional messages. For instance, it could run informative advertising on animal welfare in a magazine or on a TV channel with many readers belonging to segment 1 (e.g. *National Geographic*). And so on.

➤

Table 14.32 Five preference segments of pork customers

Name assigned to segments	Size of segment
1 Environmentally concerned and interested in animal welfare	25%
2 Almost satisfied	15%
3 Dissatisfied price sensitive	23%
4 True ecologists	20%
5 Lean pork and salmonella worry	17%

Initially (before the conjoint part of the questionnaire), all respondents were asked to rate all thirty-four attribute levels individually concerning preference. The five most significant levels were:

1. That there is an increased control of salmonella.
2. That pigs can roam indoors/outdoors.
3. That the pork is guaranteed free from medical residuals.
4. That pork quality is good for everyday use.
5. That it is lean meat with an outer fat layer.

Price came in at fourteenth place. Moreover, the current market price was preferred. However, after computing utilities based on the conjoint part, a different picture emerged. The five most significant levels turned out to be:

1. Pork on offer – 15 percent below normal price.
2. Normal price – not on offer.
3. That pigs can roam indoors/outdoors.
4. That the pigs' food is free from growth stimulants.
5. That the pigs themselves get ecological food.

According to the ordinary conjoint part of the questionnaire, price is more important than non-price attributes. This is an interesting finding that could most probably not have been revealed without the conjoint part. It seems that respondents upgrade (overestimate) the influence of ethical purchase criteria when they are asked to rank attributes separately while they tend to upgrade the influence of price when they are forced to rate full product profiles.

The findings of the study created considerable interest, both in the press and in agricultural organizations. The market potential for ecologic pork seemed bigger than expected by the clients' management. Consequently, it was decided to launch a promotional strategy targeted at conventional farmers, provided that extensive test marketing confirmed the results from the conjoint survey (it did).

Furthermore, the survey gave input to extensive product development of pork concepts. Several concepts were changed in accordance with the study findings. The importance of the price – according to the ordinary conjoint analysis – was due to further scrutiny by means of follow-up studies (Hansen and Schmidt, 1997).

The ecological pork case study represents a multifaceted commercial application of conjoint analysis. However, applications of even greater complexity have been published. An excellent example is the "classic" conjoint analysis conducted prior to launching the "Courtyard by Marriott" hotel chain (Wind et al., 1989).

Source: GfK, Denmark

14.4 A final note on conjoint analysis

Conjoint analysis is a popular technique. Searching on the exact term "conjoint analysis" on Google yields about 400,000 hits. There is a good chance that the first page will contain sponsored links emanating from companies that sell software applications for conjoint.

Well-known suppliers include: Sawtooth (www.sawtoothsoftware.com); Moskowitz-Jacobs (www.mji-designlab.com) and QuestionPro (www.questionpro.com).

Several of the companies supply a range of specialized software for gathering and analyzing data. Data gathering is usually done either via a computer or online. Data can be analyzed by way of cluster analysis, MDS, and by way of several conjoint programs.

Sawtooth's ACA is not the only conjoint program: CBC (Choice Based Conjoint) differs from ACA in that a concept is not rated or ranked but rather chosen or selected (or not) out of several competing concepts. According to some researchers, choosing among concepts is more realistic than rating or ranking concepts. CVA (Conjoint Value Analysis) focuses on price sensitivity analysis.

Textbooks by Louviere (1988) and Gustafsson, Hermann and Huber (2003) focus on conjoint analysis. Books on choice modelling usually will cover conjoint analysis in some detail. Train's book on discrete choice (2003) also covers simulation.

14.5 Summary

Whereas MDS deals with relations between existing products, **conjoint analysis** addresses alleged relationships between existing products and a new or revised product concept. Conjoint analysis is frequently applied before launching a brand. In conjoint analysis one must specify attributes (package design, price, etc.) and levels of an attribute (can, €2.35, etc.). Once attributes and levels of a hypothetical or real product have been specified, one must look for an experimental design that reduces the number of product concepts. Usually, the total number of attributes and levels that are of interest to the analyst implies a total number of concepts that by far exceeds the number a respondent can be exposed to.

A way of reducing the number of concepts is called a **statistical experimental design**.

In a conjoint analysis, the respondent is asked to rank or rate a sample of existing products or hypothetical concepts according to preference. Subsequently, the respondent's ratings or rankings are treated as observations of the dependent variable. Simultaneously, the setting of a product concept is regarded as **dummy coded observations** (1, 0, −1) of a set of independent variables.

Basically then, the conjoint model is a multiple regression where the rating or ranking score serves as the dependent measure while the dummy-coded settings of a concept are treated as observations of a series of predictor variables. A regression analysis produces a number of regression estimates or parameters. In conjoint analysis these values are called *utilities*. Utilities can be used for assessing the preference for a level. The higher the utility, the higher the preference. Also, utilities reveal how important an individual perceives an attribute to be. Utilities make up an important input to management's decisional strategy on product positioning. Since conjoint analysis is an additive model, it is possible to compare utility figures across attributes. For instance, one can estimate the effect on consumer preference for a concept caused by a shift from one attribute level to another.

Often, the preferences of consumers are heterogeneous. If this is the case, one will need to cluster analyze the matrix of utilities by respondents. A cluster analysis may help the analyst identify a small number of relatively homogenous respondents. This being the case, the company might want to aim its brand at different clusters/segments by way of different promotional and product strategies.

If a utility matrix is available, it can be loaded into a ***marketing simulator***. The simulator aims to transform the utility matrix into market shares for specified products/brands by way of a buyer behaviour model. Assuming that selected brands have been specified along the attribute levels of the conjoint design, the marketing simulator predicts how changes in the (actual) concepts transform to changes in market shares. When a new product is introduced into the simulator, the software computes the estimated share of the new brand. Moreover, it provides quantitative guesses with regard to how each existing brand's share is affected by the new product.

Questions

1. A publishing company is reconsidering the concept settings of its weekly pages, *Yellow Paper*, which carries many pages of classified advertising. It regards the four attributes in Table 14.33 as critical. The present readership is A1B2C2D2. Changing to a larger, broadsheet format would save money since the printing could be done by a big newspaper's production unit. If the paper appeared weekly, some advertisers might be interested in buying advertising space for products on sale in weekly waves in supermarkets. Appearance on Thursday fits better with the customer traffic at the multiple outlets where the paper is on sale (petrol stations, kiosks etc.). Finally, a higher price would raise profits, though with the risk of losing some sales. The reader might wonder why the paper is not distributed free. However, the publication has a lot of editorial content that generates cost, which cannot be entirely covered by adver-

Table 14.33 Critical attributes of the paper

Attribute	Level		
A	Format	1	Tabloid size (A3)
		2	Broadsheet size (A2)
B	Frequency of publishing	1	Weekly
		2	Every fortnight
C	Weekday of publishing	1	Thursday
		2	Friday
D	Price	1	75 cent
		2	95 cent

Table 14.34 Questionnaire cards

Card 01: A1B1C1D1	*Card 02: A2B2C2D1*	*Card 03: A1B2C1D2*	*Card 04: A2B1C1D1*
Tabloid	Broadsheet	Tabloid	Broadsheet
Weekly	Fortnight	Fortnight	Weekly
Thursday	Friday	Thursday	Thursday
75 Cent	75 Cent	95 Cent	75 Cent

Card 05: A1B2C2D1	Card 06: A2B2C1D2	Card 07: A1B1C2D1	Card 08: A2B2C2D2
Tabloid	Broadsheet	Tabloid	Broadsheet
Fortnight	Fortnight	Weekly	Fortnight
Friday	Thursday	Friday	Friday
75 Cent	95 Cent	75 Cent	95 Cent

Card 09: A1B2C1D1	Card 10: A2B1C2D1	Card 11: A1B2C2D2	Card 12: A2B2C1D1
Tabloid	Broadsheet	Tabloid	Broadsheet
Fortnight	Weekly	Fortnight	Fortnight
Thursday	Friday	Friday	Thursday
75 Cent	75 Cent	95 Cent	75 Cent

Card 13: A1B1C2D2	Card 14: A2B1C2D2	Card 15: A1B1C1D2	Card 16: A2B1C1D2
Tabloid	Broadsheet	Tabloid	Broadsheet
Weekly	Weekly	Weekly	Weekly
Friday	Friday	Thursday	Thursday
95 Cent	95 Cent	95 Cent	95 Cent

tising revenues. Since the experimental design is small the company abstains from using a reduced design. The sixteen cards are shown in Table 14.34 as they appeared in the questionnaire.

The page containing the sixteen concept profiles was placed on a page inside an issue of the paper. Respondents (current readers) were asked to provide the ratings (1 = best concept, to 16 = worst concept) and post the page with the responses to the publishing company. A lottery with a case of wine and free subscriptions as prizes was used as an incentive. Two weeks after publication of the page with the conjoint questionnaire, 153 usable rankings were received. The file with the rankings including a few instructions can be downloaded from www.pearsoned.co.uk/schmidt. Its name is *yellow_paper.xls*.

Now, use the procedures explained earlier in the chapter. The following are useful tools: the wine conjoint, especially Tables 14.6–14.8, Figures 14.3–14.6; the bank conjoint, especially Tables 14.13–14.14, Figures 14.7–14.9 and the file *Northern_Bank.xls*. The Excel file has several worksheets that go through much the same process as will be necessary for analyzing the *Yellow Paper* conjoint.

- Estimate the utilities by way of an OLS regression in the same way as was shown in the bank conjoint (Tables 14.8–14.10).

- How good is the model based on the aggregate data? In the bank conjoint the OLS analyses based on the aggregate data had a very low R-square – 0.07 (see the worksheet OLS_dummy_all in the file *Northern_Bank.xls*). Is the yellow paper conjoint run more successful?

- The file *yellow_paper.xls* has two background variables, gender, where female = 1 and male = 2, and born_yr, containing the year of birth (the study was conducted in spring 2004). Are there any differences in utilities between females and males? Do utilities vary across age? Use age groups (i) less than 30 years, (ii) 30–45, and (iii) 46 years and older. [Hint: in Chapter 11.2 (page 279–80) there is a seven-step procedure that shows how to select subsets of a variable in SPSS by using the "calculator" display in *[Data, Select Cases, If condition is satisfied]*. The example uses gender. But a related footnote briefly explains how to do the same selection with an age variable.]

- Do you recommend carrying out a cluster analysis based on the ranks in *Yellow Paper* conjoint?

- Based on the conjoint findings, what do you think the company should do? Should it change its concept settings? If you think they should, then how should they do it?

- Assume that the management of the *Yellow Paper* magazine considers carrying out one more conjoint analysis regarding the same problem. Can you come up with some more attributes and settings that could be included in the new study? Would you use the same procedure with regard to selecting respondents for the study?

- Could the above study have been carried out online? Inspect some of the websites of companies that supply updated conjoint software (several of them are mentioned above). Give a brief outline with regard to how the present analysis could be administered over the internet.

2. A young businessman is considering entering politics. But how should he profile himself as a brand? He is unsure about how to approach this critical question. He is convinced, though, that physical appearance plays an important role. That is, whether he wears tie and suit or rather a pullover, wears glasses, smiles, looks relaxed, etc. Thus he asks a friend who is a spin-doctor to come up with five different image profiles. The friend suggests the following: i. the macho type, ii. the bureaucrat-type, iii. the busy businessman, iv. the "guy next door" type, v. the populist. Being confident with modern marketing research, he decides to conduct a small conjoint analysis before he launches his campaign. In a conjoint analysis context the five typologies correspond to five different levels of the attribute "physical appearance". Table 14.35 shows a 5^4 Graeco-Latin with twenty-five cells. This design allows for four attributes. Thus, apart from the appearance attribute, the study can include three more attributes with five levels each. Which other levels would you recommend the potential politician to include? Assume that the politician, who is about to enter politics, is from

Table 14.35 A Graeco-Latin square – four attributes with five levels each

	A1	A2	A3	A4	A5
B1	C1D1	C2D3	C3D5	C4D2	C5D4
B2	C2D2	C3D4	C4D1	C5D3	C1D5
B3	C3D3	C4D5	C5D2	C1D4	C2D1
B4	C4D4	C5D1	C1D3	C2D5	C3D2
B5	C5D5	C1D2	C2D4	C3D1	C4D3

your country and that he wants to be elected, say, for the national parliament. Other attributes might be: marital status; bachelor, married with/without children, divorced, homosexual, etc; educational level; profession; views on political issues (say, as determined by focus groups). While attributes on political issues may be difficult to quantify, it is possible to do so using figures, percentages, indexes or intervals. For instance, public defence expenditures could be specified: level 1, 20 percent rise (per year; level 2, 10 percent rise; level 3, unchanged; level 4, 10 percent cut; level 5, 20 percent cut.

- Try to identify three other attributes that you find are the most important ones (either personal/socio-demographic characteristics or attributes based on political issues).

- Construct a questionnaire based on the Graeco-Latin square of Table 14.35. Remember to 'shuffle the profile cards' (section 14.2 dealt with a conjoint analysis for a red wine. Note that order of the cells in the 3^4 Graeco-Latin square used for the experimental design is different from the order used in the questionnaire of Figure 14.2.) Use a 1–10 scale for the rating task (1 = I would never consider voting for this politician; 10 = I would definitely consider voting for this politician).

- After you have constructed the questionnaire, hand it out to a non-representative convenient sample of co-students, friends and family members, etc. You should collect at least 20 interviews; preferably as many as 40.

- Dummy code the results using the same method as in Tables 14.8–14.9. Perform a regression analysis across all responses.

- Then run an individual regression analysis for each respondent, thereafter aggregate the utilities across respondents. Compare the results.

- Based on the interpretation of the utility levels, which political strategy would you recommend?

References

Bretton-Clark (1985) *Conjoint Designer*, Bretton-Clark, New York.

Carmone, F. (1986) "Conjoint Designer." *Journal of Marketing Research*. Vol. 23, 3. 311–12.

Cochran, W. G. and Cox, G. M. (1957) *Experimental Designs*. John Wiley, New York. 146–147.

Green, P. E. and Srinivasan, V. (1990) "Conjoint analysis in marketing: new developments with implications for research and practice." *Journal of Marketing*. Vol. 54, 4 (October). 319.

Gustafsson, A., Hermann, A. and Huber, F. (eds) (2003) *Conjoint Analysis: Methods and applications*. Springer, New York.

Hansen, L. and Schmidt M. (1997) "Revisiting conjoint. How Danish pig producers found the future road to environmentally concerned Danish consumers." *ESOMAR 50th Congress Proceedings*. 97–122.

Kerlinger, F. N. and Lee, H. B. (2000) *Foundations of Behavioral Research*. Fort Worth, TX, Harcourt. 788–799.

Kleinbaum, D. G., Kupper, L. L. and Muller, K. E. (1988) *Applied Regression Analysis and Other Multivariable Methods*. Boston, Kent Publishing. 260–296.

Levy, M. J. Webster, J. and Kerin, R. A. (1983) "Formulating push marketing strategies: a method and application." *Journal of Marketing*. Vol. 47 (Fall). 25–34.

Louvirere, J. J. (1988) *Analyzing Decision Making: Metric conjoint analysis*. Sage, Beverly Hills, CA.

Moore, W. L. (1980) "Levels of Aggregation in Conjoint Analysis: An Empirical Companion." *Journal of Marketing Research*. Vol. 7 (November). 516–23.

Ogawa, K. (1987) "An Approach to Simultaneous Estimation and Segmentation in Conjoint Analysis." *Marketing Science*. Vol. 6 (Winter). 66–81.

Schmidt, M. (1987) "An Empirical Evaluation of Some Aggregation Techniques and Estimation Algorithms in Conjoint Analysis," *EMAC/ESOMAR Symposium on Micro and Macro Marketing Modeling*, ESOMAR, Amsterdam. 135–56.

Train, K. E. (2003) *Discrete Choice Methods with Simulation*. Cambridge University Press.

Wind, Y., Green, P. E., Shifflet, D. and Scarbrough, M. (1989) "Courtyard by Marriot: designing a hotel facility with consumer-based marketing models." *Interfaces*. Vol. 19, 1. 25–47.

End notes

[1] From a model perspective we cannot even treat the levels of the price attribute as ratio-scaled or

interval-scaled. Such a scaling assumes a natural direction. While a price of €1.95 is higher than €1.65 we cannot say that 1.65 by definition implies higher *preference* ("is better") than 1.95 due to the usual assumption of negative price elasticity. Some consumers simply associate higher prices with better quality and prefer to "pay for quality."

2 In a normal regression and in almost all sorts of quantitative analysis it is *not* recommended to use 0 as an indicator of a missing observation. Computer programs like SPSS use "." (dot) to indicate a missing value.

3 Had the numerical example consisted of several respondents instead of only one, there would be data values concerning F, t, and significance levels, while R-square would be smaller than 1 and the standard error of the coefficients would be bigger than 0. Technically, the data example of Table 14.8 and Figure 14.3 consist of nine observations (the concepts) emanating from one respondent (the nine scores). Since the concepts of the design are fixed across a study – the nine concepts will be the same for all respondents – we could just copy the 8 columns*9 rows of dummy-coded data and paste them in so they are placed below the first respondent. Rows 9–18 would be concepts reserved for respondent 2, Rows 19–27 for respondent 3 and so on. Finally, we could tab in the scores of respondents 2 and 3, etc. in the corresponding lines of the score column. The reader should try doing this by tabbing in other values in these cells – they need not be ranked. Then the reader should run the analysis, based on, say, three respondents across 27 lines of data. She or he will notice that the standard errors of the non-standardized coefficients equal a constant value. This indicates that these coefficients are biased. Since t-values (and significance levels of parameters) are based on the standard error – they are biased, too.

4 This finding need not be caused by the low R-square of the aggregate but rather by the fact that respondents concentrate on the concept settings that they regard favorable concerning attributes A and B. Consequently they ignore the importance of attributes C and D.

5 It has become usual to use the part-worth utilities derived from individual level analysis as input for a cluster analysis (Moore, 1980). However, performing the cluster analysis *directly* on the respondents' rankings is more straightforward (Ogawa, 1987; Schmidt, 1987). Ranks are more 'original', or accurate than estimated part-worth utilities, and so contain more information. Normally, both methods should yield approximately the same results. But if the overall model fit is bad, i.e. when many attributes and levels are involved, then results may vary significantly. In such cases the matrix with part-worth values is plagued by loss of information – variance that could not be explained by the model. Here, the raw profiles matrix should be used for clustering rather than the matrix of estimated part-worths.

6 Note that here and in the following we ignore facilities of the program that we will not use like "Printing results", "Display color" etc. Also, we ignore page-specific instructions like "Press any key to continue", "Choose END when finished" etc.

7 A hold-out card is an extra card or profile that is not used for estimating the conjoint model. The extra profile – like all other profiles – is given a rating score by the respondent. Once the utilities have been estimated, say by way of OLS regression, we can compute the overall concept utility of the hold-out card. This estimated concept utility can then be compared with the actual preference score assigned to the profile by the respondent. If we have 100 respondents, there would be two data columns, one containing the computed score regarding the hold-out concept and one containing the original score. The two columns should correlate highly. If they do not, the validity of the estimated conjoint model must be questioned.

15 Advanced methods for categorization: CHAID and latent class analysis

Learning objectives

After studying this chapter you should be able to:

- Explain in which situations a CHAID model can be used for categorizing a data set.
- Identify the necessary scaling presumptions (dependent, dependents) for using a CHAID model.
- Run SPSS classification trees and interpret the results.
- Describe the potential pitfalls of using a CHAID model.
- Categorize a metric variable using SPSS.
- Explain in which situations a latent class model can be used for analyzing marketing problems.
- Discuss which measurement conditions favour the application of a latent class analysis.
- Perform a cluster analysis of categorical data using appropriate software such as Latent Gold or SPSS.
- Understand the output of latent class cluster analysis and a latent class regression.
- Explain the main difference between ordinary cluster analysis and latent class cluster analysis.

15.1 Introduction

In Chapters 9–14, quantitative methods were introduced that belong to a group of *multivariate statistical techniques*. All of them could be handled by Excel's Analysis ToolPak (ANOVA and regression) or by SPSS. While all programs introduced in these chapters could be run using SPSS, none of the programs covered in Chapters 15–17 are presently part of base SPSS. They either necessitate licensing an add-on module, another program, or using SPSS syntax code.

The first part of this chapter requires licensing either the SPSS add-on module called Classification Trees or the standalone program *SPSS Answer Tree*. The second part of this chapter necessitates purchase of the standalone program *Latent Gold*. If an analyst does not possess this program, SPSS *[Analyze, Classify, TwoStep Cluster]* can be used instead. However, because *Latent Gold* appears to be preferred by marketing researchers, this chapter is based on it. Chapter 16 on canonical analysis and LISREL/SEM requires an SPSS macro, a little syntax code (canonical analysis) and licensing SPSS AMOS. Chapter 17 on data mining necessitates a licence for SPSS Clementine.

Because not all readers have access to specialized SPSS modules, the way these methods are covered will differ from the approach used in Chapters 9 to 11. As before, each method will be introduced and the basic philosophy explained, though not necessarily with an example, due to two reasons:

- A detailed technical discussion of several of the methods presumes introduction of complex mathematics and statistics that are beyond the scope of this text (i.e. LISREL, canonical correlation, and latent class analysis).
- Some methods (CHAID and data mining) only make sense when the data matrix is large. These methods have been developed for analyzing huge amounts of data. Therefore, they are simply not suited for analyzing tiny matrices.

After covering the method in general, the selected software is introduced as well as an empirical data file. Next, some software screens with appropriate settings show the output based on the empirical study. As in previous chapters, all data files are available at

Table 15.1 Selected advanced marketing research methods

Method	Description	Software	Producer
CHAID (AID)	A tree-based classification procedure that aims to break down data such that the difference in measures of the dependent variable among splits is maximized by way of the predictors. The dependent variable is either interval or nominal while the predictors are nominal/categorical scaled	SPSS 13 (including licence of Classification Trees), SPSS Answer Tree	SPSS
Latent class analysis	A way to perform multivariate analyses in situations where all or some variables are nominal/categorical scaled. Can handle cluster, regression, and factor with dichotomous data	Latent Gold (SPSS TwoStep Cluster)	Statistical Innovations
Canonical correlation	A method that, unlike regression, allows for several continuous dependent variables	(Macro add-on)	SPSS
LISREL (structural equation modelling)	A procedure for modelling complex causal relations by way of a set of simultaneous regressions. Roughly a mix of regression, factor analysis and canonical regression	AMOS	SPSS
Data mining	A potpourri of methods that have been bundled to recognize patterns in a data set. Techniques involve regression, cluster analysis, factor analysis, classification tree procedures, advanced rule modelling, and artificial neural networks	Clementine	SPSS

www.pearsoned.co.uk/schmidt. Some caveats are examined and the coverage of each method closes with selected references.

Table 15.1 provides a brief overview of the methods covered in Chapters 15–17.

15.2 CHAID

CHAID (chi-squared automatic interaction detection) is a tree-based classification procedure developed by Kass (1980) that splits the data into categories. The CHAID model presumes a dependent variable and a set of predictors. CHAID is an extension and modification of a technique originally developed as AID (automatic interaction detection) by researchers in the 1960s (Morgan and Sonquist, 1963). The main difference between AID and its successor CHAID concerns the scaling of the dependent variables. While AID presumes predictors to be dichotomous involving binary splits, CHAID allows for more than two levels.

Researchers have proposed modifications to the original AID algorithm and specialized programs have been developed. Apart from CHAID, the best-known modifications are:

■ THAID Theta automatic interaction detector (Morgan and Messenger, 1973)
■ MAID Multivariate AID (MacLacklan and Johansson, 1981)
■ SI CHAID – Statistical Innovation CHAID (Magidson, 1992). SI CHAID is marked by Statistical Innovations (www.statisticalinnovations.com).

The present discussion only addresses CHAID and to some degree its predecessor AID.
AID was developed for situations where:

■ there are many observations (at least a thousand);
■ there are more than a few variables;
■ one does not make strong assumptions about relationships. AID (and CHAID) may be regarded as an explanatory technique. It is not suited for confirmatory analysis. Moreover, it may be difficult to generalize results from one empirical sample to others.

The dependent variable can be interval, ordinal or nominal, while the predictors need to be nominal/categorical-scaled. If predictors are not categorical-scaled then they must be recoded before running the analysis. Usually, two to three levels are preferred, while in CHAID more than five levels are rarely employed in empirical studies.

Assume that the dependent variable is an interval measure asking for the customer's satisfaction with his/her (primary) insurance company. The satisfaction variable is scaled from 1 (very satisfied) to 5 (very dissatisfied). Furthermore, suppose that the file containing the satisfaction measure also includes two background variables, gender (1 = male, 2 = female) and marital status (1 = married, 2 = unmarried).

The matters under investigation are:

■ satisfaction (dependent variable); and
■ gender and marital status (predictor variables).

Table 15.2 Cross-tabs of satisfaction and gender/marital status

		Gender		Marital status		Total
		Male	Female	Married	Unmarried	
Satisfaction	Very satisfied	23.2	24.7	24.0	24.1	24.0
	Satisfied	58.4	51.3	56.0	51.3	54.3
	Neither/Nor	16.8	21.0	17.4	22.6	19.2
	Unsatisfied	1.3	2.7	2.4	1.5	2.1
	Very unsatisfied	0.3	0.3	0.2	0.5	0.4
Total	Column %	100.0	100.0	100.0	100.0	100.0
n		548	746	834	460	1294
Pearson chi-square (asymptotic significance)			0.06		0.14	

An obvious way to explore this would be simply to run two cross-tabs, as in Table 15.2. Assume that all 1,294 responses emanate from a random sample of one insurance company's database. All respondents are customers of the company, called Top.

Differences exist within both the gender variable and the marital status variable:

- About 5 percent more males than females are "at least satisfied": (23.2 + 58.4) − (24.7 + 51.3) = 5.6%
- Nearly 5 percent more females than males are neither satisfied nor dissatisfied: (21.0 − 16.8) = 4.2%
- About 5 percent more of those married than of those unmarried are at least satisfied: (24.0 + 56.0) − (24.1 + 51.3) = 4.6%
- 5 percent more of those unmarried than of those married state to be neither satisfied nor dissatisfied: (22.6 − 17.4) = 5.2%

However, neither the observed difference in gender nor the corresponding one in marital status turns out to be statistically significant on the 0.05 level. As can be seen in Table 15.2, the Pearson chi-squares are 0.06 and 0.14, respectively. So, while males (married) appear to be a little more satisfied than females (unmarried) the interaction is weak and insignificant (the Pearson statistic on gender is marginally significant, though).

A general problem related to inspecting cross-tabs is that the task becomes inconvenient as the number of variables increases. To check the dependent variable for interaction with, say, nine background variables instead of only two, would need nine cross-tabs to be examined (one for each predictor). Moreover, there would be 36 possible cross-tabs *between predictors*. For instance, in the example of Table 15.2 the cross-tab between gender and marital status is ignored (simplistically, it is not significant in a monogamous society).

To summarize, for m variables there exist $m-1$ cross-tabs between dependent and predictor variable. In total there are $[m*(m-1)]/2$ cross-tabs of which $\{[m*(m-1)]/2\}-(m-1)$ will be between predictors. With ten variables (m) out of which one is a dependent and nine are predictors, this yields $[10*(9)]/2 = 45$ tables, of which nine are between the dependent and the predictors, while the remaining thirty-six tables are between predictors.

With so many cross-tabs, the researcher runs the risk of missing interactions since the task of checking must be carried out manually. In a situation like this the analyst typically will look for ways to improve insight into interaction effects. A promising research path would be to employ CHAID.

An empirical study will supply a better understanding of the applicability of CHAID. Assume that the insurance company *Top* has carried out a survey among its customers. The

Table 15.3 Satisfaction survey among customers of Top Insurance

Variable	Levels	n	%	code
Satisfaction	1 = Very satisfied	311	24.0	1
	2 = Satisfied	703	54.3	1
	3 = Neither/nor	249	19.2	0
	4 = Dissatisfied	27	2.1	0
	5 = Very dissatisfied	4	0.3	0
Gender	1 = Male	548	42.3	1
	2 = Female	746	57.7	2
Age (metric, recoded)	1 = < = 45	601	46.4	1
	2 = > 45	693	53.6	2
Household size	1 = 1	361	27.9	1
	2 = 2	527	40.7	2
	3 = 3+	406	31.4	3
Marital status	1 = Married/Cohabits	834	64.5	1
	2 = Unmarried/Divorced	460	35.5	2
Housing	1 = Owner	842	65.1	1
	2 = Non-owner	452	34.9	2
Education	1 = Elementary	363	28.1	1
	2 = Industrial	555	42.9	2
	3 = Academic	376	29.1	3
Urbanization	1 = Rural/Village	541	41.8	1
	2 = City	425	32.8	2
	3 = Capital	328	25.3	3
Personal income € (metric, recoded)	1 = 0–24,999	480	37.1	1
	2 = 25,000–39,999	487	37.6	2
	3 = 40,000 +	327	25.3	3
Household income € (metric, recoded)	1 = 0–39,999	488	37.7	1
	2 = 40,000–59,999	387	29.9	2
	3 = 60,000 +	419	32.4	3
	Total *n*	1294	100.0	

small questionnaire contained ten questions. Table 15.3 displays the variables along with the simple frequencies. (The data file used in this section can be downloaded from www.pearson.co.uk/schmidt. It is a SPSS system file called *Satisfaction_Top.sav*. It is also available as an Excel file (without labels).)

While a clear majority of the company's customers claim to be very satisfied/satisfied, about every fifth customer seems to be less than satisfied. According to a guideline that has been formulated by Top's management, 90 percent or more of customers must be at least satisfied. If one looks at the survey, however, only 78 percent of customers (311 + 703 = 1,014 out of 1,294) pass that self-imposed threshold level. A 90 percent level would necessitate $(0.90) * (1,294) = 1,164$ satisfied/very satisfied customers. These figures can be used to test whether the empirical satisfaction figure of 78 percent is significantly lower than the company goal of 90 percent. This is done by computing the chi-square statistic with $n-1$ degrees of freedom:

$$\chi^2 = \frac{(f_o - f_e)^2}{f_e} = \frac{(1014 - 1164)^2}{1164} = 19.33 \Rightarrow p \cong 0$$

Thus the empirical result is inconsistent with Top's tough, though self-enforced, guideline.

Consequently, the management wants to investigate whether the unacceptable level of overall customer satisfaction can be traced back to one or several background variables. After consulting a marketing research expert, management decides to run a CHAID analysis based on the empirical study.

The CHAID model necessitates that the predictors are categorical-scaled. So, if predictors are interval or metric-scaled, they must be recoded to, say, two to four levels before running CHAID. From Table 15.3, note that some recoding has been carried out already. Several of the background variables, such as age and personal income, by definition are metric-scaled. Since CHAID works best when predictors have a small number of levels, it was decided to recode the age variable such that all customers aged 45 years or less have been recoded as "1" while those older than 45 years have been recoded as "2". Likewise, the personal and household income variables have been recoded into three discrete levels. Note that the file includes a variable, called "sat_1_0". In this file we have recoded the original 1–5 coded satisfaction scores to a 1–0 coded variable. See also Table 15.3.

Running CHAID in SPSS

We begin by loading the file *Satisfaction_Top.sav* (from www.pearsoned.co.uk/schmidt). Next, tab *[Analyze, Classify, Tree]*. See Figure 15.1. (Note that if the *[Classify]* dropdown of procedures does not contain Tree or if it is listed but cannot be selected, either you do not have an appropriate licence or the version of SPSS is 12 or earlier.)

Once *[Tree]* is selected, a pop-up box warns about the importance of setting the proper measurement level. Select *[Define variables Properties]*.

A new dialogue box appears. See Figure 15.2 (screen 3). In this dialogue box, click the variables to scan into the "Variables to Scan field". For illustrative purposes, select the variable "Urbanization" (normally we would ask for a scan of all variables). Next click *[Continue]*. In the new pop-up, select urbanization: it says the variable has three levels.

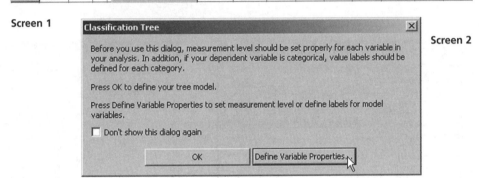

Screen 1

Screen 2

Figure 15.1 Running CHAID in SPSS

Value 1 indicates that the person lives in a village or rural environment. This holds for 541 out of 1,294 respondents (this fits with Table 15.3). And so on. The "Measurement Level" is assumed to be "Nominal," which is correct. The variable "Type" is "Numeric". (It is possible to do some recoding here. For instance, existing labels can be changed and new ones added. Also, it is possible to copy variable properties from and to other variables.) Click *[Cancel]*.

Once more, click *[Analyze, Classify, Tree]* and tab *[OK]* when the "Measurement" pop-up appears. See Figure 15.3.

The list box in screen 5 displays all variables included in the file *Satisfaction_Top.sav*. First, drag the dependent variable, Satisfaction (dummy), into the *[Dependent Variable]* field. Next drag all nominal variables except Respondent ID into the *[Independent Variables]* field. In SPSS a nominal variable is recognizable as an icon consisting of three coloured balls. Note that while the dependent variable is coded 0/1, it is treated as a scale variable – as indicated by the ruler-like icon. Because the dependent variable is defined as metric, the button *[Categories]* is not clickable.

When clicking the "Growing Method" drop-down, see Figure 15.3 (bottom) notice that SPSS's Classification Tree program supplies four CHAID algorithms:

- *[CHAID]* is the default setting.
- *[Exhaustive CHAID]* sometimes produces better fits, but necessitates more computations.

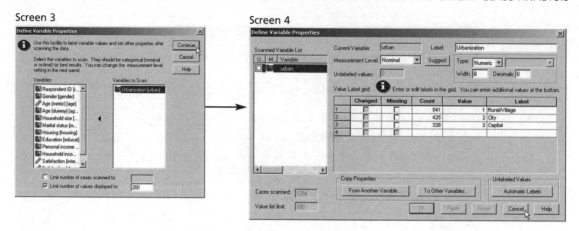

Figure 15.2 Scanning data file for proper scaling of variables

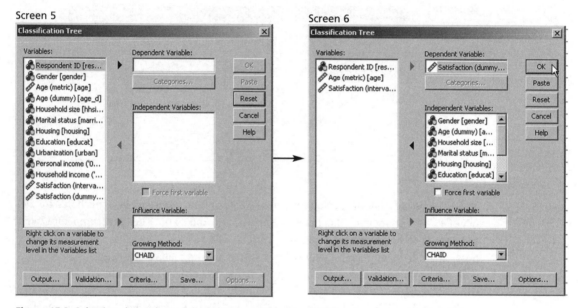

Figure 15.3 Selecting dependent and predictor variables for CHAID

- *[CRT]* Classification and regression tree is a binary tree-growing algorithm that produces more hierarchical levels and nodes than does ordinary CHAID. It is more flexible but tends to be less reliable.
- *[Quest]* acronym for *Q*uick, *U*nbiased, *E*fficient *S*tatistical *T*ree – is a method that avoids other methods' bias in favour of predictors with many categories. It can be specified only if the dependent variable is nominal.

An "Influence variable" may be employed for defining how much influence an observation is allowed to have on the growing process. Flagging the "Force first variable" implies that the first variable in the independent list will be used for the first split. For instance, in Figure 15.3 (Screen 6) gender would be used.

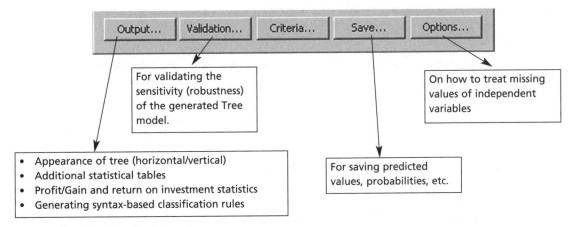

Screen 7

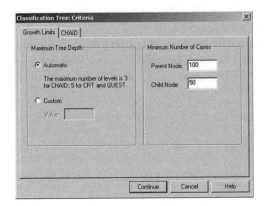

Screen 8

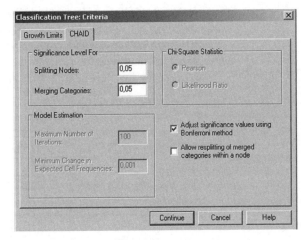

Figure 15.4 Selected options and settings in SPSS classification trees

Figure 15.4 shows that several buttons, such as *[Output]*, *[Save]* and *[Options]*, have pre-specified settings.

Classification Trees has a feature for validating a tree. This may help a researcher assess the generalizability of the results. It can be shown that the results of a CHAID/AID analysis may be highly sensitive to the way a metric variable is categorized. (See Doyle and Fenwick (1975), Magidson (1982, 1994) and the users manual for SPSS 14.)

The *[Criteria]* button shows the most important settings. Screen 7: the Parent Node is set at 100 and the Child Node at 50. In Figure 15.5 later Node 0 is a parent node with child nodes 1 and 2. Simultaneously, nodes 3 and 4 are child nodes of the parent node 1 and so on. The maximum tree depth is set at three for CHAID. The classification tree of Figure 15.5 has a depth of three levels below the dependent.

When Classification Tree splits a parent node into, say, two or three child nodes (categories), it must apply a rule that determines which among several predictors is to be used for the split. In other words, which predictor split maximizes the difference *as measured by the dependent variable*. All this becomes much clearer when looking at the output. So, we close all subscreens and click *[OK]* in Screen 6 of Figure 15.3.

In the present case the dependent variable (*Y*) is treated as a metric measure, as indicated by the 'ruler like' icon for "Satisfaction (dummy)" in the "Dependent Variable" field of screen 6, Figure 15.3. While the measure is confined to assuming two states (0 or 1) on the individual level, it is nevertheless possible to compute an average value between 0 and 1 that summarizes *Y* (i.e. 0.67 or 67 percent). Consequently, when the original data file is split into, say, two subgroups, based on a predictor such as marital status, CHAID aims to select the predictor that maximizes the difference in *Y* between the two splits. So if the data is split into two groups based on, say, gender and the average value concerning males and females is 0.61 and 0.74, respectively while an alternative split based on marital status yields averages of 0.48 for married and 0.82 for unmarried, then CHAID selects marital status as predictor for the model since the net difference between the latter pair is 0.34 which is bigger than the difference between the former (0.13). If no further split is significant on the specified alpha level the process of splitting stops, the default setting is 0.05.

Provided a predictor has more than two levels, CHAID assesses whether each level needs to be kept as a separate node after the predictor has been selected for the split. For instance, if the predictor variable is education with three categories and their average values concerning *Y* are 0.79 for Industry, 0.76 for Elementary and 0.64 for Academic then

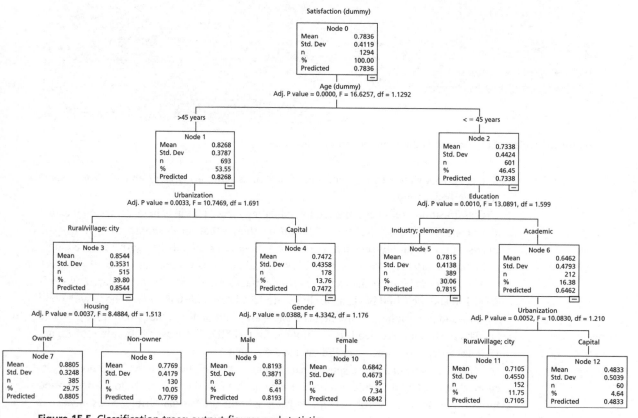

Figure 15.5 Classification trees: output figures and statistics

CHAID will (probably) merge Elementary and Industry into one category, since the difference between the two is relatively small. The merge happens if the probability value related to the split is *bigger* (i.e. 0.23) than the specified significance level for *not* merging (0.05). See screen 8, Figure 15.4. As noted, we will not change the default values. Instead we tab *[Continue]* and *[OK]*.

Now look at the output of Figure 15.5 (node 0). Notice that the (dummy coded) dependent variable has an average value of 0.7836. An average of 1.00 would imply "unanimous customer satisfaction" while 0.00 would indicate "Unanimous customer *dis*-satisfaction". The value 0.78 can be regarded as the customer satisfaction score. See the SPSS manual for more on the size of the standard deviation and the figure called "Predicted".

As for the growing of the tree, CHAID begins with splitting the data according to the (dummy-coded) predictor age. Note that the younger subgroup ($<= 45$ years) on average is less satisfied than the older one (0.73 versus 0.83). Notice also that this split is highly significant. The F-value is 16.6257 with one and 1,292 ($n-2$) degrees of freedom, corresponding to a p-value of 0.0000.

In the next level of the tree, the older subgroup is split according to urbanization while the younger group is split by education. In both cases, the CHAID algorithm merges two categories: concerning urbanization, the categories "Rural/Village" and "City" are merged while "Industry" and "Elementary school" are merged with regard to Education. These merges happen because the difference in mean among the appropriate categories is not significant on a 0.05 alpha level (screen 8 of Figure 15.4).

On the third level, rural/village/city is split according to house ownership; capital is split in relation to gender; and Academic Education is diverted according to urbanization.

Due to the selected set-up criteria, no further split is significant on the 0.05 level. To summarize, the following predictors are selected for the model: age, urbanization (twice), education, housing and gender. The remaining predictors do not enter the model, due to lack of explanatory power.

An inspection of the paths along the tree reveals some interesting findings (Figure 15.5).

Node 7 categorizes customers who come quite close to meeting management's goal of a 90 percent satisfaction score. This category covers 30 percent of the insurance company's customers.

The company's management should worry about customers who possess background characteristics corresponding to node 10, and especially to node 12. Such customers

Table 15.4 Some findings

	Node 7	Node 10	Node 12
Profile of customer subgroup	■ Older than 45 ■ Live in rural area/village or city ■ House owners	■ Older than 45 ■ Live in capital ■ Female	■ Younger than 45 ■ Academic education ■ Live in capital
Satisfaction score	0.88	0.68	0.48
Size	30%	7%	5%

deserve attention because fewer than half (48%) of node 12 customers are satisfied/very satisfied. It should be easy to send these people a questionnaire based on the node's specific profiles. While node 12 only covers 5 percent of customers, it may still contain thousands or even ten thousands of customers who appear to be quite unsatisfied with the company. Would it make sense to ask a call centre to phone these customers individually? Alternatively, they could be offered a personal visit by a company consultant, or a discount.

The company's goal should be to make customers of node 12 feel that the company cares about them because it is often easier to keep a customer than it is to acquire a new one, especially in mature markets. While node 12 might be targeted by newspaper advertisements, it is probably more cost efficient to use direct marketing.

Table 15.5 Recoded file

	Dummy coding of age	*n = 1294*
(Original) Figures 15.1 to 15.5	1 = up to 45 years 2 = older than 45 years	601 693
New coding	1 = 0–39 years 2 = 40–59 years 3 = 60 years and older	469 510 315

Screen 1:
CHAID tree. Input data as in Figure 15.5 but age predictor has been recorded to three levels instead of two

Screen 2:
CRT classification and regression tree produces more nodes and hierarchical levels

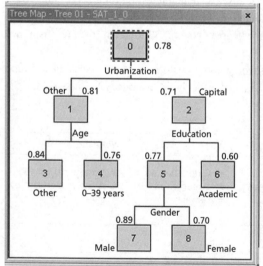

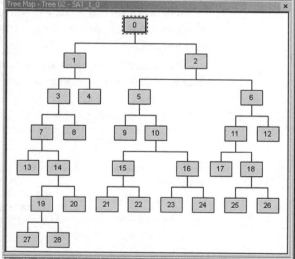

Figure 15.6 Precautions and extensions when using CHAID-type models

Some concluding remarks

The advantage of CHAID is its intuitive merits. It is relatively easy to understand and to explain. The disadvantage is that it is sensitive to minor adjustments in the input matrix. For instance, if the predictor variable age of the input file *satisfaction_top.sav* is recoded, the result is as in Table 15.5. This recoding of but one out of nine predictors affects the appearance of the tree a lot. See screen 1 of Figure 15.6.

Note the following differences from Figure 15.5:

■ changing age from two to three levels loses four nodes; and
■ age appears in a lower level of hierarchy (not shown). Moreover, splitting age into three categories is 'overruled' by the CHAID algorithm because the score difference between the two older age groups is not significant and therefore they are merged.

Similarities compared with Figure 15.5:

■ the combination of living in the capital and possessing an academic degree implies lower satisfaction;
■ younger customers tend to be less satisfied than older ones; and
■ female customers are less satisfied than males.

So, while differences are noticeable, the same directional orientation exists for the most important predictors across the tree.

As noted, CHAID presumes predictors to be categorical-scaled. The researcher should try to recode each metric variable to 2–4 'fair' levels of roughly the same size, then run the analysis and inspect the output. If patterns in the output are recognizable across runs, this points to the stability of the model. One should then choose the run with the fewest nodes as the final model. However, it is justified to choose the model that makes most sense from an applied marketing perspective. This could be a model that optimizes the differences in preference scores across nodes.

The basic problem with categorizing a metric variable is that there is no objective criteria for deciding upon the best number of levels. Therefore, under any circumstances, recoding a metric variable to a dichotomous or a nominal scale is arbitrary.

Even when recoding a nominal- or interval-scaled predictor variable to a dichotomous variable, the researcher faces trouble. If the predictor has five levels then the recoding to two levels can be done in fifteen different ways. More generally, if a variable has j categories, then the recoding can be done in $(2^{j-1})-1$ different ways. Here: $(2^{5-1})-1 = 15$.

While the problem can be solved as long as one variable has to be recoded, it becomes unmanageable as the number of variables grows. To recode, say, eight five-point Likert-scaled items, the total number of recoding options becomes 15^8 or more than two billion. Only in cases where the predictor by natural means can only assume two states, such as gender, does recoding not cause concern.

According to CHAID, the dependent variable can be either metric or dichotomous. In the above empirical example (see Figures 15.3 and 15.5) the dependent variable was treated as a metric measure although the scale was confined to two states. Consequently, the averaged measure – the score number appearing in the nodes – is a figure in the range between 0 and 1, for instance 0.7836. As long as metric figures are involved the appropriate

Table 15.6 Extra CHAID nodes

	Node 13	Node 20	Node 22
Profile of customer subgroup	■ Older than 45 ■ Live in rural area/village or city ■ House owners ■ Elementary school	■ Older than 45 ■ Live in rural area/village or city ■ House owners ■ Industrial/Academic ■ Household size 3+	■ Older than 45 ■ Industry/Elementary ■ Personal income €40,000+ ■ Male ■ Personal income (11)
Satisfaction score	0.93	0.96	0.91
Size	9%	3%	5%

test statistic is the F-statistic. Therefore, an F-test is used for assessing splits and merges of nodes. See Figure 15.5. However, if the dependent satisfaction measure is treated as a dummy-scaled dichotomous variable, then the statistical test used for separation and merging is a chi-square test. The appearance of the tree is identical to that of Figure 15.5, though. The only difference is that the F-test is replaced by a chi-square test and then the score value, i.e. 0.7836 is substituted by percentage figures 78.36 percent for satisfaction and 21.64 percent for non-satisfaction.

The procedure CRT differs from CHAID in that it produces more nodes across more levels. Screen 2 of Figure 15.6 show the output from CRT based on the same input file as was used in Figures 15.1 to 15.5.

Note though, that in the present case we have changed default settings because we wanted more nodes: The minimum number of cases concerning child node – see screen 7 of Figure 15.4 – was decreased from 50 to 30 (in accordance with the central limit theorem) while the maximum tree depth was raised from three to six.

Notice that the CRT tree has twenty-eight nodes, much more than the twelve of the original CHAID tree. With two exceptions, the nodes 1 through 12 of screen 2, Figure 15.6 are the same as in Figure 15.5. The important difference is that the CRT algorithm continues to split and produces more branches downwards. Predictors such as personal income and household size that did not enter into the solution when running CHAID now appear as nodes. Table 15.6 focuses on three nodes of screen 2 in Figure 15.6. The procedure identifies relatively small nodes that surpass the management's threshold levels concerning satisfaction of 0.90. Due to differences in default settings, the number of nodes and the appearance of the tree may look different in different versions of SPSS and Clementine (SPSS' data mining program covered in Chapter 17) – even if we use the same dataset, this illustrates the sensitivity of the technique. (Especially CRT).

Published literature on AID/CHAID is limited. Publications on AID include: Assael (1970), Martin and Wright (1974), Green (1978a), Holmes (1980) and MacLacklan and Johansson (1981). Papers on CHAID include Currim, Meyer and Le (1988), Baron and Phillips (1994) and Magidson (1994). Chaturverdi and Green (1995) provide a review of SPSS CHAID, an earlier version of classification trees. The methodological problems connected to AID and CHAID are addressed by Doyle and Fenwick (1975) and by Magidson (1982, 1994). It is important that the reader understands the pitfalls that may result from uncritical use of CHAID.

EXHIBIT 15.1 HOW TO CATEGORIZE A METRIC VARIABLE IN SPSS

It is easy to transform a metric variable into a categorical one using SPSS. See Figure 15.7. This exhibit shows how to transform the metric age variable into a variable that has three categories: 1 = up to 39 years, 2 = 40–59 years and 3 = 60 years and older.

Screen 1: the file *satisfaction_top.sav* is shown in the screen editor. First click *[Transform]* on the SPSS menu bar and scroll down to *[Recode, Into Different Variables]*. Select it.

Screen 2: in the appearing pop-up, tab the variable "Age (metric)" into the input variable field.

Screen 3: select a name for the new (output) variable, say, age_3_d. Tab *[Change]*. Then give it a name (optional), say, "Age on 3 levels" and tab *[Old and New Values]*.

Screen 4: concerning "Old Value" select "Range" and then put in "0" to "39." For "New Value" use "1." Click *[Add]*. Repeat this process where the range "40" to "59" obtains the new value "2" and finally where "60" to "120" is transformed to "3."

Finally, tab *[Continue]* and *[OK]*.

Note that the data screen now obtains a new column called "age_3_d." In this column or variable all metric values of the "age" variable are recoded either to 1, 2 or 3.

Screen 1

Screen 2

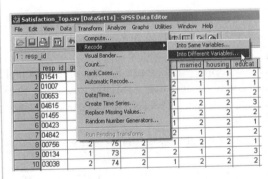

Screen 3

Screen 4

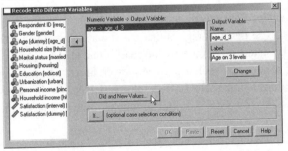
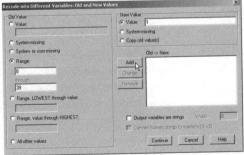

Figure 15.7 Transforming a metric variable into a categorical one using SPSS

In CHAID the predictors are assumed to be categorical-scaled. If the variable is continuous, it must be transformed to a categorical scale before being used as input. Exhibit 15.1 shows how this is done in SPSS.

15.3 Latent class (LC) models

Technically, the CHAID model is a dependence technique. The tree formation procedure begins with a top or original node – a dependent variable selected by the analyst. A dummy-coded satisfaction score was employed for this purpose earlier, in Table 15.3.

As long as the dependent variable is binary, the method resembles both two-group discriminant analysis and binary logistic regression. But whereas the latter (unlike discriminant analysis) *allows* categorical predictors, CHAID *presumes* predictors to be categorical (otherwise they must be categorized). So, logistic regression is more flexible and robust than CHAID. However, as often, greater robustness has a price: the output generated by logistic regression is more difficult to understand, whereas CHAID output is straightforward.

CHAID is an advanced **dependence method** for classification in situations where other methods do not appear appropriate or where output generated by other techniques is difficult to understand. The most important characteristic of CHAID is that predictors (and dependents) are categorical/nominal-scaled.

It turns out that there is an **independence method** that can be used for classification in cases where other techniques, like hierarchical cluster analysis or K-means cluster analysis are inappropriate. The rest of this chapter deals with this method.

In general, an analyst prefers a scale that is strong and robust. For example, a variable measuring income, price or company revenue is stronger than a variable measuring intensity of agreement concerning a lifestyle statement. This is because the former variables are ratio-scaled while the latter is interval-scaled.

However, for either ratio- or interval-scaled variables we – theoretically – can use all kinds of advanced multivariate methods.

When applying cluster analysis or factor analysis to marketing problems, measurement scales are usually interval-scaled, for instance a five-point summated scale (i.e. 1 = totally agree, 2 = agree, etc.) or a bipolar semantic differential (i.e. 1 = very modern to 7 = very old fashioned).

Such scales are created by the analyst. The advantage of such artificial constructs is that they are controlled by the analyst. The disadvantage is that cases may appear where the respondent does not understand the statement in the way the analyst intended. So one may question the validity of responses obtained by such means. Moreover, in real life, few variables follow an interval scale, let alone a ratio scale. Indeed, most variables used in surveys are categorical-scaled/nominal-scaled with a small or limited number of levels. Often they are even dichotomous (Yes/No).

However, if such "weak" or "directionless" scales are involved, we cannot use traditional factor analysis or cluster analysis as we did in Chapters 11 and 12. Chapter 11.1 briefly discussed several methods for performing factor analysis based on a qualitative input: it turns out that one of the methods, *latent class analysis*, can also conduct both factor analysis and cluster analysis in situations where the data are categorical or dichotomous.

The concept of latent class (LC) analysis was introduced in the middle of the twentieth century and belongs to a larger set of methods called *latent structure models* (Lazarsfeld and Henry, 1968). Innovative technical work on latent class has been done by Goodman (Goodman, 1974, 1979).

A latent class model treats the manifest variables as imperfect indicators or underlying traits, which are themselves unobservable (Dillon and Goldstein, 1984). With regard to making a distinction between manifest, observable variables and latent, unobservable constructs, a latent class model resembles a structural equation model (see Chapter 16).

However, unlike the standard SEM model, the latent class algorithm allows for categorical input data. Table 10.1 lists another method that can be employed in cases where both the dependent and the independent variables are categorical/dichotomous-scaled: logistic regression (simple and multinomial logit and probit). Indeed, commercial software such as *Latent Gold*, uses multinomial logistic regression to estimate parameters when the dependent variable is nominal-scaled.

The first academic publication on LC models for marketing problems was Green, Carmone and Wachpress (1976). The best, though advanced, modern marketing related book on the topic is Wedel and Kamakura (2001).

While LC algorithms were primarily intended for factor and cluster analysis of categorical data, specialized LC models and/or approaches are now available for scrutinizing other problems. The list includes:

- Multiple regression (DeSarbo and Crohn, 1988; Wedel and DeSarbo, 1994).
- Multidimensional scaling (DeSarbo, Manrai and Manrai, 1994; Wedel and DeSarbo, 1996).
- Conjoint analysis and related methods (Kamakura, 1991; DeSarbo, Wedel, Vriens and Ramaswamy, 1992; Vriens, Oppewal and Wedel, 1998; Böckenholt, 2002).
- Discriminant analysis (Dillon and Mulani, 1989).
- Analysis of missing data analysis (Winship, Mare and Warren, 2002).
- Analysis of measurement error (Hagenaars, 2002).
- Times series analysis (Collins and Flaherty, 2002).
- Analysis of Markov chains (Langeheine and van der Pol, 2002).
- Budget analysis (van der Heijden, van der Ark and Mooijaart, 2002).

This chapter covers *latent class cluster analysis* and *latent class regression*. Those who want to know more about latent class models should inspect specialized texts: McCutcheon (1987), Loehlin (1988), Bartholomew and Knott (1999), and Hagenaars and McCutcheon (2002). The reader should note, though, that most texts on latent class models assume knowledge of mathematics. McCutcheon (1987) is probably the easiest, while Hagenaars and McCutcheon (2002) is the best for new applications.

Few books contain a chapter on LC. For instance Lattin, Carroll, and Green (2003) have a chapter on logit choice models but none on LC. Likewise, Hair et al. (1998) have nothing about LC. One of the few multivariate books with a chapter on LC is Dillon and Goldstein (1984).

The motivation behind latent class analysis is the belief that the observed association between two or more manifest categorical variables is due to the mixing of heterogeneous groups. In this sense, latent class analysis can be viewed as a ***data unmixing procedure*** (Dillon and Goldstein, 1984, 491).

A potential problem concerning LC cluster analysis is that interpretation is inversely proportional to the number of variables involved. Whereas it works fine with, say, five to ten variables, it causes a problem to run a latent cluster analysis with more variables. Since it is an iterative algorithm, much time is needed for many variables and observations. Moreover, the interpretation of a problem with many variables, each having, say three to five levels, becomes unmanageable.

Go to www.pearsoned.co.uk/schmidt for a case study discussing latent class in relation to newspaper readership in New York. This is Appendix 15-A.

Latent class cluster analysis of audio equipment shoppers

The source of the following empirical example is Dillon and Goldstein (1984, 493–96) See also Dillon and Kumar (1994). However, the data originates from a study by Dash, Schiffman and Berenson (1976).

Four hundred and twelve audio equipment buyers gave answers to five dichotomous questions concerning their shopping behaviour. The first question centred on the type of shop in which the equipment was bought (department store or specialist) while the four other questions addressed aspects of pre-purchase communication and information behaviour. All questions were dichotomous-scaled. Table 15.7 lists the five questions.

The result of the study is shown in Table 15.8. The file can be downloaded as Dillon494.sav (SPSS version) or as Dillon494.xls (Excel version).

The first row ("ID1") shows respondents with the following purchase profile:

- The audio equipment was bought in a department store.
- The individual had used a catalogue.

Table 15.7 Questions for audio equipment buyers

	Variable name	*Description*
1	Store choice	Shop in which goods purchased: department store (1) or specialist (2)
2	Catalogue experience	Has the individual sought information from a manufacturer's catalogue: (1) = Yes, (2) = No
3	Previous shopping experience	Has the individual stopped in some store for audio equipment before making a decision: (1) = Yes, (2) = No
4	Information-seeking	Has the individual sought information from a friend and/or neighbours before purchase: (1) = Yes, (2) = No
5	Information-transmitting	Has the individual recently been asked for an opinion about buying an audio product: (1) = Yes, (2) = No.

Table 15.8 Buying behaviour of audio equipment shoppers

ID	Store choice	Catalogue experience	Prior shopping	Information seeking	Information transmitting	Frequencies
1	1	1	1	1	1	5
2	1	1	1	1	2	3
3	1	1	1	2	1	14
4	1	1	1	2	2	2
5	1	1	2	1	1	15
6	1	1	2	1	2	3
7	1	1	2	2	1	26
8	1	1	2	2	2	32
9	1	2	1	1	1	2
10	1	2	1	1	2	3
11	1	2	1	2	1	8
12	1	2	1	2	2	3
13	1	2	2	1	1	4
14	1	2	2	1	2	5
15	1	2	2	2	1	12
16	1	2	2	2	2	17
17	2	1	1	1	1	86
18	2	1	1	1	2	3
19	2	1	1	2	1	33
20	2	1	1	2	2	8
21	2	1	2	1	1	23
22	2	1	2	1	2	4
23	2	1	2	2	1	30
24	2	1	2	2	2	8
25	2	2	1	1	1	22
26	2	2	1	1	2	4
27	2	2	1	2	1	6
28	2	2	1	2	2	6
29	2	2	2	1	1	11
30	2	2	2	1	2	3
31	2	2	2	2	1	5
32	2	2	2	2	2	6
						Σ412

1 = Department store	1 = Yes	1 = Yes	1 = Yes	1 = Yes	
2 = Specialist	2 = No	2 = No	2 = No	2 = No	

■ Respondent had previous shopping experience.

■ Respondent had sought information from a friend/neighbour.

■ Respondent had recently been asked for an opinion on the issue.

Five out of four hundred and twelve individuals provided answers that correspond with this response profile. And so on. From an analytical perspective, five dichotomous questions yield a five-way cross-classification consisting of $2^5 = 32$ cells.

The thirty-two response categories contain between two and eighty-six cases, or on average about thirteen.

Now, how can the four hundred and twelve respondents be clustered? Or the thirty-two response categories put into, say two, three or four clusters?

First, traditional cluster analyses, be it k-means or hierarchical cluster, cannot be applied since such techniques assume that the variables that are to be clustered are ratio- or at least interval-scaled. Unfortunately, this is not the case here. However, a latent class cluster analysis can be used instead.

An example using *LatentGold* software is on the book's website at www.pearsoned.co.uk/schmidt. This is Appendix 15-B.

Latent class regression (clusterwise regression)

So far, most latent class applications within marketing have dealt with clustering problems. As noted, latent class clustering methods usually are employed instead of k-means or hierarchical cluster analysis in situations where the variables are nominal/dichotomous-scaled rather than ratio/interval-scaled. Latent class algorithms have been developed for analyzing many issues of managerial relevance. *Latent Gold*, can handle clustering, factor analysis and regression. A module supplied by its producer, Statistical Innovations, focuses on clustering choice-based preference (conjoint) data. Sawtooth Software supplies a program called Choice-Based Conjoint Latent Class Module. This module is tailored for segmentation of choice-based conjoint data.

In Chapter 14, the dependent variable in the wine study was ordinal-scaled (a ranking of concepts according to preference). As long as the dependent measure is ordinal- or interval-scaled, it is possible to employ ordinary regression analysis. But in situations where the dependent measure is nominal/dichotomous-scaled (choice between two or more brands), OLS is not an option and therefore latent class models are often used instead.

Latent class models can be applied to a regression problem. A multiple regression analysis provides a set of regression parameters, one for each predictor variable. The parameters are estimated *across all respondents*. Provided that the respondents constitute a heterogeneous group, the variance explained by the model will be low and its R-square will be disappointingly small. However, while the respondent sample appears to comprise a heterogeneous set, a hidden pattern of "homogenous subgroups" may exist within the data. Unfortunately, this pattern, if existent, cannot be properly unravelled by means of ordinary regression. This being the case, the estimation of a single set of regression coefficients across all observations may at best be inadequate and at worst misleading.

Assume that the observations (respondents) arise from a number of unknown heterogeneous groups in which the coefficients differ. This being the case it may be inappropriate to base the interpretation on a single set of parameter estimates. In such situations, latent class regression – sometimes called *clusterwise regression* – may prove advantageous to the analyst (Wedel and DeSarbo, 1994).

What follows is a brief guide to running a latent class regression (based on *Latent Gold*). The data file employed is a modified version of the empirical study based on a department store, House of Wonder. The files relating to this case (Word, Excel and SPSS file) can be found in Appendix A-4 at www.pearsoned.co.uk/schmidt. The modified version of the SPSS file that we will use is available as House_of_Wonder_lat.sav.

The following changes have been made to the original SPSS file. The original set of statements is *a1–a17*. Based on these statements, a new set of variables is established

Table 15.9 Missing values in House of Wonder case

	Valid	Missing
a1	1,298	26
a2	1,266	58
a3	1,293	31
a4	1,289	35
a5	227	1,097
a6	1,284	40
a7	895	429
a8	1,257	67
a9	1,252	72
a10	1,298	26
a11	1,301	23
a12	1,293	31
a13	780	544
a14	764	560
a15	1,285	39
a16	1,296	28
a17	782	542
Total number of respondents	1,324	

named a_1–a_17. Then, those of the a_1 to a_17 variables that possess many missing values are deleted. See Table 15.9.

It is easy to see which observations are to be excluded from further analysis: $a5$, $a7$, $a13$, $a14$, and $a17$. The remaining variables have fewer than one hundred missing values, or more than 90 percent valid responses. There tends to be a logical explanation for missing values. For instance, statement $a5$ only applies to respondents who have tried on new clothes during their visit to the department store. Since most respondents did not do so, they should not answer this question.

In the remaining variables, missing entries are exchanged with the mean, rounded to the next integer. Since the mean of the 1,298 valid responses in variable $a1$ is 4.45, the twenty-six missing responses are replaced with 4.00. And so on. So the twelve variables $a1\_1$ to $a4\_1$, $a6\_1$, $a8\_1$ to $a12\_1$ and $a15\_1$ to $a16\_1$ have been generated. For practical purposes the data set consists of interval-scaled variables (both predictor and dependents). However, it could as well have consisted of nominal/dichotomous variables.

Running latent regression resembles latent cluster. One only needs to select the regression model in the latent Gold Model menu (instead of cluster, as in the example at www.pearsoned.co.uk/schmidt seen earlier in this chapter). The only difference is that one must define a dependent variable and then use the remaining variables (or some of them) as predictors. Moreover, one needs to change the number of classes to two (or more). Like in latent cluster it is possible to save cluster membership in separate file. Table 15.10 shows an edited version of the output.

Since latent class algorithms proceed iteratively, one may obtain different results when running the analysis several times. Therefore, it is strongly recommended that the analyst performs several runs. In the present situation the authors made ten runs and obtained two different set of results. Since the R-square of the two runs was almost the same one run was selected that was the most appropriate.

Table 15.10 Output from latent regression

		Class1	Class2				
	R^2	0.43	0.63				
	Class size	0.52	0.48				
Predictors	Class1		Class2	Wald	p-value	Wald(=)	p-value
			Parameters				
a2_1 Could get service when I wanted	0.04		1.15	11.27	0.00	11.11	0.00
a3_1 Salespeople were polite	0.27		1.22	23.72	0.00	3.95	0.05
a4_1 Salespeople talking with each other	−0.16		0.04	9.42	0.01	2.00	0.16
a6_1 Difficult finding out who is customer/salespeople	0.12		−0.24	6.63	0.04	6.03	0.01
a8_1 Too few salespeople present	−0.08		0.14	4.33	0.11	3.06	0.08
a9_1 Salespeople busy rearranging products on shelves	0.07		−0.25	4.21	0.12	4.05	0.04
a10_1 Departments clean and tidy	0.04		0.41	6.94	0.03	3.33	0.07
a11_1 Allowed to inspect products before buying	0.01		−0.03	0.03	0.98	0.03	0.86
a12_1 One has to wait to get service	−0.34		0.47	40.60	0.00	9.55	0.00
a15_1 Feels like causing trouble	−0.09		0.29	2.12	0.35	1.81	0.18
a16_1 Salespeople smiling and helpful	0.25		0.18	12.30	0.00	0.05	0.82
a1_1 Dependent: overall service was satisfactory							

Scale: 1 = Strongly disagree to 5 = Strongly agree

The upper part of Table 15.10 shows that the R-square of the two classes is 0.43 and 0.63. Class 1 is a little bigger than class 2. Interestingly, an ordinary OLS regression *[SPSS: Analyze, Regression, Linear]* based on the same interval scaled data with variable a1_1 as dependent yield an R-Square of only 0.36. The reader should check this. Note that the class size here is the probability of each individual belonging to a specific class. The dependent measure was "Overall service was satisfactory" and the first listed variable "I could get service when I wanted". Notice that the parameter estimate assigned to class 2 is much bigger than that of class 1, implying a stronger influence of this predictor on the dependent. The "Wald" figure in conjunction with p-value show how significant the specific predictor is *across classes*. A small Wald chi-square value implies non-significance (probability values near 1.00). "Wald(=)" and the last column, also called p-value, indicates if the difference in parameter estimates between the two classes is significant.

Depending on the two p-values four situations are possible:

- Concerning the predictor *a2_1* the predictor on the whole is significant. Also, the difference between class 1 (0.04) and class 2 (1.15) is significant.
- *a16_1* is significant across classes (0.00) while the difference between classes (0.25 vs 0.18) is not significant (probability of 0.82). This being the case, predictions can only be made concerning the averaged parameter (not shown) whereas differences between classes are insignificant.
- The reverse situation appears with *a9_1*. Here, the overall estimate is not significant (0.12) while the difference between parameters is significant (0.04).
- With regard to predictor *a11_1*, neither of the two p-values are close to being significant.

Interpretation of a predictor estimate only appears valid for the first two situations. Of course, the first one is the preferred outcome.

Notice in the two classes that the average numeric parameter size of class 2 (0.402) is exactly three times that of class 1. Note also that the R-square connected to class 2 is much bigger (0.63) than that of class 1 (0.43). It appears that the class 2 regression coefficients are more successful predictors of the dependent than are those of class 1. Also, more than half of the predictors have opposite signs. Class 2 appears to reflect a more involved customer group or latent class than class 1.

A word of caution: Latent class models are based on an iterative algorithm called EM (Expectation-Maximization). Optimization procedures like EM tend to find different solutions. There is more about this in Appendix 15-B. When using the present dataset we find two clearly different solutions. Our discussion is based on a solution with approximately equal cluster sizes. It is essential that the analyst carries out the run (same dataset and settings) ten or so times. One should then select the solution according to stability of recovery, avoidance of very unequal cluster sizes, and size of R-square. Moreover, parameter estimates should make sense.

While most of the (significant) estimated parameters make sense, understanding the different signs (and the big positive value) presents problems concerning A_12 – "One has to wait to get service." Here, a negative sign concerning class 2 would be expected.

Usually, the analyst would like to assess whether the identified clusters vary along background criteria. This is easy to do since one only needs to inspect the appropriate cross tabs between the modal or cluster variable and the background variables. In this case, there is only limited background information (age, gender, income, etc.) and none of these variables turned out to be significant across cluster.

Cluster analysis of categorical variables using SPSS TwoStep cluster

SPSS does provide a method, TwoStep Cluster, for clustering of categorical variables (or a mix of categorical and continuous/interval/metric variables). However, the method seems to be less known in marketing research compared with *Latent Gold*. The reason for this may be that the underlying latent class algorithm of *Latent Gold* appears to be better documented. Notice also that the "classical" example, the audio equipment shopper data set, is frequently employed for illustrating the latent class model. See Dillon and Goldstein (1984), Dillon and Kumar (1994) and DeSarbo, Kamakura and Wedel (2004). Also, the parameters obtained from this data set fit nicely with the above publications using the same data.

Below is a brief explanation of how to run the SPSS method on the audio equipment shopper case (Table 15.8 and Appendix 15-B).

Since TwoStep Cluster apparently does not allow for a frequency or weight variable the data need to be structured differently in SPSS. See Table 15.11.

Table 15.11 Data format for running SPSS TwoStep Cluster

id	freq	cases	row	stchoice	catex	prishop	infseek	inftrans	2-Cluster
1	5	1	1	1	1	1	1	1	1
		2	2	1	1	1	1	1	1
		3	3	1	1	1	1	1	1
		4	4	1	1	1	1	1	1
		5	5	1	1	1	1	1	1
2	3	1	6	1	1	1	1	2	2
		2	7	1	1	1	1	2	2
		3	8	1	1	1	1	2	2
32	6	1	407	2	2	2	2	2	2
		2	408	2	2	2	2	2	2
		3	409	2	2	2	2	2	2
		4	410	2	2	2	2	2	2
		5	411	2	2	2	2	2	2
		6	412	2	2	2	2	2	2

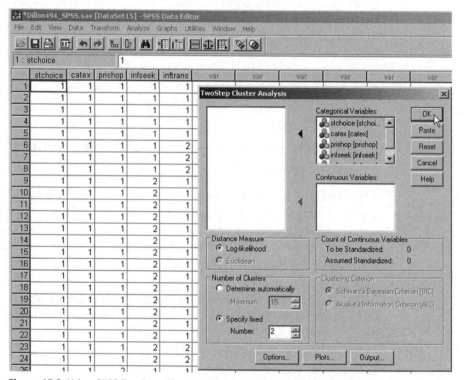

Figure 15.8 Using SPSS TwoStep Cluster analysis for categorical data

The file can be downloaded from www.pearsoned.co.uk/schmidt (Dillon494_SPSS.sav or Dillon494_SPSS.xls).

The file format of Table 15.11 can be compared with Table 15.8. In SPSS each observation or response needs to be listed separately. Note that the clustering is solely based on the five categorical variables "stchoice" through "inftrans". Thus the data used for clustering is a 5 variables by 412 observations matrix.

Figure 15.8 shows the main dialogue box in SPSS.

If one or more variables in SPSS TwoStep Cluster are categorical (in the present case all five variables are categorical) the "Distance Measure" used for clustering is set to "Loglikelihood" instead of "Euclidian." By default, SPSS automatically determines the "best" number of clusters. With regard to deciding upon the best clustering, there is a choice of two statistics, BIC and AIC (Bayes' and Akaike's information criteria – see Chapter 16 and Appendix 15-B).

In the present case, SPSS suggests five clusters. However, to compare the output with the clustering provided by *Latent Gold* (Appendix 15-B), request a two-cluster solution.

An interesting facility in TwoStep Cluster is its outlier detection procedure *[Options]*. In *[Output]* it is possible to save the cluster membership variable such that it appears at the far right of the working screen editor.

Table 15.12 compares the clustering of *Latent Gold* (see Appendix 15-B) with that of SPSS in Table 15.11 (far right column).

Table 15.12 Latent Gold and SPSS clusters

		SPSS TwoStep Cluster	
		Cluster 1	Cluster 2
Latent Gold	Cluster 1	21	203
	Cluster 2	147	41

Notice that in 85 percent of the cases, a respondent who was placed in cluster 1 according to *Latent Gold* was assigned to cluster 2 in SPSS and vice versa (recall that the cluster name or number is arbitrary).

Chapter 12 introduced a measure for assessing the stability ("recovery") of a cluster solution called the unadjusted Rand index. In the present case, the index is 0.74, which is not that bad at all (chance: 0.50). The reader should check whether the computation of the index is correct. The relevant formulae are in Chapter 12, Section 12.5.

Table 15.13 shows the cluster sizes across variables from the output of SPSS TwoStep. For illustrative purposes, the output is rearranged in order to make it comparable with the *Latent Gold* output on the website. By reversing the cluster numbers so that cluster 1 on the website becomes cluster 2 in Table 15.13, the respective cluster sizes roughly fit (SPSS output does not use the term probability). When looking at the within-variable cluster sizes of the variables (Catalogue experience and Information transmitting), the fit is almost complete.

Table 15.13 consists of ten two-by-two cross tabs (five within variable and five across class). Based on this it is possible to make twenty comparisons between the *Latent Gold* table on the website and Table 15.13 (with the order of clusters reversed). Of these, in only one case (Catalogue experience = Yes, across class) is the directional orientation – as indicated by the relation between bigger and smaller probability/size – reversed. Even in this case the divergence is marginal.

Table 15.13 SPSS cluster sizes across variables

(Probabilities)	Within variable		Across class	
	Cluster1	Cluster2	Cluster1	Cluster2
STCHOICE				
Dept	0.12	0.54	0.14	0.86
Spec	0.88	0.46	0.57	0.43
CATEX				
yes	0.82	0.64	0.47	0.53
no	0.18	0.36	0.26	0.74
PRISHOP				
yes	1.00	0.16	0.81	0.19
no	0.00	0.84	0.00	1.00
INFSEEK				
yes	0.68	0.33	0.59	0.41
no	0.32	0.67	0.25	0.75
INFTRANS				
yes	1.00	0.55	0.56	0.44
no	0.00	0.45	0.00	1.00
Cluster size	0.41	0.59	0.41	0.59

We should explain here the difference between the two clusters (Table 15.13). Cluster 1 tends to buy TV/radio equipment at a specialist store (0.88). Also, they have catalogue experience, visit several shops prior to the purchase, and transmit information. To sum up, they are highly involved customers. Within cluster 2, a small majority prefers the department store. They are less engaged in shopping and information seeking. However, two thirds of them have catalogue experience. When targeting a marketing strategy toward cluster 2, advertising in a catalogue might be successful, whereas a campaign that encourages consumers to compare prices might not be (i.e. to offer to refund the difference if a consumer manages to buy the brand cheaper from a competitor). Notice that 86 percent of those who purchased at a department store belong to cluster 2 (0.86 – in far right column).

15.4 Summary

CHAID (Chi-Squared Automatic Interaction Detection) is a tree-based classification procedure that splits the data into successive subsets of categories. The hierarchical CHAID categorization method may be an option in situations where neither *a priori* grouping methods such as discriminant analysis, nor *a posteriori* techniques such as cluster analysis are appropriate. CHAID aims at breaking down the data such that the difference in measures of the dependent variable among splits is maximized by way of the predictors. The dependent variable is either interval or nominal while the predictors are nominal/categorical-scaled.

The method works best in situations where there are:

- many observations (>1000)
- only few variables at hand (less than 20 or so)
- no strong assumptions about relationships

CHAID is an explanatory technique that is not suited for confirmatory analysis. The advantage of a CHAID model is in its intuitive merits. From Figure 15.5 it is clear that the output of the CHAID analysis based on SPSS Classification Trees is easy to understand.

The most important feature in CHAID output is the tree. The tree has a hierarchical structure and consists of several levels (branches) of nodes. Compared with nodes on the subsequent (lower) level, the (upper) node is called a **parent** node while lower-level nodes are **child** nodes. The main weakness of the method is that it is difficult to generalize results obtained via CHAID from one empirical sample to others. It can be shown that the results of a CHAID analysis are highly sensitive to the way a metric variable is categorized. Several providers supply software based on CHAID and related algorithms.

Sometimes a researcher wants to run a cluster analysis on variables that are not interval-scaled but rather dichotomous/categorical-scaled. In such situations ordinary clustering methods such as hierarchical cluster analysis or k-means cluster analysis are not appropriate since they need the input variables to be least interval-scaled. Fortunately, methods that allow for dichotomous/categorical input variables are available. One such method is called latent class analysis. In marketing, latent models are primarily used for clustering data, i.e. survey responses that are dichotomous/categorical-scaled (yes/no questions).

A latent class model treats the manifest variables as imperfect indicators or underlying traits, which are themselves unobservable. With regard to making a distinction between manifest, observable variables and latent, unobservable constructs, a latent class model resembles a structural equation model (to be covered in Chapter 16). The basic motivation behind latent class analysis is the belief that the observed association between two or more manifest categorical variables is due to the mixing of heterogeneous groups. In this sense, latent class analysis can be viewed as a ***data unmixing procedure***. According to ordinary cluster analyses (hierarchical and k-means clustering) a subject is assigned to either one cluster or another cluster. In latent class analysis each subject is assigned a certain probability concerning each cluster. Finally, the subject is categorized into the cluster with the highest probability. From a model perspective, latent class clustering represents an example of an **overlapping cluster analysis**. However, it is normally treated as a non-overlapping technique because exclusive approaches are much easier to understand and communicate. A potential problem with LC cluster analysis is that it does not work properly when the number of variables exceeds a certain level (twenty or so).

SPSS supplies a two-step cluster analysis for clustering categorical data *[Analyze, Classify, TwoStep Cluster]*. The method is also suitable for hybrid data sets (situations where some variables are interval-scaled while others are nominally-scaled).

Questions

1. Provided that you have access to SPSS Classification Trees (or comparable software for solving CHAID problems); download the file Satisfaction_Top.sav from www.pearsoned.co.uk/schmidt. The file has 1,294 observations. Split the file into two sub-samples, each having 647 observations: proceed exactly as in Figures 15.1 to 15.5. Run an analysis based on each of the two samples. Compare the results and then compare both of the runs with Figure 15.5. Discuss similarities and differences.

2. Provided that you have access to *Latent Gold*, SPSS TwoStep Cluster, or comparable software for solving latent class type problems, download the file Export_Manager_Survey_Latent.sav (the Excel version of the file has the extension *.xls*) from www.pearsoned.co.uk/schmidt. This file is a modification of the Appendix A file Export_Manager_Survey.sav. The new version of the file only contains eleven variables. Moreover, missing values have been exchanged with the series mean and thereafter several variables like number of employees and company revenue have been categorized. Table 15.14 shows the variables and labels of the actual file. More information on the export manager survey is found in the word document Export_Manager_Survey.doc on the book's website.

Table 15.14 Export manager survey – modified version for latent class analysis

Variable	Explanation	Code/level	
founded	Year of foundation	1	Before 1930
		2	1930–1960
		3	After 1960
employed	Number of employees	1	< 25
		2	25–100
		3	>100
sales02	Company revenue 2002 (€m)	1	<€5 million
		2	€5–€20 million
		3	>€20 million
act1	Export through middlemen	1 = Yes, 2 = No	
act2	Direct export (incl. agents)	1 = Yes, 2 = No	
act3	Own sales subsidiaries	1 = Yes, 2 = No	
act4	Foreign production	1 = Yes, 2 = No	
act5	Licence agreements	1 = Yes, 2 = No	
newprod	Has company developed new products (last two years)?	1 = Yes, 2 = No	
future	How many customer groups abroad will exist in five years?	1 = More, 2 = Same amount (less)	
orgforms	Organizational characteristic of company	1 = Functional, 2 = Division/Matrix	

(a) Run a latent class cluster analysis (i.e. SPSS TwoStep Cluster) on the file Export_Manager_Survey_Latent.sav.

(b) How many clusters do you recommend to use? Provide a brief description (profiling) of each cluster.

(c) Try to run the analysis based on nine of the eleven variables (exclude "employed" and "sales02"). Compare the results based on your selection of the number of clusters from above. Do the two runs look alike? If there are differences, describe them.

(d) You are an employee at the exporting association's office. The association is about to launch a promotional campaign aimed at all the country's export managers. You have access to an address file containing basic information of the manager's company (size, revenue, etc.). Could the result of the above cluster analysis be used for targeting the promotional material? If so, how?

References

Assael, H. (1970) "Segmenting markets by group purchasing behaviour: an application of the AID technique." *Journal of Marketing Research*. Vol. VII (May). 153–158.

Baron, S. and Phillips, D. (1994) "Attitude survey data reduction using CHAID: an example in shopping centre market research." In Hooley, G. J. and Hussey, M. K. *Quantitative Methods in Marketing*. Academic Press, London. 75–88.

Bartholomew, D. J. and Knott, M. (1999) *Latent Variable Models and Factor Analysis*. Edward Arnold, New York.

Böckenholt, U. (2002) "Comparison and choice: analyzing discrete preference data by latent class scaling models." In Hagenaars, J. A. and McCutcheon, A. L. (eds) *Applied Latent Class Analysis*. Cambridge University Press, Cambridge. 183–182.

Chaturvedi, A. and Green, P. E. (1995) "Software Review: SPSS for Windows, CHAID 6.0." *Journal of Marketing Research*. XXXII (May). 245–254.

Collins, L. M. and Flaherty, B. P. (2002) "Latent class models for longitudinal data." In Hagenaars, J. A. and McCutcheon, A. L. (eds) *Applied Latent Class Analysis*. Cambridge University Press, Cambridge. 287–303.

Currim, I. S., Meyer, R. J. and Le, N. T. (1988) "Disaggregate tree-structured modelling of consumer choice data." *Journal of Marketing Research*. Vol. XXV (August). 253–265.

Dash, J. F., Schiffman, L. G. and Berenson, C. (1976) "Information search and store choice." *Journal of Advertising Research*. Vol. 16, no. 3. 35–40.

DeSarbo, W. S. and Crohn, W. L. (1988) "A maximum likelihood methodology for clusterwise linear regression." *Journal of Classification*. Vol. 5. 249–282.

DeSarbo, W. S., Kamakura, A. W. and Wedel, M. (2004) "Applications of multivariate latent variable models in marketing." In Wind, Y. and Green, P. E. (eds) *Marketing Research and Modeling: Progress and prospects – A Tribute to Paul E. Green*. Kluwer, Dordrecht. 43–68.

DeSarbo, W. S., Manrai, A. K. and Manrai, L. A. (1994) "Latent class multidimensional scaling: a review of recent development in the marketing and psychometrika literature." In Bagozzi, R. P. (ed.) *Advanced Methods of Marketing Research*. Blackwell, Cambridge, MA. 190–222.

DeSarbo, W. S., Wedel, M., Vriens, M. and Ramaswamy, V. (1992) "Latent class metric conjoint analysis." *Marketing Letters*. Vol. 3, no. 3. 273–288.

Dillon, R. W. and Goldstein, M. (1984) *Multivariate Analysis: Methods and Applications*. John Wiley, New York. 490.

Dillon, W. R. and Kumar, A. (1994) "Latent structure and other mixture models in marketing: An integrative survey and overview." In Bagozzi, R. P. (ed.) *Advanced Methods of Marketing Research*. Blackwell, Cambridge, MA. 295–351.

Dillon, W. R. and Mulani, N. (1989) "LADI – a latent discriminant model for analyzing marketing research data." *Journal of Marketing Research*. Vol. 26. 15–29.

Doyle, P. and Fenwick, I. (1975) "The pitfalls of AID analysis." *Journal of Marketing Research*. Vol. XII (November). 408–413.

Goodman, L. A. (1974) "Exploratory latent structure analysis using both identifiable and unidentifiable models." *Biometrika*. Vol. 61. 215–231.

Goodman, L. A. (1979) "On the estimation of parameters in latent structure analysis." *Psychometrika*. Vol. 44, no. 1 (March). 123–128.

Green, P. E. (1978a) "An AID/Logit procedure for analyzing large multiway contingency tables." *Journal of Marketing Research*. Vol. XV (February). 132–136.

Green, P. E. (1978b) *Analyzing Multivariate Data*. Dryden Press, Hinsdale, Ill.

Green, P. E., Carmone, F. J. and Wachpress, D. P. (1976) "Consumer segmentation via latent class analysis." *Journal of Consumer Research*. Vol. 3. 170–174.

Hagenaars, J. A. (2002) "Directed loglinear modeling with latent variables: causal models for categorical data with non-systematic and systematic errors." In Hagenaars, J. A. and McCutcheon, A. L. (eds) *Applied Latent Class Analysis*, Cambridge University Press, Cambridge. 234–286.

Hagenaars, J. A. and McCutcheon, A. L. (eds) (2002) *Applied Latent Class Analysis*. Cambridge University Press, Cambridge. 234–286.

Hair, J. F., Anderson, R. E., Tatham, R. L. and Black, W. C. (1998) *Multivariate Data Analysis*. Prentice-Hall, Upper Saddle River, N.J.

Holmes, C. (1980) "AID comes to the aid of marketing management." *European Journal of Marketing*. Vol. 14, no. 7. 409–413.

Kamakura, W. A. (1991) "Estimating flexible distributions of ideal points with external analysis of preference." *Psychometrika*, Vol. 56. 419–448.

Kass, G. (1980) "An exploratory technique for investigating large quantities of categorical data." *Applied Statistics*. Vol. 29, no. 2. 119–127.

Langeheine, R. and van der Pol, F. (2002) "Latent Markov chains". In Hagenaars, J. A. and McCutcheon, A. L. (eds) *Applied Latent Class Analysis*. Cambridge University Press, Cambridge. 304–343.

Lattin, J., Carroll, D. C. and Green, P. E. (2003) *Analyzing Multivariate Data*. Pacific Grove, CAL: Thomson Learning.

Lazarsfeld, P. F. and Henry, N. W. (1968) *Latent Structure Analysis*. Houghton Mifflin, Boston.

Loehlin, J. C. (1988) *Latent Variable Models: An introduction to factor, path and structural analysis*. Lawrence Erlbaum, Mahwah, NJ.

McCutcheon, A. L. (1987) *Latent Class Analysis*. Sage, Beverly Hills, CA.

MacLacklan, D. L. and Johansson, J. K. (1981) "Market segmentation with multivariate AID." *Journal of Marketing*. Vol. 45 (Winter). 74–85.

Magidson, J. (1982) "Some pitfalls in causal analysis of categorical data." *Journal of Marketing Research*. Vol. XIX (November). 461–471.

Magidson, J. (1992) "Chi-squared analysis of a scalable dependent variable." *Proceedings of the 1992 Annual Meeting of the American Statistical Association*, section on statistical education. Additional information on SI CHAID is available at www.statisticalin novations.com.

Magidson, J. (1994) "The CHAID approach to segmentation modelling: chi-squared automated interaction detection." In Bagozzi, R. P., *Advanced Methods of Marketing Research*. Blackwell, Cambridge, MA. 118–59.

Martin, C. R. and Wright, R. L. (1974) "Profit-oriented data analysis for market segmentation: an alternative to AID." *Journal of Marketing Research*. Vol. XI (August). 237–242.

Morgan, J. N. and Sonquist, J. A. (1963) "Problems in the analysis of survey data and a proposal." *Journal of the American Statistical Association*. Vol. 58, no. 302 (June). 415–434.

Morgan, J. N. and Messenger, R. C. (1973) *THAID A Sequential Analysis Program for the Analysis of Complex Contingency Data in Survey Research*. University of Michigan Press, Ann Arbor, MI.

SPSS Answer Tree 3.0, User's Guide (2001) SPSS, Chicago.

van der Heijden, P. G. M., van der Ark, A. and Mooijaart, A. (2002) "Some examples of latent budget analysis and its extensions." In Hagenaars, J. A. and McCutcheon, A. L. (eds) *Applied Latent Class Analysis*. Cambridge University Press, Cambridge. 307–336.

Vriens, M., Oppewal, H. and Wedel, M. (1998) "Rating-based versus choice-based latent class conjoint models – an Empirical comparison." *Journal of the Marketing Research Society*. Vol. 40, no. 3. 237–248.

Wedel, M. and DeSarbo, W. S. (1994) "A review of recent developments in latent class regression models." In Bagozzi, R. P. (ed.) *Advanced Methods of Marketing Research*. Blackwell, Cambridge, MA. 352–388.

Wedel, M. and DeSarbo, W. S. (1996) "An exponential family multidimensional scaling mixture methodology." *Journal of Business and Economic Statistics*, Vol. 14. 447–59.

Wedel, M. and Kamakura, W. A. (2001) *Market Segmentation, Methodological and Conceptual Foundation*. Kluwer, Dordrecht.

Wind, Y. and Green, P. (eds) (2004) *Market Research and Modeling: Progress and Prospects – A Tribute to Paul Green*, Dordrecht: Kluwer.

Winship, C., Mare, R. D. and Warren, J. R. (2002) "Latent class models for contingency tables with missing data." In Hagenaars, J. A. and McCutcheon, A. L. (eds) *Applied Latent Class Analysis*. Cambridge University Press, Cambridge. 408–432.

16 Several dependent variables: canonical correlation and structural equation modelling

Learning objectives

After studying this chapter you should be able to:

- Explain (from a modelling and scaling perspective) the difference between multiple regression, multivariate analysis of variance and canonical correlation analysis.
- Clarify in which marketing situations a canonical analysis may be appropriate.
- Provide an interpretation of the canonical correlation coefficient.
- Give an overview of output statistics such as canonical loading, canonical cross loading, canonical pair, canonical components and the redundancy index.
- Explain the similarities and differences between canonical analysis and structural equation modelling.
- Describe the difference between exploratory factor analysis and confirmatory factor analysis.
- Show a basic understanding of the ingredients of a causal model.
- Explain what endogenous and exogenous constructs are.
- Describe the difference between latent/hidden/unobservable constructs and manifest/indicators/manifest variables.
- Explain overall/absolute fit, incremental fit, and parsimonious fit.
- Discuss the purpose of re-specifying a model and of testing competing models.
- Briefly explain the meaning of terms like recursivity, model misspecification, over- and under-identification of a model, offending estimates and measurement error.
- Determine which theoretical and empirical conditions must be present for building and testing an empirical SEM model in a marketing environment.

16.1 Canonical correlation

The techniques that have so far been covered in this book all belong to one of the following categories:

- One dependent and one predictor variable (simple ANOVA).
- One dependent and several predictors (multiple regression).
- No assumptions about dependence (factor and cluster analysis).

The task of selecting an appropriate method in Chapters 9–10 focused on the scaling of the dependent and predictor variables (Table 10.1).

- For instance, if the dependent variable is metric (e.g. sales in euros or market share) but the predictor is nominal scaled (e.g. different brands) then ANOVA is the preferred option. In cases where the predictor variable is also metric-scaled (e.g. age or household income) simple regression is the proper technique.
- If both the dependent and the set of predictors are metric-scaled, then multiple regression OLS can be used. If the data constitute a time series, different regression models such as generalized least squares are probably better suited than OLS. If the dependent is nominal-scaled, discriminant analysis is an appropriate method. If the predictors are dummy-scaled or if the assumptions of normality, homogeneity or equality of covariance matrices are not fulfilled, the knowledgeable researcher will most likely employ logistic regression instead.
- To classify variables, factor analysis is normally chosen, while cluster analysis is preferred when classifying observations.

If more than one dependent variable is involved, only one of the techniques mentioned so far, MANOVA in Chapter 9, is able to handle this situation. However, this method assumes predictors to be nominal-scaled, an assumption that limits the applicability of the technique. Moreover, MANOVA works best in situations where only few predictors are involved and where the environment of the study is controllable, as is the case in an experimental design. Also, significance tests become complex in MANOVA.

Canonical correlation can handle situations where several metric predictors *and* dependent variables are involved. The conceptual approach can be traced back to the statistician and economist Harold Hotelling (Hotelling, 1936).

First, we will show how the technique works using an example. This is followed by a large-scale analysis in *SPSS*. A technical introduction is provided in Appendix 16-A (see www.pearsoned.co.uk/schmidt).

Assume that a small sample of respondents has been exposed to four items scaled one to nine about a product. The items deal with repurchase intention, overall satisfaction, product quality and brand image (a high score implies high repurchase intention, satisfaction, etc.). The management is interested in a simultaneous assessment of how repurchase intention and overall satisfaction is influenced by product quality and brand image. The results of the analysis appear in columns I–IV of Table 16.1 (columns V–VIII will be discussed below and in some more detail in Appendix 16-A).

Table 16.1 Several predictors and dependents

	I	II	III	IV	V	VI	VII	VIII
Respondent	Y1	Y2	X1	X2	T1	T2	U1	U2
1	1	3	2	4	−1.76	−0.97	−1.58	−0.88
2	3	2	4	3	−1.58	0.35	−1.63	0.58
3	4	6	5	7	−0.37	−0.99	0.01	−0.93
4	5	3	6	4	−0.90	0.79	−0.95	1.04
5	7	5	8	6	0.03	0.77	0.11	1.01
6	6	8	7	9	0.56	−1.00	1.06	−0.96
7	9	7	6	8	0.96	0.76	0.53	−0.95
8	8	9	9	7	1.24	−0.57	0.64	0.99
9	5	7	3	6	0.10	−1.00	−0.68	−1.39
10	9	4	9	6	0.21	2.10	0.27	1.48
11	7	6	8	8	0.28	0.33	0.85	0.01
12	8	9	9	9	1.24	−0.57	1.37	−0.01

Y1 = Repurchase intention
Y2 = Overall satisfaction
X1 = Perceived product quality
X2 = Perception of brand image
Ratings: 1 = very low to 9 = very high

In terms of the management's preferred approach the appropriate model is:

$(Y1, Y2) = f(X1 + X2)$

or more formally:

$$\sum_1^p Y_i = f\left(\sum_1^q X_i\right)$$

Since there is, at present, no analytical tool for this type of model, two multiple regressions could be tried.

$Y1 = f(X1 + X2)$ and $Y2 = f(X1 + X2)$

But isolated regressions cannot show how the predictors affect the dependents *in unison*. While the numerical example is based on fictive data, situations may appear in commercial settings where it is of interest to evaluate how predictors alter several dependents at the same time.

Table 16.2 shows some bivariate correlations of the data from Table 16.1. For instance, the correlation between variables *Y1* and *Y2* is 0.57 while the correlation between *X1* and *X2* is 0.58. If the dependents (*Y1*, *Y2*) are regarded as set 1 and the predictors (*X1*, *X2*) as set 2, the *simple within-set correlations* are 0.57 and 0.58 respectively. According to the same rationale, there are four *simple across-set correlations* Y1/X1 = 0.84, Y1/X2=0.65, Y2/X1=0.47 and Y2/X2=0.88.

Table 16.2 Some correlations based on Table 16.1

			X1	X2
Y1, Y2	0.57	Y1	0.84	0.65
X1, X2	0.58	Y2	0.47	0.88
			U1	U2
T1, T2	0.00	T1	0.91	0.00
U1, U2	0.00	T2	0.00	0.70
			Canonical pair	
			T1/U1	T2/U2
Eigenvalue			0.83	0.50
Variance accounted for by component			0.62	0.38

Next, examine the correlations in the lower part of Table 16.2. They are correlations between the columns V through VIII in Table 16.1. These columns of data have been computed by means of a process that resembles the way factor score columns are calculated in factor analysis (Table 11.10, columns VII–IX), for further details, see the Eckhart–Young process in Appendix 11-A. So, variables T1 and T2 have been computed based on *Y1* and *Y2* by way of a transformation procedure. Appendix 16-A provides a technical discussion of the involved computational process.

As was the case with the variables above, the four variables are regarded as belonging to two different sets: *T1/T2* is treated as set 1 and *U1/U2* as set 2. Interestingly, the variables within a set (*T1/T2* respectively *U1/U2*) are uncorrelated. Moreover, it turns out that the off-diagonal entries of the across-set correlation matrix (*T1/U2* and *T2/U1*) are also uncorrelated. An additional issue: while the correlation *Y1/X1* (0.84) is lower than *Y2/X2* (0.88), *T1/U1* (0.91) is higher than *T2/U2* (0.70).[1] *T1/U1* is called the **first canonical function** or the **first pair of linear composites** since it has the highest correlation (0.91), while *T2/U2* is called the **second canonical function** or **linear composite set**. *T1* (like *T2*, *U1* and *U2*) is called a **canonical variate**, **component** or **linear composite**.

Computationally, a canonical function resembles a discriminant function in discriminant analysis. The output from discriminant analysis software usually contains canonical statistics either as part of the default output or as options. Recall that canonical discriminant function coefficients appeared in Table 10.4. SAS has a program that is a mixture of discriminant and canonical analysis, Proc Candisc. Also, some textbooks choose to discuss both techniques within the context of the same chapter (Green, Tull and Albaum, 1988).

Generally, in a canonical analysis one has *k* dependents and *m* predictors. Therefore it is possible to extract *min (k, m)* canonical functions. So, with three dependents and five predictors, three canonical functions can be extracted. Each canonical function has two canonical components, one for the set of dependent variables and another for the set of predictor variables.

Since there is no way to measure how *X1* and *X2 simultaneously* affect *Y1* and *Y2*, statistical techniques (Appendix 16-A) are used to transform the data matrix of columns I–IV in Table 16.1 to columns V–VIII. The latter four columns contain the same information in terms of variance as the former four. But in columns V–VIII the data have been optimally rescaled, or rather converted with respect to some statistical properties. The crux of canonical analysis now is that, say $T1$, is regarded as an optimized single indicator of ($Y1$, $Y2$). If $T1$ correlates perfectly with both $Y1$ and $Y2$ (implying that $Y1$ and $Y2$ are themselves perfectly correlated) then $T1 = f(X1, X2)$ would be a different but equivalent expression of ($Y1$, $Y2$) = $f(X1, X2)$. In reality, $T1$ never correlates perfectly with $Y1$ and $Y2$ and therefore some ($Y1$, $Y2$) correlation will be "reserved" for $T2$ (or $T3$, etc.).

Note that by using the same rationale $U1$ could be treated as an optimized indicator of $X1$ and $X2$ and the process reversed. However, since researchers are interested in how dependents are caused by predictors and not vice versa the latter approach, while equally valid, is of less practical interest.

Figure 16.1 displays the pattern of simple correlations mentioned earlier. Since all variables correlate, most of them highly, it is impossible to identify a clear pattern of causal relations between variables using simple or multiple regressions.

The purpose of canonical correlation is to convert columns containing variables to columns containing *canonical component scores*. Our numerical example has four variables ($Y1$, $Y2$, $X1$, $X2$). This implies six simple correlations (see panels (a)–(f) of Figure 16.1). By way of canonical correlation one computes a compatible set of canonical components ($T1$, $T2$, $U1$, $U2$). But out of these six correlations, four are 0.00 (panels (i)–(l)). Moreover, the non-zero correlations – panels (g) and (h) – have been transformed such that the shared variance of the first dependent and predictor component ($T1/U1$) is maximized. Thereafter the shared variance of the second dependent and predictor component ($T2/U2$) is maximized and so on.

The interpretation of canonical correlation centres on establishing a link between the canonical component(s) $T1$ (and $T2$) and:

- the predictor variables $X1$, $X2$;
- the dependent variables $Y1$, $Y2$.

When interpreting a factor analysis, high loadings (correlations) are sought between a variable and a factor and these variables are used for naming the factor. This process was explained in Chapter 11. Likewise, high loadings between a variable and a canonical component can help in profiling or "naming" the component.

However, one should be careful when interpreting canonical loadings because loadings appear to be both sample-specific and sensitive to multi-collinearity in the underlying data matrix (Lambert and Durand, 1975). Also, it may happen that several variables that load highly on a specific component do not appear to have anything in common. If, say, variables such as price and brand image load highly on a component, this only indicates that both correlate with the component and so affect it. It does not necessarily point towards the existence of a "price/image" component.

From Chapter 11, one of the core output figures in singular value decomposition is the eigenvalue belonging to a component or dimension. Recall that the size of the eigenvalue indicates how much of the variance in the variables matrix can be accounted for by the specific factor. In the present example the eigenvalues turn out to be 0.83 and 0.50 (Table 16.2).

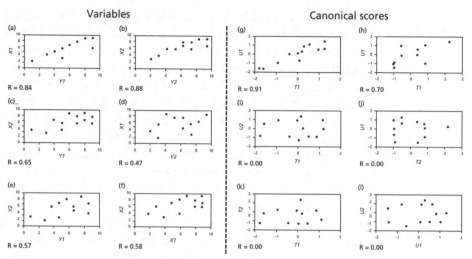

Figure 16.1 Correlation of variables and canonical scores

Now look at Table 16.1. According to canonical analysis theory, *T1* and *T2* reflect different ways of "scaling" the information of *Y1* and *Y2*, while *U1* and *U2* represent different ways of expressing *X1* and *X2*.

If the model comprises several continuous predictor *and* dependent variables it makes no sense to look at the variables individually, as in the upper part of Table 16.2. Instead, look for a pair of "super-dimensions" or "uni-factors." In this case it would be the pair *T1/U1* – the **first canonical function** or **pair of linear composites**. *T1/U1* work as a "common denominator" for the two dependents and two predictors. In the present case the first canonical function accounts for 0.83/(0.83+0.50) or 62 percent of the shared variance of dependent *T1* and predictor *U1*.

In factor analysis one can theoretically extract as many factors as there are variables. According to canonical analysis theory, as noted, it is possible to establish a number of canonical functions that equal the minimum of the number of dependents and predictors.

In the example there are two dependents and two predictors and so two canonical functions. As can be seen in Table 16.2, the second function only accounts for 38 percent of *T2/U2*'s shared variance. So, perhaps it makes sense to concentrate on interpreting the first canonical function.

Dropping a canonical function is analogous to skipping factors in factor analysis with an eigenvalue less than 1.00 or discarding factors that fall below the elbow-kink in the scree test (Figure 11.12). Dropping components of a canonical function (e.g. *T2/U2*) in canonical analysis seems justified in situations where the first canonical function (*T1/U1*) provides a proper explanation of the shared variance, which may well be the case.

So far, this discussion of canonical correlation has been based on intuitive reasoning founded on simple regression and correlation theory, combined with some analogies to factor analysis. Some terms have been introduced but without much explanation. Now, some more technical terms are necessary. It is recommended that the technically interested reader study Appendix 16-A (see www.pearsoned.co.uk/schmidt).

First, look at Figure 16.2. Panel (a) is a repetition of Table 16.1. However, due to pedagogical considerations some expositions have been provided:

Panel (a)

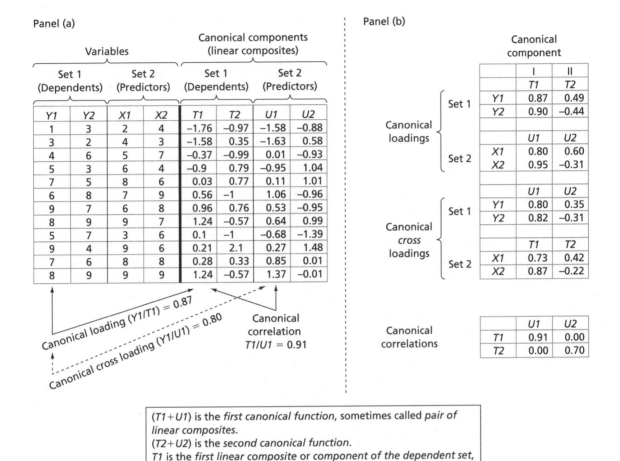

Variables				Canonical components (linear composites)			
Set 1 (Dependents)		Set 2 (Predictors)		Set 1 (Dependents)		Set 2 (Predictors)	
Y1	Y2	X1	X2	T1	T2	U1	U2
1	3	2	4	−1.76	−0.97	−1.58	−0.88
3	2	4	3	−1.58	0.35	−1.63	0.58
4	6	5	7	−0.37	−0.99	0.01	−0.93
5	3	6	4	−0.9	0.79	−0.95	1.04
7	5	8	6	0.03	0.77	0.11	1.01
6	8	7	9	0.56	−1	1.06	−0.96
9	7	6	8	0.96	0.76	0.53	−0.95
8	9	9	7	1.24	−0.57	0.64	0.99
5	7	3	6	0.1	−1	−0.68	−1.39
9	4	9	6	0.21	2.1	0.27	1.48
7	6	8	8	0.28	0.33	0.85	0.01
8	9	9	9	1.24	−0.57	1.37	−0.01

Canonical loading (Y1/T1) = 0.87

Canonical cross loading (Y1/U1) = 0.80

Canonical correlation T1/U1 = 0.91

Panel (b)

Canonical component

Canonical loadings

Set 1		I T1	II T2
	Y1	0.87	0.49
	Y2	0.90	−0.44

Set 2		U1	U2
	X1	0.80	0.60
	X2	0.95	−0.31

Canonical cross loadings

Set 1		U1	U2
	Y1	0.80	0.35
	Y2	0.82	−0.31

Set 2		T1	T2
	X1	0.73	0.42
	X2	0.87	−0.22

Canonical correlations

	U1	U2
T1	0.91	0.00
T2	0.00	0.70

(T1+U1) is the *first canonical function*, sometimes called *pair of linear composites*.
(T2+U2) is the *second canonical function*.
T1 is the *first linear composite* or *component of the dependent set*,
U2 is the second component of the predictor set and so on.
Note: T1 is uncorrelated with T2, as is U1 with U2

Figure 16.2 Terms and output figures in canonical correlation

- The eight columns of data are split into two "super-categories": variables and canonical components. Each of these categories is split into dependents (set 1) and predictors (set 2). A correlation of columns (variables/components) across super-categories but within the same set is called **structure correlation** or **canonical loading**. For instance, correlations between *Y1/T1* and *X2/U1* are canonical loadings. While *Y1* and *T1* both belong to set 1, *X2* and *U1* are both set 2 members.

- A correlation of columns (variables/components) across super-categories *and* across sets is called a **canonical cross loading**. So, correlations *Y1/U1* and *X2/T1* are examples of canonical cross loadings.

- A correlation between canonical components is called **canonical correlation**. By definition, within set correlations of canonical components are 0.00. So, *T1/T2* and *U1/U2* are uncorrelated. Moreover, the first linear composite in the first set is uncorrelated with the second linear composite in the second set and vice versa. Therefore, correlations *U1/T2* and *T1/U2* are 0.00.

- A figure of some interest is the **canonical coefficient**. Appendix 16-A shows how this is computed. Basically, it needs to be calculated before the above figures can be computed.

■ Canonical correlation *solely* aims at maximizing the shared variance or correlation of linear composites within a set. For instance, 0.91 in Table 16.2 or Figure 16.2 is simply a bivariate correlation between *T1* and *U1*. Unfortunately, it is possible to have high canonical correlations while canonical loadings between components and variables are small, implying that the canonical component – say *T1* – accounts for very little variance in the dependent set (*Y1*, *Y2*). To correct for this problem, the analyst will be interested in assessing how much variance in one set of variables (e.g. *Y1*, *Y2*) can be explained by variation in a set of canonical components (e.g. *T1* or *T2*). Such a case is somewhat analogous to the concept of variance explained in multiple regression. In regression, one calculates how big a proportion of the variation in the dependent variable can be explained by the predictors. In canonical regression **the index of redundancy**, also known as Stewart and Love's redundancy measure fulfils this need (Stewart and Love, 1968). It is possible to compute a redundancy index for each dependent and independent canonical component for each function. Only if both the canonical correlation $R_{T1,U1}$ and the redundancy index $R_{U1,(X1+X2)}$ are high for a canonical function, can the model be regarded as successful. Appendix 16-A at www.pearsoned.co.uk/schmidt shows how the index of redundancy is computed.

■ Several statistical figures have been developed for testing the significance of canonical functions. They include Bartlett's chi-square approximation, Wilks' lambda, Rao's F-test, Pillai's trace, the Hotelling–Lawley trace, and Roy's greatest root. The last five are F-tests. The first two appear as part of SPSS output. Appendix 16-A provides details on how they are computed. With regard to the other tests, the reader can consult advanced texts such as Levine (1977) and Thompson (1984).

Next, turn to Figure 16.2.

■ In panel (b) note that canonical component loadings (correlations) of all four sets are higher in column I than in II: 0.87 is higher than 0.49; 0.90 is higher than −0.44 and so on. Furthermore, the canonical correlation of the first set of linear composites (0.91) is higher than the second (0.70).

■ In essence, panel (b) displays the output of a kind of simultaneous principal component analysis of dependents (set 1: *Y1* and *Y2*) and of predictors (set 2: *X1* and *X2*). The canonical analysis transforms the variables into corresponding output columns of *T1* and *T2*, and *U1* and *U2*, respectively, last four columns in panel (a).

■ The difference between variables and canonical components is this: while variables are regarded as "equally important" with regard to explaining variance, canonical columns are not. Most correlations among canonical components are 0.00: *T1/T2*, *U1/U2*, *T1/U2* and *T2/U1*. Only *T1/U1* and *T2/U2* contain non-zero correlations. *T1/U1*, the first canonical function or set of axes, always has a higher canonical correlation (is more important, accounts for more of the shared variance between *T1* and *U1*) than the second one, which is more important than the third and so on.

■ *T1* (or *T2*) may be regarded as an effort at describing the two dependents *Y1* and *Y2* by way of one dimension. Likewise, *U1* and *U2* represent *X1* and *X2*.

- *Y1*, *Y2*, *X1* and *X2* consequently correlate higher with column I (function 1) than with column II (function 2). See panel (b) of Figure 16.2. Concerning column II, correlations on average are much lower; and while *Y1* and *X1* correlate positively, variables *Y2* and *X2* correlate negatively with column II.
- Both dimensions of the first canonical function (*T1* and *U1*) correlate a little higher with overall satisfaction (*Y2*) and brand image (*X2*) than they do with purchase intensity (*Y1*) and product quality (*X1*).
- Brand image, *X2*, has a higher canonical loading (0.87) on *T1* than product quality, *X1* (0.73).
- The correlation (loading) of both dependents with the first canonical component is high, 0.87 and 0.90, respectively, so *Y1* and *Y2* are fairly represented by *T1*. Likewise, *X1* and *X2* appear to be fairly well represented by *U1*, because their correlation with *U1* is 0.80 and 0.95.
- The second canonical function is statistically significant (not shown) but less important than the first. As noted, it correlates positively with *Y1* and *X1* but negatively with *Y2* and *X2*.

An interpretation of the statistical figures in canonical analysis appears straightforward for someone who is familiar with multiple regression and factor analysis. However, statistical analysis is one issue, managerial applicability of the results is another. Whereas publications do a good job when explaining the statistical figures in canonical analysis, good applications of the technique to marketing problems appear to be rare. Moreover, some articles trying to imply from canonical output to marketing strategy either have performed over-interpretations or have come up with recommendations based on erroneous interpretations.[2]

So, how can the figures of panel (b) be related to a marketing environment?

For a moment, ignore the fact that the data set is artificial. Also, assume that all observed differences are statistically significant. Finally, only the first canonical function (*T1/U1*) will be examined.

- *Y2* (Overall satisfaction) is the most important or most representative of the two dependents: its loading on *T1* is 0.90, which is higher than the comparable loading of *Y1* (0.87).
- *X2* (Brand image) is the most important of the predictors. Its loading on *U1* is 0.95, which is higher that the comparable loading of *X1* (0.80).
- *X2* (Brand image) is also better at explaining variance of the dependent canonical component: it has a higher loading on *T1* (0.87) than has *X1* (0.73).
- Although it represents a reversion of causality, *Y2* is better at accounting for shared variance with the predictor canonical component, *U1*, than is *Y1*: 0.82 is higher than 0.80.

Assume that a company is interested in finding a subset of the (*X1*, *X2*) predictors that is to be used for analysis of other products or for future studies. In such a case, *X2* (Perception of brand image) would probably be preferred to *X1* (Perception of product quality). Likewise, to focus on a subset of (*Y1*, *Y2*) dependents, *Y2* (Overall satisfaction) would probably be preferred to *Y1* (Repurchase intention).

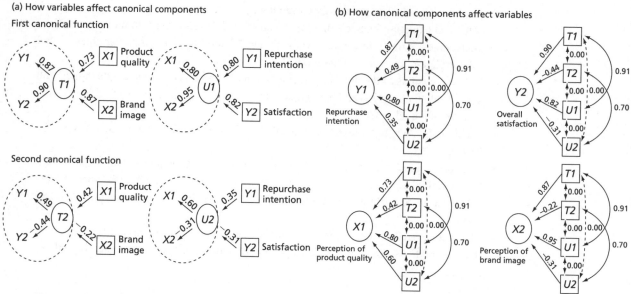

Figure 16.3 Relation between variables and canonical components

Figure 16.3 shows an attempt to model patterns of relationship between variables and components. All figures appear in panel (b) of Figure 16.2. The relationship patterns depicted in Figure 16.3 to some degree resemble the modelling structure of **structural equation modelling** or **LISREL**, which is covered in section 16.2. Therefore and because the above example is small and artificial, Figure 16.3 will not be discussed here. Also, most relations have already been discussed in connection with Figure 16.2.

In the present example the loadings of the second canonical function are clearly lower than those of the first function (compare the upper and the lower part of panel (a) in Figure 16.3). However, this need not be the case. The second function may have loadings of almost the same size than the first function. In such a case, one probably cannot justify discarding or ignoring the second component.

Appendix 16-A on the website demonstrates how the important output figures in canonical analysis are computed manually. The appendix also discusses how to run canonical analysis in SPPS and shows where all statistical figures can be found in the output from SPSS. The interested reader will need to read either the whole appendix or at least the section "Running the small numerical example in SPSS." As the reader can see, the figures discussed in the present chapter such as simple correlations, canonical correlations, canonical loadings and cross loadings (the figures in Table 16.2 and Figure 16.2), can be found in Figure 16-A.14 on the website.

Levine (1977) and Thompson (1984) are dedicated to canonical analysis.

Many multivariate texts like Dillon and Goldstein (1984), Green (1978), Lattin, Caroll and Green (2003) and Hair et al. (1998) have chapters that address canonical analysis. Hair et al. (1998) is the best non-technical introduction, Green (1978) is excellent but assumes that the reader is familiar with basic matrix algebra. The second edition of the Green book, authored by Lattin, Carroll and Green (2003) is also fine but much more difficult to read. It covers some details on statistical tests, e.g. Wilk's lambda and Rao's F-test that other texts do not address properly. Dillon and Goldstein (1984) also has a chapter on canonical analysis but it is a difficult text. The last two texts assume familiarity with mathematics and matrix algebra. It should be noted that all texts mentioned here except Hair either have an appendix or a chapter dedicated to introductory matrix theory.

Journal publications on canonical analysis are rare when compared to structural equation modelling (the next method to be covered). Most of the technical articles are unreadable by non-experts and used to appear in journals such as *Biometrika* and *Psychometrica* (deSarbo, 1981; deSarbo et al., 1982).

With regard to marketing and business related journals, technical papers include: Green, Halbert and Robinson (1966) Alpert and Peterson (1972), Lambert and Durand (1975), Fornell (1978a), Fornell (1978b), Wildt, Lambert and Durand (1982), and Watts (1995).

Concerning applied papers using canonical analysis in a business/marketing setting the following are worthwhile mentioning: Perry and Hamm (1969); Kelly (1977); Fitts and Karson (1977); Holbrook and Moore (1982); Schul, Pride and Little (1983); Schnaars and Schiffman (1984); Van Auken, Doran and Yoon (1993); Diamantopoulos and Schlegelmilch (1994).

See this book's website (www.pearsoned.co.uk/schmidt) for a large-scale application of canonical analysis based on Appendix 16-B.

16.2 Introduction to structural equation modelling (SEM)

The analysis of causal relationships among variables using the LISREL approach has seen great interest, especially within academic circles. The breakthrough in causal modelling that led to the LISREL/SEM approach can be attributed to the work of Karl G. Jöreskog and Dag Sorbom. The literature addressing or using LISREL/SEM is overwhelming and a quarterly journal, *Structural Equation Modeling*, exclusively dealing with technical issues related to the method, has existed since 1994.

So what is LISREL/SEM all about? This question is best answered in two parts:

First, the measurement model is based on a type of factor analysis, normally called ***confirmatory factor analysis***. This approach differs from the "ordinary" factor analysis introduced in Chapter 11 because one assumes that a variable only loads on one pre-specified factor (or on a few factors) while all other loadings are presumed to be 0. One can then perform statistical tests with regard to how appropriate the assumed model is. So, in confirmatory factor analysis, the analyst pre-specifies the variables that are expected to load on a given factor (in LISREL-settings factors are usually called ***constructs***) and statistical tests are used to assess whether this pattern of loadings fits the data. According to LISREL/SEM theory, a regression weight (loading) can be either fixed, say, at 1.0, at 0.0, or at some constant value, e.g. 0.5. Alternatively, it can be free, that is, it can take on any value (as long as the estimates are non-standardized, they usually fall within the interval of -2 and $+2$). Ordinary factor analysis is often named ***exploratory factor analysis*** to distinguish it from the confirmatory type.

Second, the *path model* assumes that the variables in the matrix can be arranged as a set of simultaneous multiple linear regressions. Like canonical regression, the path model allows for several dependent variables. This model is attractive because it makes it easy to explain complex causal relations between variables by way of a diagram instead of by only using statistical tables and formulae.

16.3 The measurement model

Let us start with looking at Figure 16.4. Part (a) repeats Table 11.11 in Chapter 11. The table or data matrix belonged to the example used for illustrating the mechanics of factor analysis. Table 11.11 is the unrotated factor matrix (see also Figure 11.11). Recall that *X1* and *X8* have high (numeric) loadings on factor 1 while *X4* has a high loading on factor 2. Part (b) of Figure 16.4 provides a graphical illustration of Table 11.11. In part (b) the loading pattern of the small, exploratory, factor analysis is illustrated by arrows pointing *from* factors *to* variables (it is LISREL/SEM convention to let arrows point from con- structs to indicator variables). Each arrow is assigned an estimate (weight). In the present case the weight is the factor loading.

For the moment, assume that variables *X1* and *X8 exclusively* load on factor 1 and that *X4 only* loads on factor 2. This situation is illustrated at the bottom of panel (a). *L1, L2* and *L3* indicate an expected loading in the appropriate cell. On the other hand, *X4* is not expected to load on factor 1, nor is *X1* or *X8* expected to load on factor 2.

For instance, it could be assumed that the observed loading on *X4* in the ordinary factor analysis, 0.43, represents a measurement error and that the true or unbiased value is 0. Likewise, the loadings of −0.47 (*X1*) and −0.01 (*X8*) on factor 2 may be regarded as errors

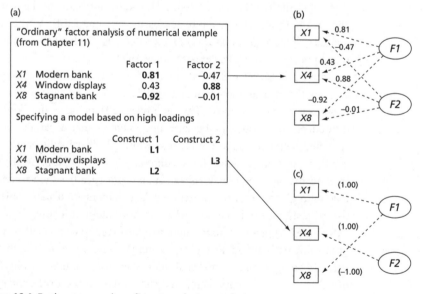

Figure 16.4 Exploratory and confirmatory factor analysis

due to the empirical analysis while the true value is 0. Panel (c) shows how the latter example would look. Because of the sampling error, the loading pattern of panel (b) has been observed. With error-free data, the result would have been "the true model" of (c) in Figure 16.4.

According to confirmatory factor analysis theory, the researcher *begins* by making a set of assumptions about causal relationships. In LISREL/SEM terminology the analyst establishes a ***hypothesized model***. For instance, *X1* and *X8* may be regarded as well-suited indicators of construct 1 (say, "Dynamic orientation"). Likewise *X4* is expected to be a good indicator of construct 2 (say, "Secondary product features"). In practical settings each construct will necessitate multiple indicators and there will be more constructs involved than just two. (A typical questionnaire would run to 50–100 items, typically on a five-point Likert scale.)

Next the researcher carries out a survey among a sample of respondents and then confirmatory factor analysis is conducted based on the data. The purpose is to find out whether the hypothesized model of panel (c) fits the empirical data of panel (b). Ideally, the modelling should be founded in theory only. This implies that the researcher constructs panel (c) *without any knowledge* of the exploratory factor analysis in panel (b). However, it would be naïve to think this is the way it works in the real world. Nothing can prevent a researcher from using the output from an exploratory factor analysis as input for establishing a confirmatory model. A researcher could look at high variable loadings on a factor in panel (b) and use this as "inspiration" for establishing the pattern of loadings for the

(a) Start up screen

(b) Building measurement model

Model-building mode button

Output mode button

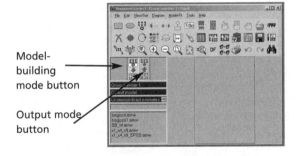

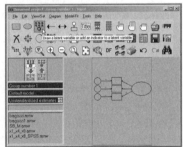

(c) Defining variables, etc.

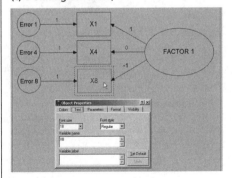

Note that AMOS has two modes, one is the *model building mode*. The other one is the *output mode*. When you load AMOS you start in the model building mode. While you build your model or while you revise it, you cannot shift to the output mode (the button cannot be clicked). After you have finished your model building or revising, you click the run button – No. 18 in Figure 16.6. Provided that your model has been properly built (in accordance with the "rules" of SEM model building), the fat arrow in the output mode button turns red. If you click it, you are in the output mode. The graphical model that you have just built now contains the coefficients estimated by AMOS. If your model has not been properly specified, say, if there are not enough degrees of freedom, if you have forgotten to name a variable or specify an input file, etc. – in such cases AMOS will not run (the output button does not turn red). Instead, AMOS will come up with an error message containing some information about what you may have done wrong.

Figure 16.5 The AMOS Program (Graphics)

confirmatory model. Using such an approach is an example of a self-fulfilling prophecy. Hair et al. warn against this procedure, which they call "data snooping" or "fishing" (Hair et al., 1998, 616), because a model generated this way has little generalizability. It simply capitalizes on the relationships specific to the sample data.

As a minimum it is recommended that one use the results from an exploratory factor analysis only for establishing the confirmatory model. The model should then be tested on a different data set.

A few screens from the AMOS program may facilitate an understanding of how the measurement model works. The program is dedicated to LISREL/SEM type problems. The website www.amosdevelopment.com lists more than 1,100 journal papers where AMOS has been employed. Most applications appear to be in psychology. AMOS is sold by SPSS as a separate module.

Figure 16.5(a) shows the startup screen of AMOS 5. The popularity of AMOS is caused by its user-friendly interface, compared to other LISREL/SEM programs. Programs like CALIS (*Ca*nonical *Lis*rel) by SAS/STAT and LISREL by Jöreskog, at least until recently, necessitated a lot of syntax coding. In AMOS one can use syntax (AMOS Basic) but one can do without.

During the production phase of this book, AMOS 6 was released. However, changes compared to version 5 are mostly cosmetic. Therefore, it is not a problem to discuss version 5.

The crux of AMOS is the toolbox shown in (a) and (b) of Figure 16.5 – the three lines or rows of icons. Figure 16.6 provides a brief explanation of all icons. Readers who want

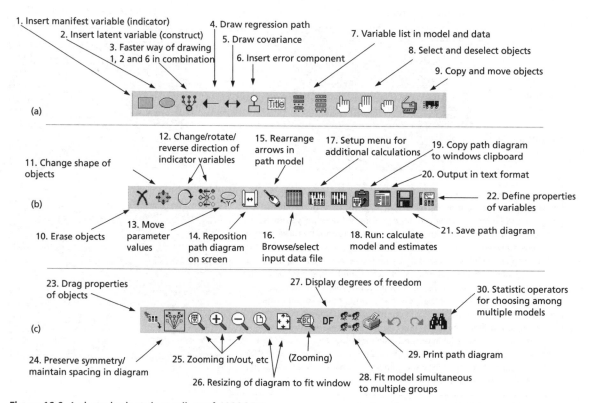

Figure 16.6 A closer look at the toolbox of AMOS 5.0

further explanation of the icons need to consult specialized sources like Barbara M. Byrne's book *Structural Equation Modeling with AMOS* (2001) or the user's guide to AMOS (Arbuckle and Wothke, 1999).

The icons help the analyst with drawing the model. AMOS resembles graphical presentation software like PowerPoint. One can draw a model just as one does in PowerPoint, with the exception that AMOS has some built-in rules for ensuring that the diagram one tries to draw is in accordance with the underlying theory of causal relations. In LISREL/SEM theory there exists a set of rules that must be obeyed. The rules concern the direction of arrowheads of a path, how errors and covariances are handled, etc. We will have more to say about these rules once we come to the path model.

Let us now return to the small numerical example. We recall from Figure 16.4(c) that our small model has three variables that load on one of two factors. In the present case it is very easy to build a simple measurement model.

1. Load the Graphics module of AMOS 5. The opening screen looks like Figure 16.5(a).
2. We begin with tabbing the icon "Draw a latent variable..." (Icon number 3 in Figure 16.6). Note that a brief explanation of an icon appears when the mouse passes the surface of the icon. Once we tab an icon it becomes highlighted while the arrow of our mouse has itself turned into a copy of the icon.
3. Now move the icon down to the empty box, click the mouse while moving it. You can now draw a circle or an ellipse and click again. The latent variable is established.
4. Next move the icon into the circle and click three times once for each of the variables *X1*, *X4* and *X8*.
5. Take the pointer back to the icon on the toolbar and click it so that it is deselected.
6. Go with the mouse to the rotation icon (number 12 in Figure 16.6 – the left one). Select it and then move the mouse to the circle or ellipse just created. Click three times until the orientation of the small measurement model looks like Figure 16.5(b). After this has been done move the mouse back to the rotation icon and deselect.
7. We can now name our variables. This is done by double clicking each of the squares. Doing this triggers a pop-up called "Object Properties." See Figure 16.5(c). In the pop-up choose *[Text]* and plug in, say, *X1* in the *[Variable name]* field. Then click the next box, tab in *X4* and so on. Once you are finished, close the window.
8. LISREL/SEM models contain a feature for measuring the error of an indicator. It appears as circles pointing at the variable (in LISREL/SEM variables are called *indicators* or *manifest variables*). We must also name the error terms. This is done in the same way as was shown with the variables: double click the circle and plug in the name of the error component.
9. Each arrow (regression weight) from error component to indicator variable by default is assigned a regression weight parameter of 1. This is the way LISREL does it. It will not be discussed here. Finally, we must give the factor a name (in LISREL/SEM a factor is called a *construct* or a *latent variable*).
10. Referring to the assumption made above, the "real" or unbiased loading (correlation) between the first construct (Factor 1) and variables *X1* and *X8* is presumed to be 1 and −1, respectively whilst the correlation between Factor 1 and *X4* is assumed to be 0. As can be seen in Figure 16.5(c) we have changed the default settings (regression

weights). AMOS by default assigns a weight of 1.00 to one of the arrows pointing at the variable (in LISREL this indicates that the variable is fixed and cannot be estimated) while no weight is assigned to the remaining variables (implying that they are free and thus due to estimation). The regression weights are changed by double clicking the respective arrow. Once again the "Object Properties" pop-up appears. Now tab *[Parameters]* and change the default value so that it fits with the presumptions.

11. In accordance with Figure 16.4 we ought to make a corresponding specification with regard to Factor 2 such that *X1* = 0, *X8* = 0 and *X4* = 1. However, since the data matrix is so small, AMOS output tells us that this second part of the model is *unidentified*, implying that the program cannot estimate this part of the model. Since the purpose of our numerical example is solely to illustrate how the method works this does not matter to us here.

12. Once the model has been established – the model of Figure 16.5(c) is almost as simple as a LISREL/SEM measurement model can be – then we must tell AMOS which data file we want to analyze. This we do by clicking the icon "Browse/select input data file" (number 16 in the tools menu of Figure 16.6). We point at the file we want to use for our analysis. See Figure 16.7(a). While AMOS can use Excel files as input we recommend using the SPSS file format (*.sav*). We tab *[View Data]*. Consequently SPSS

These correlations emanate from the small numerical example – the bank image analysis introduced in Chapter 11. The correlations appear in Table 11.10, 11.13 and in Appendix 11-A.

(a) Selecting input file

(b) Input file

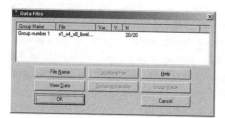

	rowtype_	varname_	x1	x4	x8
1	n		20,00000	20,00000	20,00000
2	corr	x1	1,000000		
3	corr	x4	-,006652	1,000000	
4	corr	x8	-,604508	-,324559	1,000000
5	stddev		1,000000	1,000000	1,000000
6	mean		,000000	,000000	,000000

(c) Output from AMOS Graphics

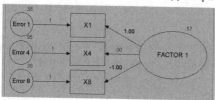

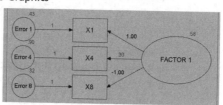

Treating *X4* as a constrained parameter
Chi-square = 3.5, degrees of freedom = 2,
Probability value = 0.17

Treating *X4* as a free parameter
Chi-square = 2.8, Degrees of Freedom = 1,
Probability value = 0.09

Figure 16.7 Running AMOS

opens and panel (b) appears. It contains the correlation matrix of our small numerical example. The first row has the number of observations. Rows 2–4 contain the correlation matrix. We have seen this matrix earlier (apart from rounding error). The first time it appeared was at the bottom of Table 11.10. Also, the matrix was used in Appendix 11-A (on www.pearsoned.co.uk/schmidt) where we show how to compute the matrix of eigenvectors in factor analysis (the so-called singular value decomposition). The last two rows contain the standard deviation and the mean. Since the input file contains the (standardized) correlation matrix and not the covariance matrix, we have set the standard deviation to 1 and the mean to 0. Note that labels and content of the first two columns must be typed in precisely as shown.

13. Once we have identified the data file that we want to use as the input file we click the *[OK]* button of Figure 16.7(a). It does not matter whether we keep the SPSS window open. However, note that if you change anything in the input file while it appears in the SPSS screen editor, you need to save the input file (*.sav*) first. Otherwise, the changes are not detected by AMOS.

14. Finally, tab the "Calculate estimates" icon (number 18 in Figure 16.6). A pop-up box may ask you to give the file, AMOS, a name. Note that the output mode button has now become active. Click it and (c) of Figure 16.7 will appear (model at left).

Figure 16.7(c) shows the graphic output from AMOS. The model at the left treats *X4* – the regression weight between Factor 1 and *X4* – as a parameter fixed at 0, while the model at the right treats the same weight as a free parameter (implying that we have removed the 0 of Figure 16.5(c)). Concerning both runs the error variance related to *X4* is bigger than that of *X1* and *X8*. The parameter related to Factor 1 (0.57, 0.58 respectively) is just the variance assigned to the factor. In the second run the weight of the free parameter of *X4* is estimated at 0.3 – somewhat lower than the corresponding loading in the exploratory factor analysis (0.43).

In both cases the model seemingly fits the data, since the probability value exceeds 0.05 (shown below). The probability value of the two model-versions is 0.17 and 0.09 respectively. In a LISREL/SEM setting a good model must *not* be significant that is H_0 should *not* be rejected. This is contrary to traditional statistical procedures where significance is what one looks for. In LISREL/SEM the direction of the test is reversed such that an appropriate model must fit the data well regarded from a statistical perspective implying that the test statistic is not significant.

Because both versions of Figure 16.7(c) fit the data, a model assuming that *X1* and *X8* are indicators of Factor 1 while *X4* is not, appears reasonable. However, the numerical example is way too small to be of any practical interest. A realistic LISREL/SEM model needs more variables and observations. Also, a certain aspect in the output of Figure 16.7(c) should make us worry: the estimated error of *X4* (0.95 and 0.90 respectively) is close to 1.0 and almost three times bigger than the other two error estimates. According to LISREL/SEM theory this indicates that there may be a fundamental problem with our model. We will have more to say on this issue later.

LISREL/SEM researchers have developed a lot of model fit statistics. Most of them are also available in AMOS. The fit measure falls into three categories:

- *Absolute fit measures.* These measures only assess the overall model fit. However, other models may fit the data better. Absolute fit measures do not express the quality of the model. If the model does not fit the data well, then absolute fit measures do not say what is wrong with the model or which part of the model is wrong (Diamantopoulos, 1994). In LISREL/SEM programs it has become practice to compare the estimated model with two models, representing extreme options, the ***independence model*** and the ***saturated model***. The independence model contains no effect parameters at all, only a constant term. In other words, it is assumed that the observed variables are uncorrelated. The saturated model on the other hand represents the most general model, given the specific correlation matrix. Since it contains all possible effect parameters, it possesses no degrees of freedom and therefore most SEM test statistics cannot be computed.
- *Incremental fit measures.* A set of statistics that compare a hypothesized model to a different model or to some baseline model. A situation may occur though, where one model fits the data better than another while neither of them fits the data well. Moreover, a model that has not been considered may fit the data even better.
- *Parsimonious fit measures.* A group of measures that aim to adjust the fit measures and provide a comparison between models with different numbers of estimated coefficients (of different complexity). For instance, a model with thirty parameters may perform worse on incremental fit measures compared with another based on twenty parameters. Parsimonious statistics appreciate "economical" models, that is, models where fewer parameters need to be estimated.

Table 16.5 groups the fit measures provided by AMOS (compare how the two versions of Figure 16.7(c) perform along these measures). Now, to explain them. Figure 16.7(c) displays the output from AMOS graphics. Normally the analyst needs supplementary details, though. Therefore, tab the "View text" icon, number 20 in Figure 16.6. This triggers a detailed text version of output from AMOS. In the file directory field at the left, tab "Model fit." The resulting page, called "Model Fit Summary" contains ten small tables with a lot of LISREL/SEM model fit statistics. Each of them will now be briefly addressed.

Because the numerical example is so small, all estimates except the p-value attributed to CMIN of the default model fail to pass the recommended threshold levels (Table 16.4). Therefore the output as such will not be discussed (apart from the competing models example of Table 16.5).

The fit statistics can be explained using a combination of figures and tables. The output appearing in Table 16.3 and Table 16.4 is based on the model at the left of Figure 16.7(c), that is, the model where all weights are fixed. Table 16.3 shows how every fit statistic in AMOS is computed by hand. The table has five columns. The first one contains an ID-number, the second one has the abbreviation, the third contains the full name of the test, the fourth column first presents the computational formula and then shows how the AMOS estimate, displayed in the fifth column, is computed manually.

Since some LISREL/SEM statistics are complex, it has been necessary in some cases to refer from Table 16.3 to figures containing further computations. All these figures are included in Appendix 16-C on the website (www.pearsoned.co.uk/schmidt):

Table 16.3 Output from AMOS and how it is computed

No.	AMOS name	Full name of measure	How the measure is computed	Estimate
1		(Figure 16.7b)	S = Sample data (Observed matrix) $$S = \begin{bmatrix} 1 & -0.006651754 & -0.604507534 \\ -0.006651754 & 1 & -0.324559188 \\ -0.604507534 & -0.324559188 & 1 \end{bmatrix}$$	
2		(Figure 16.8)	$\Sigma(\theta)$ = fitted matrix Based on the suggested or hypothesized model $$\Sigma(\theta) = \begin{bmatrix} 0.9500 & 0 & -0.5743 \\ 0 & 0.9500 & 0 \\ -0.5743 & 0 & 0.9500 \end{bmatrix}$$	
3	NPAR	Number of PARameters	3 error variances + 0 free parameters + 1 construct variance + 0 covariances (Figure 16.7c, left)	4
4	CMIN	Chi-square MINimum sample discrepancy	For a computation based on (b) (input data file) and (c) (model) of Figure 16.7 see Figure 16.8 (c), (fitted matrix) and appendix Figures 16-C.1 to 16-C.3	3.544
4a		Independence (Null) model	For a computation based on the numerical example see appendix Figure 16-C.4	12.186
5	DF	Degrees of Freedom	$DF = \frac{1}{2}\left[(p+q)\times(p+q+1)\right] - NPAR$ $= \frac{1}{2}\left[(0+3)\times(0+3+1)\right] - 4 = 2$	2
			p = number of endogenous indicators, q = number of exogenous indicators, NPAR = parameters	
6	RMR	Root Mean square Residual (RMSR)	Average residual from fitting variance-cov. matrix of hypothesized data to S Computation of RMR is shown in Panel 1 of appendix Figure 16-C.5	0.126
7	GFI	Goodness of Fit Index (Absolute value)	Computation of GFI is shown in Panel 2 of Figure 16-C.5	0.898
			$AGFI = 1 - \dfrac{q\times(q+1)}{2\times DF}\times(1 - GFI)$ $= 1 - \dfrac{3\times4}{2\times2}\times(1-0.898) = 0.694$	
8	AGFI	Adjusted Goodess of Fit Index	GFI adjusted for number of parameters (the fewer parameters, the better)	0.694
9			$PGFI = \dfrac{DF}{\left[\frac{1}{2}\times(p+q)\times(p+q+1)\right]}\times GFI$ $= \dfrac{2}{\frac{1}{2}\times(0+3)\times(0+3+1)}\times 0.898 = 0.299$	
	PGFI	Parsimony Goodness of Fit Index	GFI adjusted for complexity of hypothesized model	0.299
10	NFI	Normed Fit Index	$NFI = \dfrac{\chi^2_{Independence} - \chi^2_{default}}{\chi^2_{Independence}} = \dfrac{12.186 - 3.544}{12.186} = 0.709$	0.709

Table 16.3 continued

No.	AMOS name	Full name of measure	How the measure is computed	Estimate
11	RFI	Relative Fit Index	$RFI = 1 - \dfrac{\left(\dfrac{\chi^2\,_{Default}}{DF\,_{Default}}\right)}{\left(\dfrac{\chi^2\,_{Independence}}{DF\,_{Independence}}\right)} = 1 - \dfrac{\left(\dfrac{3.544}{2}\right)}{\left(\dfrac{12.186}{3}\right)} = 0.564$	0.564
12	IFI	Incremental Fit Index	$IFI = \dfrac{\chi^2\,_{Independence} - \chi^2\,_{default}}{\chi^2\,_{Independence} - DF} = \dfrac{12.186 - 3.544}{12.186 - 2} = 0.848$	0.848
13	TLI	Tucker–Lewis Index	$TLI = \dfrac{\left(\dfrac{\chi^2\,_{Independence}}{DF\,_{Independence}}\right) - \left(\dfrac{\chi^2\,_{Default}}{DF\,_{Default}}\right)}{\left(\dfrac{\chi^2\,_{Independence}}{DF\,_{Independence}}\right) - 1} = \dfrac{\left(\dfrac{12.186}{3}\right) - \left(\dfrac{3.544}{2}\right)}{\left(\dfrac{12.186}{3}\right) - 1} = 0.748$	0.748
14	CFI	Comparative Fit Index	$1 - \left[\dfrac{\chi^2\,_{Default} - DF\,_{Default}}{\chi^2\,_{Independence} - DF\,_{Independence}}\right] = 1 - \dfrac{(3.544 - 2)}{(12.186 - 3)} = 0.832$	0.832
15	PRATIO	Parsimony RATIO	DF(Default)/DF(Independence) = 2/3 = 0.667	0.667
16	PNFI	Parsimonious Normed Fit Index	NFI * PRATIO = 0.709 * 0.667 = 0.473	0.473
17	PCFI	Parsimonious Comparative Fit Index	CFI * PRATIO = 0.832 * 0.667 = 0.555	0.555
18	NCP	Non-Centrality Parameter	CMIN−DF = 3.544 −2 = 1.544	1.544
19	LO90_HI90	Confidence Interval for NCP	See appendix Figure 16-B.6 on how to obtain these invervals (upper limit shown)	11.050
20	FMIN	Function of MINimum Discrepancy	FMIN = CMIN/$(n-1)$ = 3.544/19 = 0.187	0.187
21	F0	Population Discrepancy Function (PDF)	NCP/$(n-1)$ = 1.544/19 = 0.081	0.081
22	LO90_HI90		For instance, HI90 is computed thus: $NCP_{HI90}/(n-1)$ =11.050/19= 0.582	0.582
23	RMSEA	Root Mean Square Error of Approximation	$RMSEA = \sqrt{\dfrac{\left(\dfrac{NCP}{n-1}\right)}{DF\,Default}} = \sqrt{\dfrac{\left(\dfrac{1.544}{19}\right)}{2}} = 0.202$	0.202

Table 16.3 continued

No.	AMOS name	Full name of measure	How the measure is computed	Estimate
24	LO90_HI90	Confidence Intervals for RMSEA	$HI90 = \sqrt{\dfrac{NCP_{HI90}}{2 \times (n-1)}} = \sqrt{\dfrac{11.050}{2 \times (19)}} = 0.539$	0.539
25	PCLOSE	Tests Null hypothesis that RMSEA < 0.05	1 – alpha test based on non-central chi-square rather than normal distribution	0.184
26	AIC	Akaike's Information Criterion	$AIC = CMIN + 2 \times NPAR = 3.544 + 2 \times 4 = 11.544$	11.544
27	BCC	Browne–Cudeck Criterion	$BCC = CMIN + 2NPAR \times \left(\dfrac{(n-1) \times \frac{p(p+3)}{n-p-2}}{p(p+3)} \right)$ $= 3{,}544 + (2 \times 4) \times \left(\dfrac{19 \times \left(\frac{3(3+3)}{20-3-2} \right)}{3(3+3)} \right) = 13.678$	13.678
28	BIC	Bayes Information Criterion	$BIC = CMIN + NPAR \times \ln(n)$ $= 3.544 + 4 \times \ln(20) = 15.527$	15.527
29	CAIC	Consistent AIC	$CMIN + NPAR \times (\ln n + 1) = 3.544 + 4 \times (\ln 20 + 1)$ $= 19{,}527$	19.527
30	ECVI	Expected Cross Validation Index	$ECVI = \dfrac{CMIN}{n-1} + \dfrac{2 \times NPAR}{n-1} = \dfrac{3.544}{19} + \dfrac{2 \times 4}{19} = 0.608$	0.608
31	LO90_HI90	ECVI confidence intervals (see also no. 18)	$[(HI90\ NCP) + DF + 2*(NPAR)]/(n-1)$ $= [11.05 + 2 + 2*(4)]/19 = 1{,}108$	1.108
32	MECVI	Maximum likelihood based ECVI	$MECVI = \left(\dfrac{1}{n-1} \right) \times BCC = \left(\dfrac{1}{19} \right) \times 13.678 = 0.720$	0.72
33	HOELTER	Critical N index	$Hoelter\ 0.05 = \dfrac{\chi^2_{0,05;2}}{\left(\frac{CMIN}{n-1} \right)} + 1 = \dfrac{5.99}{\left(\frac{3.544}{19} \right)} + 1 = 33$	33

- 4: CMIN is difficult to compute and necessitates some matrix algebra, so Figure 16-C.1 on the website gives a detailed explanation of the involved computations.
- The calculations of appendix Figure 16-C.1 assume that one knows the *determinant* of the sample correlation matrix and the fitted correlation matrix as well as the *inverse* of the fitted correlation matrix. Consequently computations of the determinants are shown in website appendix Figure 16-C.2 while appendix Figure 16-C.3 shows how the inverse of the fitted correlation matrix is computed.
- 4-a: Computation of CMIN concerning the independence model is shown in Figure 16-C.4.
- The computation of 6-RMR is demonstrated in panel (a) of appendix Figure 16-C.5 whereas the calculation of 7-GFI is explained in panel (b) of appendix Figure 16-C.5.
- Appendix Figure 16-C.6 shows how to obtain the confidence intervals of the Non Centrality Parameter.

In accordance with the approach used in Chapters 9–11, formulae for computing the different LISREL/SEM statistics are given without discussion of their rationale. Readers interested in technical details are referred to Bollen (1989). Specialized though non-mathematical discussions are offered by Byrne (2001) and Hair et al. (1998, 653–664). Since Bollen's book appeared in 1989, several recent measures are not covered. Byrne does not use any formulae, but this may make it difficult to obtain a thorough understanding. Unfortunately, a lot of LISREL/SEM statistics almost only appear in specialized journals such as *Structural Equation Models*.

Table 16.4 is structured with the first column giving an identity number; the second contains the abbreviation of the measure; and the third has the AMOS estimate based on the example (the first three columns also appear in Table 16.3). The fourth and fifth columns display the minimum and maximum of those measures that do have boundaries (ignoring the fact that some measures can, theoretically, be negative). The sixth column lists recommended values for some of the measures. Note that these values can only be regarded as rules of thumb. Moreover, some of them are disputed. In the seventh column are comments about the measures.

According to AMOS, the CMIN value of the default model (4-CMIN) is 3.544. Once this value is combined with the model's degrees of freedom, two, (5-DF) the necessary information is at hand to estimate the model's overall fit in terms of probability.[3] In the present case the model's probability is 0.170. While this value is not shown in Table 16.5, it is easy to compute.[4]

Since 0.170 is higher than 0.05, there is no reason to reject the hypothesized model. (Had the CMIN exceeded 6.000 or so, the model would be rejected because the probability would drop below the threshold level of 0.05.) However, another model may fit the data better. Theoretically, an infinite number of models may fit the data, implying that their CMIN value exceeds 0.05. (Because the measurement model is so small, NPAR=4, it is easy to try out all possible models.)

In situations where several models fit the data, which should be the preferred model? According to LISREL/SEM theory, one lets the qualified models "compete" with each other. The "winner" of the contest is regarded the best model. In most situations this makes good sense. When many variables and multiple constructs are involved it appears

Table 16.4 AMOS output: recommendations and comments

No.	AMOS name	Estimate	Min	Max	Recommended	Comments
4	CMIN	3.544	0			P-value assigned to CMIN should be higher than 0.05 (here it is 0.17). The lower the better
5	DF	2				DF may be 0 or negative. If we had wanted to treat two of the three constrained parameters as free, DF would have been 0
6	RMR	0.126	0	1	<0.05	Used with standardized estimates it can be interpreted as meaning that the fitted matrix explains correlations of S with an average error of RMR
7	GFI	0.898	0	1	n.a.	Somewhat analogous to R-square in regression (upwards inflated), the higher the better
8	AGFI	0.694	0	1	>0.90	Somewhat analogous to adjusted R-square
9	PGFI	0.299	0	1	n.a.	The higher the better
10	NFI	0.709	0	1	>0.90	Tendency to underestimate fit in small samples
11	RFI	0.564	0	1	>0.90	Like NFI biased by sample size
12	IFI	0.848	0	1	>0.90	NFI adjusted by DF, has same weaknesses as NFI and RFI
13	TLI	0.748	0	1	>0.90	>0.95 for large samples
14	CFI	0.832	0	1	>0.90	>0.95 indicates superior fit
15	PRATIO	0.667	0	1	n.a.	The higher the better
16	PNFI	0.473	0	1	n.a.	NFI where model complexity is penalized. Will be smaller than NFI
17	PCFI	0.555	0	1	n.a.	CFI where model complexity is penalized. Will be smaller than CFI
18	NCP	1.544	0			A parameter used when testing the model according to the little known non-central chi-square distribution. Also known as the Ricean or Rayleigh distribution. Chi-square actually is a special case of non-central chi-square. Non-central chi-square is used when model does not fit data. For measuring "Population badness of fit." The smaller the better
19	LO90_HI90	11.050	0			Value shown refers to HI90
20	FMIN	0.187				The smaller the better
21	F0	0.081	0			The smaller the better
22	LO90_HI90	0.582	0			

Table 16.4 continued

No.	AMOS name	Estimate	Min	Max	Recom- mended	Comments
23	RMSEA	0.202	0		<0.10	<0.05 indicates good fit, 0.05–0.08 acceptable fit, >0.10 poor fit. Tends to over-reject true models when sample is small
24	LO90_HI90	0.539	0			Possible usage: when RMSEA is small but interval is wide, the accuracy of model fit cannot be determined
25	PCLOSE	0.184	0		<0.05	"p-value" for testing the null hypothesis that the population RMSEA is not greater than 0.05
26	AIC	11.544	0		n.a.	For comparing different models. The smaller, the better
27	BCC	13.678	0		n.a.	For comparing different models. The smaller, the better. Imposes higher penalty on model complexity than AIC
28	BIC	15.527	0		n.a.	For comparing different models. The smaller, the better. Imposes higher penalty on model complexity than AIC
29	CAIC	19.527	0		n.a.	For comparing different models. The smaller, the better
30	ECVI	0.608	0		n.a.	For comparing models. The model with the smallest ECVI exhibits the greatest potential for replication. The smaller the better
31	LO90_HI90	1.108	0			HI 90 is shown (Figure 16-C.6 in Appendix 16-C)
32	MECVI	0.72	0		n.a.	For comparing models: identical to BCC, except from scale factor. The smaller the better
33	HOELTER	33	0		(200)	Estimate of a sample size that would be sufficient to yield an adequate model for a chi-square test. Note that the actual sample size ($n=20$) is smaller than 33. It ought to be higher! In real life data sets it ought to exceed 200 – according to Hoelter. Underestimates fit in small samples

reasonable to test several models. Letting models compete is not without problems, though. If the LISREL/SEM model is complex with multiple constructs and variables (and levels or layers in case of the path diagram), it becomes inconvenient to test all possible non-identical models. If this is the case, the analyst typically will concentrate on trying out a small selection of models, say three or four, that appear reasonable.

The numerical example used here is too small to allow an interesting competition among models, but a modest contest is possible. Panel (c) in Figure 16.7 shows two different runs. The only difference is that in the first model, $X4$ is fixed at 0.00 while it is a free parameter in the latter model (estimated at 0.30). Which one should be the preferred choice?

Table 16.5 compares the two models with regard to all of the AMOS fit measures. Model 1 has two degrees of freedom and Model 2 has one. Therefore, Model 1 is more

(a) Starting configuration

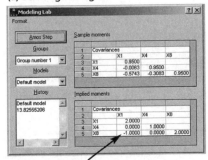

This is AMOS' starting configuration

The above screens are found thus in AMOS:
Tab [*Model Fit*] on the main toolbar and then
[*Modeling Lab*]

(b) Optimal model fit

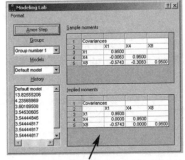

This matrix is the fitted $\Sigma\Theta$ matrix that
appears in appendix Figures 16-C.1–5 (only
the lower triangle is shown)

Panel 2 shows the result of the Maximum Likelihood
Estimation carried out by AMOS. After a few computational
steps the analysis stops, because the fit cannot be improved

Figure 16.8 How AMOS fits the data to the model

Table 16.5 Comparison of models Figure 16.7(c)

Note: model at left is Model 1 while model at right is Model 2

		Model 1	Model 2	Recommendations	Favours
Absolute fit measures:					
4	CMIN	3.544	2.837	The *smaller* the better	
4	DF	2	1		
4	PROB	0.170	0.092	>0.05	1
6	RMR	0.126	0.098	<0.05	2
7	GFI	0.898	0.915	The *higher* the better	2
18	NCP	1.544	1.837	The *smaller* the better	1
20	FMIN	0.187	0.149	The *smaller* the better	2
21	F0	0.081	0.097	The *smaller* the better	1
23	RMSEA	0.202	0.311	<0.10	1
25	PCLOSE	0.184	0.100	<0.05	2
30	ECVI	0.608	0.676	The *smaller* the better	1
Incremental fit measures:					
8	AGFI	0.694	0.492	>0.90	1
10	NFI	0.709	0.767	>0.90	2
11	RFI	0.564	0.302	>0.90	1
13	TLI	0.748	0.400	>0.90	1
14	CFI	0.832	0.800	>0.90	1
Parsimonious fit measures:					
9	PGFI	0.299	0.153	The *higher* the better	1
12	IFI	0.848	0.836	>0.90	1
15	PRATIO	0.667	0.333	The *higher* the better	1
16	PNFI	0.473	0.256	The *higher* the better	1
17	PCFI	0.555	0.267	The *higher* the better	1
26	AIC	11.544	12.837	The *smaller* the better	1
27	BCC	13.678	15.503	The *smaller* the better	1
28	BIC	15.527	17.815	The *smaller* the better	1
29	CAIC	19.527	18.186	The *smaller* the better	2
32	MECVI	0.720	0.816	The *smaller* the better	1
33	HOELTER	33	26	(200)	1

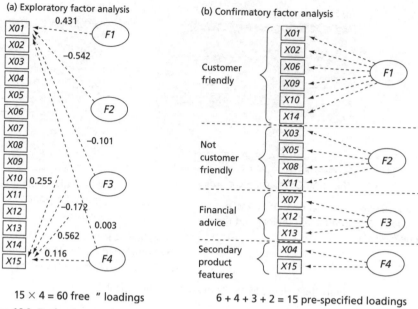

(a) Exploratory factor analysis

15 × 4 = 60 free " loadings

(b) Confirmatory factor analysis

6 + 4 + 3 + 2 = 15 pre-specified loadings

Figure 16.9 Exploratory and confirmatory factor analysis: a bigger data set

parsimonious: it "keeps" more of its degrees of freedom. Both models fit the data (their PROB value is higher than 0.05).

While several of the absolute fit measures favour Model 2, all but one of the incremental and parsimonious measures support Model 1. So, the better choice would probably be Model 1.

To make the discussion more realistic a bigger data set is used for the next measurement model. See Figure 16.9.

This data set was used in Chapter 11 (Table 11.6). It is the male subset of the bank image analysis. Panel (a) of Figure 16.9 only shows a small fraction of this data set. (Table 11.6 only displayed loadings of at least +/−0.5 – multiplied by 100 and rounded.)

The output from the exploratory factor analysis – the factor matrix – has sixty loadings (fifteen variables times four factors). Panel (b) formulates the measurement model based on the fifteen items of the bank image analysis. In the confirmatory version, the model has only fifteen loadings or coefficients.

According to theory being tested, the image of a bank is influenced by four constructs: customer friendliness (friendly); *lack* of customer friendliness (unfriendly); the quality of the bank's financial advice; and secondary product features (window displays, toys for children, etc.).

Figure 16.10(a) shows part of the original data file. Part (b) presents the precise data file with the correlation matrix used as input for the measurement model. The organization of the file is the same as panel (b) of Figure 16.7. It is just bigger. Finally, Figure 16.10(c) displays the output from AMOS graphics. The estimates of (c) are unstandardized.

Without consulting and discussing LISREL/SEM fit statistics, the constructs friendly, unfriendly and secondary features appear to behave normally: both regression weights and

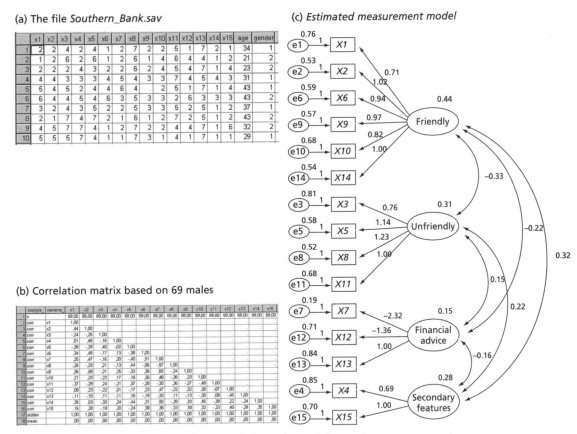

Figure 16.10 Running confirmatory factor analysis on the bank image data

error estimates appear to be within the "acceptable" range. But the parameters of the construct financial advice are unusual. Indeed, there seems to be a problem with the model.

For instance, the regression weight of $X7$ (-2.32) and to a lesser degree $X12$ (-1.36) are abnormal when compared with all the other weights. The total measurement model has fifteen regression weights of which four are fixed at 1.00 (one concerning each construct – normal LISREL practice). With the exception of $X7$ and $X12$, all free or estimated coefficients are positive. Moreover, the other coefficients are numerically smaller, ranging from 0.69 to 1.23. Also, note that $X7$'s error variance, e7, is much smaller (0.19) than all the others (ranging from 0.52 to 0.85).

Figure 16.11(a) shows the standardized regression weights of the same run (this necessitates one extra click in AMOS). Note that the standardized estimates are obtained by multiplying the unstandardized values by the square root of the corresponding construct variance. For instance:

$$-0.90 = (-2.32) \times \sqrt{0.15}$$

Once again, $X7$ behaves strangely. Its value, -0.90, comes close to -1.0.

According to LISREL/SEM theory, error variances that are either negative or close to zero (like 0.19) and standardized coefficients very close to ± 1.00 (such as -0.90) are

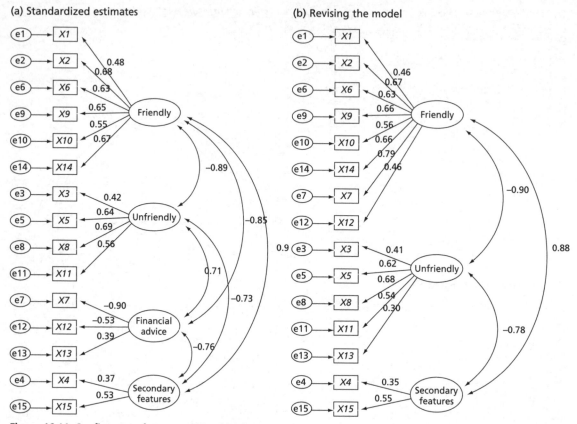

Figure 16.11 Confirmatory factor analysis of bank image data (2)

signs of an ***offending estimate***. Offending estimates now and then appear among parameters estimated by LISREL/SEM software. If they appear, remedies must be employed before the results can be interpreted for overall model fit and the individual coefficients can be examined for statistical significance (Hair et al., 1998, 582).

According to Hair et al., one should consider eliminating a construct, provided that the coefficients of one or several indicators look strange: "In many instances, such situations are the result of atheoretical models, established without sufficient theoretical justification or modified solely on the basis of empirical considerations."[5]

A possible remedy is to remove the financial advice construct and reassign the three variables (*X7*, *X12* and *X13*) to the remaining three constructs. First let us look at the underlying questions or items:

X7: Providing good advice
X12: Good housing advice
X13: No good tax advice

The directional orientation of both *X7* and *X12* is positive, whereas it is negative in *X13*. So, we reassign *X7* and *X12* to the construct friendly, move *X13* to the unfriendly construct and re-estimate the model. The result is shown in Figure 16.11(b). Like (a), standardized estimates are shown. The effect of removing a construct and reassigning the variables has a successful influence on the estimated parameters:

- The negative regression weights have vanished.
- No very small error variances are present any longer (not shown – they only appear when the unstandardized estimates are requested).
- There are no coefficients close to 1 (they range from 0.30 to 0.79).
- When comparing (a) with (b), note that (apart from *X7*, *X12* and *X13*), no coefficients have changed much.
- The pattern of covariance among constructs seems reasonable: high negative covariance between friendly and unfriendly. High positive covariance between friendly and secondary features.

So, fortunately, the model seems successful. But is it? While the statistical parameters and estimates look better in (b) when compared with (a), the model of (b) is simpler. The disadvantage of simplifying a model is that it may become less relevant or even irrelevant. In this case, there are two relatively imprecise constructs, friendly and unfriendly, that intuitively belong to opposite ends of the same scale continuum.

To improve the model, the construct financial advice was removed. Had this construct turned out to be coherent and stable, this would have been of more interest from a marketing strategy perspective. The third construct, secondary features, may be of strategic interest to management, but it has only two indicators and the parameter weight of *X4* (0.35) is small.

To sum up, while the estimated coefficients of the model now look better, the model itself has become less relevant from an operational perspective. Unfortunately, this is a situation often encountered when building causal models: better estimates imply models that are less interesting.

The suggested model of Figure 16.9 (b), as well as the input data file, can be downloaded from the book's website. The file with the suggested model is called *SB_M.amw* (AMOS graphics file format) while the input correlation file has SPSS format and is called *SB_M.sav*. Loading SB_M.amw into AMOS while using SB_M.savas input file and then tabbing the run icon (no. 18 in Figure 16.6) yields the output of Figure 16.10 (c).

16.4 The path model

Figure 16.12(a) tries to illustrate the modelling relationships in the canonical analysis of the review magazine case (on www.pearsoned.co.uk/schmidt). There were two sets of variables, one predictor set and one dependent set. Both sets were being described ("approximated" or "indicated") by a canonical component, *U1* and *T1* respectively.[6] The correlation between the first pair of linear composites was 0.601, the canonical correlation. Then there are canonical loadings like $L_{T1,Y1}$ and cross loadings like $L_{U1,Y2}$.

In canonical analysis, *T1* is treated as an indicator of (*Y1*, *Y2*). In an extreme situation *Y1* and *Y2* are uncorrelated while both correlate perfectly with *T1*. If this is the case *T1* is a perfect indicator of the dependent set ($Y1$, $Y2$). Note, though, that this situation is logically impossible if TI correlates perfectly with both $Y1$ and $Y2$, then the bivariate correlation between the latter two variables must also be 1.0.

However, by reversing the direction of causality, a variable like $Y1$ could be an indicator of the component TI: the higher the loading the better $Y1$ works as an indicator of TI. The variable $Y1$ is real or "visible" while the component TI represents an "invisible" (statistical) construct. In canonical analysis, researchers are interested in exploring the variables, especially how good a group of predictors is at explaining a group of dependents. Since this "combined" effect can only be assessed properly by way of the canonical components, TI and UI, these need to be analyzed.

In LISREL/SEM, the components – called "hidden constructs" – are of interest for their own sake while in canonical analysis they are employed as a "necessary evil" because they say something about relations between sets of variables.

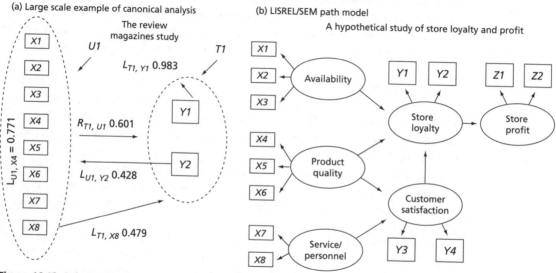

Figure 16.12 Relation between canonical analysis and LISREL/SEM

In canonical analysis there is a data matrix. From a model toolbox, it is decided that the existing data could be worthwhile analyzing by canonical analysis. In LISREL/SEM, a complex causal relation is analyzed. Right from the beginning (and before gathering data) a model is established of hypothesized causal relationships among constructs. Once the model has been formulated, the aim is to create variables that describe the constructs (for instance five-point statements on an agree/disagree scale). In other words, the variables serve as a proxy for the higher level or generalized construct.

Figure 16.12 (b) shows a hypothetical path model. The path model assumes that:

- loyalty is a function of availability, product quality and customer satisfaction;
- customer satisfaction is caused by product quality and customers' perception of service personnel; and
- store profit is a function of store loyalty.

Assume that each construct is indicated by two or three variables. For instance, *X1* could run thus: "I usually shop at supermarkets that I can reach within 15 minutes." Likewise, *X2* could run: "If I repeatedly experience problems with finding a parking space at a supermarket, I stop shopping there." All items could be scaled from one (totally agree) to five (totally disagree).

Compare (a) and (b). While paying no attention to the difference in application (review magazines on the website against store loyalty and profit) the following methodological dissimilarities can be seen between the canonical analysis (a) and the LISREL/SEM model (b). In (b):

- The predictor/indicator variables have been grouped into several categories.
- Each group of predictor/indicator variables now relates to its own component. So, while (a) has only one predictor/indicator component, *U1*, (b) has three (components are characterized by an elliptical form).
- The variables are now placed *outside* a component with an arrow pointing *from* component *towards* the predictor/indicator variable (according to LISREL/SEM theory).
- In (b) there are *several* sets of predictor constructs and dependent constructs. There are three predictor sets or constructs (availability, product quality and service/personnel) and three dependent sets (store loyalty, customer satisfaction and store profit).
- A construct can be both dependent and predictor. For example, customer satisfaction depends on product quality and service personnel. Simultaneously, customer satisfaction, together with product quality and availability, is a predictor of store loyalty.
- A predictor is not necessarily related to a dependent. For instance, there is no arrow pointing from availability towards customer satisfaction.
- There are hierarchies of dependence: store profit depends on store loyalty that depends on product quality, etc.
- If the model of (b) is treated as a regression problem, the following three (simultaneous) regressions result:
  Store loyalty = f (availability + product quality + customer satisfaction).
  Customer satisfaction = f (product quality + service/personnel).
  Store profit = f (store loyalty).

Almost all of the above methodological differences between (a) and (b) are aspects where the LISREL/SEM model represents enhancements of the canonical analysis model. For a detailed comparison see Fan (1997).

The real path model is best considered using a classic study by Bagozzi (1980). The same study is employed by Dillon and Goldstein (1984, 430–89).

A company is interested in assessing how the performance of its sales force affects job satisfaction. Also, its management is aware that the causal link between an employee's performance (say, in terms of orders gained) and the employee's job satisfaction may not be unidirectional, implying that job satisfaction also affects performance.

The management identifies three constructs that it thinks affect or cause job satisfaction and performance of an employee. They are: achievement motivation, task specific self-esteem and verbal intelligence. According to management the three constructs are defined as follows (Bagozzi, 1980):

- *Achievement motivation.* Employees possess different value systems toward specific outcomes on the job. If an employee perceives a specific reward (say, in terms of money, job advancement, etc.) as being important and attractive, the person will be motivated and work hard with the aim of obtaining the reward. Consequently, the greater the person's satisfaction will be when attaining the rewards. And vice versa.
- *Task specific self-esteem.* Individuals perform a task or job in a manner that is consistent with their self-esteem. Self-esteem influences performance through its role in an individual's internal psychological balance process. If an employee's self-concept concerning the job or task requires effective performance then the person will engage in such behaviour.
- *Verbal intelligence.* This construct is defined as the cognitive ability of employees to accurately and efficiently perceive, attend to, and process information related to conversations, written instructions, and other forms of communication associated with the job.

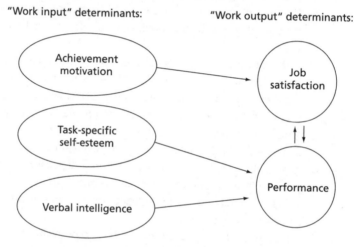

Figure 16.13 Hypothesized determinants of job satisfaction

Whereas it is assumed that motivation has a direct bearing on job satisfaction, it is presumed that both self-esteem and intelligence will first influence performance and then job satisfaction. So, the influence on job-satisfaction generated by self-esteem and intelligence will be indirect and mediated by performance.

The proposed model of interaction is displayed in Figure 16.13.

This represents a qualitative version of the causal model. The next stage, to use the LISREL/SEM term, is to **specify the parameters of the model**. This is essential because it tells the software precisely which parameters to estimate. The selected model has been described in the published literature, so it is relatively easy to do this using Bagozzi (1980) or Dillon and Goldstein (1984, 465–73).

LISREL/SEM theory has its own mathematical notation. It employs a set of Greek letters as algorithmic symbols. Figure 16-B.8 of Appendix 16-B at www.pearsoned.co.uk/schmidt lists the Greek letters used in LISREL/SEM settings. It also explains what the letters indicate.

Now turn to Figure 16.14. In (a), according to LISREL/SEM theory, a path model consist of two types of constructs: exogenous constructs and endogenous constructs.

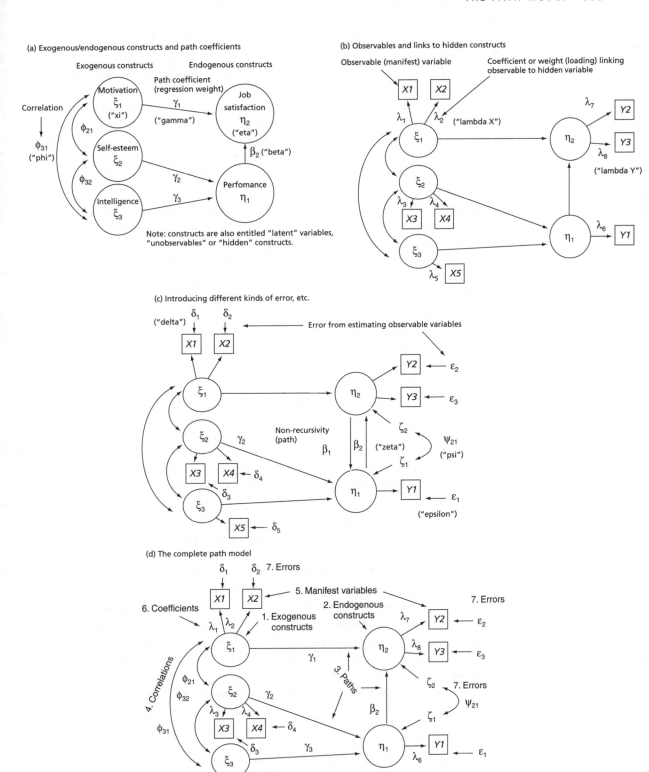

Figure 16.14 Building the LISREL/SEM path model

Constructs reflect general phenomena such as preference, sympathy, anxiety and suspicion. Phenomena symbolize higher levels of abstraction than do variables. **Exogenous constructs** differ from endogenous constructs in that they often exist independently of the specific situation that the model describes. For instance, motivation, self-esteem and intelligence are characteristics that a person possesses in a higher or lesser degree, regardless of whether she/he has a job or not. A person may have high motivation, high self-esteem and be very intelligent, yet may not work. But since such a person does not have a job, the terms performance and job satisfaction make no sense. Also, because exogenous constructs are person-specific they are mobile: a person can "carry them with her/him" once she/he leaves for a new job.

Endogenous constructs, such as job satisfaction and performance, primarily make sense in the context of a specific company (or the specific model). A person may perform well and enjoy high job satisfaction in one company. But in a new job, the same person may not perform well. Consequently, she/he soon becomes dissatisfied. Usually, the setting or loading of endogenous constructs can be manipulated by managers. Performance may become better if the reward is raised and job satisfaction may be improved when a person gets promoted.

Performance and job satisfaction can be adjusted from one day to the other, whereas exogenous constructs, such as self-esteem, are difficult to alter. Intelligence is basically unchangeable.

The correlation between exogenous constructs is called "phi" (ϕ).

According to LISREL/SEM terminology exogenous constructs are termed by the Greek letter "i" (ξ) while endogenous constructs are named "eta" (η).

Paths (regression weights) are arrows pointing *from* exogenous *towards* endogenous constructs. They are termed "gamma" (γ). Sometimes they point from one endogenous construct to another and in this case they are named "beta" (β). Note that an arrow cannot point from an endogenous construct towards an exogenous construct. (For example; differences in intelligence can cause differences in performance, but even an outstanding performance cannot raise a person's intelligence.) According to convention, exogenous constructs appear at the left side of the path diagram while endogenous constructs are on the right.

In (b), according to LISREL/SEM theory, the true nature of a construct by definition is hidden, so an individual's motivation or job satisfaction cannot be observed. What a researcher can do is to try to "approach" a construct by way of a set of variables, called *observables*, *indicators* or *manifest variables*. In LISREL/SEM it is common practice to use a set of statements that address a construct. These statements are then called the indicators of the construct. For instance, in the present case, two batteries of statements ($Y2$ and $Y3$) were used as indicators of job satisfaction. The following three statements belong to the twelve items employed for describing job-satisfaction (six concerning $Y2$ and $Y3$ respectively):

- My pay is in accordance with what others get for similar work in other companies ($Y2_1$).
- I would advise a friend looking for a new job to take one similar to mine ($Y2_2$).
- My work is challenging and gives me a sense of accomplishment ($Y3_1$).

Table 16.6 Input file for the Bagozzi (1980) study

rowtype_	varname_	y1	y2	y3	x1	x2	x3	x4	x5
n		122	122	122	122	122	122	122	122
corr	Y1	1	.	.	.	.	.	.	.
corr	Y2	0.418	1	.	.	.	.	.	.
corr	Y3	0.394	0.627	1	.	.	.	.	.
corr	X1	0.129	0.202	0.266	1	.	.	.	.
corr	X2	0.189	0.284	0.208	0.365	1	.	.	.
corr	X3	0.544	0.281	0.324	0.201	0.161	1	.	.
corr	X4	0.507	0.225	0.314	0.172	0.174	0.546	1	.
corr	X5	−0.357	−0.156	−0.038	−0.199	−0.277	−0.294	−0.174	1
std dev.		1	1	1	1	1	1	1	1
mean		0	0	0	0	0	0	0	0

All statements were scaled according to a Likert scale from one (totally agree) to six (totally disagree).

Before running the LISREL/SEM analysis one must aggregate observations from a given battery of variables. For instance, one must sum an individual's responses from the six items used for measuring job-satisfaction according to $Y2$ [$\Sigma(Y2_1 + Y2_2 + \ldots + Y2_6)$]. A special statistic known as *Cronbach's alpha* can be employed for computing the reliability of the items used for measuring job satisfaction (Nunnally and Bernstein, 1994, chapters 6 and 7).

Manifest variables vary in their capability to describe a construct. Some are excellent at describing a construct while others are less successful. The degree of success is modelled by a separate coefficient called "lambda" (λ). As long as the manifest variable indicates an exogenous construct it is called "lambda X." When it is associated with an endogenous variable it is named "lambda Y."

Motivation ($X1$, $X2$), self-esteem ($X3$, $X4$) and job satisfaction ($Y2$, $Y3$) all have two indicator sets while intelligence ($X5$) and performance ($Y1$) have only one. Intelligence is measured on a thirty-item response scale and performance is defined as the sales person's annual salary (partly paid on commission).

Part (c) focuses on errors. Every indicator or manifest variable is measured with some error. Errors point towards the indicator or towards an endogenous construct. If an error component refers to an indicator of an exogenous construct it is called "delta" (δ). If the error component relates to an indicator of an endogenous construct it is termed "epsilon" (ε). Also, endogenous constructs are measured with error (variance). This error component is called "zeta" (ζ) or "error in equation." Finally, the variance/covariance matrix of "zeta" variates (residual errors of endogenous constructs) is measured by "psi" (ψ). Note also that an arrow is pointing both to and from the two exogenous constructs in (c). This indicates that performance not exclusively causes job satisfaction but there also may be a causal effect that works in the opposite direction (if this is the case the model is said to be a non-recursive model).

To sum up, to build a path model, one must be able to:

- Differentiate between what is an exogenous construct (1) and what is an endogenous construct (2).
- Establish relevant paths (3) that point from exogenous toward endogenous constructs or from one endogenous construct towards another.
- Specify the pattern of correlations among exogenous constructs (4).
- Create manifest variables that can be used as indicators of the selected constructs (5).
- Specify how the indicators relate to constructs via coefficients (6).
- Denote the variables and endogenous constructs where error variances are expected (7).

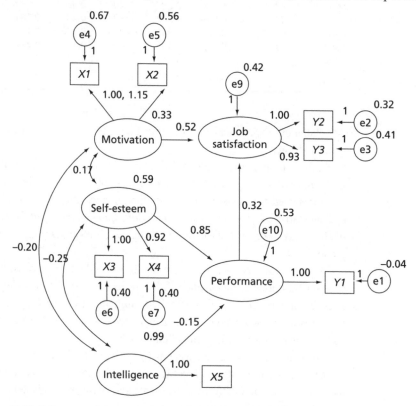

Figure 16.15 Estimates of the Bagozzi model provided by AMOS

With regard to all the Greek letters belonging to categories 3, 4, 6 and 7 in (d), LISREL/SEM will make parameter estimates.

So, how are the parameters of the model estimated by AMOS? Figure 16.15 models the Bagozzi study design in AMOS. Table 16.6 displays the corresponding input data file.

The estimates shown in Figure 16.15 fit very well with those of the original source (Bagozzi, 1980). Bagozzi used the software LISREL IV for analysis.

From comparing Figure 16.14(d) ("Theoretical model") with Figure 16.15 ("Validation"):

- Quite a lot of weights/loadings between indicators and constructs are unities ("1"): *X1*/Motivation, *X3*/Self-esteem, *X5*/Intelligence, *Y2*/Job satisfaction and *Y1*/performance. This has to do with the LISREL/SEM model that by definition, arbitrarily, fixes one weight or parameter estimate linking an indicator to a construct. This has to do with scaling (Hayduk, 1987, 103).

■ All weights (arrows) linking error variances to indicator variables according to LISREL/SEM convention are fixed at unity (Hayduk, 1987, 109).

■ AMOS does not use Greek letters, except in its manuals and help function. Note that the suggested error parameter, delta 5, pointing at *X5* in Figure 16.14(c) and (d) does not appear in the model of Figure 16.15. This is because AMOS suggested removing this component. Also, the parameter psi of Figure 16.14(c) is not estimated.

■ Note that the error estimate of *Y1* (e1) is negative. According to the above discussion, negative error variances suggest a problem with the model. However, the fits (not shown) appear to be very good so it does not appear worthwhile to investigate the nature of the negative variance.

Figure 16.15 displays the unstandardized estimates. Note:

■ A strong causal link between self-esteem and performance (0.85).

■ Moderate causal links between motivation (0.52), performance (0.32) and job-satisfaction.

■ A weak link between intelligence and performance (−0.15). The latter link is negative and not significant (not shown).

Ideally, management should use the above conclusions for an appropriate adjustment and revision of the company's reward and career policy. For instance, recruitment strategy should aim to hire people with high self-esteem and who are motivated. (Verbal) intelligence on the other hand seems not to play an important role.

Appendix 16-C on the website provides details on some technical aspects of LISREL/SEM.

Good books on LISREL/SEM are: Hayduk (1987), Bollen (1989), Bollen and Lang (1993), Hoyle (1995), Kaplan (2000), and Byrne (2001). The following have chapters on the technique: Dillon and Goldstein (1984); Diamantopoulos (1994); Hair et al. (1998); Lattin, Carroll and Green (2003). For articles, see: Bagozzi (1980), Fornell and Larcker (1981a, 1981b), and Shimp and Kavas (1984), Walters (1988) Walters and MacKenzie (1988).

As always the files that are used in this chapter are available on this book's website at www.pearsoned.co.uk/schmidt. The AMOS graphics file is called *bagozzi.amw* while the corresponding SPSS input file is called *bagozzi.sav*

16.5 Summary

This chapter has covered two statistical methods that allow for several dependent variables. Techniques that can handle multiple dependence relationships are able to model relationships between variables that are more complex than models like multiple regression and ANOVA, which only allow a single dependent variable. Disadvantages of complex models are: interpretation may be complex/tough (Canonical Correlation); model building and specification is often difficult (LISREL/SEM); and validation and generalization of the generated model becomes a problem.

Canonical correlation treats dependent and independent variables as two "sets" (e.g. *Y1*, *Y2* respectively *X1*, *X2*). Next, a parallel set of so-called canonical components (*T1*, *T2* respectively *U1*, *U2*) is computed, based on *Y1*, *Y2* and *X1*, *X2*. While variables correlate both within a set and across a set (*Y1* correlates with *Y2*, *X1* and *X2*, canonical components only correlate with components belonging to the same canonical function: *T1* correlates with *U1* and *T2* with *U2*, but *T1* does not correlate with *U2* while *T2* and *U1* are also uncorrelated. (Also, *T1/T2* and *U1/U2* are uncorrelated.) All this is shown in Figure 16.2.

T1, *U1* is called the first canonical function, *T2/U2* the second function and so on. The maximum number of canonical functions is determined by the number of dependents and predictors. The smallest number decides the possible number of canonical functions. The (first) canonical correlation is the correlation between the first linear component of the dependent set (*T1*) and the first component of the predictor set (*U1*). The correlation *T1/U1* by definition exceeds that of *T2/U2*, which is bigger than that of *T3/U3* and so on. However, the canonical correlation between *T1* and *U1* may be high, while the correlation between variables (*Y1*, *Y2*, *X1*, *X2*) generally are low. This is because canonical correlation aims to maximize correlation (variance explained) among pairs of linear composites (*T1/U1*, *T2/U2*), rather than between variables and canonical components. The so-called redundancy index may help figuring out how much variance in one set of variables (e.g. *Y1*, *Y2*) can be explained by variation in a set of canonical components (e.g. *T1* or *T2*). Only if both the canonical correlation $R_{T1,U1}$ and the redundancy index $R_{T1,(X1+X2)}$ are high for a canonical model can the analysis be regarded as successful.

Canonical correlation analysis may help the analyst to assess whether a single dependent variable suffices as the dependent measure or several dependents may help understand a problem better. In some situations, it makes sense to look at different dependent measures at the same time. Provided that both variables in the dependent set (*Y1* and *Y2*) contribute highly to a dependent component (say, *T1*) – that is when the canonical loadings are high for both variables – then both will have to be used for a proper assessment of dependence relationships. Simultaneously if cross loadings between predictors *X1/X2* and *T1* are high, none of them can be ignored as predictor. And vice versa.

Canonical correlation is normally used to analyze static data. That is, the method is used for data that exist and have not been gathered with the sole purpose of carrying out a canonical analysis. LISREL on the other side is usually (not exclusively, though) applied to data that have been especially collected. This implies that a LISREL model is typically established (formulated) before running the analysis. In general, the analyst builds ("suggests") a model of causal relationships like the one shown in Figure 16.13. Next the model is specified (Figure 16.14) and finally the model is estimated (Figure 16.15).

LISREL/SEM can be used for building two types of models, The **measurement model** and the **path model**. The former may be regarded as a special form of traditional (exploratory) factor analysis. In traditional factor analysis each variable has a loading (correlation) with each factor, whereas in confirmatory factor analysis, the analyst specifies which variables are allowed to load (correlate) with which factor. Next, the suggested model is tested and its fit with the data is assessed by output statistics. The advantage of confirmatory factor analysis is the availability of t-tests that can be used for analyzing the statistical significance of the specified factor loadings. The disadvantage is that the approach may lead to self-fulfilling prophecies.

In recent decades, the path model has become popular for analyzing complex causal relationships. In a path model, a variable may be treated as a dependent and predictor variable at the same time. For instance, *X2* and *X3* may be predictors of *Y1* while, at the same time, *Y1* itself (together with *X1*) is a predictor of *Y2*. This situation is shown in Figure 16.13.

A path model consists of **constructs** rather than variables. There are two types of constructs, exogenous constructs and endogenous constructs. In a usual path model, exogenous constructs appear at the left while endogenous constructs are on the right side of the graphical path model. Exogenous and endogenous constructs can predict/cause endogenous constructs. However, an endogenous construct is not allowed to cause an exogenous construct. Normally this makes sense. For instance in Figure 16.13 it makes sense to let intelligence predict performance while it does not make sense to assume that performance *causes* intelligence. When building a causal model it is important to use a sound theory of cause and effect combined with common sense.

According to **structural equation model** (SEM) theory, constructs themselves by definition are unobservable or hidden. Examples of constructs are "motivation," "satisfaction," "loyalty," "self evaluation," etc. Consequently, they must be circumscribed or approached by way of **manifest variables** (also called indicators or observables). Usually, a set of manifest variables is employed for describing a construct. An example of (one of several) manifest variables aiming at indicating the construct motivation could be: "When I have succeeded in a job task and I am appreciated by my boss, then I am happy" (five-point agreement scale). The ability of indicators to predict constructs is measured by separate coefficients.

Since a LISREL model entails sampling, model specification and estimation, error is involved. The size of the error is included in the model by way of an error component assigned to both manifest variables and endogenous constructs. An inappropriate model may be detected by offending estimates. Examples of offending estimates are negative error variances and coefficients (correlations) between a manifest variable and a construct that exceed 1.0.

If the model is inappropriate, the analyst should try to specify again by removing some paths (arrows) or changing their direction. For instance, in the model of Figures 16.14 and 16.15, one might alter the path from self esteem to performance so that it points from self esteem to job satisfaction, reverse the directional orientation of the path pointing from performance to job satisfaction or the like. Depending on the model, removing, changing, or reversing paths may improve (worsen) fit statistics.

In nearly every situation, an estimated model must be tested against competing models. These are theoretically justified models that differ with regard to the number of and/or direction of paths. The analyst should then select the model performing best across (the majority of) the available model fit statistics.

Unfortunately, it may well happen that about half of the statistics point towards one model while the other half favour another, making a decision based purely on fit statistics impossible.

Remember that there are three categories of test statistics: absolute fit measures of the overall fit of the measurement or structural equation model; incremental fit measures that compare the estimated model with different models or a baseline model; and parsimonious fit measures for selecting between models of different complexity, that is, comparing a model with nested or more parsimonious models.

When the suggested model has too many parameter specifications, the degrees of freedom may be negative and the model cannot be estimated. If so, the model is **under-identified** (removing one or more paths may solve this problem). A model with zero degrees of freedom is called **just identified**. Finally, if the model has positive degrees of freedom, it can be estimated without problems and is called **over-identified**. This is the preferred state, because it provides better opportunities for removing paths and making the model simpler. It has become practice to compare the estimated model with two alternatives, the **independence model** (assuming that observed variables are uncorrelated) and the **saturated model** (containing all possible parameters).

A well-specified SEM may provide insights concerning the problem under scrutiny. The advantage of such models is their flexibility with regard to modelling complex causal relationships. The disadvantages are:

- They can rarely be properly used for analyzing existing data.
- It is difficult to build powerful and realistic causal models that encompass all essential variables and causalities of the phenomenon under scrutiny.
- More often than not, one may question the generalizability of SEM models.
- A clever SEM modeller will be able to prove almost anything, or at least will be able to substantiate that any intuitively reasonable model is supported by the data set.

Questions

1. Download the file travelcost.sav from www.pearsoned.co.uk/schmidt. The file has two dependent ($Y1$, $Y2$) and four predictor variables ($X1$–$X4$):

   $Y1$ = Fixed cost of travel
   $Y2$ = Variable cost of travel
   $X1$ = Age
   $X2$ = Annual household income (€)
   $X3$ = Household size
   $X4$ = Length of trip in days

   (a) Compute the canonical correlation, canonical loadings and the redundancy index.

   (b) Provide a brief interpretation concerning dependence relationships and explained variance.

2. Consider the following six variables:

$X1$ = Satisfaction with purchase of brand A at time t-1
$X2$ = Satisfaction with purchase of brand B at time t-1
$Y1$ = Stated probability to repurchase brand A at time t
$Y2$ = Stated probability to repurchase brand B at time t
$Y3$ = Amount of purchase of brand A at time t
$Y4$ = Amount of purchase of brand B at time t

Table 16.7 Correlation matrix (n = 236)

	X1	X2	Y1	Y2	Y3	Y4
X1	1					
X2	0.534	1				
Y1	0.364	0.407	1			
Y2	0.334	0.329	0.66	1		
Y3	0.244	0.260	0.285	0.332	1	
Y4	0.142	0.211	0.292	0.363	0.432	1

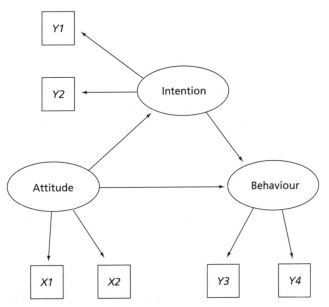

Figure 16.16 Testing a structural equation model
Source: Abridged from Lattin, Carroll and Green (2003, 384–385)

(a) Test the structural equation model suggested in Figure 16.16 using SPSS AMOS (or other appropriate software).

(b) Discuss the goodness of fit of the model (not only overall model fit but also measures on absolute fit, incremental fit and parsimonious fit).

(c) Does attitude affect behaviour? If so, how?

(d) Respecify the estimated model and test it against competing models. Compare the fit statistics and identify the best model (hint: parsimonious fit).

References

Alpert, M. I. and Peterson, R. A. (1972) "On the interpretation of canonical analysis." *Journal of Marketing Research*. Vol. 9 (May). 187–192.

Arbuckle, J. L. and Wothke, W. (1999) *AMOS 4.0 User's Guide*. Smallwaters, Chicago.

Bagozzi, R. P. (1980) "Performance and satisfaction in an industrial sales force: an examination of their antecedents and simultaneity." *Journal of Marketing*. Vol. 44 (Spring). 65–77.

Bollen, K. A. (1989) *Structural Equations with Latent Variables*. Wiley, New York. 263–305.

Bollen K. A. and Lang J. S. (eds) (1993) *Testing Structural Equation Models*. Sage, Thousand Oaks, CA.

Byrne, B. M. (2001) *Structural Equation Modeling with AMOS*. Lawrence Erlbaum, London. 72–88.

DeSarbo, W. S. (1981) "Canonical/redundancy factor analysis." *Psychometrika*. Vol. 46, no. 3. 307–329.

DeSarbo, W. S., Hausman, R. E., Lin, S. and Thompson, W. (1982) "Constrained canonical correlation." *Psychometrika*. Vol. 47, no. 4. 489–516.

Diamantopoulos, A. (1994) "Modelling with LISREL: a guide to the initiated." In Hooley, G. J. and Hussey, M. K. (eds) *Quantitative Methods in Marketing*. Academic Press, London. 105–136.

Diamantopoulos, A. and Schlegelmilch, B. B. (1994) "Linking export manpower to export performance: a canonical regression analysis of European and US data." *Advances in International Marketing*. Vol. 6. 161–82.

Dillon, R. W. and Goldstein, M. (1984) *Multivariate Analysis: Methods and applications*. John Wiley, New York. 337–359.

Etgar, M. (1976) "Channel domination and countervailing power in distributive channels." *Journal of Marketing Research*. Vol. XIII. 254–262.

Fan, X. (1997) "Canonical correlation analysis and structural equation modeling. What do they have in common?" *Structural Equation Modeling*. Vol. 4, no. 1. 65–79.

Fitts, R. L. and Karson, M. J. (1977) "Canonical correlation in a market segmentation study of commercial bank services." *Journal of Economics and Business*. Vol. 29, no. 2. 116–22.

Fornell, C. (1978a) "Problems in the interpretation of canonical analysis: the case of power in distribution channels." *Journal of Marketing Research*. Vol. 15 (August). 489.

Fornell, C. (1978b) "Three approaches to canonical analysis." *Journal of the Market Research Society*. Vol. 20, no. 3. 161–181.

Fornell, C. and Larcker, D. F. (1981a) "Evaluating structural equation models with unobservable variables and measurement error." *Journal of Marketing Research*. Vol. 18 (February). 39–50.

Fornell, C. and Larcker, D. F. (1981b) "Structural equation models with unobservable variables and measurement error: algebra and statistics." *Journal of Marketing Research*. Vol. 18 (August). 382–388.

Green, P. E. (1978) *Analyzing Multivariate Data*. Dryden Press, Hinsdale, IL. 260–289.

Green, P. E., Halbert, M. H. and Robinson, P. J. (1966) "Canonical analysis: An exposition and illustrative application." *Journal of Marketing Research*. Vol. 3 (February). 32–39.

Green, P. E., Tull, D. S. and Albaum, G. (1988) *Research for Marketing Decisions*. Prentice Hall, Englewood Cliffs, NJ.

Hair, J. F., Anderson, R. E., Tatham, R. L. and Black, W. C. (1998) *Multivariate Data Analysis*. Prentice-Hall, Upper Saddle River, NJ. 442–465.

Hayduk, L. A. (1987) *Structure Equation Modeling with LISREL: Essentials and advances*. Johns Hopkins University, Baltimore.

Holbrook, M. B. and Moore, W. L. (1982) "Using canonical correlation to construct product spaces for objects with known feature structures." *Journal of Marketing Research*. Vol. 19 (February). 87–98.

Hotelling, H. (1936) "Relations between two sets of variates." *Biometrika*. Vol. 28, no. 3–4. 321–77.

Hoyle, R. H. (ed.) (1995) *Structure Equation Modeling, Concepts, Issues and Applications*. Sage, Thousand Oaks, CA.

Kaplan, D. (2000) *Structural Equation Modeling Foundations and Extensions*. Sage, Thousand Oaks, CA.

Kelly, S. F. (1977) "Identifying innovative behaviour patterns using canonical analysis." *Journal of Business Research*. Vol. 5, no. 3. 249–59.

Lambert, Z. V. and Durand, R. M. (1975) "Some precautions in using canonical analysis." *Journal of Marketing Research*. Vol. 12 (November). 468–475.

Lattin, J., Carroll, D. C. and Green, P. E. (2003) *Analyzing Multivariate Data*. Thomson Learning, Pacific Grove, CA. 313–351.

Levine, M. S. (1977) *Canonical Analysis and Factor Comparison*. Sage, Beverly Hills, CA.

Nunnally, J. C. and Bernstein, I. H. (1994) *Psychometric Theory*, McGraw-Hill, New York.

Perry, M. and Hamm, B. C. (1969) "Canonical analysis of relations between socioeconomic risk and personal influence in purchase decisions." *Journal of Marketing Research*. Vol. 6. 351–354.

Schnaars, S. P. and Schiffman, L. G. (1984) "An Application of a segmentation design based on a hybrid of canonical correlation and simple crosstabulation." *Journal of the Academy of Marketing Science*. Vol. 12, no. 4. 177–90.

Schul, P. L., Pride, W. M. and Little, T. L. (1983) "The impact of channel leadership behaviour on intrachannel conflict." *Journal of Marketing*. Vol. 47 (Summer). 21–34.

Shimp, T. A. and Kavas, A. (1984) "The theory of reasoned action applied to coupon usage." *Journal of Consumer Research*. Vol. 11, (December). 795–809.

Stewart, G. W. and Love, W. A. (1968) "A general canonical correlation index." *Psychological Bulletin*. Vol. 70. 160–163.

Thompson, B. (1984) *Canonical Correlation Analysis: Uses and interpretation*, Sage, Beverly Hills, CA.

Van Auken, H. E., Doran, B. M. and Yoon, K. J. (1993) "A financial comparison between Korean and US firms: a cross balance sheet canonical correlation analysis." *Journal of Small Business Management*. Vol. 31, no. 3. 73–83.

Walters, R. G. (1988) "Retail promotions and retail store performance: a test of some key hypotheses." *Journal of Retailing*. Vol. 64, no. 2. 153–180.

Walters, R. G. and MacKenzie, S. B. (1988) "A structural equations analysis of the impact of price promotions on store performance." *Journal of Marketing Research*. Vol. 25, (February). 51–63.

Watts, D. G. (1995) "Understanding canonical analysis." *Journal of Quality Technology*. Vol. 27, no. 1. 40–45.

Wildt, A. R., Lambert, Z. V. and Durand, R. M. (1982) "Applying the jackknife statistic in testing and interpreting canonical weights, loadings and cross-loadings." *Journal of Marketing Research*. (February). 99–107.

End notes

[1] If there had been three dependent and predictor variables, a correlation *T3/U3* could have been computed. By definition, it could not have exceeded *T2/U2* − 0.70 and would probably have been lower. To sum up: correlations among T_i/U_i descend so that $T_i/U_i \geqslant T_{i+1}/U_{i+1}$.

[2] For instance, Fornell (1978a) has shown that a study by Etgar (1976) appears to be flawed.

[3] For the moment, ignore that CMIN – unlike 6-RMR and other LISREL/SEM measures – varies with sample size. This implies that any model will be rejected if the sample exceeds several hundred observations.

[4] In Excel: tab *[Insert]* on Excel's main menu bar, scroll down to *[fx, Function...]* and select it. Choose *[Statistics]* and *[Chidist]*. Plug in 3.544 for *X*-value and 2 for DF. Excel returns the value 0.169992663.

[5] Note that this argument is highly relevant concerning our measurement model since it is based on the empirical exploratory factor analysis of Table 11.6.

[6] Strictly speaking (a) is an overt oversimplification. Since some of the variation in *Y1* and *Y2* cannot be explained by *T1*, the dotted ellipse should intersect the squares of *Y1* and *Y2*. Likewise, the ellipse of *U1* should intersect the squares of *X1–X8*. Simultaneously, *T1* should intersect *X1* to *X8* while *U1* should intersect *Y1* and *Y2*. Moreover, the second canonical function should be included.

17 Data mining

Learning objectives

After studying this chapter you should be able to:

- Explain the difference between analytical models and data mining.
- Provide an overview of the elements of a data-mining application.
- Describe the scaling consequences of importing data from a data warehouse or database to a data-mining program.
- Explain the terms "stream canvas" and "node palette."
- Show how a rule model can be used for analyzing purchase patterns and product associations.
- Provide an overview of the ingredients of a neural network.
- Explain how expected technological improvements and market developments will influence the use of data mining.

17.1 Introduction

Since the early 1990s data mining and data warehousing have been hot topics within business. Producers of such statistical software as SAS and SPSS supply sophisticated packages for handling data mining. SAS's application is called *Enterprise Miner* while SPSS's module is *Clementine* (the latter's software will be discussed in detail below).

Interestingly, few academic journal publications on data mining have been published. While a search on "data mining" using research robots such as Proquest or Business Source Premier produces a wealth of hits, most link to non-academic and non-refereed publications. In the Winter of 2004/05, a search on *Proquest* using default fields and confined to three journals, *Journal of Marketing*, *Journal of Marketing Research* and *Journal of Consumer Research*, produced just two hits – both book reviews of books on data mining.

Why then is data mining so popular within an applied and non-academic environment whereas it seems to attract few researchers? The reason is that data mining is not an independent method or a "standalone" algorithm like multiple regression, factor analysis or latent class analysis. Rather, a typical data mining application consists of a variety of procedures and techniques bundled in a software package. Sometimes data mining is characterized as **metadata** (data about data). According to data mining theory, data are treated not as static information but as a **stream of data that has a direction**, beginning with the place where the raw data are stored, the data warehouse. The mining program then processes the data (recoding, merging, rescaling, etc.) and thereafter it performs the analysis by way of one or more statistical models (e.g. regression or factor analysis). Finally, the results are presented.

A data warehouse may be regarded as a database where vast amounts of – often heterogeneous – sources of data have been collected and stored. Some of the data may be primary data while others may be secondary data.

Provided that a company possesses a data warehouse, it may employ data mining for uncovering interesting patterns, structures, and characteristics in the data. Sometimes a warehouse contains different sources of data which, when merged and analyzed in unison, reveal relationships that otherwise could not have been detected.

A simplified and fictitious example may help to illustrate the potential value of data mining. Assume that the manager of a small company has detected a high degree of absenteeism among employees. It turns out that the worrying figures are caused by a small number of individuals. See Table 17.1.

According to accounting, absenteeism has totalled 224 days within the past twelve months, or 11.2 days on average per employee. However, it turns out that five persons (ID's 108, 161, 178, 180 and 197) account for more than half of absenteeism (127/224 or

Table 17.1 Days absent within past 12 months

Employee	Absent	ID	Department
Eleen Pearson	6	102	2
Bill Sanches	23	108	4
Florence Sipps	8	116	2
Henry Bell	0	117	3
Ron Clarke	12	122	2
Tamara Press	0	126	1
Debby Smith	7	135	4
Jackie Anderson	11	137	3
Yang Hoo	7	138	1
Susan Dale	2	153	1
V. Rao	21	161	1
Tom Banks	3	164	1
M. Agrawal	4	167	1
Rick Hawks	14	174	3
Frank Carmone	28	178	1
Gery Albaum	36	180	1
Paul Green	5	185	1
Slomo Goldstein	9	193	2
Cathy Schaffer	19	197	1
Hal Dobson	9	199	2
Total days	224		

Source: accounting department

Table 17.2 Variance of absenteeism

Department	Average days of absenteeism	n	ANOVA
1	12.5	10	
2	8.8	5	F = 0.31
3	8.3	3	p = 0.81
4	15.0	2	
Overall average:	11.2		

57%). Interestingly, four of these five individuals belong to the same department (1). But then again, department 1 has also employees with low absenteeism: ID 126 has 0 days absenteeism while ID's 153 and 164 have only been missing 2 and 3 days respectively.

The manager wants to assess whether the difference in absenteeism between departments is statistically significant. Therefore, he conducts an analysis of variance treating the department affiliation as predictor and absenteeism as dependent variable. Table 17.2 gives the results.

While there is some difference between the averages across departments, the difference is not nearly significant. Moreover, the groups sizes concerning departments 3 and 4 are very small and do not allow the manager to draw any statistical conclusions based on the data.

Instead, the manager decides to do something else. He recalls that he recently requested all employees to fill in a questionnaire on job satisfaction. The questionnaire consisted of

Table 17.3 Overall job satisfaction score

Employee	Score	ID	Department
Mary Hoffmann	3	104	3
Neil Dyson	8	120	4
Ron Clarke	7	122	2
Tamara Press	8	126	1
Andrea Horn	7	133	3
Yang Hoo	5	138	1
Tom Simson	6	141	4
Margaret Brunner	5	147	2
Susan Dale	8	153	1
Sam Field	4	159	4
V. Rao	1	161	1
Tom Banks	9	164	1
Pat Domino	3	166	3
M. Agrawal	6	167	1
Frank Carmone	1	178	1
Rolph Oldenburg	4	179	2
Gery Albaum	2	180	1
Paul Green	7	185	1
Slomo Goldstein	6	193	2
Cathy Schaffer	3	197	1

Overall satisfaction:		10 = Very satisfied	
		1 = Not at all satisfied	

Source: human relations department

Table 17.4 Second analysis

Department	Average satisfaction	n	ANOVA
1	5.0	10	
2	5.5	4	F = 0.24
3	4.3	3	p = 0.87
4	6.0	3	
Overall average	5.2	20	

a lot of statements, and concerning one statement the employee was asked to rate "overall job satisfaction" on a ten-point scale where a higher score implies higher job satisfaction. The results are provided in Table 17.3.

Once more an analysis of variance is conducted, this time treating the satisfaction score as dependent and the department affiliation as predictor. See Table 17.4.

As was the case with the ANOVA carried out on absenteeism, the new analysis is not at all significant. The average satisfaction score of department 1 is five – very close to the overall average of 5.2 – and therefore it is impossible for the manager to draw any conclusions. Had the score concerning department 1 been 2.3 or so then this might have been an indication of widespread dissatisfaction among employees of department 1.

When comparing Table 17.1 and Table 17.3 we note that some persons that appear in one table do not appear in the other. But there is an overlap of persons and 12 of them are listed in both tables.

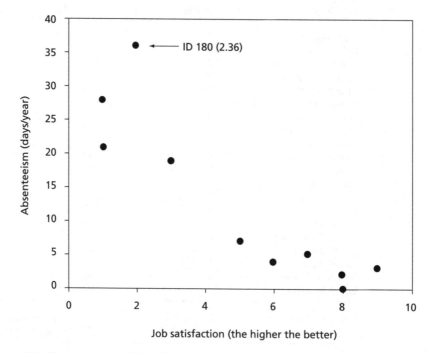

Figure 17.1 Absenteeism and job satisfaction

The manager notes that all ten employees of department 1 appear in both tables. Therefore he decides to compare their two-dimensional data person-by-person.

Regarded from a measurement perspective, absenteeism (Table 17.1) is a discrete, ratio-scaled behavioural characteristic while the satisfaction score (Table 17.3) is an interval-scaled attitudinal response profile. So, strictly speaking, the two measures are incompatible. Nevertheless, the manager performs a direct comparison of the two variables. See Figure 17.1.

Evidently, there is a strong – negative – correlation between job satisfaction and absenteeism. (Note that all ten data points appearing in Figure 17.1 can be found in Table 17.1 and Table 17.3). As the reader may check, the R-square between absenteeism and job satisfaction (based on the ten employees of department 1) is 0.80. The modelling relationship is highly significant (F = 32.9 and p = 0.0004). With job satisfaction (x) as predictor and absenteeism (y) as dependent, the parameter estimate related to job satisfaction is -3.7, implying that each time the job satisfaction score improves by one point on the $1-10$ satisfaction score, absenteeism decreases by 3.7 days.

So, by merging two heterogeneous sources of data (from accounting and from human relations, respectively) an interesting insight is gained. Based on Figure 17.1 and the regression analysis, the manager decides to conduct in-depth interviews with those employees of department 1 that appear to be especially dissatisfied with their job. He notices that IDs 161, 178, 180 and 197 have provided job satisfaction scores in the range of three or below, implying frustration with their present job. What might the reason be? And could the low satisfaction be due to a single cause?

If the manager succeeds in identifying the underlying cause(s) and provided that he is able to improve their job satisfaction markedly and immediately, there is a good chance that the absenteeism figures will drop significantly.

In many companies it is not practice to streamline all sources of internal data in such a way that they can be fused and merged. The marketing manager may succeed in making, say, foreign and native sales and consumer satisfaction data compatible, while the accounting manager may do an excellent job in rationalizing financial and monetary data flows. At the same time, the personnel manager may collect and analyze a lot of information dealing with job satisfaction of employees, command structures within the organization and so on. However, the real challenge is to combine the different sources of data. Merging and analyzing heterogeneous data structures can help improve a company's performance in several ways.

Generally, accounting data, marketing data, organizational data, etc., will be relatively homogeneous *within* a department but heterogeneous *across* departments. For instance, customer satisfaction information normally is collected via customer surveys – sampled with a margin of error. The questionnaire typically is made up of statements that are measured using interval scales, whereas accounting data normally will be instrumental figures (balance sheet figures or spreadsheets).

It is beyond the scope of the present text to provide a comprehensive coverage of data mining. Examples of suitable books are: Drozdenko and Drake (2002), Hand, Mannila and Smyth (2001), Berry and Linoff (2004), Klösen and Zytkow (2002), Pyle (2003), Giudici (2003), Han and Kamber (2000), Rud (2000), and Bigus (1996).

As noted, journal publications on data warehousing and data mining are surprisingly rare. However, two papers addressing the topic are Thelen, Mottner and Berman (2004) and Rafalski and Mullner (2003).

The screenshots shown in this chapter are based on SPSS Clementine version 8. However, where appropriate, we discuss changes and updates that appear in the new versions 9 and 10 of the program.

17.2 Data mining with SPSS *Clementine*

Data mining programs are characterized by user-friendly interfaces. However, code syntax is needed to solve complex or unusual problems.

Up to now, analysis of data has been more or less static: a data set was analyzed by way of an appropriate model and then the results were interpreted. Sometimes, data were first analyzed in one model and subsequently analyzed further by another, based on the output from the preceding stage.

Except for such combined analytical processes, every statistical model has been treated separately. Moreover, discussion of technical issues, such as the scaling of a variable, recoding or sorting, has been unsystematic. In data mining, measurement issues and a lot of other technical aspects of a data set have to be addressed in unison and simultaneously.

As noted, data mining does not represent innovation with regard to statistical models or graphical displays, but it is innovative with respect to combining input, successive processing steps, modelling and output. Also, it is inventive to work with a lot of models and processes simultaneously.

To facilitate the discussion we will show an empirical data stream as it appears in Clementine (we use version 8.0). See Figure 17.2.

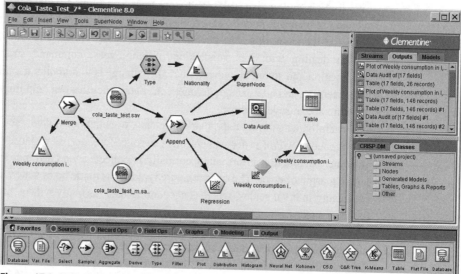

Figure 17.2 SPSS Clementine stream canvas

Clementine's main screen

The main field of Figure 17.2 is called the ***stream canvas***. Within the stream canvas many icons are shown. Each icon represents one of the following categories: an input data file, a data process/manipulation, a statistical model, a graphical display or an output table/file. *Clementine*'s manual uses the word ***node***. The authors of the present book employ the two terms "icons" and "nodes" as synonyms. If a specific node is mentioned the first letter is capitalized (Distribution node, Regression node, etc.).

Beneath the stream canvas a default selection of icons, the Favourites Palette, is displayed. In *Clementine* all icons belong to one of five groups:

- Input data files are represented by circles.
- Processes and manipulations appear as hexagons.
- Graphical displays are characterized by triangles.
- Models are represented by pentagons.
- Output appears as squares (note: graphs may also be regarded as output).

As with SEM/LISREL, some directions of arrows and arrows from some icons to other icons are not allowed:

- It is not possible to draw an arrow from so-called terminal nodes (models, graphs, and output) to other nodes. Note though that one can usually select an established model and drag the icon into the stream canvas. After having done this one can drag an arrow from this icon to, say, a graph.
- An icon may only have one arrow pointing to it, while several arrows are allowed to point from an icon towards other icons.
- An arrow cannot point towards a source icon (input file).
- Some connections imply circularity or do not make sense (e.g. from a model to some data processing icons).

If the analyst tries to draw a "forbidden" arrow, a message says this is not an option.

To the right of the stream canvas are two smaller fields. The upper one contains three tags. The first tag lists the active streams (it is possible to load and analyze several streams at the same time) while the second and third tags list the output and the models generated during the current session. Details on output and models are available by selecting the appropriate output or model from the list, right clicking the mouse and then clicking, say, display (if it is a table or a graph) or browse (if it is a model).

The other window or field provides two ways of structuring and summarizing data mining information:

- CRISP-DM. Cross-Industry Standard Process for Data Mining – A suggested "best practices" way of organizing data mining work.
- Classes. A categorical way of organizing work by the type of objects created. The *Clementine* user manual has more information on these.

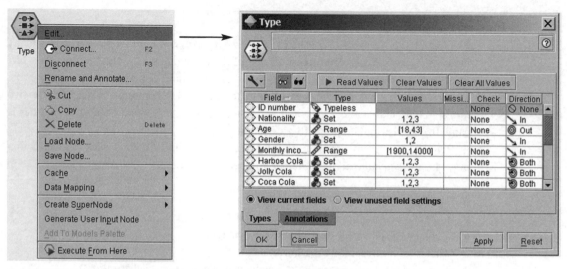

Figure 17.3 Editing data fields and defining stream settings in *Clementine*

Before proceeding, take a look at the stream canvas of Figure 17.2. First, look at the two circles. They both represent SPSS files (*Clementine* can handle other formats.) These two files are stored in the data warehouse and are now read into *Clementine*.[1] Arrows indicate the direction or flow of the data. An arrow is pointing from the SPSS files towards the merge icon.

The merge icon describes a process that joins variables from the two files by way of an ID-number variable appearing in both input files. The Merge node belongs to the group of icons called **Record Operations**. The ID variable refers to the same entity (here: an individual respondent), and in the present case both files contain a variable that is of interest to the analyst. Since the input data sets are merged, a scatter plot of the two variables can be produced. This is indicated by the triangle "Weekly Consumption." Also note an arrow pointing from one of the SPSS files toward a hexagon named "Type." This icon belongs to the group of nodes related to data processing activities (**Field Operations**).

Right-click the latter icon and see what happens. See Figure 17.3. The click triggers a drop-down with a list of options. We select *[Edit]* and the Type dialogue box appears.

The combination: right-click the icon, select *[Edit]* and then change the settings of the dialogue box is universal in *Clementine*. The dialogue boxes differ, some have more tags, but basically dialogue boxes work in the same way.

Before using the different types of data, the miscellaneous – and somewhat confusing – measurement terms used in *Clementine*, SPSS Base, and Chapter 6 above will be compared. See Figure 17.4.

Study Figure 17.4 in combination with Figure 17.3. In Figure 17.3, the Type dialogue box has six columns. The first one lists the variable's name, the second one explains how *Clementine* "understands" the scaling of the variable types:

- Range. Used to describe numeric values (ratio scale, interval scale).
- Discrete. Employed for string values (text) or when the number of distinct values is unknown.

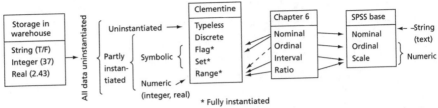

Note: Nominal is often divided into dichotomous (flag) and categorical (set). *Clementine* treats discrete as text/unknown number of levels. However, it is common to use the term discrete in order to distinguish it from a continuous variable. The number of persons in a household is discrete while household income is continuous (you can divide money but not a person).

Figure 17.4 Scale notations in SPSS and *Clementine*

- Flag. Used for dichotomous data (when there are only two levels like yes/no).
- Set. For variables that are nominal-scaled (occupation, number of brands in a product category, etc.).
- Typeless. Used when there are many levels (e.g. account number or ID number of a respondent).

When reading a file from the data warehouse or database, *Clementine* uses a default scale. If the value has no decimal points, it is read as *integer*, if it has, then it is read as *real*. Finally, if the cell/field contains terms such as "true" or "false" it is read as a *string* .[2] See Figure 17.4. Once the data enter *Clementine*, they must be ***instantiated*** or "determined." If they are uninstantiated or only partly instantiated, they can be read, but they cannot be properly "understood" by the data-mining program. By using the Type node, one can specify how each variable is to be read in the data file. If left uninstantiated (typeless), they cannot be processed in any meaningful way. Partly instantiated data are categorized into three subgroups, discrete, symbolic and numeric. These data can be processed, but still there is little that can be done with the data. For instance, one cannot know whether partially instantiated data are discrete (unknown number of levels or even text), or symbolic (nominal: dichotomous or categorical).

Before partially instantiated data can be classified as fully instantiated, the analyst first needs to either select flag, set or range (range includes both integers and reals). Once the variables of a data set are fully instantiated the data-mining program has much better knowledge about how to use the data.

A value like "1" that is stored in a file in the warehouse, obtains the storage characteristic *integer*. Then *Clementine* by default transforms this unspecific measurement value to range (integer and real). While this may apply in many cases, it need not do so in all cases. For instance, if a variable is intended to measure a characteristic that is nominal-scaled (flag/set), say, a respondent's nationality or gender, then the data-mining program should not treat the data as a range but rather as a nominal-scaled variable.

Therefore, change the default setting (range) for nationality and gender to set (since gender has two levels it could have been changed to flag). So tab the Types tag in Figure 17.3; in the Type column, click the appropriate cell and then in the drop-down menu, change from range to set or flag. (The same can be done by double clicking the source file icon in the stream canvas.)

Next click *[Read Values]*, and the min and max values of the variables (discrete levels for nominal scaled variables) appear in the values column. This is a good sign, because it shows *Clementine* has understood the range or interval of the measurement. The ID variable in Figure 17.3 is set to typeless and is not used in the analysis. It can be used for merging, filtering, sampling, sorting, etc., but is ignored in calculations and statistical analysis.

Note that the variable Nationality has three levels (in the present data file it represents the citizenship of three groups of student-respondents). Gender, of course, has two levels. The age of the respondents ranges from 18 to 43 years and their income from 1,900 to 14,000 units a month.

The missing values column is used for indicating which values are treated as blanks (choices are off – the default, on and specify *[user-defined]*.

In the check column, one can let the program check if the field values conform to a specified range. The program can provide a warning if cases appear strange (outliers, etc.). In the present case, it may be doubtful that a student is older than thirty years. Therefore, tab the cell of the age row and Missing column (Figure 17.3). Select "Specify". In the "age Values" box select *[Specify labels and values]*. Change "Upper" from 43 (years) to 31. Next tab *[Check values]* and, in the drop down, select *[Abort]* – a sign of warning/alarm. *[OK, OK]*. Finally, right click the "Type" icon in Figure 17.2 and select *[Execute from here]*. Note that a pop-up box warns you that "Age" variable has values that are out of range (that is, values bigger than 31).

The last column of Figure 17.3 addresses the direction of the data. Direction settings are *none, in, out, both in and out* and *partitioning. In* is the typical setting for a predictor field. *Out* implies that a field may be used as an output (dependent/may be predicted) field. For instance, when running a neural net model (see below) the variable that is used as dependent output node must have the direction *out*. Certain models included in *Clementine* (some of them are discussed below) necessitate that the type setting is *both in and out*. If *none* is selected the variable will be ignored with regard to the modelling process (it corresponds to the Field setting Typeless). *Partitioning* is used for splitting data into training, testing and validation groups.

After the above type changes have been carried out, the variables (except the ID-variable) are said to be **fully instantiated**.

It can be confusing when working with variables and scales in *Clementine*. From the user's guide, it seems that the terms "variables," "records," and "fields" are used interchangeably. A variable is the same as a column (or field) in the data file while a record is the same as a row or line. Depending on the circumstances, a field can probably also be regarded a cell.

Note that before proceeding we must deselect the warning due to Age being more than 31. This is carried out as follows: Right click the *[Type]* icon, *[Edit]*, click *[Abort]* in the *[Check]* column and select *[None]*, *[OK]*.

Now back to Figure 17.2. The aim is to produce a graph of the Nationality variable. This is easy to do. According to the Type settings (Figure 17.3), Nationality has three levels. Thus a simple distribution plot must be regarded a relevant graph. Therefore, tab the distribution triangle of the favourites palette and drag it to a place in the stream canvas. Then use the middle button of the mouse (or alternatively, CTRL, ALT, left button) and

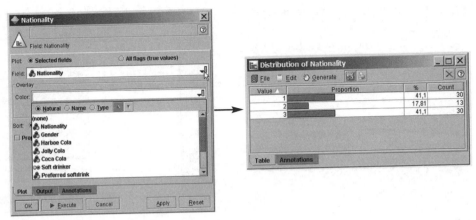

Figure 17.5 Producing a simple graph in *Clementine*

drag a connection (arrow) from the Type icon to the Distribution icon (the Distribution graph only accepts nominal – set and flag – variables). Right-click the *[Distribution]* icon, choose *[Edit]* and select "Nationality" as field variable. Finally, tab *[Execute]* and the graph is displayed. See Figure 17.5.

The distribution as such is unimportant here and is therefore not explained.

The Append node (Figure 17.2) resembles the Merge node in that it joins data from different sources but while the latter joins records from two or more files by way of a common ID number on a one by one basis, the Append node passes downstream all of the records from a source until all records have been read. Append nodes are practical for combining data sets with analogous structures but different data. For instance, assume that a researcher wants to analyze a set of pre-specified variables describing daily sales for January and February. Moreover, assume that the data are stored in two different files. January has 31 days, whereas February has either 28 or 29 days, so here an ID does not make sense.

Since the two source files of Figure 17.2 do not contain times series data the Append node is not used in any effective way.

An arrow points from the Append node towards an icon named Regression. The pentagon shape says this is one of *Clementine*'s model nodes. In the present case, a multiple regression analysis has been done based on the input files. To carry out the regression analysis, tab the Regression node (it appears among the modelling nodes in Figure 17.8), drag it into the canvas, draw an arrow from, say, the Append node to the Regression icon, select the Regression icon or node, right click, tab *[Edit]*, and indicate which variables are dependent/predictors. First, tab the fields tag, select *[Use custom settings]* and browse the Target field (dependent variable) and Input-field (predictor variables). This is done by tabbing the drop-down lists at the right end of the fields. The drop-down lists all variables. See Figure 17.6 (left box).

Once the variables have been properly selected, the job may be executed and the output appears as a couple of tables, not unlike the regression output format known from SPSS base: an ANOVA table on overall model fit, a table showing the regression estimates, etc. Since the actual output from the regression analysis is not of interest here it is not shown.

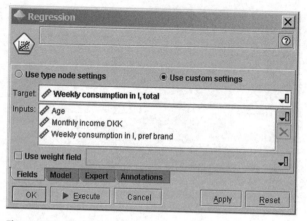 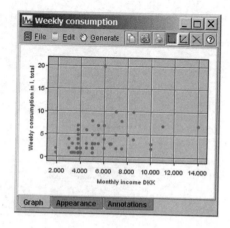

Figure 17.6 Running regression in *Clementine*

To see it select the *[Models]* tag right to stream canvas (Figure 17.2). Right click the model just created (yellow diamond shape) – Figure 17.2 only shows the outputs tab with many tables created – and, finally, tab *[Browse]*. The regression output appears. The *[Advanced]* tag has many details.

Note that whenever one tries to execute a task, such as a merge, a regression, or a graph, but where some settings have been incorrectly specified, a pop-up containing an error message will provide summary information on why the task could not be executed. Some typical examples of invalid specifications are:

- Failure to denote an ID key for the merge of two data files.
- Omitting to indicate a target key (dependent variable) in regression.
- Having specified a variable stream direction as "in" (input to the stream) when the method necessitates an "out" (output).

All executions that are successfully carried out turn green during the execution process. If the job cannot be executed, the node causing the problem turns red.

When the regression (or one of the other available models) has been run successfully, a Generated Model node appears in the Model Manager. It is not shown in Figure 17.2 but is accessible by clicking the Models tag. See the upper right field of Figure 17.2. It is possible to tab the Generated Model node, drag it into the stream canvas and draw an arrow from the Append node to the Generated Models node. This has been done in Figure 17.2 (see the cube with the tiny scatter icon).

Next, we select a Plot node, drag it into the stream canvas and draw an arrow from the Generated Model node to the Plot node. Finally, click the Plot node and specify which variables to plot. Choose a scatter plot. See Figure 17.6. (It does not seem that the two variables are highly correlated, for the R-square between monthly income and weekly consumption of soft drink is only 0.11. However, the actual size of the correlation is of no interest at this point.) Note, that by tabbing the *[Model]* tag one can select *[Stepwise Regression]*.

The stream canvas of Figure 17.2 contains some more icons that so far have not been explained. The Data Audit icon displays a simple histogram and summary statistics on

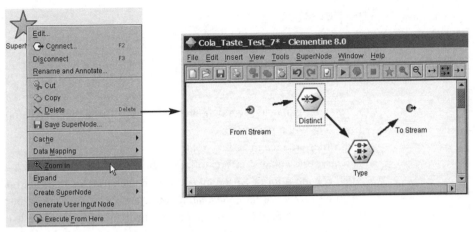

Figure 17.7 Zooming in on a SuperNode

each range variable (default: mean, standard deviation, skewness and the number of valid observations).

The SuperNode icon comprises a nested or hidden part of the stream canvas. In the present case, right-click the node and select *[Zoom In]* on the drop-down menu. See Figure 17.7.

Basically, a SuperNode is just a way to partition a data stream canvas that has become too complex to grasp. To prevent an overflow of icons and arrows, a part of the canvas is hidden. If necessary, one can zoom in on the SuperNode and analyze it separately.

The right side of Figure 17.7 shows a simple SuperNode. Normally, a SuperNode will contain a lot of individual nodes. A SuperNode may in itself enclose more nodes than does Figure 17.2. The present SuperNode contains only two nodes, a Distinct node and a Type node. The Distinct node is used in cases where the analyst wants to prevent (or ensure) duplicate records in a database. The facility may help finding multiple purchases by the same consumers in a database. For instance, the node can be used for establishing an index of all products based on bar code information, and so help detect duplicate account numbers.

In Figure 17.7, the Distinct node points at a Type node and then the data stream leaves the SuperNode canvas and returns to the main data stream canvas of Figure 17.2 where a table based on the data manipulations specified in the SuperNode is produced. The stream of Figure 17.2 is only used for illustrational purposes. A SuperNode is established by right clicking any existing node. In the drop-down select *[Create SuperNode, From Selection]* and the new "within" SuperNode canvas appears, where one can build a sub-stream. Tab the SuperNode dropdown above the canvas and select "zoom out" to return to the main canvas. In the SuperNode canvas of Figure 17.7 the flow of data points *from* the main canvas, *into* the SuperNode canvas and *back* to the main canvas. It is called a *Process Node* (other SuperNode types are Source Nodes and Terminal Nodes). For more information inspect the users' manual on the Clementine installation CD.

The palettes

The favourites palette of *Clementine* (Figure 17.2) only displays a selection of icons within each group of nodes. The complete list is shown in Figure 17.8.

First, the Sources/files palette:

- *Clementine* can read several input data formats. The authors have imported variable and fixed files without problems.
- SPSS files are recognized.
- However, the authors' efforts to import SAS files were not so successful, because these often contain a lot of SAS syntax code. In such cases it does not make much sense to import an SAS file into *Clementine*, or at least it necessitates a lot of manual editing. Sometimes, the SAS file contains only syntax while the data file is loaded separately into the program and used in the analytical process. In this case, the data file should be loaded into *Clementine* using a fixed or flat file format. Import of SAS files or importing data sets from an SQL database is for the experienced user of *Clementine*. Version 10 also includes a *Dimension* node. This node is appropriate for importing text, log files, metadata, etc.
- The User input format is a mix of fixed and variable file formats, where one then has to do a little manual coding.

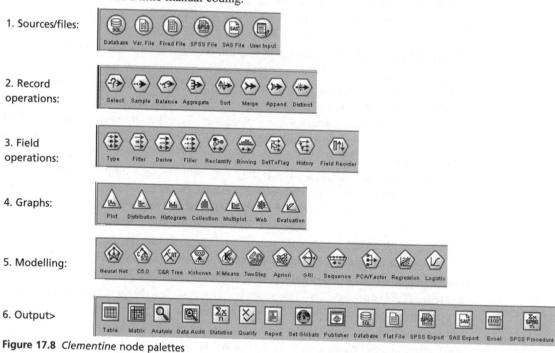

Figure 17.8 *Clementine* node palettes

Second, Record operations:

- *Select* resembles the *[Data, Select Cases, if condition is satisfied]* known from SPSS base.
- *Sample* is a powerful option in cases where the data file is huge. For instance, the authors possess a panel data file registering total purchases by 2,000 housewives of selected food and non-food products over a five-year period. The aggregate data file

contains several million records. While the file as such can be aggregated, it is too big for most purposes. By way of the Sample node, one can ask the program to draw a subset of, say, 1,000 records that constitute a representative random sample of the aggregated millions of purchases.

- *Balance* is useful for weighting data sets. Maybe some raw data in the warehouse are outdated or biased and need to be weighted by a numeric factor. Some respondent categories may be under-represented in a panel while others are over-represented. A wisely balanced weighting based on historical experience may be useful for correcting for this kind of bias.
- *Aggregate* can be used for calculating descriptive statistics on ratio and interval-scaled variables across levels of a nominal variable. For instance, one can compute mean and standard deviation regarding household income for each level of occupational status.
- *Merge* and *Append* appear in Figure 17.2 and have been briefly explained. The same holds for *Distinct* in Figure 17.7. As follows from the name, the *Sort* node performs an – ascending or descending – sort of rows, observations or records based on a sort variable. Essentially, it does the same as *[Data, Sort Cases, Sort by]* in SPSS.

Third, Field operations:

- *Type* appears in Figure 17.3 and has been explained.
- The *Filter* node can be employed for discarding or ignoring variables. For instance, one may only be interested in processing a small section of all variables with regard to a special analysis. If so, one deselects the irrelevant variables.
- With *Derive* one can create variables based on other variables. The Derive node may best be described as a recoding or data manipulation facility. For instance, one may construct a customer loyalty variable with three levels, such that customers with one or two purchases in a given period are coded as non-loyal, three to five may be coded as partly loyal and five or more as loyal. Also, one could program an estimated regression function, so that a value in one variable, for instance 5, is substituted in the regression model $y = 3.5x - 8 = 3.5(5) - 8 = 9.5$. The output or prediction estimate is then placed in a new variable. Of course, formulae can be considerably more complex than the one shown. The Derive node resembles Excel's formula editor. In many cases, effective use of the Derive facility necessitates using *Clementine* syntax code (called Clementine Language for Expression Manipulation, abbreviated CLEM). The manual on the installation CD provides an appendix on CLEM.
- *Filler* nodes exchange blank or null values with a specific data value (for instance with the mean of non-missing or valid variable-observations, or with some other value). It serves the same purpose as a find/replace utility.
- *Reclassify* resembles the Derive node but is easier to use for simpler reclassification problems. One may recode into existing and new variables. Also, it is easy to employ for handling missing values. Reclassify is similar to *[Transform, Recode, Into same/different Variables]* in SPSS.
- *Binning* is a method for constructing a histogram with a discrete number of levels (ranges/intervals) based on ratio-scaled data. It works much like Excel's *[Tools, Data Analysis, Histogram]* or SPSS' *[Graphs, Histogram]*. "Bin" refers to the number of levels and the width of a level. For instance, one may recode income observations

3,250, 6,800 and 9,100 as "€0–10000" and so on. The range "0–10000" is called bin width. If there are eight income classes then the number of bins is eight. Binning works fine with the graphical *Histogram* node (see below).

- *Partitioning* (not shown in Figure 17.8, but included in version 9 of Clementine) can be used for partitioning the data into several samples for training, testing and validating. It is most useful when working with large data sets. It gives a good indication of how well the model will generalize to different data sets that are supposed to be similar to the current data set.

- *SetToFlag* is designed for "flagging" a value if it possesses a certain characteristic. For instance, the same brand can be purchased in several areas of a shop. Normally, the bar code registers the brand name while the department's cashier lists the department where it was purchased. *SetToFlag* in combination with *Sort* and *Distribution* can be used for obtaining an easy overview of how the purchases of a brand (or product category or products on offer) are distributed across departments. If the departments' direct costs vary then the price of a brand ought to differ across departments. *SetToFlag* will normally have two states (T=True, say, for departments where the brand was purchased and F=False, otherwise).

- When analyzing times series data, the *History* node can integrate values from a sequence of previous records into the current record. For instance, one might wish to establish a measure of estimated future product sales such that sales of the preceding five periods are included in the compound measure but where the most recent sales period $(t-1)$ has a higher weight than has earlier ones $(t-5)$.

- The *Field Reorder* node is for reordering variables. If the original variable order from left to right is *x1, x2, x3* the Field Reorder node can be used for changing the order to, say, *x3, x1, x2*.

- Version 10 includes three new nodes: *Restructure* (used in combination with *SetToFlag*). Its purpose is to generate restructured fields. The *Transpose* node serves the same purpose as [*Data, Transpose*] in SPSS base. It can transpose an n*m matrix to an m*n matrix. The *Time Intervals* node can be used for building and labelling time series.

Fourth, Graph:

- The *Plot* graph can be employed for producing *x,y*-scatter plots of numeric variables. Figure 17.6 shows an example.

- The *Distribution* node is designed for making bar diagrams of nominal scaled variables. See Figure 17.5.

- Use of the *Histogram* node was explained above when discussing the Binning field operation.

- *Collection* shows the distribution of one variable relative to another. It is useful for illustrating a value whose distribution changes over time compared with others.

- *Multiplot* maps series across another series, for instance purchase in units of three related brands across time. It resembles Excel's and Power Point's [*Chart, Lines*] and SPSS [*Graph, Line, Multiple*].

- The *Web* node is a specified form of graphical display. It is discussed below (Figures 17.13 and 17.14).

- *Evaluation* represents a way to assess and compare predictive models. It helps the analyst in finding the model that best fits the data. Often, Evaluation is used in combination with Derive and, like Derive, a practical usage of Evaluation presumes knowledge of

Clementine's expression builder. The graph in a way resembles the normal probability plot – a graph that can be requested as part of the output when running regression in Excel *[Tools, Data Analysis, Regression]*. As recalled, the normal probability plot shows how well empirical data fit the normal distribution. The Evaluation node appears in Figure 17.16. The figure shows two fit functions. The one close to the diagonal line provides negligible information or poor model fit. According to a cumulative gain chart a successful model should rise steeply from left to right and then level off. If this is the case, the model markedly deviates from "random noise". This situation is indicated by the steeper line. (Generally, the interpretation of an evaluation chart depends on the type of chart.)

- Version 10 includes a *Time Plot* node. It can be used for plotting several time series over time.

Fifth, Modelling:

- *Neural Net* and *Kohonen*. Both models are neural networks – algorithms that aim at simulating aspects of information processing as it is believed to take place in the human brain. The Neural Net node can be used for prediction instead of logistic regression, discriminant analysis, etc. Like canonical analysis, the method allows for more than one dependent measure. The Kohonen node is an option to clustering methods like the k-means method. An example of using the Neural Net node and the Kohonen node is given below. Exhibit 17.2 provides a non-technical introduction to neural networks.
- *C5.0* and *C&R Tree* are decision tree models. Basically they are CHAID algorithms and both closely resemble the methods covered in the first part of Chapter 15. Version 9 of Clementine also includes a CHAID node and a Quest node (both discussed in Section 2 of Chapter 15).
- *K-means* cluster is discussed in detail in Chapter 12.
- *Two Step* cluster is a two-step clustering method. The first step makes a single path through the data, during which it compresses the raw input data into a manageable set of subclusters. The second step uses a hierarchical clustering method to progressively merge the subclusters into larger and larger clusters, without requiring another pass through the data. The method can handle categorical data and provides default settings/options for handling of outliers, and how to determine the best number of clusters. The method was covered at the end of Chapter 15.
- The *Apriori* node and the *GRI* node uncover certain association rules in a data set. Both models contain information about rules extracted from the data. The Apriori and the GRI model are **unrefined rule models** and cannot be used for generating predictions directly. A GRI node analyzes associations between items in pairs, for instance to which degree two product categories or brands tend to be purchased during the same shopping trip. An Apriori node assesses the probability that a series of items, such as specified product categories, are bought during sequential shopping trips. GRI and Apriori are explained below.
- The *Carma Node* (new for version 9) is used for predicting purchases in if/then situations. For instance, if a customer has purchased a computer on a recent visit to a TV store, he or she may be a prospect for peripherals or upgrades in the following months, provided that he or she is exposed to special offers by way of direct marketing.
- The *Sequence* node discovers patterns in sequential or time series data. A sequence is

a list of items that tend to be purchased in a predictable order. The node detects frequent sequences and creates a model that can be used for making predictions. The Sequence node is similar to the Apriori node but can be used for modelling more complex relationships. In most cases, the Sequence node necessitates some use of syntax.

- *PCA/Factor, Regression* and *Logistic*: these methods have been covered in earlier chapters.
- *The Text Extraction Node* (new for version 9) can be employed for detecting and uncovering frequently used keywords and salient concepts from structured and unstructured text data. For instance, if responses to a text field in an Internet survey frequently contain "warranty problems/issues" this might be revealed by the model and used by management for improving customer satisfaction.
- The *Feature Selection* node (new for version 10) is appropriate when hundreds or thousands of fields are to be analyzed simultaneously. It can help identify subsets of good predictor fields or variables.

Sixth, Output:

- *Table* just prints or lists the variables * observations.
- *Matrix* by default shows a cross tab of two variables (counts as well as rows and cell percentages).
- *Analysis* allows one to assess predictive models and evaluate their ability to generate accurate predictions. The feature may be useful for identifying systematic errors in prediction. For experienced users.
- *Data Audit* is a powerful, yet simple output facility that – by default – displays a small graph and descriptive statistics (mean, SD, skewness) of ratio-scaled variables.
- *Statistics* resembles the Data Audit node. It displays no graph. Instead, one may request correlation statistics.
- *Mean* node (new for version 10) can be used for labelling results as important, marginal, or unimportant based on probability grounded threshold values.
- *Quality* displays simple statistics on the number of valid observations and on missing values.
- *Report* creates formatted reports containing fixed text as well as data and other expressions derived from the data. Usage assumes some syntax code and is for experienced users.
- *Set Globals* is somewhat similar to *[Edit, Options]* in SPSS. The node makes it possible to refine output with regard to which statistics should appear in the output and how.
- *Solution Publisher* is a more powerful deployment mechanism compared with an isolated export of data or models since it publishes entire data streams including processes and generated models. Note that the Solution Publisher is not part of the *Clementine* base but requires a separate licence.
- *Excel*. The option can be used for exporting data to Excel. See Exhibit 17.1.
- When exporting the data-mining file to SPSS the same problems as when exporting to Excel are not expected.
- Saving as *Flat* file seems easy. This option is preferable to a direct Excel export. The flat file keeps variable names and by default uses a comma as separator. This file can be read by Excel (via the Import Wizard) or by SPSS and causes no problems.
- Exporting to SAS. The authors experienced problems exporting directly from

Clementine to SAS. The *Clementine* manual is not very helpful here. Try the following (easier methods may exist, though): in *Clementine*, export the data as flat file. Read this file into Excel and save it as an Excel file. Start SAS and import the Excel file into SAS using the SAS import wizard. Another method is to create a data table within *Clementine*, open SAS, and copy/paste the data from *Clementine* into SAS. (Both ways may cause problems if the file is huge.)

- *Data Base* refers to ODBC (open data base connectivity). It allows programs of various types to exchange data in a simple way. However, the data source must exist and one must have permission to access the data source. This is for experienced users.
- *SPSS procedure* allows SPSS syntax to be used (not to be confused with CLEM syntax) within *Clementine*. For experienced users.

EXHIBIT 17.1 PROBLEMS WHEN EXPORTING FROM CLEMENTINE TO EXCEL

Occasionally, one may wish to output a data-mining file to Excel. Assume one has loaded an SPSS file (.sav) into *Clementine*, merged it with another SPSS file, done some sorting, sampling, etc. But it is still a data file with variable names in the top row and then columns*rows (variables times observations) of data. Saving directly as Excel format is not an option (neither is loading an Excel file directly into *Clementine*). The options are: CSV (comma delimited); and Text (tab delimited). Right-click the Excel node, select "Create File: With specified file name," Use "File type: Text (tab delimited) (*.txt)," give it a file name and choose a folder to place it in. The decimal symbol should be "Local default." Tab [*Execute*]. Most probably this will produce an error message like "Cannot start Excel." However, the file should be created by now. Next, start Excel and choose to open the file. Excel should now launch the "Text (!) Import Wizard." Step 1: the file type "Delimited" should be selected. Step 2: "Tab" should be selected (and nothing else) should be selected. This should do it. [*Finish*]. The file appears in the Excel screen with the variable names in the first row.

Note: the authors have experienced problems using variable labels when exporting files from *Clementine* 8.0 to Excel 2000. Sometimes the far-right variables did not contain any data. The problem is prevented thus, assuming the source file is SPSS: go to the icon of the SPSS source file within the Stream Canvas. Right-click it. Be sure that both "Use variable labels" and "Use value labels" are deselected. Now you can go to the Excel node, right-click it and tab [*Execute*]. Then back to the first Step above... After completing the task, one has the variable names but the labels are gone (Excel does not support SPSS labels)!

An additional problem: assumed that the first variable (or label) – the cell in the first column and first row – that Excel is about to read is named "ID," "ID Name" or so, Microsoft Excel 97, 2000, 2002 (Standard Editions) and Office Excel 2003 refuse to read the file! Instead they come up with an error message: "SYLK: File format is not valid." This problem is recognized by Microsoft. It can be solved thus: open the file with the Microsoft Notepad. Change ID to id (small letters instead of capital ones, or to something else). Save the file and load it into Excel. This should do it. The problem may seem insignificant. However, it is not at all improbable that the first variable starts with "ID."

EXHIBIT 17.2 BASICS OF A NEURAL NETWORK

A neural network (also called ANN, abbreviated from artificial neural network) aims to simulate aspects of information processing in a similar way to the human brain. Neural nets are mostly used for prediction instead of regression-type problems. However, a specialized algorithm (known as Kohonen net) is able to categorize cases just like traditional clustering methods do. (See Beltratti, Margarita and Terna, 1996.)

Most neural nets employ so-called **supervised learning**. First, the neuron receives an input. Second, the input is processed in accordance with the algorithm and an output value is suggested. Third, the predicted value is compared with the actual or empirical figure. Fourth, the residual value (difference between predicted and actual value) is used for adjusting the parameters of the estimated model with the aim of improving the fit. Fifth, the model is re-estimated, and so on. Basically, the model is trained by trial and error. The best-known training method is the **back-propagation** algorithm. The name refers to the feedback approach since the model starts with the output and then works backwards through the network towards the input settings, which are continuously adjusted. Since the network can be constantly trained and its parameters adjusted, a neural net can approximate every functional relationship with the requested degree of precision. This makes a neural net very useful in cases where one knows very little about the true functional relationship between predictors and dependent variables or in cases where the pattern of association is complex.

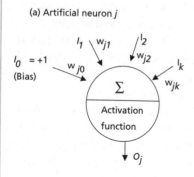

(a) Artificial neuron j

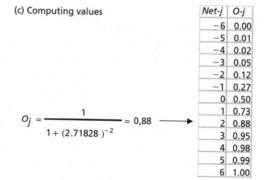

(c) Computing values

$$O_j = \frac{1}{1 + (2.71828)^{-2}} = 0{,}88$$

Net-j	O-j
−6	0.00
−5	0.01
−4	0.02
−3	0.05
−2	0.12
−1	0.27
0	0.50
1	0.73
2	0.88
3	0.95
4	0.98
5	0.99
6	1.00

(b) The estimation model

$$Net_j = \sum_{i=0}^{k} I_i \times w_{ji} \Rightarrow O_j = f(Net_j)$$

Sigmoid (logistic) function:

$$O_j = \frac{1}{1 + e^{-Net_j}}$$

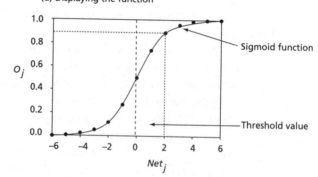

(d) Displaying the function

Figure 17.9 How a neuron reacts to input stimuli

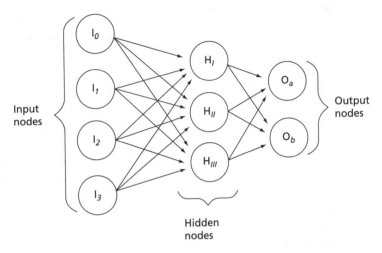

Figure 17.10 A simple neural network

The disadvantage of continuous learning is that a neural net model may become so perfectly trained to reproduce the actual data set that it becomes sample-specific and looses generalizability. ANN software and the accompanying manuals provide recommendations on preventing overtraining.

Figure 17.9 provides a very simplified model of how a brain cell (neuron) processes information. The circle of panel (a) depicts a neuron. The neuron receives impulses or inputs from k surrounding neurons. Each of these neurons 'bombards' neuron j with signals of varying magnitude (weight). Neuron j processes the input, such that the k inputs (I) are multiplied by the associated weighting (w_{jk}). A high weight implies that the signal is important.

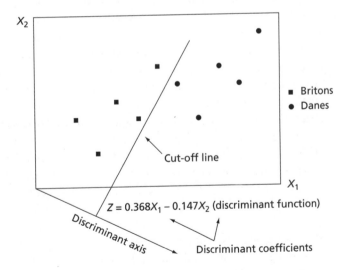

Figure 17.11 Principle of a simple discriminant analysis (from Figure 10.3)

Table 17.5 Similarities between ordinary multivariant analysis and ANN (back propagation)

Two group discriminant analysis	ANN (back propagation)
Independent variables (*X1, X2*)	Input signals (I_1, I_2)
Dependent variable (*Y*)	Output (O_j)
Discriminant coefficients	Connection weights (w_{ij})
Linear discriminant function (*Z*)	Nonlinear Sigmoid function
Cut-off line	Threshold value
Classification matrix	Residual values between input and output

Finally, all products of *w*I* are added yielding an aggregated **activation value** for neuron *j*, called *Net*$_j$. This is symbolized in (b). It is then assumed that the value of *Net*$_j$ can be regarded as an observation along an *activation function*. Often, a sigmoid function (a special, simplified case of the logistic function) is used to model the activation function. The purpose of the activation function is to transform an activation value to a binary output value (say, 1 = send signal or 0 = do nothing). From a mathematical perspective, the output (O_j) is a nonlinear function of the aggregated input (Net_j) – just like *Y* is a linear function of *X* in regression. Below, several other similarities are noted between a neural net and multivariate statistical methods covered earlier in this book.

Panel (c) shows how to compute the values based on the formula (use Excel's formula editor with the EXP function). Finally, (d) displays the sigmoid function. Provided that the estimated value passes a certain threshold value, which must be specified by the researcher, the activation function transforms the activation value to an output signal. Since the activation value, $Net_j = 2$ in (c) transforms to an output value (0.88) that exceeds the threshold level (the dotted vertical line), an output is produced. Stated otherwise, neuron *j* "fires" a signal toward the environing neuron(s). This signal then becomes an input value to them, and so on.

Neuron *j* is only one of billions of neurons in the brain. Each neuron may be connected to and exchange information with hundreds or even thousands of other neurons. A very simplified model of a neural network is shown in Figure 17.10.

A typical neural net consists of **input nodes** (nodes are also called **layers**), **output nodes** and **hidden nodes**. Hidden nodes provide the neural net with more flexibility and makes it capable of representing more complex relationships than the usual one-to-one relationship from input to output. A neural net may have more than one level of hidden nodes. However, each level of nodes automatically increases the complexity of the net. The net of Figure 17.10 has eighteen connections or arrows (twelve from input to hidden nodes and six from hidden to output nodes). An extra hidden layer with three nodes would add nine new connections. So if there are many input and output nodes as well as several levels of hidden nodes the model may become of Byzantine complexity.

Now for the similarity between multivariate methods and a neural net.

- A two-group discriminant analysis may be regarded as a single neuron with no learning involved. To illustrate this, compare the ANN model of Figure 17.9 with the simple discriminant model of Figure 17.11. See also Table 17.5. The independent variables (*X1* and *X2*) correspond to input signals (*I1, I2*), the discriminant coefficients equate to connection weights (w_{ji}), the linear discriminant function to the nonlinear sigmoid function, the dependent variable (Y) compares with the output O_j, and the cut-off line compares with the threshold value between the two groups (1/0). Finally, the classification matrix in the discrimination analysis displays the relation (difference) between predicted and actual classifications. (However, unlike in ANN, this matrix is not used for adjusting the discriminant model.)

- If the transformation of an activation value (Net_j) to output (O_j) is not binary but continuous, then the neural net is similar to a (non) linear multiple regression (apart from learning). The connection weights (w_{ij}) are conceptually similar to regression coefficients. Note also that the $I_0 = +1$ and w_{j0} (bias) in panel (a) of Figure 17.9 is similar to the intercept in regression analysis.

- A canonical analysis allows for several dependent measures. This compares with a neural net that has several output nodes.

- Hidden nodes in a neural net remind us of principal components in factor analysis and latent constructs in LISREL/SEM.

- In a neural network there may be multilayer connections: from input to hidden node 1, to hidden node 2 and to output. This is similar to LISREL/SEM where an exogenous construct (X) may predict an endogenous construct (Y) in one regression, while Y may predict endogenous construct Z in another regression.

- As noted earlier, a special class of neural network, known a Kohonen net produces an output (group membership) similar to a cluster method.

However, the neural net also in several regards differs markedly from known multivariate statistical procedures:

- No output parameters are estimated. This is unlike regression analysis where the output contains regression estimates.

- No statistical tests or inference statistics are presently available.

- The output may be difficult to understand.

The reader who wants to learn more about neural networks should turn to Bishop (1995), Fausett (1994) and Haykin (2000) as general texts on neural networks and pattern recognition; and Beltratti, Margarita and Terna (1996), Bigus (1996), Smith and Gupta (2003) and Zhang (2003) on applying neural networks to business problems.

Some research papers on ANN: Boone and Roehm (2002a, 2002b) apply the technique to marketing segmentation; Hu and Hung (1999) and West, Brockett and Golden (1997) discuss ANN in relation to consumer choice; Chatfield (1993) and Hill, Marquez, O'Connor and Remus (1994) concentrate on forecasting; Thieme, Song and Calantone (2000) deal with product development; Shards (1994) looks at management science and operational research; Kumar, Rao and Soni (1995) compare a neural network with logistic regression models.

17.3 Selected applications of data mining: rule modelling and neural networks

This section covers the applicability of two types of methods from the model toolbox of data mining software. It may not be possible to reproduce these results exactly. See www.pearsoned.co.uk/schmidt for information on the settings.

Rule modelling

Table 17.6 shows (a small part of) an empirical data file. The file contains forty-eight rows and sixteen columns of data (768 cells). Out of these 768 cells, 158 contain the character *T* and 610 the character *F*. *T* and *F* relate to a specific purchase activity where *T* means true – the product, brand or product category was indeed purchased and *F* (false) means that this was not the case (the present example deals with product categories rather than brands).

Each of the forty-eight rows represents a shopping trip, carried out by a few respondents that were members of a nationally representative British (female) consumer panel across a year. The respondents went shopping more than forty-eight times during the year, but we will be analyzing a small selection of these trips. Assume an analyst is only interested in the purchase of "high frequency" food/non-food (convenience) products. Moreover, the data of Table 17.6 have been extracted from a master file, where the following preconditions had to be met: each shopping trip (row) needed to include at least two product categories; and each product category (column) should include at least two purchases across shopping trips. The first column (id) relates to a shopping trip, but it is not known which trip was conducted by which of the respondents.

The column names (variables) and product categories are given in Table 17.7.

The first data column of Table 17.6 contains a T (true) in columns *X4* (cereals) and *X15* (butter) indicating that these two products were purchased during shopping trip ID 1. Across all the trips *X4* (cereals) was purchased twenty-three times (or almost every second time) whereas *X15* (butter) was purchased thirteen times. And so on. The file (Paneldata_SPSS_seq_NY.sav) can be downloaded from www.pearsoned.co.uk/schmidt.

Figure 17.12 shows a data stream on rule modelling. It is also available as Figure_17_12_rule_model.str

The data stream contains the following nodes:

- An SPSS source file node containing the data of Table 17.6.
- A Type node.[3]
- A Table node, to check if the data are read correctly into the stream.
- A GRI (generalized rule induction) node for generating the rule model.
- A Web node for displaying a graph of product pair purchase associations provided by the GRI model.
- An Apriori node for establishing a model of related and sequential product purchases.

Table 17.6 Purchase of 16 product categories across 48 shopping trips

id	x4	x8	x15	x57	x58	x62	x64	x65	x85	x90	x93	x94	x95	x96	x97	x99	Σ
1	T	F	T	F	F	F	F	F	F	F	F	F	F	F	F	F	2
2	F	F	F	F	F	F	F	T	F	F	T	F	F	F	F	F	2
3	T	F	T	F	F	F	F	F	F	F	T	F	F	F	F	T	4
4	T	F	F	F	F	F	F	T	F	F	F	T	F	F	F	T	4
5	T	F	F	F	F	F	F	F	F	F	F	T	F	F	F	T	3
6	F	F	F	F	F	F	F	F	F	F	F	T	F	F	F	T	2
7	T	F	F	F	F	F	F	T	F	F	F	F	F	F	F	T	3
8	T	F	F	F	F	F	F	F	F	F	F	T	F	F	F	F	2
9	T	F	F	F	F	F	F	T	F	F	F	T	F	F	F	T	4
10	F	F	F	F	F	F	T	F	F	T	F	F	T	F	T	T	5
11	T	F	F	F	F	F	F	F	F	F	F	F	F	T	F	F	2
12	T	F	F	F	F	F	T	F	T	F	F	T	F	F	T	T	6
13	T	F	F	F	F	F	F	F	F	F	F	T	F	T	F	F	3
14	F	T	T	F	F	F	F	F	F	F	F	F	F	F	F	T	3
15	T	F	T	F	F	F	F	T	F	F	F	F	F	F	F	F	3
16	T	F	F	T	F	T	F	T	F	F	F	F	F	F	F	F	4
17	F	F	F	F	F	F	F	T	F	F	F	F	F	T	F	F	2
18	F	F	F	F	F	T	F	T	F	F	F	F	T	F	F	T	5
19	F	F	F	F	F	T	F	F	F	F	F	F	F	F	F	T	2
20	F	F	F	T	F	F	F	F	T	F	F	F	F	F	F	F	2
21	F	F	T	T	F	T	F	T	F	F	F	T	T	F	F	T	7
22	F	F	T	F	F	F	F	T	F	F	F	T	F	T	F	F	4
23	F	F	T	F	F	F	F	T	F	F	F	T	F	T	F	F	4
24	T	F	F	F	F	F	F	F	F	F	F	T	F	F	F	F	2
25	F	F	F	T	F	T	F	F	F	F	F	T	F	F	F	F	3
26	F	F	F	T	F	F	F	F	F	F	F	T	F	F	F	F	2
27	T	F	F	F	T	F	F	T	F	T	F	T	F	F	F	F	5
28	F	F	F	F	T	F	T	F	F	F	F	T	F	F	F	F	3
29	F	F	T	F	F	F	F	T	F	T	F	T	F	F	F	F	4
30	F	F	F	F	F	F	F	F	F	F	F	F	F	T	F	T	2
31	T	F	F	T	T	F	F	F	F	F	T	F	F	F	F	F	4
32	T	F	F	T	F	F	F	F	F	T	F	T	F	F	F	T	5
33	F	F	T	F	F	F	F	T	F	F	F	T	F	F	F	T	4
34	T	T	F	F	F	F	F	F	F	F	F	F	F	F	F	T	3
35	F	F	T	F	F	F	F	F	F	F	F	T	F	F	F	F	2
36	F	F	F	F	F	F	F	T	F	F	F	F	F	F	F	T	2
37	T	F	F	F	T	F	F	F	F	F	F	T	F	F	F	F	4
38	T	F	F	T	F	F	T	F	F	F	F	F	F	F	F	F	3
39	T	F	T	F	F	F	F	T	F	T	F	T	F	F	F	T	5
40	F	F	F	T	F	F	F	F	F	F	F	T	F	F	F	F	2
41	F	F	F	F	F	F	F	F	T	F	F	T	F	F	F	F	2
42	F	F	F	F	F	F	F	T	F	F	F	T	F	T	F	T	4
43	T	F	F	T	F	F	F	F	F	F	F	T	F	F	F	T	4
44	T	F	T	F	F	F	F	F	F	T	F	F	F	F	F	T	4
45	F	F	F	F	F	F	F	F	F	F	F	T	F	F	F	T	2
46	F	F	F	T	F	F	F	F	F	F	F	T	F	F	F	F	2
47	T	F	T	F	F	F	F	F	T	F	F	T	F	F	F	F	4
48	F	F	F	F	F	T	F	F	F	F	F	T	F	F	F	T	3
Σ	23	2	13	11	4	6	4	17	4	6	3	29	3	7	2	24	158

Table 17.7 Product category variables

x4	Cereals	*x64*	Deodorants	*x94*	Tub_margarine
x8	Sauces	*x65*	Toilet_rools	*x95*	NA_washing_powder
x15	Butter	*x85*	Instant_coffee	*x96*	Toothpaste
x57	Cake_mix	*x90*	Washing_powder	*x97*	Shampoo
x58	Cheese_cake	*x93*	Packet_margarine	*x99*	Tea_bags
x62	Dog_biscuits				

Note: NA_washing_powder refers to non-automatic washing powder

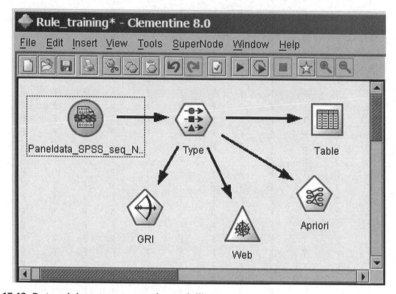

Figure 17.12 Data mining stream on rule modelling

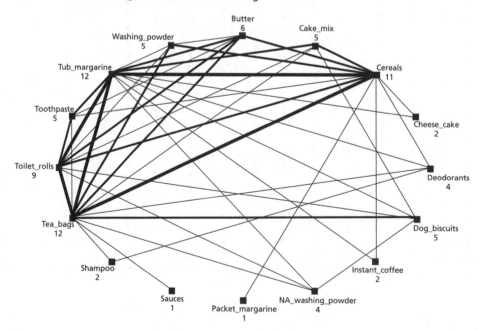

Figure 17.13 Rule-based web of product associations: circle layout

Figure 17.13 displays a rule-based web of product associations (circle layout). Let us look at this web in conjunction with Table 17.6.[4]

All sixteen products of Table 17.6 appear in Figure 17.13. Sixteen products imply one-hundred-and-twenty possible purchase pairs ($n*[n-1]/2$). However, only forty-three connections or lines of associations are shown in Figure 17.13 (adding the number of connections in the figure yields 86. Now 86/2 = 43). According to the chosen program settings, a link must represent at least two instances where both products were purchased during the same shopping trip.

The web graph is easy to understand: the fatter the line, the stronger the association. Tea bags and tub margarine were purchased together fourteen times, tea bags and cereals twelve times and tub margarine and cereals also twelve times. Consequently, their connections appear as the fattest ones.

Look at Tables 17.8, 17.9 and 17.10. They all describe weaker relationships.

Sauces (*x8*) were bought on two occasions (ID 14 and ID 34). Only one other product, tea bags (*x99*) were purchased at both events. Therefore, there is only one link between sauces and another product. And this connection is between sauces and tea bags.

Another product that has only one connection in Figure 17.13 is packet margarine (*x93*). Table 17.9 tells us why this is so. It was bought twice together with one other product, cereals (*x4*).

Finally, look at Table 17.10. It deals with shampoo (*x97*), which was purchased on two occasions (ID 10 and ID 12). In both cases it was bought with deodorants (*x64*) and tea bags (*x99*). Consequently, two – thin – lines in Figure 17.13 connect shampoo with deodorants and tea bags.

Figure 17.13 displays the web in circle layout and Figure 17.14 shows the same web in network layout. The network layout may be better at revealing 'nets' of product pair

Table 17.8

Trip	Sauces (*x8*) purchased together with ...		
ID 14		Butter (*x15*)	Tea bags (*x99*)
ID 34	Cereals (*x4*)		Tea bags (*x99*)

Table 17.9

Trip	Packet Margarine (*x93*) purchased together with ...				
ID 02				Toilet rolls (*x65*)	
ID 03	Cereals (*x4*)	Butter (*x15*)			Tea bags (*x99*)
ID 31	Cereals (*x4*)		Cake mix (*x57*)	Cheese cake (*x58*)	

Table 17.10

Trip	Shampoo (*x97*) purchased together with ...				
ID 10	Deodorants (*x64*)	Washing powder (*x90*)	NA washing powder (*x95*)	Tea bags (*x99*)	
ID 12	Cereals (*x4*)	Deodorants (*x64*)	Instant coffee (*x85*)	Tub margarine (*x94*)	
				Tea bags (*x99*)	

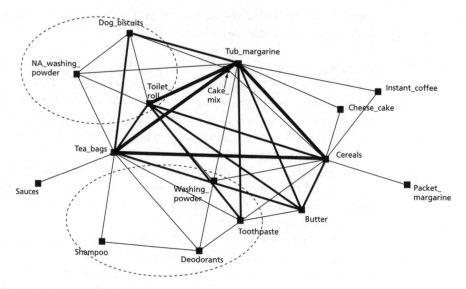

Figure 17.14 Rule-based web of product associations as a network

Table 17.11

	Current purchase (t)	t−1	t−2	t−3
(ID 1)	Cereals	Butter		
(ID 2)	Toilet rolls	Packet margarine		
(ID 3)	Cereals	Butter	Packet margarine	Tea bags
(ID 4)	Cereals	Toilet rolls	Tub margarine	Tea bags
(ID 5)	Cereals	Tub margarine	Tea bags	

associations. Notice two 'nets' of non-food products (dashed circles). The lower circle covers products that belong in the bathroom. Assume that the input data file had been big and representative. Moreover, assume that the present relations had been strong. This being the case, the findings provide interesting information for retail chain management. While shampoo, deodorants and toothpaste tend to be placed close to each other in shopping aisles, dog biscuits and toilet rolls do not. Dog biscuits tend to be placed with pet food whereas toilet rolls tend to be placed somewhere else, often with kitchen rolls.

So, it may make sense to, say, present both dog biscuits and toilet rolls in a weekly advertising flyer, on the same page. Or they could be located next to each other on the shelves.

While the GRI rule model focuses on associations between pairs of product purchases, the Apriori rule model (like the Sequence and Carma node) deals with the sequence of purchases.

To demonstrate how the Apriori rule model works, consider Table 17.11. This lists the products purchased during shopping trips one to five in Table 17.6. For illustrational purposes, assume the following:

■ Trips one to five represent five different consumers.

- The product purchases varied in time on a column basis instead of on a row basis.
- Only one product was purchased per shopping trip.
- The analysis is focused on six products: butter, cereals, packet margarine, tub margarine, tea bags and toilet rolls.
- Only the current and the preceding three shopping trips are considered.

The first row shows that consumer ID 1's actual purchase (among other products) is cereals. At a preceding shopping trip he/she (among other products) bought butter. Note that this shopping pattern resembles ID 3's. However, while ID 3 also bought other products of interest, ID 1 only bought cereals and butter. Notice also that cereals twice (ID 4 and ID 5) was preceded by tub margarine and tea bags (in that order). ID 4 also purchased toilet rolls, but according to rule modelling this purchase is ignored, because toilet rolls does not appear more than once in connection with one or several other products within the time frame. A rule model necessitates at least two (normally many more) cases of two (usually many more) products purchased in a sequence or historical order (within the time frame).

Table 17.12 provides an analysis using the rule modelling rationale from Table 17.11. However, this time the data analysis was based on the whole data file of Table 17.6.

According to SPSS *Clementine* terminology, the current period, *t*, is called ***consequent*** while period $t-1$ is called ***Antecedent 1*** and so on. Table 17.12 only shows three of the sixteen currently purchased products.

Table 17.12 Apriori (sequential) purchases of three selected product categories

Freq	Consequent	Antecedent 1	Antecedent 2	Antecedent 3
6	Cereals	**Toilet_rolls**	Tea_bags	Tub_margarine
6	Cereals	Butter	Tea_bags	
7	Cereals	Butter	Tub_margarine	
7	Cereals	Cake_mix	Tub_margarine	
7	Cereals	Butter	**Toilet_rolls**	
9	Cereals	**Toilet_rolls**	Tea_bags	
10	Cereals	**Toilet_rolls**	Tub_margarine	
14	Cereals	Tea_bags	Tub_margarine	
2	Shampoo	**Deodorants**	Tub_margarine	
2	Shampoo	**Deodorants**	Tea_bags	
3	Shampoo	**NA_washing_powder**	Tea_bags	
3	Shampoo	Instant_coffee	Tub_margarine	
4	Shampoo	**Washing_powder**	Tea_bags	
14	Shampoo	Tea_bags	Tub_margarine	
5	Toothpaste	Butter	**Toilet_rolls**	Tub_margarine
6	Toothpaste	**Toilet_rolls**	Tea_bags	Tub_margarine
7	Toothpaste	Butter	**Toilet_rolls**	
7	Toothpaste	Butter	Tub_margarine	
9	Toothpaste	**Toilet_rolls**	Tea_bags	
10	Toothpaste	**Toilet_rolls**	Tub_margarine	
14	Toothpaste	Tea_bags	Tub_margarine	

For instance, in six current shopping trips where cereals were purchased, toilet rolls were being purchased on the preceding trip (antecedent 1); tea bags were bought during the trip preceding the one where toilet rolls where purchased (antecedent 2), and so on.

Cereals typically are purchased with other food products, such as butter and tea bags. According to Table 17.12, the only non-food product preceding cereals is toilet rolls (shown in bold).

Next, look at two non-food products, shampoo and toothpaste. Generally, the purchase frequency of shampoo is lower than that of toothpaste. But whereas purchase of shampoo tends to be preceded by other non-food products, purchase of toothpaste is only preceded by one other non-food product, toilet rolls.

Assume that the findings of Table 17.12 were based on a big data file, then the following marketing decisions might make sense:

- Toilet rolls and toothpaste should be presented with conventional food products.
- Shampoo should be featured together with other non-food products, such as deodorants and washing powder. For instance, one sales flyer could feature shampoo, the following week's flyer could feature deodorants, and so on.

Exploring the neural net features of *Clementine*

As mentioned in Figure 17.8 the modelling toolbox of *Clementine* contains two different neural net models. One model is simply called "Neural Net" while the other one is named "Kohonen." (See Figure 17.15.)

Now, explore how these models work. The data file used is House_of_Wonder_neural.sav. This can be downloaded from www.pearsoned.co.uk/schmidt. All missing values of variables have been replaced by the mean.

A multiple regression has been done with a dependent variable and sixteen predictor variables. These focus on specific aspects of the service experienced during a shopping trip at a retail warehouse. All variables were scaled according to a five-point Likert scale (1 = strongly agree, to 5 = strongly disagree). Specifics on the study, including the naming of variables can be found at www.pearsoned.co.uk/schmidt in Appendix A. Look for the file called House_of_Wonder.doc.

The result is shown in the left part of Table 17.13. The R-square is 0.373, which is not good. However, in empirical studies, high R-squares of 0.7 or better rarely appear. The F-value of the overall model (48.96) is highly significant.

The right part of the table shows the result of a comparable analysis based on a neural net. With regard to the settings in *Clementine*, an attempt was made to "imitate" a multiple regression:

- 1 output layer: the dependent variable (*a_1*).
- 16 input layers: sixteen independent/predictor variables (*a_2* to *a_17*).
- 3 hidden layers (the default setting).

The model's estimated accuracy is 0.863. A neural network in some ways resembles an iterative method and, therefore, each run yields different parameters. Therefore, one

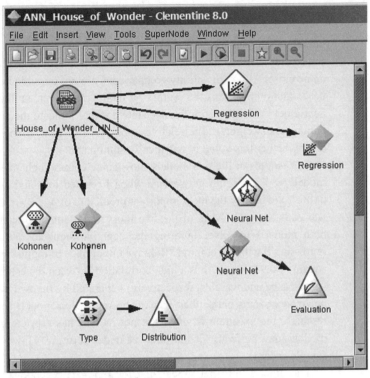

Figure 17.15 Data stream including neural net models

Table 17.13 Comparison of output from regression and from a neural net

	Regression			Neural Net	
R-Square:	0.373			Estimated Accuracy:	0.868
F	48.96			Input Layer:	16 neurons
Sig.	0.000			Hidden Layer:	3 neurons
				Output Layer:	1 neuron
				- Average of ten runs -	
Variable	Beta	t	Sig.	Relative importance of Inputs	
a_2	0.187	8.662	0.000	0.174	
a_3	0.325	9.425	0.000	0.209	
a_4	−0.065	−3.142	0.002	0.080	
a_5	0.069	2.339	0.019	0.028	
a_6	0.019	1.223	0.222	0.031	
a_7	0.045	1.558	0.119	0.033	
a_8	−0.013	−0.831	0.406	0.023	
a_9	0.008	0.366	0.714	0.017	
a_10	0.057	1.930	0.054	0.020	
a_11	−0.007	−0.202	0.840	0.036	
a_12	−0.064	−4.312	0.000	0.073	
a_13	0.011	0.212	0.832	0.033	
a_14	−0.036	−0.752	0.452	0.042	
a_15	−0.060	−2.011	0.044	0.064	
a_16	0.101	3.105	0.002	0.092	
A_17	0.097	3.396	0.001	0.066	

should conduct a sample of runs (at least ten, preferably more) and use averaged parameters. The neural net importance column of Table 17.13 is based on 10 runs. Based on the input file *House_of_Wonder_neural.sav*. While the reader will not be able to get the same parameter estimates as are shown in Table 17.13, he or she should obtain results that come close. Although validity comparisons are not possible here, it seems that the neural net model outperforms the regression model. However, unlike the regression model, the neural net model has no inference statistics that indicate the significance of the estimated parameters (weights). The relative importance of the variable a_2 is 0.174 but it is not clear whether this value is statistically significant.

The outputs of the two models show some common characteristics. According to both models, a_2 ("I could get service when I wanted to") and a_3 ("The salespeople were polite") are clearly the most important predictors of a_1 ("Generally speaking, the service was satisfactory"). Also, of the five most important/significant variables, four appear in both model's top five. Ignoring the negative signs in the column with t-values and regressing it with the column "Relative importance of inputs" gives a highly significant R-square of 0.91. So, there is a high correlation between the estimates (regression parameter significance and weights, respectively) generated by the two models. The fit of the neural net model seems better than that of the regression model. But according to theory and research, the excellent fit of neural net models has a price: generalizability. Neural net models may perfectly fit the data set under scrutiny. However, the models tend to be sample specific.

The other neural net model in *Clementine* is a Kohonen clustering model (Figure 17.15). The Kohonen node is easy to use and does not necessitate defining which variables are dependent and independent. By default, the model generates variable columns with a categorical classification variable concerning each row (subject, respondent). Figure 17.17

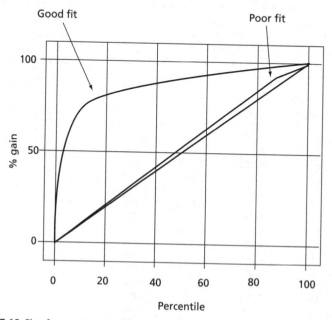

Figure 17.16 Fit of neural net model

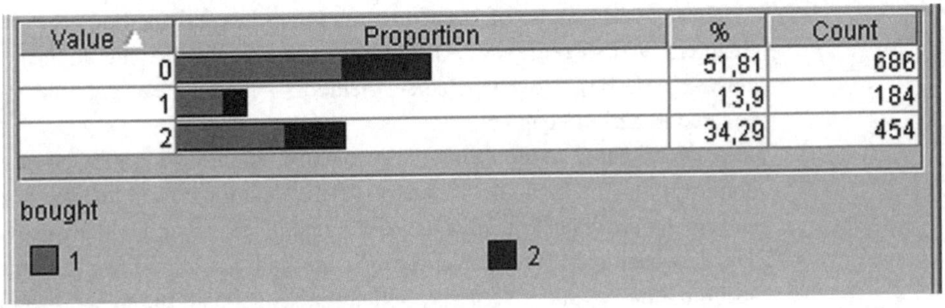

Value ▲	Proportion	%	Count
0		51,81	686
1		13,9	184
2		34,29	454

bought
◻ 1   ◼ 2

Figure 17.17 Kohonen clustering

displays a Kohonen-based clustering (three classes) across purchase activity during the actual shopping trip.

The biggest class contains 51.81 percent of the cases (686 out of 1,324). It appears that about two-thirds of respondents report purchases, regardless of class. In Figure 17.15, the generated Kohonen model was dragged from the model manager into the stream canvas. Next, a Type node was used to tell *Clementine* that the cluster membership variables generated by the Kohonen node were to be treated as nominal measures (set) and not as numeric variables. After this, the graph of Figure 17.17 can be requested (the Graph node only accepts nominal variables).

17.4 Summary

Most statistical models that are included in data mining were developed before computers came into widespread use, but interest in applying them has grown significantly as developers began to program statistical algorithms, bundle them and supply them as statistical software packages. One of the strengths of data mining is its ability to synchronize field/record operations, models, display formats and output so that it appears as a series of processes or streams of data. However, there is little that can be done in a mining program that cannot be done by SPSS.

A definite advantage of a data mining program is that it presents the data problem to the analyst in a clear way, through a kind of bird's view, the stream canvas (Figure 17.2). A typical stream canvas consists of one or several input files, operations like filtering and sorting, models like regression or clustering and display or output facilities like a graph or a table.

A stream is built by dragging and dropping nodes onto the canvas and by connecting the nodes with appropriate arrows. SPSS *Clementine* has several types of nodes: source nodes, record and field operations, graphs, models and output (Figure 17.8).

A data mining application cannot run until it has been told how to understand the data. Therefore, scaling issues are of utmost importance. As long as a variable is stored in the data warehouse, it can have one of three formats: real number, integer or text. When entering the data mining stream, the variable must be instantiated. The process of instantiation tells the data mining program which measurement scale is to be used for working with the variable. For instance, if a variable contains the gender of a person, then the selected scale should be a categorical (or nominal scale) and not a numeric scale (Figures 17.3 and 17.4).

The models palette of *Clementine* contains several methods that were introduced in Chapters 9–15 (regression, logistic regression, factor, hierarchical cluster, k-means cluster, CHAID). However, some methods – neural nets and rule models – were not covered in earlier chapters.

A neural net is an algorithm that aims to simulate information processing in the human brain (Exhibit 17.2, Figure 17.9 and 17.10). Neural nets can be used instead of regression and cluster analysis. The advantage of a neural net is that it usually provides a superior fit. The disadvantage is that the better fit is caused by continuously training the model on the specific data set under scrutiny, which may invalidate the generalizability of the model. Moreover, neural net models are nonlinear, no parameters are estimated and therefore the output may be difficult to understand.

A rule model tries to identify patterns of strong (or weak) associations between pairs (or sequences) of events or activities. A popular way of presenting such patterns is the web display (Figures 17.13 and 17.14). The stronger the link or line between two objects, the stronger the association (and vice versa). Rule models are used to help retailers figure out which products should be on display together. However, rule models and neural nets can also be used for analyzing completely different phenomena like the communication activities (phone and online) of terrorists.

Data mining programs tend to gain in popularity as the amount of available data grows and more and more heterogeneous sources of data are stored in the company's data warehouse. Moreover, the availability of online data sources will imply an increased interest in data mining. Websites can be regarded as an enormous warehouse that contains heterogeneous data sources. Also, the monitoring of website traffic constitutes a serious challenge to companies because of the growth of data.

Questions

1. A data mining program such as SPSS *Clementine* or *Enterprise Miner* from SAS, is needed to answer this question.

   Download the files Export_Manager_Survey.sav and Dream_Holiday.sav from www.pearsoned.co.uk/schmidt. Show how one can employ data mining to obtain a better understanding of the data sets. Each of the two streams should cover at least:

   - one record operation node;
   - one field operation node;
   - one graph node;
   - two model nodes; and
   - one output node.

   Try to vary the use of nodes. One of the streams should contain a supernode.

Note that none of the data sets or "streams" contains time series.

2. Data mining is being used by criminal investigators to detect fraud, such as theft of credit cards. How could a rule-based web, like the one in Figure 17.13, be used for analyzing misuse of a credit card?

Bibliography and references

Beltratti, A., Margarita, S. and Terna, P. (1996) *Neural Networks for Economic and Financial Modelling*. International Thomson Computer Press, London. Chapter 1.

Berry, M. J. A. and Linoff, G. S. (2004) *Data Mining Techniques: Marketing, sales and customer relationship management*. Wiley, NY.

Bishop, C. M. (1995) *Neural Networks for Pattern Recognition*. Oxford University Press, Oxford.

Bigus, J. P. (1996) *Data Mining with Neural Networks: Solving business problems from application development to decision support*. McGraw-Hill, Englewood-Cliffs, NJ.

Boone, D. S. and Roehm, M. (2002a) "Retail segmentation using artificial neural networks." *International Journal of Research in Marketing*. Vol. 19, no 3. 287–301.

Boone, D. S. and Roehm, M. (2002b) "Evaluating the appropriateness of market segmentation solutions using artificial neural networks and the membership clustering criterion." *Marketing Letters*. Vol. 13, no. 4. 317–333.

Chatfield, C. (1993) "Neural networks: forecasting breakthrough or passing fad?" *International Journal of Forecasting*. Vol. 9 (April). 1–3.

Clementine 7.0 *User's Guide* (2002) Integration Solutions Limited, SPSS, Chicago, IL.

Drozdenko, R. G. and Drake, P. D. (2002) *Optimal Database Marketing: Strategy, development and data mining*. Sage, Thousand Oaks, CA.

Fausett, L. V. (1994) *Fundamentals of Neural Networks*. Prentice-Hall, NY.

Giudici, P. (2003) *Applied Data Mining: Statistical methods for business and industry*. Wiley, NY.

Han, J. and Kamber, M. (2000) *Data Mining: Concepts and techniques*. Morgan Kaufmann, San Francisco, CA.

Hand, D. J., Mannila, H. and Smyth, P. (2001) *Principles of Data Mining*, Bradford Books, Cambridge, MA.

Haykin, S. (2000) *Neural Networks: A comprehensive foundation*. Prentice-Hall, NY.

Hill, T., Marquez, L., O'Connor M. and Remus, W. (1994) "Artificial neural network models for forecasting and decision-making." *International Journal of Forecasting*. Vol. 10 (June). 5–15.

Hu, M. Y. and Hung, M. S. (1999) "Estimation of posterior probabilities of consumer situational choices with neural network classifiers." *International Journal of Research in Marketing*. Vol. 16, no. 4. 307.

Klösen, W. and Zytkow, J. M. (eds) (2002) *Handbook of Data Mining and Knowledge Discovery*. Oxford University Press, Oxford.

Kumar, A., Rao, V. R. and Soni, H. (1995) "An empirical comparison of neural network and logistic regression models." *Marketing Letters*. Vol. 6, no. 4. 251–263.

Pyle, D. (2003) *Business Modeling and Data Mining*. Morgan Kaufmann, San Francisco, CA.

Rafalski, E. and Mullner, R. (2003) "Ensuring HIPAA compliance using data warehouses for healthcare marketing." *Journal of Consumer Marketing*. Vol. 20, no. 7. 629–633.

Rud, O. P. (2000) *Data Mining Cookbook: Modeling data for marketing, risk and customer relationship management*. Wiley.

Shards, R. (1994) "Neural networks for the MS/OR analyst: an application bibliography." *Interfaces*. Vol. 24 (March/April). 116–130.

Smith, K. A. and Gupta, J. N. D. (eds) (2003) *Neural Networks in Business: Techniques and applications*. IRM Press, Hershey, PA.

Thelen, S., Mottner, S. and Berman, B. (2004) "Data mining: on the trail to marketing gold." *Business Horizons*. Vol. 47, no. 6. 25–32.

Thieme, R. J., Song, M. and Calantone, R. J. (2000) "Artificial neural network decision support systems for new product development project selection." *Journal of Marketing Research*. Vol. 37, no 4. 499–507.

West, P. M., Brockett P. L. and Golden, L. L. (1997) "A comparative analysis of neural networks and statistical methods for predicting consumer choice." *Marketing Science*. Vol. 16, no. 4. 370–391.

Zhang, G. P. (2003) *Neural Networks in Business Forecasting*. Information Science Publishing, Hershey, PA.

End notes

[1] To import an SPSS file, tab the *[Sources]* tag, select the *[SPSS File]* icon and simply drag it into the stream canvas. Right-click it. Choose *[Edit]* from the drop-down menu, browse your computer to find the file (it must be a *.sav* file). Select it: Click *[Open]* and *[OK]*.

[2] *Clementine* also looks for: time, date, timestamp and unknown. Note that the program by default ignores any measurement settings (scale, ordinal, nominal) that may have been specified in the SPSS file.

[3] Two settings must be precisely specified in the Type node: the scale type should be "Flag" with levels T (true) and F (false) and the direction of the data flow must be "Both" (in and out).

[4] Figures 17.13 and 17.14 are based on Clementine 8. In versions 9 and 10, interface and default settings have changed. Consequently, the reader may be unable to recreate the results presented in Figures 17.13 and 17.14, based on Table 17.6.

18 Putting it all together: an international marketing information system

Learning objectives

After reading this chapter you should be able to:

■ Explain the purpose of a marketing information system (MIS).

■ Describe the main elements of an MIS.

■ Explain what makes an international marketing information system different from a marketing information system.

18.1 Introduction

Once research has been conducted, the data collected and analyzed, the next step is to incorporate this information into management decision-making. More and more businesses are now concerned with increasing the productivity of their marketing, especially in their research departments. Whereas functions such as sales can demonstrate their effect on the bottom line via metrics, such as number of leads generated or sales figures, marketing research departments are hard-pressed to provide such proof. Marketing research is becoming increasingly sophisticated not only through the methodologies employed, but also in terms of the statistical techniques used. Company boards are increasingly asking why they should be allocating budgets to marketing research departments. The general perception is that such departments produce voluminous studies that provide little or no actionable insights to gather dust on bookshelves.

One cause of this is that typical marketing research studies focus on variables to which most managers cannot relate. Coming from a tradition of psychology, research managers are content to measure variables such as satisfaction, agreement with statements, perceptions, and in some cases behavioural intentions. Such variables have a venerable tradition in research journals. They are used by academics because they are easy to measure (i.e., they can be administered via a cross-sectional survey) and they can be subjected to a variety of multivariate statistical techniques. Also, companies are influenced by this way of thinking. Take the case of customer satisfaction. Most companies track the overall satisfaction of customers, but few know how customer satisfaction affects repurchase behaviour (not just intentions), sales, or actual word-of-mouth behaviour. In absence of such metrics, managers work in a vacuum, having to assume that satisfaction must have a beneficial effect on the customer base. However, if they had some concrete metrics (e.g., one unit change in satisfaction score increases sales by X%), they would be more likely to use the satisfaction study in their decision process (Mittal, 2004).

A massive amount of data is available from a wide variety of sources. The trick is to transform that data, ranging from statistics and facts to opinions and predictions, into information that is useful to the decision-makers in marketing. The importance of information systems is becoming more evident with the increased need to develop closer customer relationships, the increasing costs of making wrong marketing decisions, the complexity of the marketplace, and the elevated level of competitor aggressiveness. This is one of the most crucial aspects of the research process (Wyner, 2005). All too frequently, research is conducted and a number of conclusions or implications for marketing strategy and tactics drawn, and yet these are not acted upon. Two decades ago, Alan Andreasen wrote an article for *Harvard Business Review* entitled "Backward marketing research" (Andreasen, 1985). In it, he gave practical guidelines on how to ensure that marketing research projects are used, rather then ending up on bookshelves.

In some cases, the reason is that the information does not reach the relevant decision-makers or is not readily accessible. In these instances, there is a clear solution, i.e., development of an international information system to facilitate dissemination and use of data. Such a system can deliver information to decision-makers at all levels of the organization and at different locations scattered around the world. It provides both internal links and access to external sources.

The growth of electronic information systems has accelerated the speed with which information can be disseminated throughout a cross-border organization.

18.2 Analyzing analytic capabilities: four questions

To categorize the various analytical capabilities that can be part of a Marketing Information System (MIS) or a decision support system (DSS), a classification scale related to four levels of questions is used:

- What happened?
- Why did it happen?
- What will happen if ....?
- What should happen?

"What" questions

Once there is raw data in the database of a marketing management support system, marketers first want to know what has happened ("status reporting"). This calls for descriptive analyses. The simplest analysis would be to make straightforward counts and show frequencies. Next, summary statistics such as the mean, median, mode and standard deviation can be computed. These give marketers an idea of the performance of their product and/or brands. Once certain statistics have been generated, marketers will be interested in questions such as the following: does the level of sales differ between regions? To what extent have sales changed compared with last year? One can simply compare means across different time periods and different sales areas. However, it will often also make sense to test to what extent observed differences are statistically significant. To analyze differences (e.g. between regions or segments), marketers can make use of a rich collection of both parametric and nonparametric statistical techniques. Examples are analysis of variance (ANOVA) and t-tests.

To answer the "what" question, basic analysis procedures can mostly be used. Most database systems will contain these procedures or else they will be very easy to program and implement.

"Why" questions

Determining what happened is the first step in analyzing data. However, to develop a marketing policy, marketers need to know more. They need insights into the causes and consequences of what happens in the market. Why did the international sales decline in the last quarter? Why did distribution coverage decrease, and what will be the effects of increasing advertising expenditures?

The techniques for answering such questions can be divided into two categories: *quantitative* and *qualitative* techniques.

To answer the "why" questions, marketers need to investigate relationships between quantitative variables. Correlation and regression analyses are the best-known techniques to do this. Correlation analysis determines the relationship between two variables by calculating their joint variation. Results of this analysis show the extent to which variables move up and down together or move in opposite directions. For example, what is the statistical relationship between sales and price? Multiple regression analysis can be used when the relationships between one dependent variable (e.g. sales) and several independent variables (e.g. price, advertising expenditures, and distribution) are of interest. Correlation and regressions analyses are well-known techniques, and most database packages can conduct these analyses. Regression-based econometric techniques are important in analysing marketing data. Other advanced techniques to study associations between variables are multivariate techniques such as discriminant analysis, factor analysis, cluster analysis, and structural equation modelling.

Discriminant analysis is similar to regression analysis except for the fact that the dependent variable is non-metric rather than metric. Multiple discriminant analysis handles problems that involve dependent variables with several categories. Discrete discriminant analysis may be employed when both dependent and independent variables are non-metric. An example of this would be trying to predict whether a consumer is likely to buy brand A or brand B, given his/her income (high, medium or low), education level (high school, college graduate, postgraduate) and gender (male, female). With the help of discriminant analysis one could also classify customers as loyal versus non-loyal and then try to analyze if the difference is caused by their background characteristics (e.g. education, age) and the marketing-mix efforts that were targeted at them.

Factor analysis can be used to investigate the extent to which different variables share variation that may be the result of a common underlying factor. A marketer can use factor analysis to analyze, for example, whether different buying behaviour phenomena are all caused by the same underlying factor such as risk sensitivity.

Cluster analysis can be used to classify objects (e.g. customers) in homogeneous subgroups. This classification can be performed on the basis of various variables such as, for example, buying behaviour, demographic variables, income, and psychological variables. The results of the cluster analysis can provide insights into why products do better with some buyers than with others and so form the basis for market segmentation.

Cluster analysis is widely used in segmentation studies for several reasons. First of all, it is easy to use. In addition, there are many variations of the method. Most statistical packages have a clustering option, and for the most part it is a good analytical technique. Furthermore, the non-hierarchical clustering technique k-means is particularly popular because it is very fast and can handle large data sets. Cluster analysis is a distance-based method because it uses Euclidean distance (or some variant) in multidimensional space to assign objects to clusters to which they are closest. However, collinearity can become a problem when such distance-based measures are used. It poses a serious problem that, unless addressed, can produce distorted results.[1]

In addition to these techniques, other, more advanced, methods are available to study the associations between (sets of) variables. Structural equation modelling combines factor analysis and regression analysis to study the relationships between variables that cannot be measured directly (i.e. latent constructs) but for which indicators are available. Using structural equation modelling, these analyses will be performed simultaneously. *LISREL* is a software package that can be used to perform structural equation modelling.

The data analysis techniques discussed in this section constitute a powerful set of tools for answering the "why" question.

European managers have developed a tolerance for "soft" qualitative data. North American marketers are used to "hard" data.

In the hard data approach, the research team gathers large quantities of numeric data through surveys, amassing numbers that can be manipulated statistically. Soft data is obtained from in-depth interviews with dealers and other channel members, for example.

"Hard-liners" often consider soft data as anecdotal. They maintain that soft data lead to subjective interpretations. Those who dissent from the hard-line position point out that the statistical manipulation of masses of data can be subjective in ways that are less obvious and more insidious than an acknowledged reliance on soft data.

As we have seen, marketers are obviously concerned with the collection and analysis of quantitative data on their markets and customers. Data such as market size, numbers of competitors, average purchasing prices, and so on all provide quantitative data on market facts.

The observation technique is often undervalued by researchers who lean towards heavy use of statistical analysis. Observation can be especially valuable for marketers who are entering an unfamiliar situation. The technique can be a great help in clarifying phenomena that are difficult to assess with other techniques.

Observation can have its pitfalls. For example, people in different cultures will react differently to the discovery that their behaviour is being observed. It may be necessary to deal with several languages, and this can complicate the task considerably.

Despite the need for quantitative data, marketers are also interested in qualitative data on markets and customers. Qualitative data encompass areas such as underlying customer attitudes, customer perceptions and beliefs, psychological and sociological influences on consumer behaviour. Qualitative research techniques aim to provide these sorts of information.

Marketers have tried several tools and techniques for researching these often complex qualitative aspects. Many were adapted from the psychologist and sociologist. In the 1960s, for example, marketers began to use what became collectively referred to as motivation research techniques. During the 1980s and 1990s many of these techniques fell by the wayside and motivation research in general was used less and less by marketers who felt it to be unscientific and discredited. Two techniques of qualitative research which did remain viable and have been even more widely used, are the focus groups and in-depth interviews (Chapters 4 and 5).

When conducting international research via focus groups, the researcher must be aware of the importance of culture. Not all societies encourage honest and open exchange and disagreement among individuals. Status consciousness, which has little effect on a US focus group, might have a much more potent effect in other cultures (e.g. in Asia) where the opinion of an "influential" member is adopted by other participants. Some people see disagreement as discourtesy and shy away from it, thus negating the whole point of the focus group. And then there are topics that can be discussed frankly in one society but are taboo in another.

"What-if" questions

Having determined what has happened in a market and how this can be explained, marketers next want to know what actions they have to take to reach their goals. For this, they need to have systems that can answer "what-if" and "what-should" questions. Analytical capabilities are needed that are predictive and/or normative in nature. These systems will take the form of models as far as the manipulation of quantitative data is concerned. With qualitative knowledge, such systems are called expert systems.

Decision-support models allow conditional predictions to be made. For example, what happens to sales if the price is increased by 5 percent? Besides this, decision models can contain optimization modules that help to find optimal solutions and, in a sense, provide a ready-to-implement solution.

Marketing models relate the variables the marketer can make decisions about (and that are under his or her control) to variables (objectives) he or she wants to influence. Controllable variables are marketing decision variables such as price, advertising budgets and selling efforts. If possible, the influence of non-controllable variables such as the weather and competitors' actions should be taken into account. Objectives the marketing decision-maker wants to influence are variables such as sales, market share, profit, and brand awareness. A brand manager might, for example, use a model that relates advertising expenditures to brand awareness levels. Such a model can help to predict, for example, the effect of a 10 percent increase in advertising expenditures on brand awareness.

In a similar way, a sales manager may want to have a model that relates sales efforts to sales, so as to predict the effect on sales of an increase in the number of salespeople. Such response models can differ with respect to the number of variables included, the nature of the relationship (linear or nonlinear, dynamic or static, individual or aggregate), and the level of demand (market share or sales) that is analyzed.

Statistical techniques such as regression analysis can be used to determine the value of parameters that link marketing decision variables to output variables in predictive marketing models. Predictive models can also be developed by using managerial judgement with respect to the relationship between input and output.

A technique that is especially useful for simulation purposes is conjoint analysis. *Conjoint analysis* is helpful where the dependent variables are ordinal (ranked as opposed to being truly metric). Conjoint analysis can be used to determine how customers make trade-off judgements between attribute levels of a product. If this information is known, it can be used to estimate customers' preferences for product options. A manufacturer might seek to know what level of an attribute the customer would trade for what level of some other attribute. Typically, different combinations of these features are presented to consumers who are then asked to rank the different combinations presented to them. Conjoint analysis helps to identify the relative importance of each attribute and attribute levels to the customer. Making these estimates is an attempt to answer "what-if" questions. For example, what happens to the customers' preferences for a car if we increase its maximum speed or decrease its price, and so on?

Predictive marketing models are an important type of analytical capability for marketing management support systems. Marketers can use these models to generate all kinds of decision options and predict their outcomes. This activity is called simulation. It is important to recognize, though, that someone still has to choose which decision would be the best. The model functions only as a sparring partner for the human decision-maker, providing that person with feedback on his or her ideas. It will not, however, tell the marketer what to do.

"What-should" questions

To answer "what-should" questions, decision-makers need normative or prescriptive decision models. In 1954, Dorfman and Steiner proposed a theorem with conditions that should be satisfied in order to find optimal values for marketing decision variables. Using this theorem, marketers can determine a theoretical optimal resource allocation or marketing program. With the advent of operations research/management science approaches in marketing in the 1960s, normative models started to be developed that actually determine optimal marketing decisions in terms of numerical values for marketing instruments. Most of these models solved the decision problem of one specific marketing-mix variable.

The purpose of descriptive models was to predict the outcome of different values for marketing decision variables. Normative models go a step further in that their output consists of a guideline of what the value of the marketing decision variable should be. Typically, normative models will consist of an objective function that is subject to one or more constraints. Normative models will contain an optimization part next to the descriptive part. These optimization parts are methods developed in the fields of operations research, such as linear programming, integer programming, nonlinear programming, and dynamic programming.

Analytical capabilities are especially helpful if they solve problems using either the optimizing or the reasoning mode. If a decision-maker solves a problem by means of optimizing, the use of normative marketing models that provide answers to "what-should" questions is appropriate. Solving a problem by means of reasoning can be supported with tools that answer what, why, and what-if questions.

Looking at historical developments in the use of analytical capabilities, marketing scientists have not followed a logical order in trying to develop tools that support decision-makers in their problem-solving. They did not start by attempting to answer the least complicated questions (what and why). On the contrary, researchers have started by trying to develop tools that help answer the most difficult question, the "what-should" question.

Now, it seems that researchers in marketing science are focused on developing sophisticated methodologies for measurement and estimation, and in a sense have made a step back in order to answer better the basic "what" and "why" questions. The recent data explosion is an important impetus behind this trend.

18.3 Building an international MIS

The need for current and relevant knowledge may result in the development and implementation of information systems that incorporate data management procedures involving generating data or gathering existing data, storing and retrieving data, processing data into useful information, and disseminating information to those individuals who need it. The marketing information system is an interacting organization of people,

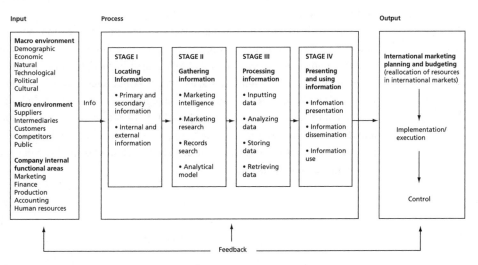

Figure 18.1 International marketing information system

machines, and processes devised to create a regular, continuous, and orderly flow of information essential to the marketer's problem-solving and decision-making activities. As a planned, sequential flow of information tailored to the needs of a particular marketing manager, the MIS can be conceptualized as a four-stage process consisting of locating, gathering, processing, and using information. Figure 18.1 illustrates the central issues to be addressed in each of the four MIS stages.

In this complete MIS model, input data flows into the system from three main sources: micro environment, macro environment, and from functional areas of the company. The output information will then be made available for analysis, planning, implementation, and control purposes. The proposed model meets the exigencies of the ever-expanding role of the MIS professional who has to provide timely, accurate, and objective information to management. Companies are increasingly developing marketing information systems to provide managers with real-time information. Companies are expanding from local to national to global operations, while consumers are becoming ever more selective in product choices.

Updating and maintaining the system

Closely related to the question of inputting data is that of updating and maintaining information. Here again greater difficulties are likely to be encountered in relation to product market data and data from internal sources than with regard to macroeconomic data.

Macroeconomic data from existing electronic sources merely require linking up and integrating into the company's system. As noted earlier these sources are typically updated continually. However, data that are not available in electronic form need to be updated regularly. While greater customization to specific company requirements will be feasible, this also requires monitoring to ensure data are appropriately updated.

Product market data are likely to pose problems where data are not available in electronic form. Where syndicated services are available, these may provide an appropriate way to monitor trends. Integration of data from other sources and diverse origins can pose problems in establishing their comparability.

In the case of internal company data, considerable attention will need to be paid to obtaining data continually and updating it. This problem may give rise to conflict if local country managers perceive this as particularly burdensome or of little value. Attention therefore needs to be paid to the ease of reporting, data access, and development of software to promote use of the data and its integration into decision-making at all levels.

Once procedures have been developed for collecting and updating information in a systematic way, procedures for analyzing these data need to be implemented. Here, an important issue is the use of the information system and in particular how it is integrated into management decisions.

EXHIBIT 18.1 THE MIS OF PEPSICO

PepsiCo is a diversified company with soft drink, snack food, and restaurant businesses. It enjoys a tradition of success based on its cost controls, innovative advertising,
aggressive promotion, and distribution power.

In the 1990s, it faced increased competition for market share. Faced with harsh
competition, PepsiCo turned to intensive advertisements and sales promotions, product
introductions and cost cuts while strengthening its distribution networks. It also tried to
transfer expertise from its successful divisions into other parts of the corporation.

Figure 18.2 illustrates various groups and sources with which a marketing manager
has to interact. These include online databases, domestic planning, promotion, international planning, distribution, and cost management. Consider these in the context of

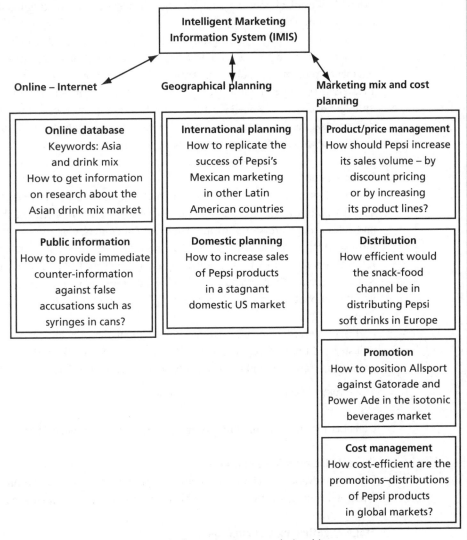

Figure 18.2 Intelligent Marketing Information System relationships

the example of PepsiCo promoting its Allsport soft drink in the isotonic beverage market (sports drinks). In such situations, marketing managers have to identify various distribution channels so that the product reaches the customers. It implies consideration of the effect of promotion on the distribution sector. The cost-efficiency of promotions has to be evaluated using a benchmark (e.g. previous promotion history). This shows the influence of the cost management group on a marketing manager's decision. However, consumer goods cannot be promoted unless they are produced, which involves a team of manufacturing, quality control, engineering, research and development, test marketers, and pricing strategists. Finally, the marketing manager has to provide adequate public information about new products to financial institutions, for example. The advantage of promoting this product in international markets, for example in tropical countries, can also be considered by marketing managers as a part of a long-term strategy.

Thus there are eight main groups within an organization that influence marketing decisions: online databases, domestic and international planning, product/price management, promotion, public information, distribution and cost management. A marketing manager should therefore consider these interrelationships before making strategic decisions. The MIS can assist in the assimilation of knowledge among the different segments. Companies such as PepsiCo can easily transfer such knowledge from successful segments of the company to the newer segments.

Input system

The input system collects data from internal and external environments. Internal data such as point-of-sale information, inventory/warehouse reports, purchase, shipment and sales orders, are stored in the database. Sometimes, this information is available through electronic data interchange. The input system for PepsiCo includes transaction information from all of its product segments such as Pepsi, Pizza Hut, Taco Bell, Kentucky Fried Chicken and Frito-Lay. In addition, sales information comes in from its international operations. A decision-support system uses the database to carry out analysis.

Data received from the external environment through online databases, such as industry and research reports, news about competition, stock markets and government policies are screened and electronically sent to the appropriate personnel.

Source: Adapted from Amaravadi et al. (1995) and other public sources

Consider the stages in the process box in Figure 18.1 (on page 587).

Stage 1: locating information

Finding relevant and useful information is predicated on having an understanding of the types and sources of information, which can be classified as either secondary or primary.

Stage 2: gathering information

The four methods of gathering information shown in Figure 18.1 are market intelligence, market research, records search, and analytical models. Marketing intelligence involves procedures for probing public and private sources or published information. Marketing research involves collecting external primary information from consumers, vendors, competitors, and the general public. Research also entails the use of scientific procedures to conduct experiments and surveys.

A records search scrutinizes internal, secondary sources of data for useful information on past, current, and planned performances and activities of the organization. Understanding existing internal operations is often a prerequisite for planning programmes and activities. Analytical models are statistical and quantitative methods used internally by researchers to generate information applicable to a particular problem or decision. These analytical techniques are used to explore relationships and test ideas by generating primary information from secondary information using quantitative procedures.

The data collection techniques of market research – interviews, focus groups, surveys, observation – are used everywhere, but their use will vary to fit the parameters of languages, cultural styles, technological levels and so on.

Stage 3: processing information

The third stage of the MIS is the processing of information. As suggested by Figure 18.1, information processing consists of inputting, analyzing, storing, and retrieving data. The goal of the processing stage is to produce marketing information that is:

- Reliable. Does the information accurately reflect what it is intended to portray? Important decisions will be made based on what is reported.
- Usable. Can the information be used to make practical decisions and solve actual problems? Data that are not useful are irrelevant.
- Understandable. Can the significant findings be grasped, interpreted, and used for making decisions?
- Meaningful. Is the information relevant to the decision or problem under consideration? Useful information addresses the issues under consideration.
- Current. Does the information reflect what is happening? New information is the lifeblood of successful marketing.

Manual processing systems are a thing of the past for most organizations. Today, the data management system of choice is electronic data processing. With computer configurations of all types and sizes readily available, electronic data processing systems can be developed for any type or size of organization. Recently, perhaps the most significant advances in the processing of information have been the use of bar codes and optical scanners to obtain data quickly and inexpensively. Electronic scanning also increases the accuracy of the data.

When presenting results from marketing research, it is as important to communicate with managers in local operations as it is with managers at headquarters.

When local managers do not get a full-fledged presentation of research results, the benefits of a multinational operation are largely lost. Researchers working with local marketers should translate results into useful information that is prioritized in terms of what is most important to the people who actually do the marketing. Board directors can contribute by ensuring that the research team does this and that the presentations are carried out in the best way possible.

Stage 4: presenting and utilizing information
Information differs from raw data in that it is useful to the marketing manager. For information to be useful it must be:

- presented in an appropriate format;
- disseminated to the appropriate user; and
- used in an appropriate way.

The reporting format for the output generated by the information processing stage of the MIS can take several forms. The primary output from the processing stage is a series of marketing research and marketing intelligence reports and a collection of current and accessible databases that marketing managers can use. These data banks are typically large and complex computer storage and retrieval systems, which provide the user with quick and easy access to electronic files. The processing stage can also yield information used to construct conceptual (why consumers prefer a certain brand) and applied (how to select a successful store location) models. Furthermore, processed information can be reported in the form of strategic and tactical plans that frame the decisions and actions of marketing managers.

Information dissemination deals with the issues of who gets what information and in what form. It is costly to locate, gather, and process information. To justify such costs, organizations strive to gain maximum internal exposure and usage by all appropriate decision-makers. Because processed information is often viewed as proprietary, organizations usually restrict its external distribution to a few, trusted, business partners. Online access to digital information is fast becoming the preferred method for distributing information.

Transnational (global) marketing learning

The international information system can also be helpful in disseminating information more broadly throughout the organization, and particularly across geographic regions and specific countries (see Figure 18.3). While data relating to performance tends most commonly to be transferred vertically within the organization, i.e. from country or local operating units to regional, area or central headquarters, information facilitates the development of more complex, horizontal, flows of information.

Local country managers can then add information relating to their operations. This might include, for example, information relating to product launches, marketing programmes, price changes or promotional ideas. This can then be filtered centrally and ideas or experience that appear to have relevance or be applicable in other countries or regions can be disseminated more broadly. This can be refined into a system of best practices. Local managers feed information concerning successful experience and programs in their own markets into the information system. A central committee examines these reports and determines which are designated "best practice" and disseminates them as such throughout the organization.

An important element for the creation of such horizontal flows is the motivation of local managers both to submit and also to access and act upon best practices there, thus incentives may be necessary. The limited time available may limit managers' willingness to access and absorb information and apply best practices. To the extent that such practices are endorsed by a central committee, the risks of unsuccessful implementation are to some extent mitigated.

Information use takes the form of making marketing decisions and initiating actions that implement those decisions. It is up to the decision-maker to determine how the information is to be used relative to a particular problem or situation. Translating facts, opinions, relationships, associations, common tendencies, unusual occurrences, and other findings into actionable marketing decisions is the central purpose of the marketing information system. If marketing managers ignore these findings, then the gathered information has no meaning or value. Information-based decisions produce better results, both in the short and long run, than decisions based on feelings.

Coming back to Figure 18.1, the two boxes at either side show some information use in the form of inputs and outputs of the proposed international marketing information system.

Tables 18.1 and 18.2 show the internal inputs and outputs of the international MIS. As opposed to internal, this external information comes from sources outside the organization.

One of the important outputs of the MIS (Figure 18.1) is that it may provide important inputs for international marketing budgeting.

For companies involved in international markets, the MIS can help assess the allocation of resources across countries or regions, product markets and target segments. This includes determining not only which geographic areas, markets and segments offer the most attractive expansion opportunities, but also whether the company should divest unprofitable operations, or shift from less profitable operations to those with higher expected rates of return.

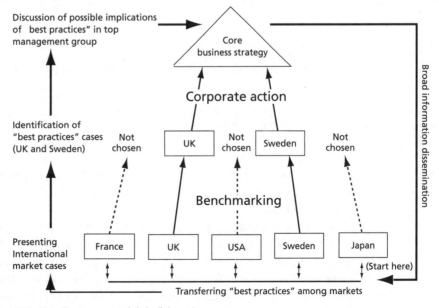

Figure 18.3 The "Bottom-up" (global) learning process

Table 18.1 Internal functional areas – from inputs to outputs in the MIS. *Source*: Adapted from O'Brian et al. (1995)

Internal functional area	Provided to the MIS (inputs)	Provided by the MIS (outputs)
Corporate planning	Corporate objectives Expansion plans	Measurement of marketing's progress towards goal attainment Data for market analysis of new products or new markets
Salesforce	Sales feedback from field	Sales analysis by sales representative
Sales-order processing	Invoices and shipments Back order status	Sales analysis of product/service lines Equivalent replacement products; Communication to the salesforce
General marketing: research, planning, promotion and administration	Types of new product/service with market possibilities Consumer response to existing products/services Planning and promotional campaigns	Plan for introducing new products and creating relationships with new customers Sales analysis of current products/services to current customers Media and lead analysis
Customer/product service	Feedback from customers and salesforce on product reliability and performance	Storage media for complaint file and product ideas
Product research and development	New product development schedules	Proper timing for new product release and phase-in
Data processing	System for organizing data files and reporting operating results	Details of what the marketing group needs in computerized reports
Manufacturing	Inventory status	Forecasts on production and inventory online updates
Personnel	Background on sales and marketing employees Salary/performance review data	Effects of learning curve for salesforce Determinants for employee selection Plan for developing selling competencies of employees
Corporate financial reporting and planning	Product pricing and costing Marketing/sales expenses	Profitability by product or sales representatives

The optimal portfolio of products will consist of a mix of products, including mature products that produce large cash flows and are used to finance products with considerable growth potential.

The same approach can be used in international markets replacing products with countries or geographic regions. A company needs to achieve a balance between high growth and mature markets (product markets and geographic areas) to ensure that a company is well placed for the future. Thus, involvement in mature product businesses has to be balanced with involvement in new, rapidly growing product businesses, and involvement in mature countries and regions of the world such as Europe and Japan has

Table 18.2 External functional areas – from inputs to outputs in the MIS. *Source*: Adapted from O'Brian et al. (1995)

External functional areas	Provided to the MIS (inputs)	Provided by the MIS (outputs)
Industry reports	Corporate data and analysis Industry news	Industry growth and trend statistics New technology and products
Competition	Products and product literature	Technology comparisons Capitalization analysis
Secondary research	Special market facts	Market segmentation and profile
Distributors, wholesalers and retailers	Market conditions Consumer analysis	Special sales programs Sales analysis Pricing policy input Market segmentation
Customers	Profile data Sales data	Customer segmentation Profile analysis Product history
State statistical data and abstracts	Corporate, competitor, and state statistical comparisons Economic/financial data	Competitive analysis Corporate profile Market-segment analysis
Information brokers	Special studies Market news	Special customer-segment identification
Database retrieval systems	News abstracts Product, market and industry news and analysis Economic news	Changes in product positions, markets and industries Economic influences on sales potential New influences on market

to be balanced with rapidly growing areas such as China and Latin America. At the same time, the company needs to assess its own performance in existing markets to ensure that this matches market growth potential and to assess whether there are opportunities for improved efficiency and performance through integrating and consolidating operations across borders.

Achieving a balance between growth and mature markets implies that for any given product market, a company needs to assess growth opportunities and risks in different countries and regions both at a macroeconomic and product market level (Craig and Douglas, 2001). Data from the international MIS can be helpful in making this assessment.

In using these criteria to evaluate and compare performance in different countries, differences in operating conditions and the market environment need to be taken into consideration.

18.4   Summary

An organization's strategy, planning and operational control will only be as good as the information that is available to the decision-maker.

An international MIS should be designed to support managers in making decisions. Rapid market development requires quick and responsive decision-making and also the ability to act proactively. An efficient MIS captures the status of and the relevant changes in the marketplace while simultaneously ridding the reporting environment of redundant information. Indeed, a properly designed MIS may solve many of the problems associated with too much information of the wrong kind, or in the wrong place.

An understanding of the entire marketing planning process is necessary to define the MIS needs of a company. Indeed, to create a strategic advantage, the MIS must not be viewed solely as a function within the organization where the individual parts generate value, but as a total system that has the power to restructure both internal and external organizational relationships.

In addition, an MIS can support managers by providing inter-linkage and integration between departments or divisions. For example, customer perceptions of products are collected by the salesforce and disseminated to development groups via the MIS. The MIS also can increase the ability to respond to a dynamic business environment. For example, based on information provided through a linkage with retail scanners, immediate price changes can be made in response to competitors' actions. The system also allows more efficient handling, organization, and storage of data. For example, data can be grouped by customer store types and/or distinct competitors present in specific markets. An effective MIS can help improve customer service directly, as a part of the product itself, or indirectly through increased responsiveness to customer needs.

Questions

1. What is meant by the socio-cultural environment in the creation of an MIS?

2. Explain the different steps in the creation of an MIS.

3. Discuss how it is possible to transform raw data into meaningful bits of information.

4. How do the variables comprising the informational and technological environment information influence the building of an international MIS?

Bibliography and references

Andreasen, A (1985) "Backward marketing research." *Harvard Business Review*. May–June. 176–182.

Amaravadi, C.S., Samaddar, S. and Dutta, S. (1995) "Intelligent marketing information systems." *Marketing Intelligence & Planning*. Vol. 13, no. 2. 4–11.

Craig, S.C. and Douglas, S.P. (2001) "Conducting international marketing research in the twenty-first century." *International Marketing Review*. Vol. 18, no. 1. 80–90.

Dorfman, R. and Steiner, P. O. (1954) "Optimal advertising and optimal quality," *American Economic Review*. Vol. 44, 826–836.

Hollensen, S. (2003) *Marketing Management: A Relationship Approach*. Harlow: Financial Times Prentice Hall.

Mittal, V. (2004) "Research and the bottom line." *Marketing Research*. Fall. 36–40.

O'Brian, T. V., Schoenbachler, D. D., and Gordon, G. L. (1995) "Marketing information systems for consumer products companies: a management overview." *Journal of Consumer Marketing*. Vol. 12, no. 5. 16–36.

Sambandam, R. (2003) "Cluster analysis gets complicated." *Marketing Research*. Spring. 16–21.

End note

[1] *Collinearity* can be defined as a high level of correlation between two variables. (When more than two variables are involved, this would be called as multicollinearity). Collinearity is a problem in key driver analysis because, when two independent variables are highly correlated, it becomes difficult to divide accurately their individual influence on the dependent variable. Two types of attributes can cause collinearity problems in segmentation that use cluster analysis: irrelevant and redundant attributes. Irrelevant attributes that contribute to collinearity have to be dealt with before starting the analysis. A good understanding of the objectives of the analysis and how the results will be used helps researchers identify the appropriate variables to use in the analysis. Two methods that Sambandam (2003) suggests for solving this collinearity problem are:

- Variable elimination. In practical marketing research, quite frequently questions are constructed that tap into very similar attitudes or slightly different aspects of the same construct. Individually, such questions usually do not provide any additional independent information. The simplest approach for dealing with this situation, if the correlations are very high (e.g. 0.80 or higher), is to eliminate one of the variables from the analysis. The variable to be retained in the analysis should be selected based on its practical usefulness.

- Factor analysis. Factor analysis can help identify redundancies in the input data because correlated variables will load highly on the same factor. However, using the factor scores directly as input into a cluster analysis usually is not recommended because the nature of the data changes when factor analysis is applied. It is possible to eliminate some variables that load on the same factor by selecting one or two variables to "represent" that factor. One situation where the use of factor analysis is not a problem is when the sample-based segmentation scheme is used for classifying the universe on the basis of variables not used in the analysis.

Index